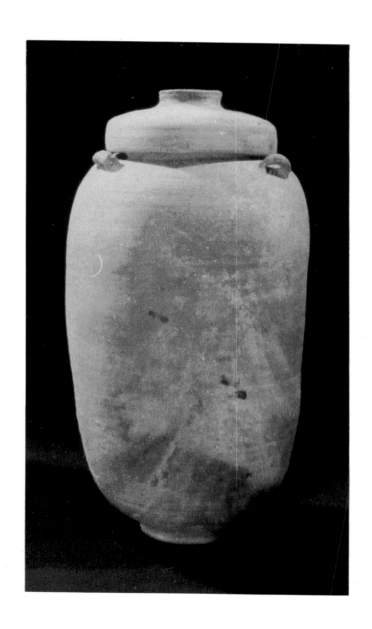

METHODS OF INVESTIGATION OF THE DEAD SEA SCROLLS AND THE KHIRBET QUMRAN SITE

PRESENT REALITIES AND FUTURE PROSPECTS

ANNALS OF THE NEW YORK ACADEMY OF SCIENCES
Volume 722

METHODS OF INVESTIGATION OF THE DEAD SEA SCROLLS AND THE KHIRBET QUMRAN SITE
PRESENT REALITIES AND FUTURE PROSPECTS

Edited by Michael O. Wise, Norman Golb
John J. Collins, and Dennis G. Pardee

The New York Academy of Sciences
New York, New York
1994

COVER ART: The photograph of lamps and pots from Khirbet Qumran was provided by Robert Donceel and Pauline Donceel-Voûte. (Photo by Garo Nalbandian)

FRONTISPIECE: The photograph is of a jar from Khirbet Qumran in the collection of the Oriental Institute of the University of Chicago.

Library of Congress Cataloging-in-Publication Data

Methods of investigation of the Dead Sea scrolls and the Khirbet
  Qumran site : present realities and future prospects / edited by
  Michael O. Wise . . . [et al.].
      p. cm. – (Annals of the New York Academy of Sciences ; v. 722)
    Includes bibliographical references and indexes.
    ISBN 0-89766-793-X (cloth : alk. paper). – ISBN 0-89766-794-8
  (paper : alk. paper)
    1. Dead Sea scrolls—Criticism, interpretation, etc.—Congresses.
  2. Qumran community—Congresses. 3. Qumran Site—Congresses.
  4. Excavations (Archaeology)—West Bank—Qumran Site—Congresses.
  I. Wise, Michael Owen, 1954– . II. Series.
  BM487.M45 1994
  296.1′55—dc20   94-16463
                                                              CIP

CCP
Printed in the United States of America
ISBN 0-89766-793-X (cloth)
ISBN 0-89766-794-8 (paper)
ISSN 0077-8923

ANNALS OF THE NEW YORK ACADEMY OF SCIENCES

Volume 722
June 20, 1994

METHODS OF INVESTIGATION OF THE DEAD SEA SCROLLS AND THE KHIRBET QUMRAN SITE
PRESENT REALITIES AND FUTURE PROSPECTS[a]

Conference Chairmen

JOHN J. COLLINS, DOUGLAS L. ESSE, NORMAN GOLB,
DENNIS G. PARDEE, and MICHAEL O. WISE

Editors

MICHAEL O. WISE, NORMAN GOLB, JOHN J. COLLINS,
and DENNIS G. PARDEE

CONTENTS

[a] This volume is the result of a conference entitled **Methods of Investigation of the Dead Sea Scrolls and the Khirbet Qumran Site: Present Realities and Future Prospects** that was cosponsored by the New York Academy of Sciences and the Oriental Institute of the University of Chicago, and held in New York City on December 14–17, 1992.

Financial assistance for this conference was received from:

Major Funder

• THE ORIENTAL INSTITUTE OF THE UNIVERSITY OF CHICAGO

Douglas L. Esse

In Memoriam

Editors' Preface

On 14–17 December 1992, the New York Academy of Sciences and the Oriental Institute of the University of Chicago cosponsored a conference on the Dead Sea Scrolls entitled "Methods of Investigation of the Dead Sea Scrolls and the Khirbet Qumran Site: Present Realities and Future Prospects." Held at the Blood Center in New York City, the conference brought together more than ninety scholars and advanced students from a dozen nations. Professor William Sumner, director of the Oriental Institute, delivered opening remarks in which he emphasized the significance of a conference of this kind, concerned with ancient manuscripts and archaeological findings, being sponsored by scientific organizations.

The New York meeting was the first major international forum devoted to the Dead Sea Scrolls since full access to all the materials for all scholars became the rule late in 1991. Thus a primary purpose of the conference was that various new texts (as well as some that had already been available) would be analyzed. As the reader will see, in this hope we were not disappointed.

A second goal of the conference was to bring together scholars of diverse – even radically diverse – views regarding the scrolls, Khirbet Qumran and the nearby caves, and to encourage open, face-to-face discussion and debate. As acknowledged by the ancient Greek rhetoricians, "the first man is right until the second man speaks." That is why we must hear the second man. The ancient Hebrews expressed a similar judgment: "As iron sharpens iron, so does a man sharpen the countenance of his friend." We feel that the 26 papers that follow – and the frequently pointed discussions appended to them – demonstrate not only the fundamental importance of this goal, but also how successfully it was met during the conference.

Professor Sumner's remarks served to highlight a unique aspect of this meeting: its conscious effort to focus on methodological approaches to the study of the scrolls and the relevant archaeology. Consonant with these remarks, a third goal of the conference was to encourage participants to assess the suitability of methods that have been used in the past, and to consider prospects for new methods and technologies. In speaking of science and of methods, we should like to make special mention of the paper submitted *in absentia* by Dr. Georges Bonani and his associates at the Federal Institute of Technology of Zurich, Switzerland, and to thank Professor Morris Shamos for presenting the paper on behalf of the Zurich team, and for his valuable comments. While no consensus emerged during the lengthy debate that followed this paper, the issues became more clearly defined, and that in itself should prove helpful to Qumran researchers.

A perusal of the papers and discussion contained in this volume may stir in the mind of the reader the notion that Qumran research is, in a sense, emblematic of scientific progress and controversy as a whole. Something of the value of the proceedings resides in their pellucid illustration of a process, that of general scholarly assessment and debate. It is our hope, *inter alia*, that these proceedings will demonstrate to the scientific community as a whole the appropriate place of philology, archaeology and related subjects within the constellation of scientific discourse.

This volume culminates three years of planning and preparation, first of the conference itself, then of the papers here published. In cheerful disregard of the proverb, we have become debtors to many, and we cannot close before acknowledging at least the greatest of those debts. We thank our sponsors, the New York Academy of Sciences and the Oriental Institute and its director, for making the conference possible. We also thank Ms. Joyce Hitchcock, associate editor with the NYAS, and Mr. Bill Boland, NYAS editor, for helping to bring this volume to completion. Mr. Anthony Tomasino, a doctoral candidate in Ancient Judaism at the University of Chicago, deserves special mention for his help with correspondence preceding the conference and with various matters afterward.

We dedicate this volume to the memory of our late colleague, Professor Douglas Esse, well known as an archaeologist of Syria-Palestine and originally one of the conference organizers. Doug played an integral part in the two years of planning and preparation, but, tragically cut short in the prime of his scholarly career, he did not live to attend the conference itself. His presence would surely have enriched that symposium, as he did our lives for the time that we knew him.

THE EDITORS
SPRING, 1994

Dougless Esse at the Albright Institute, Jerusalem, in 1987.

Note to the Reader

This volume, *Methods of Investigation of the Dead Sea Scrolls and the Khirbet Qumran Site: Present Realities and Future Prospects*, is a welcome if somewhat unusual member of the *Annals* series. For this reason a short comment on the discussions following the individual papers and on the Ethics of Publication Panel is in order.

All discussions were recorded and transcribed by a professional service, edited and pruned by the conference editors, gone over by an Academy copyeditor, corrected and edited by the author of the paper to which the discussion is appended, typeset, and then proofread. During this process, every effort was made to preserve both the content and flavor of the original debates; however, the transcripts of these debates are not published verbatim.

The panelists in the Ethics Panel saw and corrected their own presentations, as did those participants in the open discussion who made extended comments. All the panel presentations and ensuing discussions were also looked at by the chairman and the editors of the volume as well as the Academy editors. Here again, every effort was made to preserve both the content and flavor of the original.

Thus, although they are not verbatim transcripts of what went on at the Conference, it was felt that the discussions following each paper and the Ethics of Publication Panel were most worthy of inclusion and that the process by which they were edited has made them accurate renditions of the debates.

BILL BOLAND
Executive Editor
Annals of The New York Academy of Sciences

The Archaeology of Khirbet Qumran

ROBERT DONCEEL AND
PAULINE DONCEEL-VOÛTE

Ecole biblique et archéologique française de Jérusalem
Université catholique de Louvain at Louvain-la-Neuve
*[7 rue d'Aye, B.6900-Humain (Marche en Famenne) Belgium]**

INTRODUCTION

In 1986, on the initiative of the Reverend Fathers Jean-Luc Vesco, then Director of the Ecole Biblique et Archéologique Française de Jérusalem, and Jean-Baptiste Humbert, archaeologist, a team was set up and started work in order to bring new impulse to the publication of the final results of the excavations that Father Roland Guérin de Vaux directed at Khirbet Qumran in the years 1951 to 1956. Publication was interrupted in 1971 by de Vaux's death.[1]

The project did not wait for the press campaigns that have, in the meantime, raised the problem of the publication schedule of the other discoveries from the shores of the Dead Sea. Indeed, a team also set to work on the publication of another of Father de Vaux's excavations, that at Tell Far'ah North. The Centenary of the Ecole Biblique was the occasion which brought these into the limelight once again, the Khirbet Qumran excavations being about the most important undertaken by the Ecole in the past hundred years.

The site's very particular context was an ample justification for bringing its data into the scientific circuit in a form other than preliminary reports on the successive seasons, articles with a limited scope or provisional syntheses which, in French and subsequently revised in English, provided the substance of conference papers given by Father de Vaux.[2] The link which the excavator established between, on the one hand, the human group which inhabited the site and, on the other, the texts which had been discovered in the nearby

---

* Address for correspondence.
[1] Funds were provided by the French Ministry of Foreign Affairs and by the Amis de l'Ecole biblique, as well as by the F.N.R.S. and a private fund in Belgium managed by the Université Catholique de Louvain. R. Donceel, Professor at the U.C.L. is the coordinator of the publishing team, and between 1987 and 1990 nine scholars from this university worked for the project in Jerusalem and Khirbet Qumran: detailed record in notes below.
[2] R. DE VAUX, *Archaeology and the Dead Sea Scrolls, The Schweich Lectures of the British Academy*, London, Oxford University Press, 1973 (abbreviated *infra* as *Archaeology*).

1

caves, a link which the excavator pointed out as being illustrated by the relation between the archaeological finds from the one and the others,[3] asked at least to be more amply illustrated. Moreover, owing to the precise dates which Father de Vaux suggested for the successive phases of the occupation of the site, Khirbet Qumran has long been a reference site for archaeologists, a site attributed mainly to the first century before and the first three-quarters of the 1st century after the turn of the era, from which the finds could be considered as being firmly dated and thus especially useful for comparison with finds from other, sometimes quite distant, sites.[4]

When the Khirbet Qumran project was launched by the Ecole Biblique it theoretically also included the material from the other Dead Sea sites excavated by the Ecole, that is 'Ain Feshkha and the various caves. For purely practical reasons, the small team, the limited time and funds available, and the dispersion of part of the finds, the study of the caves' material was postponed; that from the 'Ain Feshkha spring area on the other hand we have worked on together with that from Khirbet Qumran mainly because the excavator himself constantly associated the two in his work and in the interpretation he gave of his results.[5]

The present report concerns the progress of our work on the material discovered in these two sites,[6] of the problems we met with, the methods we used, particularly in view of these problems, and of the steps we are foreseeing in the edition and publication of the finds and buildings from both sites.

THE EXCAVATIONS–AVAILABLE DATA

On the one hand, there are the actual artefacts and architectural structures from which they came, and on the other there are the notes and lists drawn up during the excavations and in the period immediately following.

[3] R. DE VAUX, *Archaeology*, especially pp. 102–106.

[4] The handbook by P.W. LAPP, *Palestinian Ceramic Chronology, 200 BC–AD 70*, ASOR, IV, New Haven, 1961, thus counts but two "stratified deposits" for the period which concerns us: Khirbet Qumran and the palace at Jericho-Tulul el-'Alayik (pp. 12 ff.).

[5] See R. DE VAUX, *Archaeology*, in particular p. 69. Contrary to the situation at the ruins of Qumran most of those of 'Ain Feshkha cannot be studied any more inasmuch as the archaeological zone has been turned into a recreational area (under the name of En Zuqim) from which practically all trace of ancient structures, uncovered or not, seems to have disappeared.

[6] The project of publishing the results of the excavations at Khirbet Qumran and 'Ain Feshkha, which was a joint Franco-Jordanian venture, has also received the agreement and scientific support of the Department of Antiquities of Jordan (D.A.J.) through its director Prof. Fawzi Zayadine.

The present publication offers us the occasion to inform concerned scientific circles that we are concurrently attempting to complete the documentation on the excavation at Khirbet Mird-Hyrcania, which was undertaken by a team from our university, the Université catholique de Louvain, in 1953, manned by, in particular, Prof. Jacques Ryckmans and the late Count Philippe Lippens.

The Archaeological Finds

To accomplish our aim of publishing the archaeological finds as soon as possible, we intend to provide successive short fascicles.[7] Among these different categories of finds, which we shall now rapidly review, the coins will, for a variety of reasons, be treated first.

The Coins

The inventory register records the discovery of a total of 1231 coins and fragments of coins (bronze, silver, and combinations of both) from the successive seasons at Khirbet Qumran, and of 144 from those at ʿAin Feshkha.[8] Among the items from the first, one should distinguish, for scientific as well as administrative reasons, between the all silver coins belonging to the most important hoard, found in locus 120, and the others. The hoard of coins carries three different inventory numbers (KhQ 2542, 2545, and 2547)[9] because it was found in three different vessels; in the days after its discovery it was divided into two lots, one given to the Palestine Archaeological Museum in Jerusalem (153 coins), the other to the Archaeological Museum in Amman (408 coins).[10] No particular criterion, especially scientific, seems to have governed this allotment. Father Benoit, Fr. de Vaux's successor, made repeated efforts to get the publication of these hoard coins under way, especially as their study seemed relatively easy to undertake. The information he received, in at least three different instances during the last ten years of his life, from the specialists who one after the other undertook this task in Amman, showed that

[7] They will form a series called *Novum Testamentum et Orbis Antiquus—Series Archaeologica*, Institut Biblique/Biblisches Institut, Universität Freiburg/Université de Fribourg (CH), M. Küchler, editor. The original project planned a publication by the Clarendon Press, Oxford in the series of the "Discoveries in the Judean Desert." For different reasons the E.B.A.F. chose to accept the offer of the Fribourg Université Miséricorde. The fascicles on the Finds will include: R. de Vaux's "Carnets de fouilles," The Stone Ware; The Glass Ware; The Lamps; The Common Pottery; The Metal Ware; Fine Pottery; Objects of Animal, Vegetable and Mixed Materials; Epigraphical Documents; The Coins. See below for details.

[8] One and the same inventory number was sometimes given to several coins, as in the case of the hoards and of groups that were difficult to count because they had become lumped together. It is hard to say what the exact number of coins discovered in the successive seasons is. Certain coins have disintegrated during cleaning operations, which also led to the cancellation of some other numbers given to metal pieces that turned out as not belonging to coins. On the other hand, quite recently, among the metal objects from the site, other heavily corroded coins have been identified.

[9] Other hoards have been found during the excavations such as KhQ 2009, from *locus* 103, which numbers 42 bronze coins.

[10] See the editorial note heading the article by M. SHARABANI, *Monnaies de Qumran au Musée Rockefeller de Jérusalem*, (in *Revue Biblique* (=R.B.), 87, 1980, pp. 275–284, 3 pl.) p. 274 and 275 on this apportionment and its consequent vicissitudes.

there were lacunae in the collection.[11] Owing to the help of different colleagues and especially that provided by those responsible for the numismatic
collection at the Rockefeller (*i.e.*, Palestine Archaeological) Museum, we have
at least been able to locate the 50 coins of the "Amman lot" which were
thought to have disappeared after an exhibition tour in the USA and then
Europe, in 1965.[12]

A more painful matter is that of the "excavation coins." They were entrusted by Father de Vaux for study and publication, together with all the
other coins from both sites, to the late Franciscan Father Auguste Spijkerman,
an eminent numismatist who specialized in Near Eastern mints and coins.
Those he was able to read, after treatment, finally numbered 691 items.[13] We
have been able to trace no more than 196 (2/7ths) of these, which we photographed, weighed, and described. Of the still missing coins no trace is to be
found at the Ecole Biblique or at the Rockefeller Museum; we have therefore
written, with no result as yet, to a series of numismatic collections which, in
Europe and the Near East, seemed likely to have acquired part or all of the
5/7ths still missing.[14]

We take this opportunity to appeal to anyone who might possess infor-

[11] One report was written in 1980, by a numismatist(?) whom we have not been able to
identify. The previous year, Rev. Fr. Fulco had examined the question in Amman without suc-
ceeding in creating the necessary interest for a publication. Finally in 1981 M. Christian Augé,
a fellow member of the Mission Française de Syrie du Sud, examined the Amman lot and had
new photographs made of it. Two coins were deposited in the collection of the Jordan University
Archaeological Museum. Three others were given to President Nixon by King Hussein as a state
gift on the occasion of an official visit to the country; they have been deposited at the Smithsonian
Institution, Washington, which communicated photographs and descriptions.

[12] "The Dead Sea Scrolls of Jordan," held at the National Museum of Natural History,
Smithsonian Institution, Washington, D.C., 1964. We have been able to establish that these
coins were brought back, by error, not to Amman but to Jerusalem, from where most of the
other exhibits came. Also at the request of Father Benoit, adapting his policies to the new situation between Amman and Jerusalem and the difficulties involved in working simultaneously in
both museums after June 1967, the preliminary study of the 408 coins from the same hoard kept
in Jerusalem was published (see note 10; Mrs. Sharabani does not wish to publish any further
research on the subject). A few remarks will be introduced here concerning the Amman lot of
the hoard and the surprises encountered during their examination. Intrusive coins seem to have
found their way into it (particularly Trajanic *denarii*: oral communication by C. Augé in 1989).
We were able to observe the same phenomenon on the excavation coins kept in Jerusalem. This
will not make the publication task any easier. Fortunately, we do have the autograph lists, written
out by Henri Seyrig, which should allow us, even without accompanying photographs, to at
least separate the intrusive coins from the main hoard. Also, according to C. Augé, the observations made on the coins of the Amman lot have allowed identification of traces of violent com-
bustion, evidenced by the lead having started to melt. It seems Fr. de Vaux did not integrate
this observation into his own deductions, concerning particularly the chronology of the site.

[13] The Rev. Fr. Spijkerman added a total of 21 coins to the list of those from the 1954,
1955, and 1956 digs. One silver coin was, independently, found by a visitor, R.R. Williams, who
published it.

[14] The coins that have disappeared are: all those of the 1951 season, 62 of the 1952 season,
194 from the 1954 season, 233 from the 1955 season and all the coins (6 items) of the 1956
season. All their cards are equally missing from the file in the E.B.A.F.; they seem, therefore,
to have been taken away for study. It seems unlikely that these coins from the site should have

mation on what happened to these coins. It seems, moreover, that Spijkerman, notwithstanding his intentions, as far as we have been able to understand them from the archives we have established, had totally abandoned work on the coins several years before his death, in 1973.[15]

Following the cleaning and identification work also carried out by Father Spijkerman on the 'Ain Feshkha coins, 144 items were counted, of which 74 were considered by the numismatist as being certainly or most probably identifiable and only 25 completely readable.[16] We have no information whatsoever as to the present whereabouts of these 'Ain Feshkha coins.

You will easily understand that, considering the importance which the excavator had quite logically given to the numismatic evidence, particularly for establishing a chronology, these lacunae affecting both the Khirbet Qumran and the 'Ain Feshkha coins are a serious obstacle to the publication of those we have been able to examine.[17]

Concerning the conditions of discovery of most finds the excavators usually gave but a few elements of information: the number of the locus, plus, in the best cases, two or three words about their position in relation to some topographic guidemark.[18] From the stratigraphic position of certain coins the director of the excavation drew a number of very precise conclusions, some of which have been strongly disputed.[19] Relying upon his memory and knowledge of the site, he left his readers—and the present publication team—in no position to control these.

Moreover, in the last 40 years considerable progress has been made in our understanding of coins circulating in Palestine in the first centuries before and

---

been stolen, if but for the reason that these excavation coins, often hardly legible, are far from being an attractive lot for the antiquities market. The present keepers of the numismatic material at the Rockefeller Museum, repeatedly asked to verify their card systems and their collections, are quite certain as to the absence of these coins from their collections.

[15] The archives of A. Spijkerman contain nothing that looks like the written results of his research, apart from a few words of introduction (this notwithstanding *R.B.*, 87, 1980, p. 274). They contain no trace either of the photographs of the Jerusalem part of the hoard which he (according to communication by Rev. Fr. Fulco) had ordered from the D.A.J. in Amman. On the other hand a few of the hundreds of file-cards missing from the Ecole Biblique were found in his papers. It may well be that the reason why Spijkerman seems to have abandoned the idea of publishing the numismatic evidence from Qumran is because some of the excavation coins were already missing.

[16] Eight coins were found during the 1956 season, the rest in 1958. R. DE VAUX (*Fouilles de Feshkha. Rapport préliminaire*, in *R.B.*, 66, 1959, p. 245) gives slightly different numbers, in particular for the unidentifiable coins.

[17] Our own cleaning of the Khirbet Qumran coins allowed some thirty more identifications or finer readings. The publication of the Khirbet Qumran and 'Ain Feshkha coins will be under the direction of Dr. François de Callataÿ (Curator of the Cabinet des Médailles, Bibliothèque Royale, Brussels), with the assistance of Christian Augé (CNRS).

[18] The situation concerning the numismatic evidence is no different from that concerning the other finds; see below a case in point from locus 52.

[19] See for example E. M. LAPERROUSAZ, *Qoumrân. L'établissement essénien des bords de la Mer Morte*, Paris, 1976, pp. 41 ff., with reference to previous publications.

after Christ. In reconstructing the chronology of the site, for example, de Vaux insisted upon the scarcity of coins from the period of Herod the Great; this situation and coinage are better known today and would be otherwise perceived.

Whatever the material situation of this evidence, we will close this numismatic paragraph with a remark that will have to be kept in mind for what follows and for any further syntheses: it must be emphasized that the sheer amount of coins found on both sites is to be considered as particularly, one may even say exceptionally, high,[20] to which we will add that the percentage of coins "usable" for the chronology is important even in comparison with purely Roman excavation sites in the Near East, most of them larger in size.

Concerning the other categories of archaeological material, a major venture in re-gathering, classifying, and identifying was launched by the first term of 1987, that is in the initial phase of the project, by Fr. Humbert and his team. A first check based on the inventory registers of the different seasons gave the measure of the evident lacunae,[21] and showed a state of conservation of the objects much inferior to that which the photographs give; because of the political upheavals or for other reasons the patient conservation work accomplished by the Palestine Archaeological Museum and the Department of Antiquities of Jordan was for a great part annulled.

It also appeared, as our work progressed, that the amount of artefacts collected by the excavation teams far exceeded those that had been chosen to be included in the official inventory.

This is particularly the case with the lamps and the glass ware.[22]

The Lamps

Sixty-four lamps had been listed in the inventory, including the fragments, and it seems here that the criterion Father de Vaux used was the good state of preservation. There are 172 in the publication; these include a number of small fragments, especially nozzles (about 40).[23]

---

[20] This was equally the opinion of the excavation team, judging by experience as well as by some kind of, more hazardous, relation between the quantity of earth moved and the number of coins. It will be necessary to reconcile what this abundance suggests with the hypotheses concerning the site's occupants and functions.

[21] For details on this Inventory see below.

[22] These two categories of archaeological documents will be published by Robert Donceel.

[23] The boxes containing these fragments appeared in 1989 as our stay in the E.B.A.F. was scheduled to come to an end. It was prolonged for about a year to allow for all drawings, photographs and descriptions to be made (by R. Donceel and P. Donceel-Voûte).

The quantity and variety of these inventory "complements" will obviously modify the conclusions to be drawn from each category of archaeological evidence, although we have even less information on the context of their discovery than for the items in the official inventory.[24]

Our work could have been even more rewarding had not the most elaborate and complete items disappeared: this goes for 20 lamps, and 2 out of 3 from 'Ain Feshkha. Although we have small-scale drawings of these, we are thus bereft of information concerning the clay, colors, and technical details of their manufacture which do not figure in the inventory, as already pointed out. In only a few cases did we succeed in tracing these show-pieces back to some new exhibition place (FIG. 1).[25]

Without anticipating on the results of this study, we can already offer some interesting observations. For instance, the presence at Qumran of molded lamps, thought to have appeared here around the time of the destruction of the Second Temple, is certain in levels that are neither destruction nor final levels. Some lamps, moreover, are so nearly akin to certain types found in the caves that it seems justified to suggest the same workshop for them.

The Glass Ware

The situation of the glass ware calls for similar remarks. From an original 16 inventory numbers, of which 3 have disappeared, we now have 71, which seem again to have been chosen from the best preserved pieces on the dig. We were surprised to find ourselves identifying, among the non-inventoried items, several samples of mold-blown glass, the details and quality of which can be related to those of famous workshops on the southern Phoenician coast. Considering the chronological frame proposed by Father de Vaux, certain glass discoveries from Khirbet Qumran are bound to carry weight in research on the origins of the glass-blowing technique and industry. Besides, the typology indicates imports from Italy with bottle shapes and a type of surface ornamentation that match the local glass of Herculaneum, near Pompei, the destruction dates of which are only a decade's distance from those of the fall of Jerusalem.

[24] Those artefacts that have not been included in the Inventory do however carry a short annotation in chinese ink stating the locus of origin and the date of discovery; nothing however indicates the stratigraphic position. Only the perilous game of using collateral information may in some cases help to supply some such indication; an example of this type of interplay with cross-information is provided for an object from locus 52, presented below.

[25] See LOCUS 52, AND ITS LAMP, page 22, for an example; we fear the case is not isolated. The number of 'Ain Feshkha lamps and fragments rose from 3 (in the inventory) to 18, including sherds. Our drawings at the 1/1 scale are most precious for our method of grouping fragments around the well preserved lamps, on the basis of fine technical and formal comparisons, impossible to be made on the basis of the 2/5 scale drawings that the de Vaux team used.

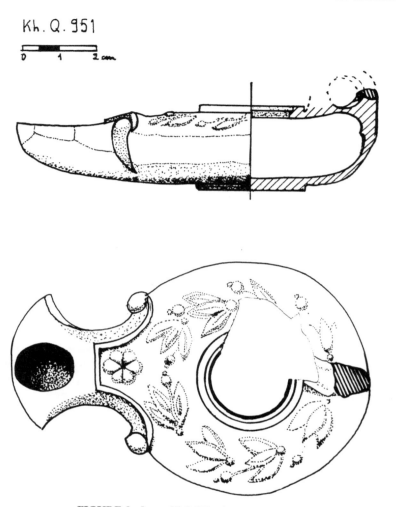

Kh.Q.951

FIGURE 1. Lamp KhQ.951 (drawing P.D.-V.).

Moreover there are traces of a local glass production, in the shape of small to medium sized lumps of light green glass which look like nothing but raw material.[26] Thus, quite unexpectedly given the excavator's silence on this category of material in his preliminary publications, Khirbet Qumran turns out to be also, to a certain degree, a "glass site" in archaeology.

[26] The glass was chemically analyzed by the laboratories of the Institut royal du patrimoine artistique, the I.R.P.A., in Brussels; it may give information on the relation of the ware with workshops, local or not. The full report on these analyses, by Ch. Fontaine-Hodiamont, will be included in the publication. The items were drawn at the 1/1 scale by P. Donceel-Voûte,

It also turns out to be an "open site," a place for which articles were purchased not only from Jerusalem[27] or Jericho but from elsewhere in the Mediterranean world.

Furthermore, and we will return to this later, the number and variety of coins and several other clues suggest that this "open site" not only received but most probably also produced and exchanged something of true commercial value.

The Pottery

The pottery represents by far the biggest category of archaeological finds to be published, also swollen by dozens of crates of non-inventoried sherds. Had the archaeologists not also chosen in this case to keep only the best and most reconstructable pieces, there would be true mounds of data to be analyzed.[28] It is particularly for this category of finds that much of the earlier patient restoration work has had to be redone, to recreate the objects' more evocative original shapes.[29] It was paralleled by a vast campaign of drawing and description.[30] The responsibility for this publication is Father Humbert's. It aims at being not just a selection in view of a global typology, but a comprehensive study bringing out not only the formal but in particular the technical aspects of local ceramics.[31] With time the reference material for these finds too has grown. The nearest comes from the Hasmonean and Herodian

---

R. Van Berwaer, and S. Verhelst in 1989–1990. The glass sherds were generally in a bad state of preservation, the entire mass of glass tending to disintegrate into mere layers of iridescent flakes; the restoration work was also done by the I.R.P.A.

[27] See below for the evidence of "Jerusalem pseudo-Nabatean painted pottery."

[28] The policy followed by the excavators with regard to the common pottery seems also to have varied according to the discoveries. Fragments of incomplete vessels seem to have been kept and partially written down in the inventory only in cases of discovery in important stratigraphic positions and in the absence of more eloquent finds. An unfinished notebook with drawings of pottery sherds dates from the 1951 season; they are reproduced in the usual but not very handy scale of 2/5 used for the bigger vessels.

[29] Thanks to the kind collaboration of the curators of the Rockefeller Museum and of its stores, and in particular of Mr. J. Zias, thousands of sherds could be transferred to the Ecole Biblique et Archéologique Française for examination and treatment. A number of vases and a lamp are the Ecole's property and were written into its collection lists then—when they were still regularly kept. Some pieces of pottery have been given to the Biblical museum of the Institut catholique in Paris.

[30] This unrewarding task could be fulfilled thanks to the collaboration of young scholars from the Université catholique de Louvain, Mr. J. Vallet followed by Miss D. Mineur, in the framework of a "pre-project" started in 1987, and of Mr. G. Humbert, Mr. A. Chambon, and Mr. and Mrs. Bedu.

[31] In this perspective the series of hundreds of vessels found together, contemporaneous and of identical shapes (see R. DE VAUX, *Archaeology*, pp. 11–12 concerning loci 86 and 89), is a great asset as it enables one to appreciate the margins of variations in clay, in color and in shape for the same product.

palace complex at Jericho.[32] Though no detailed publication of this and other comparable sites are available, it may already be said that the common pottery shapes are far from being as isolated and particular to Qumran, its caves and its neighborhood as it seemed in Father de Vaux's time, on the much more limited documentary basis then available.[33]

Clay strata around the site and upstream from the Wadi Qumran, likely to have been used by the local potters, were researched by a special mission.[34]

A small quantity of fine wares constitutes a distinctive category and will be published separately.[35] It consists of less than a dozen sherds (plus 4 from 'Ain Feshkha) of eastern sigillata, "black varnished" pottery and painted "pseudo-Nabatean" ware. For this last fine to very fine ("egg-shell") ware, of mainly bowls and plates, painted in a free style with stylized plant motifs in a black and dark and light red harmony of colors, specialists now tend to attribute the production rather to the Jerusalem area.

The Stone Ware

The stone ware from the site is typical in particular of the lathe-turned and chip-cut limestone industry very characteristic mainly of the Jerusalem region near the turn of the era (the so-called Second Temple period). With 53 new

---

[32] We are impatiently awaiting the publication of a potter's kiln discovered in the industrial area NE of the "third" Herodian palace in Jericho (J. YELLIN & J. GUNNEWEG, "The Flowerpots from Herod's Winter Garden at Jericho," in *Isr. Explor. J.*, 39, 1/2, 1989, pp. 86 ff.). The published photograph shows a batch of vessels each of a different shape inside the ruined kiln; we are inclined to bring this information in relation with our hypothesis that at least one of the Qumran potter's kilns was used only temporarily or seasonally. For a variety of reasons our working hypothesis concerning the common pottery is of itinerant potters' workshops, working according to the needs of their clients and therefore producing the same varieties of pottery in the Jericho kiln as in the Qumran kiln or elsewhere in their activity range. This would explain why not a word was said in any of the excavation reports on pottery waste levels in the neighbourhood of the kilns, waste levels which are inevitable in the case of a permanent workshop. This type of seasonal production also requires a storage area where the newly produced stocks of pottery could be stacked for the year or so to come; in this eventuality such premises should be identifiable in Khirbet Qumran; it may indeed be that loci 86–89 were just that, considering the heaps of identical vessels which had fallen with their shelves and were found broken at the south end of the room (see R. DE VAUX, *Archaeology*, pp. 11–12, pl. X, a–b).

[33] The ceramic material from the site of 'Ain el-Ghuweir (= 'Ain Ghazal), North of Engeddi and 15 km South of Kh. Qumran (P. BAR-ADON, "Another Settlement of the Judaen Desert Sect at 'En el-Ghuweir on the Shores of the Dead Sea," in *Bull. Amer. S. Or. Res.*, 227, 1977, pp. 1–25, especially p. 18), suggests the same remarks. Obviously these new finds will lead to a reexamination of the links which Father de Vaux was able to observe only between the finds in the caves, those in 'Ain Feshkha and those in Khirbet Qumran (see particularly R. DE VAUX, *Archaeology*, pp. 53 f. and 102 f.).

[34] By Mr. Pierre Francus, Lab. of Paleogeography in the Science Dept. of the Université Catholique de Louvain, in April 1990. This study should also have an impact on the data concerning the lamps from our sites (see R. DE VAUX, *Archaeology*, p. 16).

[35] See note 7.

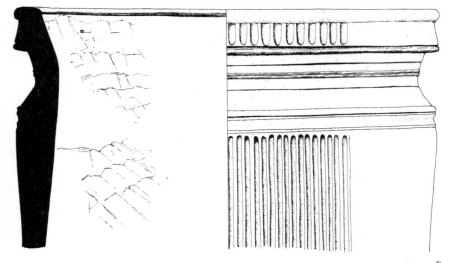

FIGURE 2. Lathe-cut and fluted stone urn, KhQ.375 (2 fragments; upper diam. 37.8 cm) (drawing P.D.-V. & V.V.D.).

items, the Khirbet Qumran material, now numbering almost two hundred pieces,[36] will make a sizable contribution to this subject.

The most spectacular pieces are the urns, lathe-turned, and with a chiseled, fluted, and gadrooned ornament on the more elaborate pieces (FIG. 2). They find parallels only with the best specimens from the Ophel hill and Tyropoeon slopes' excavations in Jerusalem, in a context of rich patrician residences.

To a good number of pieces belonging to chip-cut vessels (FIG. 3) found by the de Vaux digs were added a series of stone "mugs" found intact in the circular cistern (locus 110) by the team which realized several restorations on the site under the direction of M. Dajjani, for the Department of Antiquities of Jordan.[37]

The main series are the stoppers and lids for a variety of amphorae, jugs

[36] Eighteen numbers belong to items which have presently disappeared. There was also a small polished obsidian blade from one of the graves (n° 7). We have added to the household objects a number of elements of architectural decoration such as the pavement slabs and a few pieces of architectural sculpture, as well as non-movable items such as sunken stone vessels and other non-transportable equipment, partly absent from the inventory of certain loci. For the architectonic fragments we have the problem of their exact provenance (bases and drums of columns and a rather roughly worked piece of architrave the presence of which was hardly touched upon by R. DE VAUX, "Fouilles au Khirbet Qumran. Rapport préliminaire sur la 2e campagne," in *Revue Biblique*, 61, 1954, p. 209).

[37] The results of this campaign, which took place shortly before the 1967 events, were never published (see E. M. LAPERROUSAZ, *op. cit.*, p. 14).

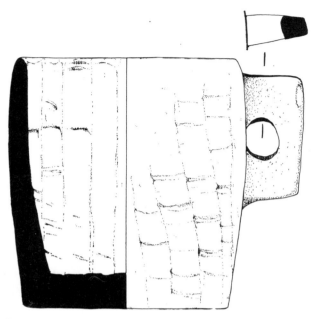

FIGURE 3. Stone mug, chip-cut, KhQ.355 (upper diam. 11 cm) (drawing P.D.-V. & V.V.D.).

and bottles. An interesting group carries a tubular orifice, of standard diameter, which may be vertical or oblique and therefore suggests not the fixing of some cord or prehension knob, but rather that the contents of the vessel it covered had to be either slightly aerated or tested at intervals by introducing some kind of straw or pipette. Pestles and mortars are particularly numerous in Feshkha.

In addition to these, marked weights and stone seals are also evidence of not only domestic but truly economic and commercial activity.

Noteworthy is also the presence of a number of colored stone slabs, carefully cut to be used in pavements of the *opus sectile* type which knew a particular vogue and style in the same period, with comparable floors to be found in the comfortable residences in Jerusalem as well as in the different Herodian palaces.

The presence of these, as well as of the sophisticated glass and stone ware is astounding considering what has been said about the "monastic simplicity" of the site.

The stone material from ʿAin Feshkha counts an impressive number of elegant lathe-turned, finely grooved bowls. Twenty-eight different new objects have been entered in the inventory, bringing it from 46 to a total of 74 numbers.[38]

Together with the lamps, the stone ware has given us unexpected information in that, in several cases, fragments discovered in two or three totally different areas and archaeological contexts were found to join perfectly. This provides us with a piece of information which will be most valuable for the reconstruction of the general stratigraphy and history of the site.

The Metal Ware

The study of the metal ware was a delicate affair, owing to the instability of the substance itself and its restoration problems.[39] The climatic conditions on both sites have allowed a great number of objects, mainly of iron and bronze, to survive. Inventoried or not, these have suffered since the time of their discovery, the worst being the fragmentation of some items, of which the different pieces are mixed up and appear as independent finds. Treatment by specialized laboratories turned out to be too costly,[40] but a small laboratory with the essential instruments was offered by the French Electricity Board and will help to restore as much as possible of the original shape of the objects.

The results that one can expect from the study of the metal objects, which vary from a key-fibula, small three-edged "arrowheads," an important series of agricultural tools, to so many other utensils, not forgetting a number of vessels, will be essential in particular for determining the function of the *loci* as well as the character of the site as a whole during the successive periods of its history.[41] Sadly enough, it seems that many of the objects of this category have also disappeared; we shall have to rely on the unsophisticated drawings that accompany the inventory.

---

[38] The fascicle on the stone ware from both sites is the responsibility of P. Donceel-Voûte, who drew all the pieces with particular emphasis on details concerning ancient techniques.

[39] This study was entrusted to Mr. Alain Chambon by Father Humbert. In quantity this material is second to the pottery, which represents two-thirds of the numbers attributed by the excavators. It counts 194 Inventory numbers of which some were given to groups of several dozens of items. The drawings will be mainly by the author, with the help of several E.B.A.F. and U.C.L. collaborators.

[40] We want, nonetheless, to express our gratitude for their proposed collaboration to the laboratory of the Musée du fer at Jarville-la-Malgrange, Nancy, and to the laboratory of the Museum of Louvain-la-Neuve.

[41] The great variety of these metal items indeed represents many facets of life on the site. In several ways it compares with the Pompeian *instrumentum* of the urban and suburban areas.

The Artefacts of Vegetable, Animal, and Other Materials

A short fascicle or part of a fascicle will contain archaeological documents that are different from those preceding either by their type or their substance: small clay artefacts, most of them unfired, objects made of wood and other vegetable substances, such as palm-leaf-work or wicker-work, of which most have no inventory number; some were photographed, few were described and many have disappeared, as in the case of one of the wooden coffins and of the large mats found in some rooms. One of the other coffins–analyzed for wood type–was made of cypress wood (*Cypressus semper virens*) and is awaiting Carbon 14 analysis.[42]

A few pieces also survived that were made out of bone or ivory, such as small styles, tool hafts and blades, spindle whorls, in all a dozen items to which four from 'Ain Feshkha should be added.[43]

A small category counts objects made out of mixed materials, mostly pieces of finery. The same volume will include stuccoed and plaster-covered pieces of various sizes such as fragments of wall revetments or of furniture.

A fascicle with the written documents from the two sites will complete the series of studies on finds. They are mainly graffiti and brief scratched or painted inscriptions on vessels, artefacts or walls.[44]

The Written and Graphic Documentation on Excavations and Finds

Excavation Diaries

Thanks to the great care taken by the Ecole Biblique to keep and pass on the intellectual patrimony of Father de Vaux, his *Journal de fouilles*, the daily record he kept of the excavation and the events on the dig, is still complete. These notebooks, written in a small, not always easily readable, handwriting

---

[42] A fragment of the coffin from grave 18 was submitted for analysis to Dr. F. Damblon and Dr. E. Gilot, respectively of the laboratory of the General Botanics Department of the U.C.L. (determination of wood species) and of the Laboratory of Inorganic, Analytical and Nuclear Chemistry of the U.C.L. (C14 dating).

[43] These include a find by Mr. Dajjani's team.

[44] Emile Puech has taken the responsibility for this publication. We have been able to establish a list of at least 70 short inscriptions from Kh. Qumran and 3 to 4 from 'Ain Feshkha; some 6 of these are in Greek or Latin, among which a weight and a legionary brick in 'Ain Feshkha. They are mostly ostraca, graffiti and dipinti, of a few signs only. These remains have suffered in years of manipulation and they have often faded, as in the case of the inscription Fr. de Vaux saw in the cartouche on the large stone urn Fesh. 207 (R. DE VAUX, *R.B.*, 66, 1959, p. 245; *Archaeology*, pp. 64–65) which was shattered and glued together twice; neither Mr. Puech nor we could find a trace of either the cartouche or the scratched inscription.

will be published integrally in a separate fascicle.[45] They will be accompanied by the typewritten text[46] which Father de Vaux produced in a second phase, preliminary to any publication. This version is not organized according to the chronology of the dig but topographically, that is per locus and per trench or sounding. For each of these the information was gathered from the day-by-day written notes from all the seasons. The pertinent finds, coins included, with their inventory numbers and some descriptions were also taken up here.[47] This typewritten work, which was not done for 'Ain Feshkha or the tombs, is not just a readable copy of the *Journal de fouilles*; compared with the first hand-written reaction of the excavator confronted with a new phenomenon or structure, it shows how the further explorations had provided enlightenment or even interpretations which led the excavator to leave out certain remarks and observations he no longer found significant.[48]

The excavation diary is usually brief.[49] Only in exceptional cases is an object precisely, that is numerically, situated in relation to some point of reference. Two days of work in a locus may be told in two words. There is no mention of measuring or drawing activities and it holds no useful references concerning the photography. In fact the diary is a combination of both archaeological data and personal thoughts which Father de Vaux wrote down at important moments of the dig, often after a discovery he considered significant. Their contents were often not included in the typewritten version, but they

[45] For convenient reference these notebooks (*Cahiers*) have been numbered "1" to "8" (excluding notebooks with accounts and with the workers' payroll). One "diary" is from another author than de Vaux (6 pages, concerning the excavation of graves 12 to 19, in March 1953). Having made contact with those of the other excavators who are still alive, we got confirmation that no other such documents can be expected from elsewhere. The notebooks cover all the seasons on both sites. The notes taken during the most important of the Feshkha seasons follow those on the Qumran dig in 1956 (*Cahier 7*) where, from 12/3 onwards, the notes were taken on both sites alternatively. This *Cahier* also holds notes on additional excavations, in the caves and on small sites in the neighborhood; at that stage the notes on the main dig become scarce or nonexistent, although the excavation was still in progress. For details, see the publication, which is nearing completion.

[46] This is *Cahier 9*, in chronological order.

[47] On a copy of notebook "9" we have added references to the coins and other items that were not in the Inventory.

[48] We plan to publish these notebooks *in extenso* making the variations between the different versions manifest. While the volumes of synthesis are still in preparation we intend this as a quick means of providing the concerned scholarly community with a maximum of information on the finds, together with data which will help to understand them in time and space.

[49] Thus locus 7 is commented upon by four lines only, locus 18 by five lines only of which one has but three words. The present remarks are not intended negatively: the conscientiousness with which the great majority of the data were stored is admirable, even in the light of modern methodology; the present remarks are simply meant to show that for any archaeologist who did not personally work on a dig, in this case with Fr. de Vaux who knew the site so excellently, the available data on which that archaeologist has to rely are never totally sufficient and satisfactory.

are of great value for us in understanding his options particularly in matters of chronology and of definition of the character of each locus.[50]

Further documents available are the Inventory register, the photographs of loci and individual finds, the drawings of ground plans, and elevations.

The Inventory Catalogue

The Catalogue or Inventory register was carefully kept from season to season. It numbers four volumes (1951, 1953, 1954, and 1955–1956 seasons) which are type-written, except for the last. The numbering of the finds is continuous throughout all the Khirbet Qumran campaigns, that is from KhQ.1 to KhQ.2673, and the same goes for 'Ain Feshkha.[51] The entries are simple and uniform: two or three short lines of description, two to four measures (according to the type of object), whenever possible a simple drawing at a scale of 2/5, a photographic print,[52] and the place of discovery (almost always with reference to the *loci*, with sometimes a precision, like "north," "centre". . .). At the entry "Level" very few if any indications are given, usually no more than: sup(érieur)," "inf(érieur)," "(près du) fond," "(près du) sol," "interm(édiaire)."[53] The date of discovery figures last, or sometimes it is the date of registration in the case of structures or artefacts which remained on the spot in their locus for some time after their discovery.[54]

Photographs

The photographs were taken systematically by Fr. de Vaux himself. In 1953 he abandoned the heavy system of glass plates, and switched over to a Leica camera and film rolls. His many negatives have been ticketed and

---

[50] Of course the chronological frame elaborated by Fr. de Vaux after the first seasons was considerably corrected by him as the clearing of the site progressed: compare for example his first articles in the *R.B.* and his *Archaeology*; one should not forget also to note a few modifications in his numbering of the loci.

[51] A few cases of double numbering and of omissions have been observed. All the Inventory numbers higher than KhQ.2673 and Fesh.250 which were the last numbers used by the excavation team, are numbers attributed by the publication team, from 1988 onwards.

[52] Usually cut out of a larger sized P.A.M. print, when it existed; the references of these P.A.M. prints are not noted in the Inventory, and we have striven to relocate these so as to have reprints and enlargements made.

[53] It seems that quite a few collaborators worked on these "Catalogues," some of whom must have had difficulties with the French language: some words have to be read phonetically, as a veritable rebus.

[54] The E.B.A.F. has a double file system with a card for each item in the Inventory, carrying an exact copy, drawing included, of the inventory contents; it allows handy manipulations and different classifications of the objects.

marked, conforming to the system that the E.B.A.F. used for its photo archive until a few years ago. Similarly, five "Qumran" albums (numbered 0 to IV), were mounted, which the excavation director annotated carefully; these brief notes concern the topographic localization of the shots and some cross-references between general and detailed views. Needless to say, these albums represent a considerable amount of work and a precious asset for us.[55] One cannot however call it a "coverage" of the excavations, the choice of shots being selective according to what Fr. de Vaux considered important. As we were checking the prints for each locus, a certain number of lacunae appeared; 34 out of the total of 144 loci were never photographed by the excavation team.[56] On the other hand the coverage was very dense for discoveries which might appear to us today of minor interest; they are, however, significant of the excavator's preoccupations: intact jars (Fig. 6), sometimes with the lid still on them, as in the case of loci 10A (for which, however, there is not one shot of the architectural and archaeological context), 13, 22, or 34.

The albums were organized by Father de Vaux so as to leave the left-hand page for the bigger prints made by the P.A.M. on the site during or immediately after the digging.[57] This parallel photographic coverage, the work of Jordanian professionals,[58] includes the objects which were registered by the Museum and had been previously restored.[59] This collection of data is of capital importance for the identification of certain documents that have been (re)broken afterwards or for which there is but an excessively summary drawing in the inventory. To bring it together we have received help from

[55] A total of about 910 "E.B.A.F." photographs exists for the excavations at Khirbet Qumran; some fifteen more were ordered by us for the albums.

[56] For thirteen other loci there is but one shot available. These lacunae do not affect any particular stage or area of the dig, although one can notice that loci 90 to 100 are particularly affected by these voids. The 'Ain Feshkha dossier was not checked for this.

[57] Thanks to this, there are finally but fourteen loci of which we have no photograph at the time of the dig. Other most welcome complements have been the documents from the archives of different visitors to the site at that time, and foremost those sent to Fr. de Vaux by Fr. J. Starcky who visited the site regularly during the campaigns and those of the Mission archéologique belge of the Université catholique de Louvain at Khirbet-Mird/Hyrcania.

[58] The pictures taken in the field usually present the place prepared and cleaned, in view of photographs that would make adequate publication material. In the Museum the objects were photographed on shelves, in glass cases or on the ground, with their written inventory numbers beside them (some errors in the numbers). There were 2 to 22 on each photograph according to their size. Some detailed shots were made, particularly for items bearing inscriptions and graffiti. Total of these P.A.M. studio pictures: 90 for Khirbet Qumran, 11 for 'Ain Feshkha.

[59] There are between 10 and 20 of such photographs from a total of 310 P.A.M. prints of the site and objects from it. It is not always easy to identify their subject in the case of the shots taken in the Museum. They include some important documents such as the print of the limestone block carrying five lines of an inscription painted in black, to which Fr. de Vaux refers (R. DE VAUX, Fouilles au Khirbet Qumran. Rapport préliminaire sur les 3e, 4e et 5e campagnes, in R.B., 63, p. 565; cf. E. M. LAPERROUSAZ, op. cit., p. 200, and n. 1) but which was never mentioned again afterwards.

scholars worldwide as well as from members of the E.B.A.F. itself;[60] this has increased the number of photographic documents from the time of the excavations and immediately after by two whole albums.

Ground Plans, Elevations, Sections

The drawings of ground plans and elevations made in the field during the Khirbet Qumran and 'Ain Feshkha excavations are kept at the Ecole Biblique on tracing paper, prints, and large blue prints. To these have been added a number of documents kept at the D.A.J. in Amman (concerning the restoration season in 1967). A few maps, drawings by some of the team's members, and air photographs of the site and its surroundings to which were added all the sketches (altogether 53) illustrating the text in the diaries, bring the total number of these various and obviously heterogeneous figured documents to 212.[61] Ground plans were constructed during the last season by the Rev. Fr. Couasnon:[62] 5 plans of the site at a scale of 1/100 (115 × 95 cm tracings). These figure in de Vaux's most recent publications.[63] They do not simultaneously represent all the structures discovered, but each sheet represents one period. They are therefore a materialization of how Fr. de Vaux saw the succession of architectural phases (Israelite, Ia, Ib, II and III) combined with the reaction *in situ* of an experienced architect, familiar with the historical buildings of Palestine, even though Fr. Couasnon did not actually take part in the dig for most of the seasons.

Besides these high quality plans, there is another collection of equally

[60] A series of color slides was taken during the 1955 season which has provided a rare polychrome illustration for the clearing of certain loci, which turned out to be extremely precious for the analysis of their stratigraphy, with soil colors changing at a certain level (in locus 130 for example). The acquisition of these slides is owed to Fr. Beauvery and to the friendly collaboration of Fr. Jean-Michel de Tarragon. It also took time and the kind help of the D.A.J. and the Amman Archaeological Museum to identify the Harding photographic archive of which only part was included in the de Vaux albums.

[61] This includes the sketches of certain plans, as well as their clean copies, and, eventually, some reinterpretative drawings that we made of them; also the plans of the buildings discovered in 1956 between Kh. Qumran and 'Ain Feshkha. On the other hand some small drawings already presented on the same page in the excavation diary have been kept together under the same number. An individual number has been given to each proof carrying some variant added by hand, most frequently colors, which seem to have been added after reflection or a discussion on the history of the buildings.

[62] We owe this and many other precious informations to Rev. Fr. Tournay, former Director of the Ecole Biblique, and to Rev. Fr. Romain Rousée who was an active and constant collaborator of de Vaux; we are most thankful to them for their help.

[63] R. DE VAUX, *Archaeology*, pl. III, IV, VI, XVII, XXIII. These plans exist in different presentations: with or without the sketched contour, with cast shadows, with water in the pools, etc. . . One such sheet covers the architectural remains at 'Ain Feshkha (see R. DE VAUX, *Archaeology*, folding pl. XLI).

good plans at the same, 1/100, scale;[64] these bring together all the structures observed, regardless of their relative chronology. They concern only the 1955 season and are limited to the North, West and South peripheral areas of the excavation, going as far as, for instance, the end of the southern terrace. The central core of the site, that is the tower and the buildings inside the big quadrilateral northeastern area, was mapped out several times during the 1951, the 1953 and the beginning of the 1954 seasons; they followed the progress of the archaeological exploration.[65] These are of uneven appearance and quality.[66]

As no large-scale vertical drawing existed, three longitudinal sections were recently made, two running parallel North-South, and one East-West, through all the still-existent structures, cisterns, tower, stairs or walls.[67]

On the other hand there were already a number of limited vertical drawings, that is of walls and sections. They had been brought together on large sheets of paper concerning a common sector.[68] Only some of them were inked in. To allow a uniform presentation of these we proceeded to transcribe them; this presented us with a whole series of difficulties, mainly the absence of reference marks, horizontal and vertical, and lacunae and errors which, with the help of photographs, could be corrected only in the best of cases.[69] However unequal, this documentation, which was made on Fr. de Vaux's re-

[64] The so-called "couverture en 6 feuilles" (numbers 136 to 141 in our system): they were made between 10 Feb. and 6 April 1955 at an intensive rhythm (only one day for some sheets!) and evidently in view of the imminent and definitive closing of the excavation. Indeed the 1956 campaign hardly concerned the site itself, where only loci 38 and 41 and the necropolis were further explored.

[65] These plans too were the result of intensive work. It seems that some of them were finished and even inked in during the year's campaign; a proof was made of them and then directly used and annotated, adding new measures and newly uncovered structures.

[66] They sometimes correct and replace each other. Some are evidently the work of nonprofessionals and show the frequent change in collaborators who were mostly the Ecole's students, of whom very few had some archaeologist's, let alone architect's, training.

[67] We owe the realization of these sections to the friendly collaboration of Mr. Michel Le Paige, ingénieur-architecte at the Service de programmation urbaine of Louvain-la-Neuve. His experience in working on archaeological sites allowed him to carry out this series of longitudinal and cross-sections in only a few days in July 1990 in difficult climatic conditions; the N-S sections run one at the height of cistern 117 and one through locus 30, and the E-W section crosses the tower.

[68] Altogether, there are 62 drawings, not including the sketches in the diaries; however, this distinction between drawings and sketches turns out to be rather arbitrary as a number of the drawings of walls are summary, incomplete or just drafts; in one case it is quite impossible to propose a locality. Their scale is mostly 1/25, sometimes 1/20 or 1/50. Some rare drawings of details are at a 1/10 scale, such as sections of a millstone, a staircase, the wood and plaster cylinder in locus 101, or certain stretches of the wall of Trench A outside the site proper. The scale is generally not indicated and sometimes very difficult to determine.

[69] With the help of Mr. Arnaud Devillers, at the E.B.A.F. in 1987–1988, we have tried to solve the problem of how to present all these, leaving them in their rough shape and just inked in or giving them a uniform treatment (for example in the way the different stratigraphic components are represented in the sections), completing them with the help of the photographs or eventually of the ruins nowadays. Decisions on this subject have been postponed until work starts on the final synthesis.

quest at a time when diggers were still quite unfamiliar with stratigraphical sections, is most precious.

The same can be said of the available horizontal plans of very limited areas, executed at a large scale.[70]

Evidently the number of detailed horizontal and vertical drawings diminished with each campaign.[71] This is most probably not due to an acceleration of work on the site but more likely to the fact that, as the clearing progressed, the excavator was sufficiently confident in his understanding of the main phases in the history of the site. Furthermore, being in possession of a number of clearly readable coins far higher than could have been expected at the time of the first spadefuls of earth, the necessity of multiplying this type of controls must have been less imperative, particularly during the last important campaign in 1955.

The Work in Khirbet Qumran

The present team's survey in Khirbet Qumran itself supplemented the work in the museums and archives; it concentrated on a comparison between the state of the architectural remains at the time of the dig and today and particularly on a systematic description of all the visible structures, which had not been done before.[72] However, after 40 years—including quite a few of invasive touristic visiting, two other excavations, and two restoration campaigns[73]—it soon became evident that not much was left of the original walls

---

[70] Twenty-five of these are known to us: 3 for the "tower," 14 for the main square building (northeastern area of the dig) and 8 for the other buildings.

[71] The quantity of vertical drawings in the loci with a number over 70 (the numbering progressing of course with the excavation) is but 7 out of the 62 drawings mentioned above, and out of these 7 there are 5 for locus 101 alone because its interior disposition, which like so many other rooms of the site suggests some type of handicraft or industrial production activity (never accounted for, however, by the excavators), had probably intrigued Father de Vaux.

[72] Every dossier per "locus" thus includes a report on this subject, as well as its bibliography, list of drawings, of photographs, of objects in or outside the official inventory, quotations from the diaries, publications, etc. No such work can now be done in 'Ain Feshkha given the present state of the ruins.

[73] One under the direction of R. W. Dajjani, as already stated, the second by the new authority. The finds from at least part of Dajjani's work (large round cistern nº 110, samples of clay and of pottery in stratigraphical order) are in Jerusalem. As to the material found by Mr. Steckoll, it was impossible to make out what their fate has been. An inkwell from Qumran in the Haifa University Museum was identified by Mr. Goranson as originating from his campaign. No notes by Mr. Steckoll seem available on the work he did in limited areas, the necropolis in particular. On the contrary, the campaign for which Prof. J.M. Allegro managed to get a permit from the Jordanian authorities, concerned a whole series of soundings, which were undertaken, in loci situated in the whole peripheral area of the site: 57 and 58, 75, 77, 107 and 108, 110, 112, 114 to 119, 126 to 130, 132 to 138, 140 to 142. The help provided by Mr. R. Reich, when in charge of the Archives department of the Rockefeller Museum, allowed us to have access to

and that little could be said about their masonry, plaster and chronology.[74] Many of the more fragile structures have disappeared, such as a series of low earthen partitions on the North of the site of which we have but one drawing[75] or an amazing set of big terracotta vats in workshops loci 115 and 116 which were photographed but never drawn, and many of the various structures in the main "industrial area," that is the west half of the site. The small potters' kiln in locus 84 can no longer be traced, the bigger one in neighboring locus 64 will not survive for more than two or three years,[76] and the kiln in locus 66 will not last very much longer either. All this must be counted as a very serious setback for the architectural synthesis and the general understanding of the site, which is scheduled to follow the publication of the finds.

An additional study is planned for the results of the explorations on *the Khirbet Qumran surroundings*. Together with our most recent information, it will include that provided by the examination of the aerial photographs, that gathered by the excavation team, that of more recent surveys, and that from the unpublished notes of the Belgian Khirbet Mird/Hyrcania excavation team whose activity developed all along the wadis to the West and above the Qumran zone and, particularly, just upstream from the *khirbeh* on the Wadi Qumran.

---

the photographs taken during that campaign; new negatives of them were taken. We owe Prof. John Strugnell, who has helped us in this case as so often before, and Prof. George Brooke, for the positive results in the search for photographs Mr. Allegro seems to have taken and which are kept in Great Britain. While their various finds in the caves seem to have been left in the Jerusalem Museum, those from Qumran were not; but it is difficult to believe that no pottery, for example, was encountered during all that clearing work. On Mr. Allegro's initiative see E. M. LAPER-ROUSAZ, *op. cit.*, p. 14 n. 2; p. 135 n. 4 (with bibliogr.).

[74] Visiting the site in 1971 with Rev. Fr. de Vaux, we took photographs of truly monumental remains, such as the staircase in locus 113, which have totally disappeared today. One wonders what would have remained had it not been for these restoration campaigns. The site is relatively well guarded today in a spirit of collaboration on the part of those responsible and of the guards of various origins.

[75] Loci 134, 140, 141, North of the "tower" and of the site, totally disappeared, some never photographed. The same goes of course for the structures discovered by the Allegro campaign, of which not one plan is known although it must have laid bare many architectural details, again in the North of the site. It must, however, be said that there would be no point for the Ecole Biblique, whose joint concession Khirbet Qumran is, to organize any excavations for any other purpose but to control a point of detail or complete the information on the necropolis. The site can be considered as totally excavated.

[76] We had hoped to have it analyzed for archaeomagnetism though no certain results were guaranteed, given the rare references from previous analyses. Adequate finances lacking, we nonetheless thank Mr. Hesse of the Centre de recherches géophysiques (C.N.R.S., ER 269) in Garchy, Pouilly-sur-Loire, for agreeing in principle to the project. Some twenty samples of plaster and mortar from the walls and floors of different loci and cisterns have been submitted for analysis to the I.R.P.A. in Brussels (see note 25); this is financed by the Belgian F.N.R.S.

SOME WORKING HYPOTHESES AND RESULTS

To illustrate the situation and the methodological problems which we are confronted with, we have chosen to present two cases: that of a find from locus 52 in the southeastern "industrial" or "workshop" area; and that of the plastered so-called "scriptorium" furniture which was found in locus 30 in the *pars urbana* of the settlement, that is the residential or domestic area.

Locus 52 and Its Lamp

The locus 52 case is not exceptional and we could have chosen dozens of other cases in point. It was raised when we came quite by chance upon a complete lamp kept on a collective farm near Khirbet Qumran, this lamp being one of the two most elaborate of the P.A.M. collection, from which it had disappeared. It carries the inventory number KhQ 951 (FIG. 1). The inventory and its card in the system on which the information from the inventory was copied carries the following data for date and place of origin «Locus 52 North, 23/4/1953»; nothing figures in the entry «Level», as is often the case. Comparing this meager piece of information with the list of the 24 other items from this same locus that were recorded in the inventory (not counting the coins) we realize that these are divided between "North," "Centre" and "South"; this means for one thing that "locus 52 North" does not stand for a neighboring locus on that side, as sometimes happens because the dig progresses in that direction with no limits available yet for a new number to be given to a next locus. There are 13 more inventory numbers for items found in "locus 52 North." Among these is a conglomerate of bronze and iron tools and an iron bill-hook, numbered KhQ 960 to 965 which have been treated, separated, and restored;[77] there also were 6 pottery objects, including our lamp, all more or less intact (which was why they were recorded in the inventory), plus a bronze belt-buckle (KhQ 902). Several of these objects are recorded as coming from the "lower level," the metal conglomerate among them. All were discovered on the same day.[78] The lamp may therefore also come from the "lower level"; but did the day's work not start with an upper level? And how were these levels removed, level by level or by vertical cuts?

Out of the total of 144 loci, number 52 is one of the 26 loci for which a drawing of a vertical element was made (FIG. 4). It represents the west face of the eastern wall, but it seems that only part of this eastern wall appears on

---

[77] See THE METAL WARE above.
[78] Apart from KhQ.870 (see below), 8 objects from locus 52 were published, including this lamp (FIG. 7) in *R.B.*, 64, 1954, fig. 1, p. 215 and fig. 3, p. 222–223.

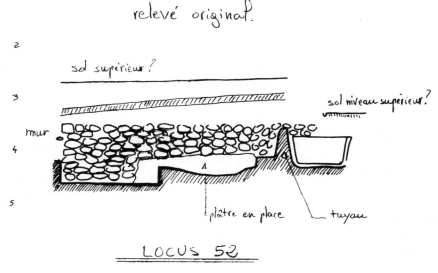

FIGURE 4. Locus 52, section on east side (E.B.A.F. document).

the drawing, and this, unluckily, is the southern part.[79] The only useful indication here seems to be that of a horizontal floor situated quite high up called "sol supérieur" represented by a horizontal line on the left and in the center of the drawing; this, however, seems not to link up with another level called this time "sol niveau supérieur" equally horizontal but more to the south and lower down, on the right. Another guess is the nature of the double line, with hatchings between, which slopes down towards the North under the upper floor.[80]

A careful examination of the room today is disappointing, incredibly so

[79] The sketch carries a 1/50 scale; comparing it with the general plans of the site (for example: R. DE VAUX, *Archaeology*, pl. VI, based on the plan n° 125 of the E.B.A.F. collection) and subsequently with the present state of the remains, one realizes that it does not reach as far as the north end of the wall, at the NW corner. As in several other cases on the site the boundaries between the loci 52 and 53 are unclear inasmuch as they are not clearly indicated by some visible and durable archaeological structure which would justify a topographical separation. The diary simply states, for the 21/4/53: "East of 49 between the N–S drain and the closing wall of the building" (which means without limits on the North), and, concerning locus 53: "Between cistern 49 and the drain closing 52 on the West" (dd. 21/4/53).

[80] It seems to be a layer of ashes which might well have been visible on the photograph PAM 40 389 (our FIG. 5 upper left) and on an EBAF photograph; this is indeed how we have interpreted it when carrying out our new drawing. The document will be submitted to further research before the final synthesis on this area. The present drawing (FIG. 4) is an orthogonal rendering of the original sketch.

when compared with the photographs of the loci during excavation.[81] It is quite impossible today to imagine in three dimensions the hydraulic system and the impressive succession of pits and basins that were there then (FIG. 5). In his *Archaeology and the Dead Sea Scrolls* as well as the *Revue Biblique* (1954) de Vaux describes it as a "washing place with stone basin"; while, for the north part of locus 52 he speaks of "a store-room or a workshop," together with the hypothesis, which he never came back to afterwards, that South of 52 the existence of an arcade could explain the presence of several architectonic fragments found strewn over this sector. None of the photographs shows the lamp, but on one of them (FIG. 6) it is possible to recognize a large jar which was also taken up in the inventory and carries the n° KhQ.870.[82] It is said to have been found in the "intermediary level." We thus know that the finds came from three, and not just two (upper and lower) identifiable levels. As the jar seems to have been found before, we will go as far as saying that this might indicate that the lamp in question came from a lower level. Two unnumbered fragments of lamps equally found in April 1953 in locus 52 are now known to us, but we have no information at all as to the level at which they were found.

The fact that we have three levels here and not just an upper and a lower one makes it clear for us that these levels concern this locus only. Why insist upon this point? Because more often the levels "upper" and "lower" concern the whole site and the two main periods of occupation that were identified (Ib and II).

This question of stratigraphy is presented here not so much for its intrinsic interest but as an illustration of our work, especially as it is nowhere commented upon in the publications.

We will also venture to resituate locus 52 as a whole in both its narrower and wider contexts.

Locus 52 is one of the many loci of the site which may be identified as a workshop. The variety of installations in the western "industrial area" as well as in this south and south-eastern complex is astonishing. The more unusual

[81] The comparison is with photograph EBAF 11783 and with PAM 40 389 which represents a more advanced stage of the excavation. Thirteen photographs, maybe 14, of the time of the dig show locus 52: 6 of these are from the PAM, 2 of the de Vaux photographs represent a close-up of jar KhQ 870, 2 prints are "Harding" photographs and one is a Beauvery slide. The present state of the ruins is so different and the drawing is so summary that we noted for this locus, southern sector, that the drawing of the east wall serves today only for giving an idea of the different levels that could be observed. The tubular channel running N–S which seems to have served for drawing the limit between the *loci* 52 and 53 has disappeared and a boardwalk serving as a visitors' path has brought further damage to this small area.

[82] This jar seems to have been discovered placed before the nook with a neatly plastered surface slightly to the left and behind the measuring rod in print FIG. 6, which is E.B.A.F. 11783, the most recent photograph taken in the locus during its excavation. Does this mean, considering that the jar came from an "intermediary level" according to the inventory, that the lamp which interests us was found at a level not yet reached at the time the other photograph (FIG. 5, PAM 40389) was taken?

FIGURE 5. Locus 52, southeast corner after excavation (photo P.A.M.40389).

FIGURE 6. Locus 52, southeast corner during excavation (photo E.B.A.F.11783).

are a series of high plastered vats of different diameters, all now destroyed, and several shallow pools with a neat mortar and plaster revetment, such as the one in locus 115, which cannot all be identified as decantation pools for the cisterns. There are also several heating installations, among which locus 125, opposite the "tower," suggests the placing of some big round vessel on the upper circle, with the fire below; a neatly plastered surface around the place for the vessel and the same careful treatment of surfaces and pools on the levels behind it, show that the process, whatever it may have been, took place in a remarkably neat, "hygienic" environment.

In our present working hypotheses concerning this area we will underline the great amount of cooking and storage pottery that was found in it, with shapes typical of the Hasmonean and Herodian period. We are also particularly interested in a peculiar type of narrow-necked, round-bellied juglet of medium to small size, which popularizing publications have named "Essenian amphorae." One such juglet was found in a cave in the near vicinity of the site;[83] it still contained a vegetal essence which was quite firmly identified as the now locally extinct balsam.[84]

Other data considered in the frame of these working hypotheses belong to the wider context of the Khirbet Qumran site. Its situation on the edge of the Dead Sea, also called by the ancient geographers the Salt Lake or the Asphalt Lake, "Asphaltites Limne," must be taken into account;[85] the excavations in Engeddi further down the shores of this "Asphalt Lake" have brought to light traces of this industry. Amongst other things, a room containing a number of jars still lined with bitumen was found,[86] which reminded historians and archaeologists alike that the embalming and mummifying of the dead in Egypt was done for millennia with Judean bitumen. We equally know that Alexander Janneus built the fortress of Machaerus on the opposite side of the "Lake" not only as a stronghold in his politics against the Nabateans and the Hellenized cities of the Decapolis but at the same time to control the trade of the Dead Sea bitumen.[87] Flowers, bushes, fruits and

[83] In cave 13, straight North from Qumran in the direction of Jericho.

[84] See J. PATRICH & B. ARUBAS, "A Juglet containing Balsam Oil(?) from a Cave near Qumran" + "Appendix: Analyses of Oil . . ."), in *I.E.J.*, 39 1/2, 1989, pp. 43–59, figs. 4 and 5, color photo in *Le Point*, #859, 6/3/1989, and ultimately in these same *Proceedings* the paper by J. PATRICH, "Khirbet Qumran in the Light of New Archaeological Explorations in the Qumran Caves," pp. 73–95. Chemical analysis of the liquid, which turned white when brought into the open air, determined that it belonged to a now locally extinct species of *Opobalsamon*.

[85] The three names are to be found written on the mosaic map in a church in Madaba, which is a compilation from several ancient geographers, different books of the Bible, *etc.* on the geography of the Holy Land in Byzantine times (M. PICCIRILLO, *Chiese e mosaici di Madaba*, Jerusalem, 1989, p. 83 inscr. n° 20).

[86] B. MAZAR, I. DUNAYEVSKI, T. DOTHAN, in *I.E.J.*, 14, 1964, pp. 121–130, and 17, 1967, pp. 133–143, and IID., *Atiqot*, 5, 1966.

[87] F. ZAYADINE, *Les fortifications pré-helléniques et hellénistiques en Transjordanie et Palestine*, in *Colloque International, Les fortifications dans le monde grec*, CNRS Colloquium 614, dec. 1982, pp. 149–156.

herbs for scents and the perfuming of balms and cosmetics were readily available and could be tended near the site, either in the direction of 'Ain Feshkha, which is a little *villa rustica* also containing an artisans' area, or up towards the Jordan valley and around Jericho, no more than 10 km away, and which, as much as Engeddi, is a site known in connection with the balsam and perfume production in this whole region.

Obviously, when one asks oneself what the economic activity or industry or handicraft at Khirbet Qumran may have been, one cannot overlook these facts—not to mention that quite a few other problematic items from the digs, for which abstruse interpretations have been ventured, could be readily explained when seen in this wider economic context, in which the neighboring sites, with their rich archaeological data, equally fit. However this, again, should be understood as a working hypothesis, no more than a basis for further research, maybe never to become a certainty.

The Plastered Furniture Found in Locus 30

We will end with another find or rather series of finds, this time from the residential area of the site, from room n° 30. Most readers have probably at some time seen pictures of the fragments of plastered furniture which had tumbled down from the first floor of locus 30, together with the ceiling, walls and all. They attracted much attention, were amply photographed and most of all commented upon.[88]

Some of the pieces of this furniture were reinforced with modern plaster; they were set up on wooden stands, in a rather unfortunate (let us say misleading) way that made them look taller than they are.

The drawings that were made by the excavators of the two biggest series of pieces are simple, using average measurements for each of the sides. Two types of shapes predominate: one higher table-like type ("P") (but no more than 50 cm high, which puts it at or below knee-level), and one lower propped-up bench-like type ("O"). Before going into the detail of the other pieces, we want to draw the attention to the plan and sketches that were made of these finds *in situ*. They show that when they were discovered the fragments "O" and "P" were but one continuous piece. De Vaux's draughtsman also made separate drawings of them, because they had come apart, but he indicated the point ("x") where they had joined with a written note: «P se raccorde à O» = «"P" joins with "O"». Restoring this link graphically and materially one finds that the curve at the foot of "P" cannot be too sharply

---

[88] See P. DONCEEL-VOÛTE, "'Coenaculum'—La salle à l'étage du locus 30 à Khirbet Qumran sur la mer Morte," in *Banquets d'Orient, Res Orientales vol. IV*, impr. Peeters, Leuven, 1992, pp. 61–84. 12 figs., for the following paragraphs.

angular—which it certainly was in the presentation of the pieces side by side in the Rockefeller Museum, but which agrees with the set-up in the Amman Archaeological Museum. As the height and weight of the so-called "tables" does not allow a restoration of them in any other position but vertical, there was but one way of restoring the original link between "P" and "O", that was at 90°, the vertical element "P" standing on the other, that is on the bench-like group of pieces which served in fact as a platform and had its oblique side away from the vertical element "P" (and not facing it). Only the edge of this platform was preserved but the amount of plaster and stuccoed revetment fallen between and under and over the identifiable pieces of furniture was considerable. That the Qumran furniture stood near to and against the walls could be inferred from its position in the destruction layers, and also from the length of platform edges available which is near to equivalent to the available length of the "table-like" elements. Moreover some of the vertical elements do not have two long flaring profiles but only one; the other was straight and vertical from the top to the level of the platform, was roughly finished and must therefore have been hidden, that is standing close to the wall.[89]

This new reading of the fragments of furniture takes into account all the excavation data; it is totally satisfying and, in particular, it solves the problem of the stability of the standing elements, as their 18–30 cm wide flaring base of stucco-covered mudbrick is shown to have been anchored deep into the mudbrick and plaster platform.

The longest vertical piece fell along the east wall of locus 30 and measured a little more than 5 meters (FIG. 7). Restoring these two features parallel to and resting against the wall one obtains the picture of a long, low bench on a platform running along it.

Now, any archaeologist of the eastern Mediterranean in the Hellenistic period will recognize the podium running along the walls on which stood the couches in the dining-rooms of common as well as palatial houses. These dining-rooms were called *triclinia* because they usually held three beds or three sets of beds or couches, the *klinai*, with one for every side of a "pi"-shaped podium on which they stood. The couches were usually made out of wood and stood free or anchored on the podiums or in the walls; more rarely, as in Qumran, they were made out of the same material as the podium, that is stone or masonry. These podiums made them stand higher: this was easier for the servants and allowed the diners to get rid of crumbs and bones on the central floor without wasting the fine draperies that were spread over the beds. The generalized custom of washing one's feet before supper was on account

---

[89] The pieces of this more and more fragile furniture in the Rockefeller Museum were quite recently "restored" for an exhibition in Berlin, but they were turned most unhappily into one long element which awkwardly mixes and sticks together the different shapes of couches as if there were but one.

FIGURE 7. Locus 30; part of the plastered furniture, the "P" and "O" type pieces recon-structed, with junction "x": the longest couch and its podium (drawing P.D.-V.).

of the street dust and dirt which one got rid of before lying down and bringing one's legs up on these, often very ornate, fabrics, and next to one's neighbor.

Triclinia can be found, with their "trottoir,"[90] which may be rock-cut just as well as set into marble floors, all over the eastern Mediterranean from Eritria to Alexandria, Petra, Jericho or the Herodion near Bethlehem.

A constant feature is the view and good ventilation these dining-rooms enjoyed: however luxurious or modest, their couches were so set that they opened up onto some kind of landscape: a small inside courtyard in Pompei, the sophisticated "hanging garden" in the Herodion or the scenery of the Wadi Qelt with the garden and landscape architecture on the opposite bank in Jericho.

Another element not to be overlooked is the little rise in the surface of the straight-backed bed found in Qumran: it is the low rest on or against which cushions were propped up for the left elbow to weigh on. The rise in the plaster surface had been seen and drawn by de Vaux's draughtsman, slightly more curved than what is left of it today.[91] He also drew a piece of the other type of couches, flaring on all sides, this time with a transverse ledge; this we propose to read as the separation which, between two diners, served to stop the second diner's cushion from sliding. A third type of rest seems to have gone unnoticed by the team's draughtsman though it is visible on the excavation photographs and found its way, only half complete, to the P.A.M., though without inventory number: it is a thin and somewhat higher rest, which looks more like a traditional head of a bed, the *fulcrum* of the Greeks and Romans.

A last, most interesting piece of stuccoed furniture is the low stand, with two compartments, in each of which is a rounded hollow.[92] Still attached to

---

[90] "Trottoir" is the term favored by the English-speaking archaeologists for the long podium.

[91] This piece is standing at the end of the row of furniture as it was set up and photo-graphed for R. DE VAUX, *Archaeology*, pl. XXI, a; the detail of the little rise is however not very visible. Detailed drawings were made by us of every fragment of plastered furniture in the Amman and Jerusalem museums; for precise drawings of the main pieces in discussion here see my article cited in note 88, figs. 4, 5, 6, 7, 9. All fragments will be taken up and illustrated in the publication catalogue of the stuccoed objects, see above THE ARTEFACTS OF VEGETABLE, ANIMAL AND OTHER MATERIALS, page 14.

[92] See R. DE VAUX, *Archaeology*, pl. XXI, b.

FIGURE 8. Banquet scene with two diners on the *kline*, wine-stand carrying two vessels, and attendant; relief from Thasos (J.M. Dentzer, R.321).

it are fragments of the plastered wall and floor against and on which it was built. Should one hesitate as to whether the room was used for sleeping or dining, this solves the dilemma: it can only be interpreted as the stand for the amphora which again and again appears on all the banquet scenes in ancient relief sculpture (FIG. 8).[93] The two hollows are meant especially for round-based footless amphorae; but they can be used for vessels with a small foot such as on the most common cylindrical type found by the dozen in the Qumran dig, as well as in the caves and in the storage areas of the Jerusalem town houses, while amphorae of a somewhat squatter rounder-bellied type are particularly stable on this stand.

Concerning the fact that the dining-room was on the first rather than the ground floor it should be remembered that this distribution of rooms and functions inside a building was so common around the Mediterranean, placing the room for supper (called *cena*) in the upper floors, that in the Roman world the name for the upper floors was simply "coenaculum." So there was nothing special in the fact that Jesus-Christ and his disciples had supper in an "upper room" the "hyperôon" of the Greek New Testament. In Pompei the inscriptions on the street facades advertise upper rooms (*coenacula*) to let. Moreover, housing around the Mediterranean and the Red Sea has always been, was then, and still is, on several floors, with the ground-floor used mainly for entrance and for storage facilities, be it of food, of tools or of water

---

[93] See J. M. DENTZER, *Le Motif du banquet couché dans le Proche-Orient et le monde grec du VIIe au IVe siècle avant J.-C.*, Rome, 1982.

(with pertinent distribution systems), or for the animals. Family and social life, on the other hand, took place in the cleaner and better ventilated upper floors.

Before leaving this subject a word must be said about the inkwells which were among the finds in locus 30 and which received a great deal of attention. They were not the only inkwells found on the site and inkwells have been found in many a contemporary town house excavated, for example, in Jerusalem.

However we will here concentrate on one point only, their relation to the stuccoed furniture: it turns out that there was none. The inventory reads as follows: «Inv. n°. 436; cylindrical inkwell; bronze; date of discovery 18/3/1953; locus 30; middle, *on the floor* = "sur le sol"»; and «Inv. n° KhQ.473: cylindrical inkwell, pottery; date of discovery 21/3/1953; locus 30, middle, *on the floor* = "sur le sol"». Indeed, the ceiling had burnt and fallen over the ground-floor and its contents, the inkwells amongst others, forming over it a thick level which contained the stuccoed floor and furniture; one can make out that this thick level and the stuccoed pieces lay sloping between 20 and 50 cm above the ground floor pavement. All these destruction layers were then buried under a new occupational stratum (contemporary with Qumran level III) which reorganized the space still determined by the upper part of the walls of room 30 into four smaller spaces.

With this identification as a whole we need have no pangs of conscience vis-à-vis the memory of Rev. Fr. de Vaux. Indeed this is one of those instances for which the comparison between his hand-written "Carnet de fouilles" and his typewritten and then published readings of the remains are most instructive as you move from one to the next and the other, with time and with hypotheses being here and there turned into statements. In his *Archaeology and the Dead Sea Scrolls*[94] he very clearly describes the furniture as having «fallen from the upper floor where the long "table" had been set up parallel to the eastern wall; they had been used there in association with a low bench fixed to this wall». In his typewritten report he suggested the furniture might have been standing «sur une sorte d'estrade» that is «on some kind of podium» and from the start he had been tempted to read the upstairs room as a dining-room, an idea he abandoned for reasons foreign to the find itself.[95]

⸻

With these first results we think we can be confident that by analyzing all the information that we have inherited from Father de Vaux and his team and by combining and confronting it with knowledge built up in the decades since

---

[94] R. DE VAUX, *Archaeology*, p. 29. However it should be underlined that the words "table" and "bench" are, even there, written within quotation marks, indicating a hesitation as to their identity.

[95] See P. DONCEEL-VOÛTE, *"Coenaculum . . ."*.

then, it will be possible to reappraise the Ruins of Qumran in the historical context of the late Hellenistic and early Roman era in Palestine they belong to and from which the world of historical and archaeological science and research has segregated them for too long.

DISCUSSION OF THE PAPER

CHAIRMAN ERIC MEYERS (*Duke University, Durham, NC*):   The Steering Committee has recommended that we slightly adjust our schedule to accommodate some discussion on this information which has come, at least to me, mostly for the first time. And, maybe we can break after that and have questions directed to Dr. Donceel-Voûte now. I might begin by saying à propos of our discussion on issues this afternoon regarding access, that the fact that it has taken 40 years to see this comes as a bit of a surprise and shock. And, spinning so many theories without having access to this material (some of which is in Belgium now) and not having been allowed to see it in the École (although I must say Emile Puech had taken me to see some of this), makes a lot of things so much more difficult. Maybe you could just comment briefly on why it's been so difficult to see this material? For example, you say the Jericho material is not available. I could take you to the Hebrew University and show you that. Anybody who has wanted to see the Jericho pottery could see it all these years; a master's thesis was done on it and anybody could see it.

PAULINE DONCEEL-VOÛTE (*Université catholique de Louvain at Louvain-La-Neuve, Belgium*):   I didn't say it wasn't available. I said it was not published.

MEYERS: But, you referred to it as if you couldn't use it, but anybody can look at that stuff.

DONCEEL-VOÛTE: We have seen it with no problem.

MEYERS: Okay. Maybe you want to comment on this matter of the difficulty in seeing your material.

DONCEEL-VOÛTE: When we arrived to work on the publication we only knew about the inventoried material. A small number of objects belong to the Ecole, to which a number of listed fragments had been brought recently for restoration and study. The rest was all (supposed to be) in the P.A.M.-Rockefeller Museum. It came as a shock to us, after a year or so, to find out that the Museum also kept those boxes and boxes of material that were not on the official, main inventory; the material was in boxes and bags marked per locus, in which everything was kept together: glass, metal, stoneware, *etc*. We had started on a very tight schedule, as the Ecole had asked us to come for only one year; we spent three years there, because of this quantity of unexpected, uninventoried material. There are a few things which are exhibited in the Rockefeller Museum, but the vast majority of the Qumran and Feshkha material is in the downstairs storage area, near the "Scrollery." Only a few pottery objects are in the Ecole Biblique museum, which anyone can look at if they want. I am absolutely not responsible, nor is Dr. Robert Donceel, for the museum of the Ecole Biblique. Some of the funds which had to go into our research have gone into installing that museum.

MEYERS: What's in Belgium now?

DONCEEL-VOÛTE: Only the glass and some wood which are being analyzed and repaired, and they will go back systematically.

MEYERS: One further question about the enormous loss of material that has occurred. It is rather shocking to me that so many coins and key data that would be critical for the reconstruction of certain levels have just disappeared. It blows my mind, frankly.

DONCEEL-VOÛTE: The coins you saw, which were part of the main hoard, are now in the Smithsonian Institution: they are the three silver coins that were given by King Hussein to President Nixon.

MEYERS: So you know where the lost material is?

DONCEEL-VOÛTE: Of the big hoard of silver coins most have been traced. The traveling exhibition in 1964–65 was a drama, because most objects came from the Rockefeller Museum but not the coins; those came from the Amman Museum. But 30 coins went back to the Rockefeller Museum and never came back to the Amman Museum.

MEYERS: What about the 5/7ths of the Spÿkerman material which are still missing?

DONCEEL-VOÛTE: We still don't know, though we have been looking everywhere. The strange thing is that for antique dealers they are not interesting. Excavation coins look terrible: they are hardly readable, they are not collection pieces. So it is very difficult to understand where they have gone. But there has been a war since then and so many upheavals. As long as things are not clear in this occupied territory we will have a difficult situation. Maybe they were "lent" to some collection, like other items, the elaborate molded lamps I reported on, for example. Though this is material which was dug up in Jordan by the French Ecole Biblique and the Jordanian Department of Antiquities.

JOHN COLLINS (*Divinity School, University of Chicago, Chicago, IL*): Do you have any comment on the shape of the structure as a whole? And, is there any light to be thrown on that from an analogy in the Eastern Mediterranean? Also, you've mentioned in your talk a residential area. Is it your working hypothesis that people lived in the site rather than in caves as we had sometimes been told?

DONCEEL-VOÛTE: One must place any hypothesis in the general context of archaeological research in the Near East. With the finding of the scrolls

Qumran archaeology just seems to have stopped. In the meantime things have progressed enormously in the neighboring countries. We know a lot more about housing in the Hellenistic-Roman Mediterranean and Near East, be it on the subject of the general lay-out or of living on the upper floors for example. Both the Qumran and Ain Feshkha plans, which are closely akin, are now much more easily readable, with the square residential area, with their twin main doors and the corner tower on one side of the Qumran settlement, while the workshops, water-reservoirs and further utilitarian areas are around it, on the South and on the West.

MEYERS: I might just demure about the lack of knowledge about houses in Israel during the Roman period. We know a great deal about this. Many things are published and may not be exactly parallel, but we know a great deal about Roman housing in the early Roman period.

DONCEEL-VOÛTE: Yes, there have been a lot of excavations, in Jerusalem or South of Mount Carmel, for example, that offer very good parallels, but they just have never been used for Qumran. That's what I want to insist upon.

ROBERT EISENMAN (*California State University, Long Beach*): I'm just surprised, Eric, that you're surprised or shocked by this information. We've been worrying about this for years. The coin data, as many will understand, is the basis of the chronology at Qumran. In my book *Maccabees, Christians and Qumran*, where I examined in detail the archaeological evidence, I asked for re-examination of the coin data. I felt this was extremely important. I, myself, in the 10 years since that book, have tried to locate some of the coins, and have found the same frustration that you have evidenced here. Now, I think I lose complete hope in ever being able to re-examine the coin data from Qumran in any kind of systematic way.

You mentioned stratigraphy. In that book, too, I call in question the stratigraphy of Qumran, and the exactness with which it was being done. I'm more shocked than I was before to hear what you're saying.

More generally speaking, there was one point I did want to make. When some people destroyed those people who were involved in the Zealot hypothesis, the argument raised particularly by Frank Moore Cross of Harvard was that Roth and Driver had "the unfortunate misfortune to come up against the greatest archaeologist of our age, Roland de Vaux." That was an exact quote from him, and I quoted that in *Maccabees*. That was taken as proof positive the Zealot people couldn't be right in any of their hypothesizing.

I think what we're hearing today might lead people to re-examine some of the early questions that were being raised in the 1950s.

I do want to say finally that we at Cal State, Long Beach, have had an expedition out in the field for three years. We have been doing surveys of the area. It is our feeling that this site was integrated in a general way into a lot of habitation all along the Dead Sea.

We have surveyed 40 kilometers south of Qumran. We have been in and out of a lot of the areas. We have felt that the wharf-like installation some 4–5 kilometers further down is part of this whole activity area. We have questioned the idea that Qumran is an isolated monastic community very strenuously. We also were involved in a radar ground scan of the area.

To add to some of the questions that you have raised here, one of the interesting points of the radar ground scan of the Qumran plateau was that we found a lot of signatures of material that had not been excavated yet. We could provide the loci for those. We found a whole water complex that had not been excavated yet. We found materials underneath the tower that had not been excavated yet. Interesting things like that.

Most interesting for our purposes was evidence that the whole earthquake hypothesis that Professor de Vaux had circulated in the late 1950s and early 1960s was not founded on the reality of the site. The radar ground scan seemed to be indicating that what he considered to be an earthquake fault in one of the stairwells was simply a local subsidence of ground. There was no signature of an earthquake fault at Qumran.

DONCEEL-VOÛTE: I hope you are going to publish your finds. And you know it is not really officially allowed to be working in that area. That is why I want to remind you that there were two other digs done in Qumran by Dr. Steckoll and Dr. Allegro. There is not one note left of that. The lost evidence is what makes our work so difficult.

MEYERS: This gets amazinger and amazinger.

DONCEEL-VOÛTE: What de Vaux published is better than 90% of the archaeologists of his time. So we shouldn't be too negative.

LENA CANSDALE (*University of Sydney, Cremorne, N.S.W., Australia*): Thank you very much for the most interesting talk. My questions also refer to an article which your husband published in the *Revue Biblique*. Three very small questions which I would love to know the answers to.

Were you able to find the source of the clay that was used in the potteries in Qumran? Question one.

Question two: Is there any possibility that the glass came from a dump of glass? (Prof.) Avigad, I think, has published glass which he found in Jerusalem, which was both blown and molded.

Question three: what do the agricultural implements tell us? What agriculture was possible near Qumran?

DONCEEL-VOÛTE: For the origin of the Qumran pottery clay we surveyed North, West and South and a few very useful clay strata have been found, especially upstream on the Wadi Qumran. We must however have Qumran pottery sherds similarly analyzed before we come to conclusions.

Next, the glass. If you remember, the Avigad finds had two very different types of raw material. They were those long rods of glass and, secondly, the same type of lumps as the ones found at Qumran. They are not just broken pieces.

Most of the glass vessel fragments are in a terrible state and had to be restored; the glass flaked off, layer by layer.

MEYERS: You're saying that they are wasters, then, and that there was a local glass industry at Qumran?

DONCEEL-VOÛTE: Yes, that's what I said. And, the last one was . . .

CANSDALE: The agriculture . . .

DONCEEL-VOÛTE: I return to the working hypothesis I spoke about. It refers to other finds. To the northeast of the palaces in Jericho a very interesting industrial area has been discovered, which links up in many ways with the one in Khirbet Qumran. There is the discovery of the balsam juglet, about which Joseph Patrich will be talking. There was a rich production of date-palms, just as today, which my husband has already underlined elsewhere. I certainly propose balsam and other resinous, odoriferous shrubs and such, which were used in combination with the Dead Sea asphalt which served to fix the fragrances.

JAMES CHARLESWORTH (*Princeton Theological Seminary, Princeton, NJ*): On one of your early slides, you showed us cases 4, 5, 6, 7, 8, 9, and 10, which you call Hellenistic glasswork. I find that hard to believe.

Number two, the tremendous hydraulic system at Qumran is well known. It is quite unlike anything we've seen. We have to analyze that, and bring that into any kind of synthesis.

The ostracon we have, with a person working on the alphabet, seems to make some sense for somebody who is going to do some writing. I think we need to look at that.

When you say that inkwells are found everywhere, I don't know that that's the case. I would like to be informed of that. Inkwells are rather peculiar and unique. I haven't found them in many places.

When you say that the glass is rather unusual, if you want to come to my office, I'll show you a whole stack of glass. Some of them are purple, which you say is very rare. Come in and I'll show you some. And, this is really from Jerusalem, from the first century.

I get the impression you are an excavator of an excavator's collection. I need to really find out, are you sure the stuff is from Qumran? Because I knew de Vaux had excavated many places, and as you well said, the stuff is not in inventory. So, how can you say it's from Qumran?

When you say that you can look at New Testament Jericho to help explain Qumran, it is the absolute opposite. When you go to Jericho, New Testament Jericho, the stones are so beautifully chiseled and carefully placed. An aristocrat, a very gifted builder has built that. When you go down to Qumran, I could do a better job. It is terrible. It is just one stone upon another. So I don't think this is an architect that's built it.

And, I think you confuse stages of Qumran. Obviously, for most of us—I think it's a consensus—the final stage is a Roman group, Roman soldiers.

When I was living in Israel in the 1960s, there was a latrine there. You can't find that anymore. You've got to go back to some of the early material.

I really want to push you on one thing. Stone vessels are very important, extremely important. We really didn't know much about them until about the last 10 years. We're finding them in the upper city of Jerusalem.

How do you know these are from Qumran, the stone vessels? And, where are they now, so I can study them?

DONCEEL-VOÛTE: I've never said Qumran was a beautifully built place. I only want to stress points which will show that it does not have the ascetic simplicity that it was supposed to have. It is absolutely certain that the glass and stone material you mention comes from there. Many pieces are in the main inventory and they have their numbers written on them; those pieces that were not in the main inventory and do not, therefore, carry an individual inventory number come from boxes and bags which carry a Khirbet Qumran locus number. Of course purple glass has been found elsewhere, but it is the least frequent color; it is expensive to produce because of the category of metal oxides that go into it.

I showed you these because to us they came as an enormous surprise. We were expecting to find what you all know, which is what we knew and no more. That is why I understand that all these unpublished small finds and all this rather luxurious material is as astonishing for you. Maybe I did insist on the luxury; of course it does not stand up to that of the palaces in Jericho.

CHARLESWORTH: And they are now at the E.B.A.F.?

DONCEEL-VOÛTE: Some of them were, for the purpose of study. But they all belong and have returned to the P.A.M./Rockefeller Museum. The nice chip-cut tureen from Feshkha was not brought to the E.B.A.F. for restoration and is now in five pieces.

During the second period of our work, on the fragments outside the main inventory, we met with another type of surprise. The largest piece of one of the, handsome, fluted urns, that I showed you, which carried an individual inventory number, was found to match and could be glued together with a piece from one of the "per locus" boxes. What was incredible is that the two pieces came from two loci more than 20 meters distant from each other. Similar unexpected links were subsequently observed. They will have to be taken into account for the general synthesis on the history of the site.

JAMES VANDERKAM (*University of Notre Dame, Notre Dame, IN*): Thank you for your paper. Two quick points. One, the terms "monastic simplicity" that you used, the two don't necessarily go together—I know. (laughter)

DONCEEL-VOÛTE: I was quoting, definitely quoting!

VANDERKAM: Okay. The more important point. You mentioned so many items having disappeared from the Qumran site that are not available anymore. Is this a highly unusual percentage of lost objects, or is this rather typical of digs from that age.

DONCEEL-VOÛTE: Absolutely. It is terrible to work on an old dig and on somebody else's excavations. Dr. Robert Donceel already had a solid experience in this type of enterprise and therefore agreed to help publish the final reports on Qumran.

Actually when you compare Qumran to other old digs, the amount of information that is available from the de Vaux seasons, notes, photographs, drawings, plans, *etc.*, is really quite reasonable and very good for his time. Subsequent events are more to blame than the excavator.

MEYERS: I think we might discuss that later. Having cleaned the Albright roof a number of times of old digs, it is surprising how well a lot of this material has survived 40–50 years. I think there is an unusually high loss of material here, and I think part of the reality is that politics have come into play, and the wars, and moving around. When you move the lots around, a lot of stuff can get lost, and apparently has. When they stay in place, the loss of material is far less.

The Community at Qumran in Light of Its Pottery

JODI MAGNESS

Department of Classics
Tufts University
321 Eaton Hall
Medford, Massachusetts 02155

Since its publication by R. de Vaux, the pottery from Qumran has served as a lynch-pin for Palestinian ceramic typology and chronology of the Hasmonean and Herodian periods. Many of the types from Qumran are illustrated in Paul Lapp's landmark handbook, *Palestinian Ceramic Chronology 200 B.C.–A.D. 70* (1961). The primary importance of this material is that it consists of assemblages of whole or restorable vessels from well-dated stratigraphic contexts. However, its value for purposes that are not strictly typological or chronological has been largely overlooked. In this paper, the ceramic corpus from Qumran will be examined with regard to the light it sheds on the character of the community that lived there. This will be accomplished by considering the internal composition of the corpus, and by comparing it with contemporary assemblages from other Judean sites such as Jerusalem, Jericho, and Herodion. This study is especially timely because a great deal of new material has been published from excavations in recent years. These include the excavations of E. Netzer at Herodion (1981), E. Netzer and E. M. Meyers at Jericho (1977), and the excavations and surveys of P. Bar-Adon at 'Ein el-Ghuweir and other sites along the northwestern shore of the Dead Sea (1977; 1989). The final (and, hopefully, forthcoming) publication of the pottery from N. Avigad's excavations in the Jewish Quarter of Jerusalem and Y. Yadin's excavations at Masada will contribute much to the comparanda.

This discussion is based entirely on a consideration of published material. Most of it comes from the site and caves at Qumran, though some of the pottery from the site at Ein Feshkha is also considered. The majority of the published types appear to date to the first century B.C.E. and first century C.E. (Qumran Strata Ib and II). Some of the first century B.C.E. (Stratum Ib) types extend back into the second century, but these subtle chronological distinctions will not be discussed here.

The only ceramic material from the site of Qumran published by de Vaux is illustrated in his preliminary reports on the excavations (1953; 1954; 1956). Some of the pottery from the caves is illustrated in the *Discoveries in the Judean*

Desert series (de Vaux 1955; de Vaux 1962; de Vaux 1977). Examples of the types found at Ein Feshkha appear elsewhere (de Vaux 1959). De Vaux reviewed and synthesized much of this information in *Archaeology and the Dead Sea Scrolls* (1973). Because these are only preliminary reports, there is no basis for determining how much pottery is still unpublished. There is also no basis for determining how representative of the entire corpus these types are, and whether examples of all of the types found at the site are published. However, Dr. Humbert repeated to me de Vaux's observation that the corpus is monotonous, limited, and very repetitive (de Vaux 1973: 17). He assured me that de Vaux published at least one or two examples of each type. With a few minor exceptions, this appears to be true of the material I examined in the basement of the Rockefeller Museum.

Most of the ceramic types found at the site of Qumran consist of cups, bowls, plates, cooking pots, jars, jugs, juglets, flasks, lids, and oil lamps. According to de Vaux, the pottery from the caves is identical with that from the site, except that it is more limited in repertoire (1973: 52, 54–55). The vessels tend to be made of smooth, well-levigated clay and have relatively thin, hard-fired walls. The clay is usually pink, red, or grey in color, and there is often a whitish slip covering the exterior. The potters' workshop discovered by de Vaux at the site indicates that at least some of the vessels were manufactured there (de Vaux 1973: 16–17). Unfortunately, petrographic analyses to determine exactly which pieces and types were made at the site have yet to be published.[1] My impression from the published descriptions and from personal observation is that most of the material found at Qumran was produced locally; although many of the types are morphologically similar to those from other Judean sites, the vessels I examined from the Jewish Quarter differ in fabric and surface treatment. The vessels from the Jewish Quarter are made of the light orange, light brown, or orange-brown fabric characteristic of Jerusalem during the Roman and Byzantine periods. They are sometimes covered with a whitish slip like that common at Qumran, but many also have a drippy red, brown, or red-brown paint or slip that is rare at Qumran.

The types of vessels found at the site of Qumran reflect the activities carried out there. The inhabitants drank out of the cups and ate from the plates and bowls. Kraters were probably used for the mixing of wine or other liquids, and cooking pots were used in the preparation of food. Jugs, juglets, and flasks served as containers or servers for water, oil or other liquids. Large jars were used for the storage of goods such as grain and oil. Oil lamps illuminated the interiors of rooms and caves.

How does this corpus compare with contemporary assemblages from

[1] Neutron activation analysis has indicated that the vessels from Qumran and 'Ein el-Ghuweir are made from different clays (see Broshi 1991: 62). I am grateful to J. Patrich for bringing this reference to my attention.

other Judean sites? Let us begin by considering those types unique to Qumran, or at least rare elsewhere. The best-known examples of such a type are the "scroll jars," so-called because some of the scrolls found in the caves were stored in them. Although de Vaux distinguished a number of sub-types (1962: 13–14), they are characterized in general by their elongated, cylindrical body, carinated shoulder, short, vertical neck, and plain rim. Most of them have ring bases and are handleless or have ledge handles. They were often covered with a bowl-shaped lid (de Vaux 1962: 14). The presence of "scroll jars" at the site of Qumran indicates that they probably also served as containers for materials other than scrolls (see, for example, de Vaux 1954: 217; de Vaux 1973: 54–55). However, the elongated, cylindrical form of the body suggests to me that these jars were originally designed to hold scrolls. The short, wide neck would have made it possible to deposit and remove scrolls easily from the jars. By way of contrast, the typical Judean storage jars of this period, which are also represented at Qumran, have a sack-shaped body, rounded base, constricted neck, and ring handles on the shoulders (see, for example, de Vaux 1953: Fig. 2:1, 3, 6). Aside from the site and caves at Qumran, the only two published examples of "scroll jars" known to me come from New Testament Jericho (Kelso and Baramki 1955: Pl. 23:A115) and Quailba near Abila (see de Vaux 1973: 54–55, footnote 1). The lids associated with the "scroll jars," which usually have the shape of a carinated bowl with a ring base, are also rare at other sites in Judea (see de Vaux 1962: 14; Lapp 1961: 181).

Another ceramic type found almost exclusively at Qumran, apparently in Stratum Ib, is a delicate cup or bowl with a flaring rim ("cyma profile") and ring base (Lapp 1961: 175, Type 51.8). At least one example is burnished, but most are covered with the usual whitish slip. The few published parallels include examples from Ramat Rahel (Aharoni 1962: Fig. 6:11) and Herodion (Bar-Nathan 1981: 63; Figs. 6:30–33; 10:25), though those from Herodion often have a drippy red or brown slip over the rim.

Among the types characteristic of the Qumran corpus are peculiar oil lamps of clearly Hellenistic inspiration (Lapp 1961: 196, Type 84). Since they occur only in Stratum Ib at the site, they should be assigned mainly to the late second to first centuries B.C.E. (see, for example, de Vaux 1956: Fig. 1:1–4). Examples also come from the caves (de Vaux 1955: Fig. 3:4, 5). In his discussion of the type, de Vaux noted that the closest parallels are found at sites outside Palestine, where they are dated mainly to the second and first centuries B.C.E. Among the parallels he cited are Corinth Type XVIII, Antioch Type 17, and Delos Group III (de Vaux 1955: 11). However, as de Vaux noted, the Hellenistic parallels are mold-made, have decoration in relief, and are covered with a black slip or glaze. The Qumran lamps are wheel-made, plain, and unslipped, although the grey color of their clay may have been inspired by the black slip.

It is thus possible to distinguish a number of ceramic types characteristic of the Qumran corpus that are rare or unattested elsewhere. It is now necessary to consider those types found at contemporary sites in Judea that are rare or unattested at Qumran. Most conspicuous by their apparent absence at Qumran are imports of any kind. There are no published examples of western terra sigillata, amphoras, or Roman mold-made lamps. Western terra sigillata was among the finest tableware of the first century C.E., while amphoras carried wine from around the Mediterranean. Of course, many of the inhabitants of Judea during the first century C.E. preferred the locally produced, plain, wheel-made "Herodian" oil lamps to the mold-made Roman ones, which often bore figured decoration on the discus. "Herodian" oil lamps are, in fact, characteristic of Stratum II at Qumran (de Vaux 1953: Fig. 3:4; de Vaux 1954: Fig. 4:8; de Vaux 1956: Fig. 4:14; for examples from the caves see de Vaux 1962: Fig. 5:2, 5, 6), apparently replacing the peculiar oil lamps of Hellenistic inspiration. Although not found in abundance, examples of western terra sigillata, imported amphoras, and Roman mold-made oil lamps are attested from Jericho (Kelso and Baramki 1955: 24, footnote 24 [western terra sigillata]; 31 [stamped amphora handle]; Fig. 25:A409 [amphora handle]; 24, Type 1 [description of a Roman oil lamp]; Netzer and Meyers 1977: Fig. 9:8 [amphora]), Herodion (Bar-Nathan 1981: 64–66; Pls. 1:16; 6:21 [western terra sigillata]; Pl. 8:6, 7 [Roman oil lamps]; Pls. 1:11, 12; 4:1, 2, 4–6; 10:1–3 [amphoras]; also note the Pompeian Red Ware in Pls. 1:17; 6:34–36), and sites in Jerusalem (see, for example, Tushingham 1985: 184; Figs. 55–58 [western terra sigillata]; 55; Figs. 21:42, 43; 22:1, 3, 4; 23:37 [amphoras]; 55; Figs. 22:5; 24:13 [Roman oil lamps]; Avigad 1980: Figs. 57, 69, 249 [amphoras]; Fig. 232 ["Megarian bowl"]; Fig. 252 [Roman oil lamp]). Amphoras are also found at the site of Qasr el-Yahud (Kh. Mazin), located at the point where the Kidron Valley empties into the Dead Sea (Bar-Adon 1989: Fig. 21:C:21–23). The absence of these types from the corpus at Qumran, combined with their presence at other sites in the area, suggests that the inhabitants could have obtained these items but deliberately refrained from doing so. Since these imports represent luxury items, their absence may also be due to financial considerations. In this context it is worth noting that Jericho and Herodion are the sites of King Herod's palaces, while the Jewish Quarter in Jerusalem appears to have served as the residential quarter for the upper classes of Herodian Jerusalem.

Much more suggestive than the lack of imports is the apparent absence of Eastern Sigillata A from the corpus at Qumran. Eastern Sigillata A was the locally produced, red-slipped fine table ware of the first century B.C.E. and first century C.E. (especially during the Herodian period). It is much more common at sites throughout Palestine than western terra sigillata (see the discussion in Hayes 1985: 183–184; for examples from Jericho see Kelso and Baramki 1955: 24, Type 1; for examples from Herodion see Bar-Nathan 1981:

64). Complete sets of Eastern Sigillata A dishes including plates, bowls, and jugs have been discovered in the Herodian houses in the Jewish Quarter (see for example Avigad 1980: Figs. 75, 230). No examples of Eastern Sigillata A have been published from Qumran, though, according to Dr. Humbert, a few fragments were recovered. The absence or rarity of this ware from the corpus at Qumran is much more suggestive than the absence of imports, as Eastern Sigillata A would have been cheaper and easier to obtain. On the other hand, there is at least one class of bowls from Qumran which appears to have been inspired by Eastern Sigillata A (see de Vaux 1953: Fig. 4:5; de Vaux 1954: Fig. 4:2; de Vaux 1956: Fig. 5:4; Lapp 1961: 180, Type 54.2). These bowls are relatively broad and shallow, and have strongly carinated walls. At the point of carination there is a sharp ridge, above which the rest of the wall rises vertically to the rim. The base is usually a disc. They are made of the local Qumran red, pink, or grey ware, sometimes with a whitish slip. At Qumran all the bowls of this type come from Stratum II. They are clearly related in form to a type of Eastern Sigillata A bowl dated by Hayes from *ca.* 50 to 70 c.e. (1985: Figs. 52:26–27; 53:1–4, 6). Another bowl from Ein Feshkha which appears to be locally made may also have been inspired by Eastern Sigillata A (de Vaux 1959: Fig. 2:10). Its rouletted decoration is otherwise un-attested in the published assemblages from Qumran, Ein Feshkha, and Ein el-Ghuweir. Like the peculiar oil lamps of Hellenistic inspiration, these imi-tation Eastern Sigillata A bowls reflect outside influence and seem to be char-acteristic of Qumran. This is an important point because it means that the inhabitants (or at least the potters) at Qumran were not isolated from contem-porary ceramic trends in Palestine and the eastern Mediterranean. However, they apparently preferred to manufacture and use their own imitations of these types.

"Pseudo-Nabataean" ware or "painted Jerusalem bowls" also appear to be unattested at Qumran, though one example is published from Ein Feshkha (de Vaux 1959: Fig. 2:7). These are delicate, thin-walled bowls decorated on the interior with red, brown, or black painted floral designs (see Avigad 1980: 185). Scientific analyses have demonstrated that Jerusalem was the center for the production of this ware (Perlman, Gunneweg, and Yellin 1986). Most of these bowls have been found at sites in Judea, in contexts dating mainly to the first century c.e. Published examples come from Jerusalem (Avigad 1980: Figs. 115, 201; Tushingham 1985: Fig. 20:36), Jericho (see Bar-Nathan 1981: 63 for a reference to unpublished fragments from Netzer's excavations at Jericho), Herodion and Masada (Bar-Nathan 1981: 62–63; she refers here to unpublished examples from Masada), and Avdat (see Perlman, Gunneweg, and Yellin 1986).

Painted decoration is common on other types of first century c.e. vessels from Jerusalem (see for example Avigad 1980: Figs. 211, 214; Tushingham 1985: Figs. 23:14, 18; 24:23; 25:1–3). The red or brown paint is usually applied unevenly, with drips, over the rim or base. Sometimes it is found over a whitish slip which, as at Qumran, covers the entire vessel. The paint occurs on open and closed forms alike. It is also found on a number of vessels from Herodion (see Bar-Nathan 1981: Pls. 1:13; 4:27; 6:24, 33; 10:20, 25), but seems to be much less common at Jericho. In fact, red slip or paint is attested only on three unguentaria published from Jericho (Kelso and Baramki 1955: Pl. 24:X96, X131; Netzer and Meyers 1977: Fig. 8:17). Either this kind of surface treatment was not common in eastern Judea, or the published comparanda from first century C.E. Jericho are inadequate. Drippy red or brown slip is also very rare at Qumran. One of the piriform unguentaria published by de Vaux has red slip or paint over the rim (1953: Fig. 3:10), and I saw one cooking ware jug in the basement of the Rockefeller Museum with splashes of red paint on the shoulder. There is also one piriform unguentarium with black painted lines published from Ein Feshkha (de Vaux 1959: Fig. 3:5).

While many of the ceramic types found at Qumran do have morphological parallels from other sites in Judea, there are some curious gaps. These include fusiform unguentaria, which do not seem to be attested at Qumran. Fusiform unguentaria, or "spindle-bottles," are the characteristic bottle form of the first century B.C.E. in Judea (see Lapp 1961: 197–198, Type 91; Rahmani 1967: Fig. 15; also see the example from Rujm el-Bahr in Bar-Adon 1989: Fig. 9A:25). During the first century C.E., they were replaced by piriform, or pear-shaped, unguentaria (see Lapp 1961: 199, Type 92). Unguentaria probably served as containers for perfumes or scented oils, or for other precious liquids. Piriform unguentaria are attested in the first century C.E. at Qumran (de Vaux 1953: Fig. 3:10; de Vaux 1954: Fig. 4:4; also see the examples from Ein Feshkha in de Vaux 1959: Figs. 2:2, 4; 3:5 and Ein el-Ghuweir in Bar-Adon 1977: Fig. 12:7–11). However, no fusiform unguentaria appear among the vessels published from the first century B.C.E. Even more conspicuous by their absence are the "cornucopia" lamps common during the Hasmonean period in Judea. These are small, wheel-made lamps with rims pinched to form a spout (see Rosenthal and Sivan 1978: 79; Rahmani 1967: Fig. 9:1–3). Fusiform unguentaria and "cornucopia" lamps have been found in Jericho, Jerusalem, and at other sites in Judea (for some examples see Lapp 1961: 192, Type 81; 198, Type 91; Avigad 1980: Figs. 58, 59, 70, 211; also see the "cornucopia" lamp from Rujm el-Bahr in Bar-Adon 1989: Fig. 10A:17). In addition, "sunburst" oil lamps, the other type characteristic of Judea during the Hasmonean period, appear to be rare at Qumran (see for example Rahmani 1967: Fig. 9:4–7; Avigad 1980: Figs. 58:2, lower one; 70, center one). These mold-made lamps have radiating lines surrounding the filling hole and are sometimes covered with a red slip (for the only published example from Qumran see Lapp 1961: 194, Type 83.2; for one from Qasr el-Yahud see Bar-Adon 1989: Fig. 21C:25). "Sunburst" lamps were inspired by Hellenistic "delphini-form" lamps, which are common at sites around the eastern Mediterranean (see Rosenthal and Sivan 1978: 13). Instead of "cornucopia" and "sunburst" lamps, the type characteristic of Qumran during the first century B.C.E. is the peculiar one discussed above.

The ceramic corpus from Qumran thus differs from contemporary sites in Judea both in terms of the types that are represented and those that are not. However, the majority of the types found at Qumran are also common at other sites in Judea. These include many of the cups, bowls, cooking pots, storage jars, jugs, juglets and flasks. While the fabric of the vessels from Qumran appears to be local, the forms are paralleled elsewhere. One of the non-Judean types represented at Qumran is jars and jugs of buff or cream colored ware. No examples were published by de Vaux, but Dr. Humbert showed me a few examples from Qumran in the basement of the Rockefeller Museum. These jars and jugs are usually decorated with combed and incised decoration, and probably served as containers for cold drinking water. They have often been mistaken for a type of buff ware characteristic of the early Islamic period. In fact, these jars and jugs should probably be associated with the Nabataeans, for they are found at sites in or near Nabataea (see the discussion in Hershkovitz 1992: 314–315). To the best of my knowledge there are no published examples of this ware from Jerusalem, Jericho, or Herodion, but it is attested at Masada (see the references to unpublished examples from Masada in Hershkovitz 1992: 319, footnote 23) and at Rujm el-Bahr (Bar-Adon 1989: Fig. 9A:26). The presence of this ware at Qumran is suggestive of contacts with Nabataea, though the better-known painted Nabataean pottery is apparently not represented.

It is now necessary to summarize and synthesize these data. First, as de Vaux observed, the repertoire of types represented at Qumran is limited and repetitive. The types found in the caves are identical in form and fabric with those from the site, but are more limited in terms of repertoire. The character of the fabric suggests, as de Vaux suspected, that the majority of the vessels were manufactured at or near Qumran. Local production would also account for peculiar types like the "scroll jars" and the oil lamps.

On the other hand, the various fine ware types found throughout Judea during the first century B.C.E. and first century C.E. are either rare or unattested at Qumran. These include western terra sigillata, Eastern Sigillata A, Roman mold-made lamps, "painted Jerusalem bowls," and red-painted wares. Thus, fine wares are almost totally absent from the corpus at Qumran. In fact, one of the striking features of this pottery is its plainness. Also unrepresented at Qumran are imported amphoras.

The absence or rarity of both imported and local fine ware types from the

Qumran corpus is suggestive of a deliberate and selective policy of isolation on the part of the inhabitants. They appear to have preferred to manufacture and use their own ceramic products. Many of these products are morphologically similar to types found elsewhere in Judea, but lack painted or relief decoration. The presence of Nabataean cream ware indicates that the inhabitants of Qumran did have access to pottery from outside sources. It seems therefore that they deliberately refrained from obtaining any kind of fine ware, sometimes substituting their own undecorated imitations. The plainness of the pottery and absence of fine wares lends an air of austerity to the corpus which contrasts sharply with contemporary assemblages from Jericho, Jerusalem, and Herodion.

Finally, I would like to return to the peculiar oil lamps. The ceramic assemblage associated with Stratum Ib at Qumran is unusual in a number of respects. Instead of these lamps, one would expect to find the "sunburst" and "cornucopia" lamps common in Judea during the Hasmonean period. The delicate cups or bowls with flaring rims are also characteristic of Qumran in this period. On the other hand, fusiform unguentaria are absent, though piriform unguentaria appear in Stratum II. Together these features suggest that the Qumran potters may have come out of a somewhat different ceramic tradition than contemporary potters in Judea. At least one strand of this ceramic tradition seems to have been influenced by different Hellenistic styles and trends than was usual in Judea. I would suggest that this influence is expressed in the peculiar oil lamps, and possibly in the delicate cups or bowls with flaring rims. The "sunburst" lamps seem to reflect a different Hellenistic source or tradition than the peculiar lamps from Qumran. That the Qumran potters did not share exactly the same ceramic traditions as other Judean potters is also suggested by the complete absence of "cornucopia" lamps. Since the "cornucopia" lamps are undecorated and wheelmade (like the Hellenistic lamps from Qumran), it is difficult to account for their absence. Their form, which recalls the Judean lamps of the Bronze and Iron Ages, may reflect the revival of an ancient ceramic tradition. Could it be that the Qumran potters did not share that same tradition, or were more familiar with another? By Stratum II, on the other hand, these differences disappeared, as indicated by the presence of "Herodian" lamps, piriform unguentaria, and types of cups similar to those found at other sites in Judea (see for example Lapp 1961: 175, Type 52.1). Thus, the earliest pottery from Qumran includes a number of types rare or unattested elsewhere in Judea, suggesting that the potters were familiar with a somewhat different ceramic tradition. By Stratum II, these differences had disappeared, and they seem to have adopted the common Judean ceramic forms.

The pottery from Qumran thus sheds a great deal of light on the character of the community. It suggests that the inhabitants practiced a deliberate and selective policy of isolation, manufacturing ceramic products to suit their own special needs and requirements. It is clear that they chose to manufacture and use undecorated pottery instead of fine wares. The great numbers of plain, repetitive, identical plates, cups, and bowls found at the site form a strong contrast with contemporary assemblages at other Judean sites, which are typologically much richer and more varied. This evidence accords well with the usual understanding of this community as communal and austere in nature. Finally, the composition of the assemblage from Stratum Ib suggests that the potters at Qumran may have come out of a somewhat different ceramic tradition than contemporary potters elsewhere in Judea.

ACKNOWLEDGMENTS

I would like to acknowledge the collegial support and assistance of Dr. Jean-Baptiste Humbert of the École Biblique et Archéologique Française in Jerusalem. Dr. Humbert is responsible for the final publication of the pottery from de Vaux's excavations at Qumran. While in Jerusalem in the summer of 1992, I discussed this paper with Dr. Humbert. He kindly shared some of his observations with me, and allowed me to examine the pottery stored in the basement of the Rockefeller Museum. Mr. Hillel Geva, who is now director of the excavations in the Jewish Quarter of Jerusalem, generously shared his time and observations with me as well. With his permission, I was able to examine some of the ceramic material from the Jewish Quarter excavations, which he is in the process of preparing for final publication. Finally, I would like to acknowledge the collegial advice and information provided by Dr. Andrea M. Berlin, who suggested to me the topic of this paper.

REFERENCES

AHARONI, Y.
  1962   *Excavations at Ramat Rahel*. Rome: Centro di Studi Semitici.
AVIGAD, N.
  1980   *Discovering Jerusalem*. Nashville, TN: Thomas Nelson.
BAR-ADON, P.
  1977   Another settlement of the Judean Desert Sect at 'En el-Ghuweir on the shores of the Dead Sea. *Bulletin of the American Schools of Oriental Research* **227**: 1–25.
  1989   *Excavations in the Judean Desert*. 'Atiqot 9, Hebrew series. Jerusalem: Israel Antiquities Authority.
BAR-NATHAN, R.
  1981   Pottery and stone vessels of the Herodian period. Pp. 54–70 in *Greater Herodion*, by E. Netzer. Qedem 13. Jerusalem: Hebrew University.
BROSHI, M.
  1991   The Archaeology of Qumran—A Reconsideration. Pp. 49–62 in *The Scrolls*

of the Judaean Desert, Forty Years of Research, M. Broshi, S. Japhet, D. Schwarz, and S. Talmon, Eds. Jerusalem: The Bialik Institute.

DEONNA, W.
1908   Les lampes antiques. *Bulletin de Correspondance Hellenique* **32**: 133–176.

DE VAUX, R.
1953   Fouilles au Khirbet Qumrân. *Revue Biblique* **60**: 83–106.
1954   Fouilles au Khirbet Qumrân. *Revue Biblique* **61**: 206–236.
1955   La poterie. Pp. 8–13 in *Discoveries in the Judean Desert I, Qumran Cave I*. D. Barthelemy and J. T. Milik, Eds. Oxford: Clarendon Press.
1956   Fouilles de Khirbet Qumrân. *Revue Biblique* **63**: 533–577.
1959   Fouilles de Feshkha. *Revue Biblique* **66**: 225–255.
1962   Archéologie. Pp. 3–36 in *Discoveries in the Judean Desert of Jordan III, Les "Petites Grottes" de Qumran*, M. Baillet, J. T. Milik, and R. de Vaux, Eds. Oxford: Clarendon Press.
1973   *Archaeology and the Dead Sea Scrolls*. London: Oxford University Press.
1977   Le matériel archéologique. La poterie. Pp. 15–20 in *Discoveries in the Judean Desert VI, Qumran Grotte 4, II*, by R. de Vaux and J. T. Milik. Oxford: Clarendon Press.

HAYES, J. W.
1985   Hellenistic to Byzantine Fine Wares and Derivatives in the Jerusalem Corpus. Pp. 179–194 *Excavations in Jerusalem 1961–1967, Volume I*, by A. D. Tushingham. Toronto: Royal Ontario Museum.

HERSHKOVITZ, M.
1992   Aroer at the End of the Second Temple Period. *Eretz-Israel* **23**: 309–319 (in Hebrew).

KELSO, J. L. and D. C. BARAMKI
1955   *Excavations at New Testament Jericho and Khirbet en-Nitla*. AASOR XXIX–XXX. New Haven: American Schools of Oriental Research.

LAPP, P. W.
1961   *Palestinian Ceramic Chronology 200 B.C.–A.D. 70*. New Haven: American Schools of Oriental Research.

NETZER, E.
1981   *Greater Herodion*. Qedem 13. Jerusalem: Hebrew University.

NETZER, E., and E. M. MEYERS
1977   Preliminary report on the Joint Jericho Excavation Project. *Bulletin of the American Schools of Oriental Research* **228**: 15–27.

PERLMAN, I., J. GUNNEWEG and J. YELLIN
1986   Pseudo-Nabataean ware and pottery of Jerusalem. *Bulletin of the American Schools of Oriental Research* **262**: 77–82.

RAHMANI, L. Y.
1967   Jason's Tomb. *Israel Exploration Journal* **17**: 61–100.

ROSENTHAL, R. and R. SIVAN
1978   *Ancient Lamps in the Schloessinger Collection*. Qedem 8. Jerusalem: Hebrew University.

TUSHINGHAM, A. D.
1985   *Excavations in Jerusalem 1961–1967, Volume I*. Toronto: Royal Ontario Museum.

DISCUSSION OF THE PAPER

LAWRENCE SCHIFFMAN (*New York University, New York*): What I would like to note I think is kind of obvious, but your presentation requires that it be noted. If in fact this profile is the one that will be reflected when all the material is available, it is very similar to a scribal and linguistic profile, and a certain kind of literary profile. The importation versus local manufacture issue exists for the very Scrolls themselves. It exists for not simply the scribal practice, but apparently the linguistic forms, and the very same issue exists for what we could call the cultural or religious forms. I simply would widen the question that your material raises. Just one little bit of food for thought. I'm wondering why the local manufacture doesn't link up to some extent with purity laws. It is obvious from what we have been hearing that there is a lot of nonlocal manufacture, and how that would all link up I'm not certain.

JODI MAGNESS (*Tufts University, Medford, MA*): Thank you. I deliberately steered clear of any issues having to do with the Scrolls, because I'm an archaeologist and I deal with pottery. But, I realize that there is a larger context to this.

ERIC MEYERS (*Duke University, Durham, NC*): I would underscore, too, Jodi, that your presentation of this ceramic corpus is in somewhat dark, if not striking, contrast with the first presentation today. That presentation would put the Qumran community much more in the mainstream and take away from the uniqueness of the community from the point of view of material culture. So, I underscore what has occurred here.

JEROME BERMAN (*California Museum of Ancient Art, Beverly Hills, CA*): You're saying that there is a tradition of pottery manufacture that's common throughout many areas of Judea at this time. And, that the people at Qumran seem to come from another tradition. What other tradition? Where did this tradition come from? It seemed, from what you were saying, to have some tie to the Nabataeans.

MAGNESS: No, no, no.

BERMAN: Well, at least a little bit.

MAGNESS: No, no. The types that are peculiar to Qumran—I used the Nabataean ware to show that was imported. That wasn't something that they imitated.

BERMAN: But, there were also local imitations of that.

MAGNESS: No, no, no. The limitations are the oil lamps. The oil lamps are the imitations that I was actually talking about. Also, the things that are peculiar are the scroll jars, those oil lamps, and the cyma profile bowls. I don't know where this is coming from. The oil lamps are actually the main thing that interested me. The inspiration for the oil lamps, as de Vaux correctly pointed out, is Hellenistic types that are found throughout the Eastern Mediterranean.

Now, those Hellenistic types are occasionally found as imports in Judea. All I'm suggesting is that a few of the local ceramic types in Qumran in stratum Ib were inspired by sources or traditions which differ from those found at other sites in Judea. Where that is coming from, I don't know. I'm just pointing it out because, as far as I know, it hasn't been pointed out before.

What bothers me the most about those oil lamps is that they are wheel-made, plain, unslipped imitations of a Hellenistic type. Now, if the people at Qumran wanted to use plain, wheel-made oil lamps, why didn't they use the "cornucopia" oil lamps, which are so common elsewhere in Judea? Why did they suddenly manufacture this bizarre, peculiar type of oil lamp that is not found anywhere else? What was the source of inspiration? Why did they do that? That's what bothers me, and that's what I was trying to point out. It does suggest that they did not share exactly the same ceramic traditions as other potters in Judea.

Can I just say something about what you said before? I obviously was handicapped in writing this paper, not being able to have access to unpublished material. Despite the fact that I was able to look at pottery that Dr. Humbert was kind enough to let me see, I had to base myself really entirely on what's been published so far. It is possible that when the final publication comes out, everything that I said here will be totally wrong. I will be interested in seeing what the percentages are of fine wares versus coarse wares. My impression from what I saw in the basement of the Rockefeller Museum (which was, I think, most of the pottery that's still around) is that there was very, very little in the way of fine wares. The vast majority is plain, undecorated pottery, and that does sharply contrast with contemporary assemblages at other sites.

MEYERS: I concur; my visits also corroborate that. I see an affirmative nod from Professor Donceel-Voûte.

Khirbet Qumran and the Manuscript Finds of the Judaean Wilderness

NORMAN GOLB

Oriental Institute
University of Chicago
1155 East 58th Street
Chicago, Illinois 60637

Khirbet Qumran had been visited by explorers considerably before the scrolls' discovery. Gustav Dalman, author of the renowned *Arbeit und Sitte in Palästina*, in 1914 had described it aptly as a place of mystery, sitting atop a promontory that jutted out toward the shore from the cliff's face and that, by its commanding situation, seemed "exceptionally well suited for a fortress."[1] Years later, in 1940, Michael Avi-Yonah had likewise perceived it as a fortress,[2] situating it among a large number of known military sites in the Judaean Wilderness whose main purpose during biblical and intertestamental times had been the defense of Jerusalem against incursions from beyond the Jordan river and the Dead Sea. It is so depicted in several maps and atlases of Israel.[3]

In December of 1951, as discoveries of Hebrew scrolls were proceeding in nearby caves, a group under Père Roland de Vaux's direction made soundings at the Khirbet Qumran site, uncovering five rooms within the largest of the buildings eventually to be excavated. Already then they noticed an aqueduct and a system of pools and cisterns at the site. One described a "main outer wall . . . constructed of large, undressed stones" and stated that the "quality of the work is very poor, and in no way resembles that of a Roman fort which we first took it to be."[4] This seemed to contradict the view of earlier explorers of the region. The further assertion – later dropped – that the "inner walls are of equally poor workmanship, being mostly of rubble and mud" only added to the growing impression that the site could have been the home of a poor ascetic community. In this same first sounding, a jar and some cooking pots and lamps were found identical in shape to some brought to light in the first

---

[1] G. Dalman, in *Palästina Jahrbuch des Deutschen evangelischen Instituts für Altertumswissenschaft des heiligen Landes* 10 (1914), pp. 9–10 (My translation).

[2] M. Avi-Yonah, *Map of Roman Palestine*, 2nd ed. (Jerusalem, 1940), map section.

[3] See, *e.g.*, *Atlas of Israel* (Jerusalem and Amsterdam, 1970), plates IX/6,A and IX/8,B.

[4] G. Lankester Harding, in *Palestine Exploration Quarterly* 84 (1952), p. 104.

manuscript cave (1Q), which already then—*i.e.*, in 1952—gave rise to the view that "it would appear . . . that the people who lived at Khirbet Qumran deposited the scrolls in the cave . . ." and that the situation fit in well "with Pliny the Elder's account of the Essenes."[5] In his *Natural History* (*circa* A.D. 77) Pliny had actually located a group of Essenes on the western shore of the Dead Sea, somewhere above the town of En Gedi, and had written that these Essenes did not marry but lived in isolation from other men, "with only the palm trees for company." Particularly since one of the first seven scrolls discovered, the *Manual of Discipline*, contained various Essene-like ideas, could not the isolated Khirbet Qumran site, close to where the scrolls were discovered, indeed have been the long-lost home of this radically ascetic group?

Then, as more manuscripts were discovered in the caves, exploring the Khirbet Qumran site in greater detail became a matter of necessity, and the archaeological team proceeded to do so in 1953 and the following three years. The results, as described by its chief investigator, were surprising: in his report on that season, he stated that "the buildings were reduced to ruins by a military action," signs of which included "collapsed walls, traces of a fire (and) iron arrows."[6] The team uncovered a highly developed system for channeling and storing a large supply of water. From Wadi Qumran, an aqueduct had carried the winter rainwaters into the settlement, entering six huge reservoirs as well as a deep cistern of much earlier date. In the northwestern portion of the settlement was another cistern, square-shaped, that was used for bathing purposes or for collecting still more water. So impressed were the excavators that Père de Vaux was moved to say that the "number and importance of the cisterns" constituted the settlement's "most striking feature."[7]

On the basis of six liters per person per day over a period of eight months—the maximal dry period in the Judaean Wilderness—over 750 people could have been sustained by the great stores of water—approximately 1127 m³—at Qumran.[8] This fit in well with the indications of a battle fought at the site, which in de Vaux's view had taken place in A.D. 68. Any defenders would have had to have just such a supply of water, for Qumran was otherwise isolated from water sources—the closest, at the nearby 'En Feshkha, being inaccessible to the Qumran inhabitants during a siege.

Besides these indications pointing to the kind of settlement Qumran had

---

[5] *Ibid.*, p. 105.

[6] R. DE VAUX, *L'archéologie et les manuscrits de la mer Morte* (London, 1961), pp. 28f. (This and all subsequent translations appearing in this study are the author's.)

[7] *Ibid.*, p. 6.

[8] I wish to thank Prof. Israel Eph'al of the Hebrew University for his aid in arriving at this figure. The actual figure of 782 individuals is arrived at on the assumption of a maximum need during the eight rainless desert months of 6 liters per person per day. Within this (generous) estimate, over the period of 240 days (*i.e.*, 8 months), 782 individuals could have been supplied by the water of the Qumran cisterns. See also B. G. WOOD in *BASOR* 256, pp. 45–60; D. AMIT, "Amot hamayim shel qumran," *Teba' wa'ares* 24 (1982), pp. 118–122.

been, the excavators unearthed still others, including remnants of surrounding walls and, most notably, substantial remains of a well-fortified tower that
had once dominated the site. The structure, "a massive tower" in the words
of de Vaux, included several interior rooms on two floors which could be
reached by a circular staircase; a second-story portal had once opened onto
a gallery facing southwestward into the interior of the settlement. The outside
of the tower formed the northeastern perimeter of the building complex, and
the main gate of the settlement had been at its base. Père de Vaux stated that
the "defensive concern was further emphasized by the isolation of this tower,
which was separated from the other buildings by two open spaces." A road
had led to this tower from the north along the plain bordering the Dead Sea.[9]

Qumran itself had originally been built as an Israelite fortress in the 7th
or 8th century B.C.; the site had afterwards apparently been abandoned, according to de Vaux, until approximately the beginning of the 2nd century
B.C., when the ancient Israelite foundations were used in erecting a relatively
modest group of buildings. This group, however, was quite soon replaced by
a more elaborate complex of buildings erected during or soon after the middle
of the 2nd century B.C., and it was then that the tower was first installed. Two
of its stories, of stone construction, were still intact when it was first uncovered in 1951, but brick remnants of a third story were found in the rubble.[10]
Père de Vaux, as Dalman before him, perceived the strategic nature of the site,
observing that "from the plateau of Qumran the view extends over the whole
of the western shore from the mouth of the Jordan to Ras Feshkha and over
the entire northern half of the [Dead] Sea."[11]

The archaeologists discovered that the buildings of Qumran had been
damaged, perhaps by an earthquake and fire. De Vaux may be justified in suggesting that the damage occurred in 31 B.C., the time of a known earthquake
in Palestine as reported by Josephus. Whatever the precise date and the cause,
archaeological evidence as described by de Vaux led him to infer that the destruction was followed by a brief abandonment of the site and its repair and
reoccupation by the same group that had previously inhabited it. Most of the
rooms were then cleared of debris, secondary structures were added, and buildings weakened by the earthquake were reinforced, some walls being doubled
in thickness and others strengthened by buttresses.[12] The greatest attention,
however, was paid to the tower: various measures to protect it were introduced, the most significant being the construction of a solid ramp of unfinished stone on all four of its sides, proceeding from its base upward at a
45° angle to the second story of the building. This ramp, de Vaux pointed out,

[9] DE VAUX, L'archéologie, pp. 4–5.
[10] Dictionnaire archéologique de la Bible (Jerusalem and Paris, 1970), p. 170 (article of A.
NEGEV).
[11] DE VAUX, L'archéologie, p. 33.
[12] Ibid., pp. 15ff.

was highest on the northern and eastern sides—those sides, that is, which faced outward and formed the salient defensive point of the settlement.[13] The buttressing of the tower showed that it was important to those who re-built the settlement and inhabited it until the battle that took place there in the first century A.D. Standing at the top of the tower, one would have had a still clearer view of the plain and over the sea as far to the southeast as Machaerus, the stronghold built by Alexander Jannaeus *circa* 95 B.C.

Relying on archaeological indications of this battle, de Vaux stated that it was characterized "by a violent destruction. . . . The tower, fortified by its ramp of stone, offered the greatest resistance. . . ."[14] Evidence was found of the burning of roofs and the collapse of ceilings and superstructures, and the presence of iron arrowheads of Roman type at the site showed that it was a troop of Roman soldiers who had attacked and eventually taken the settle-ment. For reasons not fully understood today, de Vaux failed to add a point of telling importance that was furnished by F. M. Cross, who participated in the excavations and later stated that the walls were "mined through [and] the building ruins . . . sealed in layers of ash from a great conflagration."[15] The undermining of walls by tunneling beneath them was, of course, a classic tech-nique of Roman military strategy.

From the evidence of coins found in the ruins and a statement made by Josephus, de Vaux inferred that the Roman siege and capture of the site had taken place in the summer of A.D. 68—*i.e.*, during the First Revolt, approx-imately eighteen months before the siege of Jerusalem took full effect early in A.D. 70. The actual dating of the attack is of obvious importance, but can by no means be said to have been satisfactorily solved by de Vaux. The latest Jewish coins found at the site were of Year III of the revolt (spring 68/spring 69 A.D.). The earliest Roman coins, on the other hand, were minted in and near Caesaria in A.D. 67/68. The Tenth Roman Legion, Josephus writes (*Jewish War*, IV.464), captured Jericho in the summer of 68, and Vespasian thereafter had some men thrown into the Dead Sea with their hands tied to see if they could stay afloat. De Vaux expressed the belief that, as the last Jewish coins could have been minted as early as the spring of 68, and the earliest Roman ones at virtually the same time, the summer of 68 provided an optimal time for the taking of Khirbet Qumran, particularly since Vespasian's troops had by then approached a point not many miles to the north.[16]

The scheme breaks down, however, once it is realized that during a revolt of such serious proportions as the one under way, it is unlikely that fresh Jewish coins would be found so quickly in a settlement lying in the wilderness

[13] *Ibid.*, p. 20.
[14] *Ibid.*, p. 28.
[15] CROSS, *Ancient Library*, ed. of 1958, p. 45.
[16] DE VAUX, *L'archéologie*, pp. 29–33.

and at a considerable distance from the centers of the insurrection—while one may only infer from the Roman coins that the legionnaires had some dated to A.D. 67/68 in their possession. The hidden premise in de Vaux's argument is that both the Jews and the Romans possessed newly minted coins when they fought each other at Qumran—as unlikely an event in antiquity as it would be today. In fact, in his work on Khirbet Qumran, de Vaux himself elsewhere emphasized that "silver coins remained in circulation for a long time and are of little use in dating an archaeological level except as a vague *terminus post quem*" (see note 17 below). The coins only show that the attack on Qumran could not have taken place *before* A.D. 68; as there is no evidence whatever showing that Roman legionnaires penetrated into any part of the Judaean Wilderness until A.D. 70, it is far more likely that the attack on Qumran took place as a part of the general offensive against the Jews of Judaea following the capture of Jerusalem in A.D. 70.

There were, moreover, certain facts about the nature of Khirbet Qumran that de Vaux and others working with him did not seem willing to acknowledge, and one of them was that Jerusalem and the events transpiring there might have had something to do with Qumran. This reticence heavily affected de Vaux's own treatment of the nature of the site, as well as that of his colleagues, as may be seen from their discussions of still other findings made in the course of the excavations. De Vaux uncovered evidence that the site was not simply abandoned when the Roman force overcame the defenders. Rather, a new period in its history, designated by him Period III, began. In this period, beginning with the capture of the site and extending to *at least* A.D. 74, Roman soldiers, perhaps the same ones who had wrested Qumran from its defenders, occupied and made use of it as a military post. De Vaux states that "the great tower was reutilized," but that only a part of the ruins were occupied by the Romans, and explains that they had to occupy the site for military reasons—since from it one had a superior view of the sea and surrounding region. Until the end of the war with Rome the Romans, as de Vaux observed, had to police the sea and the adjacent shore.[17]

From the evidence unearthed by the archaeologists at Qumran it thus becomes clear that this site was used for military purposes over a very long range of time. It had been a fortress in Israelite times. Then, when it was rebuilt centuries later, and while continuing to maintain its dominant geographic position, the rebuilders gave most careful attention to features of a military nature. Thereafter, in approximately A.D. 70, Roman forces fought a pitched battle there, clearly against an armed force inhabiting the site. Finally, after taking it from them, the Romans used it as a fort of their own, albeit on a smaller scale than earlier. Thus Khirbet Qumran was demonstrably a fortress.

---

[17] DE VAUX, *L'archéologie*, pp. 33ff. On DE VAUX's own assessment of the value of coin evidence, see *ibid.*, p. 15.

And yet those associated with the dig in the 1950s were unwilling to state that it had been a fortress during the crucial period when Essene sectarians were supposed to be inhabiting it—*i.e.*, in the first century B.C. and the first century A.D., until its capture by the Romans *circa* A.D. 70.

This reluctance is noticeable throughout de Vaux's writings on Khirbet Qumran, and may be perceived also in those of his colleagues. The most telling statement is that made by Frank M. Cross, who participated in the excavation and later published a book on the site as well as the manuscripts found in the caves. He writes that it is impossible to determine whether "the Essenes in whole or in part fled their settlement with the approach of the Romans, or were trapped in Qumran and slaughtered"—and then adds that "there is some likelihood that the Essenes, at least in part, put up resistance. Certainly someone resisted the Romans, using Qumran as a bastion."[18]

While admitting that Qumran was thus used, Cross as well as de Vaux and all other writers who, early on, subscribed to the hypothesis of an Essene sect living there, were unwilling to state candidly that the site, during the period in question, was in fact a fortress. De Vaux came close to admitting as much in 1954; stating that "the building was destroyed by a battle," he added the telling remark that it was possible that "the entire community departed [before the battle] and that other people retrenched at Khirbet Qumran: in the same year of 68 [A.D.], the *sicarii* were active at Masada and En-Gedi."[19] In raising the possibility these zealous warriors, who played such an important role in the revolt, had *taken the place* of the Essenes before the battle—an explanation for which there is no archaeological evidence whatsoever—de Vaux revealed a grave concern about his own findings.

This concern may be expressed as follows: how could the Essene sect, believed almost from the outset of the excavations to have been the inhabitants of Khirbet Qumran, actually have occupied a site which the excavations themselves proved was of a military nature? Ancient writers on the Essenes agree that they were the most peaceful of men, not given to waging war. Philo Judaeus, the earliest of these writers (*ca.* A.D. 20) and a contemporary witness, states of them:

> You cannot find among them any maker of arrows, spears, swords, helmets, corselets, or shields, any maker of arms or war-machines, any one busied in the slightest with military avocations or even with those which, during peace, slip easily into mischief.[20]

Josephus, who wrote his *Jewish War* approximately a half-century later,

[18] CROSS, *The Ancient Library of Quman and Modern Biblical Study*, (London, 1958), p. 45.
[19] DE VAUX in *Revue Biblique* 61 (1954), p. 234.
[20] PHILO JUDAEUS, *Every Good Man is Free*, par. 12, ed. F.H. Colson, *Philo*, vol. 9, Loeb Classical Library (Cambridge, MA, 1941), p. 54; trans. J. MOFFATT in *Encyclopaedia of Religion and Ethics*, vol. 5 (New York, 1912), p. 396.

after the revolt had ended in defeat for the Jews, does mention a certain John the Essene—clearly a singular exception—who had served as a general of the rebel force in Timna (some twenty miles due west of Jerusalem and far from the Judaean Wilderness); but he nowhere writes that actual groups of Essenes defended strongholds or fought in battles. What he does say about them is that they bore weapons only for defensive purposes while traveling.[21] Pliny the Elder's description of the Essenes living near the shore of the Dead Sea above En Gedi, written about the same time as Josephus's account (the date of the preface to his *Natural History* is A.D. 74), reinforces this impression of their peaceful ways. Nothing in his account would lead one to believe that the Essenes were a warrior group inhabiting a fortress.[22]

This troubling contradiction had to be in some way resolved by the archaeological team, and it was quite clearly for this reason that de Vaux first suggested that another group, perhaps the militant *sicarii*, had somehow taken over the site from the Essenes before the battle began. It is this same contradiction that evidently led Cross to state as a mere possibility that some Essenes had themselves defended the site while simultaneously implying that another group may have actually done the fighting. But when in 1958 other writers began raising the possibility that it was still another such ancient militant group, the so-called *zealots* of Josephus's history, who had occupied the site both well before and at the time of the battle, de Vaux rejected this interpretation out of hand—without referring to his own earlier view of possible occupation of the site by the extremist *sicarii*.[23] It was clearly of importance to the archaeological team to defend the integrity of their original identification of Khirbet Qumran as the home of Pliny's Essenes of the Dead Sea shore.

And yet other disturbing evidence had been unearthed by the archaeologists that called this selfsame identification into still further question. Also on the plateau occupied by Khirbet Qumran, less than fifty meters eastward of the buildings, was a large cemetery that had first been explored in the 1870s.[24] Then only a few of the more than eleven hundred graves had been opened, but de Vaux and his team applied themselves to exploring others.

---

[21] FLAVIUS JOSEPHUS, *War*, 2.125; ed. and trans. H. S. J. THACKERAY, *Josephus*, vol. 2, Loeb Classical Library (London, 1927), pp. 370–371.

[22] "On the west side of the Dead Sea, but out of range of the noxious exhalations of the coast, is the solitary tribe of the Essenes, which is remarkable beyond all other tribes in the whole world, as it has no women and has renounced all sexual desire, has no money, and has only palm-trees for company. Day by day the throng of refugees is recruited to an equal number by numerous accessions of persons tired of life and driven thither by the wave of fortune to adopt their manners. Thus through thousands of ages . . . a race in which no one is born lives on forever: so prolific for their advantage is other men's weariness of life." PLINY THE ELDER, *Natural History* V.xv.73; trans. H. RACKHAM (Loeb Classical Library, London, 1942) 2: p. 277.

[23] See further my *Who Wrote the Dead Sea Scrolls?—The Search for the Meaning of the Qumran Manuscripts* (New York, 1994), pp. 12–15. See DE VAUX, *L'archéologie*, pp. 91–94.

[24] See CH. S. CLERMONT-GANNEAU, *Archaeological Researches in Palestine during the Years 1873–1874*, vol. 2 (London, 1896), pp. 14–16.

They opened a total of 43 graves, finding in them the bodies of thirty men, seven women and four children, yielding a ratio for the excavated graves of more than one in four.[25] Pliny had stated, however, that the Essenes of the Dead Sea shore "had no women, had renounced all sexual desire," and that "no one is born" into their "race."

The discovery of the graves of women and children in the cemetery was thus cause for concern, which de Vaux then proceeded to ameliorate. While uncertain whether the cemetery area containing women's skeletons might legitimately be called an "extension" of the main cemetery, he found it difficult to explain how Pliny's report of a *celibate* Essenic order—recorded by that author *circa* A.D. 77—could be made to fit in with the archaeological findings. He was therefore forced in the end to suggest that the skeletons of women and children might "signify that there were different groups within the community, a main group which would have renounced marriage . . . and one or several groups which would have allowed it. . . . Clearly, the women's tombs do not strengthen the argument that the community was related to the Essenes, but they do not rule it out either."[26]

This assertion cannot be construed as being entirely candid. Of course the finding did not completely rule out the claim that the community was related to the Essenes; but at the same time it considerably reduced the probability insofar as the hypothesis had originally been built in large part precisely upon Pliny's description of a celibate community. As for Josephus, writing about the same time as Pliny, he does state that there was also a non-celibate order of Essenes, but does not place them in any particular area of Palestine.[27] This was done by Pliny, who in the same breath described the community as celibate. The archaeologists fastened upon his statement, and insisted that Qumran was the place he had in mind. And we must note that, by the time the archaeological team uncovered the women's graves, they had already dug up the evidence of a battle at Qumran, presenting a yet more serious obstacle to the identification of the site as the home of Pliny's Essenes.

---

[25] See DE VAUX, *L'archéologie*, pp. 37f., 45f., 69, 81, 96f. It may be that there were no skeletons, or else only unidentifiable remains, in two of the graves.

According to DE VAUX, the cemetery was divided into a main section, with graves oriented in a north-south direction, and other sections, an extension of the main one as well as two "secondary" ones, where the skeletons of the women and children were discovered. For DE VAUX, building on the hypothesis of Essene origins, this might "indicate that the women were not members of the community, or at any rate not in the same sense as the men buried in the main cemetery. It may also signify that a development had taken place in the discipline of the community. The rule of celibacy may have been relaxed, and marriage may have become lawful. This would explain why the tombs of women are located in what seem to be extensions of the main cemetery." This view has since been contested; see the study by Z. KAPERA in the present volume.

[26] R. DE VAUX, *L'archéologie*, pp. 96–97; idem., *Archaeology and the Dead Sea Scrolls* (Oxford, 1972), p. 128f.

[27] JOSEPHUS, *Jewish War* II.viii.13.

The evidence of the women's graves and the battle with the Romans, let alone the highly strategic nature of the site, should have been enough to dissuade the archaeologists from continuing to espouse the theory of an Essene settlement at Qumran. But as we have seen, they became committed to this interpretation almost at the very outset of their investigation, and could not be dissuaded from it. And then, at some time during the process of discovery, someone, either de Vaux himself or one of his associates, must have raised the question of the time of writing of Pliny's description. Pliny not only describes the Essenes dwelling at a place by the Dead Sea shore, but adds another statement of telling significance, namely, that

> lying below the Essenes was formerly the town of Engedi, second only to Jerusalem in the fertility of its land and in its groves of palm-trees, but now like the other place (i.e., Jerusalem) a heap of ashes.[28]

This statement could only have been written after Jerusalem had been destroyed by the Romans in the wake of its capture in the summer of A.D. 70. By this token the Essenes living above En Gedi could not have been identical with the group of people living at Qumran, who in and after A.D. 70, according to the archaeological team's very findings, were Roman soldiers, not Jewish sectarians. Pliny's Essenes would have had to be another group, living elsewhere and evidently closer to En Gedi. In addition, his statement was not pertinent to the question of identification of the people of Khirbet Qumran who lived there *before* A.D. 70, when conditions in Judaea were strikingly different. The Essenes living above En Gedi when Jerusalem already lay in ruins could have migrated there as refugees fleeing the war with Rome from virtually any area of Palestine. Jerusalem itself was known to have had a "gate of the Essenes," (Josephus, *Jewish War* V. 145) implying a relatively large number of these sectarians within the city before the revolt, and it may well be that they themselves fled to Pliny's location above En Gedi during or after the siege. But how could this "throng of refugees," as Pliny describes them, have ended up at Qumran if, as the excavation proved, it was occupied by Roman troops by, and after, A.D. 70?

The question may not have been formulated quite this way but, however put, was obviously posed and had to be answered. The response that de Vaux gave was that the text of Pliny was not the original one, but had been *altered*. He states that the thirty-seven books of Pliny's *Natural History* had been written over many years' time, that Pliny himself may never have visited the Essenes' home but only heard of it from an eyewitness, and that the words referring to En Gedi, "now like [Jerusalem] an ash-heap" were only a remark inserted into Pliny's text when it was being edited in approximately A.D. 75.

---

[28] PLINY the ELDER, *Natural History*, trans. H. RACKHAM (Loeb Classical Library, London 1942) 2: p. 277.

Thus, he explained, the original words on which Pliny later built could have been written or otherwise conveyed to him *before* the Khirbet Qumran site was captured by the Romans.[29]

All this is quite speculative, and one is reminded that students of history often emend texts to make them more consonant with their own interpretations, either by removing or changing troublesome words or putting in new ones. But particularly in view of the fact that allusions to the historical situation in Judaea *after* A.D. 70 are scattered throughout Pliny's description of Palestine,[30] there is no reasonable basis whatever for de Vaux's proposed emendation.[31] The only way to harmonize de Vaux's various explanations, adopted with enthusiasm by many writers, was to assume that the rudiments of Pliny's description were somehow recorded *many* years before the Roman attack on the site, when, by one of de Vaux's explanations, Khirbet Qumran might still have been inhabited only by celibate Essenes. But this is an obviously yet more remote likelihood. There is no evidence whatever indicating that Khirbet Qumran was at any time inhabited by Pliny's Essenes or a celibate community, and no hint in any of the scrolls of the endorsement of celibacy.

As the excavations continued, quite a few scholars began backing away from the hard and fast Qumran-Essene equation. But, although perceiving that Pliny's statement could not, minus tortuous exegesis, literally refer to the Khirbet Qumran site, most nevertheless remained intent on espousing the idea that the site had been inhabited by a *sect*. For it was located near caves where manuscripts were found, and a goodly number of these texts contained ideas and expressions that seemed notably sectarian as compared with texts of either biblical or rabbinic Judaism. The main focus of attention continued to be the *Manual of Discipline*, which revealed what was taken to be a form of heterodoxy sharing much with Essenism as described by Philo and Josephus. During the Khirbet Qumran dig, as already indicated, pottery was found—some in a potter's workshop, some elsewhere—that matched some discovered in the caves, providing what was thought to be an organic, physical bond between them.[32] Even if no statement espousing celibacy could be found in

---

[29] R. DE VAUX, *L'archéologie*, p. 103; *idem, Archaeology and the Dead Sea Scrolls*, p. 133.

[30] See for example PLINY's statement regarding Machaerus, which was an important fortress of the Jews in Transjordania before the war, but was captured by the Romans after the fall of Jerusalem in A.D. 70: "On the east [the Dead Sea] is faced by Arabia of the Romans, and on the south by Machaerus, *at one time next to Jerusalem the most important fortress in Judaea.*" Cf. further my *Who Wrote the Dead Sea Scrolls?*, pp. 15 ff.

[31] The discomfort with DE VAUX's correction of PLINY's statement is increased by the fact that DE VAUX also proposed, after the results of the excavations of the graves were tallied, that the celibate rule may have been relaxed during the course of the history of the Qumranites, or else that there were perhaps different groups, both celibate and non-celibate, living at Qumran simultaneously. Such situations are hardly reflected in PLINY's statement. For DE VAUX's additional claim that the *Copper Scroll* was a work of folklore or the product of a deranged mind, see my *Who Wrote the Dead Sea Scrolls?*, Chapter 5.

[32] Cf. DE VAUX, *L'archéologie*, pp. 40ff., 51f., 79; and *ibid.*, plates xv, xxii, xxix.

the *Manual of Discipline* or the other scrolls, even if there were additional differences between the doctrines of the *Manual* and of the classical Essenes, there was surely an intrinsic bond between Khirbet Qumran and the cave manuscripts, the texts had surely been written by people inhabiting the site, and thus one might legitimately describe them as an Essenic type of order or, that failing, at all events as a sect of some kind. Such was the reasoning of many writers. And of this view, proofs might even be furnished from evidence uncovered at the site.

That evidence has since been much debated, but remains a cornerstone of all variants of the Qumran-Essene hypothesis. It consists in the shape and appearance of certain rooms and other constructions on the site. Including the reservoirs but not the cemetery, the archaeologists numbered over 140 *loci* spread over an area of approximately 4800 meters square. The purposes of a number of these locations could not be determined; but, included among those the archaeologists claimed to be able to identify, were rooms that they designated, respectively, as a stable, kitchen, mill, oven, pottery workshop, and forge, as well as food storage areas. Clearly, a not insignificant group was living here in the 1st century B.C. and 1st century A.D., but was it a Jewish sect as so many writers maintained, or a military troop? For at such a desert outpost, the latter would have had need for all the services implied by those rooms—at least as much need, to be sure, as any communal group of Jewish sectarians.

Seeking further evidence of sectarians, however, some writers pointed to the reservoirs of water, which had steps leading down them, and asked whether some of these could not be in reality ritual baths rather than simply reservoirs. While ancient writers found notable the Essenes' practice of frequent ritual bathing, all practicing Jews of the Roman period, as far as is known, bathed ritually in consonance with biblical laws. But what is more, de Vaux and his team themselves rejected the possibility of the reservoirs serving as baths, since the steps were a characteristic feature of reservoirs of that period located elsewhere in Judaea. The steps were designed simply to facilitate the collection of water as the level decreased during the dry months. Two water-basins as well were discovered at the site that de Vaux agreed were used for baths, but he himself stated that "archaeology is powerless to say whether those baths . . . had a ritual character."[33]

The archaeological team, nevertheless believed that certain locations gave evidence of sectarian use. One hall de Vaux described as a "refectory," a term usually reserved for dining-rooms of monasteries or convents; another as a "council-hall," in allusion to the requirement laid down in the *Manual of Discipline* calling for regular meetings of the "council of the unity," a governing body of the group described in that text. However, de Vaux's identifications

[33] *Ibid.*, pp. 98–99.

were entirely arbitrary. The one hall may well have been used for dining purposes; but the circular paved area at its western end which, de Vaux asserted, "apparently marks the place where the president of the assembly held forth,"[34] may equally well have been the place where the commandant of a military camp and his officers sat during meals. Objectively speaking, this room may only be called a dining hall, not a "refectory" in particular.

The other site, the so-called "council hall," was given that designation because of a low built-in bench that ran along the walls of this relatively small room. De Vaux observed that on one wall were indentations indicating cupboards, while on another wall a basin had been hollowed out which could be filled with water from the outside. These hints, together with the encircling bench, were enough to encourage de Vaux to state that the room "appears to have been destined for restrained sessions, at which the members did not wish to be disturbed—[i.e., it was] a sort of council hall."[35]

However, a viewer not committed to the interpretation of Khirbet Qumran as the home of an Essene or other sect could say nothing else about the purpose of this room than that it was a place where a group of people met for one purpose or another. It could just as well have been a room for prayer and the recitation of the Pentateuch—that is, a synagogue, similar in character to but somewhat simpler than the chamber with built-in benches clearly used for that same purpose at Masada. There was no reason to think that those occupying the site were other than believing Jews, and any such group, sectarian or not, would have had need for a room of this kind.[36]

Thus, neither the one room nor the other offered serious evidence of sectarian use. However, de Vaux suggested that a considerably larger adjacent room, having an imposing entrance bay, "could have served for larger assemblies of people."[37] The bay of which de Vaux spoke is but one of many carefully constructed elements, in elegant Herodian architectural style, that adorn this and other areas of the site, vitiating entirely the early impression of the archaeologists that the site was of poor construction. Khirbet Qumran was designed as an important site, and the room in question may indeed have served as a gathering place for larger assemblies of people. Needless to say, however, they may as well have been troops as Jewish sectarians.

What de Vaux wished to show as more compelling evidence of sectarian activity at Qumran were the interesting elements left in the pile of debris the excavators encountered in a room adjacent to this same hall. The debris was the result of the collapse of the second story of the building, including the

[34] De Vaux, *L'archéologie*, pp. 8–9.
[35] *Ibid.*, p. 8.
[36] See plan in DE VAUX, *ibid.*, plate XXXIX, locus no. 4. Compare the plans of the Masada synagogue in Y. YADIN, *Masada, Herod's Fortress and the Zealots' Last Stand* (London, 1966), pp. 181, 185, and my *Who Wrote the Dead Sea Scrolls*, fig. 6b.
[37] See R. DE VAUX, *L'archéologie*, p. 8.

floor and whatever furnishings had been located there, at the time the Romans breached the walls and took the site. It included portions of what de Vaux claimed were three plaster tables as well as two inkwells (a third inkwell was found elsewhere in Qumran), from which de Vaux inferred that the second story had contained a kind of *scriptorium*—a term used beforehand only for medieval monasteries. In his perception, the Essenic monks or sectarians of Qumran engaged there in making copies of the works they composed.[38]

These conclusions, based upon the finding of the three so-called tables and a few inkwells, today seem astounding in their lack of caution. Already by the late fifties, a fundamental question had been raised regarding the use of the claimed tables for the purpose of copying scrolls. Not only did ancient depictions of scribes show them copying by other means than sitting at such tables, but their very height and pitch seemed unsuitable for the purposes of copying scrolls.[39] A most obvious objection, unfortunately not discussed until long after the dust of the earlier debate had settled, was that the rubble contained not the slightest hint of most of the materials that bona fide scribes used constantly in their work, such as parchment and the tools for smoothing it, needles and thread with which to bind the parchment together, line-markers to indent into the parchment for straight rows of script, and pens and styluses.[40] By the early 1990s, the continuators of de Vaux's work at Qumran had been able to prove that the "tables" of the so-called scriptorium were in

---

[38] DE VAUX, *Archaeology*, pp. 23, 81. This news of a scriptorium at Qumran was eagerly welcomed in many parts of the world where the discoveries had garnered the rapt attention of scholars. F. M. CROSS stated that the function of the room was "clear and significant," G. VERMES that "A *scriptorium* [was] found on the upper floor," C. FRITSCH that "There is little doubt that this was the scriptorium where manuscripts were copied by the scribes of the community." The most free-flowing expression of assent came from DUPONT-SOMMER, who wrote that "The remains of a *scriptorium* have been discovered, and of a very long narrow table . . . and pieces of one or two shorter tables. These were doubtless writing tables, since two inkpots were found in the same place . . . It seems therefore that this was the place in which the scrolls from the caves were copied. The copyists who bent over these tables and dipped their pens in these inkpots were not . . . just ordinary secular scribes . . . No, the copying of Essene books, which were holy and secret, required scribes recruited from among the members of the sect themselves." See F. M. CROSS, *Ancient Library*, p. 49; G. VERMES, *Discovery in the Judaean Desert* (1956), p. 14; C. FRITSCH, *Qumran Community*, p. 5; DUPONT-SOMMER, *Essene Writings* (1961), p. 63.

[39] *Cf.* particularly B. M. METZGER, "The Furniture of the Scriptorium at Qumran," *Revue de Qumran* I (1959): pp. 509–515; *idem*, "When did the Scribes Begin to Use Writing Desks?" *Akten des XI internationalen Byzntinisten-Kongress* 1958 (1960): pp. 355–362; and, in defense of his own hypothesis, DE VAUX, *op. cit.*: pp. 30 f.

[40] So shaky was the evidence for the room in question being a scriptorium that one scholar would later write that "The arguments against this being a writing table were ably marshalled by . . . Metzger and have been found convincing by many better qualified to judge than this reviewer. An examination of the supposed table in the Palestine Archeological Museum strengthens this negative attitude; yet de Vaux refused to give an inch on his previous theory. . . . The whole question of a *scriptorium* is far from decided. . . . If there is no *scriptorium*, there is no copying, or better, the wholesale copying that some writers envision does not exist . . ." (J. C. GREENFIELD in *Journal of Near Eastern Studies*, 35 [1976]: p. 288).

reality parts of benches placed along the walls of a room that served as a dining parlor, or *triclinium* (Heb. *traqlin*).[41]

The idea of a scriptorium at Qumran, based upon wholly insufficient evidence, had only resulted from the archaeologists' need to find a substantive connection between the manuscripts found in the caves and the Khirbet Qumran site. The most that can today be inferred about the room in question is that it served as a kind of headquarters or gathering-place for important individuals, and the unalloyed evidence of military activity at the site implies its use by one or more commanders charged with directing such activity. The common soldiers who could write—such as the Roman troops who occupied Vindolanda in Britain and members of the Bar Kokhba forces during the Second Jewish Revolt in Palestine—would also have had need for writing materials, and it is of interest in this respect that a third inkwell was found elsewhere within Khirbet Qumran.

No manuscript fragments written on parchment or papyrus had been found in the settlement, not even at the site of the room considered to be a scriptorium, and this posed an obvious embarrassment for the theory that Qumran had been a place where scribes copied manuscripts which were then hidden in nearby caves. De Vaux showed some sensitivity to this problem, but in dismissing it appeared satisfied with the following formula. "The conclusion cannot be resisted," he stated, "that the source of these manuscripts was the community installed in the Qumran area. It is natural that in the ruins of Khirbet Qumran, exposed as they were to the weather, texts written on skin or papyrus should have failed to survive." He had made this statement in the French version of his lectures (1961), before the results of the discoveries at Masada were known, but it remained unrevised in the English translation (1972), long after reports of the Masada discoveries had been widely published.[42] De Vaux's refusal to take into account the fact that in similar ruins at Masada, which shares virtually the same climate as Qumran, just such parchments and papyri were found in the expeditions of 1963–1965, was therefore notable. The discovery of manuscript fragments in the ruins of Masada in fact made it all the more surprising that no parchments or scribal tools whatsoever had been found beneath the rubble of a room claimed to have been the very one where the scrolls were copied.

De Vaux's additional argument for an organic connection between Khirbet Qumran and the caves was that "in the ruins of Qumran themselves inscriptions have been found written on ostraca or pots" whose "*writing is the same as that of the documents.*"[43] This remains perhaps the most enigmatic of the claims adduced throughout the years by Qumranologists defending the

---

[41] See the article by PROFS. ROBERT AND PAULINE DONCEEL-VOÛTE appearing in the present volume, pp. 1–38.

[42] See DE VAUX, *L'archéologie*, p. 80; idem, *Archaeology and the Dead Sea Scrolls*, p. 103.

[43] DE VAUX, *L'archéologie*, p. 80; italics mine.

idea of an organic connection between Khirbet Qumran and the caves. These ostraca are indeed inscribed in Hebrew, but no more can be inferred from their appearance than that the handwritings are characteristic Judaean hands of the 1st century B.C. and 1st century A.D.[44] The handwritings of the inscriptions on the ostraca match *none* of the over five hundred scribal handwritings preserved in the scrolls discovered in the caves near Qumran.

Despite the fact that no parchments or other writing materials and, what is more, no letters and virtually no autographs on parchment or papyrus had been discovered among the scrolls, de Vaux argued forcefully on still other grounds for an organic connection between Khirbet Qumran and the manuscripts found in the caves. One of his main arguments, supported by virtually all Qumranologists, was that pottery found in the caves was identical with that found at the settlement.[45]

De Vaux had himself first asserted that the cave pottery was Hellenistic, and on this basis had originally dated the hiding of the scrolls in the caves to the end of the 2nd or the beginning of the 1st century B.C. Later on, however, he had realized his error, acknowledging that the jars were not Hellenistic, but Roman, and of the second half of the 1st century A.D.[46] He had in the meanwhile found jars of the same type during the excavations of Khirbet Qumran, and also a room at the site that could be reasonably identified as a potter's workshop and another as a storage-room for the pottery.[47] This, he asserted, proved that there was an organic connection between the site and the caves: the inhabitants, so the explanation went, had filled jars made for the purpose with their precious manuscripts and hidden them in the caves, and the fact that the manuscripts once hidden in the jars included sectarian texts showed that the inhabitants of Qumran were a sect.

In making these claims, however, de Vaux did not acknowledge that pottery of the same type has been found during other excavations.[48] By refraining from dealing with this fact, de Vaux had in effect generated an unwarranted turning-point, indeed a scholarly leap of faith, in the use of pottery

---

[44] Already by 1960 a large number of scroll handwritings had become known, and even by then it could no longer be claimed that there was but one or several styles of handwriting among them. The Qumran scroll handwritings share the basic characteristics of those scroll fragments found in the ruins of Masada, but the Qumran ostraca resemble neither the ones nor the others so much as they resemble those ostraca found at Masada. What the latter share in common are documentary characteristics, as opposed to the non-documentary, scribal characteristics of the parchment and papyrus scrolls. The ostraca of Khirbet Qumran clearly prove nothing except that those inhabiting it when they were written *circa* 50 B.C.–A.D. 70 were Jews rather than Romans.

[45] See DE VAUX, *L'archéologie*, pp. 12 ff.

[46] See DE VAUX's statements in *Archaeology and the DSS*, p. 33: "The pottery of Qumran now appears less 'autonomous' or 'original' than I stated it to be at an earlier state"; and G. VERMES, *The Dead Sea Scrolls—Qumran in Perspective* (London, 1981), p. 12.

[47] DE VAUX, *L'archéologie*, p. 12 ff.

[48] See PIERRE BENOIT et al., *Les grottes de Murabba'at. Texte* (Discoveries in the Judaean Desert II, Oxford, 1961), p. 31 and note 4; and above, article of J. MAGNESS, p. 41.

for historical deductions; for it is an axiom of archaeological investigation that
if pottery of the same or similar styles is found in different locations, that does
not bespeak an organic connection between them, but only indicates simul-
taneous habitation of the sites in that period of time to which the pottery may
be dated. By ignoring the evidence of identical pottery found elsewhere, de
Vaux had made it appear that there was a unique connection between the
Khirbet Qumran site and the caves, whereas the evidence he adduced in fact
constituted no proof whatever of such a connection. Employing a modicum
of historical imagination, one might be warranted in suspecting that those
who hid the scrolls in the caves asked the inhabitants of nearby sites, including
Khirbet Qumran, for jars to aid them in their task, but that in no sense implies
that the Qumran inhabitants themselves had hidden or possessed literary
scrolls. As for the Khirbet Qumran pottery in general, the fact that, as Dr.
Magness has observed during our conference, most of it is very plain, but that,
as Dr. Donceel has observed, some of it is of very high quality indeed, is best
explained by recourse to the identification of the site as a fortress, whose garrison would have included both a relatively large number of common troops
and a much smaller number of more privileged officers.

De Vaux had at first argued eloquently that "there is only one site which
corresponds to Pliny's description, and that is the plateau of Qumran, . . .
situated some way back from the shore and at a higher level, and healthier
than the shore itself. . . . Furthermore, there is only one important group of
buildings contemporary with Pliny between En-Gedi and the northernmost
point of the Dead Sea, that is the buildings of Khirbet Qumran and
Feshkha."[49] In an additional remark in the English edition of his Schweich
Lectures, however, he stated that he had "allowed for the possibility that the
small buildings of Khirbet Mazin and 'En el-Ghuweir"–the latter some ten
kilometers south of Khirbet Qumran–"could have belonged to the same community as Qumran. In any case they would have been no more than annexes
of very minor importance."[50] Thus de Vaux had posited that Pliny's Essenes
must have possessed a serious complex of important buildings–whereas Pliny
himself had stated that the Essenes have no money and only palm-trees for
company, encouraging one to look elsewhere than to the well-built settlement of Qumran for their home. And indeed de Vaux elsewhere in the same
work had stated that "We should bear in mind that particularly during the
second Iron Age and the Roman period the west bank of the Dead Sea was
more thickly populated than we have been accustomed to imagine" (a statement not found in the earlier French edition of the book).[51]

Explorations of the area between Khirbet Qumran and En Gedi in the late

[49] R. DE VAUX, L'archéologie, p. 102.
[50] R. DE VAUX, Archaeology and the Dead Sea Scrolls, p. 135, note 3.
[51] R. DE VAUX, Archaeology and the Dead Sea Scrolls, pp. 89–90.

1960s had indeed revealed numerous places of settlement supported by agriculture in this period, thus destroying de Vaux's original idea that only the Khirbet Qumran site was susceptible to comparison with the one described by Pliny. The effort at identifying these sites, however, only illustrated how much the world of scholarship and archaeology had succumbed to the Qumran-sectarian hypothesis. Trusting fully in it, and noticing that the sites included one—at the locality known as 'En Ghuweir—with an area of graves similar in shape, style, and orientation to the graves in the Khirbet Qumran cemetery, P. Bar-Adon, the late archaeologist who discovered these interesting sites, had urged in several articles that the one at 'En Ghuweir was *another* settlement of what he called the "Judaean Desert Sect."[52] De Vaux himself, although continuing his strong support of the Essene theory, would later address this proposal with the observation: "It may perhaps be suggested that it is rash to apply the designation 'Essene' to the building excavated near 'En el-Ghuweir or to the cemetery which may have been attached to it."[53]

Bar-Adon had made this proposal after opening twenty of the graves and discovering in them skeletons of seven women and one child of approximately seven years of age, as well as those of twelve men. This was yet a higher percentage of women's skeletons than had been found at Qumran. Since no evidence of celibacy was uncovered, the statement of Pliny that the Essenes of the Dead Sea shore were celibate, rather than being acknowledged as in conflict with the findings, was tacitly set aside in favor of another idea that, as we have seen, had already come into play at Qumran itself.

A number of scholars during the 1950s and early 1960s, perceiving certain emerging conflicts between the archaeological findings and the Qumran-Essene theory, had been particularly concerned with the discovery of the graves of women and children in the cemetery adjacent to Khirbet Qumran. Committed in principle to the theory nevertheless, they suggested, as we have indicated above, slightly altering it to take account of the new findings: we should speak, they suggested, not of the "Essenes of Qumran" but rather, without being more specific, of the "sect of Qumran." It was this view, considered to be at least slightly more neutral than the original theory, that came to be reflected after 1967 in the signs erected at the site as well as in Jerusalem's Shrine of The Book. These referred consistently to "the sect that wrote the scrolls" and to its "home" at Qumran.[54]

[52] See P. BAR-ADON in *Hadashot arkheologiot* (Jerusalem), April 1968, pp. 24–28; April 1969, pp. 29–30; idem, "Another Settlement of the Judaean Desert Sect at Ein Ghuweir on the Dead Sea," *Eretz Israel* 10 (1971): 72–89.

[53] DE VAUX, *Archaeology and the Dead Sea Scrolls*, p. 89.

[54] This idea in turn became enmeshed with a growing confusion as to the beliefs and practices of the people thought by the Qumranologists to be living at the site. See the discussion in my *Who Wrote the Dead Sea Scrolls?* Chapters 3–5, 7, 9, and 10. On other manifestations of pan-Qumranism, see my "The Problem of Origin and Identification of the Dead Sea Scrolls," in *Proceedings of the American Philosophical Society* 124 (Feb. 1980), pp. 3–10.

With the discovery of graves at 'En Ghuweir identical in style and orientation to those of the Khirbet Qumran cemetery, this same logic was simply extended. While Père de Vaux insisted that Khirbet Qumran was the very site described by Pliny, no indication of celibacy at Qumran emerged, and so that portion of Pliny's statement referring to the celibacy of the Essenes of the Dead Sea shore was simply removed as a criterion of identification of Qumran's inhabitants. With this logic in play, and now having discovered graves at 'En Ghuweir identical with those at Qumran and also containing the skeletons of women, the archaeologist responsible for the dig went on to extend the new theory: Pliny's celibate "Essenes" were perhaps not really Essenes and perhaps not really celibate, and they lived not in a single habitation but in two, separated from each other by a distance of fifteen kilometers. This view further nourished the growing doctrine of pan-Qumranism.[55]

Precisely who the Jews were who garrisoned Khirbet Qumran at the time of the First Revolt remains, however, a question that still today cannot be answered with assurance. Josephus had described the war as a complex effort involving the participation of many parties and factions among the Jews. Some he called "zealots," or *sicarii*, others the factions who followed one or another leader, while still others he describes simply as the troops or forces fighting on different fronts against the Romans, and led by one or another commander. He had written that the *sicarii* captured Masada from a Roman garrison and that Eliezer B. Yair governed it for about six years while the *sicarii* conducted raids in the neighborhood. Other Jews had joined the *sicarii* at Masada before and during the course of the siege. Manuscript fragments, obviously from scrolls in the possession of the inhabitants, were found by the team of excavators under Yadin's direction who excavated Masada between 1963 and 1965. It is tempting to think that these scrolls reflect beliefs of the *sicarii*, but this cannot be proved from any of the ideas contained in the texts as they became known by 1970.

By 1958 the view had been presented by Cecil Roth[56] that the Qumran site was inhabited by Zealots and that it was to them that the scrolls found in the caves and at Masada belonged—a view later developed by G. R. Driver.[57] For this idea they relied particularly on the fact that some of the scrolls by then known, particularly the *War Scroll*, expressed a remarkably militant apocalypticism.

Because of the great variety of ideas, often conflicting ones, that are found in the scrolls, and since no firm evidence exists to connect the manuscripts found in the caves with the Khirbet Qumran site in an organic way, this thesis,

---

[55] For a yet greater extension of the logic applied to the 'En Ghuweir discovery in the wake of the finding of still more such graves both to the north and south of Khirbet Qumran as well as in Jerusalem itself, see my observations in *Who Wrote the Dead Sea Scrolls?*, pp. 26–30.

[56] CECIL ROTH, *The Historical Background of the Dead Sea Scrolls* (Oxford, 1958).

[57] G. R. DRIVER, *The Judaean Scrolls: The Problem and a Solution* (Oxford, 1965).

in the form presented by Roth and Driver, cannot be considered fully convincing. However, it had the merit of attempting to connect the contents of the scrolls with salient event of Jewish history in that period, that is, the First Revolt of A.D. 66–74. While it is clear that at least the vast majority of the scrolls was composed long before the Zealots had come into existence, there is nevertheless no reason to doubt that they would have been among the groups moved by the contents of those scrolls adopted by them as inspirational writings of their own movements. It is also quite possible that the Khirbet Qumran settlement, showing obvious military aspects, came to be inhabited by the militant *sicarii* or Zealots during the war against Rome, as had Masada. Josephus, however, is entirely silent as to the history of Qumran, and no historical documentation either proves or disproves this idea.

Unlike Masada, no manuscript fragments whatever have been discovered in the ruins of Qumran. Some of the inhabitants might have possessed scrolls, as was true at Masada. However, the massive effort to hide texts in the Qumran caves, the successful effort to hide them elsewhere as well,[58] and the fact that those that survived were copied down by several hundred scribes, not just a few, are indications of a historical phenomenon of much broader dimensions than the hiding of manuscripts possibly in the possession of some of the defenders of Khirbet Qumran. Forty years after the excavations, further archaeological investigations of the site, particularly the cemetery, are still pressingly needed for light on the question of the identity of its defenders. As of 1992 a complete scientific report on the dig was still a desideratum.[59]

For all the reasons given above, however, it is impossible to avoid concluding even in the present imperfect state of our knowledge, that the site, once divorced from the statement of Pliny the Elder, was quintessentially an ancient military fort, erected, according to the hints of architecture, at the time of stabilization of the Hasmonaean state. The First Book of Maccabees—the most historic of the Maccabaean accounts—states that Jonathan the Hasmonaean charged his most trustworthy men with "the building of fortresses in Judaea" (1 Macc. 12.35) around 144 B.C. Scholars have not hesitated to identify the so-called "fortress of the Hassidim" mentioned in one of the Bar Kokhba manuscripts of the 2nd century A.D. with Khirbet Qumran itself, and, as indicated above, some maps of Israel now so identify it. The Hassidim, or "Pietists" were that very group of "mighty men of Israel" (1 Macc. 2.42) who, of course, came to the aid of the Maccabees in their struggle against the

---

[58] On the discovery of Hebrew manuscripts "near Jericho" in both the third and eighth centuries A.D., see now my discussion in *Who Wrote the Dead Sea Scrolls?*, Chapter 4.

[59] This project, based upon DE VAUX's notes and records, is now being undertaken by Profs. Robert Donceel and Pauline Donceel-Voûte of Louvain and Father Jean-Baptiste Humbert of the Ecole Biblique in Jerusalem. In November of 1993, an archaeological team of the Israel Antiquities Authority began further excavations at Khirbet Qumran, as well as in caves near Jericho.

Syrians, and the site may well have been named after them already in the 2nd century B.C. But a strategic bastion of this kind could hardly have been handed over to a peace-loving sect such as the Essenes during Herodian times, and surely not during the period of the First Revolt of A.D. 66–73. A strong military force was stationed there during the war with Rome, as the archaeological evidence acknowledged by Père de Vaux himself indicates.

Some scholars even today insist that the twelve hundred graves lining the plateau next to the site are those of several generations of "Essenes" or related sectarians. There is, however, no stratification whatsoever to these graves, which are rather all on the same horizontal level, and their uniform exterior style shows that they were dug at one time. They are obviously better interpreted as the graves of the Jewish warriors who fought at Qumran. As we have seen, similar graves have been found elsewhere in the Judaean Wilderness, thus helping to trace the Roman army's advance after A.D. 70 toward Machaerus, Masada, and the final stand of its defenders. The very fact that the cemetery lies so close to the site of habitation proves that it could not have been an Essenic graveyard or one in the possession of the authors of the *Manual of Discipline*. No group of pious, purity-loving brethren with priests at their head could have lived in such proximity to a cemetery, as such a move would have violated fundamental principles of the Pentateuchal laws of ritual purity.[60]

From all that is now known of the site, we may conclude that Khirbet Qumran is an important archaeological testament to the First Revolt. There is nothing at the site, however, to attest to its being a monastery, a place where monks or other notable sectarians lived, or a center where scholarship, intense writing activity, or the copying of books was ever pursued.*

---

[60] See further my *Who Wrote the Dead Sea Scrolls?*, Chapter 1.

* In the spring of 1993, the Library of Congress, in association with the Israel Antiquities Authority, sponsored publication of an exhibition catalogue entitled *Scrolls from the Dead Sea*, edited and largely written by AYALA SUSSMAN and RUTH PELED of the Antiquities Authority (Washington, D.C., 1993). The exhibition for which the catalogue was prepared was one that included various artifacts as well as twelve scroll fragments, and which was held first at the Library of Congress (April 29–August 1, 1993) and thereafter at the New York Public Library (October 2, 1933–January 8, 1994) and at the M. H. de Young Museum in San Francisco (February 26–May 8, 1994). The Antiquities Authority authors attempted, in consonance with old explanations of the nature of Khirbet Qumran posted at the site itself by the same agency, to portray the writings displayed as those of a small sect living at Qumran, and to defend the interpretation of the site as a sectarian settlement rather than a military outpost. For an analysis of these efforts, see Chapter 12 of my *Who Wrote the Dead Sea Scrolls?*, and my article, "The Dead Sea Scrolls and the Ethics of Museology," in *The Aspen Institute Quarterly* vol. 6, no. 2 (Spring, 1994), pp. 79–98.

DISCUSSION OF THE PAPER

EPHRAIM ISAAC (*Institute of Semitic Studies, Princeton, NJ*): As as person who always appreciates scholarly heresies, I have followed your theory. You certainly continue to build a fortress out of your thoughts.

I was wondering whether there is any way of reconciling your theory with de Vaux's, in the sense that high places are not only outposts and military fortresses; they also can serve as religious places. I can associate Mount Zion not only with the cult, but also with the religious establishment, and many of the high places—we can go to Mount Carmel, Mount Moriah, the various high places that had very significant religious values. Cannot the two ideas be reconciled?

NORMAN GOLB (*Oriental Institute, University of Chicago, Chicago, IL*): I don't see the compelling reason for this scholarly compromise. There is no textual evidence that states that a sect was living at that site. I believe very much in the *Yahad* group, but, there is no evidence that they were living there. Of course, they were an important reality in Judea in the first century B.C. The Jews were in spiritual turmoil at this time. Look how much we find of that. The texts prove that they were. But, I don't see the sense of scholarly compromises unless they are called for by the nature of the evidence.

HARTMUT STEGEMANN (*University of Göttingen, Germany*): We discussed this theory in the past. One question: You think the Qumran settlement was some kind of fortification. How do you explain the existence of caves 7, 8, and 9? You could reach those caves only by way of the settlement.

GOLB: If I may first address the question of the proximity of these caves to the site: I have never suggested that the inhabitants of the region of Qumran did not help the hiders of the texts. I'm sure the people who brought the scrolls from libraries in Jerusalem, the cultural center, did not carry them there in jars, for example. They asked the inhabitants of the regions near Jericho, near Qumran and so on for aid in hiding these texts.

The claim that you can reach the site only from Khirbet Qumran implies a different kind of question. I do not believe that was the only access in antiquity. We must consider other possibilities, but that doesn't affect in any way the integrity of the hypothesis.

JOSEPH PATRICH (*University of Haifa, Israel*): I read your article and theories with a lot of interest, but nevertheless I have difficulties. First of all, an attack does not constitute evidence that people who were assaulted were warriors. They may have been innocent people.

Another point are the descriptions of Pliny. In this case, we should ask ourselves not just what is said in this short paragraph, but generally: Pliny's descriptions of Judea, to what period do they refer? I suggest you read the article by Menaham Stern, who claims that the descriptions refer to the Herodian period.

GOLB: I did not base the explanation of the nature of Qumran only on the attack, but on the attack (which is described by de Vaux) in combination with the other military features of the site, particularly the tower.

It is a combination of the evidence which in my view leads naturally to the description of the place as a fortress. Indeed, various scholars and archaeologists have recognized this identification, including those who put Khirbet Qumran on the map as a fortress. It is not my original identification. It was widely accepted among archaeologists and cartographers in Israel during the past 20–30 years. It was only after I expressed my doubts about the Qumran-Essene hypothesis in 1980 that scholars started suggesting that it wasn't really a fortress.

Now the other point you raise about Pliny is a matter of debate. I acknowledge the different views about the dating of Pliny's description. However, on the page before, he does describe Machaerus as also having been destroyed by the Romans. And, his description of the political regions of Palestine conform to the divisions after 70 C.E. If there is contradictory evidence, then of course it has to be investigated.

What I do criticize is the willing acceptance of the old idea that Pliny referred to Khirbet Qumran, without careful critical weighing of this assertion.

PATRICH: I have one additional point. If a garrison was stationed here, who was this garrison? Was it a garrison that was entrusted by the Romans? We're speaking of the period when Judea is a Roman province.

GOLB: I thought I answered this question very clearly. Before 70 C.E. this site was in the hands of the Jews. We know this was a Jewish site of a military nature by the findings at the site. The Romans took it from the Jews *circa* 70.

PATRICH: What was it the 200 years before 70 C.E.?

GOLB: Well, I tried to suggest in my articles that it was one of the fortresses built by the Hasmoneans, as is described in the Book of Maccabees itself, where we have Jonathan with his band going to inspect the fortresses of Judea. Archaeologists and cartographers have agreed in naming Khirbet Qumran as *Mesad Hasidim*, "the *fortress* of the Hasideans," in memory of these people.

Khirbet Qumran in Light of New Archaeological Explorations in the Qumran Caves

JOSEPH PATRICH

Department of Archaeology
University of Haifa
Haifa, Israel 31905

INTRODUCTION

In 1983, after two years of conducting an archaeological survey in the region of the Hasmonaean-Herodian fortress of Hyrcania and the monastery of Mar Saba in the Judean desert (Patrich 1993), I suggested that a new project should be started—a systematic survey and excavations of caves in the Judean desert. This was a new initiative. Since I was then a doctoral student in the Institute of Archaeology of the Hebrew University of Jerusalem, I suggested to Professor Yigael Yadin that he share with me the direction of this project, and he agreed to it with pleasure; unfortunately, he died a short time afterwards. Later on a coordinating committee was established, headed by Professor Benjamin Mazar, who had made efforts to raise funds for this project.[1] The survey continued until 1987, when the political situation in those territories brought it to a halt; the excavations are still in progress.

The team had three members, including an expert in mountaineering,[2] since an examination of the most remote and inaccessible caves was an important objective. The survey was conducted in the fall and winter of each year. Many cliffs and ravines were found to contain caves of refuge, which had been used by Jews in the first and second revolts against Rome. A number of these

---

[1] During the five years of the survey research grants were given by the Israel Ministry of Sciences (first three years), the Israel Academy of Sciences and Humanities, the Memorial Foundation for Jewish Culture, Yad Yizhak Ben Zvi Institution in Jerusalem and various private donations. However, the sums obtained enabled us to conduct the survey only on a limited scale. The plans depicted in Illustrations 2 and 5 were measured and drawn by Benny Arubas, the photograph depicted in Illustration 11 was taken by Sven Näckstrand, those depicted in Illustrations 4 and 6 were taken by the author, and all other photographs were taken by Gabi Laron. I am grateful to all.

[2] Benny Arubas was a team member throughout the survey, and his contribution both in the field work and in the processing and evaluating of the finds was a major one. The second members of the team, each an expert in mountaineering, were, for periods of various length, Shmuel Grasiani, Eyal Naor, Hanina Kali, and Benny Agur.

caves were located in places accessible only by means of ropes and ladders. In every case crevices or natural caves were enlarged and prepared by rock-cutting to accommodate the refugees; in many cases water cisterns were cut and plastered, and at one site there was even a ritual bath. These were hideouts prepared in advance by the villagers living on the fringes of the desert, for times of emergency. We found no scrolls, but at one site (Patrich and Rubin 1984; Patrich 1985a; 1985b), Jewish Aramaic inscriptions were found, inscribed in charcoal on the plaster of a cistern that served as a last hiding place. In other places the remains of hermitages and various monastic installations were revealed (Patrich 1989a; 1989b; 1990). All these were available as our comparative material for the study and proper understanding of the finds in our survey and excavations in the Qumran Caves.

THE SURVEY OF THE QUMRAN CAVES

Naturally, one of the first things in our investigation was a re-examination of the Qumran Caves, first explored in 1952 by a team of archaeologists headed by de Vaux (1953; 1962). Our survey was done mainly in December 1984 and January 1985. The territory explored, like that of 1952, was an 8 km long section of the cliffs, with Khirbet Qumran approximately halfway between the two extremes.[3] In 1952 this area was divided between seven crews, each composed of a staff member working with three or four Bedouin (de Vaux 1953: 540–541; 1962: 3–4; Reed 1954: 9). Their work lasted two and a half weeks (March 10–29, 1952). Of the soundings taken, 230 proved barren and only 40 contained pottery and other objects.[4]

Our approach was first to identify the caves marked on de Vaux's map, learn what was done by his team, explore the caves' relation to Khirbet Qumran, and determine which caves could be still further explored by means of archaeological excavations. The excavations, carried out by a large crew, marked the second stage of our exploration.

No soundings were done during the survey.[5] The method was to mark carefully each cave simultaneously on an aerial photograph and on a panoramic horizontal exposure. South of Wadi Qumran aerial photographs were of no help; the cliffs are so steep there that horizontal exposures were enough.

---

[3] During our caves survey other sections of the cliffs descending to the Dead Sea were explored, farther to the south of Khirbet Qumran and Ein Feshkha. These caves, being remote from Khirbet Qumran, are not our concern here.

[4] Site no. 16 in the survey-map, which indicates 40 sites, is the expedition camp, and no. 35 is an Iron-Age structure. But two more caves, yielding pottery and flint objects, were excavated in March 21–24, 1956, during excavation of cave 11Q. (See de Vaux 1956: 573–574; 1962: 13.)

[5] The survey team included Benny Arubas and Eyal Naor, who was later substituted by Hanina Kali. Most of the survey work was carried out by the first team.

It was realized from the very beginning that in order to proceed in this manner a new series of numbers would have to be applied as the illustrations are insufficient in de Vaux's reports and it is impossible to identify with certainty the numbers assigned to many of the caves.

Out of the 57 caves that were marked on our photographs to the north of Wadi Qumran, only 15 yielded archaeological remains, in comparison to 27 in the 1952 survey. To the south of Wadi Qumran the number was 2, in comparison to the 13 of de Vaux. It is clear that in many cases all potsherds, especially those from small cavities and crevices, were collected by the earlier investigators. On the other hand, it seems that some of our caves were not counted by de Vaux.

During our survey, special attention was devoted to trying to trace remains of huts and tents, which, according to de Vaux (1973: 56–57), constituted the dwelling quarters for the majority of the sect members. Anybody familiar with archaeological work in the desert knows that even such humble structures as tents or sheep folds would leave traces; if they existed, they should be traceable and identifiable. Ancient Bedouin encampments are easily recognizable, even though they served as temporary dwelling places instead of being in use over a period of 200 years, like the supposed huts and tents of Qumran. A dwelling place, even one of an ascetic, if intended to serve for many years, should be strong enough to survive sand storms and rain (however scanty in this region) and to give protection from the wild beasts that roam in this area even today.

If the living quarters were really outside, one would expect to find a network of constructed paths to connect these quarters with the communal center. Such paths, which create a sense of community, are seen in every Byzantine monastery of a laura type (Hirschfeld 1992: 18–33, 205–212); they run between the core, where the church, dining room and storehouse are located, and the dispersed cells (which are always well built, with masonry walls, not poor natural crevices or huts, and are appropriate to accommodate a human being for decades of seclusion). Such a network, required especially if the members had to return to their dwelling places at dusk, after the evening meal, is absent in the entire area outside Khirbet Qumran.[6] The single constructed path is the ascent leading to the Buqeia valley and to Jerusalem. We should also expect to find extensions of the aqueduct leading to the supposed dwelling quarters, but there is nothing of that kind. All these considerations

---

[6] On two separate occasions, while leading small groups of guests to visit the caves and our work therein, two persons twisted their ankles. Another point of relevance from the Byzantine sources is that Euthymius, one of the desert fathers at the beginning of the fifth century, refrained from constructing a laura in a steep terrain (similar to that in the rock cliffs of Qumran), because of the difficulties in getting from the cells to the church at dark (*Vita Euthymii* 9, edited by E. Schwartz, Leipzig 1939, pp. 16–17).

lead, in our opinion, to the inescapable conclusion that all the members of the community lived inside Khirbet Qumran. This conclusion was confirmed by the excavations as well.

THE EXCAVATIONS IN THE QUMRAN CAVES

The excavations, still in progress, constituted the second stage of our work. Since 1986 four seasons have been conducted in five caves, four to the north of Wadi Qumran and one to its south.[7] Digging a cave is not a simple task. There is the problem of light, which is neither sufficient nor as uniform as daylight. The danger of collapse and enormous amounts of dust require the wearing of helmets and filtering masks. Even so, breathing is difficult. The stay inside the cave is limited to periods of only half an hour at a time—it is then required to go out and breathe fresh air. The dust reduces visibility to zero, and there must be work breaks to let the dust settle. Sometimes heavy equipment is required to get rid of huge boulders, and the construction of a conveyer inside the cave is not always possible.

Cave 8 (=3Q, the Copper Scroll Cave)

The first cave to be excavated by us was the Copper Scroll Cave. In the 1952 survey the cave was marked as no. 8. It was explored between March 14th and 25th, 1952, by a crew headed by Henri de Contenson. The third cave to yield scrolls—fourteen fragments inscribed on parchment—it was then marked as 3Q. On March 20th two rolls of a copper scroll were found as well (de Vaux 1953: 555; *idem* 1962: 7–8; Baillet and Milik 1962: 94–104, 201, 211ff.). A plan with the exact location where the parchment scrolls and the Copper Scroll were found was not published by de Vaux, and the various descriptions he gave were not sufficiently precise in this respect (Laperrousaz 1989: 120*–122*). The plan measured at a later date and published by Pixner (1983: 362), is schematic and lacks accuracy and his reconstruction of the original layout of the cave and the location of the scroll-jars in it is hypothetical (*cf.* de Contenson's remark in Laperrousaz 1989: 122*).

---

[7] The excavations, directed by me, were undertaken on behalf of the Institute of Archaeology of the Hebrew University of Jerusalem (the 1986 and 1988 seasons), and Zinman Institute of Archaeology of the University of Haifa (the 1991 season). The staff included Benny Arubas (1986, 1988, and 1989), Hanina Kali (1986), and Benny Agur (1988, 1989). In two seasons (1986 and 1988) the work was funded and carried out by volunteers from the United States, led by Mr. V. Jones, the director of the Institute for Judaic-Christian Research in Arlington, Texas, and in one season (1989), volunteers were organized by Dr. R. Eisenman, on behalf of California State University at Long Beach. The 1991 season was funded by private donations and a research grant from the Zinman Institute of Archaeology of the University of Haifa, and the work was carried out by my students in that University. Thanks are due to all.

The French scholars were of the opinion that the ceiling collapsed at some date after the placement of the scrolls, covering more jars underneath. We decided to examine this statement by removing the huge boulders of the ceiling collapse. A large compressor and quarrying accessories, including a 100 m long air-pressure pipe, were brought to the site, being dragged for the last 200 m by 25 people since it was impossible to approach the cave by vehicle.[8]

As we soon realized that the rock was too hard to be cracked by the blows of the air-pressure hammer, the method adopted was to drill holes and pour in self-expanding cement. The next day the boulders split by themselves into a few smaller pieces, which then were further hewn to a manageable size. All we found underneath was a grey layer, less than 1 cm thick, with a few Chalcolithic sherds—not a single sherd of the Qumran type!

It is clear that the ceiling of the cave collapsed many years before the jars with the scrolls were hidden in the cave. During periods Ib and II at Qumran the shape of this cave was very much like that at the start of our excavation. It was a quite open recess, exposed to daylight, not a deep and dark cave, suitable for hiding precious writings. The jars containing the scrolls were simply heaped behind the rocks. This is quite conceivable in case of a *Genizah*. This was not a good place to choose, if the idea was to find a hiding place for an active library. For this purpose better caves could have been chosen.

Cave 11Q

The cave was not excavated nor recorded by the 1952 expedition. In 1956 the Taamire Bedouin found here several large documents, including a Psalms Scroll, an Aramaic paraphrase of Job, and presumably the Temple Scroll as well (Fitzmyer 1990: 68–75). As a consequence it was entirely cleaned out by de Vaux, who was working then at Khirbet Qumran. The finds included a small pick, a chisel, and a knife, all of iron. The amount of pottery was small, but typical of Qumran, including a jar and two lids; there were in addition pieces of linen, basketry, ropes, and several inscribed parchments (de Vaux 1956: 573–574).

Starting our dig,[9] a 20 m long conveyer was installed in the cave, half inside and half outside, conveying the dirt and stones down the terrace that was

[8] Our excavations at the site were conducted April 14–21, 1986. The excavations were undertaken on behalf of the Institute of Archaeology of the Hebrew University of Jerusalem and the Institute for Judaic-Christian Research in Arlington, Texas. The expedition resided in Kibbutz Qalia. The air compressor and accessories were loaned by Even Va-Sid Quarries Ltd. Thanks are due to all.

[9] Our work was conducted from February 29th to March 15th 1988 and a small area at the entrance was checked in March 31st and April 1st 1991. The 1988 excavations were conducted on behalf of the Institute of Archaeology of the Hebrew University of Jerusalem and the Institute for Judaic-Christian Research at Arlington, Texas. The Expedition resided in Kibbuts Qalia. I am grateful to all.

LIST OF ILLUSTRATIONS

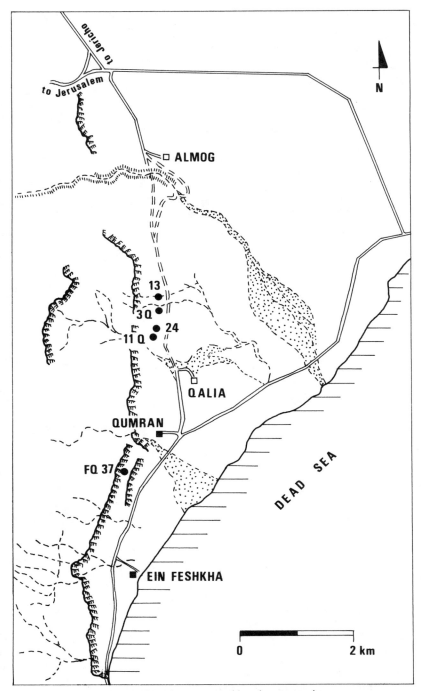

FIGURE 1. Location map, marking the excavated caves.

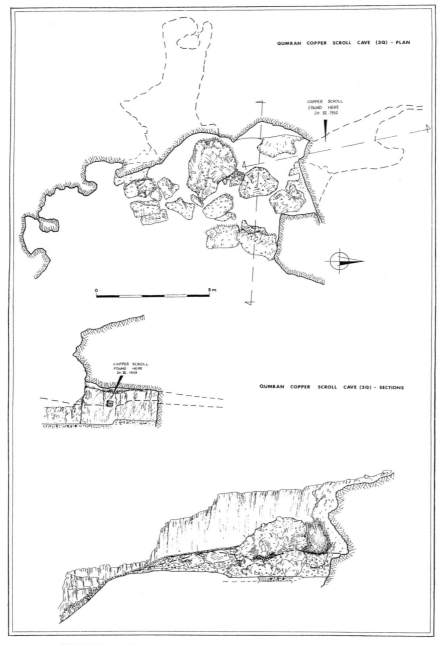

FIGURE 2. The Copper Scroll Cave (3Q). Plan and cross-section.

FIGURE 3. Volunteers pulling the compressor to the proximity of Cave 3Q.

FIGURE 4. Drilling holes in the boulders of Cave 3Q.

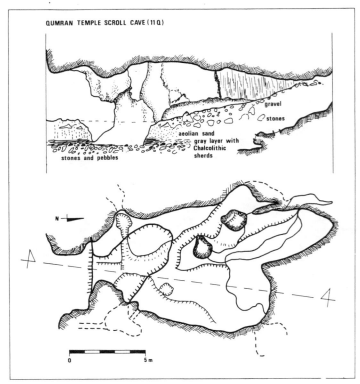

FIGURE 5. The Temple Scroll Cave (11Q). Plan and cross-section.

FIGURE 6. The conveyer at work at the entrance to Cave 11Q.

FIGURE 7. Cave 24. A cylindrical jar.

FIGURE 8. Cave 24. A bag-shaped jar with the Hebrew letter *alef* inscribed on its shoulder.

FIGURE 9. Cave 24. A cooking-pot.

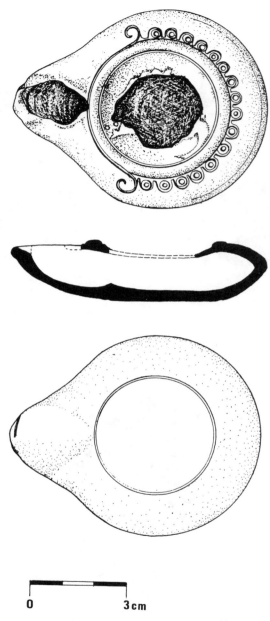

FIGURE 10. Cave 24. A Roman round-lamp.

FIGURE 11. Cave 13. A juglet containing balsam(?) oil.

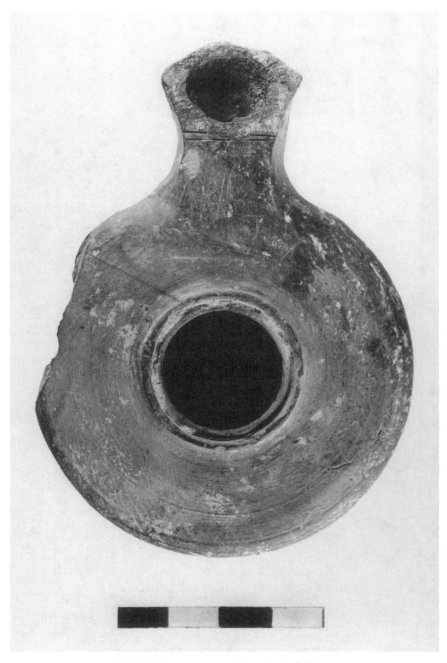

FIGURE 12. Cave 13. A "Herodian" oil lamp.

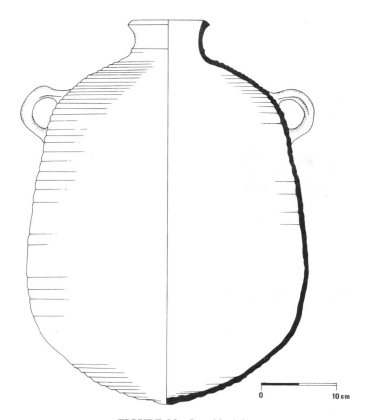

FIGURE 13. Cave 13. A jar.

FIGURE 14. Cave 13. The author and Benny Arubas sitting in front of the cave.

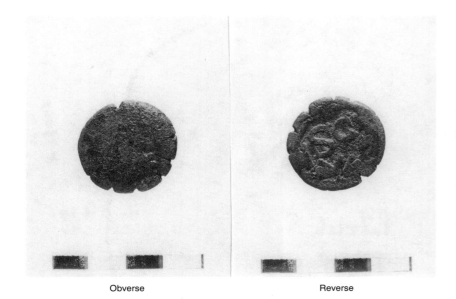

Obverse   Reverse

FIGURE 15. Cave FQ37. A Roman bronze coin.

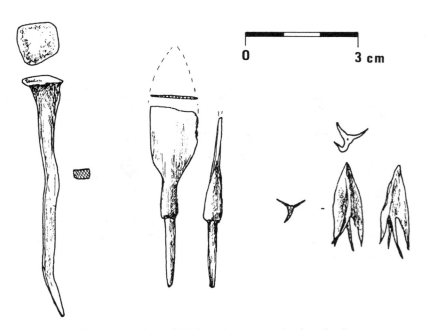

FIGURE 16. Cave FQ37. Iron Roman arrowheads and nail.

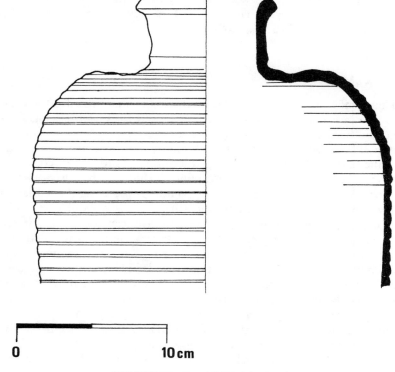

0   10 cm

FIGURE 17. Cave FQ37. A broken jar.

formed in front of the cave by the dump of the previous dig. No layer that could have been attributed to the Qumran period was found. Only four tiny Roman potsherds were retrieved by us from the dump heaped inside the cave, and two pieces of cloth were found in the innermost crevice.

It is clear that the scrolls were found by the Bedouin in the uppermost level, or in the north crevice. The crevice to the right of the entrance, cleared by us, was full of sterile aeolian sand.

Cave 24

The number was given by us during the survey that preceded the excavations. The cave is *ca.* 50 m to the north of 11Q. It faces north, being located at the southern end of a 70 m long terrace that served until recently as a sheepfold.[10] The finds belong to three main periods. The first is Pre-Pottery Neolithic B, the second is the Chalcolithic and the third, which concerns us here, is the Roman period. The Roman finds include a rich collection of pottery, some now completely restored: a cylindrical jar, a bag-shaped jar with the Hebrew letter *alef* inscribed by black charcoal on its shoulder, a cooking pot, a complete Roman round-lamp the figurative scene of which was deliberately mutilated, and a fragment of a Jerusalemite painted bowl. Most interesting is a rim fragment of a Nabataean Cream Ware vessel, a large number of which were found in post-destruction Masada. The entire ceramic corpus from this cave—jars (at least ten, of the two main types mentioned above), cooking-pots (at least six), juglets (at least five), and the oil-lamp, suggest the last phase of the Herodian period or even a post 70 C.E. date.[11] Other finds include date pits, pieces of ropes, basketry and cloth, a bronze needle with a square section, and a bronze ear- or nose-ring.[12]

The cave is large and habitable, but it is doubtful whether it ever served other than for temporary dwelling for shepherds or refugees. Fire places in various spots inside the cave, rather than in a single corner, created thick layers of ash. No installation of a more permanent nature was observed and no effort was made to narrow and block the opening in order to protect its inhabitants. A goat dung layer dated to the Roman period by radiocarbon measurements is in accord with this picture. The Roman finds may belong to some temporary inhabitants that found refuge at the site at *ca.* 70 C.E. or later.

---

[10] Two seasons of excavations were conducted in the cave: the first, on behalf of the Institute of Archaeology of the Hebrew University of Jerusalem and the Institute for Judaic-Christian Research in Arlington, Texas, from March 14th to March 28th 1988, and the second, on behalf of Zinman Institute of Archaeology of the University of Haifa, from April 1st to April 4th 1991.

[11] The pottery here and in the other caves was read by Rachel Bar Nathan. I am grateful to her.

[12] The metallurgical analysis of the bronze finds was carried out by Mr. Sariel Shalev and N. Halperin in the laboratories of the Institute of Archaeology of Tel Aviv University.

Cave 13 (The "Balsam Oil" Cave)

The number was assigned in the framework of our survey. It may correspond to cave no. 2 of the 1952 survey. A detailed report on the 1988 season has already been published (Patrich and Arubas 1989). The finds included a Herodian juglet, wrapped in palm fibers, containing viscous oil, presumably a residue of aromatic balsam oil. A second season took place in April 1991.[13] The cave has a wide opening facing to the east. Its northern part is occupied by three huge boulders that collapsed from the ceiling, while the entire area to their south is clear of any large boulders.

The main effort in the 1991 season was devoted to cleaning an inner crevice at the northwestern corner of the cave, which was not touched in the previous season. It turned out to be a pit, more than 3 m deep, filled with earth and small stones. The last 1.5 m was mixed with a large quantity of potsherds, date stones, and dry dates. One complete jar in which the dates were stored was mended, but originally there were more in use in the cave, since five jar stoppers made of lime mixed with straw were found there as well. Also found was a fragment of an oil lamp with a vertical handle made of black ware and a wood stick, *ca.* 30 cm long.

The pottery corpus is larger now, and its chronological span can be determined with greater precision. Most of it is early, representing period Ib in Qumran, although some types continued in the later period as well. As for the juglet with oil and the jars with the dates, they may date as late as 70 C.E. (or 68 C.E. in this region). It seems that at this time of emergency several people found refuge here, bringing with them jars with dates for food, and hiding behind the huge rocks. It seems that they were also responsible for the hiding of the "balsam juglet." It is doubtful if they were members of the sect, since according to the sect's laws oil defiles the body (Josephus, *Jewish Wars* II.123; Baumgarten 1967).

No effort was ever made to level the area in front of the cave and to transform it to a comfortable front terrace. This observation as well confirms our previous statement that the cave never served as a permanent dwelling.

Cave FQ37

It seems that this cave is identical to cave 37 of the 1952 expedition (de Vaux 1962: 12), but the location marked on their map is not correct. It is the largest cave to the south of Khirbet Qumran, *ca.* 1 km (not 2.5 km) distant

---

[13] The excavations, between March 31 and April 11, 1991, were conducted on behalf of Zinman Institute of Archaeology of the University of Haifa. The work was carried out by students of archaeology of that University. Benny Arubas updated the 1989 plan and cross-sections.

from it. Our excavations[14] were preceded by a survey during which a bronze
Roman coin and a fragment of a wooden plate were found. On the reverse
of the coin the Latin monogram S(enatus) C(onsultum) is inscribed inside a
wreath, while the bust of the emperor on the obverse was deliberately rubbed
away. Such coins, occurring in the first and second centuries C.E. were minted
in Antioch. Also found were a nail and two arrowheads, all of iron. One arrow
is trilobate and the second, the point of which is broken, is leaf shaped. The
trilobate arrow head has parallels in Gamla, Masada, and Nahal Hever (Gutmann 1977: 28–31; idem 1985: 36–40; Yadin 1966: 57; and idem 1971: 88).
Many potsherds, all of the same jar, were found as well. All survey finds came
from the terrace.

The cave is located high in the slope, and the ascent is quite difficult and
steep, but no ladder or ropes are required. It opens at the southern end of
a terrace (A), which faces eastward. In the terrace were found remains of a floor
made of mud mixed with palm fronds. Owing to disturbances in the entire
area caused by previous excavations, it was impossible to tell whether it should
be assigned to the Roman or to the Chalcolithic period. In cave 13 a similar
floor of mud mixed with straw was dated to the Iron Age II. But since most
finds in the terrace belong to the Roman period, it makes sense to assume that
the floor as well should be assigned to this period.

The Roman finds from the terrace, other than those already mentioned
above, include fragments of four glass plates, two of which have folded decorated rims; fragments of two stone vessels; and a variety of pottery vessels,
all fragmentary—jars (at least 5, of several types), cooking pots (at least 3), juglets (at least 12), bowls (at least 3, two of which are painted on the inside,
belonging to the Jerusalemite painted pottery), and a "Herodian" oil lamp.
The corpus as a whole belongs to the last years of the Second Temple Period,
but some types started earlier and some can be post-70 C.E. The arrow heads
attest to a period of war, indicating that the site served as a place of refuge
in emergency, rather than a place of seclusion of an ascetic.

On the other hand, the mud floor, if Roman in date, points to a dwelling
place of a more prolonged nature in time of peace. In this case we may assume
that the person who secluded himself here had some connections to the community of Qumran. This is the only place, other than the caves in the marl
plateau, that could have served as a dwelling place. If the terrace of the cave
served as a dwelling place for a prolonged period before becoming a place of
refuge, its inhabitant was probably not obliged to descend daily to the communal center in order to participate in the daily meals and prayers. He got
permission to live in seclusion. And such was, in my opinion, the case of the

---

[14] The excavations, taking place between January 1st and 19th 1989, were undertaken on
behalf of the Institute of Archaeology of the Hebrew University and California State University,
Long Beach.

one who inhabited cave 4Q. Similar phenomena occurred in the Byzantine period when distinguished members of the community were allowed to live as anchorites or recluses outside the monasteries, of both the laura and coenobium types, being exempt from the daily tasks and communal liturgy (Patrich 1990; Hirschfeld 1992: 212–222).

SUMMARY

Our survey and excavations confirmed de Vaux's statement (1973: 56–57), that the caves in the limestone cliffs, as a whole, did not serve as habitations for the members of the Dead Sea Sect, but rather as stores and hiding places (similarly Reed 1954: 12 n. 6). On the other hand, being aware that the site is of a quite small size, his other suggestion (*ibid.*), that only the administrators of the community resided inside the walls, while the majority of its members had their living quarters in huts and tents outside Khirbet Qumran should be rejected. The hut indicated by the five wooden posts found in 1952 in cave 17—a narrow crevice (Baillet and Milik 1962, Pl. VII:3), should not, in my opinion, be conceived as a place of prolonged dwelling, but a temporary refuge.

As was mentioned above, in the entire area around Qumran there are no remains of the supposed encampments of tents and huts, that should have served, according to de Vaux, the majority of the members—several dozens at least—for a period of 150–200 years during which the community existed at the site. Postulants requiring to join the community could have lived temporarily outside, in the natural crevices and caves, or in humble huts among the rocks. Violators of the Sect's laws, expelled from the community, could have found there a temporary refuge as did other members when obliged to escape in times of emergency—most probably as a result of the Roman assault in 68 C.E. And we should not forget the existence of the shepherds of the desert, who might have frequented the caves from time to time, as they did until recently.

The dwelling quarters should be sought inside the wall of Khirbet Qumran, mainly on the upper story. According to the plan of the site, the dimensions of the built area, including the cisterns, is *ca.* 60 × 80 meters. The dimensions of the Monastery of Martyrius in the Judean desert are similar, and its population was estimated by the excavator to be between 100 and 120 (Hirschfeld 1992: 78–79). Milik (1959: 97) suggested that the Qumran community counted 150–200 members, and there are also higher estimates (Laperousaz 1976: 99–107). Recently Broshi (1992: 61–62) estimated it as not more than 150, since the dining room was large enough to accommodate this number. This seems to be a reasonable figure if the members of the community shared rooms, or slept in dormitories, as was the practice in many Byzantine monasteries. But since this is doubtful with regards to the Dead Sea Sect, the population should be reduced, in my opinion, to only 50–70.

REFERENCES CITED

BAILLET, M. and J. T. MILIK
  1962 *Discoveries in the Judaen Desert of Jordan. III: Les "petites grottes" de Qumran.* Oxford.
BAUMGARTEN, J. M.
  1967 The Essene avoidance of oil and the laws of purity. *Revue de Qumran* **6**, pp. 183ff. [= idem, *Studies in Qumran Law*, 1977, pp. 88ff.].
BROSHI, M.
  1992 The archaeology of Qumran–A reconsideration, in M. Broshi *et al.* Eds., *The Scrolls of the Judaen Desert. Forty Years of Research.* Jerusalem.
DE VAUX, R.
  1953 Exploration de la région de Qumrân. Rapport préliminaire. *Revue Biblique* **60**, pp. 540–561.
  1956 Fouilles de Khirbet Qumrân: Rapport préliminaire sur les 3e, 4e et 5e campagnes. *Revue Biblique* **63**, pp. 533–577.
  1962 *Les 'petites grottes' de Qumran.* I. Archéologie. In: Baillet and Milik 1962, pp. 3–36.
  1973 *Archaeology and the Dead Sea Scrolls.* London.
FITZMYER, J. A.
  1990 *The Dead Sea Scrolls. Major Publications and Tools for Study.* Atlanta.
GUTMANN, SH.
  1977 *Gamla. The Historical Background.* The first season of excavations (Hebrew).
  1985 *Gamla. The First Eight Seasons* (Hebrew).
HIRSCHFELD, Y.
  1992 *The Judean Desert Monasteries in the Byzantine Period.* New Haven and London.
LAPERROUSAZ, E. M.
  1976 *Qumran, l'établissement essénien des bords des la Mer Morte. Histoire et archéologie du site.* Paris.
  1989 L'Établissement de Qoumrân près de la Mer Morte: Forteresse ou couvent? *Eretz Israel* **20** (Yadin Volume), pp. 118*–123.*
MILIK, J. T.
  1959 *Ten Years of Discoveries in the Wilderness of Judaea.* London.
PATRICH, J. and R. RUBIN
  1984 Les grottes de el-Aleiliyat et la laure de Saint Firmin. *Revue Biblique* **91**, pp. 379–387.
PATRICH, J.
  1985a Hiding caves and Jewish inscriptions on the cliffs of Nachal Michmas. *Eretz Israel* **18** (Avigad Volume), pp. 153–166, pls. 24–27 (Hebrew).
  1985b Inscriptions araméennes juives dans les grottes d'el-Aleiliyat, Wadi Suweinit. *Revue Biblique* **92**, pp. 265–273.
  1989a Hideouts in the Judean wilderness. *Biblical Archaeology Review* **15**, pp. 32–42.
  1989b Chronique Archéologique: Refuges juifs dans les gorges du Wadi Mukhmas, *Revue Biblique* **96**, pp. 235–239, pl. XV.

PATRICH, J. and B. ARUBAS
  1989   A Juglet containing balsam oil(?) from a cave near Qumran. *Israel Exploration Journal* **39**, pp. 43–55, pl. 6.
PATRICH, J.
  1990   The cells (*ta kellia*) of Choziba, Wadi el-Qilt. In *Christian Archaeology in the Holy Land. New Discoveries.* G. C. Bottini, Leah Di Segni, and E. Alliata, Eds. Jerusalem 1990.
  1993   *Map of Mar Saba (315).* Israel Antiquities Authority, The Archaeological Survey of Israel. Jerusalem (in press).
PIXNER, B.
  1983   Unravelling the Copper Scroll code: A study on the topography of 3Q15. *Revue de Qumran,* no. 43, tome 11, fasc. 3, pp. 323–366.
REED, W. L.
  1954   The Qumran caves expedition of March, 1952. *Bulletin of the American Schools of Oriental Research* **135**, pp. 8–13.
YADIN, Y.
  1966   *Masada.* Tel Aviv and Haifa (Hebrew).
  1971   *Bar-Kokhba. The Rediscovery of the Legendary Hero of the Second Jewish Revolt Against Rome.* Jerusalem (Hebrew).

DISCUSSION OF THE PAPER

LAWRENCE SCHIFFMAN (*New York University, New York*): Thank you. I had the privilege of visiting these and some other caves twice. I can testify from having walked back and forth that everything you said about the lack of access to the main site is true. But, I would like to ask you to speak a little bit about a cave that you didn't discuss, Cave Four. I think one of the important issues is whether or not there isn't something particularly distinctive about Cave Four, that might link it to the building complex in a way that goes beyond the pottery linkage.

JOSEPH PATRICH (*University of Haifa, Israel*): I didn't work in Cave Four, so the archaeology that was done there is what was done by de Vaux. According to my impression, and with comparison to the other caves, it is a habitable cave. I assume that it served as a place of dwelling before the Scrolls were deposited there, in a time of emergency. (That one particular person who lived there was absent from his daily duties.) I think that this is also the case with caves 7, 8 and 10 under the terraces, which are more accessible from Khirbet Qumran. I think in terms of anthropology, the comparison with anchorite cells located outside cenobitic monasteries of the Byzantine period, is very relevant.

Some Remarks on the Qumran Cemetery

ZDZISŁAW JAN KAPERA

Institute of Oriental Philology
Jagiellonian University
Al. Mickiewicza 9/11
31-120 Kraków, Poland

INTRODUCTION

The cemetery on the terrace dominating the Wadi Qumran ravine toward the north, several hundred meters from the shore of the Dead Sea and close to the ancient ruins of Khirbet Qumran, has been known to Biblical scholars for a century and a quarter.[1] However, the scrolls scholars who, for the last forty years, have been so very much interested in showing connections between the manuscripts from the caves and the ruins of the settlement have very seldom turned their eyes to the cemetery.[2] As an eminent Qumran scholar has observed in his synthesis of Qumran discoveries, "only a small number of [graves] have been investigated, because the difference between one and another of them does not seem significant."[3] I am afraid he was repeating the opinion of the excavators.

The only existing, *i.e.*, published, plan of the cemetery is the work of an outsider,[4] even though a synthesis of the Khirbet Qumran excavations was published by Father Roland de Vaux twice,[5] and the five seasons of digging

---

[1] The first exploration of the Qumran graveyard took place on 29 November 1873. One of the ancient tombs was opened in the presence of CHARLES CLERMONT-GANNEAU; *cf.* his *Archaeological Researches in Palestine*, Vol. II, London 1896, pp. 14–16 (reprinted in ANDRÉ DUPONT-SOMMER, *The Jewish Sect of Qumran and the Essenes*, London 1954, pp. 1–2).

[2] If we put aside the improbable suggestions of H. E. DEL MEDICO (*The Riddle of the Scrolls*, London 1958, pp. 84 ff.), the only valuable remarks on the Qumran cemetery were offered by E. F. SUTCLIFFE (*The Monks of Qumran as Depicted in the Dead Sea Scrolls*, London 1960, pp. 30–32).

[3] J. VAN DER PLOEG, *The Excavations at Qumran: a Survey of the Judaean Brotherhood and Its Ideas*, London 1958, p. 73.

[4] *Cf.* S. H. STECKOLL, "Marginal notes on the Qumran excavations," *Revue de Qumran* **25** (December 1969) plan on p. 38 and a revised, more detailed plan in his article "The community of the Dead Sea Scrolls" (offprint from: *Atti del Convegno internazionale sui metodi di studio della città antica*, 1973, Centro di studi e documentazione sull 'Italia Romana, *Atti* vol. V, 1973–1974, fig. 7).

[5] First in French: *L'Archéologie et les Manuscrits de la Mer Morte*, London 1961 and in revised form in English: *Archaeology and the Dead Sea Scrolls*, London 1973.

on the site were presented by him three times officially and on many more occasions in abbreviated form.[6] Every loculus can be identified in the general plan of the ruins, but it is impossible to locate even approximately the already dug ancient tombs. Not even 50 tombs of the more than 1200 were excavated in 1949, 1951, 1953, and 1956 by professional archaeologists,[7] and their contents were published only in a very preliminary form. It looks ironic that the only promising excavation of a tomb from the Qumran terrace was done by an amateur without the support or even permission of the official excavator. In return for his interesting observations published in the *Revue de Qumran*,[8] the man received the name of "the Sherlock Holmes of archaeology."[9] Father R. de Vaux's negative attitude to Solomon H. Steckoll, who eventually dug an additional 12 tombs in the Qumran area in 1965–1967 and contributed a great deal to the general interpretation of the cemetery, is indeed surprising. Since his time; *i.e.*, for the last quarter of a century, not even one new tomb has been opened. But in the last decade the Qumran cemetery has come into prominence again in connection with a dispute over Norman Golb's hypothesis of Jerusalem origins of the Dead Sea Scrolls.[10]

CEMETERIES OR A CEMETERY?

Even if Father R. de Vaux usually describes the graveyard close to Khirbet Qumran as a cemetery, in his description of tombs he immediately differentiates between a main cemetery and two other, smaller ones, one to the north and one to the south. They are called "les prolongements du grande cimetière" (extensions to the main cemetery) or "les deux cimetières secondaires" (the two secondary cemeteries).[11] E.-M. Laperrousaz, who was helping Father de Vaux in his Qumran excavations, always speaks about cemeteries ("les cimetières"); he also corrects some other data about the graveyard.[12] Father de Vaux always used the estimate concerning the main cemetery only, *i.e.*, about 1100 tombs, while E.-M. Laperrousaz adds another hundred to count

[6] *Cf.* Ch. Burchard, *Bibliographie zu den Handschriften vom Toten Meer*, I-II, Berlin 1957–1964, s.v. de Vaux.

[7] *Cf.* R. de Vaux, "Fouille au Khirbet Qumrân." Rapport préliminaire, *Revue Biblique* 60 (1953): 95, 102–103 and plates IV–V and "Fouilles de Khirbet Qumrân. Rapport préliminaire sur les 3ᵉ, 4ᵉ et 5ᵉ campagnes," *Revue Biblique* 63 (1956) pp. 569–572.

[8] S. H. Steckoll, "Preliminary excavation report in the Qumran cemetery," *Revue de Qumran* 6 (23) (February 1968) pp. 323–334.

[9] *Cf.* his article "The community of the Dead Sea Scrolls" (note 4 above) and preliminary, anonymously published information in the article "Nouvelles données sur la secte de Qumrân," *Nouvelles Chrétiennes d'Israel*, 23, No. 1(9) (1972), pp. 31–32.

[10] *Cf.* Z. J. Kapera, "Bibliography of Norman Golb's hypothesis of the Jerusalem origin of the Dead Sea Scrolls," *Folia Orientalia* 27 (1990) pp. 217–221.

[11] *L'Archéologie*, p. 46 and *Archaeology*, pp. 57 f.

[12] E.-M. Laperrousaz, *Qoumrân. L'Établissement essénien des bords de la mer Morte*, Paris 1976, pp. 19–25.

the number of all the tombs in the area. All the published descriptions of the cemetery or the cemeteries are vague, as nobody in fact has counted the tombs, or prepared a scholarly, detailed plan.

The general description of the Qumran cemetery by Father R. de Vaux was so suggestive that it was widely accepted by scholars describing the plateau; this includes three members of his scrollery team (J. T. Milik, F. M. Cross, and J. M. Allegro)[13] and other authors of general syntheses of the Dead Sea discoveries (such as F. F. Bruce[14] and E. F. Sutcliffe[15]) as well as authors of popular handbooks. Even if many of them visited the site, only Solomon H. Steckoll protested in print. During his own excavations at the graveyard in 1965–1967, he made preparations for the first plan of the area. It was done by S. Tsemel and published in the *Revue de Qumran* in December 1969, fifteen years after the last season of the Qumran excavations. To quote the words of S. H. Steckoll, the map "shows that there is a single cemetery only which follows the natural topography eastwards from the Qumran building, with four prongs marked I, II, III, IV, at the eastern edge of the plateau covered by graves." He is right in saying that "The conception of a single unified cemetery as shown on the topographic map, is of capital importance for the understanding of the Qumran Community." He adds, "that there was a single cemetery following the natural topography can also be seen from an aerial photograph . . . of the Israeli Air Force and the Israeli Department of Surveys. This is also seen on the Palestine Survey air photograph of 1936."[16] But did Father de Vaux ever study those available photographs? I am afraid not, as he never quoted them. However, except for a few negative remarks by Father R. de Vaux about S. H. Steckoll's activities there was no answer to the latter's discovery. Only August Strobel took S. H. Steckoll's suggestion seriously and pictured the cemetery as one unit on his sketch plan of the Qumran plateau. In 1974 S. H. Steckoll published a more detailed plan of the cemetery, but the article, in a rare Italian scholarly journal, escaped the notice of the Qumran scholars altogether.

INTERPRETATIONS OF THE QUMRAN CEMETERY

Father R. de Vaux never tried to evaluate, in the proper sense of the word, his own excavations at the Qumran graveyard. In all his publications it is ap-

---

[13] *Cf.* below, notes nos. 19–21.
[14] F. F. Bruce, *Second Thoughts on the Dead Sea Scrolls*, London 1961 (2nd ed.), pp. 47 f.
[15] E. F. Sutcliffe, *op. cit.* (note 2 above).
[16] S. H. Steckoll, "Marginal Notes . . . ," pp. 37–38. *Cf.* A. Strobel, "Die Wasseranlagen der Hirbet Qumrân" (*Zeitschrift des Deutschen Palästina-Vereins* **88** [1972] fig. 4 on p. 79) and J. A. Sanders, "The Dead Sea Scrolls–A quarter century of study" (*The Biblical Archaeologist* **36** [1973] pp. 118–119.)

parent that he used them instrumentally, to support some of his preconceptions.[17] At the beginning he was interested to find out if the tombs might offer him any explanation for the ruins of Khirbet Qumran and the contents of Cave 1. Later, he looked for an argument to confirm his view that unmarried Essenes had been living in Qumran. When tombs of females were found, the notion that there had been a main cemetery and annexes appeared. In his synthesis (English version), apart from a very general presentation of the main cemetery and the secondary cemeteries, he used the results of his research only in order to:

1) state that "the people who lived in the caves or in huts near the cliffs were the same as those who used to hold their assemblies at Khirbet Qumran. There they had their communal activities and their communal stores. They laboured in the workshops at Khirbet Qumran or on the farm at Feshkha. They were buried either in the main cemetery or in the subsidiary ones" in the period "which extended from the second half of the second century B.C. to A.D. 68";

2) count the number of people living in the area. To quote him: "it can be estimated that even at the period of its greatest prosperity the group would not have numbered many more than 200 members";

3) use the cemetery as an argument for identification of the Qumranites with the Essenes. According to the ancient transmissions of Philo, Pliny the Elder, and Josephus the latter abstained from marriage. The findings from the main cemetery (with one exception) fitted in very well with the texts. These tombs were burials of men. Unhappy with the tombs of females and children in the extensions to the main cemetery, Father R. de Vaux finally declared, "clearly the women's tombs do not strengthen the argument that the community was related to the Essenes, but they do not rule it out either";

4) reject K. H. Rengstorf's view that the Qumran settlement was "the temple property" which "included an agricultural and industrial estate in the area." It is hard not to agree with Father R. de Vaux's observation that "the proportions of the communal buildings of Qumran, the number of the caves made use of, and the great cemetery of more than a thousand tombs are out of proportion with the needs of the personnel attached to an estate of a few square kilometres."[18]

And that is all we know. Not very much. If we add that about forty years after the first excavations of tombs they are still not properly published and

---

[17] This opinion has been expressed by N. Golb since 1979 and was also repeated during the Graz Qumran Symposium. The proceedings of the symposium have been published by the Minorite Center in Graz: J. B. BAUER, J. FINK, and H. D. GALTER (eds.) *Qumran Ein Symposion* (= *Grazer Theologische Studien* 15, Graz, 1993) Cf. summary: M. KLINGHARDT, "Qumran Nowhere? A Symposium on the Origin of the Dead Sea Scrolls and the Khirbet Qumran Site (Graz/Austria, Oct. 17/18, 1992)," *The Qumran Chronicle* 2, no. 1 (December 1992) pp. 32 ff.

[18] All quotations from *Archaeology*, pp. 86 (twice), 129, 105–106.

that (according to personal information received from Mr. Magen Broshi) the bones have "disappeared" and cannot be found, the picture we receive of Father R. de Vaux's research is very disappointing.

Father R. de Vaux's influence on the interpretation of the Qumran cemetery by the members of his "scrollery team" is evident. J. M. Allegro, F. M. Cross, and J. T. Milik accepted the main lines of his proposals adding some marginal remarks. J. T. Milik not only stressed the atypical, systematic plan of the cemetery, but also mentioned a possibility that the annexes to the main cemetery came from a later phase of the Qumran settlement.[19] F. M. Cross agreed with the latter remark, but did not exclude that both married and unmarried Essenes had lived in the area simultaneously.[20] Only J. M. Allegro was interested in the interpretation of incomplete skeletons or in the burials with bones broken. Some of these "broken remains" were "victims of the earthquake which destroyed the monastery in 31 B.C." He did not rule out that "Essenes elsewhere, suffering violent or shameful deaths, were brought to the Qumran cemetery to find a final peace among their brothers". In his opinion "not all of the inhabitants of the cemetery had died peacefully."[21]

The research of Father R. de Vaux in the Qumran graveyard was from the beginning carefully observed by many scholars. André Dupont-Sommer presented his own interpretation of the excavations as early as 1953. According to him, "the simplicity of the graves reflects the spirit of poverty which inspired them [i.e., the Essenes] in their lifetime. The regular arrangement of the graveyard reflects the strict discipline of their communal lives, and the uniformity of the tombs is in accordance with their spirit of equality. Their particular burial rites indicate even in death the special character of their ritual, and also, no doubt, their belief in the resurrection of the body."[22]

Nobody else went so far as A. Dupont-Sommer did in his interpretation, but the main lines of Father R. de Vaux's inventions remain binding for members of the official team of publishers of the Dead Sea Scrolls to this day. The recent publications of Magen Broshi (Director, The Shrine of the Book, Jerusalem) and his public presentations, for instance at the Graz Symposium, *Qumran Nowhere*, in mid-October 1992, are a typical example.

M. Broshi defends strongly not only the Essene identification of the Qumran sect, but also the monastic character of the settlement. In this interpretation, the division into the main cemetery (for men's burials) and small ones (for females and children) plays a special role. He agrees that the existence of tombs of women and children "in a site supposed to be occupied by a

[19] J. T. MILIK, *Ten Years of Discovery in the Wilderness of Judaea*, London 1959, p. 47.

[20] F. M. CROSS, *The Ancient Library of Qumran and Modern Biblical Studies*, Garden City, NY, 1961, pp. 97 f.

[21] J. M. ALLEGRO, *The People of the Dead Sea Scrolls in Text and Pictures*, Garden City, NY, 1958, p. 49.

[22] A. DUPONT-SOMMER, *op. cit.*, pp. 7 f.[1]

monastic community has naturally raised questions." In his opinion their presence "can be explained by supposing that these were people close to the residents of Qumran," where he means a "closeness of kinship or ideological closeness."[23] As he explained more clearly in Graz, these were bodies of "relatives of the people that lived at Qumran, physical relatives or spiritual relatives."[24] He comes back to the fact that in several Qumran ditches the remains of wooden coffins were recognized, including nails. That was enough for him to state that "the coffins testify most probably that the skeletons were brought from afar." In his paper at the Haifa Colloquium (1989) he even goes so far as to say, "In three graves the skeletons were found disjointed with some parts missing, something that might indicate that these are secondary burials of people who died elsewhere and were first inhumed in a different place before they were removed to Qumran. This also might explain the fact that the cemeteries included also nonmembers." To sum up: to save the Essene working hypothesis M. Broshi admits that "part of the [Qumran] burials (and what part we do not know) are of people that were brought from the outside."[25]

This is not the place or the time to present the strongly disputed hypothesis of N. Golb concerning Jerusalem origins of the Dead Sea Scrolls. However, I should like to stress that interpretation of the Qumran cemetery figures as a major argument in the hypothesis. N. Golb's purpose is to undermine the picture of the Qumran settlement as a monastic center of the Essenes.

At the beginning, in his first paper presented to the American Philosophical Society on April 20, 1979, N. Golb observed that "no doctrine of celibacy could be located in any of the scrolls, while on the other hand—contrary to early expectations—graves of women as well as men were found in the ancient cemetery lying to the east of the ruins of the settlement."[26] In a footnote to this text he quoted a long passage from Father R. de Vaux's hesitant interpretation concerning identification of the Qumranites on the basis of the celibacy demonstrated by the cemetery and of the text of Pliny the Elder speaking about the Essenes living without sex on the edges of the Dead Sea. N. Golb noticed Father de Vaux's artificial division of the Qumran cemetery, into a main one and extensions and stressed the obviously high percentage of the female skeletons in the cemetery as a whole. He found Father de Vaux's "wording" to "appear unfortunate."[27]

[23] *Cf.* M. BROSHI, The archaeology of Qumran—A reconsideration. In *The Dead Sea Scrolls. Forty Years of Research*. Edited by D. DIMANT and URIEL RAPPAPORT, Leiden-Jerusalem 1992, p. 112. This article has already been published (early in 1992) in Hebrew. I am greatly obliged to M. Broshi for sending me a copy of the unpublished English version of his paper in 1991.

[24] As recorded during the conference.

[25] *Cf.* note 23. All quotations are from the English typescript.

[26] N. GOLB, "The problem of origin and identification of the Dead Sea Scrolls" (*Proceedings of the American Philosophical Society* **124** [1980] No. 1, p. 1).

[27] *Op. cit.*, p. 13 note 10.

For years N. Golb's view went unnoticed. Only J. D. Amusin from Russia recorded it as one of the main arguments against possible identification of Pliny's Essenes with the dwellers of Qumran.[28]

In 1985 N. Golb repeated the main lines of his original essay in the *Biblical Archaeologist*.[29] The idea attracted me so much that I organized the first of the Mogillany colloquia in 1987 specifically to discuss his Jerusalem hypothesis in a circle of Qumran scholars.[30] Of course arguments based on data from the cemetery were also taken into consideration. Particularly disputed was the problem of transportation of bodies in wooden coffins; no conclusion was reached.

An additional aspect was added to N. Golb's interpretation of the cemetery when he developed an argument to recognize Khirbet Qumran as a fortress (*American Scholar*, Spring 1989).[31] Professor John C. Trever, veteran of Qumran research, strongly attacked this vision, using among other arguments this straightforward question: "would a cemetery of over 1000 identical, austere graves be adjacent to a fortress?."[32] After the receipt of J. C. Trever's letter N. Golb replied immediately. He said that after the excavation of some tombs of females "not only did a special exegesis of the nature of Qumran Essenism follow" among leading French and American specialists in 1958–1973, but "also the excavation of all the remaining 950-plus graves was discontinued"–all that to save the Essene identification.[33] "No stratification of the graves has ever been demonstrated," he went on; "from the contents of those graves that were explored and from the uniform layout of all the graves together, and minus the Qumran-Essene identification, the cemetery appears much more likely to have been that of victims of the war with Rome." The ancient graveyard held the remains of "those who perished when the Qumran site was attacked as well as those once living in the nearby area of Judaea." He noticed that "in those days" parts of this area "were fertile farmland regions quite heavily populated."[34]

In the same year, in a paper delivered at the Groningen Qumranological congress, also F. Garcia-Martinez, who was firmly defending the Essene iden-

[28] J. D. AMUSIN, *Kumranskaya obshtshina* (The Qumran Community) [in Russian], Moskva 1983, p. 266 note 66.
[29] N. GOLB, "Who hid the Dead Sea Scrolls?" (*Biblical Archaeologist* 48 [1985] No. 2, pp. 62–82.
[30] *Cf.* Z. J. KAPERA, "An International Colloquium on the Origins of the Dead Sea Scrolls (Mogilany near Cracow: May 31–June 2, 1987)," *Folia Orientalia* 24 (1987) pp. 299–301 [esp. pp. 299 f.] and his "The present state of research on Qumran texts" [in Polish], (*Euhemer* 1989, No. 2–4 (152), pp. 33–57 [esp. pp. 39–42]).
[31] N. GOLB, "The Dead Sea Scrolls. A new perspective" (*American Scholar* 58 [1989] No. 2, pp. 177–207.
[32] Letter of Professor J. C. TREVER, dated April 17, 1989, to *The American Scholar*, printed in the September 1989 issue.
[33] *Cf.* Norman Golb replies, *The American Scholar* 58, September 1989, p. 629.
[34] *Ibid.*, pp. 629–630.

tification, underlined the question: "if the Khirbeh was a fortress, what could be the explanation for the big cemetery of more than a thousand tombs?". He recalled the argument had been used by R. de Vaux "against the theory of K. H. Rengstorf, who saw the Khirbeh as an agricultural estate" and said that it was "equally valid against N. Golb's view of the Khirbeh as a fortress."[35] N. Golb was not able to answer this criticism of his hypothesis in person, so he defended his idea again while participating in the second international colloquium at Mogilany, which came immediately after the Groningen congress in September 1989. Again, he developed his argument used previously against J. C. Trever point by point. To quote N. Golb: "From the findings that a large percentage of the exhumed skeletons were evidently of men and women under forty, that the graves included one of a woman together with a two-year-old baby and a small girl, and that the tombs were laid out closely together in regular rows and appear to have been dug and covered in haste by more or less identical processes, it would appear at least equally plausible that these graves were dug during a relatively short time and were the result of large numbers of people dying, or being put to death, in quick succession—as happened throughout Judaea in the First Revolt." Even if so positive in his statement, N. Golb did not exclude that "the cemetery may also have served as a burial ground for many inhabitants of the region, not only those connected with the fortress." Again he rejected the claim that it was "an Essene burial site" as this was an opinion based "on no more than the assumption that Khirbet Qumran was a mother-house of Essenes."[36]

In a lecture delivered at the Huntington Library in mid-July 1992 and in a German paper read in mid-October at the Graz Symposium on the Dead Sea Scrolls, N. Golb once more stressed that the bodies of women and children from the Qumran cemetery "contradicted the original identification based on Pliny."

What are we to think of these so greatly divergent opinions represented by M. Broshi and N. Golb and based on preliminary information from the first fifty-two tombs opened in the Qumran graveyard? The opponents agree only on one point: that the preliminary publications are insufficient to lead to definitive results. M. Broshi even said in Graz that only one skeleton had been published properly. (He did not mention that it was found in Q.G. 2 opened by S. H. Steckoll). However, both sides staunchly defend their stand.

[35] F. Garcia-Martinez and A. S. van der Woude, "A 'Groningen' hypothesis of Qumran origins and early history" (*Revue de Qumran* 14, fasc. 4 [April 1990] pp. 528 f.)

[36] This is a quotation from a tape recording made during the paper presented by N. Golb at the conference held in Mogilany in September 1989 Cf. N. Golb's summary of the paper, "Hypothesis of Jerusalem Origin of DSS–Synopsis," in *The Qumran Chronicle*, 1, No. 1 (August 1990) p. 37 (& 5).

To evaluate their positions I will try to answer briefly three most important questions:

1) Are tombs from the Qumran graveyard Jewish burials?
2) Are they tombs of a specific religious group?
3) Are they a post-battle cemetery?

THE JEWISH NATURE OF THE QUMRAN GRAVEYARD

Concerning the Qumran cemetery only three identifications are possible: it holds tombs of pre-islamic Arabic people, tombs of Moslems, or tombs of people of Jewish origin. The second possibility was rejected in the 19th century, when the cemetery was first discovered, because of the atypical north-south orientation, impossible for Moslem burials.[37] The possibility of it being a cemetery of pre-islamic nomadic Arabs was raised by an eminent French archaeologist, chief of the Mari expedition, André Parrot, at the Congress of Biblical Archaeology held in Saint Cloud in 1954. He stressed not only that fixed, well-organized cemeteries had existed, but also that camel transport of bodies had been confirmed. However, the type of tombs and the bent position of bodies distinguish these pre-islamic burials from those of the Qumran cemetery.[38] So only the third possibility remains, that we have here a Jewish graveyard. The fact has not been proved over the years, as we have no inscriptions from the cemetery. S. H. Steckoll's observation that some stones close to the head of the body in some tombs were covered with sacred texts, even if promising, remains unproved.[39] Fortunately, a similar cemetery was discovered in 1969 in 'Ain el-Ghuweir (by P. Bar Adon) and there, in an exactly parallel tomb, a jar was found with a small Hebrew inscription with a typical Jewish name, Jehohanan.[40] So there is no objection to identifying the Qumran graveyard as a Jewish one. Dating it to the same period as the Khirbet Qumran settlement is obvious, as in the fillings of some tombs exact parallels of pottery were found (first century B.C.–first century A.D.).[41] S. H.

---

[37] Cf. CH. CLERMONT-GANNEAU, op. cit., p. 14 (reprinted in A. DUPONT-SOMMER, op. cit., p. 1).

[38] A. PARROT, "Les Manuscrits de la Mer Morte." In La Bible et l'Orient. Travaux du Premier Congrès d'Archéologie et d'Orientalisme Bibliques (Saint-Cloud, 23–25 avril 1954), Paris 1955, pp. 63–64 and especially the discussion quoted on p. 67.

[39] Cf. S. H. STECKOLL, "Preliminary report," p. 331 and Father R. de Vaux's negative opinion, Archaeology, pp. 47 f.; but see S. H. STECKOLL, "Community," p. 241–243.

[40] P. BAR ADON, "Another settlement of the Judean Desert Sect at 'En el-Ghuweir on the shores of the Dead Sea" (Bulletin of the American Schools of Oriental Research 227 [October 1977] pp. 17, 20, and figs. 21, 23). Cf. also R. DE VAUX, Archaeology, p. 89; E. M. LAPERROUSAZ, op. cit., pp. 113; Z. J. KAPERA, "Osiedle w Ain el-Guweir" (The settlement at 'Ain el-Ghuweir) [in Polish] (Filomata [1990] No. 395, p. 37.

[41] Ibid., p. 17.

Steckoll's soundings in suspected graves close to the settlement wall also proved that the distance between the dead and the living, *i.e.*, 50 cubits, had been carefully observed, following the Jewish law of the time.[42]

ATYPICAL CHARACTER OF THE QUMRAN BURIALS AND ATTEMPTS AT THEIR EXPLANATION

Two different kinds of burials are known in the Palestine of the Hasmonaean and Herodian periods: primary burials in coffins and secondary burials in ossuaries. Both are directly or indirectly attested in the great centers nearest to Qumran, *i.e.*, Jerusalem and Jericho. However, in Jericho, Qumran and 'Ain el-Ghuweir shafts graves were found, sometimes with coffins, with at least one peculiar burial practice: broken storage jars were placed close to the graves (on top of the grave at 'Ain el-Ghuweir and at Qumran, but just next to the tomb in Jericho).[43]

The graves from Qumran and 'Ain el-Ghuweir have many features in common. First of all they are for the most part primary burials in individual graves.[44] If we leave aside a few tombs of mothers with young children, there is one body lying in one tomb. According to S. H. Steckoll's observations, "the articulation of the skeletons shows that bodies had been buried immediately after death, and the general Jewish practice of a second burial of bones was not practiced at Qumran. It is patently clear that the graves had never been reopened by the Sectarians after the burial of their dead."[45] This practice was exceptional in contemporary Palestine. Another important feature is the organized plan of the cemetery, with rows of single burials. They follow the unknown habit of a north-south orientation of tombs with the body lying in an air-pocket covered by stones or bricks, with the head to the south and face looking east. Both the unusual orientation of the tombs and the position of the corpses seem to reflect a group of people following their own religious rule, unusual for Palestine. It was natural that "these tombs in the middle of the desert were commonly accepted as the cemetery of a religious community."[46]

The rare burial habits are slowly being explained. As long ago as 1958 J. T. Milik, basing his judgment on the Enoch texts from Cave 4, elucidated the

---

[42] *Cf.* S. H. STECKOLL, "Preliminary report," pp. 327–328.

[43] R. HACHLILI and A. KILLEBREW, "Jewish funerary customs during the Second Temple period" (*Palestine Exploration Quarterly* 115 [1983] pp. 126–127). *Cf.* also R. HACHLILI, *Ancient Jewish Art and Archaeology in the Land of Israel*, Leiden 1988, p. 102, and G. J. BROOKE, "The Temple Scroll and the archaeology of Qumran, 'Ain Feshkha and Masada" (*Revue de Qumran* 13, fasc. 1–4 (49–52), [October 1988] pp. 233–234).

[44] This feature is especially underlined by R. HACHLILI and A. KILLEBREW, *op. cit.*, p. 126.

[45] S. H. STECKOLL, "Community," p. 229.

[46] The expression of A. DUPONT-SOMMER (*cf.* his *The Essene Writings from Qumran*, Gloucester, MA, 1973, pp. 64).

mysterious north-south orientation of the tombs: Paradise was located in the far north. According to one of the deciphered passages, when the dead wake up they will arise with their faces to the north and will walk straight on to the Holy Mountain, the Heavenly Jerusalem.[47] The incomprehensible position of the bodies usually in the niche in the eastern side of the grave with the face looking to the east, is to be understood as the sun-orientation of a people who prayed at dawn for the rising of the sun. And this habit was known among some dwellers of ancient Palestine. Worth noticing is also the so-far-overlooked observation of D. V. Zaitschek that the line of burials forms a right angle with the direction of sunrise at the winter solstice.[48]

All these underlined special features of the Qumran cemetery seem to suggest that the graveyard was connected with one specific religious group. The group was from the beginning of research connected with the sect of Essenes as described by the ancient texts of Pliny the Elder, Philo of Alexandria, and Josephus Flavius.

Father R. de Vaux for years forcefully imposed his view that the Essenes lived in Qumran in strict celibacy. But he did not necessarily succeed in defending his view. Unlike him, A. Dupont-Sommer saw no problem, even though some female skeletons were found in the graveyard. He used the passage of Josephus Flavius speaking about the married Essenes in *War*, II, && 160–161. What is more, according to A. Dupont-Sommer in some exceptional cases a pious woman may have been admitted "to take her last sleep in the cemetery of the holy ascetics."[49]

Another suggestive explanation of the female graves at Qumran was offered recently by Professor Shemaryahu Talmon in his paper at the Graz Symposium, *Qumran Nowhere*, in mid-October 1992. He interprets "Khirbet Qumran as the center of 'Qumranites' in which members of the group spent several years before they returned to their former places . . . Only during this part-time retreat to the desert did the members live in celibacy, the married ones leaving their families behind. The skeletons of women and children at the . . . cemetery are of the part-time retreaters' families that had been shipped to the desert during their fathers' and husbands' stay at the center."[50]

If the identification is accepted it is not necessary to explain the exceptional poverty of the male tombs. According to Pliny the Elder, the Essenes lived *sine pecunia*.[51] What is more, even female tombs contained extremely

---

[47] J. T. MILIK, "Hénoch au Pays des Aromates (Ch. XXVII à XXXII). Fragments araméens de la Grotte 4 de Qumrân" (*Revue Biblique* **65** [1958] p. 77 note 1). *Cf.* A. DUPONT-SOMMER, Essene Writings, p. 65 note 1.

[48] *Cf.* S. H. STECKOLL, Community, pp. 222–223.

[49] A. DUPONT-SOMMER, *Essene Writings*, p. 65.

[50] *Cf.* summary of this paper in M. KLINGHARDT, "Qumran Nowhere?" p. 34.

[51] PLINY THE ELDER, *Hist. Nat.*, v, xvii, 73, edited by Mayhoff (Teubner). *Cf.* A. ADAM, *Antike Berichte über die Essener* [2nd ed. prepared by Chr. Burchard], Berlin 1961, p. 38 and G. VERMES and D. GOODMAN, *The Essenes according to the Classical Sources*, Sheffield 1989, p. 32.

poor furnishings. If we know that according to ancient transmissions there were only about four thousand Essenes living in all Palestine, it is explicable why in some tombs we have wooden coffins. Some members of the sect or members of their families may have requested to be buried in a place distant from their home, *i.e.*, in Qumran, where they had first joined the sect. If we know about the peaceful disposition of the sect, it is clear why not a single one of so many tombs opened contained a sword, dagger or other piece of weaponry. Last but not least, it is worth quoting an observation by Stephen Goranson. If the Qumran settlement was a fort, or a winter villa, or a resort, we could expect "jewelry or other aristocratic or military effects." He is certainly right in saying that "Sadducees would likely rather be buried in Jerusalem than at Qumran."[52] As nothing could link the tombs with the third important sect, the Pharisees, only the Essenes (if not some Essene-like sect) remain as a possible solution.

POST-BATTLE CEMETERY

The point of view represented by the official editors concerning identification of the Qumran cemetery is rejected with conviction by N. Golb. He has stressed many times in his public lectures that "the claim that it was an Essene burial site . . . is based on no more than the assumption that Khirbet Qumran was a mother-house of Essenes."

Contrary to other scholars, N. Golb is ready to explain the regular rows of tombs, the simplicity of the shape and the burial process itself: the burials were done in haste, which could be connected with "large numbers of people dying, or being put to death, in quick succession."[53] He combines this fact with the events in Judaea during the anti-Roman Revolt of 66–74 A.D.

N. Golb has never used an anthropological argument which I must raise at this moment. According to N. Haas and H. Nathan, anatomists who worked with S. H. Steckoll, Q.G. 2 and Q.G. 3 may really have contained the bodies of massacred people.[54] If we add that similar anthropological observations were made about some other tombs discovered in the 1950s by Father R. de Vaux (but differently interpreted as secondary burials, as some parts of the bodies were missing)[55] we can say that N. Golb's suggestion gains an ad-

---

[52] S. GORANSON, "Sectarianism, geography, and the Copper Scroll" (*Journal of Jewish Studies* **43** [1992] p. 285).

[53] Statements recorded at the 2nd International Colloquium at Mogilany (1989).

[54] *Cf.* N. HAAS and H. NATHAN, "Anthropological survey on the human skeletal remains from Qumran" (*Revue de Qumran* 6, no. 3(23), [February 1968] pp. 345–352) and H. STECKOLL, "Community," p. 230.

[55] *Cf.* remarks of R. de Vaux concerning tombs 11, 24 and 37 ("Fouilles de Khirbet Qumrân," pp. 570, 572; Archaeology, p. 46). He suggested that in those three cases we could

ditional argument. At least ten percent of the Qumran graves opened so far are of this kind.

If we add, moreover, that several skeletons from the tombs opened by S. H. Steckoll have traces of burned bones,[56] we could expect that they are bodies of people who were killed by pieces of woodwork crumbling in the final stage of a siege of Qumran buildings (whether it was a fortress or not). It is very easy to imagine that the Roman soldiers (if it was really they who destroyed the settlement, which I think is only a suggestion, but not proved) deciding to stay (for a military reason, for example to watch the water transport in this part of the Dead Sea area and movements of rebel troops) simply had to clear the newly taken post of bodies of the dead. The remaining Qumran dwellers, obliged to bury their dead in a short period of time, still observed their burial habits.

As we see, N. Golb's proposal is acceptable at least as regards a part of the Qumran cemetery. Some tombs are certainly connected with the period of the Jewish Revolt. But how many?

SOME FINAL PROPOSALS

Starting again with Father R. de Vaux,[57] many scholars have repeated that all conclusions from the discoveries at the Qumran cemetery are provisional ones. The number of tombs opened so far is small, less than five percent of the total number (fifty-two graves out of about twelve hundred). However, even in this small percentage of graves, female graves (sometimes with children) and graves of children are quite frequent. This fact seriously undermines

---

have had skeletons transported from somewhere or maybe remains of the victims of an earthquake (*Revue Biblique*, p. 572). I reject the earthquake hypothesis. In the settlement at 'Ain Feshkha, which is very close, "there are no traces of a fire or earthquake" as stressed by R. de Vaux himself (*Archaeology*, p. 69). 'Ain Feshkha is only three kilometers to the south of Qumran! The strongest apparent proofs of an earthquake at Qumran, the broken cisterns, can probably be explained by a simple mistake of their builders. The capacity of the cisterns was too large. When too much water flowed in, the cisterns were destroyed. *Cf.* S. H. STECKOLL, "Marginal Notes," p. 34, quoting the summary of an interim report of T. ZAVISLOCK for the Jordan Department of Antiquities.

[56] In the graves numbered Q.G. 3, Q.G. 4, Q.G. 6 and Q.G. 10. *Cf.* S. H. STECKOLL, "Community," pp. 214–215. According to him "The Qumran Sectarians practised what we could call a form of purification or baptism by fire after death during the burial of the departed" (p. 215). However, traces of burnt wood in the filling of shafts and burn traces on bones ought rather to be connected with a great fire and destruction of the settlement, when some dwellers certainly lost their lives. In any case, during future excavations at the Qumran graveyard, it would be useful to take extreme care when digging the bottoms of shafts, to verify the observations of Steckoll.

[57] *Cf.* R. de Vaux, "Fouille au Khirbet Qumrân," p. 103; "Fouilles de Khirbet Qumrân," p. 571; and *Archaeology*, p. 47 (where he explicitly stated, for example, "The indications as to sex and age are useful, but the small number of the tombs excavated does not permit us to draw any statistics from them which can validly be applied to the cemetery as a whole").

the Essene hypothesis of Father R. de Vaux. There is also another serious argument against the hypothesis.

As Father E. F. Suttcliffe, SJ, has rightly observed "the youthfulness of the
men is surprising. One was about 16, six in their twenties, twelve in their
thirties, four about 40, and four about 50 or over. Men who live the simple,
ascetical life practiced by the Essenes are known for their longevity as in the
case of Carthusians and Camaldolese, not to mention the Fathers of the
desert. And Josephus remarks on the long lives of the Essenes" [BJ II, VIII,
10 & 151]. And he goes on to remark, "chance plays strange tricks, but it
would be against statistical probability" if Father R. de Vaux in choosing the
graves "in different parts of the cemetery had uniformly alighted on those of
the youthful members of the Community."[58] To comment on Father
Sutcliffe's remarks it is necessary to add that the percentage of young women's
graves is also very high. If I interpret the anthropological data properly not
even one female found at Qumran was over forty years old.[59] In 'Ain el
Ghuweir not even one was over thirty-four years old![60]

Let me conclude by saying that we should:

1) prepare a scholarly map of the Qumran cemetery with the exact location of already opened tombs;

2) publish all anthropological materials still in existence or rather publish
the never finally announced results of the previous research done both in Paris
and in Jerusalem;

3) undertake additional tests on any bones still preserved; we can now do
tests to ascertain, for example, whether there is any family relationship among
the buried persons;

4) include all the existing excavation notes and all photographs from the
Qumran cemetery in a final publication of the site;

5) consider new excavations in the cemetery to verify Father R. de Vaux's
and S. H. Steckoll's observations. If we take advantage of recent progress in
medicine and anthropology we can be sure that some of the mysteries of the
cemetery will finally be solved.

---

[58] E. F. SUTCLIFFE, op. cit., pp. 31–32.

[59] The main known examples: a) Excavations of R. DE VAUX: T.1–a woman about 30;
T.32–a woman about 30; T.33–a woman a little younger than 30; T.34–a woman about 25;
T.35–a woman between 30 and 40 (cf. "Fouilles de Khirbet Qumran," pp. 570–571); b) Exca-
vations of S. H. STECKOLL: Q.G.6–a woman aged 25 years; Q.G.7–a girl aged 14–16 years;
Q.G.8–a woman aged 23 years (cf. Excavation Report, p. 335).

[60] According to the research of N. Haas the women from 'Ain el-Ghuweir were between 18
and 34 years old. Cf. P. BAR ADON op. cit., p. 16.

DISCUSSION OF THE PAPER

HARTMUT STEGEMANN (*University of Göttingen, Germany*): Dr. Kapera, thank you very much for your interesting information. There is one problem. The initial idea is that all the graves which are there in the cemeteries are graves of the people who died on the site and its surroundings. We cannot know from the type of bones whether these are Jewish bones or Roman bones and so on. But, we could check how old the bones are. This should be done by radiocarbon tests. For the present, it was done by Japanese in the 1960s, but nobody knows about it.

ZDZISLAW J. KAPERA (*Jagiellonian University, Cracow, Poland*): Nobody knows.

STEGEMANN: Yes, because nobody found this article which was published by Steckoll in one small Italian journal. They are very well-known names from Japanese science. I do believe it is a matter of more or less 100 B.C.

KAPERA: Okay.

IDA FRÖHLICH (*Annenberg Research Institute, Philadelphia, PA*): Do you have any suggestions as to who could bury these people after the battle in single tombs? Because as I know the archaeology of battlefields, people are usually taken into a common tomb. It seems too irregular to me. Before the 20th century there is no evidence for this.

KAPERA: Of course, I agree. I repeat, only part of the tombs were done after a battle. It is a suggestion connected with the presence of burned wood inside the tombs. Anthropologists had so decided that these people died in a battle. So these tombs certainly are tombs of people who died during battle and were buried by some other people thereafter. Nobody would suddenly kill everybody. As you know, the Roman Army never killed everybody. The deaths occurred during the siege of some sites. The Romans were very pleased to have as many slaves as possible, so they had enough people from Qumran if the site was taken. They simply used them to bury the bodies of the people from the site any way they wished. They didn't care about it, in my opinion. They simply wanted to [clean and] use this post. I'm sure that the Roman Army used this post for some period between A.D. 68 or 69 and 74, before Masada was taken. Later on, probably not.

DENNIS PARDEE (*Oriental Institute, University of Chicago, Chicago, IL*): I have two related questions. Do you think that Roman soldiers are buried there as well as the people from the site?

KAPERA: No, no. There is no chance to find something like this. I don't believe that the fighting at Qumran was extensive. I don't believe that Khirbet Qumran was in fact destroyed by Romans.

PARDEE: What about the number of graves? We heard varying numbers yesterday about the number of inhabitants of the site. Does the number of graves coincide with your view of the number of inhabitants of the site?

KAPERA: Yes. Dr. Patrich was saying that it was between 60 and 150 people. In my opinion we should check the bones by radiocarbon again. Probably there are similar strata in the cemetery. Also, I don't believe that these tombs all belong to the same group. The cemetery was in use for a long time.

JOSEPH PATRICH (*University of Haifa, Israel*): Thank you for your presentation. I just wanted to add, in terms of comparison to the Byzantine period, we have a monastery of Hozeba with a burial chapel with a large number of inscriptions, about 300. Among them several women are attested, and we know monasteries of the time were either male or female. I think the comparison is relevant.

KAPERA: Thank you very much.

PAULINE DONCEEL-VOÛTE (*University of Louvain, Belgium*): Just two remarks. They are not hasty graves. They are deep graves. Not hasty graves and very poor graves. I think that's about all you can really say about them.

KAPERA: You mentioned yesterday that nothing was left of Steckoll's materials. So far, no one has quoted the article discovered and given to me by Dr. Hans Burgmann. It was quite long, about 25 pages. The article gives several different options. For example, the author compares this cemetery with cemeteries of Mandaean people from Iraq. I don't know how relevant it is. I didn't control it.

What is most interesting is that the author quotes scientists on some specific objects from the cemetery. There are also some photographs which are useful for future publication. And, there are also some remarks concerning some small pieces found during excavation. For example, in prehistoric times there was water in that area. It was not like today. It was not desert.

PARDEE: Can you give us the reference?

KAPERA: I must check it; one moment. It is an off-print from *Atti V CSD I R* 1973–74. It is a small journal, for a local Italian scholarly society. [It is in fact an offprint from: *Atti del Convegno internazionale sui metodi di studio della citta antica, 1973*, Centro di studi e documentazione sull 'Italia Romana, *Atti* vol. V, 1973–1974, pp. 199–244. I should like to thank Professor Robert Donceel for his kind help in solving the abbreviation. (ZJK, Dec. 1993)].

PARDEE: I'd like to ask you one point of precision here. Yesterday, Professor Golb made a major point in his lecture about the distance of the cemetery from the site. I thought I heard you say in the course of your lecture that it was . . . established by Steckoll.

KAPERA: No. I'm pretty sure this calculation was done by Professor Witold Tyloch in 1967 for Steckoll.

He asked Tyloch to find these references, and how to count the distance which was obligatory in the first century A.D. They found that it is 50 cubits. I don't know. I'm not a specialist in the law of this time. Steckoll is saying that the distance between the tombs and the site is about 30 meters. He was very anxious to get permission from the Department of Antiquities of Jordan to open two places which looked like tombs near the settlement rock. He opened them and they turned out to be only stones—no graves beneath. So apparently this law of distance was accepted. It is a Jewish cemetery according to him.

PARDEE: Any remarks on that?

GOLB: I really didn't want to inject myself into the debate since I spoke yesterday on the topic. My point yesterday was that there was a minimal distance and that it would be very strange for a purity-loving group, as described in the *Manual of Discipline*, which had priests who played an important role in the society, to put the cemetery right next to the site at a minimal distance.

ERIC MEYERS (*Duke University, Durham, NC*): I would disagree with Norman Golb on this point. I can name dozens and dozens of sites in Palestine, of a reformed, conservative, orthodox nature, where there are synagogues with contemporary tombs within 20 meters. It is very, very common. As long as it went on downwind and outside the distance, I don't think this is a problem. We have dozens and dozens of sites like that.

GOLB: Eric, we are not talking about the normal practice of the Jews, but the theory that a group of purity-loving brethren, who were extreme in their purity habits and who had priests in their society, would do this particular thing. It seems to me it was unnecessary to dig graves at Qumran at such a short distance. They had land further away, which would make it easier for the assumed purity-loving society to be at ease with respect to their distance from the cemetery.

Women in the Dead Sea Scrolls

EILEEN M. SCHULLER

Department of Religious Studies
McMaster University
Hamilton, Ontario, Canada L8S 4K1

In keeping with the concerns of this Conference for issues of methodology in the study of the Dead Sea Scrolls, I would like to situate this paper and take some methodological clues from a broader area than is perhaps usual in Qumran Studies. Today, it is acknowledged that "'women in antiquity' is now a fully established area of specialization within classical scholarship,"[1] and, more specifically, the study of women in the religions of the ancient world has developed into a sub-specialization. A feminist critical methodology has evolved which seeks to put women as well as men at the center of our study and reconstructions. Given the androcentric nature of both our ancient sources and of much modern scholarship, this has necessitated a painstaking task of reading old texts with new presuppositions about the presence and roles of women, of gathering and preserving whatever information has survived, and of using a disciplined imagination in the reconstruction of historical reality.

In an important survey article in 1983, Ross Kraemer was already able to synthesize an extensive body of primary research on women in Early Christianity and in the Greco-Roman religions; however, on turning to Judaism, she noted the contrast: "all in all, there has been very little careful scholarly consideration of women in the varieties of Judaism in late antiquity."[2] The last ten years have done much to fill this lacuna and there are now major studies on Jewish women in the Diaspora, in Philo, Josephus, in the Mishnah, and in much of the Apocrypha and Pseudepigrapha.[3] Yet there has not been, to my knowledge, similar scholarly work on women in that type (those types)

[1] SKINNER, M. 1987. "Rescuing Creusa: New methodological approaches to women in antiquity." *Helios* **13**: 1.
[2] KRAEMER, R. S. 1983. "Women in the religions of the Greco-Roman world." *Religious Studies Review* **9**: 127–139.
[3] The bibliography is now too extensive to be comprehensively listed here, but I would mention in particular: KRAEMER, R. S. 1992. *Her Share of Blessings: Women's Religions among Pagans, Jews, and Christians in the Greco-Roman World.* Oxford University Press. London; LEVINE, A-J. 1991. *"Women Like This" New Perspectives on Jewish Women in the Greco-Roman World.* Scholars Press. Atlanta; BROWN, C. A. 1992. *No Longer Be Silent: First Century Jewish Portraits of Biblical Women.* Westminster/John Knox Press. Louisville, KY; ROMNEY WEGNER, J. 1988. *Chattel or Person? The Status of Women in the Mishnah.* Oxford University Press. New York; SLY, D. 1990. *Philo's Perception of Women.* Scholars Press. Atlanta.

of Judaism reflected in the Dead Sea Scrolls; even books which claim to deal precisely with "The Jewish Woman in Greco-Roman Palestine" (to quote the sub-heading of a recent book[4]) are curiously silent on the topic.[5]

Several explanations for this state of affairs come readily to mind, not the least being the relative isolation of much of Qumran studies, and the unavailability (until very recently) of a number of key manuscripts most relevant to the study of women. Certainly the standard view which depicts the authors of the scrolls as "monks," male celibates living in isolation in the desert, has not suggested to scholars that there is anything here of particular interest for the study of women in antiquity, except perhaps by way of a negative example of misogyny carried to its logical conclusion. Given that 1QS, one of the first published and most influential of the scrolls, makes no mention of women (except for the biblical idiom "one born of a woman," 1QS xi 21) or of related issues of sexual relations, marriage and children, it was relatively easy to conclude that women were simply not part of the *yahad*, and that the authors of this rule were closely related to, if not identical with, the Essenes described by Philo, Pliny and Josephus as a group of men who lived "without women . . . with only the palm trees for company."[6] Scholars have, of course, always recognized that Josephus does speak briefly of another group of Essenes who "although in agreement with the others on the way of life, usages, and customs, are separated from them on the subject of marriage."[7] Commonly, in Qumran scholarship, texts such as the Cairo Damascus Document, which clearly talk of women and children, were assigned to this group. Again, on analogy with Christian monasticism, the "married group" has often been taken as a kind of "third order," subordinate to and of less interest than the celibate core group.

In contrast to this dominant hypothesis which postulated a male celibate group, there has been another stream of scholarship, in general less well known and popularized, which has worked from the opposite assumption, namely that the group described in the scrolls was married: that is, though we might know little of women, they were present and a part of the life of the community. Here I call to mind the oft-forgotten 1970 study of H. Hubner which demonstrated that none of the scrolls published to date need

   [4] ARCHER, L. 1990. *Her Price Is Beyond Rubies: The Jewish Woman in Graeco-Roman Palestine.* JSOT SS 60. Sheffield University Press. Sheffield.

   [5] R. KRAEMER does not treat the Dead Sea Scrolls material at any length in *Her Share of Blessings*, although she makes some very interesting observations in her article in *Signs* (1989. "Monastic Jewish women in Greco-Roman Egypt: Philo Judaeus on the Therapeutrides." **14**(2): 364–367, especially note 81). E. SCHLUSSER FIORENZA devotes less than a page to the topic in her book, *In Memory of Her: A Feminist Theological Reconstruction of Christian Origins.* 1985. Crossroad. New York.

   [6] PLINY. *Natural History.* 5.17.4 (73).

   [7] JOSEPHUS. *The Jewish War*, ii, 160.

to be interpreted as coming from a celibate community,[8] and the more recent writing on this topic by L. Schiffman and H. Stegemann, both of whom reconstruct a community in which marriage was the norm.[9]

In reviewing at least some of the vast literature on the scrolls for this paper, I was struck by the fact that whatever discussion or treatment of women I could find was, almost without exception, within the framework of this larger discussion about marriage/celibacy. And that debate goes on. Somewhat of a compromise position (a married community with an inherent impulse towards celibacy) was proposed by J. Baumgarten at a conference here in New York almost ten years ago;[10] the topic came up again, both in papers and in discussion, at the Madrid Conference in 1991.[11] I would suggest that there are a number of reasons why scholars have not been able to come to agreement on this rather fundamental question: the lack of congruity or uniformity in our sources; the difficulty in using or interpreting whatever evidence might be gleaned from the Qumran cemetery when less than five percent of the total graves have been excavated; and possible influence of a confessional bias which interpreted Qumran too readily in terms of a monastic paradigm (although, as already indicated, the married/celibate reading of the evidence does not fall neatly along Jewish/Christian lines).[12]

In this paper I want to separate the discussion of women in the Scrolls from the married/celibate debate and instead take as a focus and starting point two texts that clearly do speak of women, *i.e.*, the Damascus Document and

[8] HUBNER, H. 1970–1971. "Zolibat in Qumran?" *New Testament Studies.* **16:** 153–167.

[9] See, for example, SCHIFFMAN, L. H. 1983. *Sectarian Law in the Dead Sea Scrolls: Courts, Testimony and the Penal Code.* Scholars Press. Chico, CA, pp. 12–13; 214; STEGEMANN, H. 1985. "Some aspects of eschatology in texts from the Qumran community and in the teachings of Jesus." In *Biblical Archaeology Today: Proceedings of the International Congress on Biblical Archaeology.* Israel Exploration Society. Jerusalem, p. 410. In a more recent article, Stegemann (who identifies the community with the Essenes) attempts to explain how Josephus could so mistakenly give the impression of a celibate community (1992. "The Qumran Essenes – Local members of the main Jewish union in late Second Temple Times." In *The Madrid Qumran Congress. Proceedings of the International Congress on the Dead Sea Scrolls* – Madrid, 18–21 March 1991. J. TREBOLLE BARRERA & L. VEGAS MONTANER, Eds. Universidad Complutense/Brill. Madrid/Leiden, p. 83–166).

[10] BAUMGARTEN, J. 1984. "The Qumran-Essene restraints on marriage." In *Archaeology and History in the Dead Sea Scrolls: The New York University Conference in Memory of Yigael Yadin.* L. H. SCHIFFMAN, Ed. JSP SS 8. Sheffield University Press. Sheffield, pp. 13–24. Others have proposed the exact opposite, that is, a movement from celibacy to marriage over time (*e.g.*, MILIK, J. T. 1959. *Ten Years of Discovery in the Wilderness of Judaea.* SCM Press. London, p. 96; to quote P. DAVIES, "a century, after all, is a long time to wait for the eschaton" (1987. *Behind the Essenes.* Scholars Press. Atlanta, p. 85).

[11] QIMRON, E. 1992. "Celibacy in the Dead Sea Scrolls and the two kinds of sectarians." In *The Madrid Qumran Congress,* pp. 287–294.

[12] Although the use of the monastic paradigm was more common in the early days of scrolls study (*e.g.*, SUTCLIFFE, E. 1960. *The Monks of Qumran as Depicted in the Dead Sea Scrolls.* Newman Press. Westminster, MD), such a presentation has not disappeared, particularly in more confessional venues, see for example, DESPREZ, V. "Jewish ascetical groups at the time of Christ: Qumran and the Therapeuts." 1990. *American Benedictine Review* **41:** 291–331.

(somewhat more briefly) the Rule of the Congregation (1QS^a). Although both of these documents have been and clearly need to be studied from many perspectives, here I want to ask directly, "What do these texts say about women? Where are women mentioned, not mentioned? Can we learn anything of roles and status?" Then, in the final part of my paper, I will move from texts which speak directly of women to ask if there are more indirect questions which we might put to other types of texts which could give us some inkling of attitudes towards women.

THE DAMASCUS DOCUMENT

Without claiming to be comprehensive, and limiting myself largely to texts that are either totally published (the Cairo Damascus Document) or at least partially described (and here I am very dependent on what J. Baumgarten has released about his ongoing work on the 4QD fragments[13]), I want to draw together some of the scattered references to women in the Damascus Document. The document describes a group in which women are clearly present in the community. In addition to the general designation אשה, נשים, women servants (אמה) are mentioned twice (xi 12, xii 10), in both cases in conjunction with menservants (עבד). One 4QD text refers to women in the category of "widow" (אלמנה),[14] and another (CD xiv 15) to the category of "young girl" (בתולה).[15] References to "mothers" (אמות) parallel to "fathers" (אבות) are probably honorific titles.[16]

Although we are dealing with a community which included women (for the issue of whether they were full members, see below), the perspective and formulation of the text is androcentric (e.g., CD vii 6–7 "they take wives and beget children"; CD xii 1 "let not a man lie with a woman"). As in the biblical codes, laws are formulated in the masculine unless they apply only to women (e.g., concerning childbirth). The masculine is used even when we have every reason to assume that the law would apply also to women, and sometimes perhaps primarily to women (e.g., CD xi 9–10, a prohibition against wearing סמנים [perhaps ornamental perfume jars?] on the Sabbath;[17] or CD xi 11, a

---

[13] In particular: BAUMGARTEN, J. M. 1992. "The laws of the Damascus document in current research." In *The Damascus Document Reconsidered*. M. BROSHI, Ed. The Israel Exploration Society. Jerusalem, p. 51–62.

[14] In CD vi 16 "widows" is part of a quotation from Isa x 2, and thus not indicative in the same way of a category of women within the community.

[15] In the corresponding text in 4QD^b, the parallel word is נער, suggesting the translation "young girl".

[16] See further discussion on p. 120. Also, BAUMGARTEN, J. M. 1992. "The Cave 4 versions of the Qumran penal code." *Journal of Jewish Studies* **43**: 270–271.

[17] For this interpretation, see SCHIFFMAN, L. H. 1975. *The Halakah at Qumran*. E. J. Brill. Leiden, p. 117. C. Rabin, in contrast, translates סמנים as "medicaments" (1958. *The Zadokite Documents*. Clarendon Press. Oxford, pp. 56–57).

prohibition against carrying an infant on the sabbath). Although the address in the Admonition (CD ii 14) is formulated in the masculine ועתה בנים שמעו לי, there is no reason to presume it does not include women; thus Rabin's translation "and now, children, hearken to me" is in fact more accurate than Vermes' "hear now, my sons."[18]

In one of the most complex passages in the Admonition, a passage which has been the object of many studies, this group defines itself in opposition to others, the "builders of the wall" who are ensnared in the "three nets of Belial" (CD iv 12–v 11). Three points of conflict involve women, and thus are relevant for us. The rationale for the prohibition of marriage between an uncle and niece takes a biblical law (Lev 18:13 "you will not approach your mother's sister") which is explicitly acknowledged as written for men (v 9–10 לזכרים הוא כתוב) and states that the same is applicable for women (וכהם הנשים). Although I do not see other examples articulated in quite this way in CD, further study may indicate whether this principle was applied more broadly in the development of law.

The prohibition against "taking two wives in their lifetime" has been interpreted in various ways, all having implications for women. Although some have read this as a prohibition of polygamy,[19] most scholars interpret this very convoluted passage as a prohibition against divorce, or more specifically, remarriage after divorce.[20] If we are dealing here with a group which, in contrast with the practice among the Pharisees and Sadducees, did prohibit divorce, this raises the question whether this prohibition served to provide security for women who thus could not be cast aside, or whether it was experienced as a restriction, condemning women to a relationship we would now term abusive.[21] As is to be expected, the derivation of the prohibition is presented in terms of biblical exegesis (Gen 1:27, 7:9; Deut 17:17) rather than a concern for the rights of the woman. A minority of scholars have argued that the prohibition against a second marriage was absolute, forbidding a man to marry again even after the death of his wife.[22] If this were the case, and the law was applied equally to women, one might have expected to find mention of widows in lists of those to be cared for by community charity (CD

[18] RABIN, C. *The Zadokite Documents*, p. 9, and VERMES, G. 1987. *The Dead Sea Scrolls in English*. Third Edition. Penguin Books. London, p. 84.

[19] For the most developed argument in support of this interpretation, see VERMES, G. 1974. "Sectarian matrimonial halakah in the Damascus rule." *Journal of Jewish Studies* 25: 197–202.

[20] FITZMYER, J. 1978. Divorce among first-century Palestinian Jews. Eretz Israel 14: 103–110. Some reference to procedures for divorce (למגרש) may be implied in the fragmentary passage in CD xiii 17. Perhaps the prohibition is specifically against remarriage after divorce.

[21] For a discussion of the prohibition of divorce in terms of its practical implications for women, see BROOTEN, B. 1986. "Jewish women's history in the Roman period: A task for Christian theology." In *Christians among Jews and Gentiles*. G. W. E. NICKELSBURG, Ed. Fortress. Philadelphia, p. 22 and note 3.

[22] For example, MURPHY-O'CONNOR, J. 1970. "An Essene missionary document?" CD ii 14–vi 1. *Revue Biblique* 77: 220; see also STEGEMANN, H. *The Madrid Qumran Congress*, p. 133.

xiv 14–16), though given the high rate of female mortality in childbirth in ancient societies, the number of women who survived their husband may have been small. Perhaps it is within this context of marriage that is to be life-long that we should situate the fragment which Baumgarten has described briefly,[23] a text which speaks of mutual concern in matching couples for marriage: the defects of the bride are not to be hidden; neither "is she to be given to one who is not suitable for her"; later in the same fragment there is a listing of feminine adjectives, apparently of desirable qualities for the bride.

A number of laws regulate sexual relations. The third net of Belial in which the rest of Israel is ensnared ("profanation of the Temple because . . . [they] lie with a woman who sees her bloody discharge") implies that the group adopted a different (presumably stricter?) practice with regard to intercourse and menstruation, although, as Ginzberg concluded, we can not determine exactly what halakic controversy is at stake.[24] CD xii 1 prohibits intercourse in Jerusalem (though עיר המקדש may apply only the Temple Mount[25]). In a catalogue of sexual transgressions, reference is made to אשה הרה. Baumgarten suggests this is the conclusion of a law prohibiting sexual intercourse during pregnancy;[26] this would confirm Josephus's statement "they do not have intercourse with them [their wives] during pregnancy" (*War* ii 161). A puzzling statement in the Penal code in 4QDᵉ prescribes expulsion from the sect for the sin described as לזנות לאשתו; although the precise nature of the offense is unclear, some type of sexual activity between a man and his wife is judged serious enough to merit expulsion.[27] If sexual relations even within marriage are rigidly circumscribed, this may be a reflection of Josephus's claim "that they marry not for self-gratification but for the necessity of children" (*War* ii 161). What it would mean for the lived experience and status of women merits further reflection.

Two passages illustrate the authority which husbands and fathers exercised over women. CD xvi 6–13, which treats the group's interpretation of Num 30:3–16 about oaths and vows, follows the biblical law in assuming the husband/father's right to annul the oaths of his wife/daughter. However, line 11 may introduce an interesting limitation; the verb here (as L. Schiffman has pointed out[28]) can be pointed to read "the husband may not annul an oath

[23] *The Damascus Document Reconsidered*, p. 54.

[24] GINZBERG, L. 1970. *An Unknown Jewish Sect*. Jewish Theological Seminary. New York, p. 22.

[25] For a discussion of the complex issues around "the city of the sanctuary" see SCHIFFMAN, L. 1985. "Exclusion from the sanctuary and the city of the sanctuary in the Temple Scroll." *Hebrew Annual Review* 9: 301–319.

[26] *The Damascus Document Reconsidered*, p. 53.

[27] See the discussion by J. BAUMGARTEN. "The Cave 4 Versions of the Qumran Penal Code," p. 270.

[28] SCHIFFMAN, L. H. 1991. "The law of vows and oaths (Num 30:3–16) in the Zadokite fragments and the temple scroll." *Revue de Qumrân* 15: 199–214.

about which he does not [in]form her (וְיִןדְעֶנָה) whether it is to be carried out or annulled." Whatever the motivation here, the necessity of informing calls for a more active involvement (perhaps consent?) of his wife which goes beyond biblical law. The few passages which talk specifically of an unmarried girl (בתולה) assume that she is under the authority of her father; one passage, for instance, speaks of a girl "in her youth" (בבתוליה) who acquires a "bad name" (שֵׁ[ם רע) while in her father's house (4QD^c 1 i 13). In another passage, the בתולה who has no relatives (גואל) to look after her is to be taken care of from community funds; although the broken text in CD xiv 15–16 might suggest a special concern for young women, the corresponding passage in 4QD^b matches בתולה with נער and makes both the object of charity.

Scholars have long noted that the description of the process whereby a member enters into the group is far from clear in the Damascus Document, and difficult to reconcile with the entrance process as described in 1QS or Josephus. CD xv 5–10 speaks of the central act as "the oath of the covenant . . . to return to the law of Moses," which is sworn at the age of mustering (הפקודים). Did women take this oath? That is, is Vermes, for instance, justified in translating בניהם inclusively ("when the children of all those who have entered the Covenant . . . reach the age of enrollment") or is it only "their sons" as Rabin translates?[29] Schiffman has put forth a series of arguments to support the view that only men took the oath: he notes the military language (לעבור על הפקודים) and the parallels to 1QS^a (which we will examine in a moment), and makes an analogy with the rights of the members of the priestly family to eat the *terumah* and with membership in the Pharisaic *havurah*; thus, he goes on to conclude that "the status of women in the sect . . . was determined only insofar as their husbands took on membership."[30] This is also the judgment of Stegemann: "only men could become full members."[31] It seems that women could attain to the level which men reached after one year of initiation (*War* ii 138); that is, they were able to share in the ritual purifications, as evidenced both by the mention of the linen robe for bathing (*War* ii 161) and by the blessings connected with lustrations which were to be recited by men as well as women (in particular, 4Q512 41 where the rubric אִי[ש או אשה is added above the line[32]). The more difficult question is whether women could advance beyond this initial stage to full membership.

While I do not have any illusions that I can solve here the complex issue of membership status, I would introduce some additional points into the discussion. Following a principle which has been adopted in much of feminist history, I want to begin reading the texts with the assumption that women

[29] Comparing the translations of G. VERMES. *The Dead Sea Scrolls in English* and C. RABIN. *The Zadokite Documents.*

[30] SCHIFFMAN. *Sectarian Law*, p. 57.

[31] STEGEMANN, *The Madrid Qumran Congress*, p. 129.

[32] BAILLET, M. 1982. *Qumrân grotte 4 III.* DJD VII. Clarendon Press. Oxford, p. 274.

were full members of the community, unless there is clear evidence to the contrary—and I am still not convinced this is the case. Having seen Josephus's remark about the prohibition of intercourse during pregnancy confirmed now in 4QD, perhaps we can take more seriously his difficult phrase at the beginning of the section in *War* ii 161 "they put their wives to the test for a three-year period and only marry them after they have by three periods of purification given proof of fecundity."[33] As Baumgarten has already pointed out,[34] the same verb *dokimazo* is used for the initial testing of men in ii 138 and for the three-year probation of women in this text. Furthermore, the fact that the duration is the same three years suggests to me a probation that led to full membership.

Also, in this context, I want to consider the recent text discussed by Baumgarten which talks of "fathers" and "mothers," understanding these, as he suggests, as honorary titles.[35] The very nature of the penal code emphasizes the discrepancy between the severe penalty of expulsion for an offense against "the fathers," as compared to the much milder penalty of only ten days for an offense against "the mothers"; the text ends with the cryptic statement כי אין לאמונֶת רוקמה בתוך [העדה] (Baumgarten translates, based on the context, "for the Mothers do not have authority (?) within the [congregation]"). The obvious discrepancy and apparently lesser honor accorded to the "mothers" should not blind us to the fact that men and women are given parallel titles. Similarly, I want to recall that puzzling text 4Q502 which Baillet had entitled "Rituel de Mariage,"[36] it refers to אחיות and אחים (96 1; 9 11) and זקנים and זקנות (19 2; 24 4, 6), and describes an action undertaken by someone who stands "in the midst of" and "in the council of" זקנים and זקנות. I cannot help wondering if זקנים had appeared by itself whether it would not have been readily translated as "elders," that is, designating not so much age, but a designated role or a title of leadership within the community. Is there an implicit assumption that women would not be members of a "council of elders"?[37] But, to return to my original starting point, if women

---

[33] See the recent discussion of this text by P. W. VAN DER HORST. 1992. "Two short notes on Josephus." *The Studia Philonica Annual* 4: 59–60. He proposes that Josephus is thinking of two quite separate tests: a girl might undergo her three years of probation as young as age nine or ten, but could not be married until she had completed three menstruations. But, if the probation period for females was in any way parallel to that of males, I am less inclined to think that the age was that young.

[34] BAUMGARTEN. "The Qumran-Essene Restraints on Marriage," p. 16. I find it interesting that in a recent translation, the verb is translated "test" when referring to the men, but simply "they observe their women for three years" (VERMES, G. & M. D. GOODMAN. 1989. *The Essenes According to the Classical Sources.* JSOT Press. Sheffield, p. 49).

[35] "The Cave 4 Versions of the Qumran Penal Code," pp. 270–271.

[36] BAILLET, M. Qumrân Grotte 4, pp. 81–105. For a different interpretation of the document as a whole, see BAUMGARTEN, J. 1983. "4Q502, marriage or golden age ritual?" *Journal of Jewish Studies* 34: 125–135.

[37] We might want to think about this in the context of similar titles for women leaders in the synagogue. See BROOTEN, B. 1982. *Women Leaders in the Ancient Synagogue.* Scholars Press.

had designated titles "mothers," "sisters," "elders," this too suggests full membership within the community.

THE RULE OF THE CONGREGATION

At this point I venture to bring into the discussion some passages from another document, 1QS[a] (The Rule of the Congregation). I do so with some hesitancy because, although this Rule also assumes a community with marriage, women and children, there is much debate about the basic interpretation of 1QS[a]. Though I tend to think that אחרית הימים of 1QS[a] 1 i is the present rather than the eschatological future, the precise relationship between the Damascus Document and the Rule of the Congregation is far from clear.[38] While I do not mean to suggest that 1QS[a] can be read simply as an extension of CD (it may be a rule for a different stage or even a different community), it is instructive to note that it raises some of the same difficult questions about the extent of women's involvement as full members in the community.

1QS[a] i 4–19 is a complex passage which lists the various ages and the duties of members who attain these specific ages. The text itself alternates between passages which clearly are formulated in terms of a male subject (1. 9–10 "he shall not approach a woman to lie with her") or a female subject (1. 11 "she shall be received [תקבל unemended] to testify"); other verses use a masculine form which could be either gender-specific or inclusive (1. 7 ללמ]דהו בספר ההגי; is this "to teach them [males], or them [men and women]"?). It is the text itself that alerts us to the fact that we are not dealing only with males, for the passage begins (1. 4–5) with the explicit statement that "they shall assemble all those who come including children and women for the reading of the precepts of the Covenant. . . ." I propose that we continue reading with this same subject until the text alerts us to a change (i.e., in 1. 9–10 ולוא ינקרב] אל אשה). That would mean that both girls and boys are to be instructed in the ספר ההגי and the precepts of the covenant and, at the age of twenty, to come into the holy congregation. Then follows two parallel statements: one about men (the age of marriage) and one about women (her obligation to give witness). The manuscript copy (תקבל) is clear, and the first translators read the passage as indicating that this group within Judaism accepted the testimony of women and gave them a responsibility for ensuring obedience to the statutes.[39] How-

Chico, CA, pp. 41–55; KRAEMER, R. S. 1985. "A new inscription from Malta and the question of women elders in the diaspora Jewish communities." *Harvard Theological Review* 78: 431–438.

[38] Unfortunately, we have only one copy of 1QS[a], attached to the manuscript of 1QS. As far as I have been able to ascertain, there are no copies as part of any of the 4QS manuscripts.

[39] BAILLET, M. 1955. *Qumran Cave I.* DJD I. Clarendon. Oxford, p. 112; RICHARDSON, H. N. 1957. "Some notes on 1QSa." *Journal of Biblical Literature* 76: 106–122.

ever subsequent scholars, beginning with Baumgarten's 1957 article,[40] suspicious of the sudden shift to the feminine and the participation of women in the judicial process, simply emend the text to the masculine יקבל. I suggest that when we approach the passage in its own right, not seeking to make it conform to external understandings of the status of women, and sensitive to its basic structure (a long section which refers to both men and women, then a specific statement first about men (1. 9–10) and then one about women (line 11), it may be possible to leave the text unemended.[41]

The suggestion that women had what seems to us an unexpected status within this community is reinforced by the section 1QS^a i 27–ii 11 which describes the Council of the Community (עצת היחד). A detailed list is given of those who are excluded by reason of impurity, physical deformity, or age because "holy angels [are in their coun]cil." Women are not on the list, though it is often assumed that they are also excluded, on analogy with 1QM vii 3–4 where women are listed as shut out from the camp in the final battle because of the angels. But the point is that the authors of 1QS^a did not exclude them, again suggesting that women were considered as full members.

Having examined the main texts in the Damascus Document and 1QS^a which speak of women, I do not want to try to draw far-reaching conclusions at this point. My work has been largely descriptive; we are still at the first stage, what feminist scholars would describe as a process of recovery, simply gathering the information which is available about women. I have dealt with only two documents and with the Damascus Document incompletely; we await publication and commentary on the full text, particularly in its reconstructed form so that we are better able to see the overall contexts in which passages about women occur. Eventually we will need to expand our study to examine other similar texts which treat women, including the Ordinances in 4Q159, 4Q265, 4Q513, 4Q514, and the Temple Scroll.[42] Nor do I want to suggest a simplistic correspondence between text and social reality; again a basic prin-

[40] BAUMGARTEN, J. 1957. "On the testimony of women in 1QSa." *Journal of Biblical Literature* 76: 266–269. He has been followed by most scholars, including the major study of 1QS^a by SCHIFFMAN, L. H. 1989. *The Eschatological Community of the Dead Sea Scrolls.* Scholars Press. Atlanta, pp. 18–19; also G. Vermes in his English translation "he will be accepted . . ."

[41] In conversation at the New York Conference, George Brooke suggested the passage may refer specifically to women's testimony about their menstrual cycle and thus the observation of purity regulations. Various arguments for reading 1QS^a in unemended form were presented by Linda Bennett Elder, in a paper presented at the Society of Biblical Literature Meeting in November 1991, entitled "The Woman Question and Female Ascetics among Essenes."

[42] SCHIFFMAN, L. H. 1992. "Laws pertaining to women in the *Temple Scroll.*" In *The Dead Sea Scrolls after Forty Years of Research.* D. DIMANT & U. RAPPAPORT, Eds. E. J. Brill/Magnes. Leiden/Jerusalem, pp. 210–228.

ciple of feminist methodology cautions us against assuming that legal prescriptions written by men and from a male perspective necessarily mirrored totally or accurately the lived situation or status of women within their communities. Although it is tempting to want to move beyond straight description to pose the question of whether these texts which we are examining reflect a "high or low" status for women within this particular type of Judaism in the Second Temple period, one immediately realizes the perils and limits of such evaluative judgments—particularly since equally little, in fact less, is known about Sadducean women or Pharisaic women pre-70 as a basis for comparison.

Finally, although this paper has taken as its starting point texts of a specific genre which actually mention women, I want to raise a final question (which really points to another paper) of whether there are also other, more indirect, ways of gaining insight into attitudes toward women in the community. Here we are on even more speculative grounds and, as I will illustrate, the evidence can and has been read in quite disparate ways.

One can ask whether the simple fact of the presence or absence of certain texts in the library at Qumran is significant. For example, there are no copies of the book of Esther, and since this is the only book (if we consider Ezra-Nehemiah as a single work) of what we now know as the Hebrew canon not attested, it has sometimes been suggested that a celibate or misogynist group deliberately excluded the one biblical book with a woman as heroine.[43] However, given the relative shortness of Esther in relation to a lengthy work such as 1–2 Chronicles of which only one small fragment survives (4Q118), the absence is probably related more to statistical probability than to misogynist intent.

In contrast to the absence of Esther,[44] the presence of certain texts in the Qumran library deserves comment. In terms of biblical expansions, we can point to the extended poem describing the beauty of Sarah in the Genesis Apocryphon (20:2–8a) and the expanded Song of Miriam in the Revised Pentateuch (4Q365 6 ii).[45] In 11QPsᵃ xxi 11–xxii 1 there is an acrostic Wisdom poem, known also in a rather innocuous Greek translation in Sir 51:13–30. In its description of the psalmist's search for Lady Wisdom, his nurse, teacher and mistress who comes to him in her beauty as he burns with desire for her (xxi 15–17), much of the language is purposefully ambiguous, rich in double

---

[43] J. T. MILIK has recently published a text which he sees as closely related to Esther (1992. "Les modèles araméens du livre d'Esther dans la grotte 4 de Qumrân." *Revue de Qumran* **15**: 321–406), but the identification is less than certain.

[44] The non-appearance of Judith is more readily explained by its Maccabean, perhaps Pharisaic, roots. It has been suggested that a version of the story of Susanna is found, but again the text is probably too fragmentary to make identification certain (MILIK, J. T. 1981. "Daniel et Susanne à Qumran?" In *De la Torah au Messie: Etudes d'exégèse et d'herméneutique bibliques offertes à Henri Cazelles.* M. CARREZ *et al.*, Eds. Desclee. Paris, pp. 337–359).

[45] WHITE, S. "4Q364 & 4Q365: A preliminary report." In *The Madrid Qumran Congress*, pp. 220–221.

entendre and allowing for a more or less erotic reading.[46] J. Sanders has interpreted this poem within the context of a celibate male community at Qumran, seeing in it a reflection of the young man's effort to dedicate "his normally developing passions and desires to the pleasures of life with Wisdom" and thus "a commendable manner of sublimation in celibacy."[47] Whether such across-the-ages psychologizing can help us to understand the people at Qumran is less than convincing to me, but still the presence of a poem in praise of Lady Wisdom is worth noting.

Another text which has been variously used as a window onto attitudes toward women at Qumran is 4Q184. This poem has been read as a vivid description of the harlot (according to Allegro's problematic restoration of ה[זונ]ה as the first word[48]) and her seductions of the righteous. Even when the figure is allegorized (so that she is equated with false teaching or the evils of Rome[49]) or if she is seen as a demonic Lilit figure,[50] the fact remains that it is a female who is described so graphically and negatively. However, given that this text is probably non-sectarian in terms of its composition and stands directly in the tradition of such well-established biblical passages as Prov 7–9, Zech 5, and Isa 34:14, I am not sure that it proves that the group in whose library it was found was necessarily particularly misogynist.[51]

Finally, a feminist examination of the Qumran corpus will be alert to any passing references to women and to the use of female imagery, highlighting these precisely because of their rarity in a world-view which is so predominately androcentric. Here I can mention only a few texts by way of example of the type of approach I have in mind. In 1QpHab vi 11, the biblical text to "massacre nations mercilessly," is expanded to list (with what might be seen as a certain sensitivity) the victims of war "youths, grown men, the aged, women and children." Or, we can look at the imagery of the Hodayot which maintains the biblical precedent of speaking directly of God only as father and

[46] For a more cautious reading, see RABINOWITZ, I. 1971. "The Qumran Hebrew original of Ben Sira's concluding acrostic on Wisdom." *Hebrew Union College Annals* **42**: 173–184; MURAOKA, T. 1979. "Sir 51:13–20: An erotic hymn to Wisdom?" *Journal for the Study of Judaism* **10**: 166–178.

[47] SANDERS, J. A. 1965. *The Psalms Scroll of Qumran Cave 11.* DJDJ IV. Clarendon. Oxford, p. 84.

[48] ALLEGRO, J. M. 1968. *Qumran Cave 4 I (4Q158–4Q186).* DJDJ V. Clarendon. Oxford, p. 82. This reading is hardly possible, as pointed out by J. STRUGNELL (1970. "Notes en marge du volume V des 'Discoveries in the Judaean Desert'." *Revue de Qumran* **7**: 264).

[49] See, for example, CARMIGNAC, J. 1965. "Poème allégorique sur la secte rivale." *Revue de Qumran* **5**: 361–374; MOORE, R. D. 1981. "Personification of the seduction of evil: The wiles of the wicked woman." *Revue de Qumran* **10**: 505–519.

[50] BAUMGARTEN, J. 1991. "On the nature of the seductress in 4Q184." *Revue de Qumran* **15**: 133–143.

[51] Contra, for example, BEALL, T. A. 1988. *Josephus' Description of the Essenes Illustrated by the Dead Sea Scrolls.* Cambridge University Press. New York, p. 42; and SWIDLER, L. 1976. *Women in Judaism: The Status of Women in Formative Judaism.* Scarecrow Press. Metuchen, NJ, pp. 64–66; both see the presence of this text at Qumran as evidence of a significant depreciation of women.

not as mother (1QH ix 35) but, nevertheless, is not hesitant in drawing upon female imagery (*e.g.*, the woman in travail 1QH iii 7–12; v 30), or explicitly balancing male and female illustrations (ix 30, 35–36). In both the Pesharim and the Hodayot, the language is, of course, rooted in the biblical text and must be considered within that framework; however, both the choice and the precise reuse of this biblical language and imagery merits further study.

This paper has been exploratory and preliminary. It has sought to raise certain basic questions and to indicate some directions for further reflection. In light of the concern of this Conference for methodology in the study of the scrolls, it is my hope that this study indicates the need for the ongoing exploration of women in the scrolls to enter into closer dialogue not only with the field of Qumran studies *per se*, but also with feminist socio-historical study of women in the religions of the Greco-Roman world.

DISCUSSION OF THE PAPER

JAMES H. CHARLESWORTH (*Princeton Theological Seminary, Princeton, NJ*): For me, you have asked me to go back through some text that I thought I knew about and really struggle with the place of women in the community. Let me try to push you on a few things. First, what was once called the "Wiles of the Wicked Woman"–fortunately you did not use that title. Strugnell and I have renamed it, "Dame Folly and Lady Wisdom" and I think that to see this as simply a misogynist text is not to really understand what is going on.

Secondly, as you know, Josephus refers to *nasos ton makarion* and the importance of women there. Of course, this is coming out of the Hellenistic world. We also have it in the *History of the Rechabites* which many scholars are now recognizing is originally Jewish and in some way related to the Qumran community. I developed this in the *Nikiprowetzky Festschrift* and many scholars are now emphasizing that. It is very important, because it does talk about the place of a woman and sex with her.

Third, I'd like to push you on your reference to the community. I hear what seems to me a confusion between a lot of technical terms: '*Edah, Ha-Yahad*. *Ha-Yahad* is clearly community. But, as I read some of these scrolls, they are making distinction between community and assembly and so forth.

Fourth, can you tell me, are there different types of groups related to the Qumranites? Are we willing to talk about a monolithic group?

And, finally, all men have mothers. I think that helps us understand some of their struggle. There is no one who really can be thoroughly misogynist, it seems to me (laughter).

EILEEN SCHULLER (*McMaster University, Hamilton, Ont., Canada*): I purposely used this language of community or group in quite a general sense. It has to be within a total context of how we understand the material we have here, and particularly the relationship between various documents. I think that is a core question that we need a great deal more work on. I mean, what is the relationship between 1QS, 1QSᵃ and CD, much less the Temple Scroll. That is not a question I thought I could cover in this paper, or that I really have any solution for. So I was purposely limiting myself by picking a particular document. I took the Damascus document where it is clear that we do have some involvement of women, and tried to work within that framework.

With some hesitancy, I brought in 1QSᵃ, which either helps or confuses the situation. I do think that much of the work that needs to be done on this question has to be done within the larger framework of how we conceptualize all of this material.

I am also interested in your final point about mothers and feminine language and this type of thing. Of course, this is a question that has been much studied, even within the area of Christian monasticism, and also Buddhist monastic groups.

To imply that a celibate group is going to have a particular language when it comes to either women or female concerns: we have to be very cautious of that.

SAMUAL IWRY (*Johns Hopkins University, Baltimore, MD*): In 1989, I read a paper at the World Congress of Jewish Studies. The title of this article was, "Unambiguous Remarks in Connection with the Rights of Women in Relation to the Law in the Damascus Document." Why didn't you include it? The salient point is the question of marrying the daughter of a sister. This is one of the things that distinguishes this group and also distinguished other sectarian groups. They consider it as a sin. And, the question that they ask is very pointed. It's correct, they say, that in the incest laws, it says that a man should not marry his aunt. It means his mother's sister. Here among the sins of fornication is not only the idea of polygamy or polluting the temple, but the sin of fornication. They ask the question, "Is he not her uncle? If he is not allowed to marry an aunt, how could she be allowed to marry an uncle?" And, the Torah spoke to man. This means man dominated the document.

In your later writings or your correction, please look into it and include it. Thank you.

SCHULLER: Thank you. I did mention that text, but in a more general way. I will certainly look up your work on it.

MICHAEL WISE (*University of Chicago, Chicago, IL*): I want to push a little bit further along the lines that you already indicated are tentative. I noticed that you only referred to marrying Essenes in your discussion, and you mention an article which asked the question whether there are any documents which can be unambiguously stated to favor celibacy. As your working hypothesis here, as you're talking about "the group" and "the community" and "this group," is it your view that we are in fact dealing with Essenes, and if so, are we dealing only with marrying Essenes in these texts?

SCHULLER: The texts that I concentrated on, the Damascus document and 1QS^a, I think are dealing with marrying Essenes. That's why I took those texts. The question of whether there was some sort of a group that was celibate is a question that I have struggled with for a long time and I don't have a clear answer.

WISE: Wouldn't it strike you as strange, if we had all of these texts from one group, that it would be the minority group of Essenes, so to speak, at least according to Josephus?

SCHULLER: I think that's the point. Was that group the minority?

WISE: You're relying on Josephus for your interpretation. Isn't it true that he does give the impression this group is secondary, but he has to mention it because it is there?

SCHULLER: Well that depends—there are many different ways of reading Josephus and I don't want to say. I know Professor Stegemann has just written an article on this and it certainly made me go back and look at Josephus' text in quite a different way. Even in Josephus, I'm not sure that the language of secondary [place] is there. When he talks about the marrying group, he says they are the same as regards the laws, the customs and the practices, except for this one point. I am concerned that we are reading more of a secondary minority status into Josephus than is necessary.

WISE: I'm sure we could talk about that. Thank you.

HARTMUT STEGEMANN (*University of Göttingen, Göttingen, Germany*): I have two questions. One is regarding full membership. There is no problem that women also belong to mankind according to this text, but full membership means something more. I think from the Qumran text we must ask, do women indeed participate in the religious service? Do women participate in the common meals? And, so on. I would say no.

The problem of full membership may be the same in other religious organizations of the Jews at that time. Could women become full members with the Pharisees? With the Zealots? No. Perhaps with the Christians. And, perhaps with the Therapeutae in Egypt described by Philo. Perhaps there women were full members, but not in the other groups.

That every man must marry is, according to my mind, a command from creation. This means everybody must marry, not only Jews but all mankind. Being a Jew, you cannot escape from this. It is an order.

As far as I know, there were very few exceptions in the Talmudic literature. One scholar is mentioned who didn't want to marry. When he was urged by others, "You must marry," he said, "I am married to the Torah." The others didn't like this, but they made this exception and they allowed him to remain unmarried.

The other exception I know is in the New Testament, where Jesus says in Matthew 19 that there are three types of eunuch. This portion could mean there may be an exception not to marry, that Jesus was not married. But, these are very rare exceptions.

SCHULLER: This has been one of the questions that has been discussed for a long time, particularly because the scrolls make no exegetical argument about how they would treat the Genesis 1:28 text, if in fact they were not following it and were adopting a practice of celibacy. On the other hand, if the *Therapeutae* in Philo, were a Jewish group that did not marry (there are all sort of questions around that), that might be one precedent. I guess I still don't really know. I see the argument before us.

Certainly a number of attempts have been made particularly under the influence of Christian scholarship which has put a tremendous amount of effort into the study of female ascetic groups as providing a channel of autonomy for women – that Judaism also had an equivalent role for women. It's not so much a question of male celibacy, but was there a female celibacy at Qumran? I really started off hoping that I could find some information on that, but that's not what the texts seemed to provide.

LAWRENCE SCHIFFMAN (*New York University, New York*): I want to begin by congratulating you on doing this much better than what I tried to do with the Temple Scroll. I came up empty-handed in Haifa, with nothing more than biblical quotations. Those of you who may read that article may see some nice explanations of the Temple Scroll, but I found nothing about women – even though all the texts I dealt with concern women!

I want to just make a few comments. Is it this group of Essenes, or is it that group of Essenes? We had two questions on that point; I think, by Jim and Michael. I really would suggest that methodologically this is all backward. I think we have to let you go on with this until we find out: What do these texts say that we weren't hearing before? Then we have to go back and ask, "What about these crazy groups that we heard of in some other source, which may or may not match the Qumran Scrolls?" I would stress that we are coming with interpretative predispositions that do not flow out of the material that we are studying. Most of what we are studying is either material that didn't exist when those presuppositions were made up, or material for which there was a kind of "locked-in" assumption about what it meant. Now, as we're redoing all this work with a second group of texts, let's not fall into the trap of always trying to make it match with the presuppositions. Those presuppositions are probably in the process of passing out of existence. That's what all of the speakers in the conference seem to be sharing.

I would make one last comment. There is a Hebrew University dissertation by Tal Ilan on the subject of women in the Second Temple period, and there is a tremendous amount of material in it. I believe an English translation is in preparation. It is a very important work, and I think that it is going to be helpful as a resource.

SCHULLER: Thank you very much. I want to make one last comment. One of the ways I got into this topic was through the Canadian Society of Biblical Studies. We're involved in a five-year study on voluntary associations in antiquity. Last year we were studying women in voluntary associations. Somebody said we should have a half hour talk on women in various associations and asked if I could do something on women in the community of the Dead Sea Scrolls. I could do whatever I wanted for the other 25 minutes (laughter). That is part of the attitude that I am suggesting we reconsider.

The Copper Scroll Treasure as an Accumulation of Religious Offerings

P. KYLE McCARTER, JR.

Department of Near Eastern Studies
The Johns Hopkins University
124 Gilman Hall
3400 N. Charles Street
Baltimore, Maryland 21218-2690

The most important deficiency in his immensely erudite and durable *editio princeps* of 3Q15 (Milik, de Vaux, and Baker 1962) was Milik's failure to recognize the Hebrew expressions that refer to religious contributions deposited in several of the locations of hidden property listed in the text. In this respect Allegro's unsanctioned edition (1960, 1964) is better, and Luria's edition (1963) is much better. Manfred Lehmann, however, seems to have been the first to realize that an essential key to understanding the Copper Scroll is a correct interpretation of what he called "its technical terms" (Lehmann 1964).

The most important of these terms, because of the frequency of its occurrence (see below), is *dema'*. We are almost entirely dependent on Rabbinic sources for the interpretation of this word. It occurs once in the Bible, in Exod 22:28a, where we read *mělē'ātēkā wědim'ăkā lō' tě'aḥēr*, "Your fullness and your *dema'* you shall not withhold." The concern of this injunction is evidently the prompt payment of imposts levied on agricultural produce. *Mělē'â*, the term paired with *dema'* here, is also found in Numb 18:27, where the subject is the *těrûmâ*, the portion of produce given for the support of the Levites; there the expression "the fullness of the winevat" (*mělē'ā min-hayyāqeb*) is joined with "the grain of the threshing floor" (*dāgān min-haggōren*). From these two passages it seems clear that *dema'* has to do with religious levies on produce, if not with the specific institution of *těrûmâ* itself.

The Rabbinic writings make the association of *dema'* with *těrûmâ* explicit. Thus *b. Ḥul.* 34b, for example, describes a pottage containing *těrûmâ* as *nězîd haddema'*, and *t. Ter.* 10.16, in referring to a place set aside for the storage of *těrûmâ*, uses the expression *bêt haddema'* (*cf.* Allegro 1960: 137). With regard to *wědim'ăkā* in Exod 22:38, *b. Tem.* 4a states directly that it is *těrûmâ*, and this is echoed in the traditional midrashic interpretation of the Book of Exodus, including *Mek. Mišpaṭ.* 19 and *Yal. Exod.* 351, which identifies *dema'* as one of three names for *těrûmâ*, along with *rē'šīt* and *těrûmâ* itself. Most often, however, √*dm'* is used verbally. Thus, when said of things ordinarily exempt from the restrictions of *těrûmâ*, *nidma'* means to become subject to those restrictions in consequence of being mixed with *těrûmâ* (*e.g.*, *b. Nid.* 46b, *b. 'Erub.* 36a). Similarly, *dimmēa'* means to make such things subject to the restrictions of *těrûmâ* by mixing them with *těrûmâ* (*e.g.*, *b. Giṭ.* 53a, 53b, *b. B. Qam.* 4b, 5a, 117a, *b. Ḥul.* 41a). In short, *dema'* refers to produce that has been set apart (*hērîm*) as a special portion for the support of the Levites (*těrûmâ*), as prescribed in Numbers 18, or to other produce with which *těrûmâ* has been added in sufficient proportion to render the mixture subject to the restrictions of *těrûmâ*.

In 3Q15 *dema'* occurs twice in Columns 1 and 3 (1.9, 10, 3.3, 9), once each in Columns 5, 8, and 12 (5.5, 8.3, 12.7), and seven times in Column 11 (11.1, 4 [*bis*], 10 [*bis*], 14 [*bis*]).[1] In most cases, hidden materials are described as *kělê dema'*, "vessels of *dema'*,"–twice as *kělê kesep wězāhāb šel dema'*, "silver and gold vessels of *dema'*" (3.2–3; *cf. kl<y> ksp wkly zhb šl dm'* in 12.6–7). The expression *kělê dema'* is usually followed by some further indication of the nature of the vessels–thus plural substantives–or the *dema'* itself–singulars. The words and phrases used in this way have proven to be among the most difficult to interpret in the entire text of 3Q15. They include the following:

1) *kělê dema' bōlěgîn wa'ăpērîn*, "vessels of *dema'* polished and wrapped" (1.9). This interpretation is a departure in a very obscure passage from those of the scholars who have analyzed the sequence *blgyn* as *bêt essentiae* followed by a type of vessel–thus, *bělōgîn*, "consisting of *lôg* vessels" (Allegro 1960: 33, 137), or *bělāgîn*, "consisting of lagin(s)" (*cf.* Luria 1963: 63; Lehmann 1964: 99).[2] Hebrew √*blg*, however, means "gleam, shine," and we read *bōlěgîn*, "gleaming," thus perhaps, "polished," a description of the vessels. The second term is interpreted by Milik as *'ēpôdōt*, "vêtements sacrés," and by Allegro (1960: 33, 137) and Luria (1964: 63) as **'appôrîn*, "amphorae." Both of these readings (*'pwdt* and *'pwryn*) are graphically possible, but Lehmann's otherwise attractive proposal (1964: 99) – to relate the term to Biblical Hebrew *pědût* and Rabbinic *pidyôn*, "ransom, redemption," as a designation of ritually dedicated objects redeemed for money–stumbles on the *waw* or *yod* that follows *pe*, a spelling that would be unlikely in a noun from √*pdh*. Tentatively, I prefer to read *'pyryn* and relate the word to Biblical Hebrew *'āpēr*, "covering, bandage" (1 Kings 20:38, 41); compare Akkadian *apāru*, which means "pro-

---

[1] Milik (1962: 251–52, 293–94) finds an additional occurrence in 9.6, *viz. dm <'> ḥṣ'*, for which we should read with Luria (1963: 108) *wmḥṣ'*, "and one-half."

[2] Milik (1960:251), who believes all *dema'* in 3Q15 to be spices or aromatic woods, renders *blgyn* as "de santal [sandalwood]," comparing Sanskrit *valgu*, Syriac *'ablug*, and Biblical Hebrew *'algûmîm*, *'almŭggîm*.

vide with a headdress," and, in the stative, "be covered." Thus the meaning of *kĕlê demaᶜ* . . . *'ăpîrîn*, "wrapped . . . vessels of *demaᶜ*," is parallel to *kĕlê demaᶜ lĕbûšîn*, "clothed, swaddled vessels of *demaᶜ*" in 3.9.

2) *kĕlê kesep wĕzāhāb šel demaᶜ mizrāqôt kôsôt mēnîqî'ôt qĕsā'ôt* (3.2–3). Here the "silver and gold vessels of *demaᶜ*" are further specified as "sprinkling bowls, cups, libation cups, libation bowls."

3) *kĕlê demaᶜ lĕbûšî[n]*, "swaddled vessels of *demaᶜ*." (3.9). As noted above in connection with *kĕlê demaᶜ* . . . *'ăpîrîn*, "wrapped . . . vessels of *demaᶜ*."

4) *kā'ēlîn šel demaᶜ*, "vessels of *dēmaᶜ*." (5.5). Milik (1962: 228) makes a plausible case for an unusual *plene* spelling in an absolute form of *kē(')lîn*, "vessels."

5) *kĕlē demaᶜ ûsiprô*, "vessels of *demaᶜ* "and its record" (8.3). We read *wsprw w-*, "and its record and," for Milik's *wspryn*, "et livres." As explained below in connection with *ûkĕtābān 'eṣlām*, "and their register alongside them," the reference is probably to some kind of written document accompanying the *demaᶜ* vessels and identifying its source or destination.

6) *kĕlē demaᶜ*, "vessels of *demaᶜ* " (11.1).

7) *kĕlē demaᶜ sîaḥ demaᶜ sāpîaḥ*, "vessels of *dēmaᶜ* of (wild) growth, [that is,] *dēmaᶜ* of aftergrowth" (11.4). This passage has proved troublesome. The key to its solution lies in recognizing the term *sāpîaḥ*, "aftergrowth," in the letters *sph*, read *snh* by Milik (1962: 250), who interprets it as the herb "senna" or a related form of cassia, and Allegro (1960: 53, 164), who associates it vaguely with √*sny/sn'*, "hate"–hence, "spoilt tithes."[3] Traces of the *pe* are visible on the left side of the cut, however, and *sāpîaḥ* in Biblical and Post-biblical Hebrew refers to "spontaneous aftergrowth," comparable in a field of grain to grapes from unpruned vines (Lev 25:5, 11); the term is especially important in halachic discussions of the status of spontaneous growth in fields lying fallow during a Sabbatical Year (*e.g.*, *b. Pesaḥ.* 51b; *m. Šeqal.* 4:1, etc.). In our interpretation, then, *demaᶜ sāpîaḥ*, "*demaᶜ* of aftergrowth," is a gloss or further specification of *demaᶜ sîaḥ* (note the absence of a conjunction); the common biblical word *sîaḥ* (spelled here with *samek* instead of *śîn*) refers to an uncultivated plant (*cf. śîaḥ haśśādê* in Gen 2:5).[4]

8) *kĕlê demaᶜ 'ô demaᶜ sîaḥ*, "vessels of *demaᶜ* or *demaᶜ* of (wild) growth" (11.10). For *'w* Milik (1962: 250) reads *'z*, which he emends to *'<r>z*, "de cèdre." We follow Allegro (1960: 53) and Luria (1963: 120). For *demaᶜ sîaḥ*, see above.

9) *kĕlê de<maᶜ> mĕlē'â demaᶜ sûrā'*, "vessels of *demaᶜ* of full growth, [that is,] *demaᶜ* set apart" (11.14). In copying the sequence *dmᶜ ml'ḥ*, the scribe's eye skipped from the first *mem* to the second, leaving *dml'ḥ*. Milik

---

[3] Luria (1963: 118), who finds no satisfactory interpretation for *snh*, wonders if *dmᶜ swḥ* should be read a second time and regarded as a scribal dittograph.

[4] Compare Akkadian *šâḥu*, *šiāḥu*, "grow (high)"; *šîḫu*, "grown (high or long)."

(1962: 251) reconstructs the ʿ*ayin* and renders *l'ḥ* as "d'aloès," comparing Greek *aloē* and Jewish Aramaic *'alwā'*. Allegro (1960: 53, 164) and Luria (1963: 122) read *dm*<ʿ> *l'ḥ*, which they interpret as "liquid tithe," *l'ḥ* being a *plene* spelling of *laḥ*, "moist, fresh" in Biblical and "liquid" in Postbiblical Hebrew; being wet would render the *demaʿ* susceptible to uncleanness (*m. Kelim* 15:6; *m. Makš.* 6:4; *cf.* Lev 11:38), and this is the sense understood by Allegro and Luria, who find a number of references to impure *demaʿ* in our catalogue. When the scribe's mistake is corrected, however, we have *mĕlē'â*, which, as noted above, may refer to the fullness of the winevat, but in the Rabbinic literature is primarily the fullness of the stored grain from which the first fruits are taken (*Mek. Mišpaṭ.* 19). Thus *mĕlē'â* serves as a synonym for *bikkûrîm* (*b. Tem.* 4a) and *rē'šît*, "first fruits" (*cf. Yal. Exod.* 351). In the absence of a conjunction, the second term, *demaʿ sûrā'*, "*demaʿ* set apart" (?), ought to be a further specification of *demaʿ mĕlē'â*. The sequence *syr'*, however, is difficult to interpret. The form is apparently feminine (-*ā'*), so that it cannot be understood as a modifier of *demaʿ*. Allegro and Luria derive it from √*swr*, "turn aside," though neither attempts to account for the form – thus Luria (1963: 122), citing the description of a woman "put away" (*sûrah*) in Isa 49:21, understands *demaʿ sûrā'* "to refer to *tĕrûmâ* that was put aside because of fear of a flaw in cleanliness," and Allegro (1960: 53, 164) renders it "degenerated tithe." Tentatively, I would understand it as "*demaʿ* set aside, apart (*viz.*, from the fullness of the crop)," the form of *sûrā'* having been attracted to the preceding feminine noun *mĕlē'â*.

10) *kl* <*y*> *ksp wkly zhb šl dmʿ*, "silver vessels and gold vessels of *dēmaʿ*" (12.6–7). Five times the listing of *demaʿ* vessels is followed by a sequence read by Milik and Allegro as *(w)btkn 'ṣlm* (5.7, 11.1, 4, 11, 15). This might be understood as *ûbĕtōken 'eṣlām*, literally, "and by measurement in proximity to them," and thus, "not far away," which according to Milik is commonly used in 3Q15 to represent a new location in the general vicinity of the one just mentioned. Allegro and Luria, however, recognize that the sequence always follows a reference to *demaʿ*, upon which it should therefore be expected to have some bearing. Accordingly, they reject Milik's analysis (1962: 254) of *(w)btkn* as *(û)bĕtoken* as "(et) à peu de distance," in favor of *(û)bĕtōkān*, "(and) inside them"; they interpret the sequence *'ṣlm* as a form of *ṣelem*, "image," with prosthetic *'alep* (Allegro 1960: 148; *cf.* Luria 1963: 86–87). The point would be that the deposits thus described are religiously unfit or at least unready since coins stamped with the image of Caesar were unsuitable for religious use until they were defaced or restruck (*cf. m. Maʿaś. Š.* 1:2; *m. ʿEd.* 3:2). Though ingenious, this explanation relies heavily on a subtle interpretation of *'ṣlm* for which no corroboration has survived. Note, too, that in two of the five occurrences of this word (11.11, 15) the last letter is *nun* not *mem*, so that we should seek an interpretation that accommodates both spellings. Keeping in mind the near interchangeability of *bêt* and *kap* in our document, we may consider the

possibility of reading the first word as *wktbn*. Thus we have *úkětābān 'eslām* or *'eslān*,[5] "and their register [writing] alongside them," or perhaps, "as regards them, with respect to them." If this is correct, the meaning is probably that each of the groups of vessels to which the expression applies was accompanied by a written record identifying the contents of the vessels with regard, perhaps, to the ownership of the produce from which it was taken or for which it was redeemed and to its specific religious purpose or destination.

Let us now give special attention to location 4 (1.9–12), which contains other technical terms pertaining to religious imposts. After the mention of *kělé dema'* in 1.9, we have the statement *hakkōl šel haddema' wěhā'ōṣār haṣṣābúa' úma'ǎsēr šēnî měpúggal pithô běsúlé hā'āmmā' min haṣṣāp[ōn] 'ammôt šēš 'ad niqrat haṭṭibbúl*, "As for all of the *dema'* and the Seventh-[Year] accumulation and disqualified Second Tithe, its entrance is at the end of the aqueduct on the north, six cubits in the direction of the immersion chamber."

Of the three categories of material listed here—*dema'*, Seventh-Year accumulation, and Second Tithe—we have already discussed the first. The second is expressed by *hā'ōṣār*, "the accumulation, store," followed by *hšbw[?]'*, which Allegro, Luria and Lehmann relate to the institution of *haṣṣābúa'* or *šěbí'ît*, "the Sabbatical Year," when agricultural work was forbidden in accordance with the prescriptions of Lev 25:2–7, 20–22 and debts were forgiven as prescribed in Deut 15:1–3. Lehmann (1964: 101) cites *t. Seb.* 8.1, "which relates that the Court appointed guardians in each village to collect and dispose of any produce of the seventh year. Their instructions were to spend a part of the produce for minimal food requirements of the local population and to deliver the rest into the *'wṣr* (public treasury). It is likely that a central *'wṣr hšb'/šby'yt* (treasury of the seventh year) existed, according to this *Tosephta*, consisting of produce or money gained by redeeming the seventh year produce. . . ." Similarly, Luria (1963: 63) interprets *hšb'y* by reference to *šěbí'ît*, *i.e.*, (produce of) the Sabbatical Year, reading the phrase as "Everything (that is within [the vessels]) is *těrúmâ* and treasure, *šěbí'ît* and tithes. . . ."[6]

Following this sequence in 1.10–11 we have the third category of material, viz., *ma'ǎsēr šēnî měpúggal*, "disqualified Second Tithe." In the Talmud, *Ma'ǎsēr Šēnî* is the name of the seventh tractate of the order of *Zera'im*. The basis of the institution of Second Tithe is Deut 14:22–26, which reads as follows:

---

[5] Twice, in 11.1 and 11.4, *'ṣlm* is spelled with an anomalous form of *'alep*. This type, identified by F. M. Cross (*apud* Milik 1962: 219) as "the cursive, 'gamma-form' *'alef*," presents no obstacle to our intepetation.

[6] There is a grammatical difficulty with *hā'ōṣār haṣṣābúa'* on which neither Lehmann nor Luria comments. We expect *'ōṣār* (not *hā'ōṣār*) *haṣṣābúa'*. Allegro (1960: 33, 137), who interprets the sequence in a similar way (*wh'ṣr hšbw' w-*, "and stored Seventh-Year produce and . . ."), explains: ". . . the second word in apposition to the first, 'the store—the Seventh-Year produce'; otherwise error for *'ṣr hšbw'*. . . ." Milik (1962: 285, *cf.* 249) reads *wh'ṣrh šb' w-*, "et du trésor: sept (talents) et . . ."; this is graphically as good, but the feminine form of *'ōṣār* does not occur elsewhere.

[22] You must tithe all the produce of your seed that grows in the field year by year. [23] You must eat [it] before the Lord your god in the place he chooses to make his name dwell, a tithe of your grain, your wine, your oil, and the firstborn of your herd and flock, so that you will learn to fear the Lord your god at all times. [24] If the distance is too great for you so that you cannot carry it because the place which the Lord your god chooses to make his name dwell is too far from you when the Lord your god blesses you, [25] then you may convert it into silver, and secure the money in your hand, and go to the place which the Lord your god will choose. [26] You may spend the money for anything you desire—cattle, sheep, wine, strong drink, or anything you wish. You must eat there before the Lord your god and rejoice, you and your household.

By requiring that tithes be taken to "the place which the Lord your god chooses," *i.e.*, Jerusalem, and eaten, this passage seems to contradict the rule in Numb 18:21–24, which stipulates that tithes be given to the Levites. Modern biblical scholarship explains the contradiction by pointing out that Numb 18:21ff derives from Priestly circles, while Deut 14:22ff is Deuteronomic. The ancient solution was to posit two tithes, the first (*ma'ăśēr rī'šôn*) being that given to the priests, the second (*ma'ăśēr šēnî*) being that eaten by the tither in Jerusalem or converted into money which was brought to Jerusalem and spent for something to be eaten. This solution is already hinted at in the text of the Septuagint (*cf.* Targum Jonathan) of Deut 26:12, where, in contrast to *šēnat hamma'ăśēr*, "the year of the tithe," of the Massoretic Text, the Septuagint reads *to deuteron epidekaton*, reflecting *šēnît hamma'ăśēr*, "the second tithe." Other early authorities include Tobit 1:7, Jubilees 32:10–14, which provides (v 11) "that the second tithe may be eaten before the Lord in the place chosen," and Josephus, *Ant.* 4.8.8, where Josephus cites the divine injunction "Let there be set aside a tithe of the fruits in addition to the one I appointed to be given to the priests and Levites; let [this additional tithe] be sold at its place of origin, but let the proceeds be used for feasts and sacrifices held in the Holy City."

The purpose of *ma'ăśēr rī'šôn*, the first tithe, to which *dema'* pertains, was the support of the Levites (or with the scarcity of Levites in the Second Temple Period the priests) in return for their service at the sanctuary, and they consumed it anywhere like ordinary produce (Numb 18:30–31), though they were first required to separate an additional tenth as a "*těrûmat* of the Lord" for the (other) priests (vv 28–29). Thus *těrûmâ*, which is only for priests, cannot be bought with money derived from the sale of *ma'ăśēr šēnî*, which is for everyone (*m. Ma'aś. Š.* 3:2). On the other hand, *ma'ăśēr šēnî*, because it could be consumed only "in the presence of the Lord" (*i.e.*, in Jerusalem), was "holy to the Lord," in contrast to the secular *ma'ăśēr rī'šôn*, which could be consumed anywhere. When converted to money, the sanctity of *ma'ăśēr šēnî* was transferred to the specie, so that neither Second Tithe produce nor

Second Tithe money could be used in business transactions (*m. Maʿaś. Š.* 1:1). Produce bought with Second Tithe money could only be consumed at the sanctuary, and if the sanctuary was inaccessible, it had to be left to rot (*m. Maʿaś. Š.* 1:5–6).

Our Copper Scroll occurrence of *maʿăśēr šēnî* (note *s* for *ś*) is modified by the sequence *mpy/wgl*, which I interpret as the passive participle *měpûggal*.[7] The verb *piggēl* is denominative from *piggûl*, which according to Jastrow (1903: 1159) refers to "a sacrifice rejectable in consequence of an improper intention in the mind of the officiating priest"; thus *piggēl* means "cause to become *piggûl*, make (a sacrifice) unfit, disqualify (a sacrifice)." We have no way of knowing, of course, what it was that disqualified the Second Tithe listed in the Copper Scroll, though it may have had something to do with the relationship of the Second Tithe or the money for which it was redeemed to the *demaʿ* or First Tithe (*těrûmâ*), with which it was not mutually convertible,[8] or to the Seventh-Year accumulations, which under certain circumstances were disposed of after the fashion of Second Tithe.[9]

Note finally that the location of the entryway that provides access to the fourth location hoard is described as "in the direction of the immersion chamber." As a technical term, *ṭibbûl*, "dipping, immersion," refers to "the act which makes food subject to priestly gifts" (Jastrow 1903: 529), *i.e.*, the act which makes common food into *ṭebel*, which is food that cannot be eaten until *těrûmâ* and Second Tithe have been set aside. More generally, *ṭābal*, "dip," refers to bathing for the purpose of ritual purification and *hiṭbíl*, "immerse," refers to the ritual purification by immersion of vessels, persons, *etc.*[10] Thus our "immersion chamber" (*cf. něqîrtāʾ*, "cave, [underground] cavity") was probably a place of ritual purification, possibly the site where the vessels mentioned here were prepared for religious use.

Among other religious property listed in 3Q15, mention should be made of at least three other references to "vessels" (*kēlîn*), in 2.9, 10 and 10.11. In the last instance the specification is *kělîn kôpěrîn*; these vessels might have contained or been coated with *kōper*, "bitumen, pitch," as Milik supposes (thus "vases enduits de poix," 1962: 296, *cf.* 252), but they might also have been repositories of *kôpěrîn*, "indemnities, fines," levied for infractions of law. In three other places we have the mention of *ḥērem*, which in this period refers to property restricted for the use of the Temple or priesthood (*m. Ned.* 2:4,

---

[7] For our *měpûggal pithô*, "disqualified [Second Tithe,] its entrance," Milik (1962: 285, *cf.* 255) reads *měpî gal pithô*, "de l'entrée de sa port tournante. . . ."

[8] According to *m. Maʿaś. Š.* 3:2, *těrûmâ*, which is only for priests, cannot be bought with money derived from the redemption of Second Tithe, which is for everyone.

[9] The circumstances are described in *m. Maʿaś. Š.* 5.

[10] For *ʿd nyqrt hṭbwl*, Milik (1962: 284–85, 243) reads *ʿd nyqrt hṭbylh* (= *haṭṭěbílâ*), "dans la direction de la caverne de l'immersion," comparing *byt ṭbylh*, "une des quatres salles dans les bains du Temple," in *m. Mid.* 1:6–9; but no trace of the final *h* is now visible on the copper.

5; cf. m. 'Arak. 8:4, 7; etc.). In at least two locations (27 and 32) there is a reference to a book, viz., sēper 'eḥad, "a single book," in 6.5, and siprô, "its book," in 8.3, the former having been deposited in a qālāl (6.4), the type of vessel in which the ashes of the red heifer were said to have been preserved (m. Par. 3:3).

This list could be expanded. The point is that of sixty-four locations of hidden property in the Copper Scroll at least sixteen (or 25%) are said to have contained religious materials, most of which were restricted to Levitical, priestly or Temple use by the halachic regulations with which we are familiar. These references suggest the possibility that the Copper Scroll treasure as a whole was, in some sense, Temple property—a possibility that nothing said of the other forty-eight locations contradicts. Was it the Temple treasury itself, hidden in the wadis east of Jerusalem in anticipation of the Roman assault on the city at the time of the First Revolt? The extraordinary magnitude of the listed deposits of gold and silver favors this assumption. We recall, moreover, the tantalizing reference in Location 32 to silver bars hidden on or near the property of bêt haqqōṣ (7.9). We know from Nehemiah 3 that the běnê haqqōṣ participated in the reconstruction work in Jerusalem after the Babylonian exile alongside contingents from Jericho and it vicinity (vv 2–4) and, more generally, in company with 'anšê hakkikar, "the men of the Kikkar," the district of the Jordan Valley (vv 21–22). We also know that they were a priestly family (1 Chron 24:10), though they were among those unable after the Exile to document their eligibility for performing the sacerdotal offices in the Temple (Ezra 2:61; cf. Neh 7:63; 1 Esdr 5:38). Ezra 8:33 and Neh 10:6, when read together, suggest that it was to the House of Hakkoz that responsibility for the Temple treasury was entrusted in the Second Temple period. Finally, the reference in 1 Macc 8:17 to the appointment by Judas Maccabeus of a certain Eupolemus son of John son of Hakkoz (tou akkōs) as ambassador to Rome suggests that the family remained prominent at least as late as the Hasmonean period. It is possible, then, that the Copper Scroll treasure was removed from the Temple coffers in the mid-60s and hidden in the Judaean Desert under the supervision of the běnê haqqōṣ and other Temple officials.

Another interpretation of the nature of the Copper Scroll treasure, also compatible with the information just presented, is that it is an accumulation of religious offerings that were destined for the Temple but never reached it. Although halachic legislation permitted local distribution of dema', in actual practice it was usually taken to Jerusalem, as Second Tithe always was (Oppenheimer 1977: 30, 32). If Jerusalem was inaccessible, however, this obligation could not be fulfilled (cf. 1 Macc 3:49–50), and the reserved contributions would have to be stored or secluded (cf. Judith 11:13). Under circumstances of this kind, when contributions that had been duly set aside in accordance with Pentateuchal and Rabbinic legislation could not be transported to Jerusalem in due course, a considerable accumulation of property (converted to money) could have been amassed; and it may have been such an accumulation that was recorded in the Copper Scroll, having been hidden to prevent it from falling into unclean hands at the time of the First Revolt or another crisis. On the basis of such a possibility, Lehmann (1964) has argued that the treasure was accumulated in the period between the two revolts when the Temple was inaccessible because it no longer existed. Taking into account the preference for a mid-first century date for the script of 3Q15,[11] I have proposed the alternative view that "the Copper Scroll treasure consisted of tithes and contributions gathered in the final, turbulent years before the Roman destruction of the Temple. It is possible that the treasure arrived at the Temple shortly before the war began, then was removed from the city in secret and hidden when the Roman army appeared in Galilee. It seems more likely, however, that much of the treasure never reached the Temple. In view of the steadily growing chaos in the last years before the arrival of Vespasian's army, the Jews who had the responsibility for gathering tithes and contributions may have felt it unwise to deposit them in the public treasury. Instead they elected to divide up the treasure and hide it in a large number of different locations east of the city" (McCarter 1992: 64).

REFERENCES

ALLEGRO, J. M.
  1960 *The Treasure of the Copper Scroll.* Garden City, NY: Doubleday. 2d edition: 1964.
BAILLET, M., J. T. MILIK, and R. DE VAUX
  1962 *Les "Petites Grottes" de Qumrân.* Discoveries in the Judaean Desert of Jordan 3. Oxford: Clarendon.
JASTROW, MARCUS
  1903 *A Dictionary of the Targumim, the Talmud Babli and Yerushalmi, and the Midrashic Literature.* 2 vols. Brooklyn: Traditional Press.
LEHMANN, M.
  1964 Identification of the Copper Scroll based on its technical terms. *Revue de Qumran* **5**: 97–105.
LURIA, B. Z.
  1963 *The Copper Scroll from the Judaean Desert* [Hebrew]. Publications of the Israel Bible Research Society 14. Jerusalem: Kiryat-Sepher.
McCARTER, P. K.
  1992 The mysterious Copper Scroll: Clues to hidden Temple treasure? *Biblical Archaeology Review* **8/4**: 34–41, 63–64.
MILIK, J. T., R. DE VAUX, and H. WRIGHT BAKER
  1962 Le rouleau de cuivre provenant de la grotte 3Q (3Q15). *In* BAILLET, MILIK, and DE VAUX 1962, pp. 201–302.

[11] The conclusion of Cross (*apud* Milik 1962: 215) is that "the script is to be placed in the second half of the Herodian era, that is, within the broad limits A.D. 25–75."

OPPENHEIMER, A.
1977   *The 'Am ha-Aretz: A Study in the Social History of the Jewish People in the Hellenistic-Roman Period*, trans. I. H. LEVINE. Arbeiten zur Literatur und Geschichte des hellenistischen Judentums 8. Leiden: Brill.



DISCUSSION OF THE PAPER

NORMAN GOLB (*Oriental Institute, University of Chicago, Chicago, IL*): Dr. McCarter, could you kindly say a few words in this conference on methods of interpretation of the scrolls and about your methods of investigation? How did you arrive at your readings, what about photographs, *etc*.

P. KYLE MCCARTER (*The Johns Hopkins University, Baltimore, MD*): The Copper Scroll was opened and photographed at the University of Manchester in the 1950s. The photographs published in Milik's *editio princeps* come from that time and, by and large, were extremely good photographs for the day. They are one set of photographs taken from one light angle.

In working with the Copper Scroll, I've had several advantages. I've had opportunities to view the Copper Scroll, but I can assure you, it cannot be worked with in person, because of its fragility and because of the way it is displayed.

More important and first of all, an enhancement of the 1950s photographs is now possible by modern techniques. It considerably improves the resolution, particularly in comparison to the grainy plates published in the DJD volume.

Secondly, the Zuckerman brothers went to Amman in December 1988 and made a new set of photographs. The new set of photographs has certain advantages over the old set. In the first place, it is a record of the Copper Scroll as it looks now. The second advantage is that it represents at least two light angles in every case. Although it may not be apparent to you if you're used to working with two-dimensional media (such as a leather scroll) it is very risky to work from photographs of incised materials taken from a single light angle. In such a case certain strokes may be washed out when the camera does its work. Regardless of which light angle one chooses, certain strokes may simply disappear when the picture is taken. So you have to have at least two, and preferably more than two, light angles.

The principal advantage of the old photographs enhanced is that the Scroll was in better shape then. The surface has deteriorated somewhat, especially along the lines where the saw touched it in Manchester. The steel blade seems to have insulted the copper, so that material is retreating along the cuts and some of the marginal readings have simply disappeared. In those cases the older photographs are all we have.

JAMES H. CHARLESWORTH (*Princeton Theological Seminary, Princeton, NJ*): Just an offer of help, plus a curiosity. I'd like you to share with the group, Kyle, where you think you are in the ability to read the material. Back about maybe five years ago, you gave me a letter. You said then that in the 1950s 10%, maybe 15%, maybe 20% of the text could be read, but your estimate was you now could obtain access to something like 80% or more.

I'll be in Amman in April and maybe you can advise me. If you would give me a Xerox copy of a column where you really cannot read something, if I got a very soft charcoal pencil, maybe with some very soft rubbings I could help you resolve certain readings.

McCARTER: I wouldn't want to guess what percentage of the Copper Scroll we can read. I remind you that the problem is not always our ability to see what the scribe put there. This was an unusual scribe writing in an unusual way in what seems to be an unusual language. There are thus a number of peculiarities. Once you are certain of what you are reading then you despair of going to the standard sources and finding anything that corresponds. Very often there are aberrations in spelling, or grammar. The mistakes are common enough that they tempt the interpreter to assume mistakes where there are none. Once you begin to do that, you can read anything you want.

So this is why I have come up with what I admit are very wooden readings, such as *bōlēgín* ("shiny") for something that might refer to vessels. There are a number of difficulties involved with reading the Copper Scroll that have to do not with the condition of the document, but simply with the nature of the material on which it was written and no doubt the handicap the poor scribe was laboring under. If you or I tried to take notes with a little chisel and a metal sheet, we would probably not produce a very legible English document. He was laboring under difficulties that we have inherited from him.

I can, however, read a lot more than I could five years ago. I don't know whether that has to do with the advantage of better materials or whether it's simply that I have worked on it longer.

Certainly it is a very well preserved document, surprisingly so. It is also very obscure. As has been pointed out in the literature recently, there is language there that doesn't survive in another form. I don't mean the language itself (which is Hebrew), but features of grammar and vocabulary that don't survive elsewhere. We can only guess at them or reconstruct them from cognate languages in the usual way. It is more like reading an Iron Age inscription than a Dead Sea Scroll, which is in part why I was asked to work on it.

In 1988, I highlighted the places in the text where I either had a specific question or where there was substantial disagreement among previous interpreters.

Bruce and Kenny Zuckerman took that with them. After the first round of photographs, when they hoped they could go in and take a number of close-ups, there was some misunderstanding. They didn't want to push the people at the Museum, who had been very generous already, too hard; so that additional photographs didn't get taken.

AL WOLTERS (*Redeemer College, Ancaster, Ont., Canada*): Kyle, I'm delighted to see someone else working on the Copper Scroll. I've been thinking I've been slaving away by myself the last number of years. Thank you, too, for dealing with that very difficult issue of what those strange words after *kele dema'* mean. It is very peculiar: although most of the words in the Copper Scroll are relatively straightforward, it is precisely on half a dozen occasions after this very phrase that we get words that we don't understand.

Now, as you pointed out Milik wanted to make all of those words refer to the same type of thing. So, he ended up with some kind of incense or some kind of aromatic wood in every case. I tried to do the same thing, and decided that perhaps they're all proper names. That works in a number of cases, for example, *Sodah*, which could also be read as Serah, a proper name. Also, in the case of the reading which you take to mean *Meah* on the basis of parablepsis, that could be read as the personal name, Leah. In that case, we would have a number of names of people whose tribute was being dedicated to the temple at that point. I wonder if you had thought of that possibility?

Two other comments, or rather one comment and a question. The reading *mĕpŭggal* I owe to Michael Wise; also, I noticed later that Allegro in the second edition of his translation—there were two—had also seen that earlier.

Finally, this question. You referred to the photographs that were taken in Manchester in 1955 and 1956 and published in *DJD-3* as the only photographs we have to go by, and being only at one angle. Now, according to Baker in his account, at the opening of the Scrolls there were hundreds of photographs taken from every conceivable angle. My suspicion is that those photographs may be better than some of the ones that we have now, because they are based on an earlier state of the text. Do you know where those photographs are? I've been trying to figure out where they are. I can't find them.

MCCARTER: I can only indicate agreement in response to all parts of your question. I'm glad to know that Allegro saw the *mĕpŭggal* reference. I wasn't aware of that. I only had it in a personal communication from you that *you* had seen it. So, if it's from Michael Wise, I'm glad to know that.

The enhanced photographs that I have seen come from the Claremont set, which Bruce Zuckerman processed. They are the only ones that I'm aware of. I know the discussion that you're referring to, but I don't know of the existence of other photographs or how to find them.

Yes, the references after *'dema'* might be personal names—I have considered that. Please don't misunderstand this as a criticism of your suggestion—it is a self-criticism and probably one that you have made as well—but positing a personal name is facile unless one can find it attested in a way that it makes sense here. And, even then, it can be facile. That is, sometimes it is an easy solution to a problem that we have. We don't know what a word might mean, so we simply call it a proper noun and read it as a personal name or place name. I think that Milik did this occasionally in cases where other scholars, working from his text, discovered that the words had common meanings.

Nevertheless, you may be quite right. It would make perfectly good sense to identify the '*dema*' by the people who had set aside the contribution. I've not been able to find a pattern in that. I have found other instances where I thought '*dema*' was modified in some way that would indicate some kind of consistent pattern. One instance is in the full edition of this paper. There is a reference in one of the locations to *bêt haqqôṣ* house or the estate of *haqqôṣ*, near which something is hidden. This is an intriguing reference, because if you study the *haqqôṣ* family, you find not only that they lived in the Jericho region (as Ezra, Nehemiah and Chronicles show), but also they were a priestly family. Beyond that, they were in all probability the family that was entrusted with the temple treasury. And, in a document that has very few personal names the name of a priestly family in charge of the temple treasure seems to be very pertinent to an understanding of the nature of the treasure.

There are other ways of reading that reference, by the way. There is a midrash on Psalm 14 which identifies pagan temples by the term *battê haqqôṣ* "houses of the thorn." So *bêt haqqôṣ* might also refer to a pagan temple; that could be the meaning in the Copper Scroll reference—simply, near the pagan shrine, rather than near the estate of the Hakkoz family.

So you can see the danger that proper nouns take us into. And yet I'm very much in agreement with you that it is one possibility in interpreting these very difficult passages.

HARTMUT STEGEMANN (*University of Göttingen, Göttingen, Germany*): I have two questions. The amounts of gold, silver and so on in the Copper Scroll are very high. This may correspond to the treasures which were in the temple. On the other hand, Josephus tells that after the Romans occupied the temple, they got so much silver, gold and so on that supplies of the gold in the region went down to half of what they were before. Are both right? Secondly, why take the hidden treasures from the temple and leave others there?

McCARTER: The very large numbers—extraordinary numbers—that are used to describe the amounts of gold and silver that are hidden lead in one of two directions. One is towards the temple. It is hard to imagine there was another treasure in the country at the time that would have been large enough to be described in this way. The other is the direction that Milik took, which is to assume that the document was a fantasy, or at least that the treasure was a fantasy.

You recall that Milik cited a tradition from Jewish legend about concealed vessels from the temple of Solomon. There certainly is such a tradition. If you go to that literature, however, and read it, you find yourself in an entirely different world, I think, from that of the Copper Scroll. There you have Jeremiah or Moses hiding things. You have not only gold and silver, but you have the ark. You have the other sacred objects that presumably would have been in the Temple of Solomon. They get the emphasis. I have stressed, as I think others have, that the very dullness, the business-like quality of the Copper Scroll, argues in favor of its being an authentic treasure rather than an imaginary one.

The question of whether this text as temple treasure contradicts the statements about Roman plunder taken out of Jerusalem is another kind of question. This list doesn't seem to be a complete temple treasure in the sense that I just described. It looks like coffers of the temple having to do with religious contributions, thus funds from the temple, not the paraphernalia of the temple, which may very well have been plundered if not hidden. To my way of thinking, the Copper Scroll doesn't represent everything that the temple had, but strictly money derived from religious taxes.

GOLB: I'm fascinated by the Copper Scroll. We had a seminar at the University in 1971, I think, and since then I can't get my mind off this fascinating scroll. I congratulate you on your new readings and interesting ideas.

A few observations about the wording and some of the problems in the text. May I give these to you *seriatim*?

McCARTER: Please.

GOLB: Okay. First, *battê haqqôṣ* is to my mind much better as a term defining the possessions of the priestly family than the other you suggest. For the house to be defined by thorns, we would expect the expression *battê haqqôṣim* not *battê haqqôṣ*; the house of *a* thorn is not reasonable. That's a small matter.

David Wilmot, in his thesis on the Copper Scroll (which we still plan to publish at the University), suggested that there was more than one scribe who wrote the Copper Scroll. You refer in your talk to "the scribe" who wrote the Copper Scroll, and I think he proved by the different forms of the letters that there was more than one scribe. I was also wondering if you had some thoughts about the language as compared and contrasted with that of the MMT, which is very close to my mind to the rabbinic or Tannaitic idiom?

There was no discussion of geographical terms except one as I recall in your talk, whereas is it not the fact that the names we do know, the toponyms that we can recognize in the scroll, must play a part in deciding on the place of origin? We have a reference to *naḥal qidron*. That of course leads us out of Jerusalem and toward the desert. Then, we have Jericho. And, we have a few other wadis as well mentioned in the Copper Scroll. So we have the beginnings of a geographical configuration. I'm wondering if you've made any progress in the geography of the text, the toponymy of the text, as you have done with the artifacts.

Finally, a word about the *ketabin*. This is a very intriguing case of scholars being confused and not understanding the text. We had first Allegro saying *batokhen etslan*, didn't we? Then, Milik also wrote *batokhen*, didn't he? Then, after he edited the book, on the last page, I think he has a reference to an Israeli scholar who suggested that it was not *batokhen etslan* (which makes absolutely no sense), but *kĕtābān etslan*, "their writing," their *ketab*, is "next to them." It is more than just a possibility; it is such a straightforward reading. The writings are next to those vessels mentioned above. *Ketab* is a term used for a document or a text.

MCCARTER: We have two references. Excuse me. We have *sĕpārín*, "books," in one case, and in another we have *sēper 'eḥad*, "a single book."

GOLB: At the end, we have *mishne haketab*, showing that they used two terms for "text."

MCCARTER: Well, let me respond. A couple of your points I'll discuss with you later. As to the question of whether there are one or more scribes, I look forward to Wilmot's work for that specific reason. There is good evidence that there is more than one scribe. Let me give you a very specific example. Those of you who know the Copper Scroll know that throughout most of the text, the *'alep* is a hump-backed letter with a single diagonal stroke coming off of it—an unexceptional form of *'alep*.

Near the end of the text, though, the scribe seems to shift to a more advanced form of *'alep*, which looks like a Greek *gamma*—the so-called "gamma-form" *'alep*, which is characteristic of very late Herodian handwriting. If we had that sporadically through the text we would assume that we had a scribe who knew both forms, but the fact that the later form occurs only near the end of the test suggests strongly that perhaps a second scribe has taken over. If Wilmot has gathered more examples, I'm sure he saw that one.

On the *kĕtābān*, I've already said that we're in agreement.

HERSHEL SHANKS (*Biblical Archaeology Review*): I'd like to say at the outset, Kyle, that the question I'm about to ask reflects a conversation last night with Hartmut Stegemann and Al Wolters and Sam Iwry, so that it is not mine, and I am properly citing it lest I be sued. I don't want to be sued again.

The point concerns the Greek letters that appear after about seven of the early locations. Hartmut Stegemann said that each of these could be the beginning of a personal name recorded in Josephus. Al Wolters added that there were deposits made by private parties in the temple treasury, and that perhaps an allusion like this could be found in the New Testament. The seven examples might be deposits listed by these names or parties. I see Hartmut wants to comment on that. Maybe I mischaracterized it.

STEGEMANN: I should comment briefly. The idea that the Greek letters represent the beginnings of names was published by Pixner. But, Pixner thought the treasure of the Copper Scroll should belong to the Essenes. That's wrong in my view. The names suggested refer to people from Adiabene. It is attested that they were in Jerusalem at three palaces and they were involved in the struggle with the Romans. Some of them survived, and the money may have been theirs, given to the priests to safekeep.

ROBERT EISENMAN (*California State University, Long Beach*): I want to throw one point at what Hartmut is saying about the Adiabene family. There is some indication that the Zealots in the 60s and 70s were very interested in this family. Each was a sort of opposition king. These were the kings that the Zealots were really interested in, not the Roman-sponsored kings that were there. So that suggestion for the Copper Scroll really may tie in very nicely.

McCARTER: I'll make a very brief comment on that, expressing caution about the very small number of Greek letters that we have. I sometimes despair of the final answer to the question of the Greek letters. There are so few that it would be fairly easy to impose a solution on them that would work consistently but would not have enough information behind it to convince any significant number of people. Since the letters don't correspond to any known system of abbreviation, if we assume one which works, we're not likely to be able to assemble enough evidence to make us confident about it.

The Place of the Damascus Document

MICHAEL A. KNIBB

Department of Theology and Religious Studies
King's College London
Strand
London, England WC2R 2LS

≈ I ≈

The Damascus Document is one of the most important sources of information for the origins and early history of the Qumran community.[1] Of its two
constituent parts, the Admonition is one of the few documents from Qumran
to refer explicitly to the teacher of righteousness and to the origins of the
group associated with him, while the Laws contain material that casts an important light on the character of the group which produced it. But there are
considerable problems in making use of all this material. The historical statements within the Damascus Document are notoriously opaque and have been
interpreted in widely different ways. There are questions over the unity of the
Damascus Document, and, in addition to the problem of the internal coherence of the Admonition, the question of the relationship of the Laws to the
Admonition—and, by implication, that of the relationship of the groups that
lie behind these two sections of the Damascus Document—remains to be resolved. There are uncertainties over the dating of the Damascus Document
and of the various elements contained within it. Finally, there is the question
of the relationship of the Damascus Document to the Community Rule, and
of the Laws to other similar collections. My purpose in what follows is to take
up some of these questions and to try to suggest some possible ways forward.
It is, I believe, an appropriate moment to do so in view of the helpful new
edition by Qimron of the Cairo Genizah manuscripts of the Damascus Document (CD) that was published earlier this year in the volume entitled *The*

---

[1] For recent surveys of research on the Damascus Document, see CALLAWAY, P. R. 1988.
The History of the Qumran Community: An Investigation. Sheffield Academic Press. Sheffield,
England, pp. 89–133. VAN DER WOUDE, A. 1992. *Theologische Rundschau* **57:** 49–56. See also
GARCÍA MARTÍNEZ, F. 1992. "Damascus document: A bibliography of studies 1970–1989." In
The Damascus Document Reconsidered. M. BROSHI, Ed.:63–83. The Israel Exploration Society and
the Shrine of the Book, Israel Museum. Jerusalem, Israel.

Damascus Document Reconsidered,[2] and in view of the increased knowledge that we now have of the Cave 4 manuscripts (4QD[a–h]).

At the outset I ought to make clear that I accept the view that the Damascus Document in more or less its final form dates from approximately 100 B.C.E.[3] Part of the evidence for this view lies in the dating of 4QD[a], which is written in a semi-cursive Hasmonean hand that has been assigned to the first half of the first century B.C.E.[4] It has been argued that it is difficult to date such a script with precision, and in view of this Brooke has suggested that "it may be preferable to acknowledge that it is more likely that all extant copies of the Damascus Document date from the end of the first century B.C.E. or later."[5] But even if this were accepted, there is internal evidence which points to a date for the composition of the work at the beginning of the first century B.C.E. The Damascus Document twice refers to the death of the teacher of righteousness, apparently as a fairly recent event (see XIX,35b–XX,1a; XX, 13b–15a), and these references occur in a section (XIX,33b–XX,22a) which seems to belong to the latest layer within the work. However little we know about the teacher, it is clear that he belongs in the second century B.C.E., and this suggests a date of composition at the end of the second century or the beginning of the following one.

≈ II ≈

In an article entitled "The Laws of the Damascus Document in Current Research," which appeared in the volume *The Damascus Document Reconsidered*,[6] Baumgarten has given us the fullest account so far available of the contents of the Cave 4 manuscripts of the Damascus Document and has provided an outline of the probable structure of the entire work in which he has tentatively placed the 4Q fragments in relation to the Genizah text. There are two points that he makes that I wish to refer to here. The first is his confirmation that "aside from sporadic modifications of Qumran spelling, the Genizah texts, as far as they extend, are likely to emerge as substantially reliable copies."[7] The second is his observation that, when the Genizah texts and the 4Q fragments are combined, the laws and communal rules form about two-thirds of the entire work, and that in the light of this the Admonition is to be seen essentially

---

[2] QIMRON, E. 1992. "The Text of CDC." In *The Damascus Document Reconsidered*, pp. 9–49.
[3] See, *e.g.*, VAN DER WOUDE, A. 1992. *Theologische Rundschau* 57: 52, 55.
[4] BAUMGARTEN, J. 1992a. "The laws of the Damascus Document in current research." In *The Damascus Document Reconsidered*, p. 57.
[5] BROOKE, G. J. 1991. "The Messiah of Aaron in the Damascus document." *Revue de Qumran* 15: 216.
[6] BAUMGARTEN, J. 1992a. pp. 51–62.
[7] BAUMGARTEN, J. 1992a. p. 62.

as an introduction to the Laws.[8] However, as he also indicates, it is the Admonition rather than the corpus of laws that has attracted the greatest attention from scholars since the Scrolls were discovered.

If the implication of Baumgarten's comments is accepted, then it is clear that research on the Damascus Document in the immediate future ought to begin with, and to concentrate on, the Laws. But in this case two questions immediately arise: What is the relationship of the Laws to the Admonition? And what is the relationship of this corpus to other collections of laws and to other documents that have a legal character?

So far as the first question is concerned, the views of scholars have varied considerably. At the one extreme Stegemann, in an article published in 1990, has denied that there was any literary connection between the Admonition and the corpus of laws and has argued that the latter represents the oldest rule book of the Essenes and was composed in the second quarter of the second century B.C.E.; he attributes its origin to the Hasidim, whom he believes came into existence as a properly organized community in 172 B.C.E.[9] Murphy-O'Connor had earlier maintained–as part of his theory of the Babylonian origin of the Essene movement–that the legislative material in the Damascus Document "was designed for a community living in a gentile environment" and belonged to the period in Babylon, whereas the Admonition was composed–in successive stages–after the members of the movement had returned to Palestine in the early years of the Maccabean revolt.[10] To mention two other recent examples, Callaway has considered the possibility of the literary independence of the Laws from the original Admonition,[11] and Strugnell has raised the question whether the nucleus of the legal code in the Damascus Document does not go back to the pre-Qumranic period.[12] At the other extreme Dimant has argued that although the Damascus Document, as represented by the Genizah texts and the 4Q fragments, may include various sources, the work is a unity and expresses the intention of an author.[13] In a very different way Davies has maintained that the Laws belong with what

[8] BAUMGARTEN, J. 1992a. pp. 52, 55, 61.
[9] STEGEMANN, H. 1990. "Das Gesetzeskorpus der 'Damaskusschrift'" (CD IX–XVI). *Revue de Qumran* **14**: 409–434.
[10] MURPHY-O'CONNOR, J. 1974. "The Essenes and their history." *Revue Biblique* **81**: 215–244. See the references there to the author's earlier articles, on which the synthesis given in *Revue Biblique*, vol. 81 is based. See also MURPHY-O'CONNOR. 1985. "The Damascus Document revisited." *Revue Biblique* **92**: 223–246.
[11] CALLAWAY, P. R. 1988. *The History of the Qumran Community*, pp. 97–98.
[12] STRUGNELL, J. 1991. "The Qumran scrolls: A report on work in progress." In *Jewish Civilization in the Hellenistic-Roman Period*. S. TALMON, Ed.:102–103. Sheffield Academic Press. Sheffield, England.
[13] DIMANT, D. 1984. "Qumran sectarian literature." In *Jewish Writings of the Second Temple Period*. M. E. STONE, Ed.:490–497. Van Gorcum. Assen, the Netherlands. Fortress Press. Philadelphia, PA. *Cf.* VAN DER WOUDE, A. 1992. *Theologische Rundschau* **57**: 54–55.

he regards as the original layer of the Admonition, which terminated at CD VII,9a, but also included material at the end of CD XX.[14]

The legal corpus of the Damascus Document consists of a loosely structured collection of rules and laws for a community that is conceived, like Israel in the wilderness, to be living in "camps." We now have the end of this corpus in fragments of two of the 4Q manuscripts (4QD^a and 4QD^c), while another fragment of 4QD^e appears to belong to some form of introduction.[15] The material is divided up by a series of headings of various kinds[16] and is arranged topically, but the topics follow no particular order; in this respect, and in its general character, Baumgarten has suggested that the closest analogy to the Laws is provided by 4Q159.[17] It seems more than probable that there are different layers within the corpus, and Boyce in his unpublished dissertation has maintained that CD X,10–XII,18, which contains rules for the inhabitants of the cities, stems from a different source from that for the inhabitants of the "camps."[18] The question of the literary unity of the legal corpus can, however, only effectively be taken up when all the 4Q fragments have been properly published. More important for our present purposes is the fact that the community for which the Laws were intended does seem to have had some kind of clearly defined structure. It is regularly spoken of as an עדה, a "congregation,"[19] but it is also described in CD XII,8 as an "association" (חבור). It had a number of officers at its head: there are frequent references to the "overseer" (מבקר), who is also called the "overseer of the camp" and the "overseer of the many";[20] there are references to judges and to priests,[21] and it is stated that each group of ten must include a priest;[22] in addition there is mention of the "overseer of all the camps" and of the "priest who enrolls at the head of the many."[23] It is also clear both from the existence of a penal code[24] and from the injunction against revealing the rules of the "congregation" to applicants for membership before they had sworn the oath of

[14] DAVIES, P. R. 1983. *The Damascus Covenant: An Interpretation of the "Damascus Document."* JSOT Press. Sheffield, England.

[15] *Cf.* BAUMGARTEN, J. 1992a. p. 53.

[16] *Cf.* (1) CD XVI,6; IX,2; (2) XVI,10, 13; IX,8; X,10, 14; (3) X,4; XII,22b–23a; XIII,7, (20); XIV, (3), 12; (4) XIV,17, 18; (5) XII,19; (6) XII,20b–21a; XIII,22.

[17] BAUMGARTEN, J. 1992a. p. 56.

[18] BOYCE, M. 1988. *The Poetry of the Damascus Document.* Unpublished Ph.D. dissertation, University of Edinburgh. (Not seen.) *Cf.* VAN DER WOUDE, A. *Theologische Rundschau* **57**: 55.

[19] *Cf.* CD X,4, 5, 8; XIII,10, 11, 13; XIV,10; see in addition the 4QD^a text corresponding to XIV,11.

[20] (1) CD XIII,7, 13, 16; (2) XV,8.

[21] (1) CD XV,4; XVI,19; IX,10; X,1, 4; XIV,13; (2) XVI,14; IX,13, 15; XIII,2, 5; XIV,3, 5, 8.

[22] CD XIII,2b–3a.

[23] (1) CD XIV,8b–9a; (2) XIV,6b–7a, *cf.* the text of 4QD^b.

[24] For the penal code see now BAUMGARTEN, J. 1992b. "The Cave 4 versions of the Qumran penal code." *Journal of Jewish Studies* **43**: 268–276.

the covenant (XV,10b–13a) that it was concerned to preserve its identity vis-à-vis outsiders.

Against this background it is possible to take up the question of the relationship of the Laws to the Admonition. In fact there seem to be good grounds for the view that the law code is somewhat older than the Admonition and stems from a pre-Qumranic and pre-teacher community. There are a number of obvious differences which immediately suggest this. The corpus of laws lacks any historical perspective, whereas such a perspective is characteristic of all parts of the Admonition. Callaway has drawn attention to differences in vocabulary and observed that some expressions in the Laws never occur in the Admonition (משכיל, מושב, ספר ההגו), and that the use of some others is confined almost entirely to the Laws (מחנה, עת, סרך).[25] There is a difference in attitude to the temple in that whereas the Laws assume that members of the "congregation" would both send offerings to the temple and themselves offer sacrifice (XI,17b–21a), the Admonition forbids visiting the temple (VI,11b–14a). But more important than these considerations is the whole difference in attitude reflected in the two sections of the Damascus Document. Baumgarten has pointed out that "the bulk of the CD laws, including the largest topical collection on the sabbath, is not formulated in polemical fashion," and he has referred to the "objective manner" in which the organizational and the penal rules are presented.[26] Although it is a question of degree, rather than an absolute difference,[27] the attitude of the Laws stands in sharp contrast to that of the Admonition, where a polemical approach is apparent not only in those sections that seem to belong to the latest layer in the Admonition and are concerned with the "scoffer" or "liar" and his followers, or with other real or potential apostates (CD I,13–18a; IV,19c–20a; VIII,12c–13; XIX,333b–XX,22a), but also in the main body of the Admonition, namely in the section on the three nets of Belial (CD IV,12b–V,15a), in the summary presentation of the laws (CD VI,11b–VII,4a), and in the critique of the princes of Judah (CD VIII,2b–21a). Thus although there is now a clear literary connection between the Laws and the Admonition, in the light of the above it is difficult to believe that they were both composed at the same moment.

If this is accepted, it is possible to consider the relationship of the corpus of laws to the works that have been seen to have the closest affinities to it. General considerations would seem to confirm the view that it belongs between Jubilees and the Temple Scroll, on the one hand, and *Miqṣat Maʿaseh*

---

[25] CALLAWAY, P. R. 1988. p. 98. CALLAWAY also refers to גורל האור, but the evidence in relation to גורל is not clear cut.

[26] BAUMGARTEN, J. 1992a. p. 56.

[27] My doctoral student, Charlotte Hempel, has pointed out to me that the passages referring to the בני השחר (XIII,14) and to the "blindness" of Israel (עורון ישראל, XVI,2b–3a) do have a polemical character. But these on the whole are exceptional in the Laws.

Ha-Torah (4QMMT), the Admonition, and the Community Rule (1QS), on the other.[28] The closest affinities are perhaps with the book of Jubilees, which is referred to by title in the Laws (CD XVI,3b–4a), and from which a passage is quoted (CD X,8b–10a, *cf.* Jub. 23:11); but whereas Jubilees is addressed to Israel and is not sectarian in character, the Laws reflect the ideology of an עדה, whose identity they are concerned to preserve. Similar considerations apply to the relationship of the Laws to the Temple Scroll, which, as VanderKam has shown, has close connections with Jubilees.[29] On the other hand, the "distinct polemic nature"—as the editors have described it—of 4QMMT suggests that this work is later than the Laws of CD, or that the two stem from different groups; the character of 4QMMT is evident both from the polemic formulae that are used and from the explicit statement in the epilogue that the group which lies behind it had separated from the majority of the people.[30] The Admonition and the Community Rule are also both later than the Laws, but more will be said about this below.

General considerations of this kind need to be substantiated by detailed comparison of specific passages where the same topic is treated in the Laws and in one of these other writings. Schiffman has recently devoted just such a study to the treatment of the law of vows and oaths (Num.30:3–16) in the Zadokite Fragments—to use his preferred title for the Damascus Document—and in the Temple Scroll.[31] He notes that the Zadokite Fragments reflect a higher degree of sophistication and of legal development than the Temple Scroll, and suggests that this could be explained either on the basis that the two works stem from related but separate groups or in terms of chronological development. It is the latter view which he prefers, and this seems to me right. Where I would disagree with Schiffman is in his view that sources such as 4QMMT and the Temple Scroll are appropriately to be described as Sadducean, and—in part—in his view that the Zadokite Fragments date from after the formation of the sect and "after the coming of the teacher."[32] Thus, whereas the Admonition knows of the Teacher, there is nothing in the Laws that presupposes his coming. So far as the actual date of the corpus is concerned, the use of the book of Jubilees, which can be dated to about 170 B.C.E., points to a period after this, perhaps around the middle of the second century B.C.E.; but since the material seems to be composite, individual sec-

---

[28] Cf. STEGEMANN, H. 1990. *Revue de Qumran* 14: 430.

[29] VANDERKAM, J. C. 1989. "The Temple Scroll and the Book of Jubilees." In *Temple Scroll Studies.* G. J. BROOKE, Ed.:211–236. Sheffield Academic Press. Sheffield, England. *Cf.* DAVIES, P. R. 1989. The Temple Scroll and the Damascus Document. *In* Temple Scroll Studies, pp. 201–210.

[30] QIMRON, E. & J. STRUGNELL. 1985. "An unpublished halakhic letter from Qumran." In *Biblical Archaeology Today.* J. AMITAI, Ed.:402. Israel Exploration Society. Jerusalem, Israel.

[31] SCHIFFMAN, L. H. 1991. "The Law of Vows and Oaths (Num. 30,3–16) in the Zadokite Fragments and the Temple Scroll." *Revue de Qumran* 15: 199–214.

[32] SCHIFFMAN, L. H. 1991. p. 213.

tions could be older—and some may be younger. In any case this material will have represented the law code of the "root of planting" which is said in column I of the Genizah text of the Admonition to have groped for the way like blind men for twenty years until the appearance of the teacher of righteousness.

≈ III ≈

The fragments of the Damascus Document from Cave 4 have altered our perception of the Admonition to a much smaller extent than they have our perception of the Laws. It is true that what appears as the introduction in the CD text was preceded by "a teacher's first person call to the Sons of Light to separate from transgressors,"[33] but apart from this the Admonition in the 4Q fragments was substantially as it was known to us from the Genizah manuscripts.

The Admonition in its final form refers explicitly to the teacher of righteousness (מורה צדק) in two places (CD I,11; XX,32); it also twice refers to a figure called "the unique teacher" (מורה היחיד (XX,1), יורה היחיד (XX,14)) or—reading היחד for היחיד—"the teacher of the community," and this figure is commonly identified with the teacher of righteousness. In addition, it has often been maintained—and also denied—that the teacher is referred to in VI,7 as "the interpreter of the law" (דורש התורה). As it now stands, therefore, the Admonition serves as an introduction to the Laws from the viewpoint of the community associated with the teacher, and it is likely that the Laws are referred to in the final section of the Admonition (XX,27b–34) as "these rules" (XX,27b) and as "the first rules" (XX,31). It has, however, been argued in two recent literary-critical studies, by Murphy-O'Connor and by Davies, that the references to the teacher belong to a secondary stage in the composition of the Admonition, and the question at issue is whether the teacher is integral to the Admonition, or whether the Admonition in its present form represents a revision of a source or sources that were in origin pre-teacher and pre-Qumranic. Linked to this question are those of the meaning of "Damascus" and the relationship of the Admonition (and of the Damascus Document as a whole) to the Community Rule.

Literary seams are apparent throughout the Admonition, and it is probable that it has been built up from a number of smaller units, some of which may be older—or represent older exegetical traditions—than the Admonition itself. But this does not mean that it does not form essentially a unity, as both Dimant[34] and Van der Woude[35] have recently maintained, and it seems to

---

[33] Cf. BAUMGARTEN, J. 1992a. p. 53.
[34] DIMANT, D. 1984. "Qumran sectarian literature," pp. 495–497.
[35] VAN DER WOUDE, A. 1992. Theologische Rundschau 57: 52–55.

me doubtful whether it is possible to isolate a pre-teacher version of the Damascus Document. The issue really stands or falls on the identification of the interpreter of the law in CD VI,7, and the relationship of the passage in which he is mentioned (V,20–VI,11a) to the "historical" introduction to the Damascus Document (I,1–II,1).

It is appropriate to begin consideration of the references in the Admonition to the teacher of righteousness at the end. The final section of the Admonition (XX,27b–34), which was clearly written to form a conclusion, provides an assurance of salvation to faithful members of the community, who are described, amongst other things, as those "who obey the teacher of righteousness" (XX,32), and as those "who obey the teacher" (XX,28)—although in the second case it is not certain whether the reference is to the teacher of righteousness or to God. This final section of the Admonition has been attributed by Murphy-O'Connor to the compiler of the work and is regarded by him as later than the main sources he has identified.[36] In contrast, Davies argues that the nucleus of this section did form the original conclusion of the pre-Qumranic Admonition and was intended to form a transition to the Laws, but that it was subsequently reworked by the addition of a small number of phrases which reflect the ideology of the Qumran community; the references to the teacher in XX,28 and to the teacher of righteousness in XX, 32 form part of this reworking.[37]

It seems to me that Davies is right in his view that the conclusion is integral to the Admonition, however the Admonition is defined, and I see no reason for regarding it as later than the main body of the work. The question whether the references to the teacher are secondary is quite another matter. It cannot be answered on the basis of this passage, but depends on what view is taken of the reference to the teacher in column I. If that is original, there is no reason to regard the references here as secondary.

The conclusion to the Admonition is the place where the Damascus Document intersects with the Community Rule. There are similarities between the confession in CD XX,28b–30a and that in 1QS I,24b–II,1a. But more important than this, the linguistic similarities between CD XX,31b–32a ("who have been instructed in the first rules by which the men of the community were governed") and 1QS IX,10b ("but they shall be governed by the first rules in which the men of the community began to be instructed") are such as to suggest literary interdependence. The statement in the Community Rule belongs in a section which seems clearly to represent the oldest layer in the Rule, namely columns VIII–IX, the Program for a New Community. This, if anything, has been regarded by most scholars as representing the teaching of the

---

36 MURPHY-O'CONNOR, J. 1972. "A Literary Analysis of Damascus Document XIX,33–XX,34." *Revue Biblique* 79: 556–562.
37 DAVIES, P. R. 1983. *The Damascus Covenant*, pp. 194–197.

teacher of righteousness and has been associated with the withdrawal of the teacher group to Qumran. It is a reasonable assumption that the same group was responsible both for this material and for the conclusion of the Admonition, certainly as it now exists. But this is a point to which we shall need to return.

The two references to the teacher of the community (XX,1, 14) both occur in the context of a section of the Admonition (XIX,33b–XX,22a) which does indeed seem to be secondary in comparison with the main body of the work, and they may for that reason be dealt with fairly briefly here. (Murphy-O'Connor regards the *Grundschrift* of this section as one of the four documents used by the compiler of the Admonition,[38] while Davies holds that XIX,33b–XX,34 – apart from the nucleus of XX,22b–34 – is a Qumranic addition to the original work.[39]) This material stems in fact from the critical period immediately after the death of the teacher, when the community faced the threat to its existence posed by real and potential apostasy. It belongs with a number of other passages (I,13–18a; IV,19c–20a; VIII,12c–13) in which opposition to the community is seen to be focused in a particular individual, called "the scoffer" or "the liar," and his supporters, and it probably dates from a slightly later period than the rest of the Admonition.

Links with 1QS VIII–IX can also be observed in this section of the Admonition, notably in the use of the expression "the men of perfect holiness" (אנשי תמים הקדש, XX,2, 5, 7) and of the expression היחד (XX,1, 14, *cf.* 32 – assuming it is right to emend היחיד to היחד) to refer to the community. (This happens also to be the only section of the Admonition where עדה is used to refer to the community (*cf.* XX,2, 3), other than in the title "the prince of all the congregation" (VII,20).) The expression אנשי תמים הקדש has close parallels within 1QS VIII–IX in VIII,17, 20, 23; IX,8, and תמים is used repeatedly in these columns, while היחד is characteristic both of 1QS VIII–IX and of the Community Rule as a whole. These parallels point to a continuing overlap between the community of the Admonition and the community of 1QS VIII–IX. In a recent detailed comparison of CD XIX,33b–XX,34 and 1QS VIII–IX Davies has drawn attention both to the parallels between these blocks of material, and also to certain differences, which in his view militate against the identification without further qualification of the communities behind them.[40] It is not possible to discuss these differences here, but while I accept that they need explanation, I think in view of the parallels that there is a real overlap between the community at least of the final part of the Ad-

---

[38] MURPHY-O'CONNOR, J. 1972. *Revue Biblique* 79: 544–556, 562–564.
[39] DAVIES, P. R. 1983. *The Damascus Covenant*, pp. 173–190.
[40] DAVIES, P. R. 1991. "Communities at Qumran and the case of the missing 'Teacher.'" *Revue de Qumran* 15: 275–286.

monition and the community of 1QS VIII–IX, the oldest layer within the Community Rule.

The references to the teacher of the community occur in the context of a passage which twice mentions the new covenant made in the land of Damascus (XIX,33b–34a=VIII,21; XX,12; cf. VI,19), and it seems likely that this covenant is the covenant made by the teacher group. If this is so, and if it is right to associate the teacher group at all with Qumran, then whatever Damascus means elsewhere in the Admonition, it is here used as a symbolic name for Qumran.

The last explicit reference to the teacher of righteousness occurs in the account of the origins of the group behind the Damascus Document, which forms the introduction to the Damascus Document in the Genizah text; according to this introduction the group had already been in existence for a twenty-year period when the teacher arrived in it. This reference to the teacher has, however, been regarded as secondary by both Murphy-O'Connor and Davies. Murphy-O'Connor argued that both the "historical" introduction (I,1–II,1) and the following "theological" introduction (II,2–13) were added at a secondary stage to the source which he identified within the Admonition as a "Missionary Document" (II,14–VI,1) in order to adapt this to a new purpose, namely that of stemming defection from the community.[41] In contrast, Davies maintained that both introductions were integral to the plot of the admonition, but argued instead that the presence of the teacher in CD I,11 was "a product of Qumranic recension."[42] However, whatever may be thought about the chronological references in CD I, there are no literary grounds for removing the teacher from this passage, and it is arbitrary to do so, as Boyce has shown.[43] There is more to be said for the view of Murphy-O'Connor inasmuch as the existence of multiple introductions–with the 4Q material we now have three–raises the possibility that one or other is secondary. But the presence of the historical introduction as an integral part of the Admonition seems to me to be confirmed, apart from anything else, by the parallel passage in CD VI,2–11a, which, as Van der Woude has pointed out, and as the similarities in vocabulary indicate, is to be understood as a commentary on I,7ff.[44] The interrelationship of the two passages both shows that the interpreter of the law is properly to be identified with the teacher of righteousness, and not with a figure of the past, such as Ezra,[45] and confirms that the reference to the teacher in column I is original.

[41] MURPHY-O'CONNOR, J. 1970. "An Essene missionary document? CD II,14–VI,1." Revue Biblique 77: 225–229.

[42] DAVIES, P. R. 1983. The Damascus Covenant, pp. 63–64, 200.

[43] BOYCE, J. M. 1990. "The poetry of the Damascus Document and its bearing on the origin of the Qumran sect." Revue de Qumran 14: 615–628.

[44] VAN DER WOUDE, A. 1992. Theologische Rundschau 57: 250.

[45] CALLAWAY, P. R. 1988. The History of the Qumran Community, pp. 107–111. Cf. CALLAWAY. 1990. "Qumran origins: From the Doresh to the Moreh." Revue de Qumran 14: 642.

The identification of the interpreter of the law is linked to the question of the significance of "Damascus," and in conclusion I would like to comment briefly on this. The Damascus terminology is confined to the Admonition and represents a particular exegetical tradition preserved by the group behind this work. The tradition is based on the interpretation given to Damascus in the Amos-Numbers midrash (VII,14b–21a); this seems to underlie all the references to Damascus in the Admonition, even though the midrash itself is secondary in its context.[46] The key thing about Damascus in the midrash is not its geographical location, but that it is associated with the revelation of the meaning of Torah;[47] this understanding was no doubt influenced by Zech. 9:1, which speaks of Damascus as the resting-place of the word of the LORD, and to which many scholars have drawn attention. But the revelation of the meaning of Torah is the counterpart of its intensive study (cf. III,12–17a), and it is as a place devoted to the study of Torah that Damascus is mentioned in VI,2–11a, the Well midrash. The statement in this midrash referring to "the converts of Israel who went out from the land of Judah and sojourned in the land of Damascus" (VI,5) and the abbreviated version of this in IV,2b–3a, "the converts of Israel who went out from the land of Judah," are, as Stegemann indicated twenty years ago,[48] to be read alongside the passage in 1QS VIII–IX which speaks of going into the wilderness to prepare the way of God, a way which is defined as the study of the law (VIII, 12b–16a). The difference between the documents is that whereas 1QS VIII–IX is a program for the future, the Admonition is looking back on past events. "Damascus" was thus a name derived from scripture and had a symbolic significance; it is not to be interpreted literally, and the context for its interpretation is not so much provided by the exile,[49] as by the understanding of it as the place devoted to Torah study. In practice it seems to me that as a geographical location it is still to be understood as a symbolic name for Qumran. According to the Well midrash (VI,2–11a) the interpreter of the law (i.e., in my view the teacher of righteousness), whose supporters are responsible for the Damascus Document in its final form, is associated with Damascus. It seems clear that the teacher group did ultimately settle at Qumran, and in this case, in addition to the references to the "new covenant in the land of Damascus" (VI,19; XIX,33b–

---

[46] Cf. KNIBB, M. A. 1991. "The Interpretation of Damascus Document VII,9b–VIII,2a and XIX,5b–14." Revue de Qumran 15: 243–251.

[47] Cf. SCHIFFMAN, L. H. 1975. The Halakhah at Qumran. E. J. Brill. Leiden, the Netherlands, pp. 31–32.

[48] STEGEMANN, H. 1971. Die Entstehung der Qumrangemeinde, pp. 240–241. Dissertation, University of Bonn.

[49] Cf. MURPHY-O'CONNOR, J. 1974. Revue Biblique 81: 219–223. MURPHY-O'CONNOR. 1985. Revue Biblique 92: 224–226. DAVIES, P. R. 1983. The Damascus Covenant, pp. 122–123. DAVIES. 1990. "The birthplace of the Essenes: Where is 'Damascus'?" Revue de Qumran 14: 509–512.

34a = VIII,21; XX,12), the references to Damascus in the Well midrash (VI,5) and the Amos-Numbers midrash (VII,15, 19) are to be understood as references to Qumran.

~~~~~~

Discussion of the Paper

HARTMUT STEGEMANN (*University of Göttingen, Göttingen, Germany*): You cited me sometimes regarding the problem of the relationship between the Admonitions and the Laws. In the past I have said there is no true relationship. The Admonitions and the Laws are divergent from a critical point of view. In the meantime, I have worked extensively on the Damascus Documents with Professor Joseph Baumgarten for his future edition. The problems are still considerable. I worked particularly on the question of how to reconstruct the Cave 4 documents. One result is there is indeed at least one manuscript which bridges both parts. It is a big manuscript, formerly called 4QD[b] now 4QD[a]. This manuscript originally had 32 columns, each column of about 25 lines. When one asks how this manuscript is related to the Cairo Genizah documents: what remains from the beginning, from the Admonition, stops at the top of column 10. What remains of the Laws starts in column 23. Between columns 10 and 23, you have scattered fragments from several manuscripts. This is a problem of reconstruction, but it is clear in spite of the different hands that all the fragments belonged to one scroll. That is, one text, not two. One can measure it very exactly as the final column is there. You will find a small picture of this column in the new volume by Michael Wise and Robert Eisenman. You can see that a worm has eaten through the layers of the scroll. The same hole recurs again and again in this very nice sheet. On that basis you can measure very exactly from one turn of the scroll to the next. You will arrive at a distance of about 16 cm, and that's just what we have in the first 2–3 columns of this manuscript. That is the best evidence to show it is one book.

One could say (and it has already been stated by Joseph Baumgarten) that 1QS is used in the Damascus Covenant. 1QS is an older book. It is used at least for the final part, for Punishments. Other parts of the Laws are older than 1QS, and also older than the Qumran community of the Essenes or whatever we call it. They come from earlier times. On this point I haven't changed my mind; it is not the whole book which is older, only some parts of it.

MICHAEL A. KNIBB (*Kings College London, London, England*): Thank you very much for that comment. It did seem to me that 4QD[a], and to some extent 4QD[b] must show that they belong to a common document. I think it still leaves open the critical question of the age of the material and its evolution. I have seen that article on the penal code by Professor Baumgarten, which only just came out. At the end he does say, as I read him, that he thinks that 1QS is younger than the Laws in some of these punishments.

STEGEMANN: *Serek ha-Yaḥad* is older.

KNIBB: Well, he doesn't say that explicitly in that article. In the final paragraph discussing the relationship he seemed to me to say the opposite.

SAMUEL IWRY (*Johns Hopkins University, Baltimore, MD*): You tried to say how difficult the whole situation with the Damascus Document is; we have to take it more seriously than you and I and others think. This is the cardinal document. Solving the questions of what the Damascus Document is, what its relation to the law is, what its relation to the other scrolls is, like the Discipline Scroll and others, is very important. Don't forget that the Damascus Document was the catalyst that opened up the mystery of the scrolls. Without the Damascus Genizah copy that was by some kind of a miracle preserved, we wouldn't be able to find ourselves on our way in this whole scroll business. The latest findings of Dr. Baumgarten also show that every step is very difficult and fraught with dangers.

For 20 years, I fought (and I still fight) and I said it clearly: Ginzberg, Segal, and Rabin and, finally, all others have been mistaken in their understanding of the Hebrew *shabe yisrael ha-yotsim*. The question of its meaning is crucial for the whole text. I think the connection between the Admonition and the Law section is correct. I don't know yet whether the longer piece of Dr. Baumgarten does or doesn't belong to the Damascus Document. It has to do with the priests who knew how to deal with sicknesses of the skin. And they elaborated greatly. Its inclusion, or the opposite, does nothing to affect the Damascus document.

Another mistake was to collate the A and B versions. Actually, one is earlier, the other later. They must be treated separately.

PHILLIP CALLAWAY (*Jonesboro, Georgia*): I think it is appropriate that I speak after Professor Iwry. This is a conference on methods, and for three-fourths of your paper I thought you and I were moving in the same direction. Suddenly, you discovered more historical information than I've ever discovered.

I would like to ask two very simple questions concerning exegesis, which I think is a preliminary stage in writing history. Number one, why are you permitted to take the reference to Damascus as symbolic when you don't do that to Judah? Number two, how do you relate the *Doresh ha-torah* to the *Yoreh ha-tsedek* in the last days? I don't think you answered these questions in your paper.

KNIBB: Thank you for those questions. I agree with you that not much history is to be derived from these documents. I'd also agree that this is a very enigmatic work which defies interpretation in places.

On your second question, I have actually discussed it elsewhere. That's why I didn't talk about it here. I do think that you can make a distinction between the Teacher in the past and the one who is prophesied to come in 6:11. One just has to agree to disagree on this. I think it is proper to make a distinction between the two. There is no doubt that the figure in column one is a figure of the past, and that the one in column six is a figure of the future and can be linked up with other messianic figures in the scrolls.

On your first point, why am I permitted to treat Damascus as a symbolic term but not Judah, I could put the question the other way around. Why have people in the past thought that Judah can be interpreted literally but not Damascus? As for Damascus, I think it may well have been interpreted in different ways at different times. I'm not sure that we have the evidence to speak with certainty about the earlier stages. One can only talk about the way it is in the document now. As it is used now, it is a place devoted to Torah study and the revelation of the meaning of Torah. A great deal is made of Damascus, but I think it has to be borne in mind: the term is only used seven times, four of which concern the new covenant in the land of Damascus. And, those usages reflect a later stage of interpretation. Three of them come in column 20; I think there are good reasons for dating column 20 later. One of them comes in the summary passage on the Laws, where it may or may not be secondary. But, four of them are really concerned with the new covenant in the land of Damascus.

There have been endless arguments about the relationship of manuscript A to manuscript B and how the text has evolved. I would argue that that midrash is secondary. So I'm quite willing to admit that it may have had different meanings in the earlier stages. But I think now Damascus is used as the place of Torah study. Probably what's ultimately understood is Qumran, however it may have been understood previously.

The Aramaic "Son of God" Text from Qumran Cave 4

JOSEPH A. FITZMYER, S.J.*

The Catholic University of America
Washington, D.C. 20064

The Aramaic text, which was discovered in Qumran Cave 4 in 1952 and employs the titles "Son of God" and "Son of the Most High," figures in the account of a recent notorious book by Baigent and Leigh, *The Dead Sea Scrolls Deception*.[1] They base their account of it on a brief article, which Hershel Shanks, the editor of the *Biblical Archaeology Review*, wrote, having heard me lecture on the Dead Sea Scrolls at the Johns Hopkins University in 1989. Shanks quoted some of the lines of the text,[2] which I had published sixteen years before,[3] after Milik had publicly lectured on it at Harvard University in 1972 and it was judged to be in the public domain. According to Baigent and Leigh, some "unnamed scholar, whose conscience was troubling him," had leaked the text to *Biblical Archaeology Review* only in 1990! Worse still, they think that this is the document to which John M. Allegro alluded in one of his letters to Roland de Vaux, written in September 1956. There Allegro spoke of the Essene belief in their Davidic Messiah as a "'son of God', 'begotten' of God. . . ."[4] Baigent and Leigh were ignorant, of course, of a passage in the Hebrew Appendix A of the Manual of Discipline of Qumran Cave 1, which, according to Allegro and some other scholars, speaks of God's "begetting the Messiah." From it Allegro had concluded that there was an Essene belief in a Davidic Messiah as Son of God. This Cave 1 text had been published only

* Address for correspondence: Jesuit Community, Georgetown University, 37th & O Streets, NW, Washington, DC 20057.

[1] BAIGENT, M. & R. LEIGH. 1991. *The Dead Sea Scrolls Deception*. Jonathan Cape. London. Summit Books. New York: 66.

[2] ANONYMOUS. 1990. "An Unpublished Dead Sea Scroll Text Parallels Luke's Infancy Narrative." *Biblical Archaeology Review* 16(2): 24.

[3] FITZMYER, J. A. 1974. "The Contribution of Qumran Aramaic to the Study of the New Testament." *New Testament Studies* 20(4): 382–407, esp. 391–94.–Reprinted in a slightly revised form in *A Wandering Aramean: Collected Aramaic Essays*. Society of Biblical Literature Monograph Series 25 (1979). Scholars Press. Missoula, MT: 85–113, esp. 92–93.

[4] *The Dead Sea Scrolls Deception:* 56.

shortly before in 1955,[5] and Allegro was really referring to it. Moreover, Baigent and Leigh were also ignorant of the fact that this Aramaic "Son of God" text from Qumran Cave 4 had not yet even been acquired by the Palestine Archaeological Museum in East Jerusalem. It was, in fact, among the last eight pieces of Cave 4 material that were bought from Kando on 9 July 1958,[6] the day before I left Jerusalem to return to the U.S.A., after the first year of work on the infamous concordance of Cave 4 nonbiblical texts, now being "bootlegged" by B. Z. Wacholder and M. G. Abegg.[7] Such misinformation about this Aramaic "Son of God" text is only part of a larger pattern of errors and uninformed statements that make the Baigent and Leigh book itself *the* deception par excellence about the Dead Sea Scrolls!

The "Son of God" text was entrusted to J. T. Milik for publication, but he never published it. He made references to it in two of his other writings.[8] On the basis of my publication of seven lines of the text, a number of other studies appeared, chiefly those of D. Flusser[9] and F. García Martínez.[10] Most recently, with Milik's approval, E. Puech has at length published the text in full,[11] and J. J. Collins discussed it at the last annual meeting of the Catholic

[5] BARTHÉLEMY, D. & J. T. MILIK. 1955. *Qumran Cave I*. Discoveries in the Judaean Desert 1. Clarendon Press. Oxford: 110, 117 (1QSa [1Q28a] 2:11–12). It reads *'m ywlyd ['l] '[t] hmšyh 'tm*, a highly contested reading, which Barthélemy originally translated as "au cas où *Dieu mènerait le Messie avec eux*," because he preferred to interpret *ywlyd* as *ywlyk*, believing with Milik that *ywlyd*, "la lecture . . . pratiquement certaine," was actually "une faute de lecture du scribe." ALLEGRO himself, in his first publication of part of 4QFlorilegium (1956. *Journal of Biblical Literature*: 174–187, esp. 177) refers to this text and says that the "implication of 'sonship' of the Messiah has obvious NT parallels, and has, perhaps, to be connected with the *ywlyd* of 1QSa." He goes so far as to admit "a special infra-red photograph taken then [Summer of 1955] leaves no doubt as to the correctness of the editor's reading" (n. 28). So Allegro certainly understood the mention of "the Messiah" in 1QSa as implying divine sonship. Why we never heard more from him in this regard, once the contents of 4Q246 became known, is a mystery. In his later book, *The Dead Sea Scrolls and the Christian Myth* (1979. Newton Abbot, Devon. Buffalo. Prometheus), he makes no mention of it, tinder though it would have been for his thesis.

[6] This date is now officially confirmed by the editor of the *editio princeps* (see n. 11 below, p. 104 n. 22).

[7] "Bootleg" is the word used for their work in *The New York Times*. 5 September 1991: A1. See WACHOLDER, B. Z. and M. G. ABEGG. 1991. *A Preliminary Edition of the Unpublished Dead Sea Scrolls: The Hebrew and Aramaic Texts from Cave Four: Fascicle One*. Biblical Archaeology Society. Washington.–1992. *Fascicle Two*.

[8] MILIK, J. T. 1976. *The Books of Enoch: Aramaic Fragments of Qumran Cave 4*. Clarendon Press. Oxford: 60, 213, 261; and in 1992. "Les modèles araméens du livre d'Esther dans la grotte 4 de Qumran." *Revue de Qumrán* 15(3): 321–399, esp. 383–384.

[9] FLUSSER, D. 1980. "The Hubris of the Antichrist in a Fragment from Qumran." *Immanuel* 10(1): 31–37.–Reprinted in his book, 1988. *Judaism and the Origins of Christianity*. Magnes Press. Jerusalem: 207–213.

[10] GARCÍA MARTÍNEZ, F. 1983. 4Q 246: ¿Tipo del Anticristo o Libertador escatológico? in *El misterio de la Palabra: Homenaje a L. Alonso Schökel*. V. COLLADO & E. ZURRO, Eds. Ediciones Cristiandad. Madrid: 229–244. In English (1992), "The Eschatological Figure of 4Q246." *Qumran and Apocalyptic: Studies on the Aramaic Texts from Qumran*. Studies on the Texts from the Desert of Judah 9. Brill, Leiden: 162–179.

[11] PUECH, E. 1992. "Fragment d'une apocalypse en araméen (4Q246 = pseudo-Dan^d) et le 'royaume de Dieu'." *Revue Biblique* 99(1): 98–131.

Biblical Association of America, in Washington in mid-August 1992.[12] Now we can discuss it further, since more has still to be said about it. The text appears on page 166.

COMMENTARY

Milik had dated the text to the last third of the first century B.C., and Puech agrees: between 4QSam[a] and 1QIsa[b] or 1QM—hence *ca.* 25 B.C. There is no reason to contest this palaeographic dating of the copy, and it thus gives us precious firsthand information about pre-Christian Palestinian Jewish beliefs. The importance of this text for the tenets and theology of the Qumran community cannot be underestimated. Its language reveals it to be apocalyptic: it speaks of distress that will come upon the land, of the disastrous reign of enemies, which is to be, however, short-lived; it will only last "until there arises the people of God, and everyone rests from the sword." But it also promises the appearance of some figure called "Son of God" and "Son of the Most High," who will rule in peace and with everlasting prosperity. The apocalyptic stageprops are clear. There is little difficulty in reading and interpreting col. 2; the problem is the reconstruction of the beginnings of the nine lines of col. 1. I have given above my attempt to reconstruct them. The justification of the reconstructed text and notes on both columns has been published in *Biblica* 74 (1993) 153–174. Here I shall concentrate on the major thrust of the document.

The broken text begins with a fragmentary narrative sentence: When something happened, someone, possibly a seer, fell before the throne. This prostrate person addresses an enthroned king, using the second singular independent personal pronoun and pronominal suffix (-*k*). The enthroned king is described as shaken by the evils that he has seen in a vision or been made to realize are coming in his time, evils that are described in the fragmentary lines 4–6 of col. 1. Among such evils is the "king of Assyria" and "Egypt." That description may continue on to line 7, "[   ] will be great upon the earth." That line, however, may just as easily announce a change that is being promised to the enthroned king: "he/it will be great," will be served by all, will be given lofty titles, and will be guaranteed divine favor. In col. 2, which is completely preserved, the first part of line 1 continues this promise, and mentions the titles that will characterize the figure who is expected. The end of line 1 and line 2 tell of the short-lived duration of the enemy's reign (with plural suffixes and plural verbs, which clearly refer to some persons or people

---

[12] COLLINS. J. J. 1992. "The 'Son of God' Text from Qumran" in *From Jesus to John: Essays on Jesus and Christology in Honour of Marinus de Jonge.* M. DE BOER, Ed. JSOT Press, Sheffield. Forthcoming.

Col. 1

1 [וכדי דחלה רבה ע]לוהי שרת נפל קדם כרסיא

2 [אדין אמר למלכא חיי מ]לכא לעלמא אתה רגז ושניך

3 [זיו אנפיך ועלי]בא חזוך וכלא אתה עד עלמא

4 [תמלך ויהוון עבדיך ר]ברבין עקה תתא על ארעא

5 [ולהוה קרב בעממיא]ונחשירין רב במדינתא

6 [די יעבדון גדודי]מלך אתור   ומצרין

7 [להוה עמהון ברם אף ברך]רב להוה על ארעא

8 [וכל עממיא שלם עמה י]עבדון וכלא ישמשון

9 [לה והוא בר אל ר]בא יתקרא ובשמה יתכ נה

Col. 2

1 ברה די אל יתאמר ובר עליון יקרונה כזיקיא

2 די חזותא כן מלכותהן תהוה שנין] ימלכון על

3 ארעא וכלא ידשון עם לעם ומדינה למד[ינ]ה

4 (vacat) עד יקום עם אל וכלא ינוח מן חרב

5 מלכותה מלכות עלם וכל ארחתה בקשוט ידי[ן]

6 ארעא בקשט וכלא יעבד שלם חרב מן ארעא יסף

7 וכל מדינתא לה יסגדון אל רבא באילה

8 הוא ועבד לה קרב עממין ינתן בידה וכלהן

9 ירמה קדמוהי שלטנה שלטן עלם וכל תהומי

Col. 1

1 [when great fear] settled [u]pon him, he fell down before the throne.

2 [Then he said to the king, "Live,] O King, forever! You are vexed, and changed

3 [is the complexion of your face; de]pressed is your gaze. (But) [you shall rule over] everything forever!

4 [And your deeds will be g]reat. (Yet) distress shall come upon the earth;

5 [there will be war among the peoples] and great carnage in the provinces

6 [which the bands of] the king of Assyria [will cause]. [And E]gypt

7 [will be with them. But your son] shall also be great upon the earth

8 [and all peoples sh]all make [peace with him], and they shall all serve

9 [him, (for)] he shall be called [son of] the [gr]eat [God], and by his name shall he be named.

Col. 2

1 He shall be hailed (as) son of God, and they shall call him son of the Most High. Like comets

2 that one sees, so shall their rule be. For (some) years they shall rule upon

3 the earth and shall trample everything (under foot); people shall trample upon people, province upon [pro]vince,

4 (*vacat*) until there arises the people of God, and everyone rests from the sword.

5 (Then) his kingdom (shall be) an everlasting kingdom, and all his ways (shall be) in truth. He shall jud[ge]

6 the land with truth, and everyone shall make peace. The sword will cease from the land,

7 and all the provinces shall pay him homage. The great God is himself his might;

8 He shall make war for him. Peoples He shall put in his power, and all of them

9 He shall cast before him. His dominion (shall be) an everlasting dominion, and none of the abysses of [the earth shall prevail against it]!

other than the one who bears the titles, Son of God and Son of the Most High. Their reign will last only "until there arises the people of God" (line 4). Its rule, or possibly his rule, is then extolled: respite from war, an everlasting kingship, and paths of truth and peace with all provinces in submission. For the Great God will be with him (or it), and He will subject all enemies to him (or it).

The difficulty of interpreting the text is sixfold. (i) Who is the speaker and whom does he address? (ii) Are the references to the "king of Assyria" and to "Egypt" and the plurals being used allusions to historical figures, or are they references similar to "the Kittim of Assyria" and "the Kittim in Egypt" in the apocalyptic War Scroll (1QM 1:2, 4)? (iii) If they are to be taken in an apocalyptic sense rather than in a historical sense, can one say to whom they refer? (iv) Who is X, the person to whom the titles are applied? (v) Is X to be understood in a positive or a negative sense, as an enemy who arrogates to himself such titles or someone favored by God? (vi) To whom does the third singular masculine in 2:5–9 refer? Is it the "people of God" (2:4) or X, the expected figure of 1:9?

There are also six different interpretations that have been given to the text.

1) Milik was originally of the opinion that God, seated upon a divine throne, was being addressed, but now thinks that the text refers to a historical king of Syria (מלך אתוד, 1:6), whose reign would be disastrous, and whose supreme blasphemy was that he would proclaim himself Son of God and would be called Son of the Most High by his followers.[13] This would then refer to the last Seleucid king, whose reign would be followed, according to this text, by an eschatological rule of the people of God. Because Alexander Balas (150–145 B.C.), the pretended son of Antiochus IV Epiphanes, who became king of Syria on the defeat and death of Demetrios I Soter, used the Greek title Θεοπάτωρ on coins of his realm,[14] the titles "Son of God" and "Son of the Most High" in this Qumran text would refer to him.

This interpretation is problematic, first, because one may wonder whether such a Palestinian text of clearly Jewish provenience would tolerate such laudatory appellation of a pagan king with the titles "Son of God" and "Son of the Most High." Second, would a Jewish writer refer to the king of Syria

---

[13] "On y décrit le règne désastreux d'un roi de Syrie (MLK 'TWR, 1 I 6), dont le blasphème suprême semble être le fait qu''il se proclamera Fils de Dieu et (qu')on appellera Fils du Très Haut', BRH DY 'L YT'MR WBR 'LYWN YQRWNH, 1 II 1" ("Modèles araméens" [n. 8 above], 383).

[14] E.g., βασιλέως Ἀλεξάνδρου θεοπάτορος εὐεργέτου. See IMHOOF-BLUMER, F. 1883. Monnaies grecques. Koninklijke Nederlandse Akademie van Wetenschappen, Afdeeling Letterkunde, Verhandelingen 14. J. Muller. Amsterdam: 433–434 (§102, pl. H 13).–Also 1890. Catalogue des monnaies grecques de la Bibliothèque Nationale: Les rois de Syrie, d'Arménie et de Commagène. E. BABELON, Ed. C. Rollin et Feuardent. Paris: cxxx et fig. 29, 101–119 and pl. XVII §8,10.–KÜTHMANN, C. 1954. Münzen als Denkmale seleukidischer Geschichte des II. Jahrhunderts vor Chr. für die Regierungen von Demetrius I. bis Tryphon. Blätter für Münzfreunde und Münzforschung 78: 51–55.

as *mĕlek 'attûr*, "King of Assyria"? Third, how would one then account for the mention of "Egypt" in this interpretation? Fourth, no matter who the speaker is, he is addressing a human king who needs reassurance about the continuation of his rule, about someone who will succeed him and who is related to "the people of God." Whether that person is his son, as I once understood the text and still prefer to, or some other human successor may be debated. In any case, this seems to be the message that the prostrate seer is trying to give the enthroned king, as he also tells of the disaster that is to come upon the land before that reign of peace is established. Fifth, as F. García Martínez has pointed out, it was Alexander Balas through whom Jonathan became the high priest.[15] Would he then be regarded as an enemy of Israel, arrogating to himself such titles, as Milik's interpretation would presuppose? Hardly.

2) The text has been subjected to a different interpretation by D. Flusser, who regards it as apocalyptic.[16] He maintains that the *vacat*, with which 2:4 begins, starts a new topic about the rise of the people of God. Accordingly, what precedes the *vacat* would describe "the king or the leader of this horrible kingdom" who will bring all the distress; it also tells of those who worship and serve him and the way they regard him. For Flusser the text refers not to a historical figure, but to an Antichrist, an idea which "is surely Jewish and pre-Christian," *i.e.*, a "human exponent of the Satanic forces of evil." He compares 2 Thess 1:1–12 with its description of "the man of lawlessness," and three other texts: a) *Ascension of Isaiah* 4:2–16, which tells of an incarnation of Beliar, "a lawless king and a matricide," in whom all the people of the world will believe: "they will sacrifice to him and serve him";[17] b) *Oracle of Hystaspes*, preserved in Lactantius, *Divinae Institutiones*,[18] which describes a king who will arise from Syria, "a destroyer of the human race . . . a prophet of lies" who "will constitute and call himself God and will order himself to be worshipped as the Son of God"; and c) *Assumption of Moses* 8, which tells of a "man who rules with great power," who will persecute the Jewish people.[19] Hence in this Qumran text too one would read of the same sort of "*hubris* of the Antichrist."

Although the parallels are striking, much of Flusser's interpretation depends on his highly questionable understanding of the Aramaic verb *y'bdwn*

[15] See JOSEPHUS, *Antiquities* 13.2.2 §45. *Cf.* GARCÍA MARTÍNEZ, F. 1983. 4Q 246: ¿Tipo del Anticristo o Libertador escatológico? (see n. 10 above): 229–244, esp. 235. Or 1992. "The Eschatological Figure of 4Q246." In *Qumran and Apocalyptic: Studies on the Aramaic Texts from Qumran*: 162–179, esp. 169.

[16] See n. 9 above. *Cf.* FLUSSER. 1982. "D. Hystaspes and John of Patmos." In *Irano-Judaica: Studies Relating to Jewish Contacts with Persian Culture throughout the Ages.* S. SHAKED, Ed. Ben-Zvi Institute, Jerusalem: 12–75; repr. in *Judaism and the Origins of Christianity* (see n. 9 above): 390–453.

[17] SPARKS, H. F. D., Ed. 1984. *The Apocryphal Old Testament*. Clarendon Press. Oxford: 791.

[18] 7.17.2–4; Corpus scriptorum ecclesiasticorum latinorum **19**: 638–639.

[19] See H. F. D. SPARKS, *Apocryphal Old Testament* (n. 17 above): 611–612.

(1:8) as a Hebraism, "they will worship." Further, even though he insists that the idea of an Antichrist is Jewish and pre-Christian, the evidence that he uses is from Christian texts, as F. García Martínez has also noted. That Qumran texts envision some eschatological opponent of Melchizedek or even of a Messiah can be admitted, but that does not make the figure an Antichrist.[20] Nor is it obvious that all that precedes the *vacat* is to be understood in a negative sense, since we may be encountering here the kind of repetitious treatment of a topic that is characteristic of apocalyptic writing.

3) Still another interpretation of the text has been given by F. García Martínez,[21] who also understands the text as apocalyptic, but thinks that the mysterious personage is an eschatological savior of angelic or heavenly character, someone "designated in other texts [11QMelchizedek; 4QVisAmram, 4Q175] as Michael, Melchizedek, Prince of Light (*1QM* XIII 10) and proclaimed in this text as 'Son of God' and 'Son of the Most High,'" whose intervention ushers in the end-time. He finds an intelligible context for this text in what is said in 1QM 17:5–8, where Michael is promised to come in the end-time to bring low the Prince of the dominion of wickedness.

That there are such heavenly figures in the Qumran texts is clear and that they form part of the Qumran community's eschatological teaching is also evident, but that they supply the key to the interpretation of this text and to the identification of the mysterious figure who is to be called "Son of God" and "Son of the Most High" is the problem. For such titles are never used of those heavenly figures. And, as Collins has noted,[22] this text depicts God as "the might" or source of strength of the mysterious figure. Would that be said of a heavenly figure? The thrust of the text, however, is such that one would expect these titles to be ascribed to a human being. García Martínez has called my attribution of the titles to a successor or son of the king gratuitous; but that can be said with much more reason of the heavenly eschatological savior that he has proposed.

4) M. Hengel has suggested that the titles may be interpreted collectively "of the Jewish people, like the Son of Man in Dan. 7.13."[23] This suggestion

[20] HINNELLS, J. R. 1973. "The Zoroastrian Doctrine of Salvation in the Roman World: A Study of the Oracle of Hystaspes." In *Man and His Salvation: Studies in Memory of S. G. F. Brandon*. E. J. SHARPE & J. R. HINNELLS, Eds. Rowman and Littlefield. Totowa, NJ: 125–148. Collins notes that Hinnells defends the Persian origin of the *Oracle* and does not include this passage of Lactantius among the fragments. *Cf.* also JENKS, G. C. 1991. *Origin and Early Development of the Antichrist Myth*. Beihefte zur Zeitschrift für die neutestamentliche Wissenschaft **59**. De Gruyter. Berlin: 30–32, 41–43, who notes that among the earliest patristic writers who discuss the Antichrist myth Hippolytus of Rome traces it to Daniel, especially chaps. 10–12, without, of course, using the term. But otherwise all the witnesses to the myth that Jenks discusses are Christian.

[21] See n. 10 above.

[22] "The 'Son of God' Text" (n. 12 above).

[23] HENGEL, M. 1976. *The Son of God: The Origin of Christology and the History of Jewish-Hellenistic Religion*. Fortress Press. Philadelphia, PA: 45.

exploits the unclarity of the third person singular reference in some of the sentences of col. 2. Though not impossible, it is unlikely, given the parallels to those sentences in other writings that point rather to an individual person.

5) In the *editio princeps*, E. Puech has questioned some of these interpretations and has proposed a forthright messianic interpretation of this Aramaic document.[24] For him the text is apocalyptic and titles are to be ascribed to an expected "Messiah." In this he follows H.-W. Kuhn,[25] and is supported by J. J. Collins[26] and by S. Kim.[27] This sort of interpretation was also mentioned by authors who had not even seen the text.

I find this messianic interpretation, however, questionable. That there was, indeed, a lively messianic expectation in the Qumran community is beyond doubt; that it was dyarchic or bipolar, expecting both a Davidic and a priestly messiah, is also accurate.[28] But such an interpretation of this text encounters several problems.

a) The word "messiah" does not occur in this text, and to import it is gratuitous.

b) It is far from clear that the titles "Son of God" and "Son of the Most High" are without further ado to be understood as "messianic." These titles have a distinct Old Testament background.[29] Although the king on the

---

[24] He does, however, toy with the interpretation of the text in a negative sense, that the mysterious person could be a Seleucid ruler, either Alexander Balas, as Milik interprets it, or even Antiochus IV Epiphanes (Fragment [n. 11 above], 127–130). Obviously, Puech, who was allowed by Milik to publish this text in full, does not want to reject outright Milik's interpretation. Yet his otherwise wide-ranging discussion of the document in a messianic sense reveals where his preference lies.

[25] KUHN, H.-W. 1984. "Röm 1,3f und der davidische Messias als Gottessohn in den Qumrantexten." In *Lesezeichen für Annelies Findeiss zum 65. Geburtstag* . . . C. BURCHARD & G. THEISSEN, Eds. Heidelberg: 103–113.

[26] COLLINS, J. J. 1992. "The 'Son of God' Text from Qumran." (n. 12 above). He considers the use of "Son of God" as an "early interpretation of the 'one like a son of man' in Daniel 7, who also stands in parallelism to the people," without, however, being "simply an exposition of Daniel 7."

[27] KIM, S. 1983. *"The 'Son of Man'" as the Son of God.* Wissenschaftliche Untersuchungen zum Neuen Testament 30. Mohr (Siebeck). Tübingen: 20–22, esp. n. 33.

[28] See 1QS 9:11. For secondary literature on Qumran messianism, see FITZMYER, J. A. 1990. *The Dead Sea Scrolls: Major Publications and Tools for Study: Revised Edition.* Society of Biblical Literature Resources for Biblical Studies 20. Scholars Press. Atlanta, GA: 164–167.

[29] For the long history of these titles in the ancient Near East, see HENGEL, M. 1976. *The Son of God* (n. 23 above): 21–23. – FITZMYER, J. A. 1989. *Paul and His Theology: A Brief Sketch.* Prentice Hall. Englewood Cliffs, NJ: § PT49–50; also 1979. *A Wandering Aramean* (n. 3 above): 104–107. – WETTER, G. P. 1916. *Der Sohn Gottes.* Forschungen zur Religion und Literatur des Alten und Neuen Testaments 26. Vandenhoeck & Ruprecht. Göttingen. – DE BOER, P. A. H. 1973. "The Son of God in the Old Testament." In *Syntax and Meaning: Studies in Hebrew Syntax and Biblical Exegesis.* Oudtestamentische Studiën 18. A. S. VAN DER WOUDE, Ed. Brill, Leiden: 188–207. De Boer significantly finds the title used of a) heavenly beings; b) the king; c) the people of Israel; and implied in d) theophoric names. The singular is used only of the king, but in not one instance does de Boer speak of a messiah, though he mentions Cyrus as "the anointed of Yhwh." – E. LOHSE (1972). Huios, in *Theological Dictionary of the New Testament.* G. FRIEDRICH, Ed. Grand Rapids. Eerdmans, vol. 8: 361: "Thus far there is no clear instance to support the

Davidic throne is often said to be God's son (*e.g.*, 2 Sam 7:14; Ps 2:7–8), the titles are never used there of the king as a "messianic" figure.[30] In Christian writings of the New Testament they are so used of him who is the Messiah, but that is an entirely different matter. *Per se*, the titles do not connote "messiah" in the Old Testament. Only a naive interpretation, stemming more from a traditional understanding than from critical thinking, espouses that connotation.

c) Puech's messianic interpretation of this Aramaic text depends on how he has read certain Old Testament passages as speaking of "un messie roi du judaïsme."[31] But by what right does one call 2 Sam 7:12–16 and 23:5, Gen 49:10–12, Psalms 2, 89, and 110, Isaiah 9–11, Zech 3:8; 6:12 "messianic" within pre-Christian Jewish tradition?[32] The Old Testament often calls *historic* figures *māšîaḥ*. Thus, a king (generically), in 1 Sam 2:10,35; 16:6; Ps 2:2;[33] 20:7; 28:8; 84:10; Saul, in 1 Sam 12:3,5; 24:7bis,11; 26:9,11,16,23; 2 Sam 1:14,16,21(?);[34] David, in 2 Sam 19:22; 22:51; 23:1; Ps 18:51; 89:39,52; 132:10,17; Solomon, in 2 Chr 6:42; Zedekiah, in Lam 4:20; Cyrus, in Isa 45:1; possibly the patriarchs of old, in Ps 105:15; 1 Chr 16:22;[35] the high priest, in Lev 4:3,5,16; 6:15; and even the people of Israel as a whole, in Hab 3:13; Ps 28:8. There were undoubtedly other kings in Israel's history, who had been anointed and put on the Davidic throne, but they were not all accorded the title מָשִׁיחַ, much less "messiah" in the proper sense.

Some of the foregoing passages, especially 1 Sam 2:10,35; Ps 132:17, refer to the dynasty that will eventually develop as Davidic; but they have to be understood generically of a guarantee of the future Davidic household or dynasty, or of what has been called "restorative monarchism."[36] The person

---

view that in pre-Christian times Judaism used the title 'son of God' for the Messiah. The Messiah is 'my son' in Eth. En. 105:2, but this v. was added later, since it is not in Gr. En. and has thus to be disregarded."

[30] It should be needless to point out that, although Ps 2:2 uses *mĕšîḥô*, it cannot be translated there "his Messiah." The *KJV, RSV, NRSV, NAB, NJV, NEB, REB, NIV* all translate it "his anointed (One, king)," because the psalm refers to one who already sits on the Davidic throne.

[31] Fragment (n. 11 above): 98; see also p. 127.

[32] That some of these passages were understood in a messianic sense in later Judaism is clear. See LEVEY, S. H. 1974. *The Messiah: An Aramaic Interpretation: The Messianic Exegesis of the Targum*. Hebrew Union College–Jewish Institute of Religion. Cincinnati, OH. Most of the passages are conveniently listed here. But note the reviews of this book in *Biblica* 56(1975): 421–424; *Journal of Biblical Literature* 94(1975): 473–477.

[33] Puech contests my denial of a messianic understanding of Psalm 2 in pre-Christian Judaism (Fragment [n. 11 above]: 127 n. 60), appealing for proof to *Ps. Sol.* 17 and 1QSa 2:11, as if these passages showed that that psalm were indeed messianic. He also appeals to a non-critical article by TOURNAY, R. 1966. "Le Psaume (*Ps* 2): Le Roi-Messie" in *Assemblées du Seigneur* 88: 46–63. However, to see that I am not alone, *cf.* BECKER, J. 1980. *Messianic Expectation in the Old Testament*. Fortress. Philadelphia, PA: 28 n. 8, 68; COOKE, G. 1961. "The Israelite King as Son of God." *Zeitschrift für die alttestamentliche Wissenschaft* 73(1961): 202–225, esp. 205; TREVES, M. 1965. "Two Acrostic Psalms." *Vetus Testamentum* 15(1965): 81–90, esp. 85.

[34] See the *apparatus criticus* on this passage; the form may be plural.

[35] But see the commentators; this may refer to prophets.

[36] See BECKER, J. *Messianic Expectation* (n. 33 above): 54–57.

mentioned as "messiah" is not necessarily part of the continuation or restoration of the monarchy. In other words, these passages may express eschatological hopes, but *not directly eschatological messianism*. Usually they refer to persons who have been "anointed," or perhaps are anointed agents whom God *has* appointed, but they are not Messiahs (with a capital M), *i.e.*, future, expected anointed figures *to be raised up* by God for the good or the salvation of his people. Hence, in none of these instances is the adjective "messianic" truly applicable.

d) From such Old Testament passages, however, especially those with a vague or generic future reference, there developed in time the promise of a "future David," one, however, who is not yet called "messiah." Thus in Jer 30:9, "They shall serve the Lord, their God, and David, their king, whom I shall raise up for them." See also Hos 3:5; Ezek 34:23–24; 37:24–25 (in these Ezekiel passages a future David is promised who will be a "shepherd" [*rō'ēh*] or a "prince" [*nāgîd*], one who is not yet called *māšíaḥ*.)[37] Other relevant passages would be Jer 23:5–6; 22:4; 30:21; 33:14–17; Ezek 29:21; Amos 9:11. These texts clearly refer to the renewal of the Davidic dynasty.[38]

e) The first clear reference in the Old Testament to *māšíaḥ*, used in the sense of an expected, future anointed agent of Yahweh to be raised up for the good of his people is found in Dan 9:25–26, "From the utterance of a word about the rebuilding of Jerusalem until one is anointed, a leader (*māšíaḥ nāgîd*) there shall be seven weeks. . . . After sixty-two weeks (the) anointed one shall be cut off." Here one could well substitute "Messiah." Written in final form *ca.* 165 B.C., this passage provides the context for the Qumran belief in expected messianic figures.[39]

f) The Qumran messianic passages are clear. The principal one is: "until the coming of a prophet and the Messiahs of Aaron and Israel" (1QS 9: 11). See also 1QSa 2:11–12,14,20; CD 19:10–11; 20:1; 12:23–13:1; 14:19; 4QPBless 1 i 3–4; 4Q161 (4QpIsaiah[a]) 7–10 iii 15–19; 4Q174 (4QFlorilegium) 1–2 i 11; 4Q175 (4QTestimonia);[40] possibly also 1Q30 1:2; 4Q285.[41]

---

[37] I cannot agree that *nāśí'* is a "terme ézéchiélien pour le messie," as Puech maintains (Fragment [n. 11 above]: 100). It may be used of some shepherd or prince, as part of the book's monarchic expectation, but it does not denote or connote "messiah."—Nor does *šěnê běnê hayyishar* (Zech 4:14), often translated as "two anointed ones," mean "two Messiahs." See J. BECKER, *Messianic Expectation* (n. 33 above): 62–63.

[38] *Ibid.*, 58–63.

[39] In other words, "there is no evidence for true messianism until the second century B.C." (J. BECKER, *ibid.* 50). *Cf.* GRELOT, P. 1962. "Le Messie dans les Apocryphes de l'Ancien Testament" in *Le Venue du Messie: Messianisme et eschatologie*. Recherches bibliques 6. E. MASSAUX, Ed. Desclée de Brouwer. Bruges: 19–50.

[40] Of disputed interpretation; see BROWN, R. E. 1990. Dead Sea Scrolls in *The New Jerome Biblical Commentary*. Prentice Hall, Englewood Cliffs, NJ: art. 67 §91; *cf.* SKEHAN, P. W. 1957. The Period of the Biblical Texts from Khirbet Qumrân. *Catholic Biblical Quarterly* 19: 435–440.

[41] VERMES, G. 1992. "The Oxford Forum for Qumran Research: Seminar on the Rule of War from Cave 4 (4Q285)." *Journal of Jewish Studies* 43(1992): 85–90.

That some of these passages allude to 2 Sam 7:14 or Isa 11:1 no one will deny. But it remains noteworthy that none of them ever uses the title "Son of God."

g) To the foregoing Qumran passages one could possibly add the following references, which may have some relation to Qumran theology: *T. Levi* 8:13–14 (possibly an allusion to a priestly and Davidic Messiah); *T. Reuben* 6:8 ("until the fulfillment of the times of an anointed high priest");[42] *T. Simeon* 7:1–2;[43] *Ps. Sol.* 17:32 (χριστὸς κυρίου), which may not be an Essene composition.

There are, however, other passages in the *Testaments of the Twelve Patriarchs*, which speak of a coming kingdom or priesthood, but make no mention of an anointed figure or of an anointing. Hence they cannot be "messianic." Similarly, there is no reference to a Messiah in *1 Enoch* 105:2, even if it does depict the Lord saying, "I and my son will join ourselves to them forever."[44] The occurrence of a "messiah" in *4 Ezra* 7:28–29 is questionable, because it speaks of *filius meus Jesus* and *filius meus Christus*, whereas 14:9 uses only *cum filio meo*, without any mention of an anointed figure.[45] In all of this matter one should be aware of the difference of messianic expectations among various groups who depend on what we call the Old Testament: Jews, Samaritans, the Qumran community, and Christians.[46]

Hence I continue to question the importation of messianism into the interpretation of this text,[47] and continue to insist that there is as yet nothing in

---

[42] The Greek text reads, μέχρι τελειώσεως χρόνων ἀρχιερέως χριστοῦ. A footnote in M. de Jonge's translation reads: "Or 'of Christ, the high priest'." See SPARKS, H. F. D., Ed. *The Apocryphal Old Testament* (n. 17 above): 520.

[43] The Greek reads ἀναστήσει γὰρ κύριος ἐκ τοῦ Λευὶ ὡς ἀρχιερέα, καὶ ἐκ τοῦ Ἰούδα ὡς βασιλέα, θεὸν καὶ ἄνθρωπον, which may be a Christian interpolation.

[44] The chapter is not extant in Greek. KNIBB, M. 1978. *The Ethiopic Book of Enoch* [2 vols.; Clarendon Press. Oxford. 2.243) speaks of it containing a "Messianic reference." But that is not justified. *Cf. Jubilees* 31: 8–20.

[45] *Pace* J. J. COLLINS, "The 'Son of God' Text" (n. 12 above). He appeals to STONE, M. E. 1990. *Fourth Ezra.* Hermeneia. Fortress. Minneapolis, MN: 207–208. Stone compares the various versions that have rendered the verses concerned; yet even he speaks generically only of a "redeemer figure." *Cf.* VIOLET, B. 1910. *Die Esra-Apokalypse (IV. Esra): Erster Teil. Die Überlieferung.* Griechische christliche Schriftsteller 18. Leipzig. Hinrichs: 140–141.

The Syriac text of *4 Ezra* 7:28–29 does have *bĕrî mĕšîḥā'*, but that of 14:9 does not. Moreover, there is no mention of a "messiah" in chap. 13, even though vv. 32, 37, and 52 speak of *filius meus* or *bĕrî*. See ROBINSON, J. A., Ed. 1895. *Texts and Studies 3/2: Liber Esdrae Quartus* (text prepared by R. L. BENSLEY). Cambridge University Press. Cambridge: 27, 69.–BIDAWID, R. J. 1973. *4 Esdras.* The Old Testament in Syriac according to the Peshitta Version 4/3. Brill. Leiden: 16, 45.–GRY, L. 1938. *Les dires prophétiques d'Esdras (IV. Esdras).* 2 vols. Geuthner, Paris. *Cf.* S. GERO. 1975. "'My Son the Messiah': A Note on 4 Esr 7,28–29." *Zeitschrift für neutestamentliche Wissenschaft* 66: 264–267.

[46] See the wise remarks of TALMON, S. 1971. "Typen der Messiaserwartung um die Zeitwende" in *Probleme biblischer Theologie: Gerhard von Rad zum 70. Geburtstag.* H. W. WOLFF, Ed. Kaiser, Munich: 571–588.

[47] I have mentioned the non-Qumran passages in the preceding paragraph only to state where I stand in reference to them, since they have entered into the discussion of this text by both Puech and Collins. The latter admits that "we are now well aware that texts found at

the Old Testament or in the pre-Christian Palestinian Jewish tradition that we know of to show that "Son of God" had a messianic nuance.

6) Consequently, I consider this apocalyptic text to speak positively of a coming Jewish ruler, perhaps a member of the Hasmonean dynasty, who may be a successor to the Davidic throne, but who is not envisaged as a Messiah. The text should be understood as a sectarian affirmation of God's provision and guarantee of the Davidic dynasty. But just as not every king of old who sat on David's throne was given the title "messiah," even in a historical sense, so too it is not clear that the successor to the enthroned king will necessarily be an expected Messiah, even though the text grants that he will be "Son of God" and "Son of the Most High." When one uses the messianic interpretation of this text, one is importing the same kind of eisegetical "messianic" interpretation of the "Son of Man" in Dan 7:13, which was standard for many centuries, but which even Collins admits "has fallen into disfavor in recent times."[48]

However one wants to interpret the character of this apocalyptic Qumran writing, it makes it clear that such titles were "not completely alien to Palestinian Judaism."[49]

In my earlier discussion of this text I called attention to the pertinence it has for the interpretation of the Lucan infancy narrative, and especially to the Palestinian Jewish background that it provides for the words of the angel Gabriel to Mary in the annunciation scene.[50] Here I need only list the pertinent parallels:

οὗτος ἔσται μέγας (1:32);	compare 4Q246 1:7
υἱὸς ὑψίστου κληθήσεται (1:32)	compare 4Q246 2:1
κληθήσεται υἱὸς θεοῦ (1:35)	compare 4Q246 2:1
βασιλεύσει . . . εἰς τοὺς αἰῶνας (1:33)	compare 4Q246 2:5

A problem remains, however, since we cannot say whether we are faced with a perchance coincidental use by Luke of Palestinian Jewish titles known to him or whether "Luke is dependent in some way, whether directly or indirectly, on this long lost text from Qumran."[51]

In any case, the debate over this important sectarian Qumran text is far from over.

Qumran do not all necessarily pertain to one coherent system" ("The 'Son of God' Text"). But if that is so, then why try to impose a "messianic" interpretation on this text? The attempt reminds me of that of A. Schalit, who wanted to consider Herod the Great a "Messiah" and establish his Davidic descent. See SCHALIT, A. 1969. *König Herodes: Der Mann und Sein Werk*. Studia judaica 4. De Gruyter, Berlin: 450–482.—*Cf.* KELLERMANN, U. 1971. *Messias und Gesetz*. Biblische Studien 61. Neukirchener Verlag. Neukirchen-Vluyn: 55–57.

[48] "The 'Son of God' Text" (n. 12 above).
[49] HENGEL, M. The Son of God (n. 23 above): 45.
[50] The Contribution (n. 3 above): 394.—*A Wandering Aramean* (n. 3 above): 93.—*Cf.* 1981. *The Gospel according to Luke*. Anchor Bible 28. Doubleday. Garden City, NY.: 205–207, 347–348.
[51] COLLINS, J. J. "The 'Son of God' Text" (n. 12 above).

DISCUSSION OF THE PAPER

JOHN COLLINS (*Divinity School, University of Chicago*): Do I understand you to claim that a figure like the branch of David in Jeremiah, who was a future eschatalogical Davidic king, would not be anointed? And, if so, on what do you base that?

JOSEPH A. FITZMYER (*Catholic University of America, Washington, D.C.*): I would not say he would not be anointed.

COLLINS: But, you did say that you define Messiah as a future, expected anointed figure.

FITZMYER: Yes.

COLLINS: So, if you say that the branch of David in Jeremiah is not a Messiah, then why not? Or, is your point purely the insistence on whether the word 'Messiah' is used?

FITZMYER: Well, that's part of it. The tendency always is to use that word 'Messiah' as a sort of "rubber band" concept. Everything gets into it.

COLLINS: Come in the morning (laughter).

HARTMUT STEGEMANN (*University of Göttingen, Göttingen, Germany*): Professor Fitzmyer, I agree that the Messiah is not intended here, but the genre of the text is very similar to some passages in the book of Daniel, especially Daniel 11. This could be a hint that this son of God is none other than Antiochus IV Epiphanes. This is a reference to his claim to be a god. He calls himself "Son of God." What do you think of this idea?

FITZMYER: Well, I would not deny that that title is clear. That's in the background of it. But, I would hesitate to say that the text is speaking about either Antiochus IV or Alexander Jannaeus. In other words, it is over against that kind of use of the titles that I think this Jewish text is applying it to somebody else, who will take the place of the king on the throne, and who will be the leader of the people of God.

STEGEMANN: I understand, but why not the king himself?

FITZMYER: Well, if for example the unknown X were the king who was sitting on the throne, I would have no difficulty with that, because I think it's a Jewish king.

STEGEMANN: Not a Jewish king. . . .

FITZMYER: No I don't think it is Antiochus in this text. I would have difficulty with that suggestion. If the titles are to be applied to him, I cannot imagine a Jewish text applying such titles to somebody like Antiochus IV Epiphanes. That would be abomination, I think.

STEGEMANN: But, it is that close to Daniel 11.

HERSHEL SHANKS (*Biblical Archaeology Review, Washington, D.C.*): If the Messiah in one sentence is a restorative monarch coming back in a temporal setting, I understand that that's an early Hebrew Bible/Old Testament usage.

Christian messianism, "the Messiah" with a capital M, is something different. But, you concede that this text is apocalyptic. Now what is there in addition.

If an apocalyptic Messiah is not enough to be a Messiah with a capital M, what do you need in addition?

FITZMYER: I have no difficulty with an apocalyptic Messiah with a capital M.

SHANKS: If it is apocalyptic, then isn't it *per se* messianic?

FITZMYER: I don't understand why it has to be.

SHANKS: What is the additional element that is required?

FITZMYER: The additional element would be the reference specifically to such an anointed figure. I can have an apocalypse, for example, that would make no reference whatsoever to a Messiah.

SHANKS: If you have a person coming back at a future date, in the apocalyptic setting, and ruling and bringing salvation to his people, but it doesn't use the word 'Messiah', is it still messianic?

FITZMYER: That's the same kind of question that John Collins asked. I would have no difficulty with that, but my point here is I could understand an apocalyptic piece of writing even mentioning a coming Messiah, but it doesn't necessarily mean that that person is the son of God. That's the point. This text is talking about a son of God figure, the son of the Most High. It is not *ipso* talking about a Messiah. I think, given the fact that these titles come out of the Old Testament, they represent independent strains; we should respect them. When they come into use in the New Testament, they are all predicated of Him, whom Christians call the Messiah, the Christ. Now, because that's what happened in the New Testament, we tend to retroject that back into pre-Christian Judaism. That's the thing that I find questionable about so interpreting this text.

You used the phrase "restored monarchism," which is a phrase that I used. That comes from Joachim Becker's book on messianism, which is a very interesting book. I looked up H. L. Ginzberg's article on the Messiah in the *Encyclopedia Judaica*. He claims that there is no Messiah in the Old Testament, believe it or not. He uses the expression "a biblical protohistory" for the Messiah, and says that the Messiah only comes in to Jewish belief at the time of the Romans. That's a Jewish scholar writing about this kind of a problem. To a certain extent, I was very happy to see that.

JAMES H. CHARLESWORTH (*Princeton Theological Seminary, Princeton, NJ*): Joe, have you seen the collection of studies on the Messiah that's just been published by Fortress? No? It is entitled *The Messiah*, and it has about 40–50 major studies by almost everybody you would recommend should be writing in the field. In full support of you are most of the articles, pointing out that our nomenclature has got to be cleaned up. In most of the texts in the pseudepigrapha and in other Jewish writings, people are putting the term

"Messiah" on would-be messianic figures, yet it is demonstrable that there are "eschatological figures that are not clearly Messiahs." One has to be very clear. Are you going to refer only to a text that refers to and contains the name "Christos" and "*mashiah*" as messianic? I think I am in full agreement with everything you say.

I find it interesting that such very distinguished scholars as you've mentioned, whom we all admire, still do not use terms precisely, and never even explain what they mean by the term "Messiah." So, I find your work very helpful.

FITZMYER: We'll hear more tomorrow from Dr. John Collins.

EPHRAIM ISAAC (*Institute of Semitic Studies, Princeton, NJ*): I'm not sure I'm really convinced by your dismissing Martinez's argument that this text may refer to an angelic figure or Michael, particularly in view of a possible connection to pseudo-Daniel. And, although in the singular form we may not have this son of God conception, we do have *bene 'elohim*, of course referring to the descent of angels, the plural form. Angels are so referred to. I am also thinking of certain *haggadic* traditions from *Midrash Ha-Gadol*, where Michael is often so regarded . . .

FITZMYER: Yes, but when was the *Midrash Ha-Gadol* written? When do you date that? Fourteenth century?

ISAAC: Yes, but the tradition is earlier.

FITZMYER: I will not buy that argument. That's extrapolation.

ISAAC: As a matter of fact, the *Midrash Ha-Gadol* proved to be one of the most important works, possibly containing material from the Tannaitic period.

FITZMYER: Personally, I date the Tannaitic period to Rabbi Judah the prince: 200 C.E., not before that.

ISAAC: What about your suggestion that the son of God in the plural does appear? It is not in the singular.

FITZMYER: That's used for angels and so on. I can understand that, but this text is using it in the singular. This text is talking about a very specific person. To say that Michael would be called the Son of God, I find very difficult.

Admonition Texts from Qumran Cave 4

TORLEIF ELGVIN*

Caspari Center
Hebrew University, Jerusalem

This paper introduces some sectarian sapiental writings from the group 4Q410–4Q426[1] ("sectarian" is in this paper used as meaning "belonging to the Qumran community"). Theological themes, phraseology and orthography place these compositions among the writings of the Qumran community. One of these writings, Sap. Work A, demonstrates a specific vocabulary and characteristics of its own, clearly different from other sapiental writings found in Qumran, whether they are of sectarian or non-sectarian origin.

I will discuss the relationship of these texts to the overall Qumran corpus and sectarian literature and present some of the central themes in Sap. Work A. Further studies of these compositions are needed to supplement my preliminary conclusions.

Discussed here are the following texts: 4Q413; Sap. Work A (4Q415/416/417/418/423/1Q26) and 4Q420/421 (4QWays of Righteousness). I have been assigned 4Q420/421 and 4Q423 for publication, but I shall relate to all the above-mentioned texts in this paper.

The composition most closely related to Sap. Work A and 4Q413 is 1Q/4Q Myst, which reflects much of the same phraseology. 1Q/4Q Myst does not, however, have the long, wordy admonition passages on different areas of human life characteristic of Sap. Work A. The term רז נהיה, the Mystery of Being, which is central in Sap. Work A, is less frequent in 1Q/4Q Myst, which more often than our texts uses terms like רז, רזים, רזי עד or רזי פלא. 1Q/4Q Myst should therefore probably be seen as related to, but separate from, Sap. Work A. Some of the phrases characteristic of Sap. Work A are found in the biblical paraphrase 4Q422 (4QparaGenExod), which has been assigned to me and Emanuel Tov for publication.

* *Address for correspondence:* Åsterudsletta 45, 1344 Haslum, Norway.

[1] I am indebted to Profs. John Strugnell and Daniel Harrington for valuable feedback for the final version of this paper, and would like to express my thankfulness to Prof. Emanuel Tov of the Hebrew University for his faithful support. Together with Prof. Moshe Weinfeld he guides my dissertation, entitled "An Analysis of Admonition Works from Qumran Cave 4." Financial support from The Norwegian Research Council for Science and Humanities enabled my participation in this conference.

LITERARY OBSERVATIONS ON SAPIENTAL WORK A

I started my investigation of these writings with the presupposition that Sap. Work A existed in four copies, 4Q416/417/418/419, and that 4Q415 and 4Q423 were separate works. The affinities between 4Q415, 4Q423 and Sap. Work A seemed to indicate a genre of admonition writings. These presuppositions were revised through the investigation of the texts.

My study seems to indicate that 4Q419 is not another copy of Sap. Work A. It has some phrases in common with the latter composition, but does not represent the same text.[2] 4Q419 frg. 1 is concerned with the status and duties of the Aaronic priests, a theme not found in the other texts.[3] It seems therefore more reasonable to consider 4Q419 as a separate composition.

In my view Sap. Work A is represented by six copies from cave 4, in addition to one known copy from cave 1, 1Q26. The same passage is found two or three times in two different fragments in the big collection of fragments 4Q418,[4] which means that 418 preserves remnants not of one, but of two copies of Sap. Work A. All fragments of 418 seem to have been written by the same scribe.

The text of two different fragments from 4Q423 duplicates the text of two fragments from 4Q418: The words of the small piece 423 8 are found in 418 81 2–4,[5] and 423 9 overlaps the text of 418 188. As pointed out in note 4, the text of 415 11 is found in two or three fragments of 418. 4Q415 and 4Q423 seem therefore to be copies of Sap. Work A, and not separate compositions. The possibility that the fragment from 415 which duplicates the text known from 418, is wrongly attributed to 415, ought to be discarded. All 415 fragments reflect the same hand and come from a scroll where another composition (4Q414) was written on the rear side, which means that they definitely belong to the same text.

---

[2] The phrase (בשר) אם יקפוץ ידו ונאספה רוח כול, "if he shut his hand and the spirit of all flesh be gathered in," appears both in 419 8 ii 7 and 416 2 ii 2, but the context is different.

[3] Cf., however, priestly coined terms in 4Q421 frgs. 11 and 13, and in 1Q/4QMyst; 4Q299 frgs. 52 and 75.

[4] The letters שלם from the word ישלם of the text of 416 1 13 appears in two different fragments of 418 – frgs. 2 and 213. Both fragments definitely preserve the text known from 416 1. This overlap therefore demonstrates without any doubt that 418 preserves remnants of two copies of Sap. Work A. A similar doublet can be shown on the words לעומר ועומר from 415 11 2. These two words are preserved both on 418 167 and on the following fragment of three lines from PAM 41.909, which is not found in the preliminary concordance of J. Strugnell and H. Stegemann: אשר לוא /יחד למשקלמה / לעומר ועומר (the text of 415 11 can thus be supplemented with these fragments from 418). The text of 418 38 possibly overlaps with two words from 418 167 of this same text.

[5] After comparison with 418 81 the last word in 423 frg 8 4 which looks like כבוך should be read ככבור.

4Q423 overlaps with 1Q26, which therefore proves to be another copy of Sap. Work A (423 3 overlaps the text of 1Q26 2, 423 4 the text of 1Q26 1).[6]

The different copies of Sap. Work A can thus be designated as following: Sap. Work A^{a,b} (418), Sap. Work A^c (416), Sap. Work A^d (417), Sap. Work A^e (415), Sap. Work A^f (423), Sap. Work A^g (1Q26).

The large fragments from 4Q416 and 417, which partly overlap one another, enable us to reconstruct the sequence of seven different columns: 417 2 i; 417 2 ii (417 frgs. 3 and 4 possibly belong to this column); (after a possible break) 417 1 i (=416 2 i); 416 2 ii (=417 1 ii); 416 2 iii; 416 2 iv; (and after a possible break) 416 1.

Different editorial stages of Sap. Work A seem to be reflected by 416 and 418. If my analysis of two of the photographs of 418 8 is correct, the text of almost a full column is absent in 418 where (compared with the running text we know from 416) we would expect to find it. Part of this text is found in 418 but placed elsewhere.[7]

The fact that seven copies of this composition are found in Qumran does not necessarily demonstrate a sectarian origin of the work, but certainly its popularity within the community. Most of the copies of Sap. Work A are written in early Herodian script, and one or two seem to be late Herodian.

DESCRIPTION OF THE ADMONITION COMPOSITIONS

Sap. Work A is a long composition. Its main contents are admonition passages pertaining to different areas of human experience. The instruction is re-

---

[6] Some of the readings in DJD I can now be corrected: 1Q26 2 4 should read פרי בטנכה, not פרי בידכה. 1Q26 3 2 should be read as כי אתה לו לבן בכור, not כי אתה לי לבן יחיד, cf. 416 2 ii 13; 418 81 5. The proposed ונקלחתה in 1Q26 1 6 cannot be sustained, as the last letter before ה in the parallel text in 4Q423 is מ.

[7] 418 frg. 9 (a column seen on photograph PAM 42.759) demonstrates that the columns of 418 had approximately 51–56 letters per line, and at least 18 lines per column. The photograph PAM 41.907 seems to fit accurately this same column (frg. 9, here called col. ii) to the left margin of the preceding column (frg. 7, here called col. i), which ends with the words כול חסרי (= 416 2 ii 1). This column would then have had at least 21 lines, the three bottom lines reaching below the last line of the following column. The first legible words on col. ii in PAM 41.907 (418 9) are פקדו לכה (= 416 2 iii 3), which leaves out a full column of the running text of Sap. Work A which we know from 416.

It is impossible to squeeze the text of a full column into the missing top of col. ii on PAM 41.907 (418 9). The (missing) text of 416 2 ii 2–13 is represented by another fragment of 14 lines on PAM 42.759 (418 8). This problem can be solved in two ways: either by rejecting the joint proposed on PAM 42.759, which looks perfect, or to accept this joint as I tend to do. Then it would be clear that 416 and 418 represent different editorial stages in the development of Sap. Work A: the text of almost a full column is absent in 418 where (compared with the running text we know from 416) we would expect to find it, and part of this text is found in 418 but placed elsewhere. The weakness of this assumption is that it places the lower margin of col. ii three lines above that of col. i in the middle of a composition. This would be an irregular phenomenon, but not unique in the Qumran scrolls.

lated to sectarian theological concepts and especially to the knowledge of God's mysteries, רז נהיה. At times eschatological material is woven into the parenetic discussion, at other times we meet more comprehensive eschatological passages on God's endtime judgment in the presence of the heavenly hosts, in, for example, 416 1 and 418 69. The eschatological passages seem to put the admonition into perspective: One day God's righteousness will triumph, in the meantime one should live according to his instructions.

Many of the fragments of Sap. Work A^e, 4Q415 (previously designated Sap. Work B) talk about God who measured out the universe, and now is testing and judging man on the scales of righteousness, מוזני צדק,[8] using phrases from Isa 40:12, Job 31:6 and 28:20–28:

]בם כי כמוזני צדק ישקולמה ...]כֹי יחד למשקלקלֹמֹה [...] אשר לוא [ולאיפה וֹ]איפה
לעומר ועומר [וישקלו ... בֹנֹהֹןֹ מֹבֹינים כי לפיא רוחות יתֹנֹהלכו   הארץ]תכנתה ביחד
רוחכֹה [כֹוֹל מׁיֹמׁיֹה ספר לו ובנוותיה הביﬞנﬞ [...] עם משקל תכינה רוחם ביוֹן]^9

. . . them, for like scales of righteous[ness he will weigh them . . .,]for together with their weights . . . as neither according to ephah and ephah nor according to omer and omer [will they be weighed . . .] they have understanding of riches, because they wa[lk] according to the spirits . . . Together with Your spirit You measured out [the earth]. All her waters were counted for Him, and her bodies He knew[. . .] with scales He will test their spirits . . .

Many of the fragments of Sap. Work A^f (4Q423) refer to the agricultural sphere; to man being placed by God in charge of the earth,[10] the yield of the fields (we often meet the words אדמה and תבואה), the firstborn of the cattle, the farmer's obligation to keep the agricultural set times, *etc.*[11] References to Gen chs. 1–3 and 8–9 are obvious in many passages.[12]

The judgment on Korah (Num 16) is referred to by 423 5 1, which continues with the theological expression ואשר גלה אוזנכה ברז נהיה, "as he opened your ears for the Mystery of Being." The next line talks about רא]שׁ אבותיכה ... ונשיא עמכה, "the leader of your fathers . . . and the prince of your people." נשיא עמכה is found only here in the Qumran corpus; in this context it is more probably a reference to Moses[13] than to the Messianic prince or a present ruler. The text continues (with proposed reconstructions):

---

[8] כין באוֹנֹכֹי אמת ומשקל צדק תכן אל כול ;3 126 418 .*cf* ,12 9 415 ;5–6 6 415 ;8 ,02 11 415 בֹנֹי אדם.

[9] Excerpts from 4Q415 11, supplemented with two fragments from 4Q418 (see note 4).

[10] המשילכה לעבדו ולשמרו, 4Q423 2 2.

[11] ואתה אֹ]יש אדמה פקוד מועדי הקיץ ואסוף תבואתכה בעתה ותקופת[ן, 4Q423 5 5.

[12] 423 1 9; 423 2 1–3; 423 5 6; 423 9 1–2; 423 13 4.

[13] The expression ביד משה is found in 419 1 2, possibly in 423 11, and in 418 184.

הוֹא פלג ונֽחֹלת כל מושלים ויצר כלן מעשׂנֽה בידוֹ והוא פעולת

[אנוש הכין 14 וישׁפֹטֹ כולם באמת יפקוד לאבות ובנימן לנרינֹם עם כל אזרחים ודבר

]   5   ואתה אֽנֽיש אדמה 15 פקוד מועדי הקיץ ואסוֹף תבואתכה בעתה ותקופת

וֽהזרע למועדוֹ 16 הֽבֹנֽונך בכל תבואתכה ובעֽבֽדֽותכה השׂכֽל לדעת הֽנֽוֹב עם הרע

אֽנֽיש שכל את בעל אולת הֽנֽבדיל מכֽלֽן חפץ הקורֽשֽים כן איש

He shared out[17] the inheritance of all rulers. He formed each deed by his
hand, and [established] the work of [man. He will judg]e everybody in truth
and visit upon fathers and sons, on strangers and all native born. And He spoke
[   ] You are a man of the earth. Keep the set times of the summer and collect
the crops in their set time and the season [of sowing in its right time. L]ook
upon all your crops and your labor, be wise and know both the good and the
evil [. . .] a man of knowledge. K[eep] the fool [away] from the property of
the holy ones. Thus a man [

418 frg. 81, which overlaps the text of 423 frg. 8, does not refer to agricultural matters. 418 81 preserves almost a full column with admonition in
a lofty style, emphasizing the holiness of the community unlike other admonition passages.

Only the first 4–5 lines of 4Q413 are preserved. The photograph places
together two fragments which seem to preserve the upper right and the upper
left part of the same column. If this connection is correct, the composition
starts with the words מזמר שֽיר, and continues דעתן וחוכמה אלמדכמה, "I will
teach you knowledge and wisdom." The proposed connection seems questionable. Close investigation of the fragments reveals that they can hardly belong
together, and the texts in the two fragments cannot easily be fit together. The
main fragment brings the words of a teacher who instructs "those who understand" about the ways of men and the truth of God. Line 4 ends with the
words כאשר גלה אל, which can be emended to כאשר גלה אל]אוזן מבינים ברז
נהיה. The expressions כאשר גלה אל אוזן מבינים ברז נהיה, "as God opened
the ears of those who understand to the Mystery of Being" and כאשר גלה
אוזנכה ברז נהיה, "He has opened your ears to the Mystery of Being" are
common in Sap. Work A, and not found in other compositions.

The teaching style of 4Q413 with instruction in the 1st person singular
is also found in the opening phrases of 4Q298 and 4Q525 1. 4Q413 links
this way of sapiental instruction to Sap. Work A and thus to the Qumran
community.

---

[14] For the reconstruction, cf. 1QH i 9; xv 22.

[15] For the reconstruction, cf. 423 26; אֽנֽיש אדמה אתה. This phrase refers to Noah, Gen 9:20
(I am indebted to Moshe Bernstein for this observation).

[16] For the reconstruction, cf. 1QS x 7.

[17] We find a similar use of פלג in 418 81 20, אל פלג נחלתן בכֹל חי; in 418 55 6, הוא פלג
פלנתה עבודתם בכול דוריהם; cf. 1QH i 16, פלג שכלם; in 4QMyst (299 8 2), לנוחלי אמת.

Two fragmentary copies of 4Q420/421 (4QWays of Righteousness) are preserved, listing in sapiental style the characteristics of the righteous (a similar style is found in 4Q424): the knowledgeable man . . ., the humble man . . ., the steadfast man . . . We encounter the image of the wise man, איש משכיל ונבון, that can receive admonition and keep a careful profile in public discussion (similar motifs are found in Sir 5:10–14; 4Q424 2, lines 1 and 5 and 4Q525 14 ii 20–28):

ללכת בדרכי אל לעשות צדקה̇ן [oȯת לוא ישיב בטרם ישמ̇ע ולוא ידבר
בטרם יבין באר̇ך א̇נפי̇ם ישיב פתגם ידרש אמת משפט ובמחקר צדק ימצא
תוצאותיה י̇ן̇דר̇ן̇ש̇]לדעת וא̇נ̇י̇ש̇ן ענוו ונכי שכלו לוא ישוב אחור עד [...
איש]נאמן לוא יסור מדרכי צדק וישמ [...]מ̇̇ותיו וכפיו בצדק נגאלו̇ [בבינ̇ה]כו̇ל̇ [
...]ש̇דותיו גבולן[18]

Following the way of God, being righteous, . . . He will not answer before he has listened, nor speak before he has understood, with patience will he pass judgment. He will seek justice, and through the study of righteousness earn its rewards and seek knowledge. A meek man, humble in his knowledge, will not turn back but . . . A steadfast man will not turn away from the ways of righteousness and put [. . .] His hips and his hands will be redeemed by righteousness, in understanding all . . . the border of his fields[

In 4Q421 frgs. 13 and 11 we unexpectedly encounter sacrifices and the courts of the temple:

כ̇ו̇ל העולות והזבחים א̇ן ...] דברי קודש כחוק[ ] ... [ב̇ב̇ו̇ן̇ל̇ הק̇ר̇נ̇בנים
o[וכול עבד ואמה לוא יוכל בו̇ן ...]א̇ ואל יבא בשער חצרו ובשע̇ן̇ר

all the holocausts and the sacrifices . . . the holy things according to the law . . . with all the offerings;
no slave or maid should in[. . .] and not enter the gate of its court and the gate . . .

The term רז נהיה does not occur in the preserved fragments of this composition. The term לאכול ולשתות ממנו, "to eat and drink from it," 421 6 12, reminds us of similar phrases in Sap. Work A.

QUMRAN TERMINOLOGY

It was asserted above that our writings are "Qumranic" enough to have clearly come from the Qumran community, although they have characteristics of their own. The designation for God is consistently אל.

4Q420/421 (Ways of Righteousness) clearly demonstrates terminology that is known from the Rule of the Community and other sectarian writings:

---

[18] 4Q 421 1 ii 12–17, supplemented with 421 14 and 420 1.

לסרוך, muster/set in order; לסרך הכול איש לפני רעהו, "to muster every-body, each man before his neighbour," 421 1 3–4, cf. 1QS v 23.

גורל, lot, יצא הגורל הרישון וכן יצאו, "the first lot will fall and then they will go out," 4Q421 1 i 4, cf. CD xiii 4; 1QM i 14.

יביא את כול ח[כמתו ודעתו ובינתו וטובו]ביחד אל, "he will bring all] his wisdom and knowledge and understanding and good things [into the com-munity," 421 1 i 2, cf. 1QS i 11–12.

We meet the term גורל, lot, in another (also sectarian) meaning in 4Q413 2–3: [19]הרבה לו נחלה בדעת אמתו וכפי גורלו, (possibly to emend with the words בעצת אל), "multiplied his inheritance in the knowledge of His truth, and ac-cording to his lot [in God's design," cf. איש כגורלו בעצת אל, "each man accord-ing to his lot in God's design," 1QS i 9–10. These words from 413 2–3 are almost identical with 1QH x 28–29: הרביתה נחלתי בדעת אמתכה ולפי דעתו, which is a strong indication of the sectarian provenance of 4Q413.

If we go to Sap. Work A, the terminology is not so obviously sectarian. Neither is the structure of the יחד, which we know from 1QS, reflected in Sap. Work A. If, however, 4Q413 is sectarian, the presence of the phrase כאשר גלה אל]אוזן מבינים ברז נהיה (413 4–5), which is common in Sap. Work A, points towards a sectarian provenance for Sap. Work A as well. The closest parallels to this phrase are found in the (sectarian) Hodayot.[20] Also other phrases indicate some kind of knowledge of sectarian terminology:

להתהלך תמים, to walk in perfection, 415 2 i 3; 417 2 i 12; 417 2 ii 5, cf. CD i 20–21; vii 4–5; 1QS i 8; ix 19.

לערב הון, "mix the property," 416 2 ii 18, cf. 1QS vi 22, vii 24, viii 23, ix 8.

The term מחוקק, "lawgiver," which occurs twice in 417 2 i 14–15, links our text to the early community described in CD vi.[21]

אנשי רצון, 418 81 10 reminds us of בני רצונו, 1QH iv 32–33 and בני רצונכה, 1QH xi 9.

אביון, poor, a well-known term from biblical as well as sectarian writings, is a common designation for the addressee of Sap. Work A: אביון אתה....

The term מטעת עולם, eternal planting, 418 81 13, which is known from 1QS xi 8 and 1QH vi 15, seems to me to presuppose the sectarian com-munity as the *ekklesia* of the writer.

It has been proposed that this "sectarian" terminology could be pre-sectarian or is reflecting a wider usage in Judea in the second and first centuries

---

[19] The scribe of 4Q413 erroneously wrote נועלו for גורלו.

[20] כיא גליתה אוזני לרזי פלא, 1QH i 21; from the Hodayot frgs.: גליתה אוזני]למוז[סרך, 1QH vi 4; ואתה גליתה אוזני, frg. 4 7; ואוזן בשר גליתה, frg. 5 10; חויכה גליתה, frg. 6 5.

[21] Cf. DAVIES, P. R. 1983. *The Damascus Covenant. An Interpretation of the "Damascus Docu-ment."* JSOT Press. Sheffield: 121–125.

B.C. I see, however, the Qumran community as the most probable background for our texts.

משכיל is a common word for a man of knowledge both in our texts and in other sectarian writings (and in the Bible as well). In light of the admonition texts it becomes clear that משכיל in sectarian literature more often has the meaning *the knowledgeable* (as in CD xii 21; 1QS ix 12, 21; 1QH xii 11) than *the authoritative teacher* (as in 1QS iii 13; 1QSb iii 22, v 28; 4Q288 1; possibly CD xiii 22).

THEOLOGY: ETHICS BASED ON
THE ORDER OF CREATION

Sap. Work A and 4Q422 (4QparaGenExod) seem to be the only sectarian texts which use Gen chs. 1–3 and 8–9 as well as Ps 8 as the basic texts of reference for their thinking on man's place in God's creation and his tasks on earth.[22] 4Q422 frg. 1 reads as follows:

1 השמים והארץ וכול]צבא֗ם עשה בדב֗ר֗ו וישבת ביום השביעי [
    מכול מלאכתו אש֗ר עשה ורוח קודש֗ו[
    עשה כל נפ֗ש החיה והרמש֗ת אשר שרצו המים למינהם
    ועשה האדם   ]ע֗ המשילו לאכול פרני האדמה
5   ]ל֗נ֗בלתי אכול מעץ הד֗עת טוב ורע
    ]י֗קום עליו וישכחו֗ן מצוותיו
    ]ב֗יוצר רע ולמעש֗֗י

heavens and earth and all] their hosts he made by his word. [And he rested on the seventh day from all his work whic]h he had been doing. And his holy spirit[. . . He made every]living being and all which abounds [in the waters according to their kinds. He made man . . .] put him in charge [of the earth] to eat its frui[t . . . and decreed]that he should not eat from the tree that gives know[ledge of good and evil. . . . and [he rose against him and they forgot [his commandments . . .]in evil inclination and deeds [of injustice.

Central in this paraphrase on Gen ch. 1 is the assertion that God has placed man (as he did with Adam and Noah) in charge of the earth, to eat its fruit, המשילו לאכול פרני האדמה. The text continues talking about the eating from the tree of knowledge and man's sin and rebellion against God.

This passage from 4Q422 introduces a number of phrases and concepts which recur in the admonitions of Sap. Work A: God has placed man in charge of creation, the knowledge of good and evil, the evil inclinations.

Sap. Work A and 4Q422 possibly provide the earliest allusions to what later

---

[22] *Cf.* VERMES, G. 1992. "Genesis 1–3 in Post-Biblical Hebrew and Aramaic Literature before the Mishnah." *JJS* **XLIII**(2): 221–225. Vermes' discussion on Gen 1–3 in early post-biblical Judaism needs to be supplemented with the material presented here.

became the rabbinic concept of "the good and evil inclinations," ביוצר רע יצר:, טוב ויצר רע "in evil inclination," above, 422 1 7; יצר בשר, "the inclination of the flesh," 416 1 16; מחשבת יצר רעוה, "the thoughts of evil inclination," 417 2 ii 12. Cf. יצר in neutral meaning; 417 2 i 9; 417 2 i 9,11.

The phrase המשילו/המשילכה is central in our admonition genre and describes man's place under God and above creation. 416 2 iv 1–3 makes it clear in a paraphrase on Gen 2:24 that God has placed the husband to be in charge of his wife, אותכה המשיל בה.

Ps 8 fits well with the theological thinking reflected in our compositions. Ps 8:7 has one of three cases of משל in *hiphil* in the O.T., תמשילהו, "You set him to rule," on God giving man the task of ruling over his creation, as in our texts. Dan 11:39 uses המשילם, "he set them to rule," on the blasphemous king who sets the ungodly to rule over others. I propose that these two biblical references (and possibly Sir 17:2, 4 and Jub 2:14) were essential for the use of the term המשיל in Sap. Work A. The idea of God setting man to rule creation is found in biblical, pre-sectarian, and sectarian texts. Sap. Work A elaborates and blends this motif with other theological themes in a unique way.

The 2-Spirit Treatise in 1QS uses different terminology to express a similar thought: והואה ברא אנוש לממשלת תבל, 1QS iii 17–18, "He created man to rule the world." We also find similar expressions on Adam and Eve in the non-sectarian psalm 4Q381 (probably from an earlier date) which paraphrases Gen 1: ובכלן וברוחו העמידם למשל בכל אלה באדמה, "and by His spirit he set them to rule all these, the earth and all . . ." 381 1 7. This fragment demonstrates more parallels to 4Q422 (4QGenpara) frg. 1 and to Sap. Work A.[23] The Hebrew original of the phrase we find both in Sir 17:2 and Jub 2:14 (either the latter is literarily dependent on the former, or they both use the same source), "He gave him authority over everything on earth," possibly used the term המשיל.[24]

Sap. Work A is twice addressing the listener with the word איש אדמה אתה, "you are a man of the earth," an allusion to Noah, Gen 9:20. Gen chs. 8–9, which describe man and his tasks in the post-flood situation, are suitable as reference texts for this kind of *Schöpfungsethik*.

We note that in 4Q422 frg. 1 the eating from the tree which gives knowledge of good and evil introduces man's rebellion against God. The admonitions of Sap. Work A, by contrast, portray the man of knowledge that positively can discern between good and evil. We possibly encounter here a "realized eschatology" that perceives the enlightened, to whom God's mysteries have been revealed, as partaker of God's knowledge, described in Gen chs. 1–3. A

---

[23] SCHULLER, E. M. 1986. *Non-Canonical Psalms from Qumran: A Pseudepigraphic Collection.* Scholars Press. Atlanta, Georgia: 71.

[24] Segal uses וימשילם in his translation of Sir 17:2. SEGAL, M. S. 1972. ספר בן סירא השלם. Bialik Foundation. Jerusalem: 102.

radical exegesis of Gen 3:6, ונחמד העץ להשכיל, "the tree was desirable to give knowledge," and 3:22, הן האדם היה כאחד ממנו לדעת טוב ורע, "lest man be like one of us to know good and evil," connected with wisdom concepts from the book of Daniel (see below), seems to provide the background to this way of thinking. Do the enlightened members of the Community already have a share in the glory of Adam, כבוד אדם (CD iii 20, 1QS iv 23)?[25] Sap. Work A does not stress the sinfulness of man—including the men of the Community—as do the Hodayot and the hymn in 1QS x–xi; its admonitions seem to express a more optimistic anthropology.

4Q423 2 1–6 interweaves a paraphrase on Gen ch. 3 and admonition for human life.

1]וֹכל פרי תנובה וכל עץ נעים נחמד להשכיל הלוא גן נן
]ל וֹבֹכֹול מֹועשׂ]בֹה ובו המשילכה לעבדו ולשמרו vac יֹן
] o קוץ וֹדֹרֹדֹר תצמיח לכה וכוחה לא תתן לכה [
] במועלכה vacat [
5] vac ילדה וכל רחמי הורֹ]וה [לֹן o]הֹשׂן
]בכל חפציכה כי כל תצמיֹן[ח לכה

every good fruit and every pleasant tree that is desirable to give knowledge. Is not this a garden . . . and in all your works. He put you in charge of it to work it and guard it . . . It will produce thorns and thistles for you. It will not give you of its strength . . . in your toil . . . she will give birth, and every mother's womb . . . in all your possessions, for everything it will produce for you . . .

4Q423 frg. 9 repeats the term כי נחמד הוא]להשכיל (Gen 3:6) and continues to talk about man's walking in the ways of holiness, דרכי קודש, and about seeking God's covenant.

The admonition passages of Sap. Work A describe (and prescribe) man's role in the world created by God, in the different fields of human experience: family, agriculture, wealth, property, finances, relation to God and fellow men etc.

416 2 iii–iv describes family relations. After an admonition to honor his parents, the wise and enlightened is told (with proposed emendations):

אשה לקחתה ברושכה קח מילדֹי]וישע אשר נפשמה מלטון[26 מרז נהיה בהתחברכה יחד התהלך עם עזר בשרכהן בנחֹ[ם ענֹל כן יעוב אישן את אביו]וֹאֹת אמוֹ וֹדֹבֹק באשתו והיו לבשר]אֹחד אותכה המשיל בה ותשׂן   אביהן לא המשיל בה
מאמֹה הפרידה 27

When you take a wife in your poverty, take her from among the children [of salvation whose souls are saved] by the Mystery of Being. In your union together walk with your helpmate in [graceful]ness f[or it is said: Man shall leave]

---

25 Cf. Sirach 49:16 and Targum Neofyti and Targum Pseudo-Jonathan on Gen 3:21.
26 For the reconstruction, cf. אשר נפשמה מלטו מרו נהיה, 1Q27 1 4; מולדי ישע, 4Q417 1 i 11.
27 416 2 iii 20–iv 3, supplemented with one fragment from 418, 41.907.

his father and mother and cli[ng to his wife, and they will become]one flesh. (God) put you, . . . not her [father] in charge of her. From her mother he separated her . . .

4Q417 1 i 17–26, which basically is a short sermon on Prov 6:1–5, gives sound financial advice to the poor man who is obliged to take a loan from the wealthy: "If you borrow riches from men when in need, do not slumber day or night and do not give your soul rest until you have given back to your lender. Do not lie to him lest evil and shame be done to you. . . . and he will lift his hand while you are in need and chastise you . . . do not hide from your lender lest he reveal your shame."

THEOLOGY: THE MYSTERY TO COME OR THE MYSTERY OF BEING

רז נהיה is the central theological concept in Sap. Work A, occurring more than 20 times. It also occurs in 4Q413 (according to my emendation), 1Q/4QMyst and once in 1QS. נהיה is more probably *niphal* perfect (nihya) than participle (nihye) of היה. The meaning of the term רז נהיה is not easy to comprehend.

רז, mystery, occurs in the Bible only in the Aramaic part of Daniel (9 times). Six of the references, all connected to Nebuchadnezzar's secret dream in ch. 2, connect רז with the verb גלה, to reveal: God can reveal secrets to his elect.

רז is a central phrase in the vocabulary of the Qumran community for the mysteries or secrets of God, see *e.g.* 1QH i 11; viii 5–6, 11; ix 23; xii 13, 20; רזי פלא, "wonderful mysteries," 1QS iv 6; ix 18; xi 5; 1QH i 21; ii 13; vii 27; xi 10. It is often used about the knowledge of God and his ways, which now is revealed to the members of the community.

The term רז is common in 1Q/4QMyst (9 occurrences). It is also found in our texts: כי משכיל התבונן ברזיכה, "the wise shall look into your mysteries," 417 2 i 25; רזי פלא, 417 2 i 13.

1QS xi 3–4 contains רז נהיה in the following context: כי ממקור דעתו פתח אורו ובנפלאותיו הביטה עיני ואורת לבבי ברז נהיה והווא עולם משען ימיני, "He let his light shine (upon me) from the source of his knowledge. My eye has beheld his wonders, and the light of my heart the Mystery of Being. The everlasting Being is the support of my right hand."

Wernberg-Møller and Licht discuss the meaning and temporal aspect of רז נהיה in 1QS xi in light of 1QS iii 15 and CD ii 10. Wernberg-Møller translates 1QS xi 3–4 "my heart has beheld the secret of what happens and will happen for ever." Both he and Licht interpret רז נהיה and the following words והווא עולם as parallel terms. רז נהיה is for Licht the mystery of the universe, the mystery that gives the rules of the universe (of what has come into being, נהיה), and possibly the mystery of the future. The author of 1QS knows the rules of the universe, also those secrets of God's world which now are revealed to the community. Bardtke proposed to understand רז נהיה והווא עולם as "das Geheimnis alles Sein und Geschehen."[28]

רז נהיה is found twice in 1Q/4QMyst (1Q27 i 3; i 4). Milik translates רז נהיה in 1Q26 and 1Q27 "le mystère futur," the mystery to come (DJD I pp. 102–103).

The most frequent context of this phrase in Sap. Work A is הבט ברז נהיה, "Look into the Mystery of Being," and אשר גלה (אל) אוזנכה/אוזן מבינים ברז נהיה, "as he opened your ear/the ear of those who understand to the Mystery of Being."

The term has a clear revelatory meaning. The wise and enlightened have gazed (הביט) into God's mysteries and are admonished to continue to do so; יום, ולילה הגה ברז נהיה ודרוש תמיד ואז תדע אנת, "Meditate day and night on the Mystery of Being. Search always (the Scriptures), and then you will know truth," 417 2 i 6. God has revealed his secrets to the men of the community, cf. CD iii 13–14. God's revelation gives knowledge: הבט ברז נהיה ואז תדע, "Gaze into the Mystery of Being, and then you will know . . ." The phrases ואז תדע/ואז תבין/ואז יראה, "and then you will know/understand/see," often recur in this context.

Milik's proposal to understand רז נהיה as "the mystery to come," or alternatively "the mystery which is about to come into being" is attractive. The use of the expression in Sap. Work A, however, makes a future meaning of נהיה difficult. 418 123 ii 3–4 clearly uses נהיה about the past in a context where רז נהיה appears: כול הנהיה בה למה היה ומה יהיה ... אשר גלה אל אוזן מבינים ברז נהיה, ". . . everything that was in it with what is and will be . . . as God opened the ears of those who understand to the Mystery of Being." The expression וכול נהיה עולם, "everything that ever came into being," 418 69 6, also clearly points to a meaning of נהיה in the past tense. 4Q298 1 iii 9–10 has a similar phrase where תביט is used for looking back into the past: בעבור תבינו בקץ עולמות ובקרן[מ]זניות תביטו לדעת, "so that you understand the era of eternity and look into the things of the past, to know . . ." As said above, Sap. Work A often uses this same verb, הביט, in connection with רז נהיה.

רז נהיה is the mystery of God, revealed to the man of the community. It might be an alternative expression for the knowledge of God. With this understanding in mind, I translate רז נהיה "the Mystery of Being."

Sap. Work A takes the concept רז נהיה as a starting point for instructing the enlightened how he shall "walk" in his everyday life. התבונן and התהלך

[28] WERNBERG-MØLLER, P. 1957. *The Manual of Discipline. Translated and Annotated with an Introduction.* E. J. Brill. Leiden: 38, 68, 151. LICHT, J. 1965. מגילת הסרכים ממגילות מדבר יהודה. סרך היחד-סרך העדה-סרך הברכות. Bialik Institute. Jerusalem: 90, 228. BARDTKE 1952. *Die Handschriftenfunde am Toten Meer.* Evangelische Haupt-Bibelgesellschaft. Berlin: *ad locum.*

are often used in connection with רז נהיה. The analogy to a central theme in parenetic passages in New Testament epistles is not far away; "you are called and saved/raised up with Christ, therefore walk according to your calling."[29]

QUMRAN ORTHOGRAPHY AND MORPHOLOGY

Both 4Q420/421, 4Q413 and Sap. Work A are written in the so-called Qumran system of orthography and morphology.[30] For pronominal suffixes we find כה-, מה-, המה- and כמה-. כול and לוא (also written לוה and לו) are written plene in most of the manuscripts. Prima/media מ at times occur in final position (and once פ), and we find alternation between forms such as מואדה/מודה/מאודה, תאומר/תומר/תמר, ראש/רוש, הוא/הואה. Occasionally forms such as ידורשוהו (423 9 2) can be found.

If one follows Tov's assertions, the fact that these writings demonstrate the Qumran orthography indicates that they were copied by scribes of the Qumran community, without necessarily having their origins in this community.

RELATIONSHIP OF SAP. WORK A TO OTHER
QUMRAN WRITINGS

The terminology of Sap. Work A reveals close links with the Rule of the Community, the Damascus Document and some of the Hodayot (especially 1QH i, xi and xv), 4Q424[31] and possibly to 4Q426 frg.1.[32]

Apart from 1Q/4QMyst, the closest relative as to phraseology seems to be the Rule of the Community, especially the 2-Spirit treatise in 1QS iii 13 -iv 26. The 2-Spirit dualism typical of the treatise[33] is not adopted in our

---

[29] Cf., e.g., Col. 3:1–17.

[30] See Tov, E. 1986. *The Orthography and Language of the Hebrew Scrolls found at Qumran and the Origin of These Scrolls.* Textus 13. Jerusalem: 31–57; *idem*, 1988. "Hebrew Biblical Manuscripts from the Judaean Desert: Their Contribution to Textual Criticism." *JJS* **XXXIX**(1): 5–37. *Cf.*, however, recent cautious remarks from E. C. Ulrich and E. Qimron, who think this system can reflect a wider or earlier usage in Judean Hebrew: ULRICH, E. C. 1992. "Pluriformity in the Biblical Text, Text Groups, and Questions of Canon." In *Proceedings of the International Congress on The Dead Sea Scrolls, Madrid.* 18–21 March 1991. J. T. BARRERA & L. V. MONTANER, Eds. Leiden. Brill. 23–41: *31.* QIMRON, E. 1992. "Aspects of Qumran Hebrew." In *Abstracts*, The New York Academy of Sciences, December 14–17, 1992.

[31] A common link between 4Q424 and our texts might be אט in 424 1 6, which seems to be identical with the enigmatic אוש, often occurring in Sap. Work A. The context could indicate that this word means either *secret* (fits in 424 1 6) or *property/resources.*

[32] Of the 4Q426 fragments, at least frgs. 1 and 2 represent another admonition text. For the relation to our texts, compare, *e.g.*, 426 1 ii 3–4 with 413 1.

[33] *Cf.*, SEKKI, A. E. 1989. *The Meaning of* Ruah *at Qumran.* Scholars Press. Atlanta, Georgia: 194–219.

texts,[34] which concentrate on positive admonition to the enlightened and do not elaborate the ways of darkness as does the treatise.

The manuscripts of the Rule of the Community from cave 4 seem to confirm the view that 1QS is an edited compilation of different literary units.[35] The 2-Spirit treatise was probably inserted into 1QS at a late stage of its editorial development.[36] The fact that Sap. Work A shows more similarities to the 2-Spirit treatise than to the rest of 1QS could indicate that it derives from a time before this treatise was editorially inserted into 1QS towards the end of the 2nd. cent. B.C.[37]

This would mean that the author of Sap. Work A was familiar with material from the early version of the Rule, but was more dependent upon the separately existing treatise. Material later incorporated into the Damascus Document and the Hodayot scroll would also have been accessible at this early period of the Qumran movement. The "unorthodox" features of our text compared to other sectarian writings might also point to an early date of composition, in a period when the theology of the nascent community was still fluid.

The other possibility is to postulate only a literary dependence between the final edition of 1QS and Sap. Work A. In this case the author of Sap. Work A would be dependent upon 1QS in a more or less final form, when the 2-Spirit treatise already was included in the Rule of the Community. This would provide an easy explanation for the fact that he utilizes material from all parts of 1QS.

USE OF SCRIPTURE

It was stated above that Gen chs. 1–3, 8–9 and Ps 8 are important reference texts for Sap. Work A. The author draws inspiration, vocabulary and themes from a wider body of biblical texts, pentateuchal, prophetic and sapiental. Only once do we find a direct quote from the Hebrew Bible; Gen 2:24 is quoted in 416 iii 20–iv 1 (see above). Other times biblical passages are alluded to (as with "the tree that is desirable to give knowledge") or exposed in a paraphrastic way, as Prov 6:1–5 in the example quoted above.

---

[34] See, however, לפי רוחות יתנהלכו, 415 11 4.

[35] See the forthcoming critical edition of the Rule of the Community by J. C. B. MOHR, Tübingen (J. H. CHARLESWORTH, Ed.).

[36] LICHT, J. 1958. *An Analysis of the Treatise of the Two Spirits in DSD.* Scripta Hierosolymitana IV: 88–100. *Cf.* MURPHY O'CONNOR, J. 1969. "La genèse littéraire de la Règle de la Communauté." *RB* 76 (1969): 528–549. POUILLY, J. 1976. *La règle de la communauté de Qumran: Son évolution littéraire.* Gabalda. Paris.

[37] MURPHY O'CONNOR, *op. cit.* Cross dates the oldest manuscript of 1QS to approximately 100–75 B.C., CROSS, F. M. 1961. "The development of the Jewish scripts." In *The Bible and the Ancient Near East.* G. E. WRIGHT, Ed. Doubleday. New York: 198, note 116.

The book of Daniel seems to have special importance for the conceptual world of the writer of these admonitions. Both the holy and righteous community (Dan 7:15–27; 8:24; 11:32–35; 12:7) and those who are given wisdom and revelation from above (2:20–23; 9:22; 12:3, 10) in the midst of a hostile world, would fit well into a Qumran worldview, as would the idea of the fellowship of the enlightened with the holy angels (8:13, *passim*) and eschatological motives in this late biblical book.

A number of phrases from Daniel chs. 1 and 8–12[38] occur again and again in Sap. Work A. The book of Daniel was obviously an important source for its author, even more than for sectarian writers in general. Possibly it could indicate a closeness in time and milieu between the writer of these chapters of Daniel, from the Maccabean period, and our text, although I tentatively tend to date Sap. Work A to a period later than the beginnings of the Qumran community. In this case there would only exist a literary dependency between our writer and the book of Daniel.

INSTRUCTION FOR THE QUMRAN COMMUNITY OR FOR ESSENE CAMPS IN JUDEA?

We have seen that the instruction in Sap. Work A pertains to many different aspects of human life, including family ethics, finances, relation to wealth and property, agriculture, *etc.* These broad instructions presuppose a social life in an ordinary social context and cannot fit the closely knit community at Qumran.

The centrality of family life in these admonitions points in the same direction. It is usually postulated that only men lived in the community center at Qumran, probably for considerations of purity. The excavation of the main cemetery points in this direction. Only one of 26 skeletons excavated in the main cemetery by de Vaux's team was of a female, although at the expansions of the cemetery four out of six skeletons were of women and one of a child.[39] The preoccupation with family life in our texts makes it more probable that they are intended for the "camps" (*cf.* CD vii 6–9, xix 2–5) of the Essene movement outside Qumran.[40] The presence of terms known from the Rule of the

---

[38] The most important are: השכיל/שכל/משכיל: 1:4, 17; 8:13, 25; 9:13, 23, 25; 11:33; 12:3, 11. להבין/מבין; 23 cases. דעת/יודע: 1:4; 9:25; 12:4. חרפה: 9:16; 11:18 (2×); 12:2. קודשים/קודש/קדוש; 16 cases. ברית: 11:22, 28, 32. נכשל: 11:19, 33, 34, 41. קץ: 8:17, 19; 10:6; 11:13, 27, 35, 40; 12:4, 6, 9, 13.

[39] DE VAUX, R. 1959. *Archeology of the Dead Sea Scrolls.* Oxford University Press. Oxford: 46–48.

[40] *Cf.*, RUBINSTEIN, A. 1952. "Urban Halachah and Camp Rules in the Cairo Fragments of a Damascene Covenant." In *Sefarad* 12: 283–296. WEINERT, F. 1974. "4Q 159: Legislation for an Essene Community outside of Qumran?" *JSJ* 5: 179–207. DAVIES, P. R. 1983.

Community combined with the absence of the structure of the יחד in Sap. Work A give further support to this hypothesis.

CONCLUDING REMARKS

In Sap. Work A we have an admonition writing with characteristics of its own, which reflect a specific school within the sectarian community. Both the "unorthodox" features compared to other sectarian writings and the broad spectrum of social life covered in these admonitions point to a use within the wider Essene movement in Judea. Might we suggest an independent Essene thinker and teacher not residing in Qumran, who put his stamp on this text before it was finally edited (or only copied) in the community center at Qumran? Further investigation is needed to ascertain the relationship between 1Q/4QMyst and Sap. Work A.

~~~~~~~~~~~~~~~~~~~~~~~~~~~~~~~~~

DISCUSSION OF THE PAPER

JOSEPH A. FITZMYER (*Catholic University, Washington, D.C.*):   On page 4 of your handout, you have a quotation from 4Q416 fragment 2, columns 3 and 4, about family relations. I'd just like to ask, what is the basis of your reconstruction of the first line of the quotation, "When you take your wife, take her from among the children of salvation, whose souls are saved by the mystery of being." What is that based on? I find that a very strange reconstruction.

TORLEIF ELGVIN (*Caspari Center, Jerusalem*):   There are two phrases here I have emended. One is *miyalde yesha'*, found in another place in the same composition a couple of columns away (4Q417 1: 11). And, then I have a phrase from the Book of Mysteries, 1Q27, '*ašer nafšemma milletu miraz nihyah*. That is, "were saved by the mystery of being." I agree these are daring emendations, but I think there is a reason for them. The second is possibly safer than the first.

FITZMYER: Well, it is the "of salvation, whose souls are saved," that's the part that puzzles me.

ELGVIN: The words, "whose souls are saved by the mystery of being" are found in the *Book of Mysteries*, 1Q27, fig. 7, line 4.

HARTMUT STEGEMANN (*University of Göttingen, Göttingen, Germany*):   I know this text since I worked together on it with Strugnell for a very long time. It was one of his major unpublished texts. When I worked on these texts in the past, I had the idea that this is wisdom of the third century B.C.E. and therefore background for the Book of Daniel.

You put it in the formative phase of the sect, after Daniel, and you don't discuss the other possibility. Apparently you do so because you think you can find Qumran terminology. I am not so convinced. What do you think of the possibility of third century wisdom?

ELGVIN: I know that Strugnell and Harrington have a working hypothesis that this text might be presectarian; that is, early second century B.C.E., a little before the beginnings of the Qumran community. They believe that sectarian writings are dependent on these writings. I tend to see it the other way around and see a sectarian community as a more likely background for these writings. It would seem somewhat strange to me if already in the third century B.C.E. we found so many of the typical sectarian phrases and concepts. Surely we have to move out into the second century B.C.E. Whether you place it before or after *Serek Ha-Yaḥad*, that is another question.

MOSHE BERNSTEIN (*Yeshiva University, New York*): In the text that you quoted from 4Q423 fig. 5 some of the language strikes me as deriving from Noah material in Genesis. Noah himself is called an *'ish 'adamah*. I don't know if anybody else is in the Bible, but Noah certainly is. And, then the instruction to this *'ish 'adamah* reminds me of God's promise to Noah after the Flood of Gen 8:22. I see *zera*, seed, in your reconstruction, as well as ingathering, and it just looks a little like that complex of material. I wonder whether it is merely stylistic imitation, or do you think a person is being addressed here? Is the *'ish 'adamah* the reader? Or is it possibly talking about some ancient figure?

ELGVIN: I think the person addressed in our writings is the enlightened member of the Qumran community. There is interweaving with the topics from the Book of Genesis, especially from the first three chapters. I think Noah is used here as one kind of prototype for the instruction. Thank you for the reference.

LAWRENCE SCHIFFMAN (*New York University, New York*): As to the translation of *raz nihyeh* as "the mystery of being," in my work on 1Q27 and the 4Q mysteries texts, I have come to feel that it is the *raz* which is coming into being, rather than "the secret of being."

In modern times, certainly in this country, when you talk about "the secret of being," "being" itself becomes a kind of religious value with certain Eastern overtones. I think that unless you mean that, I would avoid it. Whether you accept my view that it's the secret which comes into being is another matter. Certainly "secret of being" comes off, at least in American English, as having certain connotations that I don't think you want.

The second comment is more general. We now have recovered – I think Wacholder is right when he says this in his introduction – a literature that we didn't know existed. Most of us in this room until very recently had no understanding, even from the few little bits that we have seen, of what the wisdom literature of the Qumran corpus was, be it sectarian or be it presectarian, or both. There is a whole new world that we're starting to learn about; how that world connects up with what we knew about before, I don't know. I would caution against deriving general conclusions when we've got to evaluate this new world in a wider context. These wisdom texts are really substantial, and they fall into both the real sectarian group of texts and also apparently into the nonsectarian. So, I think that we've got a long way to go before we ought to guess about what they mean.

The final thing is a question. Do you have that strange word *molade/moladim* in your text or not, for "creatures" or whatever it means?

ELGVIN: Yes, Sap. Work A contains the phrase *beth moladim*.

SCHIFFMAN: How do you interpret that?

ELGVIN: It seems to be "those who are born," but I am not sure.

SCHIFFMAN: Time of birth? Is that a possibility? It occurred to me because I do know one place in Genesis where Pharoah had his "birthday," which is understood by some to mean "the day of his conception." Some of the sources refer to it as *bate valdah*. So it occurred to me that maybe it does mean that:

ELGVIN: I think *beth moladim* might be a designation for the community in some sense or another. I thank you for your suggestions.

MATTHIAS KLINGHARDT (*Universität Augsburg, Augsburg, Germany*): You distinguish in your handout between nonsectarian and sectarian texts. You refer to 4Q381 as a nonsectarian psalm and mention the *Hodayot* and the *Serek* as sectarian texts. Can you tell me the criteria for these distinctions, please?

ELGVIN: Some of my categorizations might be somewhat arbitrary. I need to work more with that. But the main criteria were the Qumran morphology and orthography as well as sectarian concepts. It is often difficult to discern clearly which texts are sectarian and which are not.

Methods for Determining Relationships between Manuscripts, with Special Reference to the Psalms Scrolls

PETER W. FLINT*

Department of Theology
University of Notre Dame
Notre Dame, Indiana 46556

INTRODUCTION

This paper is directed towards those of us who deal with more than one exemplar of a book from Qumran, whether Biblical or non-Biblical. When working with several manuscripts or copies of a work, it is important to determine the relationships between them. In order to attain this goal, one needs to consider the similarities and differences between the documents involved. For example, if all copies of a particular Biblical book found at Qumran are very similar to the Masoretic Text ($\mathfrak{M}$), one could plausibly surmise that it existed there only in a proto-Masoretic form. If very similar forms of the work are also evident in Versions such as the Septuagint ($\mathfrak{G}$), the Old Latin (La), the Aramaic Targums ($\mathfrak{T}$), the Syriac ($\mathfrak{S}$), and the Vulgate ($\mathfrak{V}$), it is reasonable to propose that there was only one basic form of this book in antiquity. However, if substantial differences exist between manuscripts of the same Book at Qumran, it would be reasonable to think in terms of different editions, expansions, or later corrections. If similar textual diversity is also evident in the Versions, the notion of different editions or groupings of texts is lent further impetus.[1]

PURPOSE AND BACKGROUND

In order to understand the relationships between manuscripts, it is necessary for scholars working with different exemplars of a book to focus on the

---

* *Present address*: Department of Biblical Studies, Southwestern College, 2625 E. Cactus Road, Phoenix, AZ 85032. All document extracts in this article are reproduced from the author's original paper. See note 5.
[1] The theory of text-types or textual families arises precisely from the fact that particular groups of texts share specific readings or arrangements in opposition to other groups of texts.

variants or differences between them. In this paper, I offer a methodology for identifying, collating and categorizing such variants, with the object of employing them to determine several kinds of relationship between the manuscripts concerned. These procedures have been developed in the course of research on the largest group of documents from the Judaean Desert, namely the Psalms scrolls. Although many of these are very fragmentary, several are rather substantial, the best known being 11QPsalms[a]. The large number of manuscripts involved renders it imperative to establish a methodology that enables one to control and manipulate the hundreds of variants that arise, rather than becoming overwhelmed by such a vast array of data.

In order to situate this paper in a wider context, the pertinent details of my research on the Psalms scrolls are provided. First of all, the systematic collation and analysis of variant readings has arisen from two enterprises: my dissertation on the Dead Sea Psalms Scrolls and the Book of Psalms,[2] and my work on the critical edition of twenty-one of the Psalms manuscripts.[3] Secondly, the techniques for evaluating variant readings have been developed over the past five years in my capacity as Assistant to Professor Eugene Ulrich, Chief Editor of the Biblical Scrolls from Cave 4.[4] Finally, it will soon become apparent that the proposed methodology makes extensive use of the computer; this is closely connected to our work at Notre Dame in preparing and formatting camera-ready editions of the scrolls for the series *Discoveries in the Judaean Desert*.[5]

TWO TYPES OF DOCUMENT

In order to work effectively with large numbers of variants, two types of document need to be created by the researcher: the Permanent Record and the Working Document.

a) *The Permanent Record.* The function of this document is to preserve in-

---

[2] PETER W. FLINT, "The Dead Sea Psalms Scrolls and the Book of Psalms." Ph.D. Dissertation, University of Notre Dame (1993). Director: Eugene Ulrich. Forthcoming in the series *Studies on the Texts of the Desert of Judah* (Leiden: Brill).

[3] P. W. SKEHAN, E. ULRICH & P. W. FLINT, *Qumran Cave IV:* The Psalms Manuscripts from Qumran Cave 4 (DJD series; Oxford University Press, forthcoming).

[4] I am grateful to Dr. Ulrich, who has taught me so much regarding precise and careful methodology.

[5] A brief comment is appropriate on the approach to computer technology that has been adopted in the present paper. While many scholars are impressed with the results of some computer-related studies, they often feel unable to utilize such methods owing to the degree of complexity that characterizes many such projects. Although computer work features prominently in this study, the level of sophistication is not particularly high. A practical approach has been adopted, which entails methods that can be mastered in a few hours by anyone with a working knowledge of computers and equipped with the appropriate software. The original paper was prepared on a Macintosh SE, using MicroSoft 5.1 and three fonts (Times, Hebraica, Graeca).

formation that will need to be checked or reused in the future. Once it has been entered into the computer, the information contained in the Permanent Record is no longer needed for the immediate research at hand. However, it will later become necessary to consult this document, in order to establish how certain readings were arrived at, and to confirm that errors have not been made. Without such Permanent Records (there can be several), one often ends up repeating tasks that were done months before.

b) *The Working Document.* It is important for the researcher to have only one Working Document at all times. The objective is to avoid two pitfalls: duplication of effort and the confusion that arises when multiple copies of a document are being used. Consequently, the temptation must be resisted to use several working documents as well as scattered notes at the same time. We all know just how easy it is to end up wasting many valuable hours in trying to sort out notes, references, and scribblings written on diverse pages, envelopes, and scraps of paper. This problem is largely solved when the researcher firmly resolves to include all relevant data on the Working Document. As more information is gathered, successive versions of the Working Document will need to be made; this is accomplished by transferring all current data to the new Working Document, thus rendering previous versions obsolete.

NINE PRINCIPLES OR STEPS FOR DETERMINING RELATIONSHIPS

Step 1. Identify the Relevant Manuscripts

In order to determine the relationships between manuscripts in a comprehensive manner, broadness of vision is required. By this I mean that "unconventional" scrolls as well as "conventional" ones must be taken into account. For instance, most of the Psalms scrolls preserve only compositions that are found in the Masoretic Text, but some of the manuscripts also contain (so-called) "Apocryphal" Psalms. Some scholars who define the Book of Psalms strictly in Masoretic terms would not recognize the second category as constituting true Psalms scrolls, and thus might exclude readings from this group of manuscripts when collating variants or conducting other research. However, this outlook is a retrojection from the post-Biblical era, and does not accord with the evidence from the Qumran period. A comprehensive treatment of the Psalms scrolls needs to take into account all documents that include Psalms from the received Psalter (whether found alone or together with other compositions), as well as *pesharim* and other works that quote specific Psalms.

The principle of inclusiveness extends to the collation of variants for the Psalms and all other books, whether Biblical or non-Biblical. This means that every scroll from the Judaean desert that contains the work in question (or parts of it) will have to be taken into account. In the case of Psalms, most of the relevant manuscripts were found at Qumran; two more were discovered at Masada, and parts of a third at Naḥal Ḥever and Wadi Seiyal. In the collations that will be presented and discussed, Psalms readings from all of these sites have been included. The full listing of Psalms scrolls or scrolls containing Psalms falls into the three groups shown below.

PSALMS SCROLLS FROM THE JUDAEAN DESERT

a) *Manuscripts in which only Biblical Psalms are preserved:*[6]

(1) 1QPs^a (1Q10)	(13) 4QPs^j (4Q91)	(25) 4QPs89 (4Q236)
(2) 1QPs^b (1Q11)	(14) 4QPs^k (4Q92)	(26) 5QPs (5Q5)
(3) 1QPs^c (1Q12)	(15) 4QPs^l (4Q93)	(27) pap6QPs (pap6Q5)
(4) 2QPs (2Q14)	(16) 4QPs^m (4Q94)	(28) 8QPs (8Q2)
(5) 3QPs (3Q2)	(17) 4QPs^n (4Q95)	(29) 11QPs^c (11Q7)
(6) 4QPs^a (4Q83)	(18) 4QPs^o (4Q96)	(30) 11QPs^d (11Q8)
(7) 4QPs^b (4Q84)	(19) 4QPs^p (4Q97)	(31) 11QPs^e (11Q9)
(8) 4QPs^c (4Q85)	(20) 4QPs^q (4Q98)	(32a) 5/6ḤevPs
(9) 4QPs^d (4Q86)	(21) 4QPs^r (4Q98a)	(32b) Wadi Seiyal 4
(10) 4QPs^e (4Q87)	(22) 4QPs^s (4Q98b)	(33) MasPs^a (M1039–160)
(11) 4QPs^g (4Q89)	(23) 4QPs frg. 1 (4Q98c)	(34) MasPs^b (M1103–1742)
(12) 4QPs^h (4Q90)	(24) 4QPs frg. 2 (4Q98d)	

b) *Manuscripts which contain Biblical Psalms and other compositions*

(35) 4QPs^f (4Q88)
(36) 4QPs122 (4Q522)
(37) 11QPs^a (11Q5)
(38) 11QPs^b (11Q6)
(39) 11QPsAp^a (11Q11)

c) *Manuscripts which quote or allude to specific passages from the Psalms*

(40) 1QpPs (1Q16)
(41) 4QpPs^a (4Q171)
(42) 4QpPs^b (4Q173)
(43) 4QFlor (4Q174)
(44) 4QTanh (4Q176)
(45) 4QCatena (4Q177)
(46) 11QMelch (11Q13)

There are thus thirty-nine manuscripts that may be termed Psalms scrolls, together with seven more that quote or allude to specific passages, which gives a total of forty-six documents.

[6] The sigla "32a" and "32b" indicate that different parts of one manuscript were found at two locations, Naḥal Ḥever and Wadi Seiyal.

Step 2. Collect and Assemble the Relevant Texts

Collecting all the relevant texts is often a formidable task and should not be underestimated. Sometimes, the researcher is fortunate enough to find all of these documents in the form of final editions, or at least in preliminary editions. Of course, this does not mean that all the pertinent readings are accurate; many of us have had the experience of trying to decide between conflicting readings of the same text in different printed editions. Sometimes no edition exists for a particular work, which means that the researcher must then work with photographs or consult the scrolls themselves, most of which are housed in the Rockefeller Museum in Jerusalem.[7] Finally, it may be necessary to correspond with the editors of some of the relevant manuscripts in order to determine certain readings or variants.[8]

Step 3. Collate all Variant Readings against a Standard Text (Permanent Record I)

As far as is possible, the initial collation must be done against a standard or complete text. In the case of Biblical scrolls, this complete text is the Masoretic Text ($\mathfrak{M}$). However, an important distinction made by Eugene Ulrich should be emphasized: $\mathfrak{M}$ is not an *ideal* standard against which other texts are judged to be correct or incorrect, but rather a *practical* or *working* standard, since it is the only complete text of the Hebrew Bible that has survived. In the case of non-Biblical manuscripts, collations should also be done against a complete text if at all possible, even if this text exists only in another language.[9] The document that results from this initial collation is termed *Permanent Record I*, which contains the differences between the Standard Text and the manuscripts being assessed.[10]

---

[7] With respect to the Cave 4 Psalms scrolls, Dr. Ulrich and I carry out most of our work during the academic year using photographs and the preliminary edition of the late Patrick W. Skehan. Since 1989 we have spent part of two summers at the Rockefeller in order to verify readings and check leather questions, and expect to make a final visit in the summer of 1994.

[8] In connection with certain Psalms scrolls, I have corresponded with several editors, all of whom have been most cordial and helpful. They are Prof. F. García Martinez (concerning some of the Cave 11 manuscripts) and Prof. S. Talmon (the Masada Psalms scrolls).

[9] Two examples are the Ethiopic versions of Enoch and Jubilees.

[10] This Record typically consists of several pages containing the transcriptions of the manuscripts involved, with all variant readings against the Standard Text being highlighted in a distinctive color to make them easily recognizable.

Step 4. Enter the Variants for Each Manuscript and Print the New Working Document

The variants identified in Step 3 are now entered from *Permanent Record I* onto the computer. It is important that only one large document be created, with all variant readings appearing in one place. Therefore, if one is working with several texts, the groups of variants involved are brought together in a single consolidated list. This inclusive listing is termed the *Working Document*, which is then printed out. A short extract from such a document appears below, containing the collation of part of 4QPs^e (frg. 26 cols. i and ii) against the Masoretic Text:

Frg. 26, col. i

Psalm 125:2	סביב לעמו 4QPs^e] לע[מ]ו סביב tr 𝔐
Psalm 125:3	ידם 4QPs^e*] ידים 4QPs^e corr] ידיהם 𝔐
Psalm 125:4	בלב 4QPs^e] בלבותם 𝔐
Psalm 125:5	עקלק– 4QPs^e*] והמטים עקלק– 4QPs^e corr 𝔐
Psalm 125:5	עקלקולים 4QPs^e*] עקלקולתים(?) 4QPs^e corr; עקלקלותם 𝔐
Psalm 126:1	בשוב 4QPs^e*] שיר המעלות pr 4QPs^e corr 𝔐
Psalm 126:1	שבות 4QPs^e 𝔐^mss] שיבת 𝔐; שבית 𝔐^ms
Psalm 126:2	בגויים 4QPs^e] בגוים 𝔐 [ORTH]
Psalm 126:2	הגדיל 4QPs^e*] יהוה + 4QPs^e corr 𝔐
Psalm 126:4	שבה 4QPs^e] שובה 𝔐 [VAR. or ORTH?]

Frg. 26, col. ii

| Psalm 130:1 | ממ[עמקים] 4QPs^e*] שיר המ[ע(ו)]ל[ו]ת pr 4QPs^e corr 𝔐 |
| Psalm 130:6 | כש[ומרים] 4QPs^e] שמרים 𝔐 |

Step 5. Collate Variants from Other Scrolls and the Versions (Permanent Record II)

Using the Working Document that was obtained in Step 4, readings from other manuscripts and versions are added to the collation, in the following order: 𝔔 (other Psalms scrolls), 𝔊 (Septuagint), La (Old Latin), 𝔗 (Aramaic), 𝔖 (Syriac), and 𝔙 (Vulgate). As many scholars are all too aware, working out such collations is necessary, but also tedious and time-consuming if a large number of manuscripts is involved. The resultant document is termed *Permanent Record II*.[11]

[11] In appearance this Record would contain the collations from the Working Document together with hand-written entries representing readings from various Psalms scrolls and the Versions.

Step 6. Enter the New Collations and Print the New Working Document

When the entries from Step 5 are entered onto the computer and printed out, a new *Working Document* emerges, since the earlier one from Step 4 has been superseded and no longer exists. The collation that was given in Step 4 has now been transformed as follows (4QPs[e], frg. 26, cols. i and ii):

Frg. 26, col. i

Psalm 125:2	סביב לעמו 4QPs[e]] לע[מ]ו סביב tr 𝔐 𝔊 La 𝔗 𝔖 𝔙 Hier —11QPs[a]
Psalm 125:3	ידם 4QPs[e]*] ידים 4QPs[e corr] ידיהם 𝔐 𝔊 La 𝔗 𝔖 𝔙 Hier —11QPs[a]
Psalm 125:4	בלב 4QPs[e] 11QPs[a] 𝔊(τῇ καρδίᾳ)] לבותם 𝔐 𝔗 𝔖
Psalm 125:5	והמטים עקלק– 4QPs[e]* 11QPs[a]] עקלק– 4QPs[e corr] 𝔐 𝔊 La 𝔗 𝔖 𝔙 Hier
Psalm 125:5	עקלקולים 4QPs[e]*] (?)עקלקולתים 4QPs[e corr]; עקלקלות 11QPs[a]; עקלקלותם 𝔐 𝔊 La 𝔗 𝔖 𝔙 Hier
Psalm 125:5	את כל פועלי 11QPs[a]] את פ(ו)עלי 4QPs[e] 𝔐 𝔊
Psalm 126:1	בשוב 4QPs[e]*] שיר המעלות pr 4QPs[e corr] 11QPs[a] 𝔐 𝔊
Psalm 126:1	שבות 4QPs[e] 𝔐[mss] 𝔊] שיבת 𝔐; שבית 𝔐[ms] La 𝔗 𝔖 𝔙 Hier —11QPs[a]
Psalm 126:1	כחלמים 4QPs[e] 𝔐] כחלומים 11QPs[a] [VAR. or ORTH?]
Psalm 126:2	בגויים 4QPs[e] 11QPs[a]] בגוים 𝔐 [ORTH]
Psalm 126:2	הגדיל 4QPs[e]*] יהוה + 4QPs[e corr] 11QPs[a](?) 𝔐 𝔊(?)
Psalm 126:4	שבה 4QPs[e]] שובה 𝔐 𝔊 La 𝔗 𝔖 𝔙 Hier [VAR. or ORTH?]

Frg. 26, col. ii

Psalm 130:1	ממ[עמקים] 4QPs[e]*] שיר המ[ע](ו)ל[ות] pr 4QPs[e corr] 11QPs[a] 𝔐
Psalm 130:6	כש[ומרים] 4QPs[e]] שמרים 𝔐 𝔊 La 𝔗 𝔖 𝔙 Hier; מש(ו)מרים= 𝔊 —11QPs[a]

It is evident from the above collation that the Working Document has been expanded to contain readings from other Qumran scrolls and from the Versions.

Step 7. Enter Notes, Comments and Queries onto the Computer and Print

In the course of research, all scholars write down meanings, roots, notes, and queries, which serve as reference tools or supplementary comments to the documents they are working with. In Step 7, all such notes and comments are to be entered into the electronic version of the *Working Document*. There are two reasons for this strategy. First, it is important to avoid supplementary documents and messy notes as far as possible, since these only cause confusion when one is working with many texts and processing a large amount of data. Secondly, the Working Document is now becoming a resource file, whose usefulness is enhanced by the addition of notes and comments. The significance of a resource file and the purposes it serves will be explored in Steps 8 and 9 below. The expanded Working Document now appears as follows (4QPs^e, frg. 26, cols. i and ii):

Frg. 26, col. i

125:2 (Line 1) לע[מ]ו סביב 4QPs^e] לעמו סביב tr 𝔐 𝔊 La 𝕮 𝕾 𝔙 Hier —11QPs^a

125:3 (Line 3) ידם 4QPs^{e*}] ידים 4QPs$^{e\,corr}$ (= יָדִים or יָדַיִם [?], cf. 125:5); ידיהם 𝔐 𝔊 La 𝕮 𝕾 𝔙 Hier —11QPs^a

125:4 (Line 4) בלב 4QPs^e 11QPs^a 𝔊(τῇ καρδίᾳ) pure in heart [𝔊La Sanders]] בלבותם 𝔐 𝕮 𝕾

125:5 (Line 4) עקלק– 4QPs^{e*} 11QPs^a] –והמטים עקלק 4QPs$^{e\,corr}$ 𝔐 𝔊 La 𝕮 𝕾 𝔙 Hier

125:5 (Line 4) עקלקולים 4QPs^{e*}] עקלקולתים(?) 4QPs$^{e\,corr}$; עקלקלות 11QPs^a; עקלקלותם 𝔐 𝔊(εἰς τὰς στραγγαλιὰς) [Also σ′ et al. Sanders; > suffix 𝔊 P R 𝔙 Sanders; 𝔊 La 𝔙 Skehan; cf. Jdg 5:6. Maybe עקלקלולים, with ה inserted above ם]

125:5 (Line 4) את פ(ו)עלי 4QPs^e 𝔐 𝔊(μετὰ τῶν ἐργαζομέων) La 𝕮 𝕾 𝔙 Hier] את כל פועלי 11QPs^a

126:1 (Line 5) בשוב 4QPs^{e*}] שיר המעלות pr 4QPs$^{e\,corr}$ 11QPs^a 𝔐 𝔊

126:1 (Line 5) שבות captivity (√ שבה) 4QPs^e 𝔐^{mss} 𝔊(αἰχμαλωσίαν)] שיבת (√ שוב return [or √ ישב reside]) 𝔐; שבית captivity (√ שבה) 𝔐^{ms} La 𝕾 𝕮 𝔙 Hier —11QPs^a [but שבית = שבות captivity!]

126:1 (Line 6) כחלמים 4QPs^e 𝔐] כחלומים 11QPs^a [VAR. or ORTH?]

126:2 (Line 7) בגויים 4QPs^e 11QPs^a] בגוים 𝔐 [ORTH]

126:2 (Line 7) הגדיל 4QPs^{e*}] יהוה + 4QPs$^{e\,corr}$ 11QPs^a(check) 𝔐 𝔊(check)

126:4 (Line 8) שבה 4QPs^e] שובה 𝔐 𝔊 La 𝕮 𝕾 𝔙 Hier [VAR. or ORTH?]

Frg. 26, col. ii

130:1 (Line 2–3) ממ[ע]מקים] 4QPs^{e*}] pr [שיר המ(ע)(ו)ל]ות 4QPs$^{e\,corr}$ [vid] (עול[) 11QPs^{a}𝔐

130:6 (Line 7) כש[ו]מרים] 4QPs^e] שמרים 𝔐 𝔊 La 𝕮 𝕾 𝔙 Hier; מ(ו)ש מרים = 𝔊 —11QPs^a

It should be obvious by now that, since only one Working Document can exist at all times, this expanded document supersedes and replaces the previous one illustrated in Step 6. This new Working Document is not intended to be in finished form, since it contains all manner of notes, queries, meanings, roots and comments.

Step 8. Regard the Working Document as a Resource File or Data Bank, rather than as a Collection of Variants

The expanded collations arrived at in Step 7 are but a small sampling of the complete variants for the 46 manuscripts that were specified in Step 1; the full document comes to no less than 44 pages! A tremendous amount of time and labor has obviously been expended on this assembling of the primary data; however, the question must be posed whether the results warrant all the effort involved. It will be demonstrated in Step 9 that the information collected in the Working Document can be profitably used for several purposes. The value of the notes, comments, and queries added in Step 7 now becomes apparent, because they help to transform a long list of variant readings into a resource file or data bank.

Step 9. Put the Working Document or Resource File to Many Uses

The Working Document—which may be titled *Variants by Manuscript*—contains a vast array of information that can be used to address specific issues in relation to the Psalter in general and to the Psalms scrolls in particular. This Document as a whole, or categories of data that may be extrapolated from it, provides the primary data for several research topics. Details of six such topics or projects are given below:

a) *The Cave 4 Psalms Edition.* In keeping with the principle of having only one Working Document at all times, the variant readings to be listed in the DJD Edition of the Cave 4 Psalms scrolls will be excerpted from the full list of *Variants by Manuscript*. However, these collations will not appear exactly in the form shown in Step 7 for three reasons: Professor Ulrich and I are in the process of checking and refining several of the readings; supplementary notes and other extraneous matter will need to be removed; and the material must be reformatted in conformity with the DJD style.

b) *Orthography of the Psalms Scrolls.* The orthographic character of manuscripts is of interest to several scholars, especially those who subscribe to Emanuel Tov's theory of "Qumran orthography."[12] From the Working Document, a comprehensive *Orthography List* has been compiled, thus facilitating an

[12] E. Tov, "Hebrew Biblical Manuscripts from the Judaean Desert: Their Contribution to Textual Criticism," *Journal of Jewish Studies* 38/1 (1988) 5–37, esp. 23–25.

overview of the orthographic character of the 39 Psalms manuscripts specified in Step 1. This list will provide the primary data for an investigation or assessment of the orthography of the Psalms scrolls at Qumran. In the sample from 4QPsᵉ that has been used in this paper[13] to illustrate successive versions of the Working Document, three possible orthographic variants are evident:

Frg. 26, col. i

Psalm 126:1	כחלמים 4QPsᵉ 𝔐] כחלומים 11QPsᵃ [VAR. or ORTH?]
Psalm 126:2	בגויים 4QPsᵉ 11QPsᵃ] בגוים 𝔐 [ORTH]
Psalm 126:4	שבה 4QPsᵉ] שובה 𝔐 [VAR. or ORTH?]

c) *Textual Affiliations among the Psalms Scrolls.* In comparison to 𝔐, several of the Psalms scrolls contain additional compositions or radical differences in arrangement of material, or both of these major variations (which I term "macro-variants"). From the Working Document, a complete listing of these variants has been extracted under the heading *Macro-Variant List*. This information features prominently in a paper and forthcoming article on Textual Affiliations or Groupings among the Psalms Scrolls.[14] Some examples of these large-scale variants are as follows:

Psalm

145:1	pr Catena 11QPsᵃ] pr Ps 144 𝔐 𝔊[143]
146:1	pr Ps 105 11QPsᵃ 4QPsᵉ] pr Ps 145 𝔐 𝔊[144]
146:1	pr Ps 105 [reconstructed] 4QPsᵉ 11QPsᵃ] pr Ps 145 𝔐 𝔊[144]
147:1	pr Ps 106 or Ps 134 4QPsᵈ] pr Ps 104 11QPsᵃ 4QPsᵉ [reconstructed]; pr Ps 146 𝔐 𝔊[145]
147:1	pr Ps 104 [reconstructed] 4QPsᵉ 11QPsᵃ] pr Ps 106 or Ps 134 4QPsᵈ; pr Ps 146 𝔐 𝔊[145]
148:1	pr Ps 146 11QPsᵃ] pr Ps 147 𝔐 𝔊[146–147]
149:1	pr Ps 143 11QPsᵃ] pr Ps 148 𝔐 𝔊
150:6ᶠⁱⁿ	+ several compositions 11QPsᵃ] end of Psalter 𝔐 MasPsᵇ; + Psalm 151 𝔊
Ps 151A	pr Ps 134 11QPsᵃ] pr Ps 150 𝔊; > 𝔐
Catena	pr Ps 136 11QPsᵃ] pr Ps 117 4QPsᵇ[reconstructed] 𝔐 𝔊[116]; sequence unclear 11QPsᵇ
Apos. Zion	pr Ps 109 4QPsᶠ] pr Sir 51:1-23[13-30] 11QPsᵃ; > 𝔐 𝔊

[13] So far, the sample collations have all been for frg. 26 (cols. i and ii) of this manuscript.
[14] P. W. FLINT, "The Psalms Scrolls from the Judaean Desert: Relationships and Textual Affiliations," presented at the Congress of the International Organization for Qumran Studies (IOQS) held at the Sorbonne (Paris), 19 July 1992. Publication will be in the *Proceedings* of the Congress, GEORGE BROOKE, Ed. (STDJ series; Leiden: Brill, forthcoming 1994).

d) *The Psalms Scrolls and the Septuagint.* The scrolls sometimes contain Hebrew words, phrases or lines that are supported by the Septuagint (in their Greek equivalent) but not by the Masoretic Psalter. A complete listing of readings shared by specific manuscripts and the Septuagint against 𝔐 has been extracted from the Working Document, under the heading *Readings Common to the Scrolls and the LXX.* This information formed the basis of a paper and forthcoming publication,[15] which explore the implications of the Psalms scrolls and these shared variants for the *Vorlage* of the Old Greek of the Psalter. Some extracts from this list of common readings are as follows:

MT	LXX	
		(i) *Substitutions of verbal or nominal root*
49:13	48:13	יבין 4QPs^c 𝔊(συνῆκεν; cf. v 21)] ילין 𝔐
		(ii) *Addition of superscripts or Halleluyahs*
104:1	103:1	לדויד 11QPs^a 4QPs^e(?) 𝔊(τῷ Δαυιδ pr [L^{pau} add.] ψαλμός L$^{a'}$ [nonHe])] > 4QPs^d 𝔐
		(iii) *Addition of phrases or strophes*
145:13	144:13	נאמן אלוהים בדבריו וחסיד בכול מעשיו 11QPs^a 𝔐^{ms}(Ken #142) 𝔊(πιστὸς κύριος ἐν [+ πᾶσιν = בכול* 𝔊$^{RL''}$ $^{1219s'}$] τοῖς λόγοις αὐτοῦ καὶ ὅσιος ἐν πᾶσι τοῖς ἔργοις αὐτοῦ)] > 𝔐 α' θ' σ' ε' ς' Ἑβρ
		(iv) *Translation on the basis of onomatopoeia*
88:16	87:16	א[פ]ורה 4QPs^s 𝔊(ἐξηπορήθην); cf. Isa 24:19 𝔐 𝔊] אפונה 𝔐

e) *Corrections in the Psalms Scrolls.* Corrections made in manuscripts should always be taken into account by the researcher. This is because corrected readings can differ in significance: whereas some merely constitute the putting right of minor errors, others are due to the deliberate alteration of an earlier or original text. From the Working Document, all corrected readings found in the Psalms scrolls have been extrapolated to form the *Correction List.* An extract from this list, which is given below, contains the relevant readings from the sample collation (4QPs^c frg. 26, cols. i–ii) that has featured repeatedly in this paper. In this case the corrected readings are particularly interesting, since they seem to indicate that 4QPs^c was systematically corrected towards the proto-Masoretic Text.[16]

---

[15] P. W. FLINT, "The Psalms Scrolls from the Judaean Desert and the Septuagint Psalter," presented at the VIII Congress of the International Organization of Septuagint and Cognate studies (IOSCS) held at the Sorbonne (Paris), 18 July 1992. The paper will be published in the *Proceedings* of the Congress, L. GREENSPOON & O. MUNNICH, Eds. (Septuagint and Cognate Studies series; Atlanta: Scholars Press, forthcoming 1994).

[16] It may be argued that several of the collations point to a systematic correction towards 11QPs^a as much as to the proto-MT. However, the second collation in particular shows that 4QPs^c has been corrected to conform with the proto-MT (and not 11QPs^a) by the insertion of והמטים.

Frg. 26, col. i

Psalm 125:3 ידם 4QPs^{e*}] ידים 4QPs^{e corr}; ידיהם 𝔐 𝔊 La 𝕮 𝕾 𝕯 Hier —11QPs^a

Psalm 125:5 עקלק– 4QPs^{e*} 11QPs^a] והמטים עקלק– 4QPs^{e corr} 𝔐 𝔊 La 𝕮 𝕾 𝕯 Hier

Psalm 125:5 עקלקולים 4QPs^{e*}] עקלקולתים(?) 4QPs^{e corr}; עקלקולות 11QPs^a; עקלקלותם 𝔐 𝔊 La 𝕮 𝕾 𝕯 Hier

Psalm 126:1 בשוב 4QPs^{e*}] pr שיר המעלות 4QPs^{e corr} 11QPs^a 𝔐 𝔊

Psalm 126:2 הגדיל 4QPs^{e*}] + יהוה 4QPs^{e corr} 11QPs^a (?) 𝔐 𝔊(?)

Frg. 26, col. ii

Psalm 130:1 ממ[עמקים] 4QPs^{e*}] pr [שיר] המ[ע(ו)ל]ות 4QPs^{e corr} 11QPs^a 𝔐

f) *A Textual Commentary on the Book of Psalms.* When the material in the 44 page Working Document is rearranged, another major document is produced, under the heading *Variants by Chapter and Verse.* This is a powerful resource file, since it provides in Biblical order for Psalms 1 to 150 every variant reading found in the 39 Psalms scrolls, plus the seven manuscripts that quote the Psalms. Not only are all the variants for each Psalm presented in one place, but the accompanying notes and comments help provide the textual data for a commentary on individual Psalms or on the entire Psalter. The sample expanded collation given below lists the complete variants (with notes and comments) for Psalm 125:

125:1 (col. IV/3) שלוא 11QPs^a] לא 𝔐 𝔊

125:2 (col. IV/4) לו 11QPs^a (NB לו in reference to Jerusalem found also in Ps 122:3 [col. III/9])] לה 𝔐 —4QPs^e

125:2 (col. IV/4) יהוה 11QPs^a (haplography?)] ויהוה 𝔐 𝔊 La 𝕮 𝕾 𝕯 Hier —4QPs^e

125:2 (frg. 26 i/1) לע[מ]ו סביב 4QPs^e] סביב לעמו tr 𝔐 𝔊 La 𝕮 𝕾 𝕯 Hier —11QPs^a

125:3 (frg. 26, i/3) ידם 4QPs^{e*}] ידים 4QPs^{e corr} (= יָדִים or יָדִים [?], cf. 125:5); ידיהם 𝔐 𝔊 La 𝕮 𝕾 𝕯 Hier —11QPs^a

125:4 (frg. 26 i/4) בלב 4QPs^e 11QPs^a 𝔊(τῇ καρδίᾳ) pure in heart La] בלבותם 𝔐 𝕮 𝕾

125:4 (col. IV/7) בלב 11QPs^a 4QPs^e 𝔊(τῇ καρδίᾳ, pure in heart) La] בלבותם 𝔐 𝕮 𝕾

125:5 (frg. 26 i/4) עקלק– 4QPs^{e*} 11QPs^a] והמטים עקלק– 4QPs^{e corr} 𝔐 𝔊 La 𝕮 𝕾 𝕯 Hier

125:5 (col. IV/7)   עקלקפ‎ 11QPsᵃ 4QPsᵉ*] pr והמטים‎ 4QPsᵉ corr 𝔐 𝔊 La
                    𝔗 𝔖 𝔙 Hier

125:5 (frg. 26 i/4) עקלקולים‎ 4QPsᵉ*] עקלקולתים‎(?) 4QPsᵉ corr; עקלקולות‎
                    11QPsᵃ; עקלקלותם‎ 𝔐 𝔊 (εἰς τὰς στραγγαλιάς)
                    [Also σ′ et al. Sanders; > suffix 𝔊 P R 𝔙 Sanders;
                    𝔊 La 𝔙 Skehan; cf. Jdg 5:6. Maybe עקלקולים‎, with
                    ת inserted above ם]

125:5 (col. IV/7)   עקלקולות‎ 11QPsᵃ] עקלקולים‎ 4QPsᵉ*; עקלקולתים‎ (?)
                    4QPsᵉ corr; עקלקלותם‎ 𝔐 𝔊 (εἰς τὰς στραγγαλιάς)
                    [Also σ′ et al. Sanders; > suffix 𝔊 P R 𝔙 Sanders;
                    𝔊 La 𝔙 Skehan; cf. Jdg 5:6. Maybe עקלקולים‎, with
                    ת inserted above ם]

125:5 (frg. 26 i/4) עלי‎ 4QPsᵉ(/)את פ(ו)עלי‎) 𝔐 𝔊 (μετὰ τῶν ἐργα-
                    ζομέων) La 𝔗 𝔖 𝔙 Hier] את כל פועלי‎ 11QPsᵃ

125:5 (col. IV/8)   פועלי‎ את כול פועלי‎ 11QPsᵃ] את פעלי‎ (כל >) 4QPsᵉ(/את פועלי‎)
                    𝔐 𝔊 La 𝔗 𝔖 𝔙 Hier

125:5 (col. IV/8)   און‎ 11QPsᵃ 𝔐ᵐˢ(Ken); cf. Ps 141:9b [col. XXIII 5]] האון‎
                    𝔐 et al. hebr.; τὴν ἀνομίαν 𝔊 —4QPsᵉ

CONCLUSION

This paper has presented a comprehensive methodology for investigating
the relationships between manuscripts, with special reference to the Psalms
scrolls. The nine steps that have been outlined, as well as the creation of a
Permanent Record and Working Document, are intended to be practical
strategies for scholars dealing with more than one exemplar of a book from
Qumran, whether Biblical or non-Biblical. Of course, individual researchers
may wish to adapt or modify some of these proposals to their particular requirements; nevertheless, when a systematic approach such as this is adopted,
two benefits will accrue. First, the scholar will avoid confusion and the duplication of effort by exerting control over the primary material – instead of being
overwhelmed by it. Secondly, he or she will be able to use this research as a
Resource File from which several articles, studies, or lectures can emerge – thus
yielding tangible results from an enterprise that is usually time-consuming and
tedious. To borrow an idea from the Business World, where "effective time
management" is encouraged in order to increase productivity, the central
theme of this paper may be termed "effective Scrolls management."

DISCUSSION OF THE PAPER

MOSHE BERNSTEIN (*Yeshiva University, New York*): I am humbled by this, but I have a couple of questions and they're meant to be constructive. Number one, why do you keep the minor Greek versions out until a later stage? They come in with your notes, comments and queries. I would have thought that if you are collecting ancient versions all in one place, it might have been logical to put them in at the earlier stage, where you're entering ancient versions.

Number two: what you have begins to look in a certain way like the apparatus of the Hebrew University Bible Project, let's say the edition of Isaiah that they've been producing, except that you were able to separate out the material by calling your different databanks up. I was wondering if you have a way to elicit specific kinds of exegetical material, things you've marked or noted as exegetical features. Can they be pulled out of this mass of notes?

I would warn you that if you're doing Psalms, you have to be very careful in using the material from the Aramaic Targum, because there isn't any edition which correctly reflects the manuscript tradition of that document.

PETER FLINT (*Southwestern College, Phoenix, Az*): You have raised some important points. With respect to the minor Greek versions, there are some I haven't mentioned. In fact, one could have three or four stages of the working document. The important thing is to retain control of the data. It is accordingly easier to start off with the critical Greek text, the Latin text, one of the Targum manuscripts and in the next round to incorporate variations within these traditions. In today's presentation I have given you just a few steps in this process. Two or three more steps would make no difference methodologically because we end up still with one working document. The important thing is for one to be in control of the data and not to become confused by dealing with too much information at one time.

With respect to extrapolating exegetical interpretations or readings, I'm not sure if I fully understand the question. However, I do believe that the computer may be helpful for gathering such readings. Let me refer you to the Correction List given in Step 9 (part e). Did you notice that the examples listed there all have an asterisk?

Using the computer, one systematically searches for such asterisked readings, and that's how one ends up with a complete collation. In other words, you don't only rely on your own eyes to spot these things. You tag it to a symbol. On the basis of the few corrected readings listed in Step 9, I was able to conclude that 4QPs^c was deliberately corrected towards the proto-Masoretic Text.

With respect to actual exegetical readings, it may be possible to proceed in a similar manner. If there is a clear way of identifying exegetical readings, these could be tagged by a distinctive siglum and then gathered in a separate list.

RAYMOND EDGE (*University of Texas at Austin*): Are you saying that when you get to Working Document one, that you don't make a hard copy? Sometimes if you don't have a hard copy and you start working on your only copy, you can lose it. Are you saying that you did not keep a hard copy at all? Then I have another quick question concerning paleography.

FLINT: You do have a hard or printed copy, but the idea is that it becomes obsolete.

EDGE: You keep one at all times as the stages go through, just from a computer point of view?

FLINT: You have Working Document one, you print it out, and then, when you get to Working Document two and you add material to number one, you don't keep an electronic version anymore. You keep a print-out. The idea is to have a latest working document which supersedes all previous ones. Otherwise, you end up with many manuscripts and two years later you have to go back and spend 3–4 weeks working through them to see if you have lost some information.

EDGE: Is there a way in this particular scheme of things to allow for the difference in how they wrote the name of God? And, do you have a font for that? I know that Emmanuel Tov had to create his own for the 8th volume in DJD.

FLINT: That's a very nice question. The *tetragrammaton* is sometimes written in paleo-Hebrew letters in the manuscripts, and in fact I've been drawing up a *tetragrammaton* list that I didn't put up on the board. It is very interesting that sometimes scribes write the Divine Name in the Aramaic square script, but at other times in ancient Hebrew letters. In one manuscript the paleo-Hebrew *tetragrammaton* has been corrected using square script. The whole notion of the Divine Name at Qumran is a very interesting topic. I refer you to an article by Patrick Skehan, which he wrote shortly before his death for the *Bulletin for the International Organization of Septuagint and Cognak Studies*. The precise reference is: "The Divine Name at Qumran, in the Masada Scroll, and in the Septuagint," *BIOSCS* 13 (1980) 14–44.

EDGE: Will the writing of God's name be part of this particular edition?

FLINT: No. The Psalms edition can only give some of this information, but I have been gathering the data for a later study.

Messiahs in Context:
Method in the Study of Messianism
in the Dead Sea Scrolls

JOHN J. COLLINS

Divinity School
University of Chicago
1025 E. 58th Street
Chicago, Illinois 60637

The study of messianism in the Dead Sea Scrolls has vacillated between two poles. On the one hand, the standard treatments which have dominated the study of the Scrolls for the last forty years have generally assumed a high level of doctrinal consistency, and have tended to fit the various messianic allusions into a coherent system.[1] On the other hand, there has been a growing tendency to accuse such systematic treatments of "harmonization" and to take the individual texts in isolation.[2] It is my contention that the latter tendency has been taken to excess in some recent studies. While real differences between texts must certainly be respected, we must also recognize the signals that link one text with another and so provide a context for interpretation, if we are not to miss the forest for the trees.

At issue in this discussion is the nature of the Qumran corpus. No one, to my knowledge, has ever claimed that everything found at Qumran was produced there, or was a product of the same sect. It has been common, however, to claim that non-sectarian material must be pre-Qumran, and that the community was effectively screened off from outside influence for most of its history. This position is difficult to maintain, in light of the abundance of material from Cave 4. Nonetheless it remains true that there is a core group of interrelated texts, with overlapping terminology and common subject

[1] See, for example, G. VERMES, "The Qumran Messiahs and Messianism," in E. SCHUERER, *The History of the Jewish People in the Age of Jesus Christ* (revised and edited by G. VERMES, F. MILLAR and M. BLACK; Edinburgh: Clark, 1979) 2.550–2.554; S. TALMON, "Waiting for the Messiah – The Conceptual Universe of the Qumran Covenanters," in *The World of Qumran from Within* (Jerusalem: Magnes, 1989) 273–300.
[2] The pioneer in this regard was MORTON SMITH, "What is Implied by the Variety of Messianic Figures?" *Journal of Biblical Literature* 78(1959) 66–72. See recently L. H. SCHIFFMAN, "Messianic Figures and Ideas in the Qumran Scrolls," in *The Messiah. Developments in Earliest Judaism and Christianity* (J. H. CHARLESWORTH, Ed.; Minneapolis: Fortress, 1992) 116–129; M. O. WISE and J. D. TABOR, "The Messiah at Qumran," *Biblical Archeology Review* (Nov./Dec. 1992) 60–65.

matter, which show that the Qumran corpus is not just a random sample of the Jewish literature of the time.[3] This core corpus includes, on any reckoning, the Rule books and the biblical commentaries. In evaluating the Qumran evidence on a particular subject such as messianism, it is important to discriminate between the different kinds of documents involved. Rule books presumably had some authoritative status in the community or communities they represented. We have nothing to indicate the status of fragmentary compositions from Cave 4. Of course the interpretation of fragmentary texts requires great caution, and we should be especially wary of arguments based on the omissions in such texts.

The study of messianism in the Dead Sea Scrolls presents some further problems of its own, most fundamentally in the matter of definition. Here again there has been vacillation between a very loose approach, which includes any kind of eschatological savior figure, and an excessively narrow approach that restricts discussion to actual occurrences of the word מָשִׁיחַ.[4] In modern, and indeed in traditional Jewish and Christian usage, "messiah" is an eschatological term, nearly always referring to the King messiah at the end of days. In the Scrolls, the term can also refer to figures from the past, notably the prophets, and to various eschatological figures, including at least a priest as well as a king, and possibly also a prophet. The term "messiah," then, does not yet have the technical sense it would later acquire. It is of fundamental importance that the figures who are called "messiahs" or "anointed ones" in the Scrolls can also be referred to in other terms. The royal messiah is simply the eschatological king, whether he is called "messiah" or "Branch of David." The priestly messiah, equally, is simply the eschatological High Priest, whether or not he is called "messiah of Aaron" in a specific text.

The role of messianism in the Scrolls must also be kept in perspective. The claim in the recent Eisenman and Wise volume that the Scrolls represent "the messianic movement" is very misleading, if that expression implies that messianism was the *raison d'être* of the movement.[5] There is no mention of messiahs in 4QMMT, and they do not figure among the hidden things revealed to the remnant in the third column of the Damascus Document. They appear in the Rule books by way of allusion; they are not the subjects of doctrinal exposition. Messianic expectation is widely attested in the Scrolls,

[3] For an attempt to distinguish between sectarian and non-sectarian material in the Scrolls, see CAROL A. NEWSOM, "'Sectually Explicit' Literature from Qumran," in *The Hebrew Bible and Its Interpreters* (W. H. PROPP, B. HALPERN, and D. N. FREEDMAN, Eds.; Winona Lake, IN: Eisenbrauns, 1990) 167–187.

[4] See, *e.g.*, J. H. CHARLESWORTH, "From Messianology to Christology: Problems and Prospects," in *The Messiah*, 25.

[5] R. EISENMAN and M. WISE, *The Dead Sea Scrolls Uncovered* (Rockport, MA: Element, 1992) 11.

and is certainly important, but it does not appear to have been a subject of
sectarian controversy, and does not enjoy the kind of centrality that it did in
early Christianity.

THE BRANCH OF DAVID

Many of the methodological issues in the study of messianism in the
Scrolls can be illustrated from the recent controversy over the fragment labeled
4Q285, better, though inaccurately, known as the "Dying Messiah" text. The
controversy has by now been essentially resolved. Initial claims reported in the
media, that this text reported the death of a messianic figure,[6] have been
shown to be unwarranted.[7] What is decisive in this case is not the grammar
or syntax, which can be construed in different ways, but the context. The fragment begins with a reference to "Isaiah the prophet" and line 2 contains the
beginning of Isa 11:1: "there shall come forth a shoot from the stump of Jesse."
The third line reads ". . .]the Branch of David and they will enter into judgement with [. . ." The Branch here is surely the fulfillment of Isaiah's prophecy.
Branch and shoot are closely related images in any case. The passage then continues with the controversial line

וֹהמיתו נשׂיא העדה צמ‍ח דויד[

Even though the mem of צמח is only partially visible, the restoration seems
very probable, so that the Branch of David is further identified with the Prince
of the Congregation. In view of the association with Isaiah 11, where the
shoot of Jesse will strike the earth with the rod of his mouth, and kill the
wicked with the breath of his lips, it seems beyond reasonable doubt that
the Prince/Branch is the subject of the verb to kill, not its object.[8]

Twenty years ago, J. T. Milik identified 4Q285 as a fragment of the War
Rule.[9] The identification is suggested by the reference to killing, and by an

---

[6] *New York Times*, Nov. 8, 1991, *The Times*, Nov. 8, 1991, *The Chicago Tribune*, Nov. 11,
1991 and *The Independent*, Dec. 27, 1991. The claims were attributed to R. Eisenman and M. O.
Wise. Eisenman and Wise are more tentative in their subsequent publication, *The Dead Sea Scrolls
Uncovered*, 24–27, but they still defend their original interpretation as possible.

[7] G. VERMES, "The Oxford Forum for Qumran Research Seminar on the Rule of War from
Cave 4 (4Q285)," *Journal of Jewish Studies* 43(1992)85–90; M. BOCKMUEHL, "A 'Slain Messiah'
in 4Q Serekh Milhamah (4Q285)?" *Tyndale Bulletin* 43(1992) 155–169. The objections of JAMES
D. TABOR, "A Pierced or Piercing Messiah?–The Verdict is Still Out," *Biblical Archeology Review*
(Nov./Dec. 1992) 58–59 are easily refuted by Vermes, *ibid.*, 59.

[8] G. VERMES, "The Oxford Forum," 88–89.

[9] J. T. MILIK, "Milikî-sedeq et Milkî-rešaᶜ dans les écrits juifs et chrétiens," *Journal of Jewish
Studies* 23(1972) 143. M. G. ABEGG has reconstructed the place of this and other fragments at
the end of the War Rule in a paper presented to the Society of Biblical Literature in San Francisco,
November 22, 1992.

apparent reference to "the slain of the Kittim" in line 6. The other fragments on the plate, which come from the same hand and most probably from the same document, make further reference to the Kittim, to the archangel Michael and to the Prince of the Congregation, all of whom are mentioned in the War Rule. The War Rule had a complicated literary history, and it is not yet clear how 4Q285 should be related to the Scroll as found in 1QM.[10] But it is surely clear that the two are related, and that 4Q285 is part of a tradition about the eschatological war. Presumably these fragments belong towards the end of the War, since the figure who is killed is evidently a figure of importance, possibly the king of the Kittim (who is mentioned in 1QM 15:2).[11]

As Vermes has noted, there is a significant parallel to 4Q285 in a fragmentary pesher on Isaiah, 4QpIs[a].[12] The commentaries on Isaiah are characterized by lengthy citations, followed by very short interpretations, many of which refer explicitly to the end of days. 4QpIs[a] is based on Isaiah chapters 10 and 11. There are several parallels to the War Rule. Fragments 2–6, col. 2, line 18 reads "when they return from the wilderness of the p[eopl]es," recalling 1QM 1:3. The following line mentions "the Prince of the Congregation."[13] This passage gives little information about him, except that "afterward he will depart from [them]." Fragment 7, col. 3 line 11 refers to the battle of the Kittim, and there are several other mentions of the Kittim in the context of battle. Fragment 7 goes on to cite Isa 11:1–5. The interpretation is fragmentary. Only two and a half words are preserved on the first line: ‪[דויד עומד באחן‬. The line is plausibly restored to read:

‪פשר הפתגם על צמח] דויד העומד באחרית הימים‬

"The interpretation of the matter concerns the Branch of] David, who will arise at the en[d of days . . ."[14]

Whatever the precise wording, there can be little doubt that the reference is to an eschatological Davidic king. The pesher goes on to speak of a throne of glory and (victory over) Magog and says that his sword will judge the

---

[10] See the fragments from Cave 4, published by M. BAILLET, *Qumrân grotte 4* (Discoveries in the Judean Desert 7; Oxford: Clarendon, 1982) 12–45, which show considerable divergence from 1QM.

[11] G. VERMES, "The Oxford Forum," 89.

[12] *Ibid.*

[13] M. P. HORGAN, *Pesharim. Qumran Interpretations of Biblical Books* (Catholic Biblical Quarterly Monograph Series 8; Washington: Catholic Biblical Association, 1979) 79, restores the line to read ‪השבט הוא] נשיא העדה‬ "the rod is the Prince of the Congregation," in light of CD 7:20, where the prince is identified with the ‪שבט‬ of Num 24:17. The text being interpreted here is Isa 10:24–27, which mentions how the Lord's rod (‪מטה‬) will be over the sea. The word ‪שבט‬ also occurs in the passage with reference to the rod with which Assyria will smite Israel. ‪מטה‬ rather than ‪שבט‬ would seem to be the more apt restoration here.

[14] M. P. HORGAN, *Pesharim*, 80, following the suggestion of J. Strugnell.

peoples. The pesher clearly envisages a role for the Davidic messiah in the final battle against the Kittim.

The controversy over 4Q285 shows clearly the danger of interpreting a fragmentary text in isolation, without due attention to its context. On the other hand, Wise and Eisenman at least deserve credit for recognizing that the figure in question is messianic, although the word משיח does not occur.[15] The Branch of David (צמח דויד, mentioned clearly in the third line of the fragment) cannot be other than an anointed eschatological king, and is in fact explicitly called "the righteous messiah" (משיח הצדק) in 4QpGen (=4QPatriarchal Blessings). In fact, the correlation of various epithets and titles that may be applied to the same figure is an essential step in the interpretation of the Scrolls.

4Q285 invites such correlation, since the Branch of David is also called נשיא העדה, Prince of the Congregation. This title is also used, in a fragmentary context, in 4QpIsᵃ. The messianic connotations of this title are shown in another Qumran document, the Scroll of Blessings, 1QSb. This scroll contains a series of blessings, apparently intended for the messianic age. The first blessing applies to all the faithful; the second to an individual priest (perhaps the messiah of Aaron); the third to "the sons of Zadok, the priests." Finally there is a blessing for "the Prince of the Congregation," that God will raise up for him the kingdom of his people (1QSb 5:21). The blessing that follows is heavily indebted to Isaiah 11:

> . . . to dispense justice with [equity to the oppressed] of the land (Isa 11:4a).
> (May you smite the peoples) with the might of your hand and ravage the earth
> with your sceptre; may you bring death to the ungodly with the breath of your
> lips! (Isa 11:4b) . . . and everlasting might, the spirit of knowledge and of the
> fear of God (Isa 11:2); may righteousness be the girdle (of your loins) and may
> your reins be girded (with faithfulness) (Isa 11:5).

The blessing goes on to compare the Prince to a young bull with horns of iron and hooves of bronze, and (probably) to a lion (cf. Gen 49:9).[16] Also notable is the phrase כיא אל הקימכה לשבט (1QSb 5:27), an allusion to the "sceptre" of Balaam's oracle in Num 24:17.

In view of the clear application of Isaiah 11 to the Prince of the Congregation in 1QSb, and there can be little doubt about the identification with the "Branch of David" in 4Q285 and 4QpIsaᵃ. All three texts have the same scriptural base, and share a common view of a warrior messiah.

---

[15] J. H. CHARLESWORTH, "Sense or Sensationalism? The Dead Sea Scrolls Controversy," *The Christian Century* (January 29, 1992) 97, denies that the text is messianic.

[16] Only the first letter of וריה א, lion, is legible, but the word טרף (prey) occurs on the next line.

Both "Branch of David" and "Prince of the Congregation" appear in a number of other texts.

The "Branch of David" appears in the "Patriarchal Blessings" (4QpGen), in an interpretation of Genesis 49:10, where he is identified as "the righteous messiah." This verse of Genesis is also given a messianic interpretation in the Targumim and in midrashic and Talmudic sources.[17]

The Branch also appears in the Florilegium. There 2Sam 7:14 ("I will be a father to him and he will be a son to me") is interpreted as referring to "the Branch of David" who will arise with the interpreter of the law in Zion at the end of days. This text is further correlated with Amos 9:11 ("I will raise up the tent of David that is fallen"): "the fallen tent of David is he who shall arise to save Israel."[18]

The expression "Prince of the Congregation" has its background in the Priestly writings of the Pentateuch (*e.g.*, Exod 16:22; Num 4:34) where it refers to leaders of the tribes. The use with reference to a future figure, however, is determined by Ezekiel, who uses the term נשיא for the Davidic ruler: "and I the Lord will be their God, and my servant David shall be prince among them" (Ezek 34:24; *cf.* 37:25, and the use of נשיא in Ezek 40–48).[19] In at least some of the major Scrolls, the "congregation" in question has a new reference. It is the congregation of the new covenant in the Damascus Document, and the congregation of the "end of days" in the War Rule and the Messianic Rule (1QSa). In these contexts, the Prince of the Congregation becomes a distinctively sectarian title for the branch of David, or Davidic messiah.

The Prince of the Congregation also appears with messianic overtones in CD 7:19, in an extremely complex passage.[20] The passage begins with the citation and interpretation of Amos 5:26–27, but then introduces Num 24:17: "The star is the Interpreter of the Law who shall come to Damascus; as it is written, A star shall come forth out of Jacob and a sceptre shall rise out of Israel. The sceptre is the Prince of the whole congregation, and when he comes he shall smite all the children of Sheth."

The messianic interpretation of Balaam's oracle is well attested. Perhaps the most famous attestation is in the legend of Akiba's recognition of Bar

---

[17] S. H. LEVEY, *The Messiah: An Aramaic Interpretation. The Messianic Exegesis of the Targum* (Cincinnati: Hebrew Union College, 1974) 7–11. Messianic interpretations are found in Targums Onkelos, Pseudo-Jonathan, and in Genesis Rabbah 98:8. In Sanhedrin 98b שילה (to whom it belongs) is taken as the name of the messiah.

[18] See the discussion of this passage by G. J. BROOKE, *Exegesis at Qumran. 4QFlorilegium in its Jewish Context* (Journal for the Study of the Old Testament Supplement **29**; Sheffield: Journal for the Study of the Old Testament, 1985) 197–205.

[19] H. NIEHR, "נשיא," *Theologisches Wörterbuch zum Altes Testament* **5**(1986) 647–657; M. A. KNIBB, "The Interpretation of Damascus Document VII, 9b–VIII, 2a and XIX, 5b–14," *Revue de Qumran* 57–58(1991) 250.

[20] For a recent discussion see M. A. KNIBB, as cited in the note above.

Kochba.[21] The messianic interpretation of Num 24:17 was also current in Greek-speaking Judaism. The LXX read "man" (ἄνθρωπος) for sceptre, and Philo interprets this "man" as a warrior, who "leading his host to war, will subdue great and populous nations."[22] A similar interpretation appears in Test Judah 24:1–6.[23] There can be little doubt that the Prince who is identified with the sceptre in CD 7 is also a messianic figure. Balaam's oracle is also cited without interpretation in the Testimonia, which is apparently a collection of passages with eschatological significance, and in 1QM 11:6–7, again in an eschatological context.

It is now clear that the Davidic messiah/Branch of David had a role in the traditions about the eschatological war at some stage. The title "Prince of the Congregation" also occurs in 1QM 5:1, where his name is written on his shield as part of the preparation for battle, and Balaam's oracle (Num 24:17–19) is cited without interpretation in 1QM 11:6–7. In view of the clear identification of the Prince with the sceptre in the Damascus Document, and his messianic role in 4Q285, the burden of proof falls on anyone who would claim that the Davidic messiah was absent at any stage of the War Rule tradition.

The appearance of the Branch of David/Prince of the Congregation in the War Rule is of some significance for our understanding of the extent of messianic expectation. In a major survey of Jewish practice and belief between 63 B.C.E. and 66 C.E., E. P. Sanders writes that "What is most striking about the sect's messianic expectation is that there is no Davidic messiah in the *War Rule*, where one would expect him to take the leading role."[24] He goes on to offer explanations for this absence: the ambiguous attitude towards kings in the Hebrew Bible, and the fact that "the stage had become too large for a mere king." Such speculation can now be seen to be needless. The Dead Sea sect did indeed have its own distinctive attitude to messianism, and did indeed look for supernatural deliverance in the final war, but the Davidic king had a well-established place in their expectations.

Thus far we have confined our attention to the titles "Branch of David" and "Prince of the Congregation" which are juxtaposed in 4Q285. What we have found is a network of overlapping references, involving two major rule books, the Damascus Document and the War Rule, several exegetical texts

---

[21] "Rabbi Akiba interpreted, 'A star has come forth out of Jacob' as '[Kosiba] has come forth out of Jacob.' When Rabbi Akiba saw bar [Kosiba] he said: This is the King Messiah. Rabbi Yohanan ben Torta replied: 'Akiba, grass will grow out of your cheek-bones before the son of David comes.'" yTaanith 68d. G. VERMES, *Jesus the Jew: A Historian's Reading of the Gospels* (Philadelphia: Fortress, 1981) 134.

[22] De Praemiis et Poenis, 95. On the LXX see P. VOLZ, *Die Eschatologie der Jüdischen Gemeinde* (Tübingen: Mohr, 1934; reprint, Hildesheim: Olms, 1966) 188.

[23] For further, Christian references see H. W. HOLLANDER and M. DE JONGE, *The Testaments of the Twelve Patriarchs* (SVTP 8; Leiden: Brill, 1985) 228.

[24] E. P. SANDERS, *Judaism. Practice and Belief. 63 BCE–66 CE* (Philadelphia: Trinity, 1992) 296. Compare P. R. DAVIES, "War Rule (1QM)," *Anchor Bible Dictionary* 6.875.

(pesharim on Isaiah and Genesis 49, the Florilegium),[25] and a liturgical collection of benedictions (1QSb). The references are tied to a few biblical texts sometimes linked together, sometimes separately. Chief of these passages are Isaiah 11 and Num 24, and the expression צמח דויד from Jeremiah 23 and 33 all of which occur several times. Genesis 49, 2 Sam 7 and Amos 9 are also interpreted with reference to a Davidic messiah at least once. These passages by no means exhaust the references to the Davidic messiah in the Scrolls. We should also take into account messianic references in the Community Rule and the so-called Messianic Rule, and some other texts such as 4Q246 (the "Son of God" text). My concern for the moment, however, is with the network of overlapping references, and the light they shed on the study of the Scrolls. Specifically, I would like to focus on two questions. The first concerns the consistency of exegetical traditions relating to the Davidic messiah, and the second concerns the distinctiveness of messianism in the Scrolls.

EXEGETICAL TRADITIONS

Joseph Fitzmyer concludes his thorough study of biblical quotations in the Scrolls with the declaration that "There is no evidence at Qumran of a systematic, uniform exegesis of the Old Testament. The same text was not always given the same interpretation (see the variants in CD 7 and 19 and compare the use of Nm 24:17 and Am 9:11 in different contexts)."[26] That there is some variation is certainly true. Amos 9:11 provides a clear example that bears on our subject. In the Florilegium, the booth of David which is fallen is equated with the Branch which will arise to save Israel at the end of days. In CD 7:15–16, however, the booth is identified with the books of the Torah.[27] Another pertinent example is the מחוקק (staff) of Num 21:18, which is variously interpreted as the Interpreter of the Law (CD 6:7) and as "the covenant of the kingdom" (4Q252, Pesher on Genesis). We have fragments of two distinct commentaries on Isaiah.

To say that there was variation, however, is not to deny that there were any fixed traditions. Isaiah 11:1–5 is cited with reference to a Davidic messiah in 4Q285, 4QpIsa[a] and 1QSb, and no non-messianic interpretation is at-

---

[25] I do not understand how Charlesworth can say that "None of the Pesharim contains messianic exegesis," especially as he goes on to recognize the allusion to the Branch of David in the Pesher on Isaiah (*The Messiah*, 25).

[26] J. A. FITZMYER, "The use of explicit Old Testament quotations in Qumran literature and in the New Testament," in *Essays on the Semitic Background of the New Testament* (Missoula: Scholars Press, 1974) 55. *Cf.* F. M. CROSS, *The Ancient Library of Qumran* (Garden City: Doubleday, 1961) 229.

[27] This passage begins with Amos 5:26–27, which refers to "the booth of your king," but introduces Amos 9:11 as a supporting citation.

tested. Moreover, the same passage is echoed in Pss Solomon 17:22–24, where "their king, a descendent of David" is endowed "with the wisdom of righteousness to drive out sinners from the inheritance, to destroy the pride of sinners as a potter's vessel; with a rod of iron to shatter all their substance, to destroy godless nations by the word of his mouth."[28] The Psalms of Solomon are roughly contemporary with the Scrolls, but are conspicuously absent from the caves. If sectarian scrolls such as the pesher on Isaiah and the War Scroll share a common understanding of Isaiah 11 with the Psalms of a different group, it is reasonable to assume that this interpretation was widespread. The same text is reflected in the account of the messianic "man from the sea" in 4 Ezra 13, who "sent forth from his mouth as it were a stream of fire, and from his lips a flaming breath" (4 Ezra 13:10).[29] It is also applied to the "Chosen One" in the Similitudes of Enoch (1 Enoch 49:3–4; 62: 2–3).[30] It is routinely referred to "the king messiah" in the Targumim and Midrashim,[31] although there was also a tradition that related Isaiah 11 to the historical Hezekiah.[32] Here again there is some variation: the messiahs in the Similitudes of Enoch and 4 Ezra are rather different figures from the king in the Psalms of Solomon. There is, however, a very strong and widespread tradition that interpreted Isaiah 11 with reference to a Davidic, messianic king, and this tradition is already reflected in the Scrolls.

The same is very probably true of Balaam's oracle in Numbers 24, which Fitzmyer cites as an example of variation in interpretation. We have already noted the explicit identification of the sceptre with the "Prince of the Congregation" in CD 7:19. Num 24:17–19 is cited without interpretation in 1QM 11:5–7. The context emphasizes that victory in battle is by the power of God, not of human beings. Fitzmyer infers that "the promise of messianic figures, which is the normal understanding of the verse, is here completely set aside in the new context."[33] I see no basis for this statement. The power of God may be exercised through a messiah. While the messianic interpretation of Balaam's oracle is not explicit in 1QM 11, there is nothing to exclude it, and this interpretation now seems more likely in view of the role of the Branch of David in 4Q285. Balaam's oracle is also cited without interpretation in the Testimonia, but the context has generally been taken to imply a messianic

---

[28] G. DAVENPORT, "The Anointed in Psalms of Solomon 17," in J. J. COLLINS and G. W. NICKELSBURG, Eds., *Ideal Figures in Ancient Judaism* (Missoula: Scholars Press, 1980) 72–74.

[29] For further allusions see Volz, *Die Eschatologie*, 176.

[30] J. THEISSEN, *Der auserwählte Richter* (Göttingen: Vandenhoeck & Ruprecht, 1975) 58–63.

[31] LEVEY, *The Messiah*, 49–52 (T. Jonathan), *Midrash Rabbah: Genesis* (trans. H. FREEDMAN and M. SIMON; London: Soncino, 1939) 2.902; *Midrash on Psalms* (trans. W. G. BRAUDE; New Haven: Yale, 1959) 1.36–37; *Pesikta Rabbati* (trans. W. G. BRAUDE; New Haven: Yale, 1968) 2.641–2 (Piska 33); *Pirke de Rabbi Eliezer* (trans. G. FRIEDLANDER; New York: Hermon, 1965) 19.

[32] KLAUSNER, *The Messianic Idea*, 464. This tradition is attested in Justin's *Dialogue with Trypho*, 43, 67, 68, 71, 77.

[33] FITZMYER, "Old Testament Citations," 43.

interpretation. The oracle is not without ambiguity. Since it refers to both a star and a sceptre, it may on occasion refer to two messiahs rather than one. The interpretation of both CD 7 and the Testimonia is disputed in this respect. When the passage is cited without interpretation, as in 1QM and the Testimonia, there is no way to be sure whether it was taken to refer to one figure or two. In the Testaments of the Twelve Patriarchs we find the star related to Judah in T. Judah 24, but it is also said of Levi that his star will rise in heaven like a king (T. Levi 18:3). Here again we may speak of a strong and widespread tradition that identified the sceptre with the Davidic messiah, but not of strict exegetical orthodoxy that would exclude all variation.

The exegetical traditions pertaining to the messiah were surely not confined to Isaiah 11 and Numbers 24. Genesis 49 and 2 Samuel 7, both cited at Qumran, later enjoy an illustrious history in messianic exegesis. Other texts such as Psalm 2 which are important both in the New Testament and in later Jewish tradition may also have been used more widely around the turn of the era. It is unfortunate that the pesharim on the Psalms are not more fully preserved. The extant evidence, however, lends support to the position of Vermes that there were exegetical traditions relating to the Davidic messiah, which were known across sectarian lines by the first century B.C.E.[34] Whether we may therefore speak of a "general messianic *expectation*,"[35] is another matter. We do not know how important these traditions were to the populace at large; interest probably fluctuated with historical circumstances. When interest in messianic expectation arose, however, there was at hand a body of tradition which could be used to articulate it.

THE DISTINCTIVENESS OF THE SCROLLS

Vermes has argued that expectation of a Davidic messiah was part of the common stock of Judaism in the centuries before and after the turn of the era.[36] It is attested in such diverse sources as Philo, the Psalms of Solomon, the Scrolls and the Eighteen Benedictions, and is tied to the interpretation of a few recurring biblical texts, such as Isaiah 11 and Numbers 24. It should be noted that the evidence from the first century B.C.E. and later contrasts

---

[34] "The disclosure of a body of interpretative tradition prior to, and free from any sectarian bias is one of the most important contributions made by Qumran literature to our knowledge of Palestinian religious thought," VERMES, *Post-Biblical Jewish Studies* (Leiden: Brill, 1975) 47. The fact that even Philo seems to be familiar with a messianic understanding of Balaam's oracle shows the widespread diffusion of such exegesis in the first century C.E.

[35] So VERMES, *Jesus the Jew*, 130. Vermes also cites the "Blessing concerning David" from the Eighteen Benedictions, but it is not clear that this can serve as evidence for the period before 70 C.E.

[36] See especially his *Jesus the Jew: A Historian's Reading of the Gospels*, 130–134.

sharply with the earlier Hellenistic period in this regard. Messianic expectation is conspicuously lacking in the writings of the early second century B.C.E.
(Sirach, Daniel, the early Enoch books).[37] The resurgence of messianic expectation appears to have occurred after the restoration of the monarchy by the
Hasmoneans.

The continuity with common Jewish expectations must be balanced
against the distinctive features of the documents found at Qumran. One such
feature is the prominence of the title "Prince of the Congregation," which is
not otherwise picked up in post-biblical Judaism, and which, as we have seen,
has a specific, sectarian connotation in the Scrolls. (Bar Kokhba was called
נשיא ישראל, Prince of Israel).[38] Another is the fact that the Davidic messiah
will not have sole authority in the eschatological period. In 4QpIsaᵃ, the biblical phrase, "He shall not judge by what his eyes see" (Isa 11:3) is taken to
mean that the messiah will defer to the teachings of "the priests of renown."
4Q285, line 5, after the reference to the Prince of the Congregation, reads
"and a priest will command . . ." In the Florilegium 1:11, the Branch of David
is accompanied by the Interpreter of the Law; similarly in CD 7:18 the Prince
of the Congregation is linked with the Interpreter. In the Messianic Rule
(1QSa) the presiding priest takes precedence over the "messiah of Israel," and
in the Scroll of Blessings (1QSb) the blessing of the High Priest precedes that
of the Prince of the Congregation. Most scholars regard the priest in 1QSa,
and the Interpreter of the Law in the Florilegium and CD 7, as a messianic
figure,[39] but in any case he qualifies the authority of the royal messiah. There
is clear reference to a priestly messiah in 1QS 9:11: "they shall be judged according to the former precepts, in which the men of the community were instructed at the start, until the Prophet and the Messiahs of Aaron and Israel
come."[40] This coupling of the Davidic messiah with a High Priest, indeed
subordination of the king to the priest, has its biblical warrant in Zech
4:12–14 (cf. Zech 6:11–12),[41] but it is distinctive in the Hasmonean and
Roman periods.[42]

Michael Wise and James Tabor have recently questioned the consistency

---

[37] J. J. COLLINS, "Messianism in the Maccabean Period," in J. NEUSNER, W. S. GREEN and
E. FRERICHS, Eds., *Judaisms and their Messiahs* (Cambridge: Cambridge University Press, 1987)
97–109.

[38] B. ISAAC and A. OPPENHEIMER, "Bar Kokhba," *Anchor Bible Dictionary* 1.600.

[39] See, *e.g.*, VERMES in the revised Schuerer, *The History of the Jewish People* 2.550–552.

[40] This passage is missing from the oldest copy of the Community Rule. In view of the retro-
spective reference to the start of the community, it is likely to be an addition.

[41] S. TALMON, "Waiting for the Messiah at Qumran," in *The World of Qumran from Within*
(Leiden: Brill, 1989) 290–293.

[42] The Book of Jubilees, which is closely related to the Qumran sect, singles out Judah and
Levi for leadership in Chap. 31, and may be said to lay the groundwork for dual messianism. See
J. VANDERKAM, "Jubilees and the Priestly Messiah of Qumran," *Revue de Qumran* 49–52(1988)
353–365.

and centrality of the doctrine of two messiahs in the Scrolls, and argued that
the expectation of a single messiah is more the rule than the exception.[43]
They claim that "there is not much evidence in the previously published
scrolls that straightforwardly supports a putative doctrine of two messiahs,"
and that not one of the newly released texts from Cave 4 speaks of two messiahs (granted that references to any messiah are sparse). They call for care in
the matter of method, and for vigilance against harmonizing different texts.

There are in fact several methodological issues here. The first is a matter
of terminology. Just as the royal messiah is the eschatological king of Israel,
by whatever name he is called, so the priestly messiah is the eschatological
High Priest. The use of the term משיח with reference to this figure in the
phrase "messiahs of Aaron and Israel" implies that his rank in the eschatological period is at least comparable to that of the King Messiah. The issue, then,
is not how many texts speak explicitly of two messiahs, but how many involve
the presence of another figure of authority equal to or greater than that of
the Davidic messiah. If the issue is viewed in these terms, the evidence for a
"priestly messiah" is considerably more extensive than Wise and Tabor allow.
It includes any text that subordinates the King Messiah to priestly authority,
such as the Pesher on Isaiah and apparently 4Q285. We should note that the
Temple Scroll, which Wise regards as the Torah for the end of days, clearly
subjects the king to the authority of the High Priest: "on his instructions he
shall go out and on his instructions he shall return home."[44]

A second issue concerns the different kinds of documents in which the
messianic references are found. In fact all the major Rule and Law books,
the Community Rule, the Messianic Rule, the Damascus Document and the
Temple Scroll, support the bifurcation of authority in the messianic era (if
indeed the Temple Scroll is written for the "end of days" as Wise and others
have argued). In the War Scroll, too, the High Priest enjoys greater prominence than the Prince of the Congregation.

The main point in dispute here is the nature of messianic expectation in the Damascus Document. Debate has centered on the expression
משיח אהרון וישראל which occurs in four passages (CD 12:22–13:1; CD 14:
18–19; CD 19:10–11 and CD 19:33–20:1). Louis Ginzberg's view that the reference was to two messiahs rather than one seemed to be confirmed by the
plural in 1QS 9:11 (משיחי אהרון וישראל),[45] but several scholars have argued

[43] M. O. WISE and J. D. TABOR, "The Messiah at Qumran," *Biblical Archeology Review*
(Nov./Dec. 1992) 60–65.

[44] Temple Scroll 58:19. For the eschatological character of the Scroll see M. O. WISE,
A Critical Study of the Temple Scroll from Qumran Cave 11 (Chicago: The Oriental Institute of the
University of Chicago, 1990) 167–194.

[45] L. GINZBERG, *An Unknown Jewish Sect* (New York: Jewish Theological Seminary, 1976,
trans. of the German 1922 edition) 209–256. See also K. G. KUHN, "The Two Messiahs of Aaron
and Israel," in K. STENDAHL, Ed., *The Scrolls and the New Testament* (New York: Harper, 1957)
54–64; TALMON, "Waiting for the Messiah–The Conceptual World of the Qumran Convenanters," in *The World of Qumran from Within*, 288.

instead that the two documents reflect different stages in the messianic devel-opment of the sect.[46] The expression משיח אהרן וישראל is a somewhat shaky foundation, however, on which to base a theory about messianic devel-opment, since it is admittedly ambiguous. Grammatically, it may refer to either two messiahs or one.[47] The strongest argument in favor of the single reference here is found in CD 14:18–19, where the reference to the coming of the messiah of Aaron and Israel is followed by the singular verb יכפר. This could, arguably, be translated as a passive (pual), so "atonement will be made," but it is more natural to translate it as an active (piel) "he will atone."[48] This would imply that the subject is a single figure, and that he is a priest.[49] This datum, however, is difficult to reconcile with other considerations. If the phrase "messiah of Aaron and Israel" refers to one messiah rather than two, it must nonetheless presuppose an expectation of two messiahs: it would be too much of a coincidence if the sectarians had first coined the reference to "Aaron and Israel" and only later developed the notion of a dual messiahship. Nowhere outside of the Scrolls do we find messiahs associated with Aaron and Israel. This consideration argues strongly that the original reference of the phrase was dual rather than single. Moreover, the Damascus Document, as preserved, has a clear reference to the Prince of the Congregation in col. 7. Both the biblical background of the phrase and the other occurrences in the Scrolls argue strongly that this figure should be identified as the Davidic mes-siah. If CD 14 attests a stage at which only a priestly messiah was expected, this can only be one redactional stage of the document. It represents neither the original expectation of the sect nor the final redaction of the document.[50]

---

[46] J. STARCKY, "Les quatres étapes du messianisme à Qumrân," *Revue Biblique* **70**(1963) 481–505. *Cf.* A. CAQUOT, "Le messianisme Qumrânien," in M. DELCOR, Ed., *Qumrân. Sa piété, sa théologie et son milieu* (BETL 46; Paris-Gembloux: Duculot/Leuven University Press, 1978) 231–247.

[47] A. S. VAN DER WOUDE, *Die messianischen Vorstellungen der Gemeinde von Qumrân* (Assen: van Gorcum, 1957) 29; R. DEICHGRÄBER, "Zur messiaserwartung der Damaskusschrift," *Zeitschrift für Alttestamentliches Wissenschaft* **78**(1966) 333–343.

[48] See however F. M. CROSS, "Some Notes on a Generation of Qumran Studies," in J. TREBOLLE BARRERA & L. VEGAS MONTANER, Eds., *The Madrid Qumran Congress* (Leiden: Brill, 1992) 1.14, who insists on the passive reading.

[49] Caquot, "Le messiaisme Qumrânien," 241. See the discussion by VAN DER WOUDE, *Die messianischen Vorstellungen*, 32.

[50] The reference to the Prince of the Congregation is complicated by the fact that it belongs to the material that overlaps between MSS A and B, and that a reference to the "messiah of Aaron and Israel" occurs in the parallel passage, 19:10–11. The context is a warning about future punish-ment. Both MSS have midrashic passages at this point, but they cite different texts. MS A cites Isa 7:17, followed by Amos 5:27a (with two phrases from 26) and Numbers 24:17. MS B cites Zech 13:7 and Ezek 9:4. Mention of the Prince of the Congregation occurs in MS A in the Numbers midrash, while there is reference to "the messiah of Aaron and Israel" in MS B at the end of the midrash on Zechariah. Only the reading of MS A is attested in the fragments from Qumran. There is no consensus as to what the original text read. S. A. WHITE, "A Comparison of the 'A' and 'B' Manuscripts of the Damascus Document," *Revue de Qumran* **48**(1987) 537–553 has argued that both readings were original and that each suffered loss through haplography. While this explanation is less than certain, it is attractive in so far as it rests on mechanical con-

While the expectation of two messiahs may not be invariable in the Rule books, it is predominant.

A third issue concerns the inferences that may be drawn from fragmentary texts. I agree with Wise that the "Son of God" figure in 4Q246 should be identified as a Davidic messiah, and that the extant fragments of this composition contain no reference to any priestly figure.[51] Correspondingly, 4Q Aaron A speaks of an eschatological priest with no reference to a Davidic king.[52] 4Q521 speaks of a messiah whom heaven and earth will obey, again with no reference to a priest.[53] (In this case it is not clear that the messiah is a king). Do these texts count as evidence against a doctrine of two messiahs in the Scrolls? I think not. *First*, some of these texts are extremely fragmentary, and so it is dangerous to argue anything on the basis of their omissions. 4Q Aaron A has some affinities with the Testament of Levi, which speaks of an eschatological priest from the line of Levi (T. Levi 18) but which is now part of the same book as the Testament of Judah, which envisages a royal messiah from the line of Judah (T. Judah 24). It is hard to have confidence that the few surviving scraps of 4Q Aaron A give us a full exposition of the author's messianic expectations. *Second*, it is unreasonable to expect a full exposition in every individual composition. Wise and Tabor draw attention to the exalted nature of the messiah in 4Q521, whom heaven and earth obey, and contrast him with the messiah of 1QSa, who takes second seat to the Priest. I am not at all sure, however, that the messiah of 4Q521 could not still be subject to a priest, or even that he is necessarily a Davidic, royal messiah. Much remains uncertain here. It is true that texts which do not mention two messiahs provide no support for that doctrine, but they do not necessarily provide counter-evidence either. None of these texts from Cave 4 is incompatible with the doctrine of a dual messiahship. Finally we must ask whether all these texts belong to the same movement as the Community Rule and Damascus Document. Everyone now grants that the Scrolls include some texts that are not distinctively sectarian. This possibility has in fact been suggested in the case of 4Q521, because of its lack of points of contact with the major sectarian documents.[54]

Methodological care, then, should guard not only against harmonizing

---

siderations rather than hypothetical redactional intentions. If White is right, then in this passage, at least, the משיח אהרון וישראל must refer to a Davidic as well as a priestly messiah.

[51] See my essay, "The 'Son of God' Text from Qumran," *From Jesus to John. Essays on Jesus and Christology in Honour of Marinus de Jonge* (M. DE BOER, Ed.; Sheffield: *Journal for the Study of the Old Testament*, 1993) 65–82.

[52] E. PUECH, "Fragments d'un apocryphe de Lévi et le personnage eschatologique. 4QTest Lévi c–d(?) et 4QAhA," in J. TREBOLLE BARRERA & L. VEGAS MONTANER, Eds., *The Madrid Qumran Congress* 2. 449–501.

[53] WISE and TABOR, "The Messiah at Qumran," 62.

[54] G. VERMES, "Qumran Forum Miscellanea I," *Journal of Jewish Studies* 43(1992) 303–304.

but also against indiscriminate evaluation of different kinds of text, and against the distortion that comes from considering texts in isolation. I believe that the evidence supports the view that a core group of sectarian texts affirmed a bifurcation of authority between Priest and King in the messianic age. It is certainly possible that some texts that did not share this view were preserved at Qumran. In the case of the fragmentary texts from Cave 4, however, much depends on the larger context in which they are read.

CONCLUSION

We have noted above that messianic expectation was conspicuously lacking in texts from the early second century B.C.E., but is attested in very diverse sources thereafter. Several documents among the Scrolls share the common understanding of the centuries around the turn of the era, that such texts as Isaiah 11 and Numbers 24 should be interpreted with reference to the Davidic messiah. The Qumran texts, however, put their own twist on this common expectation, in so far as they typically subordinate the royal messiah to an eschatological priest, presumably in protest against the combination of kingship and High Priesthood by the Hasmoneans. While there may have been some variation in the history of the sect, it is difficult to trace, because of the uncertainty of the dating of the individual documents. The dual messiahship, or the Davidic messiahship qualified by priestly authority, is, in any case, widely attested.

All of this suggests that the messianic expectations of the Scrolls have a profile that has considerable coherence and is also distinctive over against other strands of Judaism of the time. I am not, of course, suggesting that everything found in the caves should be fitted into a single system. Everyone now agrees that many scrolls contain texts that are either older than the Qumran sect or not distinctively sectarian. Neither am I suggesting the messianism was the main principle of coherence for the sect revealed by the Scrolls. The primacy of halachic considerations is shown decisively by 4QMMT, and indeed could be inferred already from the Damascus Document. I do submit, however, that the network of overlapping messianic references we have found in several Scrolls supports the view that the Scrolls contain a nucleus of closely related sectarian material and are not simply a cross-section of Jewish opinion at the turn of the era.

DISCUSSION OF THE PAPER

JOSEPH A. FITZMYER (*Catholic University, Washington, D.C.*): Two comments, John. In general I like what you were saying about the two Messiah problem, but there is something that ought to be considered beyond what you've said. Does the text in CD column 14, the one that seems to suggest a single Messiah, or at least it's been so interpreted, turn up in any of the 4Q documents? The point is, in other words, we get that from a late medieval copy of CD which we all know has sometimes misinterpreted things (for example, *yahad* becoming *yahed*). It may very well be that a single Messiah in CD column 14 represents something that had developed in Judaism way beyond Qumran itself.

JOHN J. COLLINS (*Divinity School, University of Chicago, Chicago, IL*): I think it does turn up. One could perhaps entertain the idea that you have a title that refers to both of them, but the action is only relevant to one; but that becomes a bit difficult.

FITZMYER: The other point I wanted to make is your paper all too easily presupposes that in 4Q285 the line that has the Prince of the Congregation, then *tsemah*—I don't agree that it's *tsemah*. The length of the preserved half character that's there cannot possibly, in my opinion, be a *mem*.

NORMAN GOLB (*Oriental Institute, University of Chicago, Chicago, IL*): You said at the beginning that the Qumran corpus is not just, I quote, "the random literature of the time," and people have said that idea characterizes the hypothesis of Jerusalem origin. That isn't my view. [Allow me to quote from my *PAPS* article of 1980:] "These manuscripts stem from first century Palestinian Jews, and are remnants of the literature, showing a wide variety of practices, beliefs and opinions, *etc*. Determination of the nature of the concepts and practices described in the scrolls may best be achieved not by pressing them into the single sectarian bed of Essenum, but by separating them out from one another through internal analysis, into various spiritual currents that characterized Palestinian Judaism. While I don't share the view of colleagues who uphold the Qumran-Essene hypothesis, I offer this interpretation with admiration for the brilliant work done by them on these texts." I believe very much in the Yahad group, as in other groups that are now emerging from 4Q; it's just that I don't think we can place them—any of them, including the Yahad group—by logic or by evidence of the texts on the Qumran plateau.

COLLINS: You will be relieved to know that I do not attribute that view to you.

HARTMUT STEGEMANN (*Göttingen University, Göttingen, Germany*): Two points, one regarding the Damascus document. Whatever is the solution for the understanding of column 14, there's a quotation of Numbers 24 in column 7, and there the roles are clearly divided. One is a political leader. I think that's clear evidence, whatever the evidence is elsewhere in the Damascus document. And secondly, you said rightly: in MMT there is no Messiah. Perhaps there is at least the title *nasi'*. In the final part, according to the numbering of Strugnell and Qimron, about C line 4, they read *nashim*, but that is only guesswork. You have no *mem*; and you can read an *aleph*, which is much better for the context. If there is *nasi'*, one may propose that when there is *nasi'* or *nesi' ha-'edah*, it's not always for the future, but also for the present. People can have this title; it's similar to what we have later on, with *Shimon ben Kosiba*.

COLLINS: Thank you.

MOSHE BERNSTEIN (*Yeshiva University, New York*): I'd like to make one point which I think applies not just to the Messianism issue, but to the whole question of the use of biblical material at Qumran. Wherever we find texts being used over and over again, regardless of the fact that they may not be interpreted exactly the same way, it implies that this is a text which is on the mind of the community. It doesn't necessarily have to be that the interpretation is going to be parallel. It's a text which they took very, very seriously in terms of their own ideology. If I'm not mistaken, either the beginning of Isaiah 11 or the very end of Isaiah 10 is also found in one of the other *pesharim*. That fact indicates that this text is very, very fundamental. Now obviously it lends itself to a messianic interpretation. In general, we should try to collect those passages which are employed in different contexts by the group. It may give us a better overall picture of which biblical material is motivating a variety of aspects of their ideology.

COLLINS: Thank you.

Samaritan Origins and the Qumran Texts

FERDINAND DEXINGER

Institut für Judaistik
University of Vienna
Ferstelgasse 6/12
Vienna, Austria A-1090

Shortly after the publication of the first Qumran texts scholars recognized significant similarities between certain doctrines in Samaritanism and Qumran. But from the beginning scholarly efforts were characterized by methodological inaccuracies. These resulted from the lack of sufficient insight into the very nature of Samaritanism as well as into the nature of the Qumran material. It is the main purpose of this paper therefore to review the steps of research in this field and to highlight several aspects of the Qumran material which can be considered as relevant for research into Samaritan origins. I am not going to reveal new facts or texts, but to evaluate the results of different studies presented till now.[1] A review of this material will make possible a fresh look at Samaritan origins and early Samaritan history and will perhaps contribute to a clearer insight into the general nature of the Qumran material. It is however interesting to mention that Epiphanius (*ca.* 370 C.E.) in his *Panarion* I,10 describes the Essenes as a Samaritan sect.[2] We recognize that there must be some confusion behind this statement without being able to see the underlying historical realities.

THE BIBLICAL TEXT AS A STARTING POINT

In 1955 Patrick W. Skehan analyzed the Exodus Scroll from Qumran cave 4 (4QExᵃ=4QpaleoExᵃ). Two different characteristics of these fragments led to a comparison with the Samaritan Pentateuch.

Paleo-Hebrew

At first sight the paleo-Hebrew script of this fragment reminds one of the actual Samaritan script, but after inspecting it closely Skehan came to the con-

---

[1] *Cf.* PUMMER, *Einführung.* (See bibliography at end of article.)
[2] *Cf.* ISSER, *The Dositheans*, 40;184f.

clusion, that this fragment cannot "by any stretch of the imagination be called Samaritan."[3] A turning point was Purvis's comparative study of the Samaritan script which he undertook on the basis of Qumran paleography.[4] He reached the conclusion that the Samaritan script as well as the Samaritan Pentateuch originated from the 2nd century B.C.E. Ben-Hayyim regarded this a too far-reaching conclusion on the narrow basis of paleography.[5] But since then many detailed studies of various other aspects of Samaritanism have shown that Purvis was headed in the right direction. Purvis did not on this occasion develop a theory of Samaritan origins in general but one of the Samaritan Pentateuch in particular.

The Proto-Samaritan Text Recension

Since its discovery the most important aspect of comparison between Samaritanism and Qumran material has always been the text of the Pentateuch itself. Skehan noticed similarities between the Samaritan recension and the paleo-Exodus fragment from Qumran "with all the essential characteristics of that (*i.e.*, the Samaritan) fuller text . . ."[6] This fact shed new light on the authenticity of the Samaritan Pentateuch, which according to Skehan, has "been preserved with a measure of fidelity from a time somewhere near the origin of the recension."[7] Without overlooking the secondary features of the extant Samaritan recension, 4QpaleoEx[a] is in Skehan's opinion "new evidence for the antiquity and for the constancy of transmission of the Samaritan recension."[8] He later made it clear that the paleo-Hebrew Exodus from Qumran "is not a Samaritan sectarian document, though it does offer the type of text the Samaritans have preserved as their own."[9] He however did not draw any conclusion as far as Samaritan origins are concerned.

Maurice Baillet some fifteen years later[10] without mentioning Skehan, carefully analyzed the different fragments of Exodus found in Qumran, comparing the variant readings. After detailed analyses he summarizes and states that 4Q158 (=4QBibParaphrase), 4Q174 (=4QFlorilegium) and 4Q175 (=4QTestimonia) quote the Samaritan text whereas 4QEx[a] and 4QEx[m] represent the Samaritan text itself.[11] Regardless of this particular theory he thinks,

---

[3] SKEHAN, *Exodus* 182.
[4] PURVIS, *Pentateuch*.
[5] BEN-HAYYIM, *Review*. C
[6] SKEHAN, *Exodus* 182.
[7] SKEHAN, *Exodus* 183.
[8] SKEHAN, *Exodus* 187.
[9] SKEHAN, *Qumran* 23.
[10] BAILLET, *Exode*.
[11] BAILLET, *Exode* 373 and 380: "L'étude des variantes et des divisions de l'Exode invite donc à penser que certains manuscrits de Qumrân contiennent, non seulment des éléments samaritains disséminés, mais le texte samaritain lui-même.

as already Skehan did, that the Qumran material confirms the authenticity of the Samaritan Pentateuch. Generally speaking, it had become clear at this stage of research that the biblical fragments from Qumran proved the antiquity of the Samaritan version, but it had not yet been made clear how the Qumran and the Samaritan texts were related. In an up-to-now final step of research, Emanuel Tov has made an important contribution to the understanding of the relationship[12] between the biblical texts from Qumran and the Samaritan version, but without treating the question of Samaritan origins in particular. He carefully describes the characteristics of the Samaritan Pentateuch such as harmonizing alterations, linguistic corrections, content variants, phonological changes, orthographical usage, and last but not least sectarian changes. Now there is a group of textual fragments from Qumran, which have in common the occurrence of harmonizing elements such as found in the Samaritan Pentateuch. These fragments are 4Q158, 4Q364, 4QNum^b, 4QDeut^n and last but not least 4QpaleoEx^m. It is perfectly clear that the Samaritan Pentateuch is based on such a textual form which can therefore be called proto-Samaritan. ". . . these proto-Samaritan texts share a sufficient amount of significant detail with the Samaritan Pentateuch in order to recognize the close relationship with that text."[13]

4QpaleoExod^m written in paleo-Hebrew has recently been studied by Judith E. Sanderson.[14] She was interested in the text itself, not the paleography. She clearly had in mind also the relevance of this material for the study of Samaritan origins and drew conclusions regarding the origins and nature of Samaritanism. The exact dating of 4QpaleoEx^m is not possible (225–175 B.C.E. or 100–25 B.C.E.). In spite of the uncertainty whether this text was written before or after the Qumran community came into existence, it seems to be clear that texts of that sort were used in different groups "during the last centuries of the Common Era."[15] As far as the typical sectarian Decalogue-expansion in Ex 20 is concerned, she states that "unfortunately we cannot know whether the Gerizimites' use of Scripture as a weapon preceded or followed the Hasmoneans' use of military weapons against them."[16]

As long ago as 1977 I tried to make clear in my study of the Samaritan Decalogue[17] that this expansion of the Exodus text has something to do with the origin of the Samaritans itself. I think that Sanderson did not sufficiently stress this very fact, although she made an important contribution to this view by recognizing explicitly that Scripture was being used as a weapon against

---

[12] Tov, *Proto-Samaritan Texts.*
[13] Tov, *Proto-Samaritan Texts* 406.
[14] SANDERSON, *Exodus Scroll.*
[15] SANDERSON, *Exodus Scroll* 317.
[16] SANDERSON, *Exodus Scroll* 319.
[17] DEXINGER, *Garizimgebot. Cf.* the later dating suggested by BEN-HAYYIM, *Tenth Commandment* and SCHWARTZ, *Destruction.*

other communities. She states: "The weapon was not, be it noted, the interpretation of Scripture, but the actual text of Scripture."[18] The importance of the paleo-Hebrew script for the Samaritans can be understood in a parallel way and fits exactly into the chronological framework of the Hasmonean period. Used by several groups and under different circumstances in the Second Temple period, this script was kept by the Samaritans and finally became an essential and distinguishing part of their tradition.

According to Tov only one of the doctrinal differences between Jews and Samaritans, namely the central place of worship, was inserted into the biblical text.[19] There cannot be any question that the insertion of the Garizim commandment into the Exodus-Decalogue is of the greatest importance. But one should take into consideration that other Samaritan doctrines were based on scriptural passages which are ancient variant readings. This is in my opinion a very important methodological instrument for determining the antiquity of Samaritan doctrines. The origin of some of these Samaritan doctrines therefore should be seen in the light of the Qumran material.

DOCTRINES COMMON TO THE SAMARITANS AND QUMRAN

As long ago as 1957 John Bowman asked the question "Contact between Samaritan Sects and Qumran?"[20] Bowman in his short note tried to establish links between sectarian Samaritanism and Qumran. He pointed to a variety of ritual and doctrinal aspects of Samaritanism reminiscent in one way or another of what we know from Qumran.

Once the idea of some sort of relationship between the Qumran material and Samaritan traditions was established, the scholarly investigation of possible connections continued.[21] Josephine Massingberd Ford in 1967 put the question: "Can we exclude Samaritan influence from Qumran?"[22] asking in particular, "what Samaritan thought is discernible in the Qumran writings?"[23] She pointed to many elements common to Qumran and the Samaritans. Unlike Bowman she attributes these common elements to Samaritan influence on Qumran, thus committing a major methodological error. This however does not invalidate her list of observed common aspects. It is the way of explaining these facts that must follow other lines.

[18] SANDERSON, *Exodus Scroll* 318f.
[19] Tov, *Proto-Samaritan Texts* 403.
[20] BOWMAN, *Contact*.
[21] BAILLET, *Exode* 363–366, summarizes the different elements enumerated by BOWMAN, FORD and by JOHN MACDONALD, Theology of the Samaritans.
[22] MASSINGBERD-FORD, *Samaritan Influence.*
[23] MASSINGBERD-FORD, *Samaritan Influence* 111.

In accordance with Bowman she stresses the importance of Deuteronomy for the Samaritans and at the same time guesses that Deuteronomy could have been a "good basic document" for Jewish sectarians who welcomed Samaritan thought. "Especially after the desecration of Jerusalem it might have appeared to some Jews that the Samaritans might be right after all . . ."[24] Another parallel between Qumran and the Samaritans can be seen, according to Bowman, in the common structure of a "priestly theocracy."[25] According to Ford it is the Zadokite priesthood that links Qumran and the Samaritans. This leads Ford to the statement that the "sectarian movement by the Dead Sea should not entirely be equated more with the Essenes,"[26] who were not a priestly caste, thus neglecting the priestly element obviously represented in Qumran. As "perhaps the most concrete connection between the Qumran community and the Samaritans" Ford regards their common use of the solar calendar.[27] As far as the liturgy is concerned it has to be noted that Purim and Hanukkah are neither celebrated by the Samaritans nor by the Community of Qumran.[28]

Bowman mentions the importance of the ritual bath for the Dositheans and Qumran without assuming a direct influence of Qumran on the Samaritans.[29] He then compares fundamental doctrines still kept by the present orthodox Samaritans which he considers the result of an influence by the sectarian Dositheans, such as the use of the term "Belial" in the Malef[30] or the name "children of light" given to the Samaritans in the same Samaritan source and very often used in the Qumran literature. He furthermore considers the idea of "God having hid His face from the land" expressed in CD II,9 as a parallel to the belief of the Samaritans that God has hidden his face in the time of Fanuta, the time of Divine Disfavor in which mankind is living now.

As a further common feature of Samaritan and Qumran tradition Ford notes the strong emphasis laid on the figure of Moses instead of Abraham.[31] She further on points to some parallels between the Samaritan Taheb and the "Teacher of Righteousness," who makes, in her opinion, ". . . a better Taheb than a pre-Christian Jesus of Nazareth!"[32]

In a more detailed argument Ford points to the interpretation of Gen 49, 10 in 4QPatrBlessings and 2Sam 7,10–14 in the 4QFlor. In both cases not the Davidic or priestly Messiah but the Teacher of Righteousness is the expected

[24] MASSINGBERD-FORD, *Samaritan Influence* 114.
[25] BOWMAN, *Contact* 187.
[26] MASSINGBERD-FORD, *Samaritan Influence* 117.
[27] MASSINGBERD-FORD, *Samaritan Influence* 123.
[28] MASSINGBERD-FORD, *Samaritan Influence* 124.
[29] BOWMAN, *Contact* 188.
[30] *MS Gaster* 1169.
[31] MASSINGBERD-FORD, *Samaritan Influence* 115.
[32] MASSINGBERD-FORD, *Samaritan Influence* 127.

eschatological figure. Ford concludes in accordance with her methodological approach: "It seems therefore, that there is a Samaritan element in these Testimonia."[33]

CRITICAL METHODOLOGICAL REMARKS

Ford in fact has pointed to most of the elements common to Samaritan tradition and Qumran. The starting point of her investigation is the presupposition that in spite of the comparably late date of Samaritan texts they preserved much older traditions, which can be compared with the Qumran material. Ford furthermore reckons with the presence of people whom we later include among the Samaritans in Qumran and does not exclude the possibility that "the Essenes were a branch of the Samaritans,"[34] thus following the statement of Epiphanius quoted above. Only the lack of precise methodological principles can induce, for example, the following hypothesis: "The Rule of the Community could be written for a group of Samaritan-Jews."[35] She regards her paper "a plea not to forget the Samaritans at Qumran."[36] But, in my opinion, it was a fundamental methodological mistake to consider all the elements enumerated as an argument in favor of Samaritan influence in Qumran. Her error is due to the fact that within the field of Qumran studies itself it never became clear enough which elements must be regarded as specific for the Qumran community and which ones belong to the common Jewish heritage. Qumran studies could according to my view gain some methodological accuracy from their correct application to Samaritan studies.

METHODOLOGICAL CONSIDERATIONS

There cannot be any doubt as to the great importance of the Qumran material for Samaritan research. Qumran material contains elements rooted in the common Jewish heritage on the one hand and aspects typical for the Qumran-group on the other. This very structure helps us in an unprecedented way to understand Samaritan tradition as well. Looking back to the first period of Samaritan research, we notice the tendency to interpret all the elements common to Qumran and the Samaritans as Samaritan or Qumran *influence*. In the light of the study of the biblical texts from Qumran this view has clearly to be abandoned. It has become clear that various biblical texts without specific sectarian affiliations were in existence and used by different

[33] MASSINGBERD-FORD, *Samaritan Influence* 120.
[34] MASSINGBERD-FORD, *Samaritan Influence* 129.
[35] MASSINGBERD-FORD, *Samaritan Influence* 121.
[36] MASSINGBERD-FORD, *Samaritan Influence* 129.

Jewish groups. The structure of the Samaritan Pentateuch is, generally speaking, represented in Qumran textually as well as graphically. This clearly identifies the Samaritans simply as a Jewish group of the pluriform Judaism of that age. As long as this unity was felt and was ideologically possible we should call this specific Jewish group Proto-Samaritans, and only after the overstressing of separating doctrines such as the exclusivity of the Garizim should we call them Samaritans. This renders obsolete all theories of a pagan and syncretistic origin fostered in rabbinical tradition. In spite of all later developments, Samaritanism preserved in many ways an older structure of the religion of Israel than that represented by the later strata of rabbinical Judaism.

It goes without saying that one has to avoid any generalization as far as the antiquity of Samaritan traditions is concerned. As a possible methodological approach to make use of Qumran material for research in Samaritanism I suggest the following.[37]

The fact that a Samaritan tradition has an old parallel is obviously not proof that the tradition within Samaritanism is of the same antiquity as the external parallel. The similarity between medieval Samaritan and New Testament eschatology, for example, does not prove that such a Samaritan tradition dates to the first century. A conclusion like this can only plausibly be drawn if there exists at least one indirect old support, Samaritan or non-Samaritan, by which it can be shown, that a specific Samaritan tradition in fact has ancient roots. Such a support seems to be given whenever in later Samaritan sources the textual and/or exegetical arguments used presuppose such an ancient tradition, which is attested for example in Qumran material.

In the following I should like to give some examples of that sort connected with the Qumran material. One must not overlook that all the different examples taken together make clear that there is a certain amount of nonsectarian Second Temple tradition common to the Samaritans and the Qumran material.

THE DECALOGUE

For the Samaritans as for Jews (cf. Philo, *De Decalogo*) and Christians the Decalogue has a special significance. The text of the Decalogue was for liturgical purposes transmitted independently from Bible scrolls (cf. the Jewish Nash Papyrus and the Samaritan Decalogue inscriptions[38] discovered in various places of Samaritan settlement). In antiquity and still today stones on which the Decalogue was engraved, served as mezuzot in Samaritan synagogues and private homes. This parallels the earlier Jewish custom testified, *e.g.*, by the mezuzah 4Q149 (=4Qmez[a]) found in Qumran (DJD VI,80),

---

[37] Cf. DEXINGER, *Eschatology* 292.
[38] Cf. for this chapter DEXINGER, *Garizimgebot*.

which contains the Decalogue (Ex 20). The Samaritans as well as the Jews obviously understood Deuteronomy 6:9 as referring to the Ten Commandments to be written on their doorposts. Another testimony for the importance of the Decalogue is the fact that it was used as well in phylacteries[39]: 1Q13 (Deut 5), 4Qphyl[d] and 10Qphyl[3]. In Judaism the liturgical use of the Decalogue was reduced at the end of the Second Temple period (cf. jBer 1,8(3c); bBer 12a).

The Masoretic Exodus-Decalogue (Ex 20,1–21) is expanded in the Samaritan Pentateuch by the insertion of Ex 13,11a; Dtn 11,29b; 27,2b–3a.4–7; 11,30 (after Ex 20,17MT) and Dtn 5,24–27 (after Ex 20,18MT) and Dtn 5,28b–29, 18,18–22; 5,30–31 (after Ex 20,21MT). The Fragments 4Q158 and 4Q175 (=4QTest) from Qumran have a similar expansion of the text, without the verses mentioning Mount Gerizim. The inclusion of the Gerizim-verses (Dtn 27,2b–3a.4–7; 11,30) meets Samaritan interests alone. This typical Samaritan expansion of the text cannot have taken place after the 2nd century C.E. because the earliest known Decalogue inscriptions already contain it. The "Sitz im Leben" for the insertion of the Gerizim-Commandment probably was the situation shortly before or after the Maccabean destruction of the Samaritan cultic center in the 2nd century B.C.E. The preceding non-sectarian expansion of the text may go back as far as the 4th century B.C.E.

THE TAHEB

It can be debated whether the insertion of Dtn 18,18 in the Samaritan Decalogue, mentioning the "Prophet like Moses" is a sectarian reading. The expectation of an eschatological prophet with reference to Deuteronomy 18,15.18 is not a specific Samaritan idea but a common Jewish one dating back to the 2nd century B.C.E. The Taheb[40] is identical with the eschatologically conceived "Prophet like Moses" of Deuteronomy 18,18 and has preserved the basic traits of this figure. In the specifically Samaritan expansion of Exodus 20 the "Prophet like Moses" appears closely associated with Gerizim. The Aramaic designation of the "Prophet like Moses" as "Taheb" which stems from the Aramaic-speaking period of the 4th century C.E. assumes that this prophet is a "Returning One." But the idea of the Taheb as the expected echatological prophet is much older than its Aramaic designation. The antiquity of the idea of a coming eschatological prophet preceding the Messiah(s) is clearly attested in Qumran 1QS IX,11. The Samaritan tradition can plausibly be regarded as an old one common or at least wide-spread in Second Temple Judaism.

---

[39] YADIN, *Tefillin* 34: "From this, one can conclude that the inclusion of the Decalogue in tefillin at Qumran was regular, in both the first centuries B.C. and A.D."
[40] Cf. for this chapter DEXINGER, *Taheb*; and *id.*, "*Prophet wie Mose*."

THE ESCHATOLOGY

A central idea of Samaritan eschatology[41] is the "Day of Vengeance and Recompense" (*jwm nqm wšlm*). The evidence for the Day of Vengeance and Recompense in Samaritan sources is strong in all epochs. This terminology does not, however, appear in the Mishnah. As far as Samaritan literature is concerned we encounter this concept in the 4th century Tibât Mârqe (IV,12). How far can we trace back this terminology and is it typical sectarian?

The concept *jwm nqm* is found in the Masoretic Bible only in Isaiah 34:8; 61:2; 63:4 and Proverbs 6:34 but not in the Pentateuch which, alone, is of relevance to the Samaritans. But Deut 32:35 (SP) offers together with LXX an important variant reading. Instead of the Masoretic text's *lj nqm wšlm* "vengeance is mine . . ." SP adds two letters (*wm*) to the Hebrew word for "mine" (*lj*) making the word *lywm*, "for the day." This part of the verse in the Samaritan version then reads, "For the Day of Vengeance and Recompense . . ." In Qumran (lQS 9:23) the concept (*ywm nqm*) is used similarly in an absolute sense without particular reference to a Biblical passage. When we look to the LXX we notice that the parallelism favors the term "*lywm*" corresponding to "*l't*" as more authentic. So the variant reading of the SP in Deut 32,35 parallel to the LXX and the eschatological use of this concept in Qumran point to the 3rd/2nd century B.C.E. as the date of origin of this now specifically Samaritan but at that time obviously more common Jewish doctrine. The text of MT could easily be the result of an ideologically based change.[42] The LXX in any case proves that the text of Dt 32,35 in SP is not the result of a Samaritan sectarian textual emendation. From this we may assume that the eschatological interpretation of the term "*ywm nqm*" in Qumran is not typical for this group but part of a common Jewish heritage which has been preserved by the Samaritans.

THE FEAST OF THE SEVENTH MONTH

In the context of our methodological considerations as far as the relationship between Samaritanology and Qumranology are concerned we must turn to the festival calendar. Is it possible to find in the existing Samaritan liturgical tradition hints of the date of the separation of both the Samaritan and the Jewish liturgical traditions? And in what way can the Qumran material be helpful in this field of research? But first we have to ask if this is a legitimate question at all. Reinhard Pummer in an unpublished manuscript states: "If at all, the Samaritans can only with great caution testify for pre-rabbinic Jewish

---

[41] *Cf.* DEXINGER, *Eschatology.*
[42] *Cf.* MARGAIN, *Samaritain-Pentateuque.*

TABLE 1. Comparison between Samaritan and Jewish Festivals

Samaritan Festivals	Jewish Festivals
Simmut ha-Pesach	—
—	Purim
Mazzot	—
Pesah	Pesah
Mazzot	—
Hag ha-Kazir	Shavuot
Simmut ha-Sukkot	—
Feast of the 7th Month	Rosh ha-Shana
Yom Kippur	Yom Kippur
Sukkot	Sukkot
Shemini Azeret	Shemini Azeret
—	Hanukka

usage." He builds this methodological warning on the argument, "that biblical rituals could be revitalized after they had not been practiced for ages.[43]

The starting point of our deliberations is the obvious fact that the Samaritan calendar compared to the Jewish has its pluses and minuses. Without astonishment we register the fact that Jews and Samaritans share the feasts Pesah, Shavuot and Sukkot all mentioned in the Pentateuch. A certain difference exists as far as the Mazzot-feast is concerned which is celebrated by the Samaritans as a feast distinct from Pesah.[44] I won't pursue this question but turn to another biblical feast, namely the "Feast of the Seventh Month" as mentioned in Lv 23,24 and celebrated in the Jewish calendar as Rosh ha-Shanah.

TABLE 1 shows a comparison between the Samaritan and the Jewish festivals as published by Cowley[45] and printed in the Mahzorim. The "Feast of the 7th Month" can be seen as another example of an ancient, that is, Second Temple tradition within Samaritanism.

Both the Jewish and the Samaritan liturgical texts connect, although in totally different wording, various religious ideas based on biblical texts with the Feast of the Seventh Month. Some of these are given major importance (in TABLE 2 printed with capital letters) whereas others are obviously considered as being of minor relevance. The role of the Shofar can according to my view be helpful to gain some insight into the historical development of this feast. Again the Qumran material will be useful for this purpose.

The blowing of the Shofar is an integral part of the Jewish Rosh ha-Shanah Liturgy, but it is not mentioned in Lv 23,24. The biblical proof for the Shofar as the instrument of the T^{c}ru^{c}a can only be obtained by reference to another

---

[43] Unpublished Manuscript 48.
[44] *Cf.* POWELS, *Kalender* 110; *id.*, *Calendar* 730f.
[45] COWLEY, *Liturgy*.

TABLE 2. Comparison between the Feast of the Seventh Month and Rosh ha-Shana

	Feast of the Seventh Month	Rosh ha-Shana
	Creation	zkrwn lywm r'šwn
	Atonement	–
	Gan Eden	–
	–	Day of Judgment
	–	Akeda
	Moses	–
	SEVENTH	–
	–	MALKUT
	REMEMBRANCE COVENANT	ZIKARON
	–	SHOFAR
	TEN WORDS	–
	Priestly Blessing	Priestly Blessing

biblical passage, namely Lv 25,9. Regarding the blowing of the Shofar as a command of this feast, the Amidah quotes the three existing pentateuchal verses mentioning the Shofar as part of the Sinai story.[46] In spite of introducing by these texts the theme of the Decalogue, the Decalogue itself is not recited in the Jewish Rosh ha-Shanah Musaph, whereas this is the case in the Samaritan Shaharit. This reminds us of what was said before in connection with the Decalogue. Num 10,10 as the concluding pentateuchal verse is contained as a biblical text in the Samaritan liturgy of this day. This verse however does not speak of the Shofar but of the Hṣwṣrwt. This reminds us that mention of the Shofar is lacking in mRH 3,3–4. Heinemann concluded therefore, that the Mishnah here describes a practice dating back to the times of the Second Temple.[47] This part of the Amidah using Num 10,10 therefore was part of the Jewish Temple Liturgy.

The Samaritan Shaharit does not contain the Shofar-verses at all,[48] whereas the hṣwṣrwt are mentioned several times. The "Shofar" is not connected with the Samaritan Feast of the 7th Month.[49]

Comparing this material with the Temple Scroll (11QTemp 25,3) mentioning the Feast of the 7th month and also based on Leviticus, we observe that the Shofar is not mentioned either, though one has to admit that the text of Column 25 is very fragmentary.

If one does not assume that the Samaritans at some unknown date started

[46] Ex 19,16; Ex 19,19; Ex 20,18.
[47] HEINEMANN, *Prayer* 80.
[48] Cf. *SamLit* (R. ZADAKA & A. ZADAKA, Eds.) 116 and BAGULEY, *New Year Liturgy* LIX.
[49] Cf. the information given by PUMMER, *Rituals* 686: "No shofar is used by the Samaritans, since the use of the shofar and trumpets was restricted to the time when the temple was in existence. However this may be a recent view" (B. ZADAKA 1983).

the celebration of their Feast of the 7th Month[50] one has to look for some chronologically reasonable starting point.

Taking into consideration that the Samaritans do not favor the use of the Jewish names of the month[51] but use the ordinal numbers instead, the assumption seems to be plausible that the proto-Samaritans did not follow the Jewish calendar from the time when the Babylonian names for the months were finally introduced together with the Autumn Calendar. An additional support for this dating is the fact that the Samaritans do not celebrate the Jewish Feasts Purim and Hanukkah introduced in the Maccabean period.[52] This is once again a parallel to the Qumran Festival-Calendar. I therefore come to the conclusion that beginning with the Maccabean period the Proto-Samaritans stopped developing their religious and liturgical traditions within the common biblical heritage of the Jews.

ZADOKITE PRIESTHOOD AND THE HALAKHAH

Josephus (*Ant.* XI,302–347) reports that a dissident priest from Jerusalem founded the sanctuary on Mount Gerizim in the 4th century B.C.E.[53] It is a fact that Samaritanism is up to this day a priest-dominated group. Again looking at the Qumran material we notice common structural and halakhic elements with Samaritanism. When Shemaryahu Talmon describes the founding members of the community of Qumran "as a group of millenarian messianic Jews who had figured out the advent of the 'Kingdom to Come' by attaching a real-historical interpretation to a biblical prophecy,"[54] he does not according to my view highlight strongly enough the priestly element in Qumran.

That there is such a priestly element has always been noticed. One specific text from Qumran which illustrates this fact is 4QMMT, explicitly describing the Qumran halakhah.[55] This is very important for the history of Judaism because it enables us to distinguish between Tannaitic halakhah, Sadducaean halakhah, and typical Qumran halakhah, which was not possible till now. At the same time one can see more clearly how far Samaritan halakhah is typical Samaritan or Sadducaean. Likewise in Qumran and in Samaritanism it is the

---

[50] As for the function of the Bible in the early liturgical service *cf.* ELBOGEN, *Gottesdienst,* 241f: "Das gemeinsame Bekenntnis hatten bereits die ältesten gottesdienstlichen Versammlungen, es fand seinen Ausdruck in der Rezitation von Schriftstellen; daß sie sämtlich aus dem Pentateuch entnommen waren, weist darauf hin, daß sie in einer Zeit vereinigt wurden, wo noch kein anderer Teil der Heiligen Schrift kanonische Geltung hatte."

[51] *Cf.* PUMMER, *Samaritans* 20.

[52] This fact was already observed by POWELS, *Kalender* 25.

[53] *Cf.* DEXINGER, *Ursprung* 102–116.

[54] TALMON, *Emergence* 606.

[55] *Cf.* DOMBROWSKI, *4QMMT.*

general tendency of 4QMMT to interpret biblical law very strictly.[56] The halakhah of Qumran is, as has been shown recently by Lawrence Schiffman and Jacob Sussman[57] not Pharisaic but Sadducaean.

Schiffman looks at this text as evidence for the halakhic discrepancies between Qumran and the Sadducaean priests in Jerusalem. After pointing to parallel views in the Temple Scroll, Schiffman discusses the origin of the Qumran group. Schiffman,[58] like Sussman, finds evidence for a Sadducaean halakhah in 4QMMT and 11QTemp and Schiffman comes to the conclusion: "The earliest members of the sect must have been Sadducees who were unwilling to accept the situation that came into being in the aftermath of the Maccabean revolt (168–164 B.C.). The Maccabees replaced the Zadokite high priesthood with their own priests, reducing the Zadokites to a subsidiary position for as long as Hasmonean rule lasted."[59] Schiffman therefore thinks "that we must abandon theories that seek to link this sect and its origins with the Hasidim, supposedly a second-century B.C.E. group that was opposed to Hellenism and devoted itself to a strict observance of ritual law."[60] Unlike Sussman he is skeptical as far as an identification of the Qumran group and the Essenes is concerned. Only if one looks at the Essenes as Sadducaean sectarians would it be possible to call the Qumranians Essenes.[61]

Josephus's report of the role of priests among Samaritans is very similar to the dominating function of the priestly element at Qumran. One could imagine that like 4QMMT Samaritan halakhah has Sadducaean roots. This is exactly the result of Boid's study of Samaritan halakhah: "It seems that the Sadducean and Samaritan view of the theory of the relationship between Torah and tradition is largely identical."[62] Obviously, Samaritan halakhah was later influenced from many sides, but its origin in the Second Temple period was never totally lost.

It is methodologically interesting to note what Schiffman said about the relations between Qumran and Samaritan halakhah: "Even if a large number of affinities between the halakhah of the Dead Sea sect and the Samaritans were found, the most that could be concluded would be the influence of the Dead Sea group on the Samaritans."[63] According to my view one must not speak of "influence" but of the common tradition that connects both groups.

---

[56] Cf. SUSSMAN, History 27.

[57] Cf. mPara III,3 and 4QMMT B 13–17; mJad IV,7 and 4QMMT B 55–58, where the difference between the Pharisaic and the Sadducaean halakhah is emphasized. (SUSSMAN, History 28f.) As far as Qumran is concerned BAUMGARTEN, Laws 57, states that Sadducaean as well as proto-rabbinic halakhot can be found there.

[58] SCHIFFMAN, Letter.

[59] SCHIFFMAN, Letter 69.

[60] SCHIFFMAN, Letter 71.

[61] SUSSMAN, History 40, does not consider it a contradiction to identify the Qumranians as Essenes and to qualify their halakhah as Sadducaean.

[62] BOID, Halachah 646.

[63] SCHIFFMAN, Halakhah 17.

CONCLUSION

Bowman noticed that "direct points of contact between Samaritan sects and Qumran probably never existed, but both grew out of a similar background."[64] What Frank Moore Cross said about the text of the Samaritan Pentateuch can be applied to Samaritan religion in general. "The Samaritan text-type thus is a late and full exemplar of the common Palestinian tradition, in use both in Jerusalem and in Samaria."[65] The religion of the proto-Samaritans was essentially the religion of Jerusalem. It is the common Jewish heritage, then, which forms the similar background of Qumran and the Samaritans as well. And it is the Qumran material that enables us to reach a fresh scholarly view of Samaritan origins. At this point I have to mention Eileen Schuller's interpretation of 4Q 372 1. Although I don't think that this text can be called anti-Samaritan,[66] I fully agree with Schuller's proposed connection of this text with Second Temple Judaism.[67] The two biblical clusters of Joseph texts (Joseph as an individual–Joseph as a tribe) need not be separated. 4Q 372 1 interprets, according to my view, the history of the tribe of Joseph in post-exilic times along the biographical lines of Joseph in Gen 37. Thus lines 13–14a seem to recall Esr 4,1 whereas lines 14b–17a describe the situation of the descendants of Joseph in Shechem (*i.e.*, the proto-Samaritans) in the early Persian period.[68] In any case this text[69] must be taken into consideration as an interpretation of post-exilic Jewish history relevant to the prehistory of Samaritanism.

I think it appropriate at this point to add one remark on Norman Golb's theories about Qumran origins[70] at the end of this paper. From the viewpoint of Samaritanology Golb's explanation has a certain relevance as Reinhard Pummer in his introduction to Samaritan research has already mentioned.[71] Without entering into a discussion of whether he is right or wrong, I think that his theory in any case draws our attention to the fact that there is more common Jewish heritage in Qumran than we often are aware of, and it is exactly this sort of material which is extremely important for Samaritanology and Qumranology as well.

---

[64] BOWMAN, *Contact* 189.
[65] CROSS, 209.
[66] *Cf.* SCHULLER, *Joseph* 371.
[67] *Cf.* SCHULLER, *Joseph* 375.
[68] *Cf.* DEXINGER, *Ursprung* 96–100.
[69] SCHULLER, *Joseph* 350.
[70] GOLB, *Scrolls.*
[71] PUMMER, *Einführung* 44 n. 181.

BIBLIOGRAPHY

BAGULEY, EDWARD C.
1956   *A Critical Study and Translation of the Samaritan New Year Liturgy with a Comparison with the Corresponding Jewish Rite.* MA thesis. Leeds University.
BAILLET, MAURICE
1971   "Le texte Samaritain de l'Exode dans les manuscrits de Qumran." In *Hommages à André Dupont-Sommer.* A. CAQUOT & M. PHILONENKO, Eds.:363–381. Paris.
BAUMGARTEN, JOSEPH M.
1992   "The laws of the Damascus Document in current research." In *The Damascus Document Reconsidered.* MAGEN BROSHI, Ed.:51–62. Jerusalem: Israel Exploration Society.
BEN-HAYYIM, ZEEV
1971   *Review: J. D. Purvis, The Samaritan Pentateuch . . .* , *Biblica* **52**: 253–255.
1993   "The Tenth Commandment in 'the Samaritan Pentateuch'." (Heb.) In Mehkere Talmud II: 33–38. M. BAR-ASHER & D. ROSENTHAL, Ed. Jerusalem: Magnes.
BOWMAN, JOHN
1957   *Contact between Samaritan sects and Qumran?* VT **7**: 184–189.
BOID, I. R. M.
1989   "The Samaritan halachah." In *The Samaritans.* ALAN D. CROWN, Ed. :624–649. Tübingen: Mohr.
CROSS, FRANK MOORE
1966   *Aspects of Samaritan and Jewish history in Late Persian and Hellenistic times,* HTR **59**: 201–211; (*cf.* the reprint in *Die Samaritaner* (WdF 604). FERDINAND DEXINGER & REINHARD PUMMER, Eds. Darmstadt (Wiss. Buchges.) 1992, pp. 312–323.
DEXINGER, FERDINAND
1977   "Das Garizimgebot im Dekalog der Samaritaner." In *Studien zum Pentateuch. W. Kornfeld zum 60. Geburtstag.* GEORG BRAULIK, Ed.:111–133. Wien: Herder.
1985   "Der 'Prophet wie Mose' in Qumran und bei den Samaritanern." In *Festschrift M. Delcor.* AOAT **215**: 97–111.
1986   *Der Taheb. Ein "messianischer" Heilsbringer der Samaritaner.* Salzburg: O. Müller.
1989   "Samaritan eschatology." In *The Samaritans.* ALAN D. CROWN, Ed. :266–292. Tübingen: Mohr.
1992   "Der Ursprung der Samaritaner im Spiegel der frühen Quellen." In *Die Samaritaner* (WdF 604). REINHARD PUMMER, Ed.:67–140. Darmstadt: Wiss. Buchges.
DOMBROWSKI, BRUNO W. W.
1992   *An Annotated Translation of Miqsat Ma^{a}seh ha-Torah (4QMMT).* Weenzen.
ELBOGEN, ISMAR
1967   *Der jüdische Gottesdienst in seiner geschichtlichen Entwicklung.* Hildesheim: Olms. (Reprint 3rd edit. 1931.)
GOLB, NORMAN
1989   "The Dead Sea Scrolls: A New Perspective." *The American Scholar* (Spring): 177–207; (Autumn): 626–632.
HEINEMANN, JOSEPH
1966   *Prayer in the Period of the Tannaim and the Amoraim.* Jerusalem. (Heb.)

ISSER, STANLEY
  1976   *The Dositheans. A Samaritan Sect in Late Antiquity.* Leiden: Brill.
MACDONALD, JOHN
  1964   *The Theology of the Samaritans.* London: SCM.
MARGAIN, JEAN
  1990   *Samaritain-Pentateuque.* DBS **XI** (Paris): 762–773.
MASSINGBERD FORD, JOSEPHINE
  1967   *Can we exclude Samaritan influence from Qumran?* RQ **6**: 109–129.
POWELS, SYLVIA
  1977   *Der Kalender der Samaritaner.* Berlin.
  1989   "The Samaritan calendar and the roots of Samaritan chronology." In *The Samaritans.* ALAN D. CROWN, Ed.:691–742. Tübingen: Mohr.
PUMMER, REINHARD
  1987   *The Samaritans.* Leiden: Brill.
  1989   "Samaritan rituals and customs." In *The Samaritans.* ALAN D. CROWN, Ed. :650–690. Tübingen: Mohr.
  1992   "Einführung in den Stand der Samaritanerforschung." In *Die Samaritaner* (WdF 604). FERDINAND DEXINGER & REINHARD PUMMER, Eds.: 1–66. Darmstadt.
PURVIS, JAMES D.
  1968   *The Samaritan Pentateuch and the Origin of the Samaritan Sect.* Cambridge, MA.
SANDERSON, JUDITH E.
  1985   *An Exodus Scroll from Qumran: 4QpaleoExod^m and the Samaritan Tradition.* Atlanta (Scholars Pr.) (Harvard Sem. St. 30).
SCHIFFMAN, LAWRENCE
  1990   *The new halakhic letter (4QMMT) and the origins of the Dead Sea sect.* BA **53**: 64–73.
  1975   *The Halakhah at Qumran.* Leiden: Brill.
SCHULLER, EILEEN
  1990   *4Q372 1: A text about Joseph.* RQ **14**(Nr.55): 349–376.
SCHWARTZ, SETH
  1993   *John Hyrcanus I's destruction of the Gerizim Temple and Judaean–Samaritan relations.* Jewish History **7**: 9–25.
SKEHAN, PATRICK W.
  1955   *Exodus in the Samaritan recension from Qumran.* JBL:182–187.
  1959   *Qumran and the present state of Old Testament text studies: The Masoretic text.* JBL **78**: 21–25.
SUSSMANN, JACOB
  1990   *The History of Halakha and the Dead Sea Scrolls—A preliminary to the publication of 4QMMT.* Tarb **59**: 11–76. (Heb.)
TALMON, SHEMARYAHU
  1987   "The emergence of Jewish sectarianism in the early Second Temple period." In *Ancient Israelite Religion. Essays in Honor of Frank Moore Cross.* P. MILLER, PAUL HANSON & S. DEAN MCBRIDE, Eds.:587–616. Philadelphia: Fortress.
TOV, EMANUEL
  1989   "Proto-Samaritan texts and the Samaritan Pentateuch." In *The Samaritans.* ALAN D. CROWN, Ed.:397–407. Tübingen: Mohr.
YADIN, YIGAEL
  1969   *Tefillin from Qumran.* Jerusalem: Israel Exploration Society.
ZADAKA, RAZON and ABRAHAM ZADAKA, Eds.
  1958   *Tefillot mo'ed hodesh hashebi'i.* Holon (polycop.). (= *SamLit*).

DISCUSSION OF THE PAPER

MICHAEL WISE (*University of Chicago, Chicago, IL*): I have a question for you with regard to the concept of common Jewish heritage. I'm specifically thinking here of the calendar texts from Qumran. As you know, there are a group of them which set up a concordance between a lunisolar calendar (a form or version of it, or so it seems) and the 364 day calendar familiar to us. The thing that's interesting to me about this concordance is that the lunisolar version calculates for the day on which the month ends. This fact seems to me to imply that the new moon is calculated and is the equivalent of the modern astronomical new moon, rather than being a new moon determined by observation. In other words, it's when the conjunction between the sun and the moon occurs, rather than when the first portion of the moon is visible, that the new moon is designated.

I see the same thing in the Samaritan lunisolar calendar. That is to say, a calculated new moon: not based on observation, but an astronomical new moon. In your opinion, does this then represent one of the elements of a common Jewish heritage, possibly going back to the Second Temple period?

FERDINAND DEXINGER (*University of Vienna, Vienna, Austria*): I'm not an expert in calendrical research, because that has to do with mathematics, but as far as Samaritan studies are concerned, Sylvia Powels wrote about the Samaritan calendar. Coming to your question, I think that this has something to do with this common heritage. Experts like you and others should try to get the exact comparison. The calendar is of utmost importance for the life of a community. In spite of all the medieval changes, the calendarical computation remained conservative. My answer is yes.

EPHRAM ISAAC (*Institute of Semitic Studies, Princeton, NJ*): When we speak about the distinctions between the *Samaritan halakha* and later Jewish *rabbinical halakha*, what do we really mean? We are talking about a period during which time the halakha was evolving, growing, and developing. It's somewhat anachronistic to be so sure about things that are really so limited, particularly during the particular period with which we are dealing. The very expression *halakha* sounds somewhat anachronistic.

DEXINGER: I agree with you. I don't use this word *halakha* in the later technical sense, but to describe the fact that everyday life is regulated according to interpretation of biblical law. It is a fact that we have regulations; we have such in Qumran, obviously, and we do have it in later Samaritan law. One must compare between the biblical prooftexts of individual laws in Samaritan tradition and in Qumran. If we come to the conclusion that there is similarity in the halakhic outlook and the biblical reference, then that points to a common Jewish heritage. This is what I intended to say.

LAWRENCE SCHIFFMAN (*New York University, New York City*): I of course have fallen into the trap of using the word *halakha* and I was trying to refrain from it. I found all kinds of problems using other English words. The problem is there's simply no word. I tried "law," I tried "legal," that implies all kinds of things in our society . . .

DEXINGER: Well, we have a word in German that could be useful–"Religionsgesetz," but I didn't use it here.

SCHIFFMAN: We sometimes say religious law. This immediately, to the English reader, eliminates the idea of laws of damages and things like that. So it's a very difficult problem. But I wanted to make some other comments. First of all, in Sussman's work, he basically takes the view that there are two systems of *halacha* possible in the whole development of Jewish sectarianism. You can go the way of what we call the Pharisees/rabbis, or you can go the way of what exists in the Sadducean, *etc.* trend. One can therefore throw the Samaritans into this second trend, with Bethusians, Karaites, *etc.* He doesn't do it to that extent, but he moves in that direction.

This raises a wider question, and you talked about it yourself, about medieval Karaite influence. There are numerous laws which seem to be shared by the Dead Sea sect and the Karaites (Professor Golb wrote on some of this many years ago), and the Samaritans as well. Here we always face a mixture of causes. Some of the commonalities are inheritance from the old days, some of them are influences, and some of them are a combination. Simplistic answers like, "These guys copied from those guys" or, "It all is ancient" don't seem to work. On the other hand, as you pointed out, the notion of saying, "Well it's all medieval influence" would be inappropriate. We have to do what you said, go on a law-by-law basis. When you do that you come up with this mixed notion of what really happened, but apparently this generally Sadducean trend is being reflected.

The final point: I wanted to make one brief comment about the calendar. Rabbinic sources claim that the Tannaim already had similar means of calculating the dates on which the calendar should synchronize, or at least when the new moons should occur. They would then supposedly know when to make the leap years. Most of us have tended to think that this is a later exaggeration, because by somewhat later (the 4th, 5th century) this was the norm. In light of the Qumran material, which shows that whoever it was that put these calendaric texts together knew how to make these calculations, maybe we have to reassess our nonbelief.

We seem to be finding that a lot of people knew how to calculate calendars. Maybe the rabbis knew how to do it also; then the Samaritans would have known how to do it later on, and everybody would have known how to do it, in the same way that certain aspects of our culture that have to do with mathematical calculations are known to us. It's speculation, admittedly, but our skepticism may simply not be appropriate any more, in light of the material emerging and the calendar text that Michael was alluding to.

HARTMUT STEGEMANN (*University of Göttingen, Göttingen, Germany*): Dr.

Dexinger, let me add one statement and put one question. The statement is regarding the use of biblical texts. We have a lot of scrolls of books of the Pentateuch which to a high degree correspond to the Samaritan Pentateuch. We have also quotations from such versions, which demonstrate that this text was not only handed down, but was at the same time used. The best example is 4Q Testimonia, where we have four quotations. The first quotation, regarding the future prophet, is not taken from different places in Deuteronomy, but from Exodus 20 in the Samaritan version.

And now the question. You said, and I agree, those correspondences demonstrate a common path – but when was this path? I had the idea (from the examples you mentioned) you think the Hellenistic period, 3rd century or 2nd century. I think this would be impossible. This common path must date to the 5th century or 4th century at the latest, which means the Persian period.

DEXINGER: This is a very important question, because it gives me the chance to explain in a few words what I think of Samaritan origins. First, it's not easy to say that the Samaritan tradition reflects the northern Israel tradition. This is an old idea that has to be abandoned. But on the other hand, remnants of ancient Israel continued living in Samaria, and they kept their religion, the pagans taking part in it especially in the Hellenistic period. It was a scandal in the eyes of Jerusalem. The tension between Samaria and Jerusalem is already obvious from the first testimony in Ezra (4,1 ss) where these people from the north are mentioned. I don't think that these were all pagans who tried to join Jerusalem. These Proto-Samaritans were not against Jerusalem totally, but they worshipped on Gerizim. So I agree with you that the Persian period was essential for the further development. I can't say when these expansions, and this sort of use of the Bible known to us from the Samaritan Pentateuch and Qumran, came into use.

But it is not a problem for my view of Samaritan origins if it began in the Persian period. It would be problematic before the Exile, but after the return it can have happened at any time. A specific question is at what time the Samaritans thought it appropriate to insert the Gerizim commandment. I have thought it would be sometime before John Hyrcanus destroyed the temple because they insisted on that temple. The time of John Hyrcanus seems to be a plausible situation for the Samaritans to insist on the biblical foundations of the cult on Mount Gerizim. In any case I think this is the *terminus post quem non* for the insertion of the Gerizim commandment.

The Manual of Discipline in the Light of Statutes of Hellenistic Associations

MATTHIAS KLINGHARDT

Institut für Evangelische Theologie
Philosophische Fakultät I
Universität Augsburg
Universitätsstrasse 10
D-86135 Augsburg, Germany

Research on the Dead Sea Scrolls and related problems over the past 40 years has achieved a far-reaching *communis opinio* about their origin and general background: It is widely acknowledged that the scrolls stem from a somewhat sectarian, probably Essene, community that lived in a community center in the Judean desert, thus separating itself from the Jerusalem Temple and its priesthood and leading a cenobitic life in a monastery-like setting. This basic view which, of course, has taken a variety of forms, is derived first of all from the sectarian character of the Manual of Discipline (1QS) and related texts, such as the Order of the Congregation (1QSa) and the Damascus Covenant (CD).[1] Even the archaeological identification of the Khirbet Qumran site as a monastery-like community center with a *refectorium*, a *scriptorium* and so on, is primarily based on these texts. Given the great importance the sectarian character of these texts had for establishing the general view on the scrolls and the archaeological data, it is surprising how little effort has been made to seek historical analogies to those texts that might explain their genre as well as their contents.

On the other hand, any criticism of the *communis opinio* about the origin of the Qumran scrolls, for example, the suggestion of a Jerusalem origin as claimed by K.-H. Rengstorf and, more recently, by Norman Golb,[2] must be able to explain to what sort of group these alleged "sectarian" texts could possibly apply.

It is the purpose of this article to shed some light on this problem. Owing to the limited space available I will concentrate on the Manual of Discipline only, providing parallels to its genre as well as to its contents. I will present

---

[1] Examples of general surveys of an academic nature include SCHÜRER (1979), 575–590, and BIETENHARD (1979).

[2] RENGSTORF (1960); GOLB (1980; 1985; 1989).

my thesis first and then discuss it and draw some conclusions. The thesis is: The closest parallels to the Manual of Discipline in regard to genre and contents are statutes of *Hellenistic associations*. The similarities between those statutes and 1QS make it most likely that the group to which 1QS applies was such a religious association, rather than a cenobitic "sect." I presume that it was a synagogue community.

1QS AS A STATUTE OF AN ASSOCIATION

It is widely acknowledged that Jewish life, culture, and religion not only in the Diaspora but also in Palestine was deeply influenced by Hellenistic culture in the aftermath of the Greek conquest.[3] In contrast to the vast literature on Qumran and its problems, only little has been said about the Greek influence on the Dead Sea Scrolls in general[4] and about the organizational similarities between Hellenistic associations and the *yachad* as described in 1QS.[5] In regard to this latter aspect of the organization, the recent and highly instructive study by Moshe Weinfeld on *The Organizational Pattern and the Penal Code of the Qumran Sect* represents a decisive improvement.[6] Weinfeld provides detailed analogies to most of the organizational and penal regulations in 1QS and CD from several Hellenistic associations. The analogies stated by Weinfeld relate to the following issues:

1) *Procedure of admission*, which includes prescriptions about a probationary period for the initiant, about the examination of the candidate (*dokimasia*), about his registration and an entrance-fee (*eisēlysion*), and about an initiation oath.
2) *Disciplinary regulations about the gatherings*, such as: disloyalty, seating and speaking in fixed order, disturbances of various kinds during the gatherings, insults and violence against members and priests, and absence from the assembly.
3) Many issues of the more general *ethical teaching* are paralleled by statutes of Hellenistic associations, such as: the prohibition against appealing to an outside court; the obligation of mutual aid between the members of the association (in CD); the general requirement of purity.
4) *Regulations of jurisdiction within the group*, pertaining to such matters as: membership in the court of the association, witnesses and proof, the modality of re-applying for apostates and reconciliation, different kinds of penalties, and so on.

---

[3] *Cf.* HENGEL (1988).
[4] *E.g.*, SCHNEIDER (1963); HENGEL (1978).
[5] *Cf.* BARDTKE (1961); TYLOCH (1967); DOMBROWSKI (1966); KOFFMAHN (1961); WERNBERG-MØLLER (1969).
[6] WEINFELD (1986).

Thus Weinfeld not only proved that most of the detailed regulations contained in 1QS have close analogies in the statutes of pagan associations, but also demonstrated that the whole organizational structure of the *yachad* was nearly identical to those associations: the structure of offices and office-holders is identical[7] as is the groups' self-designation.[8]

Yet, Weinfeld did not draw the one necessary conclusion: the identity between the statutes of Hellenistic associations and the groups represented by 1QS and CD did not lead him to the obvious suggestion of identical kinds of groups. He limits the similarities to the "external form and structure" and claims a uniqueness of the "sect's" basic ideology and nature.[9] For Weinfeld, the group to which 1QS applies remains a "sect" and does not become an association. Weinfeld supports this clearly ideological refusal to identify the community of 1QS as an association by stating several differences. It is worthwhile to discuss at least those differences related to matters of organization, because, in my opinion, these differences are due to the fact that Weinfeld takes only very few pagan statutes into account for his comparison, thus neglecting the majority of Greek and Roman material.[10]

1) *Sacrifices, oblations and gatherings in temples are mentioned in pagan statutes, but not in 1QS or CD*. Weinfeld explains this absence with the commonly acknowledged hypothesis of the "Qumranites'" separation from the Jerusalem Temple and its sacrificial cult. But I think one does not have to go so far. There existed many associations—actually, probably the majority—which obviously did not perform any sacrifices, although a libation in honor of the eponymous deity was usually connected with the communal gathering that followed the communal meal and preceded the symposium.[11] Almost no association in Hellenistic-Roman times existed without some kind of religious ceremony, but sacrifices (combined with sacrificial meals) were performed primarily by public rather than private cult-associations, which usually had a social rather than a particular cultic function. Although communal meals were a regular

---

[7] The co-existence of religious (priests, Levites) and "secular" (president, treasurer, elders) functionaries is typical for pagan associations as well as for 1QS.

[8] The Hebrew terms *yachad* and *ha-rabbim* are paralleled by the Greek *koinon* and *hoi polloi/ hoi pleinones*: WEINFELD (1986), 10–19; DOMBROWSKI (1966).

[9] WEINFELD (1986), 7f. *Cf.* also his summary, p. 104: "All these formalities common to the religious guilds and associations of the Hellenistic and Roman period do not affect the nature of the Judeo-Christian sects which was altogether different from its contemporaneous sects."

[10] Differences listed in WEINFELD (1986), 46f. His list of pagan statutes being compared to 1QS contains several Demotic and Greek statutes from Upper Egypt, and only three codes from Greece (among them the famous code of the Athenian Iobacchi). Thus he completely neglects the Roman texts and almost completely the Greek texts (*cf.* below, n. 23).

[11] I give only a few of the well known examples: The code of the Zeus Hypsistos association only mentions a *posis*, a drinking party, but no sacrifices (for text and commentary see ROBERTS, SKEAT & NOCK: 1936). The famous statutes of the worshippers of Diana and Antinous, a *collegium funeraticium* from Lanuvium in Italy, mention various kinds of gatherings; but even on festive days they only have a symposium which is accompanied by the libation *"ture et vino,"* without sacrifices, although the gatherings take place in the temple of Diana and Antinous: DESSAU (1892ff), no. 7212 (col. II, lines 23–30).

part of the life of pagan associations, they were not necessarily linked to sacrifices. The fact that the *yachad* obviously did not perform any sacrifices is therefore not a "Qumranic" peculiarity to be explained by the opposition to the Jerusalem Temple.

2) *No mention of burial and funeral regulations is made in 1QS, whereas such ordinances were an important part of pagan statutes.* Again, Weinfeld explains this difference by invoking the remote, cenobitic situation of the sect in the Judean desert.[12] At first glance this is an important argument, since not only the Demotic statutes from the Fayyûm mentioned by Weinfeld have specific burial regulations, but also the major part of private *collegia* from Rome, the so-called *collegia funeraticia*. But again, many statutes of private associations do not mention burial regulations at all.[13] Whether an association took care of its members' burials or not was primarily dependent on its social level: only people of a low social level, who could not privately secure their own burial for financial reasons, were in need of the support for funerals provided by an association.[14] The Roman *collegia funeraticia* are found among the *collegia tenuiorum* which were formed completely, or at least to a great part, of slaves and *libertini* of a low social level. Therefore, the lack of burial regulations in 1QS is rather an indication of the *yachad's* social level than an argument for its sectarian character.

In this respect, it is interesting to see that the obligation of mutual aid (*i.e.*, financial support) does not appear in 1QS, whereas the statutes of the Damascus Document include such regulations (VI 20ff; XIV 12ff). At least one difference between the *yachad* of 1QS and the "people of the camp" in CD seems to be the social level of their members.

3) *The lack of ordinances concerning the payment of membership fees and pecuniary fines* in 1QS is explained as the result of the sect's joint participation in property and thus serves as an argument for the sectarian, cenobitic character of the Qumran *yachad*. But the suggestion that there ever existed joint participation in *all* possessions—be it in 1QS or in pagan antiquity—must be seriously doubted. I give only a few hints:

a) There existed many associations whose members did not have to pay regular fees. This is not only true for those associations that were based on an endowment,[15] but for many others too, for in many cases the entrance-fee

---

[12] WEINFELD (1986), 46: ". . . in a sect whose members live within a common framework, *in the same place*, there is no need to propound and encourage participation in mourning rites and their like" (my italics).

[13] *E.g.*, the statutes of a private association in Philadelphia/Lydia: SOKOLOWSKI (1955), no. 20; the code of the Zeus-Hypsistos association (P. Lond. 2710): ROBERTS, SKEAT & NOCK (1936); the Milesian Molpoi: SOKOLOWSKI (1955), no. 50. This list could easily be expanded.

[14] *Cf.* BÖMER (1957), 466.

[15] *E.g.*, the association of Epicteta in Thera (HILLER VON GAERTRINGEN [1907] no. 330); the association of Diomedon in Kos (DITTENBERGER [1898/1901], no. 734); the deed of foundation of the association of Antistheros in Thera provides that the interest of the endowment should pay for the costs of assemblies (*synagōgai!*): HILLER VON GAERTRINGEN [1907], no. 329, line 15. See in general LAUM (1914).

was sufficient to provide for further expenses.[16] But it is not necessary to assume that regular fees besides the entrance-fee had to be mentioned in the statutes proper. Prescriptions about regular fees are mentioned only in statutes that were valid for one year only, as is the case with most of the Egyptian associations. The lack of such regulations in 1QS and many other Greek and Roman statutes does not necessarily mean that there were no such regular fees; there might have been further documents settling this matter.[17]

b) Since the submission of private property to the *yachad* is mentioned only in connection with the initiation, this is most likely what is called in Greek associations the "*eisēlysion*," the entrance fee. There is a famous early Christian parallel for this submission of property to the community at the occasion of conversion: The story of Ananias in Acts 5 does not deal with the problem that he retained part of his property,[18] but that he lied about it: this is exactly the problem of the ordinance 1QS VI 24f (in a modern context, it is like lying about one's tax report). It is very unlikely that the initiant had to submit *all* his possessions to the *yachad*, because otherwise the regulation about financial liability for damages (1QS VII 6–8) would make no sense at all. Besides, there exists no reference whatsoever that supports the idea that *everything* was submitted to the community. The very common ideal of sharing possessions, the famous "*koina ta philōn*,"[19] does not mean submitting everything to the community. The especially numerous instances of this ideal relating to philosophers sharing possessions[20] make clear that it is realized as communal property of an association, in this case of philosophical circles. There does not exist a hint that even Pythagorean associations, which served as the *exemplum* par excellence for very close friendship and relation in Hellenistic-Roman antiquity, understood the ideal of sharing possessions other than putting together part of their private money.

c) The lack of pecuniary fines sanctioning disciplinary offences in 1QS, as can be found in many pagan associations, is not quite as clear as maintained. The penalties of the laws on communal judgment (1QS VI 24ff) designate different periods of time that are usually understood as temporary (or, in severe cases, absolute) exclusion from the community. Yet, the first of these regulations sanctioning lying about property to be submitted to the community

---

[16] *E.g.*, the Milesian Molpoi: SOKOLOWSKI (1955), no. 50; for details and further examples *cf.* the instructive commentary by VON WILAMOWITZ-MOELLENDORFF (1904), *ad loc.*

[17] This is the case with accounts for the supply of assemblies of associations: There is a wax-tablet (MOMMSEN [1873], p. 953 [*tab. cerat.* XV]) mentioning different kinds of food. Tebtunis Papyri 118 177 224 (GRENFELL, HUNT, SMYLY & GOODSPEED: 1902/07) are accounts for the supply of assemblies of associations from Tebtunis, containing the amounts of individual contributions; these texts are accounts, but not the statutes of those associations.

[18] *Cf.* CAPPER (1986).

[19] *Cf.* KLAUCK (1982).

[20] Plato, Leg 739C; Rep 424A; Aristotle, EthNic 1159B; 1186B; Diogenes Laertius, VIII 10; X 11; Jamblichus, Vita Pythag. 30,167ff; Diodorus Siculus V 9,4 and so on.

(VI 24f) names a temporary exclusion from the purities of the "many" and besides that a reduction of a quarter of the portions of the meal. The following regulations only stipulate a temporary fine; it is not clear whether this is related to an exclusion or to a diminution of meal portions. If the latter is the case, this would come very close to the pecuniary fines of pagan associations, because in many statutes money is equated with naturals (e.g., wine, bread, and oil) both in regard to the contributions for the assemblies or to the honors granted to members of merit.[21] Therefore, the diminution of portions of the communal meal in 1QS as a disciplinary sanction is very similar to pecuniary fines.

So far, the differences in organizational structure between 1QS and the statutes of Hellenistic associations as stated by Weinfeld are not convincing. His concentration on only a few Egyptian associations has misled him into assuming an overall uniformity concerning even details which at least partially are due to the very peculiar organization of Egyptian associations.[22] But if one takes into account the abundant epigraphical evidence for Hellenistic associations in general[23] (of which the statutes form only a very small part) it is evident that the description of the communal life in 1QS perfectly fits into the general structure of those associations. Clearly, the group to which the *serekh* of 1QS applied was organized exactly like an association. That means that the so-called "sect" was a private association in a legal sense. The accuracy with which the statutes, the *serekh*, are formulated does not allow any doubt that its members understood themselves to be anything other than members of an association, not of a cenobitic sect (if this social form can be determined at all). The often claimed religious uniqueness of the so-called Qumran sect, that would diminish its compatibility with Hellenistic associations,[24] must therefore be understood differently: the particularly Israelite theological (and social!) concepts, such as covenant, purity, holiness, *etc.* were, under the altered circumstances of the Hellenistic culture, realized in the categories of

[21] One example among many others is the designation *chous* (pitcher for wine), which was used in various ways: In the association of the Attic *eranistai* of Men it means the monthly payment (*cf.* Hegesander, in: Athenaeus, Deipnosophists VIII 365D; POLAND [1909], 263 etc.); in the statutes of the Milesian Molpoi, *chous* is used for the public support for the association (SOKOLOWSKI [1955], no. 50, line 21); in the statutes of the Orgeones of Amynos from Piraios, *chous* means the regular fee, from which members of merit are exempt (*ateleia tou chou*: DITTENBERGER [1898/1901], no. 725, line 11). In none of those cases is it clear whether *chous* means money or wine.—For the exemption from regular payments (*ateleia*) *cf.* POLAND (1909), index *s.v.*

[22] *Cf.* SAN NICOLO, M. (1972).

[23] For Egyptian associations *cf.* DE CENIVAL (1972); SAN NICOLO (1927); SAN NICOLO (1972). For Greek associations *cf.* POLAND (1909); ZIEBARTH (1896). For Roman associations *cf.* LIEBENAM (1890); WALTZING (1895/1900).—A more recent summary of research on Greek and Roman associations is HERRMANN, WASZINK, COLPE & KÖTTING (1978). A more thoroughgoing description of Hellenistic associations that takes into account the evidence published in the last 70 years is still a *desideratum*.

[24] Of course, not only Weinfeld made this claim; the same is true for BARDTKE (1961), KOFFMAHN (1961), SCHNEIDER (1963), HENGEL (1978), and many others.

religious associations and thus achieved innovative social concretion in a new political and social setting.[25]

Before turning to the question of what kind of association the *yachad* might have been, it may be useful to add two conclusions at this point:

1) The first conclusion is of methodological importance. Taking seriously the Hellenistic culture as the all-encompassing area in which comparative study with the Qumran texts must be done, one has to take early Christian instances into account as well. The fact that early Christian congregations were organized like pagan associations has been well known for more than 100 years, although recent research does not pursue this lead. This organizational analogy must imply sharing the same cultural and economic world, rather than simply depending on earlier (Jewish or pagan) congregations. In this respect, Paul's first letter to the Corinthians (1Cor) can be seen as a first attempt to give this community an organization similar to other associations.[26] The Didache (Did), a church order from the 1st century C.E., appears to be the earliest instance of a fully formulated *nomos* or code of a Christian association.

If one takes early Christian congregational rules as further examples of Hellenistic-Roman statutes, other first-glance differences between 1QS and Hellenistic associations as stated by Weinfeld lose their significance. One of them is the *"religious-moralistic rhetoric"*[27] adjoining the ordinances in 1QS and CD, a feature which is not found in pagan statutes. The existence of such theological legitimation for ordinances in 1QS marks the difference between Jewish-Christian associations on the one hand and pagan ones on the other, but it is certainly not a "Qumranic" particularity. The early Christian statutes (*i.e.*, 1Cor and the Didache) certainly contain "religious-moralistic rhetoric" along with ordinances, and the dualistic teaching about the two ways in Did 1–6 is clearly similar to the passage about the two spirits in 1QS III 13–IV 26. Further "unique" features of the Qumran statutes can easily be explained in this way, such as the hymn at the end of 1QS (paralleled, for instance, by the prayers provided by Did 9f) and the eschatological character (*i.e.*, the formulation of the code "not only for the present but also for the ideal future"[28]): eschatology is certainly no Qumranic peculiarity, but a feature common to all Jewish and Christian apocalyptic groups.[29]

---

[25] This is, by the way, another analogy to the Greek associations in particular: The general structure of Hellenistic-Greek associations (different functionaries in contrast to the whole body of the assembly) reflects the political structures of the *polis*; although this adaptation of *polis*-structures by the associations reaches back to the earliest examples, an enormous increase can be observed in Hellenistic times, when the *polis* had lost its predominant importance for structuring public life, *cf.* LEVINE (1985).

[26] The proof of the identical organizational structure of early Christian communities and pagan associations is a *desideratum*, although important preliminary work was done more than 100 years ago: HEINRICI (1876; 1881). See also KÖTTING (1978).

[27] WEINFELD (1986), 47.

[28] WEINFELD (1986), 47.

[29] Characteristically, both 1Cor and the Did end with an eschatological outlook (1Cor 15; Did 16) that serves as a motivation to obey the regulations of the statutes given before.

2) A second conclusion is related to the Qumran texts: The *non-uniform literary character of 1QS* has often been stated.[30] Indeed, not only the teaching about the two spirits (1QS III 13–IV 26) seems to be a later, originally independent interpolation, but also the repetition of many single regulations and the clearly recognizable sections beginning with "these are the regulations" *etc.* disprove the literary integrity of 1QS; the same is true for CD. Without going into details, it is worth noting that many of the statutes of associations show the same literary non-uniformity, which results from changes that have been made through the years. There exist, for instance, several statutes of the Suchos-association of Tebtunis,[31] where later versions replace earlier ones that were valid for one year.

In the case of this Suchos-association, the annual statutes were single documents, but there exist other examples where the replacing statutes are redactionally connected with the earlier ones.[32] In other cases, replacements and enlargements of earlier stages of the statutes are not due to the principle of annuity, but to changes concerning the contents of the statutes.[33] Likewise, it seems to imply that 1QS consists of several originally independent statutes or parts of statutes. This would apply not only to the different parts within 1QS, but also to the relationship between 1QS and 1QSa: 1QSa is certainly not simply an "appendix" to 1QS with an eschatological motivation for communal meals, but a completely different code.[34]

THE *YACHAD* AS A SYNAGOGUE COMMUNITY

In a second step we turn to the question of what kind of association the *yachad* of 1QS might have been. As I stated in the beginning, I assume it was a synagogue community. Unfortunately, our knowledge of the organization of Palestinian synagogue communities of the Hellenistic period is very meager and limited either to later (Rabbinic) sources or to archaeological evidence.[35] On the other hand, we know quite a bit about the organization of Diaspora synagogues.[36]

---

[30] *E.g.*, MURPHY-O'CONNOR (1979); STEGEMANN (1988) *etc.*

[31] P. Dem. Cairo 30605; 30606 in: SPIEGELBERG (1906/1908).

[32] *E.g.*, P. Dem. Berlin 3115: DE CENIVAL (1972), 103–131.

[33] Next to the statutes of the Delphic Labyades (DITTENBERGER [1898/1901], no. 438) see in particular the Roman *fratres Arvalium*, for whom statutes of several years are preserved that contained their cultic calendar: HENZEN (1874).

[34] This is clear from the completely different groups of people participating in this meal, *cf.* 1QSa II 17ff to 1QS VI 4ff.

[35] KRAUSS (1922); SAFRAI (1976); SCHÜRER (1979), 423–463.

[36] KRAUSS (1922); GOODENOUGH (1953/1969), vol. II, 70–100; APPLEBAUM (1974). The great amount of epigraphical evidence from Rome permits a more detailed reconstruction of the local circumstances, *cf.* LEON (1960).

It is obvious that Diaspora synagogues were organized in very much the same way as pagan associations. The designation "*synagōgē*" is not limited to Jewish communities, but also occurs for pagan associations.[37] Titles, offices and functions that are known from synagogue communities occur in pagan associations as well, first of all the *archisynagōgos* (which is exactly the same as the Hebrew *ro'sh ha-knesset*), but also titles like *archōn*, *phrontistēs*, *hyperetēs*, *diakonos* and so on.[38] In fact, it is impossible to distinguish between Jewish and pagan references to associations only on the basis of titles; Jewish origin of synagogue inscriptions can very often be ascertained only by particular Jewish names or by symbols such as the *menorah* or the *shofar.*

Since pagan associations form the general social and organizational background for both the *yachad* of 1QS and for synagogue communities, the most obvious suggestion is to identify the *yachad* as a *Palestinian synagogue community.* This has several consequences among which I will mention only a few.

It has already been stated that 1QS, being a code of an association, can be seen as a composition of several originally independent statutes. If so, other texts and fragments from the Qumran caves can be interpreted in the very same way. This relates not only to CD and 1QSa, but also to further texts and fragments from the Qumran caves: **4Q255–263** (= 4QS[a–i])[39] are not necessarily (fragments of) copies of 1QS, but may as well represent similar statutes of different groups.[40] The same is true for the halakhic texts **4Q513** and **514,**[41] since the regulations given in those texts would fit perfectly into the setting of the communal meal of an association.[42]

---

[37] *Cf.* the guild of barbers (*synagōgē tōn koyreōn*) near Heraclea Pontica from the first century C.E.: WALTZING (1895/1900), vol. III, no. 208, line 5f. There are many more references for *synagōgē* designating the assemblies of pagan associations rather than the group itself, only a few of which are listed in SCHÜRER (1979), 430 n. 13; see further the indices *s.v.* συναγωγή in POLAND (1909) and WALTZING (1895/1900), and above, n. 15.

[38] For officers in pagan associations *cf.* POLAND (1909), 337–423 and the index for the titles mentioned above; for Jewish references *cf.* the brief sketch in SCHÜRER (1979), 433–439.

[39] I refer to the list of unpublished texts by Tov (1992).

[40] Some readings in the preliminary publication of parts of 4QS[b] and 4QS[d] (VERMES, 1991) differ significantly from 1QS.

Further disciplinary texts from cave 4 (**4Q265 266 270**), briefly discussed by BAUMGARTEN (1992), show the same kind of differences regarding the penalties for disciplinary cases. The synopsis of penalties given by BAUMGARTEN (*ibid.* 275–276) does not permit a final conclusion about the relationship between **4Q265 266 270** and 1QS; the analogies, however, concern problems that are *typical* for disciplinary regulations of associations. Since these topics are unspecific for the *yachad*, it seems to be more likely that, in view of the differences, those new texts from cave 4 relate to different groups.

[41] 4Q513 514 = Ord[b c]: BAILLET (1982), 287ff.

[42] Although the texts are very fragmentary, the regulations about amounts of money (4Q513, fr. 1), purity of food and eating (**513** fr. 2; **514** fr. 1) together with a dating on a Sabbath (**513** fr. 3/4), mentioning a memorial (*ibid.*), oil and incense (**513** frs. 12/13) could be understood as part of a statute of an association; for parallels *cf.* P. Dem. Cairo 30605 30606 31179 31178 30619 (SPIEGELBERG, 1906/1908), P. Dem. Prague (ERICHSEN 1959) and many Greek and Roman references.

The same could be true for 4Q477, labeled "Decrees of Sect" by Tov (1992) and recently published by EISENMAN & WISE (1992), 269–273.

But even if the 4QOrd texts do not belong to such a social setting, and even if the alleged copies (4Q255–263) are indeed copies of one original, the suggestion that the *yachad* of 1QS was a synagogue community rather than a "sect" permits a determination of the relationship between this *yachad* and similar groups mentioned by Josephus and Philo: Both the Essenes (especially in Josephus' description: *Bell.* II 119–161) and the Therapeutae (Philo, *De Vita Contemplativa*) have been seen as sectarian movements similar to the "Qumranic" *yachad*. But the similarity between those groups, which is basically their close community, can be explained more easily as characteristics of synagogue communities, even if the Essenes and the Therapeutae had some special features not common to other synagogues. The organizational features of the Essenes, such as their initiation ceremony with a probationary period, their assemblies and communal meals, the judgments and disciplinary regulations, are paralleled not only by the *yachad* of 1QS, but by many pagan associations as well. The same is true for Philo's description of the Therapeutae. The comprehensive and harsh apologetic sections about pagan *symposia* (*VitCont* 40–63) are necessary exactly because the Therapeutic assemblies and meals are so similar to their pagan counterparts. What Philo's Therapeutae and Josephus' Essenes have in common is not a particular sectarian character, but the typical characteristics of religious associations, which most probably were synagogue communities.

There is one important objection to this perspective I must deal with: It can be – and it has been – claimed that these three groups – the *yachad*, the Essenes, and the Therapeutae – share not only a similar organizational pattern, but also the cenobitic life in some sort of community center which, in the case of the *yachad*, would be the Khirbet Qumran site.

As far as the Therapeutae are concerned, it is worth noting that they did not live together; instead, Philo stresses the point that they lived solitary each in a house of his or her own and that they gathered only on Sabbaths for their assemblies (*VitCont* 21–24). Since Josephus nowhere mentions a center of cenobitic life for the Essenes, only Pliny's statement remains that the Essenes near En-Gedi are a "solitary tribe."[43] I cannot see that *gens sola* should mean that they lived in a monastery-like, cenobitic center.

It might be important to recall the fact that, except for the claim that has been made for the "Qumranites," there exists no reference whatsoever to cenobitic life in antiquity prior to the Egyptian monks of the 4th century C.E. And even those earliest forms of cenobitism did not emerge from a group that retreated to seclusion *as a group*. Instead, this cenobitism was the result of a unification of many solitary hermits that, gradually, led to a com-

---

[43] Pliny the Elder, *Nat. Hist.* V 73: *"gens sola et in toto orbe praeter ceteras mira."* *Gens sola* means that the Essenes' moral or ethical standards in regard to marriage and possessions are unique in the ancient world.

munal, cenobitic life.[44] In this perspective, the suggestion of the existence of any cenobitic community in pre-Christian Judaism is against all historical probability.

Once the possibility is granted that texts such as 1QS are statutes of associations, it would be possible to expand the range within which such associations could have existed. We know from countless Greek, Roman, and even Palmyrenian references that religious associations often were attached to temples and were entrusted with service and maintenance of the cult.[45] In those associations that were cult-associations in a narrow sense usually the priests of the cult were organized, but there were others that included laymen as well.[46] Without going into any detail, I want to point to the possibility that statutes found in the Qumran caves might possibly belong to assemblies of priests or Levites attached to the Jerusalem Temple.[47] If that could be proved, we would have first-hand evidence about the priestly organization in *mishmarôt* and *ma'amadôt*.[48] Although highly hypothetical, this idea is of importance in view of the many references to cultic language, concepts, and matters in the Qumran scrolls. If it could be affirmed, those references would not have to be interpreted as a "spiritualization" of cultic ideas, but could indeed relate to the real cult.

A final and more tangible conclusion I want to draw from this understanding of 1QS is related to the communal meal mentioned in 1QS VI 2f, which has attracted a lot of attention among scholars of Christianity because of its similarity to the early Christian eucharist. The claim has been made that the three references to communal activities—"together they shall eat, together they shall bless, together they shall take counsel"—relate to three different kinds of gatherings.[49] If the group behind 1QS is an association or a synagogue community, this is very unlikely, because what all associations of the Hellenistic-Roman world have in common is the way they assemble: this is probably the steadiest feature of all in the life of associations. The assemblies always consist of three parts: they begin with a communal meal (Gr. *deipnon*, Lat. *cena*) that was followed by the libation. The religious ceremony of the libation, originally the concluding part of the meal, was usually accompanied by the *paian*, a religious hymn that was sung in unison. What followed was the *symposium* proper, a drinking party. This was generally the most important part of the meeting in which the actual life of the community took place. The

[44] *Cf.* BACHT (1956); SCHNEEMELCHER (1964).
[45] For the Greek cults *cf.* STENGEL (1920); for Rome: LATTE (1960). For Palmyra *cf.* MILIK (1972) and the inscription of the association of Bêl-priests published by TEIXIDOR (1981). For the Semitic institution of the *marzeah cf.* BRYAN (1980).
[46] *E.g.*, the private Lydian cult at Philadelphia: SOKOLOWSKI (1955), no. 20.
[47] One could consider 1QSa and 4QOrd^a (= 4Q159: ALLEGRO [1968], 6–9) as being related to the Jerusalem Temple.
[48] For the *mishmarôt* and *ma'amadôt cf.* SCHÜRER (1979), 237–313 (with bibliography).
[49] SCHIFFMAN (1983), 191.

symposium provided the opportunity for honoring members of merit, for coun-seling disciplinary cases (actually a very important part of communal life),[50] and for entertainment, which often consisted of learned conversation and teaching. It is obvious that the three communal activities of 1QS VI—even in correct order—relate to this very kind of assembly. The particular character of the "Qumran meal" must be determined in this perspective: it is "sacral," meaning it is not an everyday meal. The requirements of purity, of priestly domination, of certain disciplinary prescriptions do fit perfectly into the set-ting of the meal of any religious association. It is, therefore, not even necessary to determine the religious character of this meal in the light of the messianic meal of 1QSa, although this religious aspect cannot be excluded for certain.[51]

The question is then: Can it be that those activities of eating, blessing and taking counsel refer to the worship service of the *yachad* synagogue? There are some hints that this might be true. It is well known that the architecture of Second Temple synagogues is very similar to the *triclinium*, the assembly hall for common meals and *symposia*; the synagogue in Masada was actually built in a *triclinium*.[52] The architectural resemblance between *triclinia* and syna-gogue buildings is not at all surprising, if synagogue communities not only shared the organizational form of associations, but also led a similar life, which took place in the *triclinia*. Besides, it is not surprising that scriptural readings could have taken place in such a setting. I already mentioned the conversation at the occasion of the *symposium*. This conversation was such an important fea-ture that a whole literary genre emerged from it, the symposia literature. This literature, which existed from Plato to the Middle Ages, was primarily a *didactic genre*, often in the form of the *erotapocrisis*—that is, questions and answers.[53] If these questions and answers were related to biblical writings, as is the case with Philo's *Quaestiones in Genesim* and *in Exodum*, the result would be exactly what Philo says about the teaching in the assemblies of the Therapeutae—an allegorical interpretation or exegesis in the setting of a symposium-meeting.[54]

I will stop here, since proving these suggestions is beyond the scope of this paper. But it is important to recognize their possibility, as it could shed light on the pre-Rabbinic origin and history of synagogue worship.

Let me finally point to the general importance of interpreting 1QS and the group to which it applies in the light of Hellenistic associations. Although there is no question about the intensive encounter of Greek and Jewish reli-

---

[50] Still the most instructive study is SAN NICOLO's description of disciplinary jurisdiction of associations in Ptolemaic Egypt (1927).

[51] *E.g.*, SCHIFFMAN (1983), 191ff.

[52] *Cf.* FOERSTER (1982); NETZER (1982); YADIN (1982). The same could be said about some of the older Diaspora synagogues, *e.g.*, in Delos.

[53] MARTIN (1931); STEIN (1957).

[54] Aulus Gellius states several times that interpretation of texts and discussion of exegetical problems took place at *symposia*: These are the *symposiaka zētēmata* (NoctAtt II 22; II 27; III 19 etc.).

gion and culture in Hellenistic Palestine in general, it has not yet been spelled out what consequences this could have. The Qumran writings must be seen much more in the light of Greek-Hellenistic culture than has been done so far, because this is the only reasonable way to provide productive historical parallels to them that are able to break up the isolation of a "sectarian" setting. Comparing 1QS to statutes of pagan-Hellenistic associations is of great *methodological importance*: these analogies are the only ones relative to the organization of the *yachad* we have so far—no matter how convincing they are in particular. In my opinion, the burden of proof lies with the critics of this perspective: any criticism must provide historical analogies that are more convincing than the statutes of Hellenistic associations.

If, however, the Qumran texts are put into this wider context of Hellenistic culture, they might seem to lose the outstanding singularity partially responsible for the attention they have attracted. But this is not true. It is only Hellenism as the historical and cultural context of the Qumran writings that provides the means for understanding and evaluating 1QS. For if 1QS is seen in this cultural context of Hellenism—and if the statutes of Hellenistic associations are acknowledged to be the closest analogies—then 1QS gains a unique importance: It is the only documentary testimony about the organization of a Palestinian synagogue community in the second Temple period, thus shedding some light upon the crucial questions of origin and early history of synagogue communities in general. Beyond that, 1QS illuminates the way in which Hellenistic Judaism realized traditional religious values (such as purity, election, priestly orientation, *etc.*) in an altered cultural situation by adopting the social form of associations, thus bearing witness to the vital powers of Hellenistic Judaism and to its ability to accommodate itself to a new cultural and political situation without abandoning its religious identity.

REFERENCES

ALLEGRO, J. M.
1968   Qumrân Cave 4. Vol. I (4Q158–4Q186). *DJDJ* V. Oxford.
APPLEBAUM, S.
1974   The Organization of the Jewish Communities in the Diaspora. In *The Jewish People in the First Century: Historical Geography, Political History, Social, Cultural and Religious Life and Institutions. Vol. I.* S. SAFRAI & M. STERN, Eds. Assen :464–503.
BACHT, H.
1956   Antonius und Pachomius. Von der Anachorese zum Cönobitentum. In *Antonius Magnus Eremita 356–1956: Studia ad antiquum monachismum spectantia cura B. Steidle.* :66–107. Rome.
BAILLET, M.
1982   Qumrân Grotte 4. Vol. III (4Q482–4Q520). *DJD* VII. Oxford.

BARDTKE, H.
1961   Die Rechtsstellung der Qumran-Gemeinde. *Theologische Literaturzeitung* **86**: 93–101.
BAUMGARTEN, J. M.
1992   The Cave 4 Versions of the Qumran Penal Code. *Journal of Jewish Studies* **43**: 268–276.
BIETENHARD, H.
1979   Die Handschriftenfunde vom Toten Meer (Ḥirbet Qumran) und die Essener-Frage. Die Funde in der Wüste Juda (Eine Orientierung). In *Aufstieg und Niedergang der Römischen Welt. Vol. II 19/1.* W. HAASE & H. TEMPORINI, Eds.: 704–778. Berlin–New York.
BÖMER, F.
1957   Untersuchungen über die Religion der Sklaven in Griechenland und Rom. Part 1. In *Abhandlungen der Akademie der Wissenschaften und der Literatur in Mainz. Geistes- und sozialwissenschaftliche Klasse 7.* :374–580. Wiesbaden–Mainz.
BRYAN, D. B.
1980   *Texts Relating to the Marzeah: A Study of an Ancient Semitic Institution.* Dissertation, Johns Hopkins University, Baltimore, MD (1973). Ann Arbor.
CAPPER, B. J.
1986   "In der Hand des Ananias . . ." Erwägungen zu 1QS VI, 20 und der urchristlichen Gütergemeinschaft. *Revue de Qumran* **12**: 223–235.
CENIVAL, FR. DE
1972   *Les associations religieuses en Égypte d'après les documents démotiques.* Cairo.
DESSAU, H., Ed.
1892ff *Inscriptiones Latinae Selectae. Vols. I–III.* Berlin.
DITTENBERGER, W.
1898/1901 *Sylloge Inscriptionum Graecarum. Vols. I–III.* 2nd edit. Leipzig.
DOMBROWSKI, B. W.
1966   היחד in 1QS and τὸ κοινόν. *Harvard Theological Review* **59**: 293–307.
EISENMAN, R. and M. WISE
1992   *The Dead Sea Scrolls Uncovered.* Shaftesbury–Rockport–Brisbane.
ERICHSEN, W.
1959   Die Satzungen einer ägyptischen Kultgenossenschaft aus der Ptolemäerzeit. Nach einem demotischen Papyrus in Prag. In *Historisk-Filosofisk Skrifter Videnskabernes Selskab 4 No. 1.* Kopenhagen.
FOERSTER, G.
1982   The Synagogues at Masada and Herodium. In *Ancient Synagogues Revealed.* L. I. Levine, Ed.: 24–29. Jerusalem.
FREY, J. B., Ed.
1936   *Corpus Inscriptionum Judaicarum: Recueil des inscriptions juives qui vont du IIIe siècle avant Jésus-Christ au VIIe siècle de notre ère. Vol. I, Europe.* Rome (= repr. New York 1975).
GOLB, N.
1980   The Problem of Origin and Identification of the Dead Sea Scrolls. *Proceedings of the American Philosophical Society* **124**: 1–24.
1985   Les manuscrits de la Mer Morte: Une nouvelle approche du problème de leur origine. *Annales: Economies Sociétés Civilisations* **40**: 1133–1149.
1989   The Dead Sea Scrolls: A New Perspective. *The American Scholar* **58**: 177–207.
GOODENOUGH, E. R.
1953/1969 *Jewish Symbols in the Greco-Roman Period. Vols. I–XIII.* New York.

GRENFELL, F. P., A. S. HUNT, J. G. SMYLY, and E. GOODSPEED, Eds.
1902/1907   The Tebtunis Papyri I/II. London–New York.
HEINRICI, G.
1876   Die Christengemeinde von Korinth und die religiösen Genossenschaften der Griechen. Zeitschrift für wissenschaftliche Theologie 19: 465–526.
1881   Zum genossenschaftlichen Charakter der paulinischen Christengemeinde. Theologische Studien und Kritiken 54: 505–524.
HENGEL, M.
1978   Qumran und der Hellenismus. In Qumrân, sa piété, sa théologie et son milieu. M. DELCOR, Ed.: 333–372. Paris–Leeuven.
1988   Judentum und Hellenismus: Studien zu ihrer Begegnung unter besonderer Berücksichtigung Palästinas bis zur Mitte des 2. Jh.s v. Chr. 3rd, enlarged edit. Tübingen.
HENZEN, W.
1874   Acta Fratrum Arvalium quae supersunt restituit et illustravit. Berlin (= repr. 1967).
HERRMANN, P., J. H. WASZINK, C. COLPE, and B. KÖTTING
1978   Art. Genossenschaft. Reallexikon für Antike und Christentum 10: 84–155.
HILLER VON GAERTRINGEN, F., Ed.
1907   Inscriptiones Graecae Vol. XII: Inscriptiones Insularum Maris Aegaei, fasc. 3. Berlin.
KLAUCK, H. J.
1982   Gütergemeinschaft in der klassischen Antike, in Qumran und im Neuen Testament. Revue de Qumran 11: 47–79.
KOFFMAHN, E.
1961   Rechtsstellung und hierarchischer Charakter des יחד von Qumran. Biblica 42: 433–442.
KRAUSS, S.
1992   Synagogale Altertümer. Berlin–Wien (= repr. Hildesheim 1966).
LATTE, K.
1960   Römische Religionsgeschichte. Handbuch der Altertumswissenschaften. Vol. V/4. München.
LAUM, B.
1914   Stiftungen in der griechischen und römischen Antike: Ein Beitrag zur antiken Kulturgeschichte. Vols. I/II. Berlin.
LEON, H. L.
1960   The Jews of Ancient Rome. Philadelphia.
LEVINE, D. B.
1985   Symposium and the Polis. In Theognis of Megara: Poetry and the Polis. T. J. FIGUEIRA & G. NAGY, Eds.: 176–196. Baltimore–London.
LIEBENAM, W.
1890   Zur Geschichte und Organisation des römischen Vereinswesens: Drei Untersuchungen. Leipzig.
MARTIN, J.
1931   Symposion: Die Geschichte einer literarischen Form. Paderborn (= repr. New York–London 1968).
MILIK, J. T.
1972   Dédicaces faites par des dieux (Palmyre, Hatra, Tyr) et des thiases sémitiques à l'époque romaine. Paris.
MOMMSEN, TH., Ed.
1873   Corpus Inscriptionum Latinarum vol. III: Inscriptiones Asiae, provinciarum Europae Graecarum, Illyrici Latinae. Berlin.

MURPHY-O'CONNOR, J.
1979   La genèse littéraire de la Règle de la Communauté. *Révue Biblique* **76**: 528–540.
NETZER, E.
1982   The Herodian Triclinia – A Prototype for the "Galilean-Type" Synagogue. In *Ancient Synagogues Revealed*. L. I. LEVINE, Ed.: 49–51. Jerusalem.
POLAND, F.
1909   *Geschichte des griechischen Vereinswesens.* Leipzig.
RENGSTORF, K.-H.
1960   *Hirbet Qumrân und die Bibliothek vom Toten Meer.* Studia Delitzschiana 5. Stuttgart.
ROBERTS, C., T. C. SKEAT, and A. D. NOCK
1936   The Gild of Zeus Hypsistos. *Harvard Theological Review* **29**: 39–88.
SAFRAI, S.
1976   The Synagogue. In *The Jewish People in the First Century: Historical Geography, Political History, Social, Cultural and Religious Life and Institutions. Vol. II.* S. SAFRAI and M. STERN, Eds.: 908–944. Philadelphia.
SAN NICOLO, M.
1927   Vereinsgerichtsbarkeit im Hellenistischen Ägypten. In *Epitymbion H. Swoboda dargebracht.*:255–300. Reichenberg.
1972   *Ägyptisches Vereinswesen zur Zeit der Ptolemäer und der Römer. Erster Teil: Die Vereinsarten; Zweiter Teil: Vereinswesen und Vereinsrecht,* 2nd edit. J. HERRMANN, Ed. Münchener Beiträge zur Papyrusforschung und antiken Rechtsgeschichte 2/I–II. München.
SCHIFFMAN, L. H.
1983   *Sectarian Law in the Dead Sea Scrolls: Courts, Testimony, and the Penal Code.* Chico, CA.
SCHNEEMELCHER, W.
1964   Erwägungen zu dem Ursprung des Mönchtums in Ägypten. In *Christentum am Nil.*:131–141. Recklinghausen.
SCHNEIDER, C.
1963   Zur Problematik des Hellenistischen in den Qumrantexten. In *Qumran-Probleme*. H. BARDTKE, Ed. Deutsche Akademie der Wissenschaften zu Berlin. Schriften der Sektion für Altertumswissenschaft **42**: 299–314.
SCHÜRER, E.
1979   *The History of the Jewish People in the Age of Jesus Christ* (175 B.C.–A.D. 135). A New English version revised and edited by G. VERMES, F. MILLAR & M. BLACK. Edinburgh.
SPIEGELBERG, W.
1906/1908   *Catalogue général des antiquités égyptiennes du Musée du Caire. Die demotischen Denkmäler 30601-31270.50001-50022.* Die Demotischen Papyrus I/II. Straßburg.
SOKOLOWSKI, F.
1955   *Lois sacreés de l'Asie Mineure.* Paris.
STEGEMANN, H.
1988   Zu Textbestand und Grundgedanken von 1QS III,13–IV,26. In *Mémorial J. Carmignac.* F. GARCÍA MARTÍNEZ and E. PUECH, Eds.:95–131. Paris.
STENGEL, P.
1920   *Die griechischen Kultusaltertümer.* Handbuch der Altertumswissenschaften. Vol. V/3. 3rd edit. München.

STEIN, S.
    1957   The Influence of Symposia Literature on the Literary Form of the Pesah
            Haggadah. *Journal of Jewish Studies* **8**: 13–44.
TEIXIDOR, J.
    1981   Le thiase de Bêlastor et de Beelshamên d'après une inscription récemment
            découverte à Palmyre. In *Comptes rendus des séances de l'académie des inscriptions
            et belles lettres* :306–314. Paris.
TOV, E.
    1992   The Unpublished Texts from Caves 4 and 11. *Journal of Jewish Studies* **43**:
            101–136.
TYLOCH, W.
    1967   Les thiases et la communauté de Qoumran. In *Fourth World Congress of Jewish
            Studies: Papers I* :225–228. Jerusalem.
VERMES, G.
    1991   Preliminary Remarks on Unpublished Fragments of the Community Rule
            from Qumran Cave 4. *Journal of Jewish Studies* **42**: 250–255.
WALTZING, J. P.
    1895/1900 *Etude historique sur les corporations professionelles chez les Romains I–IV.* Paris.
WEINFELD, M.
    1986   *The Organizational Pattern and the Penal Code of the Qumran Sect.* Novum Tes-
            tamentum et Orbis Antiquus 2. Fribourg–Göttingen.
WERNBERG-MØLLER, P.
    1969   The Nature of the YAHAD According to the Manual of Discipline and Re-
            lated Documents. In *Dead Sea Scrolls Studies 1969.* Annual of Leeds Univer-
            sity Oriental Society **6**: 56–81. Leiden.
WILAMOWITZ-MOELLENDORFF, U. VON
    1904   Satzungen einer milesischen Sängergilde. In *Sitzungsberichte der Preussischen
            Akademie der Wissenschaft* :619–640. Berlin.
YADIN, Y.
    1982   The Synagogue at Masada. In *Ancient Synagogues Revealed.* L. I. LEVINE,
            Ed.: 19–23. Jerusalem.
ZIEBARTH, E.
    1896   *Das griechische Vereinswesen.* Stuttgart.

DISCUSSION OF THE PAPER

DENNIS PARDEE (*University of Chicago, Chicago, IL*): I wonder if you'd say
a few words about the relationship between the given synagogue community
with its rule and a broader community. Just to take two examples, I believe
one of the classical sources refers to several thousand Essenes; also, the early
Christian groups would have been very widespread. Would they have had a
common rule for each synagogue, geographically spread apart, or would they
each have had an individual rule? What would have been the relationship between a given synagogue and a much broader community?

MATTHIAS KLINGHARDT (*Universität Augsburg, Augsburg, Germany*): The question of whether there existed an overall organization for Jewish synagogues in the Second Temple period or not is a much-belabored issue. It is debated especially for Rome where we have an abundance of epigraphical evidence; yet the existence of this alleged organization (the *gerousia*) can not be confirmed (see LEON, 1960). Therefore, it is more probable that each synagogue community had its own individual statutes and organization.

The evidence we have from the Demotic associations (which were very much alike) and from early Christianity points into the same direction: Each single community or association had statutes of their own which, however, were very much alike: If we did not have the name of the eponymous deity or the founder of many of the Demotic associations, we could hardly confirm the existence of different groups. In early Christianity the existence of a common rule for several congregations is the result of a longer process that did not start prior to the end of the 2nd century C.E.

HARTMUT STEGEMANN (*University of Göttingen, Göttingen, Germany*): The community of the *yachad* which is behind 1QS is a group which has some connection with everything, and yet clearly different local groups. That's clear from column 6, which you have recorded. Also there is the idea here they are at different places. How can you arrange this clear finding in column 6 with your idea of synagogue community? On the other hand, you commented on *yachad*, a term which is used in these manuscripts very often. It gives a special idea of their organization. If you look for their characteristics, a central one is that they designate themselves as *berit 'or*. They are the representatives of this *berit*; at the same time, this *berit* is for all of Israel. Is it possible to think something like the synagogue community covered all of Israel?

KLINGHARDT: Since I discuss the possibility of 1QS being a composition of several statutes, I have no problems with the idea that 1QS applies to several groups which, of course, would have assembled in different places. I think this is a fair possibility.

But even if 1QS is related to only one group, different meeting places would not be unusual, for there exist many analogies. I give a few examples: Most of the Egyptian associations assembled in different places; the famous statutes of the Zeus-Hypsistos association (ROBERTS, SKEAT & NOCK, 1936) mention "outings," and the Demotic codes frequently imply that assemblies were held in at least two different places, the regular meeting room and the funeral sites where the *perideipnon* was to take place. In Rome, the *fratres Arvalium* (HENZEN, 1874) assembled and performed their religious and social activities in three different places.

The variety of meetings and meeting places mentioned in 1QS can, therefore, be explained in two ways: The statutes of 1QS could either belong to different groups (which means different meeting places), or they could apply to only one group that assembled in different places and at different occasions.

Frankly, I find the second question much harder to answer: Whether the *yachad's* claim to represent all of Israel can be attributed to a synagogue rather than to a "sect." We tend to think that the claim of exclusive representation implies a sectarian character, since it denies the legitimacy of other, similar groups. But the idea of exclusive representation is not unparalleled: We can find it among the numerous Dionysiac associations, and here this claim implies that there should be only one Dionysiac association at one place or in one city. Since these Dionysiac *technitai* were guilds of craftsmen and performing artists, the claim of exclusivity has far-reaching social and economical consequences.

The same would be true for early Christian analogies: Paul's denying the legitimacy of his opponents in Galatia and Corinth and his claim that his gospel is the only true one (Gal 1,8!) reflect social and economical tensions as well as religious. But Paul does certainly not want to say that there did not exist any legitimate congregations beside those founded by him.

Therefore, I think that the idea of a limited, local competition between synagogues could also apply to the *yachad* (as a synagogue) and explain its claim to represent all of Israel.

JAMES VANDERKAM (*University of Notre Dame, Notre Dame, IN*): It was not clear to me how you related, if you did, the community of the *Serekh Ha-Yachad* to Qumran. And second, could you summarize the range of dates for your parallel associations?

KLINGHARDT: Firstly, I do not connect the *Serekh Ha-Yachad* to Qumran at all. The only connection I see is that 1QS was found in one of the caves near Khirbet Qumran. I wanted to make clear that the idea of cenobitic life—which means living under one roof day and night—does not exist in antiquity prior to the Egyptian monks of the 4th century C.E. Since it is, therefore, not very probable that there ever existed a monastic group in Qumran, and since there is no need to postulate one in order to explain 1QS, my idea tends to support Professor Golb's suggestion of an origin of these writings elsewhere, be it in Jerusalem or wherever.

Secondly: We have evidence for associations that were similar to 1QS in regard the legal status and the social organization from the 5th century B.C.E. to the 2nd and 3rd centuries C.E. But most of what I rely on in my paper stems from the Hellenistic-Roman world between 200 B.C.E. and 100 C.E.

VANDERKAM: It's interesting that the Serekh says a group went to the wilderness to prepare the way of the Lord.

KLINGHARDT: Yes, many groups were linked to or had their origins in the wilderness—but nevertheless lived in cities. A famous example is John the Baptist and his followers in Ephesus (Acts 19), not to speak of the earliest Palestinian Christians. But I am not really dealing with the origin of the Qumran texts. This is not the purpose of my paper.

PAULINE DONCEEL-VOÛTE (*University of Louvain, Humain, Belgium*): I was of course very interested in many ways in your talk and I think I totally agree with everything. It all links up very well with the general Hellenistic ways of life. Apart from that I wanted to draw your attention to a rather important enterprise of linking Hellenism with Jewish antiquity in Palestine and around it, which started with the translation by Etienne Nodet of Josephus's *Jewish Antiquities*. There is a group of students, more or less contemporary with you, who are working on the relations between temple furniture and the Jewish Temple in Jerusalem, *etc.*

EPHRAIM ISAAC (*Institute of Semitic Studies, Princeton, NJ*): I subscribe to many of your very interesting original interpretations. I especially appreciate your disabusing us of this expression "sect," although the terminology might be very old. You made a statement that we don't have an example of a cenobitic community in antiquity before the fourth century monks. I assume you are specifically referring to the ancient Near East, you're not including Asia . . .

KLINGHARDT: No, I'm not . . .

ISAAC: I see . . .

KLINGHARDT: I'm only referring to the range where our real proven historical relations lie: Greece, Rome, and the Near East.

ISAAC: Okay, fine.

Morphological and Philological Observations: Preparing the Critical Text and Translation of the *Serek Ha-Yaḥad*

JAMES H. CHARLESWORTH

Princeton Theological Seminary, CN821
Princeton, New Jersey 08542-0803

As experts on the Dead Sea Scrolls have known for some time, the Princeton Theological Seminary Dead Sea Scrolls Project was launched in 1985. The need for a comprehensive edition of the Dead Sea Scrolls was stressed by Professor Elisha Qimron and published by Professor Lawrence Schiffman in 1990. Both of these distinguished scholars, and many others in this symposium, are heavily involved in the Project.

Meetings of the subeditors have been held during the SBL annual meetings. The subeditors are from the United States, Israel, Canada, Great Britain, and Germany. The Board of Editorial Advisors is made up of Professors Frank Cross, Noel Freedman, James Sanders, and Shemaryahu Talmon. The first publication was *The Dead Sea Scrolls: Graphic Concordance*, which appeared in 1991. Now, the first two volumes of texts, translations, introductions, and notes have been sent to J.C.B. Mohr (Paul Siebeck) in Tübingen for publication.

After seven years of work, the critical text of 1QS, with an *apparatus criticus*, and the critical texts of all Cave IV fragments of the *Rule of the Community*, have been prepared, corrected, printed out, and shipped to the publisher. Professor Qimron submitted to the editorial team not only the critically revised and improved text of 1QS but also the transcriptions of the 4Q fragments of the *Rule of the Community*. Thanks to improved photographs of all the data, and improved understandings of the morphology and philology of Qumran Hebrew, many readings have been improved. The revised methodology for presenting the text, which was developed in dialogue with others, especially Professor Qimron, intends to present more faithfully what the scribe, and the correcting scribes, left on the leather. Sections of 1QS once considered unclear have been discerned and comprehended.

Sigla and signa have been developed for the preparation of texts on the IBYCUS Computer System. Professor Richard E. Whitaker, one of the most distinguished experts in the field of Semitics and computer technology, developed software so that the IBYCUS system can present both on screen and on hardcopy the peculiar forms found in the Dead Sea Scrolls. It was necessary, of course, to devise methods to represent supralinear letters, and to present these not only with the scribal dots for errors but also the editorial notations that indicated the degree of certainty for each consonant. This was a difficult task, especially when supralinear words needed to be shown above consonants that had been erased, and which had earlier received supralinear and sublinear dots by a corrected scribe. The labor intensive work was successful; the critical texts reveal the state-of-the-art method for presenting what the scribe wrote, what other scribes corrected, and what an editor discerned to be readable, and with what certainty.

This task was difficult enough. Then, it increased astronomically with the additions of the *apparatus criticus* demanded by the inclusion of readings from the Cave IV fragments of the *Rule of the Community*. Prior to the inclusion of the apparatus the page was filled with text; and it represented on one page what was in one column of a scroll. The size of an apparatus sometimes filled one-fifth of a page. The problems encountered should be easy to imagine. The results can now be seen in the first two volumes of texts, translations, and introductions to the rules of Qumran. These volumes will be available this summer and are published by Mohr (Paul Siebeck) and distributed in the United States by Westminster/John Knox Press.

The introductions, translations, and notes to 1QS and to the 4Q fragments have gone through the same cycle as all of the texts. Assisted by Professor Qimron and Michael T. Davis, I have assumed responsibility for this work.

PREPARING THE *SEREK HA-YAHAD* IN THE NEW EDITION

In the following pages I will present some reflections on preparing the *Rule of the Community* for publication. The first, and most obvious, problem relates to nomenclature. No longer should a scholar refer to 1QS as synonymous with the *Rule of the Community*. 1QS is one copy of the document called the *Rule of the Community*. The 4Q fragments of the document present a text that is often markedly divergent from that represented in 1QS. It is now clear that 1QS is by no means a perfect copy of this document; but it is the only one which is extant in a full form. Not only are the readings in 1QS often inferior to the readings in the other exemplars, but these versions have been transmitted through diverse means. 1QS was not copied from earlier manuscripts like it; it incorporates different documents that had separate histories of transmission.

What is the title of this document? It used to be called the *Manual of Discipline*, which was the name given to it by Professor Millar Burrows, who admitted it reminded him of the Methodist book of discipline. Fortunately, the title of 1QS is preserved in a fragment that probably was used to cover this copy. In 1Q28 is preserved the Hebrew words סר]ך היחד (*cf.* DJD 1, Plate 22). These facts indicate the title given by the Qumranites to this document; hence the title of this document is the *Rule of the Community*. The document may be mentioned in 1QM 15.5, in which we find the phrase ספר היחד, which obviously means "the document (or book) of the Community"; this same phrase appears also in 4QS MS A.

THE PREAMBLE TO THE *SEREK HA-YAḤAD*

How does the *Rule of the Community* begin? The published translations of 1QS do not adequately represent the philology of the opening column and the Preamble of 1.1–15. In order to present a smooth idiomatic translation, scholars have understandably chosen to use finite verbs to represent the string of infinitives.

In the new translation these infinitives are taken seriously and literally. The Preamble, in only 15 lines, contains no less than 22 infinitive constructs; each has a prefixed Lamed, denoting the purpose of the actions; there is only one finite verb. It becomes clear that these infinitives were chosen to clarify the purpose of entering the covenant before God by means of the statutes in this document, the *Rule of the Community*. The leading infinitives are translated "in order to." Those infinitives dependent on the leading infinitives are translated as English participles, following the rule of Semitics that Hebrew infinitives often carry the force of English participles (see Waltke and O'Connor, pp. 598–610).

By carefully crafting the Preamble with a string of infinitive clauses, the author pointed to the purpose of the *Rule of the Community*. He was also able to summarize the high points contained in the remaining columns. Note these purpose clauses:

> In order to seek God . . . and in order to love all that he has chosen, and to hate all that he has rejected, . . . and in order to perform truth and righteousness and justice upon the earth; . . . in order to receive all those who devote themselves to do the statutes of God into the covenant of mercy, . . . and in order to love all the Sons of Light . . . and to hate all the Sons of Darkness . . . and in order not to deviate from any single one of all the commands of God. . . .

Thus, all those who are Sons of Light and intend to live according to such purposes may now "cross over into the covenant before God," which is the first sentence after the Preamble. How can they cross this sociological barrier? It is, in the words of the rest of the sentence, "by the Rule of the Community." Hence, the Preamble clarifies the purpose of entering the New Covenant and the means, specifically referring to this document and its contents.

THREE EXAMPLES OF IMPROVED TRANSLATIONS

What are three examples of new and improved translations? The first example is from column one, lines 21 and 22:

> (21) Then the priests shall report the righteousness of God along with its wondrous works, (22) and recount all (his) merciful acts of love towards Israel.

Verse 21 is almost always translated as if the suffix to "wondrous works" is an odd form of the third masculine singular suffix or an error for it. Note Leaney's translation (p. 123): "The priests recount the righteous acts of God in the deeds of his power and recite all the gracious acts of mercy towards Israel; . . . ." The Hebrew for his translation "in the deeds of his power" is במעשי גבורתום.

Perhaps the suffixed form -*wm* in *gbwrtwm* is neither an error for *w* ("his") nor denotes a putative singular suffix "his," which would refer to '*l* (a singular noun). The plural form, "their," refers back to the plural noun *sdqwt*, "righteousness," (as Brownlee noted in *BASORSS* 10–12 [1951] 9). Thus, I take this pronominal suffix to be the Qumran form of the third plural, "their." That meaning is the one recognized by specialists when this form occurs elsewhere in 1QS; see 1QS 5.20 which has *hwn(w)m* and means "their property" (note the erasure). Also see 5.21 and 9.14 which have *rwḥwm* and denote "their spirits."

The form -*wm* does not appear elsewhere in 1QS. The clear evidence that phonetics caused the pronunciation of a Mem at the end of some syllables is not questioned, but if 1QS 1.21 is the only passage in which the suffix -*wm* means "his," and not the expected "theirs," then it is highly doubtful that this suffixal form meant "his" in 1QS or anywhere in Qumran Hebrew.

I am therefore led to disagree with Qimron (*HDSS*, p. 27–28). This position developed gradually, since it is unwise to differ with one who not only has devoted his life to Qumran philology and grammar, but is also–in my judgment–one of the finest Hebrew philologians in the world. Qimron thinks that in Qumran Hebrew -*wm* denoted not only the third plural masculine suffix but also the third singular masculine suffix. The only examples he knows are 1QS 1.21 and 5.21; but I am not convinced that context demands this explanation for either passage.

The suffix -*wm*, "their," may also conceivably denote the plural Godhead (*cf.* Gen 1) or the divine beings working with God in heaven (*viz.* the *'elim*, angels, archangels, Word, Voice, Wisdom). Perhaps "their" in 1QS 1.21 comes from the memorization of Gen 1:1 which indicates that the plural noun for God was associated with the act of creation. Also, the apocalyptic imagery of more than one hypostatic being who helped God in creation, or the numerous divine beings in heaven (*cf.* the *Angelic Liturgy* [4Q400–407]) may explain the use of "their."

The second example of an improved translation in 1QS is found in column seven, which contains "the penal code"(see Weinfeld, pp. 26, 31). Here is the translation of lines 12–14:

(12) . . . Whoever walks naked before his fellow without being forced shall be punished (for) six months. (13) And a man who spits into the midst of the session of the Many, shall be punished (for) thirty days. Whoever causes his penis to come out from under his garment, or it (has) (14) holes so his nakedness is seen shall be punished (for) thirty days.

Almost all translators take the Hebrew literally so that יד = "hand": Lohse and Maier translate *yādhô* as "seine Hand." Brownlee (*BASORSS* 10–12 [1951] 30), Vermes, and Knibb offer "his hand." Dupont-Sommer (*EE*) and Pouilly follow the consensus for translating *yādhô*: "sa main." Moraldi follows the trend: "la sua mano."

But it is now clear that יד in Qumran Hebrew obtains the extended euphemistic meaning "penis." See especially 11Q Temple 46.13 in which מקום יד denotes not "the place of the hand," but the latrine, or literally the "place for the penis." In Ugaritic *yd* also clearly can mean "penis" (consult M. H. Pope, *El in the Ugaritic Texts* [SupVT 2; Leiden: Brill, 1955] p. 38, and C. H. Gordon, *Ugaritic Textbook* [AO 38; Rome: PIB, 1965] p. 409).

Note the excellent comments by Guilbert (*TdQ*, p. 51): "Celui qui fait sortir son 'membre' de sous son vétement, ..." Leaney also chose the word "member." Dupont-Sommer, Moraldi, and Knibb translate with "main," "mano," or "hand" but rightly state that "hand" is "a euphemism for the male sexual organ" (Dupont-Sommer, *EE*, p. 104 [also see Dupont-Sommer in *EcInt*, p. 30; Moraldi, p. 156; Knibb, p. 127]). An excellent discussion of the semantic range of meanings for *yd* has been published by M. Delcor (*JSS* 12 [1967] 234–40 [= Delcor, *Ancien*, pp. 143–49]) and Ackroyd (in *TDOT*, vol. 5, pp. 399–403).

Contrast Vermes' interpretative translation: "Whoever has been so poorly dressed that when drawing his hand from beneath his garment his nakedness has been seen. . . ." Vermes has probably understood the passage correctly, but decides to avoid the vulgar meaning; but the protrusion of the penis, not the hand, or nakedness from under the garment is what has apparently disturbed the leaders of the Community, probably the Council of the Community, and caused the addition of another regulation.

Contrast the present interpretation and translation with Wernberg-Møller's translation. He defends the rendering "one who stretches out his hand from under his cloak so that, he being clad in rags, his nakedness is seen. . . ." Wernberg-Møller (p. 118) concludes that the passage "alludes to the reaching out for food" which is proscribed according to Sirach 31 (34): 14, 18. Note again the translation of 1QS:

Whoever causes his penis to come out from under his garment, or it (has) (14) holes so his nakedness is seen shall be punished (for) thirty days.

The word translated "holes" is a restored Hebrew פוחה; the text reads פוח which seems to be an error. The emendation was first suggested by Brownlee who was influenced by discussions with M. Burrows and H. L. Ginsberg (in *BASORSS* 10–12 [1951] 31). In Mishnaic Hebrew the noun פּוֹחֵחַ is a Qal participle which derives from the verb פָּחַח; it denotes holes in one's garment (*cf.* Jastrow, p. 1152). In *Soph'rim* 14.15 a *pōhēaḥ* denotes someone whose garments are full of holes so that "his knees" or "legs" (*kr'yw*) protrude. There are no fragments from Cave IV or V that can help us confirm this emendation, but the scribal error in the next word (see *apparatus criticus* to the critical edition) strengthens the probability that פוח is an error. Grammatically the antecedent of the emendation פוחה is "his garment."

Some translators and exegetes may find this section of the *Rule of the Community* problematic; they may presuppose that the Qumranite emphasis on purity and perfection would demand a clean and well tailored garment. This supposition is incorrect. If in the first century C.E. the Qumranites were a strict form of the Essenes—as most specialists conclude—then there is a remarkable confirmation of our interpretation in Josephus' *War*, book 2, line 126 (noted also by Brownlee, *BASORSS*). In this passage the erudite Josephus describes the garments of the Essenes. This group of Jews are said to resemble children under strict discipline. They do not change their garments (*esthesis*), but wear them until they are worn out and full of holes (*diarragēnai to proteron pantapasin ē depanēthēnai tō chronō*). If the Essenes garments are shredded and full of holes, then it is easy to understand why at Qumran legislation was necessary to prohibit the exposure of the genitals through the clothing. Such an action, whether deliberate or accidental, would have been as disconcerting to the פקיד or מבקר as spitting into the midst of the session of the Many, proscribed in 7.13, or one who guffaws improperly, proscribed in 7.14.

The third, and final example of an improved translation is from the last column of 1QS. Note the translation of lines 20–22:

> What, indeed, is the son of Adam among your wondrous works?
> (21) Born of a woman, how can he dwell before you, he whose kneading (is) from dust and whose corpse (is) food for maggots? He is (but) a discharge, (mere) (22) pinched-off clay whose urge is for the dust.

The last sentence in this excerpt has frustrated the best translators. Guilbert (*TdQ*) could not solve the problem and concluded that מצירוק is "qumrânien, de racine inconnue." Lohse left it unpointed and put a question mark in his translation (pp. 42–44). Guilbert (*TdQ*) and Wernberg-Møller also place question marks in their translations.

Both 1QS and 4QMS J read מצירוק, which as Guilbert noted is an unattested form. Earlier some scholars separated the words, but such an attempt or any emendation is now less likely. Perhaps מצירוק is a composite form which consists of two words. In Mishnaic Hebrew, as is well known, רוק means "spit," and is a euphemism for "semen" (m.Niddah 16b). In Syriac *rûqâ'* denotes "spit" and "ignominia" (*Thesaurus Syriacus* 2,3973). Leaney notes this meaning and aptly cites Aboth 3:1, which calls semen "a putrid drop." Perhaps *msy-* is a contraction of the Hiphal participle of the root *ys'*, written *defectiva* (as one would expect in a contracted form with the shifting of the accent to the last syllable); it would then probably mean "coming forth." I conclude, therefore, that this unknown noun may be from two separate roots, and a contracted composite noun analogous to the well-known *ṣalmāweth* in Ps 23:4.

The translation presented is suggestive; it depends on the possibility that מצירוק means "discharged semen." The parallel with the pinched-off clay is important to observe. The meaning may well be simply ejected saliva, or spit. Vermes does not struggle with the problem; and presents the following translation: "He is but a shape, but moulded clay, /and inclines towards dust."

The tradition preserved in Aboth 3:1 is important. It is early and even assigned to Akabya b. Mahalaleel, a pre-70 Rabbi. The contiguous words and the context is a major help in solving the meaning of the ending of 1QS, and apparently the *Rule of the Community*. There is a well-crafted conceptual linkage between the coming forth of the human from "a putrid drop" and his going to "the place of maggots." Hence, perhaps the scribe of this hymn was denoting euphemistically the semen emitted in an ejaculation.

The proposal here, and the translation in the new edition of the *Rule of the Community* is greatly indebted to many specialists. Of special importance in research on 1QS is the work by Wernberg-Møller. He, however, presented long ago a rendering appreciably different from the one now defended. He translated the passage as follows: "he, who is saliva which has been emitted. . . ."

These three examples help the reader perceive that the new comprehensive edition of all the non-biblical Dead Sea Scrolls contains something familiar; but it will also present to the reader some challenging new renderings worthy of discussion and debate.

SELECTED BIBLIOGRAPHY OF PUBLICATIONS NOT OBVIOUS TO THE SPECIALIST

BROWNLEE, W. H.
  1951   *The Dead Sea Manual of Discipline: Translation and Notes.* BASOR Supplementary Studies 10–12. New Haven: American Schools of Oriental Research.
BURROWS, M.
  1955   *The Dead Sea Scrolls.* New York: Viking.
CHARLESWORTH, J. H., *et al.*, eds.
  1991   *The Dead Sea Scrolls: Graphic Concordance.* Tübingen: J.C.B. Mohr (Paul Siebeck); Louisville: Westminster/John Knox Press.
DUPONT-SOMMER, A.
  1980   *Les écrits esséniens découverts près de la Mer Morte.* Bibliothèque historique. Paris: Payot, (4th ed.). [=*EE*]

GUILBERT, P.
    1961   "La règle de la communauté," in *Les textes de Qumran traduits et annotés*,
            J. CARMIGNAC, *et al.*, eds. Paris: Letouzey et Ané, vol. 1, pp. 9–80. [=*TdQ*]
KNIBB, M.
    1987   *The Qumran Community.* Cambridge Commentaries on Writings of the
            Jewish and Christian World 200 BC to AD 200. Cambridge, New York:
            Cambridge University Press.
LEANEY, A. R. C.
    1966   *The Rule of Qumran and its Meaning.* New Testament Library; London:
            SCM; Philadelphia: Westminster.
LOHSE, E.
    1981   *Die Texte aus Qumran: Hebräisch und Deutsch.* Munich, Kösel, (3rd ed.).
MAIER, J.
    1960   *Die Texte vom Toten Meer*, 2 vols. Munich, Basel: Reinhardt.
MORALDI, L.
    1971   *I manoscritti di Qumrān.* Classical delle religioni. Turin: Unione Tipografico–
            Editrice Torinese.
POUILLY, J.
    1976   *La règle de la communauté de Qumrân: Son évolution littéraire.* Cahiers de la *RB*
            17. Paris: Gabalda.
QIMRON, E.
    1986   *The Hebrew of the Dead Sea Scrolls.* Harvard Semitic Studies 29. Atlanta:
            Scholars Press.
QIMRON, E.
    1990   "The Need for a Comprehensive Critical Edition of the Dead Sea Scrolls,"
            in *Archaeology and History in the Dead Sea Scrolls: The New York University Con-
            ference in Memory of Yigael Yadin*, L. H. SCHIFFMAN, Ed. JSPS 8 and JSOT/
            ASOR Monographs 2. Sheffield: Sheffield Academic Press, pp. 121–31; also
            see Charlesworth's "Concerning the New Comprehensive Edition of Pre-
            viously Published Qumran Documents," on pp. 132–33.
VERMES, G.
    1987   *The Dead Sea Scrolls in English*, 3rd edition. London: Penguin; New York:
            Viking Penguin.
WALTKE, B. K. and M. O'CONNOR
    1990   *An Introduction to Biblical Hebrew Syntax.* Winona Lake: Eisenbrauns.
WEINFELD, M.
    1986   *The Organizational Pattern and the Penal Code of the Qumran Sect.* Novum Tes-
            tamentum et Orbis Antiquus 2. Göttingen: Vandenhoeck & Ruprecht.
WERNBERG-MØLLER, P.
    1957   *The Manual of Discipline.* Studies on the Texts of the Desert of Judah 1;
            Leiden: Brill.

APPENDIX

The Rule of the Community, Isaiah 40:3, and Qumran Theology

Qumran theology is developed biblical theology. By that I mean it is fundamentally an exegetical expansion of the Hebrew scriptures, especially Isaiah.[1]

From the scrolls which survived in Cave IV we might be able to discern what were the most important biblical scrolls for the Qumranites. The most numerous copies were of Deuteronomy (14 copies), followed by Isaiah (12 copies), and then the Psalter (10 copies).[2] These statistics seem to indicate some of the scriptures which were most formative for the self-understanding of the Qumranites. Hence, it would follow that one of their favorite scriptures was the book of Isaiah, with its dreams for a better future in which God's promises are fulfilled, and with its means of preparing the way for this fulfillment. The means for prophetic fulfillment, according to the Qumranites, was found in Isaiah 40:3.

The large *Isaiah Scroll* (1QIs^a) is copied so that 40:3 is preceded by a *vacat*. Perhaps this open space was to draw attention to the supreme importance of the verse: קול קורא במדבר פנו דרך יהוה.[3] These words are usually interpreted by Jews and Christians today to mean, "A voice is calling in the wilderness, 'Prepare the way of the Lord.'"

The Qumranites, however, understood this verse to mean, "A Voice is calling, 'In the wilderness prepare the way of the Lord (Yahweh).'" They had left the Temple, claiming to be the only legitimate priests (Aaronites [Sons of Zadok] or Levites). More importantly, they had gone into the Judaean *wilderness* (במדבר)[4] to obey the Voice and to prepare the way of the Lord.[5] The document called *More Precepts of the Torah* (4QMMT) certainly helps us understand more of the halakhic rationale for this movement from Temple to wilderness.

---

[1] These additional comments were added to the published form of the lecture. They are intended to serve as a response to a question from Professor Golb (see the DISCUSSION which follows).

[2] F. M. Cross pointed out this fact in the fifties. See his *The Ancient Library of Qumran & Modern Biblical Studies*, revised edition (Grand Rapids: Baker, 1980 [a reprint of the 1961 edition]) p. 43.

[3] See the color photographs in *Scrolls from Qumrân Cave I*, edited by F. M. CROSS, D. N. FREEDMAN, J. A. SANDERS [from photographs by John C. Trever] (Jerusalem: Albright Institute of Archaeological Research and the Shrine of the Book, 1972) Plate XXXIII p. [81]. The tetragrammaton is written in square script (so it is not penned in Paleo-Hebrew or represented by four dots).

[4] במדבר is, of course, the name of "Numbers" in the TANAKH. See my note 37 to 1QSa in the first volume of the PTS DSS Project.

[5] As G. J. Brooke states, pointing to 1QS 8.14 and 9.19, the Qumran exegesis of Isaiah 40:3 is "so important for the self-understanding of the Qumran community." Brooke, *Exegesis at Qumran: 4QFlorilegium in its Jewish Context* (Journal for the Study of the Old Testament, Supplement Series 29; Sheffield: University of Sheffield, 1985) p. 104.

Here are some major texts which help us understand the way the Qumranites understood themselves, their reason for living in the wilderness, and their exegesis of Isaiah 40:3. In the comprehensive edition the translation of 1QS 8.12–14 is as follows:[6]

> When these become the Community in Israel [13] they shall separate themselves from the session of the men of deceit in order to depart into the wilderness to prepare the Way of the Lord (?);[7] [14] as it is written: "In the wilderness prepare the way of the Lord,[8] make level in the desert a highway for our God."

According to these verses the Qumranites separated themselves from "the men of deceit"–surely the "wicked" priests in the Temple–in order to prepare the "Way of the Lord" as Isaiah had prophesied (40:3).[9]

Note also 1QS 9.18–20:

> He shall guide them with knowledge, and instruct them in the mysteries of wonder and truth in the midst of [19] the men of the Community, so that they may walk perfectly each one with his fellow in everything which has been revealed to them. That is the time to prepare the way [19] to the wilderness.

It seems obvious, in light of 1QS 8.12–14 – probably one of the oldest sections of the *Rule of the Community*[10] – that in 1QS 9.18–20 Isaiah 40:3 is being interpreted to mean that the Qumranites went במדבר to prepare the way of the Lord. Khirbet Qumran – in my judgment – is obviously the place in the wilderness of Judaea in which the Righteous Teacher settled with the priests who followed him into the wilderness. They went במדבר "to prepare the way of the Lord."

The Qumran movement began as an eschatological acting out of a literal interpretation of Isaiah 40:3. The sectarian works, especially the *Rule of the Community* and the *Pesharim* (which reveal the eschatological and pneumatic exegesis of the Qumranites), clarify why the Qumranites were living in the wilderness.

The importance of the book of Isaiah for the Qumranites is now further confirmed by some additional observations. The *Scroll of Blessings* (1QSb) con-

---

[6] All translations of the Dead Sea Scrolls are according to the Princeton Theological Seminary Project. 1QS, 1QSa, and 1QSb are found in volume 1.

[7] "Lord" is written הואהא.

[8] "Lord"–the tetragrammaton–is written with four dots. This technique warns the Qumranite not to pronounce the divine name. This technique appears eight times in 4Q176 and in 4QTest 1.1. The punishment for pronouncing the tetragrammaton was severe, though it is now lost due to a lacuna (see 1QS 6 at the end of the column; cf. CD 9.5).

[9] D. Flusser is of the opinion that not only 1QS 8.12–14 but also the *Ascensio Isaiae* interpreted Isaiah 40:3 "as a literal command to go out into the wilderness in order to found there a new way of life." Flusser, in *Judaism and the Origins of Christianity*, ed. B. Young (Jerusalem: Magnes Press, 1988) pp. 36–37.

[10] See the arguments by J. Murphy-O'Connor in "La genèse littéraire de la Règle de la Communauté," *Revue Biblique* 76 (1969) 528–49.

cludes with words reminiscent of Isaiah 11:2–5. Two *Pesharim* were attributed to this prophetic book: *Isaiah Pesher 1* (4Q161–165) and *Isaiah Pesher 2* (3Q4). Also indicating the importance of Isaiah for the Qumranites is the unpublished document named the *Isaianic Fragment* (4Q285).

In conclusion, I am convinced that one of the most important biblical books for shaping the self-understanding of the Qumranites was the book of Isaiah. I am also persuaded that one of the reasons that led the Righteous Teacher to leave the Temple and to go into the wilderness was a literal exegesis of Isaiah 40:3; but then it is possible–indeed probable–that this meaning dawned with pellucid clarity only after he and the other priests with him were actually במדבר. Their interpretation of Isaiah 40:3 is certainly obvious in their collection of rules, namely the *Rule of the Community* (especially in columns 8 and 9).

DISCUSSION OF THE PAPER

MOSHE BERNSTEIN (*Yeshiva University, New York City*): You're publishing 1QS with an apparatus from the 4QS materials. Isn't that very dangerous for later scholars who are going to be employing this as the standard edition, presumably, of the text that you're publishing, being unaware of the problems of stematics that exist, because you've put it all together on one page? Are these independent documents, 4QS and whatever else we're going to call them, going to be printed someplace in your series, separately, so that a scholar can sit down with 1QS and with a complete text of whatever these other documents are in order to look at them independently? I think you're correct about *yad*, but I don't think that the passage from 11Q Temple that you've cited is an appropriate parallel. A *mqwm yd* describing a latrine is probably based on the passage of Deuteronomy where there shall be a *yad* for you outside the camp. I think you may be correct in that last passage, and it might be fruitful to consider other descriptions of the insignificance of human existence.

JAMES H. CHARLESWORTH (*Princeton Theological Seminary, Princeton, NJ*): I thoroughly agree with everything you said. 1QS will appear and then readings, all the readings, not just the variants are given for the text. Secondly, in the facing English translation you will receive a discussion of what the English translator considers the major variants. Then, on the left side of the page the text of every fragment is presented. So there are three places where you can look for variant readings. We are setting up a reference work; we are not making judgments. What we are doing is giving you the data; we want to give you a major reference work that will not be dated.

On the second point I really do need to doublecheck the Temple Scroll.

Three, yes. You know where most of this stuff is! Such deprecating comments abound in *Syriac colophons*; but it would take me 30 years to explore that terrain adequately.

NORMAN GOLB (*Oriental Institute, University of Chicago, Chicago, IL*): Dr. Charlesworth, I congratulate you on this project, and I look forward to reading the results during the coming summer eagerly. In the past I've criticized editors of the Qumran scrolls, including editors of the Oxford series, for working into the translations and the commentaries their particular interpretations of Qumran origins.

Now, there is a famous passage which quotes Isaiah 40:3; then they say, *zeh midrash ha-torah*, "this is the expounding of the Torah." In other words, they are using the words of Isaiah in a metaphorical way. Now this passage has often been used, it was used by my colleague VanderKam, to show that the people were going into the desert. We don't have that in the words. It's an interpretation foisted upon the text in order to support a particular theory of Qumran origins. Would you be able to divulge to us how you translate that passage, or is that an unfair question?

CHARLESWORTH: I hear two questions. The first one is, "Are interpretations going to be intrusive?" We have deliberately spent almost a decade doing our best to make this a noninterpretative translation. We are trying to publish something that will not be out of date, but does bring us together to study and discuss the data.

Now in terms of your second question, on Isaiah 40:3: I concur with you on one point, I differ with you on another. This, to me, is a very important passage. It becomes clear from the Isaiah scroll, where you have the space (*vacat*) before it. What does it mean? I think it's important to hear your suggestion. I have an interpretation and I have a right to say what my interpretation is. I think from my own reading this means to prepare in the wilderness a way for *the Community* (see APPENDIX).

GOLB: They're using the words of Isaiah in a metaphorical way, to espouse the doctrine of study of the Torah.

PETER FLINT (*Notre Dame University, Notre Dame, IN*): I think what we've seen today is the coming of age of scholarship with respect to the computer. By this I mean that when you think of a Qumran text, we have the Hebrew, we have dots, we have circlets, we have midline circlets, we have scribal correction dots, we have superlinear letters, we have sigla below. If you think about it, this is not merely a page of text, this is a work of art. If you submit such a work of art to any journal in the world, even the most scientific, it is inevitable that they will make mistakes. We've all had problems where journals cannot handle such a technology, for after all the artist asks a journal to redraw the work of art. I think what you're doing with the IBYCUS computer shows us the way ahead, that you're able to submit your painting, as it were, and have it reproduced. Now my question is with respect to the IBYCUS. Most of us here today use the MacIntosh or the IBM technology. What led you to the IBYCUS? Is it a powerful instrument; what are its advantages?

CHARLESWORTH: Why did we choose the IBYCUS computer? Remember we started in 1985. The IBYCUS computer at that time was the state of the art. We have numerous windows, we have use of the CD-ROM, we had absolute access to an incredible amount of material. We have worked with it; it is fantastic. We have two of them in the laboratory and two of them in the next building. Unfortunately you cannot purchase these at the present time. But they are absolutely invaluable for the kind of work we are doing. But remember, we are also creating hardware and software. We are going to give you a CD-ROM so you can study these texts perhaps more conveniently.

HARTMUT STEGEMANN (*University of Göttingen, Göttingen, Germany*): I have a question about the title of what we usually call the *Serekh Ha-Yaḥad*. Indeed, the title *Serekh Ha-Yaḥad* is in one of the manuscripts, column 1 line 1 of 1QS; but this title relates only from there to column 3 line 12. After that we have the spirits, and what is following in column 5 is not only a separate book, but a book which is called, at least in some manuscripts from *Cave* 4, not a serekh but a midrash. The full title for this could be *midrash ha-torah*, like *midrash ha-torah ha-'aḥaron* is the title of what we call today the Damascus Document. *Serekh Ha-Yaḥad* is nothing but a rhetorical agenda with a preamble and some concluding remarks.

CHARLESWORTH: I am in thorough agreement with what you said.

History and the Copper Scroll

AL WOLTERS

Redeemer College
Ancaster, Ontario, Canada L9K 1J4

By the title *History and the Copper Scroll* I mean to signal my intention to discuss two topics: the historicity or authenticity of the treasure listed in the Copper Scroll, and the historical *Sitz im Leben* of the Copper Scroll itself. In a secondary sense, the title also alludes to the history of the scroll's interpretation.

Forty years ago this year, on March 20, 1952, the Copper Scroll was discovered in a cave about two kilometers north of Qumran. The discovery was announced in the pages of the *Revue Biblique* in the following year,[1] but it was not until 1956 that the complete scroll was cut open and read, and not until 1962 that Milik's *editio princeps* of the Hebrew text, together with his French translation and commentary, was published. The nine years separating the first announcement of the discovery from Milik's edition were a period of wild speculation and bitter controversy. A brief account of this colorful early history will be illuminating for the present state of scholarship on the Copper Scroll. It can be conveniently subdivided into three periods of three years each.

From 1953 to 1956 the two rolled-up pieces of the Copper Scroll remained unopened, and its contents could only be guessed at from the letters which showed through on the outside. Roland de Vaux, the leader of the joint expedition which had discovered the scroll, wrote that "the most probable hypothesis is that it contains some rule or regulation which was posted in the central building of Khirbet Qumran."[2] Later that year he expressed himself even more positively: the scroll "had been attached flat to a wall" and "could only have been affixed in one of the rooms of the central building of the community whose ruins are found in Khirbet Qumran."[3] De Vaux had no doubt that the Copper Scroll, together with the pottery and parchment fragments that were found with it in Cave 3, belonged to the Qumran community.

Originally, there was no doubt about its date either. William Reed, who had participated in the expedition as director of the American School of Oriental Studies in Jerusalem, and who reported on the discovery in *BASOR* in 1954, stated flatly, on the basis of the archeological evidence, that it was "certain that the rolls were placed on the floor of the cave prior to 70 A.D."[4]

[1] DE VAUX, R. 1953. Fouille au Khirbet Qumrân. *RB* **60** (1953) 84–85.
[2] DE VAUX, Fouille, 85.
[3] DE VAUX, Exploration de la région de Qumrân. *RB* **60** (1953) 558.
[4] REED, W. L. The Qumrân Caves Expedition of March, 1952. *BASOR* **135** (1954) 10.

Unlike De Vaux, he was not certain about the connection with Qumran; the unknown contents of the two rolled-up pieces would have to make clear "whether they were originally on display in the Jerusalem temple or in the buildings of the Qumran community."[5]

A third hypothesis about the unopened Copper Scroll in these years was put forward by the German scholar Karl Georg Kuhn, and this later proved to be correct. On the basis of the letters that were visible on the outside of the rolled-up copper sheets Kuhn correctly deduced that the Copper Scroll was a catalogue of treasures.[6] Kuhn initially assumed that the treasure was connected with the Qumran community.[7]

The cutting open of the Copper Scroll was completed on January 16, 1956 in Manchester,[8] but in the following three-year period the full text of the Copper Scroll was still not made available to the broader scholarly world. Instead, only two scholars had the opportunity to study the Hebrew text: John Allegro in Manchester and J. T. Milik in Jerusalem. From the outset, these two men took opposing views of the Copper Scroll, Allegro regarding it as an authentic inventory of buried treasure, and Milik considering it a piece of Jewish folklore.

Unfortunately, their disagreement about the Copper Scroll soon became part of an acrimonious dispute during the course of 1956. In order to understand this, we need to take into account two other factors: Allegro's public statement that the Dead Sea Scrolls might contain a reference to a crucified Messiah, and the rise of Arab nationalism in Jordan. The former infuriated Allegro's colleagues in Jerusalem (including Milik and De Vaux), who took the unprecedented step of publicly disavowing Allegro's statement in a letter to the London *Times* on March 16, 1956, just two months after the Copper Scroll had been opened. On the other hand, Arab nationalism led to King Hussein's sudden dismissal, on April 2, 1956, of the British military commander John Glubb, followed in July by the dismissal of G. Lankester Harding, the British Director of Antiquities in Jordan, whom Allegro had persuaded to let the Copper Scroll be cut open in Manchester.[9] Both men were replaced by Jordanian nationals. It was also Arab nationalism which fed the suspicion in Jordan at the time that "scheming Western Christian scholars were passing off the treasure list as fictitious so that they could steal the treasure themselves."[10] It was in this tense and highly politicized atmosphere, further complicated by the archaeologists' legitimate fear that the contents of the Copper Scroll would lead to uncontrolled treasure hunting expeditions,

   [5] REED, "Qumrân Caves Expedition," 12.
   [6] KUHN, K. G. Les rouleaux de cuivre de Qumrân. *RB* 61 (1954) 193–205.
   [7] KUHN, "Les rouleaux," 202–204.
   [8] See ALLEGRO, J. M., *The Dead Sea Scrolls* (Hammondsworth: Penguin, 1956) 184.
   [9] ALLEGRO, *Dead Sea Scrolls*, 181–182.
   [10] BROWN, R. E., in a review of *Discoveries in the Judaean Desert of Jordan*, Vol. III in *CBQ* 26 (1964) 252.

that the initial public statements on the nature of the scroll were made in 1956.[11]

The first such statement was the press release of June 1, 1956, based on a preliminary translation prepared by Milik, which was put out by Lankester Harding, then still Director of Antiquities, and which was simultaneously presented in Paris by De Vaux.[12] This press release, which represented the quasi-official view of the Western scholars in Jerusalem, stressed the legendary nature of the scroll, and included three short excerpts of Milik's translation. In the following months, Milik himself became the chief spokesman for this legendary interpretation. In an article in the September issue of *The Biblical Archaeologist* he states quite emphatically: "It goes almost without saying that the document is not a historical record of actual treasures buried in antiquity."[13] However, he still assumes that it was "associated with the Essene community," and can be dated to the mid-first century C.E.[14]

Allegro meanwhile, who had arranged for the Copper Scroll to be cut open in Manchester, and who was himself present as adviser while the operation was carried out, took quite a different view. He had made a preliminary transcription and translation of the scroll as it was being opened, and was convinced that it was authentic. In his popular book *The Dead Sea Scrolls*, which was published later in 1956, he writes that Kuhn's earlier hypothesis had been dramatically vindicated: "It is indeed an inventory of the Sect's most treasured possessions, buried in various locations."[15] Furthermore, in an article published shortly thereafter, he suggested that the treasure might still be recoverable with the help of modern technology.[16]

In the three years following the opening of the Copper Scroll, during which everyone but Allegro and Milik had access only to the three short excerpts published in the press release,[17] scholarly opinion tended to favor its authenticity. Allegro's view was supported by Chaim Rabin,[18] K. G. Kuhn,[19] C. Roth,[20] A. Dupont-Sommer,[21] and H. Bardtke,[22] while Milik's opinion

[11] On this fear, see WOLTERS, A., Apocalyptic and the Copper Scroll. *JNES* **49** (1990) 145.
[12] The text of the press release is found in H. WRIGHT BAKER, Notes on the Opening of the "Bronze" Scrolls from Qumran, *Bulletin of the John Rylands Library* **39** (1956–57) 56. For the French version presented by De Vaux, see *CRAIBL* (1956) 224–225.
[13] MILIK, J. T., The Copper Document from Cave III. *BA* **19** (1956) 63.
[14] MILIK, "Copper Document," 63 and 62.
[15] ALLEGRO, *Dead Sea Scrolls*, 184.
[16] ALLEGRO, J. M., Science and the Dead Sea Scrolls. *The New Scientist*, January 3, 1957, p. 20.
[17] These were supplemented by one more extract in MILIK, J. T., L'édition des manuscrits du désert de Juda, *SVT* **4** (1957) 22. MILIK there also gives the Hebrew original of these extracts.
[18] RABIN, C., The Copper Scroll, *The Jewish Chronicle*, June 15, 1956, p. 19.
[19] KUHN, K. G., Der gegenwärtige Stand der Erforschung, *TLZ* **81** (1956) 541–546.
[20] ROTH, C., *The Historical Background of the Dead Sea Scrolls* (Oxford: Blackwell, 1958) 44.
[21] DUPONT-SOMMER, A., Les rouleaux de cuivre trouvés à Qoumrân. *RHR* **151** (1957) 22–36.
[22] BARDTKE, H., *Die Handschriftenfunde am Toten Meer* (Berlin: Evangelische Haupt-Bibelgesellschaft, 1958) 176–181.

was seconded by S. Mowinckel,[23] and F. Cross.[24] All agreed that the scroll should be dated to the first century, and should be associated with the other Qumran finds, although Rabin, Kuhn and Roth suggested that the enormous treasure belonged not to the sectarian community but to the Jerusalem temple. During this time Allegro was also invited to publish his own edition of the Copper Scroll by the Jordanians who succeeded Harding as Director of the Jordan Department of Antiquities.[25]

It was in the third period, from 1959 to 1962, that the full text of the Copper Scroll was finally published. In September 1959 Milik submitted his completed translation and commentary to the Clarendon Press, but it did not see the light of day until late 1962, ten years after the initial discovery.[26] In the meantime, since there was widespread impatience with the long delays, he also published his French translation in the *Revue Biblique* in 1959, and an English version of this in the *Annual of the Department of Antiquities of Jordan* in 1960.[27] In addition, he prepared a critical edition of the medieval Jewish midrash called *Masseket Kēlîm*, which he regarded as a striking parallel to the Copper Scroll.[28] Allegro, for his part, with the full authorization and cooperation of Jordanian officialdom, committed what to his Jerusalem colleagues were two unforgivable sins: he published his own edition and translation of the Copper Scroll in 1960, and organized two archeological expeditions to look for the buried treasure in 1959–1960.[29] For De Vaux this was the last straw, and provoked him to write a scathing critique of Allegro's book and excavations in the pages of the *Revue Biblique*.[30] By this time relations between Allegro and Milik were so strained that neither acknowledged the work of the other in their respective editions of the Copper Scroll.[31]

Although the two book-length commentaries by Allegro and Milik continued to reflect their opposing views with respect to the authenticity of the

[23] MOWINCKEL, S., The Copper Scroll–An Apocryphon. *JBL* 76 (1957) 261–265.

[24] CROSS, F. M., JR., *The Ancient Library of Qumran and Modern Biblical Studies* (Garden City: Doubleday, 1958) 16–18. An idiosyncratic variant is found in DEL MEDICO, H. E., *L'énigme des manuscrits de la Mer Morte* (Paris: Plon, 1957) 259–261.

[25] ALLEGRO, J. M., *The Treasure of the Copper Scroll* (London: Routledge & Kegan Paul, 1960) 6.

[26] MILIK, J. T., Le rouleau de cuivre provenant de la grotte 3Q (3Q15), in *Discoveries in the Judaean Desert of Jordan, Vol III: Les "petites Grottes" de Qumran* (Oxford: Clarendon, 1962).

[27] MILIK, J. T., Le rouleau de cuivre de Qumrân. *RB* 66 (1959) 321–357, and The Copper Document from Cave III of Qumran. *ADAJ* 4/5 (1960) 137–155.

[28] MILIK, J. T. Notes d'épigraphie et de topographie palestiniennes, *RB* 66 (1959) 567–575. The same comparison was made independently in SILBERMAN, L. H., A Note on the Copper Scroll. *VT* 10 (1960) 77–79.

[29] The edition and translation are found in ALLEGRO, *Treasure*, 32–55; the excavations are discussed in WILSON, E., *The Dead Sea Scrolls* (New York: Oxford University Press, 1969) 172–173.

[30] *RB* 68 (1961) 146–147.

[31] See MILIK's comment in *DJD* III, p. 299.

Copper Scroll, they each contained evidence of a major shift in their authors' interpretation in other respects. Allegro had now come around to the view that the treasure had belonged to the Jerusalem temple, and that it had been hidden, not by the sectarians of Qumran, but by the Zealots who were in control of Jerusalem in 68 c.e.[32] Milik, on the other hand, suggested for the first time that the Copper Scroll was to be dated *later* than the other Qumran materials, and that it had been deposited in Cave 3 around 100 c.e.[33] He came to this conclusion in the last stages of preparing his commentary,[34] and De Vaux accepted it with great reservation.[35] Ironically, Milik's change of mind meant that he and Allegro now agreed that the Copper Scroll had nothing to do with the Qumran community.

Only a few other scholars made contributions during this period. F. F. Bruce opted for Allegro's revised position.[36] K. H. Rengstorf argued in 1959 that all of the Dead Sea Scrolls, including the Copper Scroll, emanated from the temple in Jerusalem. Like Allegro, he maintained that the treasure of the scroll was real, and represented part of the fabulous wealth of the temple.[37] E. M. Laperrousaz, in an essay published in 1961, also defended the factual nature of the Copper Scroll, but (taking his cue from Milik) dated it later than the other Dead Sea Scrolls—in fact considerably later, to the time of the Bar Kokhba revolt in 135 c.e.[38]

By 1962 the scholarly world finally had at its disposal the *editio princeps* of the Copper Scroll, but oddly enough this did not provoke a flood of new studies or fresh interpretations of the long-awaited text. In fact, apart from reviews of Milik's edition, there were only three substantial contributions to the study of the Copper Scroll in the years 1962 to 1965, after which there was a deafening scholarly silence on the scroll for fifteen years. These three are a book by Ben-Zion Luria in 1963, an article by M. R. Lehmann in 1964,

---

[32] ALLEGRO, *Treasure*, 120–129. In effect, Allegro was adopting the view of C. ROTH, who had presented his interpretation of the Copper Scroll at the University of Manchester in February 1957 (ROTH, *Historical Background*, vii).

[33] MILIK, *DJD* III, 283–284.

[34] See DE VAUX, R., *L'archéologie et les manuscrits de la Mer Morte* (London: British Academy, 1961) 84. MILIK's change of mind may have been prompted by H. H. ROWLEY, who had put forward the same hypothesis in a review of CROSS's book *The Ancient Library of Qumran* in the *JSS* 4 (1959) 86. The first published indication of Milik's new dating is found in his article Le rouleau de cuivre de Qumran, in *RB* 66 (1959) 322.

[35] DE VAUX, *L'archéologie*, 83–84.

[36] BRUCE, F. F., *Second Thoughts on the Dead Sea Scrolls* (2nd Edit.; London: Paternoster, 1961) 26–28.

[37] RENGSTORF, K. H., *Hirbet Qumran und die Bibliothek vom Toten Meer* (Stuttgart: Kohlhammer, 1960) 26–28. As the "Vorwort" explains, this publication is the German version of lectures which Rengstorf delivered in Leeds in 1959.

[38] LAPERROUSAZ, E. M., Remarques sur l'origine des rouleaux de cuivre découverts dans la grotte 3 de Qumrân. *RHR* 159 (1961) 157–172, esp. 165–172.

and a chapter by G. R. Driver in 1965. Luria's book, published in Hebrew, came independently to a position much like that of Laperrousaz: the treasure of the Copper Scroll belonged to the Jewish rebels under Bar Kokhba.[39] Driver simply aligned himself with what was by that time a British consensus on the Copper Scroll: its treasure belonged to the temple in Jerusalem, and was hidden around 68 C.E. by the Zealots.[40] Lehmann came with an entirely novel view: the treasure of the Copper Scroll represented the regular Jewish contribution to the temple, which continued to come in during the decades after the destruction of the temple in 70 C.E.[41] We might also mention a long Portuguese study published in 1963 by M. A. Rodrigues, but this is so slavishly dependent on Milik that it hardly counts as an independent contribution.[42]

After these publications a strange silence descended on Copper Scroll studies for a decade and a half.[43] Since no substantially different interpretation of the scroll was put forward after the revival of scholarly interest in the scroll in 1980, it will be useful at this point to take stock of our survey of the first dozen years of Copper Scroll studies. With respect to the basic question which concerns us, the relation of the Copper Scroll to history, it emerges that there have been six basic paradigms of interpretation, four of which accept the historicity or authenticity of the scroll, and two which do not. These can be summarized as follows:

A. *The treasure is historical*
1) It belongs to the sectarians in Qumran. So Kuhn (before 1956), Allegro (before 1958), and Dupont-Sommer.
2) It belongs to the temple around 68 C.E. So Rabin, Kuhn (after 1956), Roth, Rengstorf, Allegro (after 1958), Bruce, and Driver.
3) It belongs to the rebels under Bar Kokhba around 135 C.E. So Laperrousaz and Luria.
4) It represents the temple contributions after 70 C.E. So Lehmann.

[39] LURIA, B. Z., *The Copper Scroll from the Judean Desert* (Jerusalem: Kiryath Sepher, 1963) [in Hebrew]. Unlike LAPERROUSAZ, however, LURIA argued that all the treasure derived from the temple, which was briefly restored during the Second Revolt.

[40] DRIVER, G. R., *The Judaean Scrolls. The Problem and a Solution* (New York: Schocken Books, 1965) 30–36.

[41] LEHMANN, M. R., Identification of the Copper Scroll Based on its Technical Terms. *RevQ* 5 (1964) 97–105.

[42] RODRIGUES, M. A. Aspectos linguísticos do documento de cobre de Qumran (3Q15). *Biblos. Revista da Faculdade de Letras* 39 (1963) 329–423. RODRIGUES is so dependent on MILIK that his Portuguese translation of the Copper Scroll sometimes makes sense only as a misunderstanding of MILIK's French (for example, "ângulo" in I,7 and "obstruída" in II,1).

[43] An apparent exception to this general rule are two publications by LAPERROUSAZ (review of *DJD* III in *REA* 68 [1966] 530–537, and Chapter 2 of his *Qoumrân. L'établissement essénien des bords de la Mer Morte* [Paris: Picard, 1976] 131–147), but these are simply restatements of the argument of his 1961 article.

B. *The treasure is unhistorical*
1) It was recorded by the sectarians of Qumran. Before 1959, this was the position of Milik, De Vaux, Harding and Cross. Similarly Mowinckel and Silberman.
2) It was recorded by persons unknown around 100 C.E. So Milik and De Vaux after 1959, as well as Rodrigues.

The view that the treasure is unhistorical was too much the product of the polemical and political circumstances in which it was born, and too heavily dependent on the authority of Milik, to carry conviction today. It is perhaps not surprising that it has found very few supporters in the last twenty-five years.[44] Moreover, as I have argued elsewhere, Milik's suggestion that the Copper Scroll represents some kind of folklore cannot withstand serious scrutiny.[45]

Nor is Milik's last-minute attempt to lower the date of the Copper Scroll very persuasive. As Pixner has shown, the archaeological evidence counts quite decisively against it,[46] and it is telling in retrospect that De Vaux considered Milik's second dating proposal to be only a theoretical possibility.[47] But if the archaeological evidence rules out a date later than about 68 C.E., then the positions of Luria, Laperrousaz, and Lehmann must also be disallowed, and it is not surprising that no one but Laperrousaz and Lehmann themselves have defended these positions since the early 1960s.[48]

Consequently, of the six paradigms which emerged in the first dozen years of Copper Scroll study, only two remain as viable contenders in contemporary scholarship. A scholarly consensus seems to be emerging that the Copper Scroll is an authentic record of ancient treasure, to be dated around 68 C.E., and that its treasure belonged either to the sectarians of Qumran or the temple in Jerusalem. The recent work of Pixner and Goranson supports the former option,[49] while that of Golb and Wilmot supports the latter.[50] For my own

[44] A rare exception is MURPHY-O'CONNOR, J., in *Early Judaism and its Modern Interpreters* (R. A. KRAFT and G. W. E. NICKELSBURG, Eds.; Atlanta: Scholars Press, 1986) 135.

[45] WOLTERS, Apocalyptic and the Copper Scroll, 147–154.

[46] PIXNER, B., Unravelling the Copper Scroll Code: A Study in the Topography of 3Q15. *RevQ* 11 (1983) 334–335.

[47] DE VAUX, *L'archéologie*, 83–84.

[48] For LAPERROUSAZ, see his book *Qoumrân*, 131–147, and his article Note sur l'origine des manuscrits de la Mer Morte, in *Annales ESC* (1987) 1305–1320; for LEHMANN, see Emperor Nerva: A Mystery Solved in *Allgemeiner Journal*, January 10, 1992, and Where the Temple Tax Was Buried, *BAR* 19 (Nov.–Dec. 1993) 38–43.

[49] See PIXNER, Unravelling the Copper Scroll Code, and S. GORANSON, Sectarianism, Geography, and the Copper Scroll, *JSS* 43 (1992) 282–287.

[50] GOLB, N., The Problem of Origin and Identification of the Dead Sea Scrolls, *Proceedings of the American Philosophical Society* 124 (1980) 5–8; *idem*, Who Hid the Dead Sea Scrolls? *BA* 48 (1985) 79–81; *idem*, The Dead Sea Scrolls, *The American Scholar* 58 (1989) 195–197. For WILMOT, DAVID see *Abstracts AAR/SBL 1984* (Atlanta: Scholars Press, 1984) 214.

part, I have followed the example of Kuhn and Allegro before me, and have moved from the first option to the second.[51]

Against the background of this overall *Forschungsbericht* on the topic *History and the Copper Scroll*, let me turn now to some new evidence that I believe bears on the question. In the first place, I would like to point out that the presence of cultic items is much more prominent than is commonly believed. In a forthcoming paper entitled *Cultic Terminology in the Copper Scroll*, I argue that cultic terms are almost three times more frequent than Milik's treatment would lead us to expect.[52] In my own forthcoming edition and translation of the Copper Scroll, there are 32 places where cultic terms occur, all but five of them in descriptions of treasure. This compares to 12 in Milik's edition. Most of the items in question have a direct connection with the temple worship service, especially sacred vessels of various kinds. Needless to say, these statistics strengthen the hypothesis that the treasure of the Copper Scroll derives from the fabled wealth of the temple in Jerusalem.

It should also be mentioned in passing that the late David Wilmot's dissertation, which was done under Norman Golb at the University of Chicago, and which is to be published posthumously, also supports this hypothesis. As we know from a published abstract which appeared in 1984, Wilmot has discovered parallels with the genuine Greek temple inventories of sacred treasure.[53]

In the remainder of this paper let me draw your attention to two further bits of evidence that can help us situate the Copper Scroll more firmly in its historical context. The first of these has to do with the occurrence, on my reading, of the first person singular suffix in three places in the Copper Scroll text. Since all three of these are readings which occur only in my own forthcoming edition, let me hasten to add that they are based on the direct examination of the copper segments which I was able to carry out in Amman in June 1991. At that time I also prepared a more extensive essay entitled *Textual Notes on the Copper Scroll*, in which I give an account of the more than seventy places where my text differs from that of Milik. For the present I will simply refer to this commentary for a justification of the readings I have adopted.

The three places where I read the first person singular pronominal suffix are the following:

1) III,9 *kly dm' lbwšy*, "vessels of tribute, my garments."[54]
2) VIII,3 *kly dm' wspry w'lt ks[p]*, "vessels of tribute, and my scrolls, and a bar of silv[er]."
3) XI,9 *thwrty bw kly dm' 'z dm' swḥ*, "my pure things are in it, vessels of Az's tribute, Suah's tribute."

[51] Contrast WOLTERS, A., The Last Treasure of the Copper Scroll. *JBL* **107** (1988) 423–424 with *idem*, Cultic Terminology in the Copper Scroll (forthcoming).
[52] Forthcoming in Volume II of the MILIK *Festschrift*.
[53] *Abstracts AAR/SBL 1984*, p. 214.
[54] See also WOLTERS, A., Notes on the Copper Scroll, *RevQ* **12** (1987) 593–594.

The words which have the first person singular suffix have a number of things in common. For one thing, they could all be either singular or plural; I have assumed that they are plural because most of the other treasure items are plural. More significantly, all three suffixed words are nouns which constitute part of a treasure description, and are associated with the phrase *kly dm'*. With most interpreters of the Copper Scroll, I take the latter to be a cultic term referring to vessels containing a "heave-offering," that is, a tribute or tithe offered to the priesthood.[55] The regular association of the three "my" words with the *kly dm'* suggests that the former may likewise refer to cultic items. This is certainly true of *thwrty*, and may also be true of *lbwšy* and *spry*. In that case, the latter terms designate someone's sacred vestments and religious books.

What is significant about these three cases of the first person singular suffix is that they suddenly give us a glimpse of the author of the scroll. In the midst of the dry and impersonal enumeration of buried items, we hear a reference to the author himself. Evidently the writer of the Copper Scroll (not the engraver of the text, but the person who composed it) is not just some clerk or bookkeeper, but an important personage who has valuable belongings which must also be hidden and recorded. It is also noticeable that the author's possessions are quite different from most of the rest of the treasure, which consists overwhelmingly of items of silver and gold. If we are justified in suspecting that the three possessions in question are cultic in character, then this would suggest that the author's belongings needed to be preserved, not primarily because of their monetary value, but rather because of their *religious* value. In short, it seems probable that the author of the Copper Scroll was a high-ranking religious official, perhaps the High Priest.

My second bit of new evidence has to do with the dramatic discovery in 1988 of a juglet of oil less than 200 meters from the place where the Copper Scroll was found. According to the published report by J. Patrich and B. Arubas, the juglet was buried about a meter under the floor of the cave, and belongs to the Herodian period.[56] Other pottery in the same cave is similar to that found in Qumran, and one cooking pot "is more characteristic of the end of the third quarter of the first century C.E. than of the first half of the century."[57] The oil which the juglet contained was made from a plant which no longer exists, quite possibly the famous balsam trees of the Jericho Valley and En Gedi.[58] In that case the contents of the juglet would have been worth a small fortune when it was buried, and would constitute a considerable

---

[55] See WOLTERS, "Notes on the Copper Scroll, 590, and *idem*, The Copper Scroll and the Vocabulary of Mishnaic Hebrew. *RevQ* 14 (1990) 488.

[56] PATRICH, J. and B. ARUBAS, A Juglet of Balsam Oil (?), *IEJ* 39 (1989) 43–59, specifically 49–50.

[57] PATRICH and ARUBAS, A Juglet, 48.

[58] PATRICH and ARUBAS, A Juglet, 51–55.

treasure in its own right.[59] Since the Copper Scroll is a list of buried treasure, and the juglet is a buried treasure which comes amazingly close in date and location to the Copper Scroll, it is only natural to inquire whether the juglet of oil might be part of the treasure described in it.

As far as I can see, there are four expressions in the treasure descriptions of the Copper Scroll which might reasonably be taken to include a reference to a juglet of precious oil. These are the following:

1) *kly dmʿ*. This phrase and its variants occur 13 times in the Copper Scroll (I,9; III,2; III,9; V,6; VIII,3; XI,1; XI,4 *bis*; XI,10 *bis*; XI,14 *bis*; XII,6). As we saw above, it is probably a cultic term meaning "vessels of tribute." As Lehmann points out, since *dmʿ* sometimes refers to liquids, the vessels in question may have contained oil or wine.[60] It is possible, therefore, that the *kly dmʿ* included a juglet of oil. Another interpretation of the phrase is that of Milik, who translates it as "vase d'aromates," connecting it with the etymological meaning "tear."[61] It is a remarkable fact that Laperrousaz, on the basis of Milik's interpretation, suggested a connection between the *kly dmʿ* of the Copper Scroll and the product of the famous balsam trees of En Gedi, the very trees from which Patrich and Arubas hypothesize the oil of the juglet was made. Laperrousaz made this suggestion in a book published in 1976, twelve years before the juglet was discovered.[62] It is also remarkable, as Patrich and Arubas point out, that balsam oil was grouped among the aromatics in antiquity, and that it was sold in drops known as *lacrimae*, *i.e.*, "tears." On either interpretation of the phrase *kly dmʿ*, the treasure it describes would fit the juglet of oil.

2) *blgyn* (I,9). This is a notoriously difficult sequence of characters in the Copper Scroll. It has received no fewer than six quite distinct interpretations, including an adventuresome attempt of my own.[63] One of the proposed interpretations is that of Luria, who sees here an example of the Greek loanword *lāgín*, meaning "bottle."[64] This interpretation, which is adopted by Lehmann,[65] Sharvit,[66] and Greenfield,[67] could also be taken as a description of our juglet.

3) *kwzyn* (XII,1). Milik here reads *bydn*, but both the original in Amman and two of the published facsimiles clearly support the reading *kwzyn*,

[59] PATRICH and ARUBAS, A Juglet, 53–54.
[60] LEHMANN, Identification of the Copper Scroll, 98.
[61] See MILIK, *DJD* III, 250 (C 122).
[62] LAPERROUSAZ, *Qoumrân*, 144.
[63] See WOLTERS, Notes on the Copper Scroll, 590–592. To the five interpretations there listed should be added that of LEHMANN, Identification of the Copper Scroll, 99, n. 3.
[64] LURIA, *Copper Scroll*, 62–63.
[65] LEHMANN, Identification of the Copper Scroll, 99.
[66] SHARVIT, S., Investigations concerning the Lexicon of the Copper Scroll. *Beth Mikra* 31 (1967) 134 [in Hebrew].
[67] GREENFIELD, J. C. The Small Caves of Qumran. *JAOS* 89 (1969) 138–139.

"juglets." This was in fact the reading adopted by Allegro and Luria in their books on the Copper Scroll, and it is also accepted in my own edition of the text. This section of the Copper Scroll therefore reads as follows: "Under the black stone: juglets." Apparently one cache consisted of nothing but a number of juglets, and the recent find may well be one of these.

4) *mšḥwtyhm* (XII,12). This expression is usually rendered "their measurements," but could also be taken to mean "their portions."[68] A third possibility is that it means "their oils," and could refer to different types of oil in the last treasure of the Copper Scroll. In that case a reference to the juglet of oil is also possible.[69]

For the purposes of this essay it is not necessary to decide which one of these four expressions, found in a total of 16 places in the Copper Scroll, is most likely to refer to the recently discovered juglet of oil. It is enough to note that each of the four are reasonable candidates for such a reference. In that case we are left to calculate the probability that the juglet of oil is *not* part of the items described in the Copper Scroll, if it meets the required specifications not only in date and location, but also in value and manner of concealment. I would guess that that probability is fairly remote. In other words, I consider it likely that the juglet of oil is part of the long lost treasure of the Copper Scroll. If so, it is the first tangible evidence that has come to light that the scroll is indeed a genuine historical document.

DISCUSSION OF THE PAPER

PAULINE DONCEEL-VOÛTE (*Université Catholique de Louvain, Louvain-la-Neuve, Belgium*): Yes, the oil that was found wasn't identified as balsam oil. This type of juglet is very common; you find a great number in the excavations of Khirbet Qumran itself, of Jericho, Herodian, and the Hasmonean palaces as well. It would be very easy to have a few hundred of these in a treasure. So just one juglet wouldn't be much of a treasure.

AL WOLTERS (*Redeemer College, Ancaster, Ont., Canada*): You're entirely right. It's not certain that it is a balsam oil. I guess the only thing that has been determined is that it might be. Now if it is balsam oil, which is a possibility, and balsam oil was only produced in one locality (well, really two) in all of the world, the Jericho valley and En Gedi, then it did in itself constitute a treasure. It would have been worth double its weight in silver. And

[68] See WOLTERS, The Last Treasure, 422–424.
[69] See WOLTERS, Vocabulary of Mishnaic Hebrew, 492–493.

in that case it's not surprising it was only one juglet. But it could be one juglet which happened to be buried very deeply. The others, which are in fact mentioned in my reading of the Copper Scroll, could have been found by people in the course of the few thousand years since it was buried.

JOSEPH PATRICH (*University of Haifa, Haifa, Israel*): I would be pleased, if I could, to confirm that this juglet was part of the treasure of the high priest. But I cannot. About the archeology I wanted to add that, as much as I could judge from the cave, there is nothing against the possibility that the Copper Scroll was deposited later than the parchment scrolls.

As to your suggested reading, why should the author identify his items as his? If I'm making a list of things that belong to me, I'll write simply garments, vessels, *etc.* If it is my list and I'm writing it why should I add that it is mine? I find this a difficulty in your interpretation.

WOLTERS: The archeological evidence I cannot judge for myself. The initial archeological finding by Reed and de Vaux and everyone concerned assumed until 1959 that they all belong together. That was confirmed by Pixner when he investigated this matter and had Emile Puech interview the leader of the expedition that actually discovered the treasure. I noticed you very carefully phrased your opinion, to say there's nothing in the archeological evidence that opposes later dating of the Copper Scrolls. In other words, it's a theoretical possibility. Pixner apparently disagrees; he also investigated the cave, but of course not as extensively as you have. I guess I would have to bow to the archaeologists, that it's not absolutely ruled out; but it's certainly not the first assumption that one would make.

As to why the author of the scroll would identify certain things as his own, the answer is I don't know. I only discovered that there are three places in the text where apparently this reading is there. I haven't gone into a comparison with the other readings, but they are quite improbable. For example, in the case of Allegro, it involves the assumption that there was a final *nun* precisely on the cut where the saw went through. According to Baker, who did the sawing, there were no letters which were eliminated. In the case of Milik he takes the following *waws* as the final *nun*. As you see in my second little facsimile here in my handout, there's a circle around what I'm interpreting as a *waw*. This is a copy from my own personal working copy. I've circled it because when I was in Amman I wanted to see exactly what it looked like on the original. Well, on the original it looks exactly like the transcription. It's a peculiar feature of the paleography of the Copper Scroll that the little triangular head at the top is never used for final *nun*. It's regularly used for a *waw* or a *yod*. So it's extremely improbable that the letter can be interpreted as a *nun*.

I don't want to get into all the details of paleography, but I think I have made a good case in the other articles that I have written. In all these cases the reason why the obvious reading wasn't taken was because it simply went against people's expectations. I could speculate as to why the author of the Copper Scroll designated certain things as his own property. It could be that he was designating things which belonged to him in his capacity as an official, as a high priest or some other kind of official, and he wanted to distinguish those from the common property of the temple at large. But I'm speculating. I'm simply saying the text in fact has that suffix—quite clearly in at least two cases.

HARTMUT STEGEMANN (*University of Göttingen, Göttingen, Germany*): Dr. Wolters, I'm very glad that you have made the point that the treasure may be the treasure of the Temple and is real. The implications of your suffixes, first person singular, are very weighty for the theory. This is a list, and when you have this person three times it means that what is in this list is his property, or he is responsible for it. Perhaps he sat down and wrote the list or some text which was copied in copper, but it is his personal register. How many mistakes are there in this part of the scroll, according to your observations? Could it be possible that final *nuns* are dropped, or very extremely, is it possible we have here curious plural forms?

WOLTERS: It is possible because in other respects the Copper Scroll has mistakes; final *nun*'s could have been dropped. That's possible, but I think one would have to have fairly strong arguments for assuming that. As far as I know, there are no other cases in the Copper Scroll where a final *nun*, or any other final letter has dropped off, with the one exception that you will see in the middle example that I give here at 8:3.

As for other mistakes, in my opinion the statements by Milik and Allegro that the document is riddled with mistakes are too strong. There are mistakes, and there are some peculiarities of orthography to be sure, *alef* for *heh* and that sort of thing, but it's not the product of a "semi-literate crank," the expression that Milik used in 1956. One other thing to take into account is that presumably the person who engraved the letters was not only different from the person who composed them, but may have been illiterate himself. The reason for thinking so is that there are a whole series of letters which are not distinguished at all, like *kaph* and *beth*, look-alike letters which normally are just slightly different. In the Copper Scroll, they are absolutely indistinguishable. I've done a chart where I put all the *beth*'s on a page and all the *kaph*'s, and I've asked people which is the *kaph* sheet, which is the *beth*, but they can't tell.

Presumably what this means is that it was a secret document given to a craftsman who couldn't read for security reasons. This is the hypothesis of Thorion, who wrote in the *Revue de Qumran* a number of years ago. That may also account for some of the grammatical and orthographic lapses.

ABRAHAM TERIAN (*Andrews University, Berrien Springs, MI*): I'm happy to hear about the forthcoming publication of David Wilmot's posthumous work. With regards to your first person suffixes, I think you've demonstrated them very well. Since we're dealing with theoretical possibilities, if not speculations, I'd like to toss this one in and see what you think about it. I'd like to draw an analogy with the fall of the First Temple, namely, worshipers continue to come and to bring their gifts to the sacred site. As we read in the book of Lamentations, curiously enough the first person singular, the speaker, is most frequently Jerusalem or the temple. In other words, while you're dealing with first person singular suffixes, I'd like to suggest that there may be a possibility that this usage is impersonal. It could be the temple, could be the city. And if we were to further speculate about the possible date of the Copper Scroll, one would think that possibly after the fall of the Second Temple there was some such practice, however short-lived it may have been. Perhaps pious people continued to bring their gifts to the site and eventually they ended up in some form of treasure.

WOLTERS: That's a very interesting suggestion. Just off the top of my head I see the following objections to it. This would be a highly poetic figure, as in Lamentations. Lamentations, of course, is composed in an extremely intricate way, involving alphabetical acrostics and so on. It's a highly poetical text. The Copper Scroll by contrast is a very prosaic text. Moreover, the suggestion would not explain, it seems to me, why the suffix occurs in only three places, and then in places where unusual treasure is being described. But that's just an initial reaction; I think it's a creative suggestion. As to whether the scroll may list contributions to the temple which continued to come in after the fall of Jerusalem, that is in fact the hypothesis of Lehmann. Lehmann just recently, in 1992, published an article in which he claims that he can date the Copper Scroll on the basis of a coin put out by the Roman Emperor Nerva, having to do with the Romans putting a stop to continued contributions. That of course depends on the archeological point we were talking about earlier, whether or not the Copper Scroll was a later deposit. If it was, then yes, it's possible, although if it's contributions to the Temple, the enormous treasure would again be difficult to account for.

The "Qumran Library" in the Light of the Attitude towards Books and Libraries in the Second Temple Period

YAACOV SHAVIT

Department of Jewish History
Tel-Aviv University
Tel-Aviv, Israel

The phenomenon of the DSS is an illuminating test-case for the study of the genesis, evolution, and crystallization of different and contradictory historical world views and disciplines as well as their interrelationship. This is yet another historical and intellectual domain in which speculations and creative imagination inevitably serve as tools to create and defend theories, particularly when scholars involved in the debate wish to present a general historical picture.

Qumran as a "historical problem," comprises three sets of facts: the external textual evidence, the archeological evidence, and the scrolls themselves. Since there is no unanimity between these three sets, and since they can be interpreted in various ways, they can serve as a basis for the construction of diverse general theories. The problem is that every such theory is like a small blanket—it is capable of covering only part of the problem, while leaving some other part uncovered. Similarly, in every theory like this, we can discern the loose threads with which it has been sewn.

Despite the intensive debate on the "Qumran problem" and the diverse theories put forward, there still remain a number of central issues which have not been adequately addressed. I will attempt to discuss the methodological aspect of the subject, by considering the question of "the Qumran library."

Regarding the question of the origin of the library that was found in the Judean Desert, three main paradigms have been proposed during more than 45 years of research.

1) The library belonged to the "Qumran Sect." Members of the sect are those who wrote the books and preserved them in their library in Qumran; they are also the ones who concealed the books in the caves.

2) The library belonged to the members of the "sect" or the "community," to be used by them as a study-library. Qumran did not serve as a center for writing and copying, but rather as a center of learning. The library contained about one thousand scrolls, some of them in a few copies. Before the enemy's arrival, the entire contents of this library were hidden in caves.

3) The scrolls did not come from Qumran itself, but from outside it, and therefore include both sectarian and non-sectarian works.

Among those who advocate the first two paradigms, two explanations have been set forth regarding the contents of the "library." One camp maintains that we are dealing with a "textual unit" of a decisively homogeneous nature; the second camp believes the books were of a more complex character, and were not made up entirely of "sectarian literature." Supporters of the latter view believe that the literary corpus found in the caves of the Judean Desert, consists of a rather broad corpus, in its genre and content. It is also not singular in its nature or its design. It also is not representative of all the literature written by Jews from the Hasmonean period up to the Great Revolt and thereafter. For example, no distinctively historical texts were found among the manuscripts, and there is no literature representative of the Pharisaic stream. Alas, there is no way of knowing what the totality of the hidden manuscripts contained or did not contain in the first place. If this is the case, undoubtedly a great deal of what was written up to the time of the destruction is simply not known to us. In any case, the corpus that had been preserved was also not homogeneous, and therefore, a commonly accepted assumption is the notion that the DSS are indeed a diverse corpus, but that it was collected and preserved by a defined group espousing a clear world outlook. If one takes this view, one ought to find in this corpus a clear distinction between what might be called its "canonical" or "primary" literature and what might be called "secondary literature," i.e., literature introduced by new convenanters who joined the "community," or manuscripts that were written or copied in other parts of Palestine and brought to the Qumran library. According to this view, there is actually a clear criterion of classification between "canonical" manuscripts and "less canonical" manuscripts in the community's library: manuscripts that were composed by the community members and manuscripts that were copied elsewhere but studied and deposited in its library.[1] This criterion is determined according to the relationship the scholar finds between the content of the texts and what is known to us about the Qumran sect from external sources, particularly Josephus. However, in my view, any

---

[1] EMANUEL TOV, "The Biblical Scrolls from the Judean Desert and their Contribution to Textual Criticism," in MAGEN BROSHI et al., Eds. The Scrolls of the Judean Desert: Forty Years of Research, Jerusalem, 1992, pp. 63–98 (Heb). Esther G. Chazon offers four criteria for determining the sectarian or non-sectarian authorship of the scrolls found at Qumran; see her article, "Is Divrei HaMe'orot a Sectarian Prayer?" in DEVORA DIAMANT and URIEL RAPPAPORT, Eds., The Dead Sea Scrolls—Forty Years of Research, Brill-Leiden, 1992, pp. 3–17.

such criterion is basically an arbitrary one, because we lack knowledge about the full extent of the texts and there is no evidence that the members of the sect made any such classification themselves.

The logic in the claim that the authors of the texts and those who hid them belonged to the same defined group is that the "secondary" books, those not written by the members of the sect itself, were not copied in Qumran, since it is not very likely that the "community scribes" would engage in copying writings that were not an integral part of their spiritual-cultural world! However, these books were not rejected by the sect or the community and were considered to at least merit a place in their "library." According to this view, one can find in the caves a methodical and deliberate organization of the material according to its origin. But at the same time: "We do not know whether all of the texts found in Qumran were kept in a 'library,' and the people in their daily lives used only one textual group [. . .]."[2] This thesis assumes, first, that there was a "textual group," that was used in daily life, and second, that before the books were hidden at some time in the caves of the Judean Desert, they had constituted the "library," the treasury of manuscripts, that was in their possession or was available for the use of members of the Qumran sect. It is not clear whether the intent here is to assert that the caves were the "library" from the outset or that the books of the "second category" were first hidden in them, because they were not an integral part of the sect's world, or that they were part of the library found in the central building in Khirbet Qumran itself, and later transferred to hiding places along with the important books "as one unified whole."

In any case, as a foundation for this theory, which regards Qumran or the members of the specific community residing there or belonging to it and also living elsewhere as the sole source of all or most of the texts, several explanations were offered for the diverse nature of the Qumranian literature. Briefly, these are:

1) Those who came to live with the community brought with them various works, which were not an integral part of the sect's library, and hence were placed for safekeeping in the library.

2) Members of the "community" also read, studied, or collected non-sectarian literature, which therefore was also kept in their "library." These manuscripts were hidden together with the sect's main writings when the "sect" tried to save its manuscripts by placing them in the caves for safekeeping. Therefore Qumran is indeed a center of learning and its "library" the collection of a large portion of "Jewish literary writing" of the Second Temple period.

3) For reasons which are not clear, books belonging to members of the community living in other, sometimes distant, places, were also sent to the

---

[2] EMANUEL TOV, *ibid.*, p. 95.

Judean desert caves for storage and safekeeping. The argument in principle, in contrast to the widely held (until recently, at any rate) view, is that in Qumran, writing and copying were not carried out intensively, but books were intensively collected for the purpose of study![3]

Against the background of these assumptions, we may ask: Are we dealing with a "library" (in the Hellenistic sense) or with a "collection of books"? Is it possible to discover any logic in the corpus' contents, or is it made up of different sources? Is the organized effort made to safeguard these books a single instance of a Jewish library in the Second Temple period known to us, arising from the nature of the community and its attitude towards the written word, or is this perhaps a cultural custom that prevailed in the Jewish society of the time, which the Qumran community also adopted? If indeed books were hidden at one specific time, when an enemy was approaching or because of some dramatic political occurrence, even if we assume this occurred over a period of two years, that would mean that most of this great number of texts—certainly many hundreds and probably more—were kept until then in some "library" at the sect's headquarters in Qumran or in other places where there was a concentration of sect members. If we assume that the members of the community did indeed collect and preserve many books, we have to try and understand what motivated them to do so. The accepted premise that they had a compelling interest in keeping the books, because of the message they contained or the codification of the way of life set forth in them, is also an *a priori* assumption. It presupposes that all of the manuscripts were re-garded as sacred texts that must be saved from destruction, even when the community itself and Jerusalem were on the verge of annihilation. Can we assert that this attitude was a part of the prevailing cultural tradition or norm which the sect also shared and were part of, or that the people of Qumran were the only ones in their time to demonstrate such an attitude towards books? Does the very act of hiding the writings imply that books had in the eyes of their owners an eternal existence beyond that of humans, or the Messianic (or natural) expectation that a day would come when the members of the community would return and need these texts?

—————

This leads us to the first question to be considered: Were there libraries in Jerusalem or in other Jewish cities, as there were in many Hellenistic cities as well as in the pagan temples in the ancient and the Hellenistic-Roman world? Libraries as a cultural institution were a Hellenistic phenomenon. In

[3] One of the problems with this theory is that many of the scrolls do not constitute "study material," like the Temple texts, and thus one must assume that this library was no more than a reading room.

these *bibliotekhe*, "qualified" librarians handled the books, which were kept in niches on shelves carved into the wall or in rounded boxes (*capsa*) in reading rooms with catalogs (*pinakes*).[4]

Professor Golb posits this kind of attitude towards books by Jews, and therefore in speaking about the "act of removal of manuscripts from Jerusalem during the revolt," states "that indicates that Hebrew literary texts were deemed precious enough to warrant rescue during periods of danger."

Golb speaks about the existence of "libraries" in Jerusalem, and hence about an organized operation of their removal elsewhere since they were regarded as no less than treasures of the Temple.[5] The problem with this thesis is that although it has a great deal of internal logic, we have no evidence attesting to the existence of libraries in Jerusalem, although it is reasonable to assume that there were collections of books in that city. Nor do we have any evidence or indication that a central library existed in the Temple in Jerusalem.

What does Josephus tell us about books and libraries? When Josephus in *The Wars of the Jews* speaks about the removal of the Temple's treasures with the approach of the Roman soldiers, he does not explicitly mention the removal of books or a library, just as he does not enumerate manuscripts among the "Temple treasures." It is hard to assume that Josephus, a scholarly author, who by his own testimony appreciated and understood the value of books and libraries, would have failed to explicitly mention the existence of a library or allude to the thousands of books among the "Temple treasures." Josephus does not speak about the removal of treasures from Jerusalem itself and from his descriptions it appears that until the final stages of the siege, treasures were left in the Temple (*Wars of the Jews*, V, XIII, 6; IV, VIII, 3) in *Against Apion* C Ap (II, 11). Josephus makes references to history books and chronicles kept in the temples or public archives in the cities of the Hellenistic East, but does not mention the existence of such a collection in Jerusalem. In the fifth chapter of *Wars of the Jews*, he describes the Temple in detail, without making any mention of a library. In *Antiquities of the Jews* (Book V, chapter 5, as well as in book XV which relates to the construction of the Temple), there is no reference to books but only to an archive ("בית הפקדות").

As for the possibility that we are dealing here with a "Temple library," there is no hint in the sources as to the existence of a library in the Temple. In pagan

---

[4] LUCIANO CANFORA, *The Vanished Library: A Wonder of the Ancient World*, translated by MARTI RYLE, University of California Press, 1989; and F. G. KENYON, *Books and Readers in Ancient Greece and Rome*, Oxford, 1951.

[5] NORMAN GOLB, "Khirbet Qumran and the Manuscripts of the Judean Wilderness: Observations on the Logic of Their Investigation," *Journal of Near Eastern Studies*, Vol. 49, No. 2, pp. 103–114. One can assume, for example, that in the *beit midrash* of Hillel the Elder in Jerusalem, and in Shamai's as well, there were collections of a quantity of books. We also know of the literature of the Sadducees and other groups, from which the writings known as "apocryphal" were preserved.

temples (in Egypt, for example), there was a library, usually the library of the priests; however, in Jewish sources of that time, as well as in later periods, there is no suggestion that the Temple priests engaged in writing of any kind or in the organization and operation of a library in the Temple in Jerusalem. In the listing of priestly duties, there is no mention of priests being responsible for the "library." The "scribes" of the Second Temple period were not writers of books but rather clerks and administrators. There was an archive in the Temple (the "house of the archives," (בית ספריא) (Ezra 6, 1,2), but it housed official documents of various types. However, it is difficult to assume that a library containing literature pertaining to rules and regulations, eschatological literature and wisdom texts existed there. On the other hand, in the "Qumran Library," no remnants were found of literature that could be designated as "Pharisaic," which makes it difficult to establish a connection between Qumran and the Temple.[6] Furthermore, Josephus relates how the archives were burned by the rebels in Jerusalem, who set fire to בית גנזי הכתבים (*Wars of the Jews*, Book VI, chapter 6), but makes no mention of books destroyed or rescued from the destruction. In all the descriptions of Jerusalem in the Hellenistic-Roman literature, as well as in the writings of Philo, no mention is made of a "treasury of books," nor is Jerusalem praised as a city renowned for its libraries.

The *Damascus Rule* speaks about the treasures of the Temple, but it is quite clear that the reference is not to tainted books "[. . .] They shall separate from the sons of the Pit, and shall keep away from the unclean riches of wickedness acquired by vow or anathema or from the Temple treasure [. . .]."

Even from a later period, we have no evidence of the existence of collections of books or of the attribution of sanctity to books that were not Torah scrolls.[7] The Talmudic sources refer to the fact that the authoritative source of the Pentateuch was kept in the archives of the Temple (*Mishnah, Moed Katan*, [Minor Festival] C,D) and that other versions were in public hands, as well as various books copied by professional copiers (*librarius*). Certainly books of laws and other books (*Megillat Ta'anit*, for example, which was not found at Qumran) were disseminated in quite a few copies.[8] However, again there is no allusion to a general central library that one might assume had been kept by "secular" elements (in the courts of Herod or Agrippas, for example). It is reasonable to assume that there were also private libraries in Jerusalem.

In the Qumran texts, only the *Copper Scroll* lists sixty-four hiding places where gold and silver aromatics and scrolls are said to be deposited, but we

[6] There is no doubt that there was written Pharisaic literature, regardless of whether it was literature of rules and regulations or another type, for example, liturgical literature.

[7] Every time a Talmudic source speaks of scrolls (in plural), the reference is not to collections of books, but mainly to the Pentateuch.

[8] It was only after the Destruction that the Sages began to compile traditions of laws, and one can assume that not everything was compiled from memory.

have no clue as to who wrote the scroll, even if we accept the premise that its authors did indeed list in it the true hiding places of treasures and books.

If in fact books were removed from Jerusalem and hidden outside the city when the Roman Legions approached, it is likely that this was done by those who appreciated their importance in their own time, and perhaps also for future generations. It is therefore reasonable to assume that the existence and removal of hundreds or thousands of parchment scrolls, encompassing the greater part of "Second Temple literature," would have merited some mention and that at least some intimation of it would have been retained in the collective memory. It is well known that from the beginning of the revolt, Jerusalem became the focus of a ruthless struggle in a factional war that erupted in the opening stages of the Roman siege, and the atmosphere in the city was one of Messianic self-confidence mingled with terror. It is extremely unlikely—although not inconceivable—that it would have been possible, in the midst of this mad furor, to carry out an orderly removal of hundreds of sealed jars containing parchment scrolls. It would have been necessary to make hundreds of jars, since the books were not kept in jars in the "libraries" before their removal. Josephus tells us that even before the siege was laid, "no one thought of anything but his own safety" (I, C, 5), and writes that people were fleeing from Jericho and the Jordan Valley to Jerusalem—not in the opposite direction.

It is not clear which of the diverse groups in Jerusalem had either the interest or the ability to carry out an act of removal of this scale. Even if it were carried out over a short span of two years (68–70 A.D.), it would have been a well-organized rescue operation requiring many participants. The only place in which Josephus mentions caves is in the fourth book (Chapter 8, 4) in which he relates that Simeon Bar Giora widened many caves in the Valley of Paran, some of which he found already prepared, and hid the treasures of his loot in them. It is highly unlikely that his booty also included jars containing scrolls. Then, who in Jerusalem would have endangered his own life, in such catastrophic times, in order to rescue not just a few valuable or sacred texts, but all of the books in the city, or a large portion of them? And who could have felt certain that a hiding place like the caves near Khirbet Qumran was a place no one would know about or succeed in uncovering? After all, during a period of civil strife, of starvation and plunder, no hiding place was safe—certainly not in the environs of Jerusalem. Caves in the nearby Judean Desert or in the area of Jericho are not safe hiding places in any case, particularly for invaluable treasures and hundreds of manuscripts. It seems to me that in this instance also, Golb's thesis makes an *a priori* assumption in order to explain the existence of manuscripts at Qumran and other places and to postulate the existence of many others, in an unknown location. He makes this assumption, based on the experience of later generations (the Cairo Geniza) that Second Temple Jews attributed sanctity and value to every written text. The fact that manuscripts were found in Masada, for example, is not evidence of this, since the few found there might have been part of a really "small library" rather than remnants of manuscripts placed in hiding.

Let us return to the question of the libraries. It appears that in every major Hellenistic city, there were official public libraries (as Josephus tells us in the *Wars of the Jews*, Book VII, Chapter 3: "It happened that a fire destroyed the Square Market, the City Hall, and the Law Courts [. . .]," as well as large, wealthy private libraries. In the sources, however, there is no allusion to a Jewish library as a public institution. One can infer from the Talmudic source that deals with the issue of which books are worthy of being saved from fire on the Sabbath (Mishnah *Shabbat* 16a; Babylonian Talmud *Shabbat* 116a) libraries which included diverse types of texts existed. However, it may also be true that the issue discussed in this source is a fundamental one presented in a rhetorical fashion. The Sages recognize the existence of secular books (Sifrei Hamiros, סִפְרֵי הַמְרֹם) and the Apocrypha (those that sully the hands and those that do not sully the hands) but they do not allude to the existence of sizable collections of books that contain both of these types.

There is no doubt that larger or smaller collections of books could be found in the synagogues for the use of those who came there to study, as we know from the Gospels, or in various institutions, but there is no mention of that. In various sources of the Sages, there are allusions to the reading of books and commerce in books, usually Torah scrolls ("Wealth and riches shall be in his house, and his righteousness endureth forever, the one who writes Pentateuch, Prophets and Hagiographa, and lends them to others [הון ועשר בביתו וצדקתו עמדת לעד — זה הכותב תורה נביאים וכתובים ומשאילם לאחרים נ כתי]). In most cases, not in all, the reference is to the Bible. There is no doubt that the Sages also knew of other literature, but their attitude towards it was negative. It is to that kind of literature that the verse "By these my son be admonished: of making many books there is no end" (Ec 12:12) refers, which the midrash relates to the "Apocrypha" that create turmoil in the home of the reader (Ec Rabah 12; Jerusalem, Sanhedrin 10:1) *etc*. The Sadducee tradition places an emphasis on the oral culture even in an era of "book culture." It can be argued that the existence of book collections was self-evident, and needed no mention. Nevertheless, it is worth noting that in the sources there is no reference to the significance and practice of preserving books and how that should be done.

In other words, the historical sources confront us with a dilemma that is far from simple: there can be no doubt that Jews in the Second Temple period wrote many books, a few of which were preserved as "Apocrypha," while others were lost.[9] But the sources mention only isolated names out of a wide corpus, and we have no evidence at all that there were collections of books, and even less, that there were public libraries, such as existed in Hellenistic

---

[9] Jews wrote in both Hebrew and Aramaic in this period.

centers of learning. It is clear that in order to dispute beliefs appearing in the "Heretical books," the Sages had no need to keep the books in their possession, and could learn the main principles of these beliefs and contentions through oral discourse. If that is the case, the fact that there is no reference in the literature of the Sages to the wide literary corpus that predated the destruction of the Temple can indicate either a break in the literary sequence, apathy toward the corpus, or a conscious and diversified attempt to cover up and expunge its existence.[10]

There is no doubt that a "book culture" flourished during the Hellenistic period. Books were written, copied and sold, and obviously were also kept in various collections.[11] However, all of the evidence presented for this argument comes from Hellenistic Egypt or from the Hellenistic society in general, but does not relate directly to the Jewish society and its reading public. If there is any reference to books, it is, as already stated, to a limited canon. Even if we assume that books were bought and sold, there is still a substantive difference between that and a collection of hundreds of books. We may agree there was a library attached to every Hellenistic *gymnasium*, but one cannot infer from this that there was a large collection of books in every synagogue or *beit midrash*. The spread of literacy does not necessarily contradict the centrality of the oral culture. Jesus, for example, is described as a preacher, and no mention is made of any books he read (except for the Book of Isaiah) or any parables or adages he put into writing! Jesus certainly read books, but the writers of his story had no interest in mentioning them.

On the other hand, it is very difficult to accept the view that the only place books were written or kept was the site of Qumran – the *Civitas Litterarum* of Palestine, and it is equally hard to accept the view that Qumran was a central place of learning – where people came from all over the country to read and study books, a sort of *beit midrash* of the Essenes.

And what about the possibility that the "sect" possessed a large collection of books for its own use? It is well known that archeological research has failed to identify such a special storage place for parchment scrolls. In fact, there is no way of identifying the location of a library unless one finds a clear inscription indicating its existence. However, in our case the most striking fact is that the written sources contain no reference to the existence of a library in Qumran, despite the assumed central role that the copying and collecting of

---

[10] As expressed in Rabbi Akiva's famous diatribe against heretical literature, and the deliberate – and successful – attempt to expunge the apocryphal writings from memory.

[11] MICHAEL O. WISE, "Accidents and Accidence: A Scribal View of Linguistic Dating of the Aramaic Scrolls from Qumran, *Abr-Nahrain*, Supplement 3, 1992 (Louvain, 1992), pp. 124–167. In this regard, see *ibid*, pp. 138–141, and particularly note 54.

books played in the community's life, at least according to the accepted
theory, and despite the importance of written literature in the Jewish culture
of the Second Temple period. It is very hard to accept Stegemann's theory that
almost one thousand scrolls were preserved in baskets or jars in the main
building; this theory has its logic, but he cannot present any solid evidence
for its validity.

In the literature on Qumran, there is no allusion—either directly or
indirectly—to a library or to books.[12] Josephus relates that the Essenes were
"[. . .] studying the writings of the ancients, and chose out of them what
is most for the advantage of their soul and body [. . .]" (*Wars of the Jews*,
Book II, Chapter 8) and this is the only reference. But there is no mention
of new books being written, of books being collected, or of the intense and
assiduous work of copiers. Philo (about 20 A.D.) relates that the members of
the sect "had a storehouse, common expenditure, common raiments,
common food [. . .]" but he does not mention "common books." From his
description of the requisite spiritual activity, we learn that it comprised
reading and interpreting the Bible. Josephus states that the Essenes applied
themselves to different arts, but does not mention the art of writing or copying books, and there is no suggestion of special times devoted to reading
books of any sort. Therefore, it is difficult to accept the claim that "Nowhere
is there a relationship of community to scriptures so tangibly attested as in
the case of the Qumran sect and the Scrolls [. . .]."[13] Even in the Qumran
texts themselves, there is no mention of writers or copiers, or of a big library
which serves as a center of learning. It seems to me that in a closed sect that
held books in such high esteem, it is reasonable to expect some reference to
the organization of a library and to the copiers and writers, or to the Hellenistic practice of copying books and differentiating between "old copies" and
"latest correct editions." The *Damascus Rule* describes the "Rule of the assembly of the camps" but mentions only that "[. . .] the Priest who enrolls
the Congregation shall be from thirty to sixty years old, learned in the Book
of Meditation and in all the Judgement of the Law so as to pronounce them
correctly." He is not required, however, to know the broad literary corpus included in the "Qumran library," but only a limited number of works. From
the corpus, we can conclude that the members of the community did not
differentiate between the Oral Law and the Written Law, but this conclusion
stems from the character of the corpus and not from a written provision of
any kind.[14]

In conclusion, it is possible to argue that there is no point in searching

---

[12] Again, whenever there is a mention of scrolls or copper scrolls, it does not refer to a large
collection of books.

[13] A. POWELL DAVIES, *The Meaning of the Dead Sea Scrolls*, New York, 1956, p. 42.

[14] SHEMARYAHU TALMON, "Between the Bible and the Mishna in the World of Qumran"
from Within, *Collected Studies*, Jerusalem-Leiden, 1989, p. 28.

for any mention of libraries in the sources, if indeed they were a common cultural phenomenon. I believe, however, that it is precisely because we are dealing with a common and well-established phenomenon during the period under discussion, and because a "library" is an institution entailing organization, resources and skills, one could expect to find some sort of reference to it. Of course, this does not mean that the Jews had no libraries, only that the fact of their existence, if they did indeed exist, is not alluded to in the sources; hence perhaps they did not attribute any basic cultural or religious value to libraries. This calls for an explanation particularly due to the extent of the "Qumran corpus" from which we can deduce the richness, the scope and the diversity of literary creation during the Second Temple period. In other words, there is no evidence that the "Qumran library" exemplified a widespread practice, just as there is no evidence that various Jewish groups had libraries as permanent institutions to any marked degree. Nevertheless, it is clear that there was a considerable Jewish reading public in Palestine which consisted of much more than small elite enlightened groups, but we have no data regarding its extent or its reading patterns.

The fact that we have no evidence of this special regard, which almost everyone considers self-evident, does not entirely eliminate the possibility that those who hid the corpus were indeed motivated by the strong desire to preserve their intellectual world for future generations. To claim that the corpus is heterogeneous and therefore could not belong to a single group – the Essenes, for example – ignores the fact that the gnostic corpus, for instance, is also heterogeneous in character.[15] A heterogeneous content and genre are characteristic of the spirit of syncretism of those times. Such a claim, naturally, also establishes unequivocally that the authors and copiers were the ones who hid the texts.

⸻⸻⸻⸻⸻

At this point, we should deal with the general attitude towards the literary product of the period.

The writings in the DSS included works that presented relatively anomalous points of view. The one positive assumption we can make about them is that the urge to collect and to save the books came from a specific group within the Jewish society of the period. If indeed this is the case, which of the groups in Jerusalem would be interested in preserving the heterogeneous totality of these writings – the Zealots, the Pharisees, the Sadducees, or some other unidentified group?

---

[15] GIOVANNI FILORANO, *A History of Gnosticism*, translated by ANTHONY ALOK, Cambridge, MA, 1992, pp. 7–19. One should draw comparisons between the Qumran sect and the Hellenistic Associations (thiasoi) as well as between it and the Gnostic communities.

Let us discuss the hypothetical possibilities:

There is no evidence that the Pharisees, who held the Oral Law in high esteem, placed much value on collecting and preserving books; neither are there accounts of such an attitude on the part of the Sages after the Destruction. During the period we are dealing with, we can assume that their understanding was similar to that of Horace, as quoted by Hieronymus, that "*delere licebit quod non edideris; nescit vox missa reveti.*" An echo of the same view is found in the Jerusalem Talmud (*Pe'ah* 2:17b; *ibid. Hagigah* 1:76d), which makes a distinction between Israel and the nations of the world, in that the Jewish people do not find their law (Torah) in books.[16] In the Qumran library, in any case, sections of the corpus are missing, just those sections which characterize the Pharisee way of thinking (and the Christian, *e.g.*, sayings and proverbs).[17] The Sadducees, on the other hand, ascribed great importance to the Written Law, but there is no evidence that they attributed any value to post-Biblical literature, and certainly not to literature which promulgated ideas far from their own world outlook. It is difficult to assume that they would make a supreme effort to preserve works whose spiritual world so contradicted their own. If we consider the "Essenes" an all-inclusive name for not only the settlers of Qumran, but a wider, relatively heterogeneous circle, then it is possible to assume that the members of this circle could preserve diverse works toward which they felt a spiritual affinity. However, this would not apply to works which were remote from their world. In any event, we do not have a glimmer of evidence of such a practice, which would have had to continue over a long interval.

One possibility is "radical" Hassidean circles—part of the Jewish people, whatever their identity—who placed great value on written literature and were among those who wrote it. As is well known, "marginal circles" or "avant-gardists" place a paramount value on their own literature or that which is akin to it. This is particularly true because they are on the fringes of consensus, and their literature is the basis and unifying force of their shared world—even, and primarily, when they are dispersed in many places. Their "spiritual territory" does not consist only of the literature of religious regulations, but is rather a sum total of a much wider literary picture. Written literature is their foremost means of expression and experience, as well as their means of communication. Through literature, they create a new world, which encompasses the world of imagination; they interpret reality and react to it. Perhaps a suggestion of this can be found in later Jewish tradition, which views the hiding of books in the ground as characteristic of heretics, a practice usually ascribed to the Karaites, but to the Hellenistic-Egyptian Hermetic tradition as well.

---

[16] SHAUL LIEBERMAN, "Light on the Cave Scrolls from Rabbinic Sources," *Proceedings of the American Academy for Jewish Research*, Vol. XV, New York, 1951.

[17] And in the Qumran literature there are no rules and regulations pertaining to the people's "ephemeral life"!

Another possibility is that first-century Christianity evolved out of oral traditions, but had a written body of literature that served as a basis for study and was disseminated among the members of the community. Colossians 3:16 states: "Let the word of Christ dwell in you richly in all wisdom; teaching and admonishing one another in psalms and hymns and spiritual songs [. . .]." In other words, they possessed written religious literature for daily use. In Timotheus II 6:13, Paul requests: "Bring with thee the books but especially the parchments [. . .]." In Corinthians 4:7–9, it is written: "But we have this treasure in earthen vessels, [*ostrakinois skeuesin*] that the excellence of the power may be of God, and not of us. We are troubled on every side, yet not distressed; we are perplexed, but not in despair; persecuted, but not forsaken [. . .]." In the metaphoric language of apocryphal literature, an expression like "חתום הספר עד-עת קץ" may perhaps give a hint of the philosophical outlook that advocated the hiding of books, which was characteristic of these circles and not those of the "establishment."

This does not mean that the documents were Christian works, but only that the early Christians were interested in preserving them, in their strong desire to prove that they grew out of a long-standing traditional – therefore valid – literary (and revelatory) base.[18] A group like this, at the beginning of its way, under the influence of diverse traditions, is not yet fully consolidated, has not yet written its own history and the history of its messiah and has not yet begun its canonization. Such a group would typically be interested in preserving texts, especially during periods of internal crisis and bitter persecutions which forced its members to flee and hide (like those that characterized Judaeo-Christian history in the first century). Therefore, we need not search the corpus for works of a clear-cut Christian nature, like the Evangelistic writings or a mention of Jesus and his pupils, since there is no need to presume that the works were written by Christians. There is also no need then to search for direct textual or conceptual links between the scrolls and Christian literature as evidence of contact – or the absence of contact – between the early Christians and the "Qumran sect" or "Jewish sectarian literature."[19] There is no doubt that there was some sort of contact, but there is no way to reconstruct the nature of these contacts between the diverse streams and substreams, against the broad syncretic backdrop of contemporary intellectual and spiritual history. In any event, I must re-emphasize that if any group were interested in preserving a relatively heterogeneous collection of works which approximated their world view it would be just such a new group. Such a group would be interested in preserving books, since its spiritual world had

---

[18] There is no doubt that in its short existence until the Destruction of the Temple, the Judeo-Christian community could not have written such a large number of literary works.

[19] R. Eisenman's theory on the nature of the "Christians" and their status is totally groundless, in my view.

still not been conclusively crystallized or institutionalized; it was aware of the innovations within it, while at the same time it emphasized its continuation of an ancient tradition which formed the basis for its spiritual world. Let me stress that this does not mean that the Judaeo-Christian hypothesis is valid. I have suggested it only in order to elucidate my view that we are dealing with the literature of a group, not the literature of the Second Temple in its entirety, and that this group must be a body with a special self-consciousness and with a special regard for books.

In this connection, it is important to emphasize that as far as the Sages were concerned, apocryphal literature, including that written by the Hassidean sect, was identified with the works of the heretics. The existence of hidden works and hiding places in the Judean Desert and the like, were known in the third century A.D. (to Origen, for example) and later, which proves that the sages realized that the sort of books found in the Judean Desert were associated with heretical views. There is an additional point worth mentioning here. Almost without being aware of it, research follows the typology of Josephus, by identifying in the Jewish community of the Second Temple period a limited number of well-defined and well-characterized groups. Jewish society, however, was more stratified and also included other groups and sub-groups. Even more pertinent, scholarship has made an indispensable and exclusive connection between "organized groups" and "written literature," thus conveying the impression that "literature" was in every instance a product of well-defined groups and could not be the works of individual anonymous authors reflecting streams of a *Zeitgeist*; there is a difference between a messianic-popular mood and a well-defined messianic theology, often versed in a language that is incomprehensible to many. Nor could it be the work of similar-minded people (with a similar style) who were not part of a specific, cohesive socio-spiritual framework.

To sum up, we can state that according to the information available at present—and perhaps in the future as well—we can date many of the Scrolls, but unfortunately, cannot know with certainty where they came from and when, and who brought them to the Judean Desert caves, a place which may not have been such a deep secret at the time, and was frequented by people who took books from it. All one can say with certainty is that their spiritual world reflects much more than the restricted and exclusive world of one particular sect.

With this background in mind, what conclusions can we reach about the contents of the corpus itself? Moreover, if we exclude the process of publishing, deciphering and final reprinting the texts, as well as the interrelationship between the different texts, what questions should scholars address?

Research on the Qumran corpus, in its historical and literary-historical context, is troubled by two central issues:

1) the attempt to identify the members of the sect with the authors of the texts through parallels between the world reflected in the corpus and what we know of the sect and kindred groups, from other sources. This has generated a great deal of speculation in an effort to decipher clues in the literature which conform, in one way or another, to what we have learned elsewhere. Scholars, on the basis of radical speculation, even try not only to determine precise identities and relationships, but to reconstruct (as it were) the events and incidents involving the sect and to fit them into the known historical narrative.[20]

Such an attempt in this case, I believe, is an unproductive one. The sources which deal with Qumran are of a typological nature, not historical or narrative. We have not even a hint, for example, of the confrontation between the people of Qumran and the Temple[21] in Jerusalem (which does appear in the New Testament) although such a confrontation was almost inevitable, in light of the attitude of the Qumran people to the Temple. In other words, the sources do not mention even one event pertaining to the history of the "sect." And if we are indeed referring to a "sect" that functioned for many years, there is no doubt that its internal life, as well as its relations with the world around it, would be filled with events, confrontations and a complex dynamic. If indeed various groups were in contact with the "people of Qumran," then it is remarkable that we find not the slightest intimation of such contact in literature.

2) the attempt to determine the literary and spiritual links between Qumran literature and the works of other circles, including the influences of one group on its contemporaries.

The first attempt uncovered hints and reports of historical events, but we must point out that these hints make it possible to establish with certainty only when a text was *not* written, but not exactly when it was written. Therefore, a reconstruction that seems to present a complete picture of events, but which interweaves fragmented and vague information, is a mere figment of the imagination. All the texts in our possession are theological, halachic or literary texts, some of them utopian or eschatological. Despite the similarity between the way of life in *Manual of Discipline* and the *Damascus Document* and what we learn from Josephus and others, we may wonder whether we are dealing with a set of rules according to which life was actually lived, or

---

[20] Regarding the way to draw an historical conclusion from apocalyptic literature, see P. J. ALEXANDER, "Medieval Apocalypse as Historical Course, *American Historical Review* 73 (1960), pp. 997–1018.

[21] ITHAMAR GRUENWALD, "From Priesthood to Messianism: the Anti-Priestly Polemic and the Messianic Factor," in I. GRUENWALD, S. SHAKED and G. G. STRONMSA, *Messiah and Christos: Studies in the Jewish Origins of Christianity*, Tulingen, 1992, pp. 75–93.

a utopian depiction of a utopian society. The allusion to historical events in a non-historiographic text calls for utmost caution in anything that relates to the "historical validity" of the event, since literary texts "use" historical events in different ways: as a paradigm, a symbol, "authentic background" and the like.

The second attempt ignores the fact that although we speak of the socio-spiritual life of the period, there was a broad and multifaceted mosaic of groups and circles, and a diverse and wide range of literary works being written, that were not necessarily linked to an organized and unified group. Nevertheless, studies try to use clear-cut group typology to relate each literary corpus to one specific group. This diversified literature was written in a climate of viewpoints and a common cultural environment, and without doubt, there existed within it a migration of ideas and motifs, even without direct contact or organized group cooperation. It therefore seems correct to argue that the similarity between ideas and motifs does not necessarily prove a direct connection between two texts or two groups, and might be the result of cooperation in one great heterogeneous and syncretistic intellectual-literary-semantic domain. Certainly it does not prove that this cooperation was extensive and thorough. The social history of ideas in more documented periods clearly shows that a similarity of semantics, or even of ideas or literature, is not necessarily the aftermath of cooperation and unity. There is a fundamental difference in the way in which ideas, symbols and terminology get their meaning and the way in which they are interpolated or internalized into a text. Since the Qumran texts were not single copies (there is no evidence of this, even regarding texts ascribed to the "community" and that guide its way of life), it is reasonable to assume that they were influenced from diverse directions, and could in turn, be influential in diverse ways.

Even if we agree that the DSS embody the contents of one large library, it still does not mean that the library was homogeneous in character or that it was the only library of its kind. Any attempt to reconstruct the entire contents of a library cannot be thorough; and this is all the more so in regard to the attempt to reconstruct the position and status of the "library" within the sum total of written literature. Much has been written of the affinity and relationship of the Qumran literature to Biblical literature and to the works of various groups in the Jewish community, but in the absence of the full corpus, any such reconstruction will be partial and deficient, because we are missing many important links in the chain. On the other hand, if the Qumran library represents more than a subordinate or even marginal stream, or if it was interrelated with other segments of the contemporary cultural-literary life, we might ask where its traces can be found in generations after the Destruction. Its influence on the New Testament—or its affinity to it—and on the Karaites has been extensively discussed. It is known that scrolls were taken from Qumran, over circuitous paths to many locations, but there is no way of knowing by whom they were taken, when and to what destinations. However, if the Qumran library represented more than a marginal stream it is logical to suppose that there are corresponding ideas and manners of expression in the literature written after the Destruction. And if it was a marginal stream, we can assume that the Destruction decreed its end; however, if we are dealing with a stream that was firmly fixed in the contemporary *Zeitgeist*, the destruction of the Temple would not necessarily have caused its demise.[22]

We must remember, therefore, that the existence of an extensive literary corpus does not necessarily testify to its place and status in its contemporary culture – certainly not in a culture that was in the main an oral one – and at times, it is precisely this corpus which can represent a subordinate stream rather than a central one. The influence of such a corpus must be tested both in the context of its own time and also in the context of later generations – and there is not necessarily a correspondence between the two. Frequently, a corpus, which is subordinate in its own time, can be very influential through different channels, in later generations, which may be times of deep schism, of ferment, and of new creativity. Written literature cannot in any way provide the key for a thorough reconstruction of the course of contacts and influences and of the various routes through which ideas travelled from one place to another, one group to another, one text to another, and one age to another. Ideas and motifs can travel and permeate in a diversity of forms, and literary and intellectual parallels found in different texts are not sufficient evidence for reconstructing patterns of influence and contact. Therefore, we can only say that the Qumran library provided a unique key to recognizing the existence of the spiritual complex, but did not furnish us with the key for charting its complete map.

---

[22] As stated, the attitude of the Sages to apocryphal literature testifies to the fact that they were aware that in Palestine there were many heretics with an extensive literature. There are those who regard anything in post-Destruction literature bearing a resemblance to ideas or exegetic techniques in the "Qumran literature" as evidence of the direct influence of the specific Qumranian corpus. However, in my view it is more reasonable to assume that the literature of the Sages, as well as the Jewish literature of the second century A.D., could have "absorbed" or even developed ideas defined as "Qumranian," not necessarily through familiarity with the "literature of Qumran," but through similar ideas found in Jewish literature that has not come into our hands.

DISCUSSION OF THE PAPER

RAYMOND EDGE (*University of Texas at Austin*): You mentioned that Jesus probably never read any text. I think we're told that he read from Isaiah when he was in the synagogue at Nazareth, so there was one incidence of reading. I would suggest that he probably knew how to read and read others as well. Based on what we heard this morning concerning the Hellenistic or possible Hellenistic influences in Judaea, why not accept that there was also a library in Jerusalem?

YAACOV SHAVIT (*Tel Aviv University, Israel*): I'm sure that Jesus read the Bible. What I suggested is that the New Testament writers put no importance on the fact that he read or wrote something. The early Christians, of course, had their own library; it's written somewhere that Paul said, "Come, and bring with you the scrolls, mainly the parchment scroll." We don't know if it was a small library or a big library but they had their own collection of books.

The question of Hellenistic influences on Judea during this period is very complicated. I'm convinced that there were libraries somewhere and that Jews read books. They also read history books. History books were the most popular in the Hellenistic-Roman period. But in Qumran we could not find even one fragment of any so-called "secular" historical book. So there were libraries somewhere, but the sources are silent about them. This is a very interesting question of the so-called collective memory, which somehow neglects to mention their existence.

LENA CANSDALE (*University of Sydney, Cremorne, N.S.W.*): If biblical Judaism was witness of the various sects, and it was their writing from the third century onwards which we have, is it possible that what we know about a Second Temple period is what the Pharisaes and rabbis wanted us to know?

What happened on the other side of the fence, namely the Sadducees and Hellenistic writers with their own books, their own libraries, is what (following Professor Golb's idea) we have got in Qumran. Would you agree with or comment on that?

SHAVIT: I would be very happy to find, instead of the Copper Scroll, a catalogue of books. I think a catalogue of books, or even a receipt for a printer somewhere, that he charged this amount of money for schemes or ledger or ink, would be very useful for us in order to decide where the scrolls were written and so on. But we don't have a catalogue and we don't have a receipt from a printer.

Again, my main notion was that, if indeed libraries in the Hellenistic period were such an important institution, then why don't we have any indication or reference, or any evidence, that libraries were indeed such in the social, cultural and educational life of the Jews in Palestine? I really don't know the answer.

NORMAN GOLB (*Oriental Institute, University of Chicago, Chicago, IL*): I said before, the trouble for those of us who work in the field of Jewish history, especially ancient and medieval Jewish history, is that we don't have the history, we just have little pieces and shreds of the history. We have to learn; that's why we're manuscript scholars, we're trying to learn from the sources, to make inferences about the nature of the ancient culture of the Jews. We only have certain pieces of the culture, certain pieces of the books.

We're confronted with this phenomenon of 850 scrolls; just in the caves of Qumran. We know that scrolls were discovered in the third century near Jericho and in the eighth century near Jericho. They were found also at Masada. So we have a bigger picture building up of many, many books, and the question is how best to interpret; what inferences can we make, what proper conclusions can we draw about the source of those books? I acknowledge we don't have a source which says we had libraries in Jerusalem; that's the way historians have to work, with what we have.

SHAVIT: You know better than me that the corpus of the Geniza has a totally different nature than the corpus of Qumran. The corpus in the Geniza, which was kept for different reasons, can give us a picture of the social and cultural life of the Jews in the Middle Ages. Here in Qumran we have literary books, and literary books are hard to interpret in historical terms.

GOLB: The reason we have that kind of a construction in the Cairo Geniza is that when various people died, their literary remains, all their manuscripts, regardless of whether they were documents or not, were put into this storage because they had the name of God written on these papers. In the case of the library at Qumran, we have a selective group of literary sources, as opposed to documentary sources that the Geniza naturally included.

SHAVIT: This is my point, that during the Second Temple period, this type of Jew or sect of Jews was interested mainly in keeping a certain selected corpus of books and not the entire archives of that period. That causes us all there troubles, which may last forever without any real solution.

DENNIS G. PARDEE (*Oriental Institute, University of Chicago, Chicago, IL*): One aspect of Professor Golb's hypothesis that I've always wondered about was its "Jerusalemocentricity," if I may put it that way. Would you be any more sympathetic to a hypothesis that would see those manuscripts coming from all over Palestine?

SHAVIT: I think so, not only from Palestine, but maybe even from the Jewish diaspora; why not? We have a lot of evidence that a so-called community had connections with communities elsewhere, outside Palestine. If we take the example of Paul, who was traveling with these scrolls from synagogue to synagogue, I can't see why members of a so-called community couldn't do so as well.

Language of the Copper Scroll in the Light of the Phrases Denoting the Directions of the World

PIOTR MUCHOWSKI

Department of Comparative Linguistics and Oriental Studies
Adam Mickiewicz University
5 Miedzychodzka Street
PL-61-712 Poznań, Poland

The question of language classification is one of the relevant controversies about the Copper Scroll. It is important for the study of Hebrew as well as for the historical interpretation of 3Q15. The dissension concerns two issues:

• the typological identity of M3Q15 (= Copper Scroll Mishnaic); some scholars maintain that it should be identified with classical Mishnaic Hebrew (CMH)[1] and others claim that it should be regarded as a distinct Mishnaic dialect;[2]

• the Qumranic authorship; according to some scholars, we are dealing with a text written in the Mishnaic used by the authors of the Qumran scrolls,[3] and according to others with a text of external provenience.[4]

In previous publications, scholars expressing their opinions on the subject mainly adduced two elements of M3Q15 – the orthography and the vocabulary.

The orthography seems to have been the most important reason for the separation of M3Q15. The most essential, distinctive features of the M3Q15

---

[1] *Cf.*, *e.g.*, SHARVIT, S. 1967. Investigations Concerning the Lexicon of the Copper Scroll [in Hebrew]. *Beth Mikra* **31**, p. 135: "We are allowed to say that the Scroll was written in the language nearest to the language of Tannaim and Amoraim."

[2] *Cf.*, *e.g.*, MILIK, J. T. 1962. Le Rouleau de Cuivre Provenant de la Grotte 3Q (3Q15), Discoveries in the Judean Desert III, Oxford: Clarendon Press, pp. 222–223: "Au lieu de voir dans les particularités linguistiques du cataloge les idiosyncrasies du language personel de l'auteur, il vaut mieux considérer le rouleau de cuivre comme le monument d'un dialect mishnique, celui de la vallée du Jourdain sans doute;".

[3] *Cf.*, *e.g.*, WOLTERS, A. 1990. The Copper Scroll and Vocabulary of Mishnaic Hebrew, *Revue de Qumran* **14**, p. 494: "The likelihood seems strong that the Copper Scroll will continue to be the Qumran document with the clearest affinity to MH" [MH = Mishnaic Hebrew of the Tannaitic and Amoraitic literature].

[4] *Cf.*, *e.g.*, TOV, E. 1986. The Orthography and Language of the Hebrew Scrolls Found at Qumran and the Origin of These Scrolls, Textus 13, Jerusalem: The Magness Press, pp. 31–57.

orthographic system are an extensive usage of the graphemes *alef* (instead of *he*) to represent final $[\bar{a}, \bar{e}]$ and *nun* (instead of *mem*) in the nominal masculine plural suffix. Milik's interpretation of M3Q15 as a distinct Mishnaic dialect is founded, to a great extent, on those features.[5] Likewise, Sh. Morag pointed to the *-yn* suffix, when linguistically classifying M3Q15 as a separate category and distinguishing between it and Qumran Mishnaic (QM), *i.e.*, the variety that he defined as the language "of those texts which show an affinity to classical MH."[6] The hypothesis of the uniqueness of such an orthography in Hebrew was, however, criticized by J. Greenfield. Indicating its presence in the "good" manuscripts of Mishna, he defined M3Q15 as ". . . clearly related to Mishnaic Hebrew"[7] [*i.e.*, "the language of Mishna and other products of the Tannaic period . . ."].[8]

Without considering here the question of origin and status of the orthographic system used in 3Q15, I would like to make two remarks:

1) A similar orthography (with respect to *alef* and *nun*) can be found in Bar Kokhba Mishnaic (BKM); *cf.* Naḥal Ḥever 12, where the masculine plural suffix occurs 7 times with *nun* (with *mem* not even once) and the feminine singular suffix twice with *alef* (with *he* not even once). This suggests that the orthography of 3Q15 may be placed within the limits of the orthographic system of BKM, *sensu largo*.

2) In the first column of 3Q15 there are corrections[9] which should be, in my opinion, interpreted as a clue that the scribe knew another, seemingly more normative, orthographic system and probably regarded it as more convenient to annotate the 3Q15 text. In view of it, my thesis is that the features in question are not necessarily integral, inseparable parts of M3Q15 and should be regarded as indicators of a stylistic variety rather than dialectal individuality.

The fact that a considerable number of the words attested in 3Q15 are known only from CMH,[10] has been used as a basic argument for the iden-

---

[5] MILIK, J. T. 1962, pp. 224–226.

[6] MORAG, S. 1988. Qumran Hebrew: Some Typological Observations. *Vetus Testamentum* (=VT) **38**, p. 149.

[7] GREENFIELD, J. 1969, "The Small Caves of Qumran," *Journal of the American Oriental Society* **89**, p. 135.

[8] GREENFIELD, J. 1969, p. 136.

[9] Corrections of graphic signs in the first verses of the document may be interpreted as a proof of the scribe's hesitation when choosing the orthographic system. In the first verse he changed *alef* (suffix of 3rd person feminine) to *he*. In the seventh and tenth *sin* to *samekh*. In the fourth one, in the *šbʿśrh* syntagm he noted $[ś]$ by *sin* and final $[\bar{e}]$ by *he* (differently than, *e.g.*, in the analogical syntagm in 2,8: *tšʿśr*). In the subsequent verses he almost regularly recorded $[ś]$ by *samekh*, final $[\bar{a}, \bar{e}]$ most often by *alef*. The correction *sin* to *samekh* is rather untypical. Correction of *alef* to *he*, and then the recording of the final $[\bar{e}]$ by *he* and $[ś]$ by *sin* in the first note, indicate that the scribe began copying with the intention of using traditional orthography. Correction of *sin* to *samekh* in the final $[\bar{a}, \bar{e}]$ suggest that he gave up his attempt and began to use a more phonetic orthography, with which he was probably more familiar.

[10] So for instance, S. SHARVIT, (1967) selected 24 such lexical items and A. WOLTERS 50 (1990). According to my reading of the 3Q15 texts there are 25.

tification of M3Q15 with CMH. An obstacle to this hypothesis is, however, that a relatively large number of the 3Q15 words were also documented exclusively in the Old Testament and in the Qumran texts.[11] Furthermore, the fact that CMH is the only variety of Mishnaic possessing such extensive sources does not support it, either. It is characteristic that the word "opposite," occurring in CMH in the form *kngd*, in 3Q15 appears in the same variant as in the Old Testament and the Qumran texts, *i.e.*, *ngd*. Similarly, the feminine ordinal number "second" was probably used in 3Q15 in the form *šnyt*, as in Biblical Hebrew (BH) and Qumran Hebrew (QH) and differently than in CMH (*šnyyh*). Seemingly, these two divergences should be classified as dialectical rather than stylistic. In Mishmarot, *i.e.*, in the text held to be written in a literary variety of Mishnaic, the number "second" occurs in the variant *šnyt*,[12] *i.e.*, in the same form as in M3Q15.

Looking for linguistic evidence which could contribute to the solution of the problem under discussion and especially which could shed some light on the relation of M3Q15 to the hypothetical Mishnaic vernacular of the Qumran texts authors, I assumed that a source of additional information may be the comparative analysis of the directive and locative phrases designating the directions of the world. The idea of using these phrases resulted from their high frequency in 3Q15 and in the Temple Scroll, whose language is held to be heavily influenced by Mishnaic. I put forth a thesis that the system of the phrases in question attested in the Temple Scroll, can, at least to a degree, reflect the system functioning in the vernacular of the author.

The material with which the phrases from the Copper Scroll were compared was restricted to the phrases documented in Hebrew and Aramaic sources contemporaneous with 3Q15–Qumran texts, Bar Kokhba texts, and Mishna (the material attested in Mishna is representative for the whole CMH). The only aim of the comparison was an attempt to find out any essential differences between the systems of such phrases in M3Q15 and CMH, BKM, and QH. Consequently, the comparative corpus consisted of about 300 phrases. From this number, 35 are attested in the Hebrew Qumran texts (Temple Scroll–31, 2Q23–2, 4QMMT–1, 4QMishmarot–1), 17 in the Hebrew texts from Murabbaʿat (Mur 22–7, Mur 30–10), 24 in the Aramaic Qumran texts (Enoch–5, Genesis Apocryphon–13, Description of the New Jerusalem–4, Testament of Levi–1, Leviticus Targum–1), 12 in the Aramaic Bar Kokhba texts (Mur 25–3, Naḥal Ḥever 45–5, Naḥal Ḥever 46–3) and over 200 in Mishna.[13]

[11] I identified 17 such lexemes.
[12] *Cf.*, *e.g.*, Bª fragment 1, column 2, 5.
[13] The corpus includes only the material from the officially published texts, except for 4QMMT and 4QMishmarot. In the following I used Latin terms to denote particular sememes of the directive and locative.

In 3Q15 the phrases in question occur 24 times. I classified them into six main types according to their construction:

1) *mn ḥxxx* – the preposition min + a determined w.d.d.w. (= a word denoting the direction of the world = *xxx*)
meaning: *inessivus*

1,11	*mn ḥṣpwn*	"on the north"
5,2	*mn ḥṣpwn*	"on the north"
2,10	*mn ḥmzrḥ*	"on the east"
12,1	*mn ḥm(ʿ)rb*	"on the west"

Apparently this construction does not have any distinctive value. Its usage was attested in all varieties of Hebrew. The fact that in all three examples in the Temple Scroll and the only one in the texts from Murabbaʿat it appears with the preposition "from" in the form *m(h-)*, for instance *wmḥmʿrb* (Temple Scroll 31,13), is probably of no importance. In the language of the Temple Scroll, as in BKM, the usage of the prepositions *mn* and *m-* with a determined word seems to be alternative. The latter variant was also attested in 3Q15, *i.e.*, *mḥnḥl ḥgdwl* (10,3).

2) *lxxx* – the preposition lamed + w.d.d.w.
meaning: *illativus*

1,2 *lmzrḥ* "eastward"

Structures of this type are common. They were attested in all the sources, except in the Bar Kokhba texts (this absence, however, seems casual as the phrases expressing *illativus* do not appear at all in these texts).

3) *bxxx, bxxxw, bxxx st.c. N* – the preposition b + w.d.d.w. (or + a suffixed w.d.d.w., or w.d.d.w. in the relation status constructus with the following word/s/)
meaning: *inessivus*

8,11	*bdrwm*	"on the south"
3,8	*bṣpwnw*	"on its north"
4,2	*bṣpwnw*	"on its north"
2,13	*bmzrḥ kḥlt*	"on the east of . . ."
4,11	*bṣpwn kḥlt*	"on the north of . . ."
9,14	*bṣpwn py ḥṣwq*	"on the north of . . ."
12,10	*bṣpwn kḥlt*	"on the north of . . ."

Likewise, these structures occur in the Qumran texts and in Mishna, but are absent from the Bar Kokhba texts (Hebrew and Aramaic). In this case, however, their absence does not seem casual. Instead of them, the parallel phrases without the preposition *b* appear (see the following type).

4) *xxx, xxx st.c.* N—w.d.d.w. without a preposition, or in the relation
   status constructus with the following word(s)
   meaning: *inessivus*

10,1	*drwm*	"on the south"
12,10	*spwn*	"on the north"
5,6	*mzrh 'ṣyh šlwmw*	"on the east of . . ."
8,1–2	*mzrh byt 'ḥṣr*	"on the east of . . ."
8,2	*mzrh 'ḥzr*	"on the east of . . ."

In Mishna, this construction probably appears in the phrase *r'šw drwm*.[14]
In the Temple Scroll it occurs only once.[15] In the texts from Murabbaʿat it
is documented 14 times.[16] It is also present in the Aramaic Dead Sea Scrolls
(more frequently in those from Murabbaʿat and Naḥal Ḥever, rarely in these
from Qumran[17]). It seems that this type should be regarded as characteristic
of the spoken language. Its usage in BKM, 5 examples against 7 of the parallel
construction with the preposition *b* in 3Q15, suggests that with respect to
style M3Q15 comes closer to the literary language than BKM.

5) *ṣwp' (l)xxx*—the active participle of the verb ṣ.p.h. + w.d.d.w. (once
   with the preposition lamed)
   meaning: facing to, *e.g.*, east

6,2	*ṣwp' mzrh*	"facing east"
6,8	*hṣwp' lmzrh*	"facing east"
8,10–11	*hṣwp' m'rb*	"facing west"
8,12	*hṣwp' spwn*	"facing north"
9,4	*hṣwp' mzrh*	"facing east"
9,7	*hṣwp' ym*[18]	"facing west"

This structure was not documented in any source. The only similar usage
of the verb ṣ.p.h. seems to be attested in BH in Cant. 7,5: *kmgdl hlbnwn
ṣwph pny dmśq*. In CMH, as well as in the Temple Scroll language and in
Qumran Aramaic (QA) and Bar Kokhba Aramaic (BKA), in place of it a phrase
ptwh 1- "open to" appears.[19] The *lamed* in the example in 6.8 *hṣwp' lmzrh*
was presumably used as a mark of the accusative.

[14] *Cf.* Yoma 3,8, Tamid 4,1, Para 3,9.
[15] 31,10 *ngb mzrh*.
[16] *Cf.*, *e.g.*, Mur 22 1,3: *spwn*.
[17] *Cf.*, *e.g.*, Naḥal Ḥever 45,4 *spn*; Genesis Apocryphon 21,12: *mdnh ḥwrn*.
[18] I assumed that this word was used here in the meaning "west" (it is suggested by the constant occurrence of a w.d.d.w. after the participle *ṣwp'*). *ym* = "west" functioned in BH (*e.g.*,
Gen. 13,14). In QH it appears 5 times in the Temple Scroll (*e.g.*, 38,14). In Mishna it was not
attested. In the Bar Kokhba texts the word *ym* does not occur at all.
[19] See Temple Scroll 31,6; Description of New Jerusalem 3,2; Naḥal Ḥever 45,4; *e.g.*,
Midot 4,5.

6) As a separate type I classified the segment in 3,11–12, consisting of two words denoting the directions of the world, read by me as *mzrḥw bṣpwn*.[20] Similarly to Milik and Pixner I assumed that we are dealing with a phrase designating intermediate direction.[21] Such phrases appear in QH, QA, and in CMH. They are absent from the Old Testament and the Bar Kokhba texts. In QH they occur 4 times in the Temple Scroll:

> 30,7   *ḥm'rb spwnw*
> 31,10 *ngb mzrḥ*
> 39,14 *lmzrḥ spwn*
> 46,14 *lspwn ḥm'rb*

In QA they are attested twice: in Genesis Apocryphon 21,20 – *klmdnḥ spwn* and Enoch 32,1 – *klspwn mdnḥḥwn*.

In all these cases both words were connected with the relation *status constructus*. In Mishna there are apparently 4 occurrences of phrases denoting the intermediate directions:

> Tamid 4,1:   *mzrḥh spwnh*
>   *m'rbh drwmh*
> Para 3,1:   *spwnh mzrḥh*

They seem to be constructed by an ordinary juxtaposition. Each word terminates with a (*h*) expressing the locative. From the above it is evident that a structure like that in 3Q15 was not documented in any source. This fact may seemingly be interpreted in two ways: the phrase in question may be regarded as a deviating dialectical construction or simply as having been faultily written. In the second case, which appears to me more probable, the error would consist in a metathesis, *i.e.*, instead of *mzrḥw bṣpwn* it should be *bṣpwn mzrḥw*, as in the Temple Scroll 30,7. Assuming that my identification is correct, as

---

[20] The other proposals of its reading are as follows:
J. T. Milik: *mmzrḥw bṣpwn*
J. M. Allegro: *byrydtw bṣpwn*
B. Z. Luria: *mzrḥw mṣpwn*
B. Pixner: (to the north east of)
M. Mishor: *mmzrḥw bṣpwn*
A. Wolters: *mzrḥy bṣpwn*

[21] The thesis that this is one phrase is supported by the context, requiring rather only information of location of the grave. In other notes referring to the graves no data are given concerning the side on which the deposit is cached in the grave (*cf.* notes 25, 55, 56). I decided to reject the proposal of J. T. MILIK that the grapheme mem should be identified as the preposition *m-, i.e., mmzrḥw bṣpwn*. Supposing that the mem does not belong to the preceding toponym (*i.e., mlḥ m-*), in the analogous phrase where this toponym appears, *i.e.*, in 15th note, we should read the following phrase as *mbspwnw* (instead of *bṣpwnw*). The fact that it would be the only example of such a compound preposition *mb-* in 3Q15 simply does not favor that solution. The proposal of WOLTERS, *i.e., mzrḥy bṣpwn*, seems to be dismissed by the lack of the definite article in front of *mzrḥy* (assuming that *mlḥm* is a proper name) and the fact that in the 15th note this toponym occurs individually.

far as the attested examples show, the phrase in 3Q15 was constructed in the same way as in the Temple Scroll and the Aramaic Qumran texts and otherwise than in Mishna.

From the above it follows that the system of 3Q15 differs from that in Mishna in 3 items: i) in the usage of the constructions without prepositions (*e.g.*, *mzrḥ*), ii) in the presence of the phrases with the verb *ṣ.p.ḥ.* (analogous to the phrases with the verb *p.t.ḥ.* in Mishna), and iii) in the way of constructing phrases denoting intermediate directions (if of course my reconstruction is correct). Taking into account that the Mishnaic system has been extensively documented, these divergences should be considered very meaningful. Concerning the system functioning in QH and particularly in the Temple Scroll language, it seems that the most significant difference may be the lack of constructions with the verb *ṣ.p.ḥ.* The single example of the construction without a preposition suggests that such constructions were in use in the spoken language of the scribe. Besides, it should be noted that both in the Temple Scroll and in Mishna we find constructions with the suffix *he*, expressing the location, which are absent in the Copper Scroll and the Bar Kokhba texts (it seems probable that they were characteristic of the literary style). In the case of BKM, the number of attested types is of course too small to permit a reliable conclusion, but as regards the structures without prepositions, it shows significant similarity to M3Q15 (although their usage in 3Q15 is not so frequent and they occur side by side with the parallel structures with prepositions).

Connecting the results of the comparison with the aforementioned lexical data it seems reasonable to reject the hypothesis identifying M3Q15 with CMH. Such an opinion is confirmed by two other linguistic facts, which have not been pointed to above, *i.e.*, the presence of the temporal construction of the type *bqtlw* in 3Q15[22] and the way of noting the particle *šl* with the determined *nomen rectum*.[23]

---

[22] It occurs probably once, *i.e.*, in 10,5: *bbw'k*. Such constructions are characteristic of the late BH. They are also attested in QH and QA; *cf.*, *e.g.*, Temple Scroll 32,12: *bbw'm*, Targum of Hiob 28,25: *bm'bdh*. In CMH they do not appear, nor was I able to find them in the texts from Murabba'at and Naḥal Ḥever. Their presence in 3Q15 seems to suggest a chronological proximity between M3Q15 and QH.

[23] In 3Q15 the particle *šl* occurs 24 times. In 7 cases *nomen rectum* is preceded by the definite article. As it follows from that, the particle *šl* was noted separately and the phenomenon of the *he* elision did not take place. In CMH *šl* appears written also continuously as well as separately. Nowhere, however, was the form with *he* attested. In BKM the particle *šl* occurs 13 times, 9 times with the space and 4 without. In 4 cases *nomen rectum* is preceded by the definite article. In the Qumran texts, as far as I know, there is one example of *šl* followed by *nomen rectum* (noted continuously): Temple Scroll 6,1.: *šlnḥwšt*. According to that, as regards the way of notation of *šl* with the determined *nomen rectum*, M3Q15 shows agreement with a variety of Mishnaic presented by some texts from Murabba'at and Naḥal Ḥever (*i.e.*, Mur 45,46, Naḥal Ḥever 5) and disagreement with CMH. Only one example in the Qumran texts does not permit any conclusion.

In light of the similarly distinctive material attested in 3Q15 and in the
Bar Kokhba texts, it seems that BKM is the nearest known variety of Mishnaic
to M3Q15 (this is manifested by such relevant linguistic evidence as, *e.g.*, the
orthography, and the way of noting *šl* with the determined *nomen rectum*). At
the same time, however, it appears that some differences existed between them
(this finds expression, *e.g.*, in the frequent use of the preposition *mn* before
not-determined words in BKM). I am not sure, however, if these distinctions
are more basic than those between different Bar Kokhba texts.

A reliable definition of the relation of M3Q15 to the hypothetical Mishnaic vernacular used by Essenes does not seem possible.[24] The absence of a
linguistic phenomenon similar to 3Q15 among the Qumran texts may not,
however, in my opinion, be utilized as proof that M3Q15 was not a language
used by the same people who wrote the Qumran texts. Considering the structure of the Essene movement, I do not believe that, as far as the spoken language is concerned, the linguistic situation inside the Essene society was significantly different from that in Judea. I do not suppose that Essenes used
only one specific variety of Mishnaic vernacular, either. Such linguistic phenomena common to M3Q15 and QH as, *e.g.*, the structures *bqtlw*, the forms
šnyt, *ngd*, seem to make the hypothesis plausible that M3Q15 was the spoken
language of the Essenes. The notation of original final *he* by *alef* attested in
QH may be interpreted as traces of an orthographic system parallel to that in
3Q15. The results of this comparative analysis of phrases designating the
directions of the world do not disprove such a possibility, although they do
not completely confirm it, either. My final conclusion is that, to our present
knowledge, a safe definition of M3Q15 should be restricted to the statement
that this language is a specimen of the Mishnaic vernacular used in Judea, probably in the first century c.e.

<hr />

DISCUSSION OF THE PAPER

RAYMOND EDGE (*University of Texas at Austin*): I'm intrigued by your classification of classical Mishnaic Hebrew, in that we know that there are two
different types of Mishnaic Hebrew, that of the Tannaim, and that of the later
period. Which one are you talking about here? Second, we don't have much

---

[24] Concerning the supposition that the language of 4QMMT might have been the spoken
language of the Essenes, I would like to note that in my opinion its value as an informant of
the vernacular of Essenes is limited. I am inclined to consider it a result of a literary adoption
of an originally Mishnaic text to the norms of QH. The presence of the Mishnaic vocabulary
I attribute to stylistic reasons.

information on the development from Biblical Hebrew to a classical Mishnaic Hebrew. Could this text fall right in the line of development, not only of spoken, but also of written Hebrew, since we have a written text?

PIOTR MUCHOWSKI (*A. Mickiewicz University, Poznań, Poland*): By classical Mishnaic Hebrew I mean Mishnaic Hebrew of the Tannaim and Amoraim. Concerning the second question, the problem is that our knowledge of Mishnaic Hebrew before Mishna is very limited. The Copper Scroll Hebrew seems to represent an earlier stage of development of the same variety of non-literary Mishnaic Hebrew which was attested in the Bar Kokhba documents.

DENNIS PARDEE (*Oriental Institute, University of Chicago, Chicago, IL*): Regarding the semantics of your first category, where you have *min* plus a word, you gave the example I believe of *mitsaphon*. Is that followed in turn by *lamed*, or is it all by itself?

MUCHOWSKI: It appears separately.

PARDEE: I see. Do you see any difference in the semantics of the phrase between *mitsaphon* and *betsaphon*, for example? Do the *min* and the *beth* seem to play different roles or not?

MUCHOWSKI: In my opinion they play the same role.

TONY TOMASINO (*University of Chicago, Chicago, IL*): I'm probably kicking against a long-standing scholarly convention in suggesting that doing comparisons between Mishnaic Hebrew and the Hebrew of either the Dead Sea Scrolls or the Bar Kokhba letters gives me some difficulties, not so much with regard to the Dead Sea Scrolls in general, but particularly with regard to the Copper Scroll. Most people seem to assume that the Copper Scroll is written in a Hebrew closer to an epistolary language, as are the Bar Kokhba letters. They're written in something closer to the spoken language of the society, whereas Mishnaic Hebrew is clearly a literary dialect. It seems that to compare the elements of this literary dialect with the elements of the spoken language is like comparing apples and oranges.

MUCHOWSKI: The reason for my analysis was disagreement as regards the question of classification of the Copper Scroll Hebrew. My only aim was to find out which one of the contradictory opinions should be accepted. My intention was not to compare different varieties of Hebrew. I took into account the possibility of stylistic character of the considered distinctive elements; however, most of them seem to have a dialectical nature.

The Exegetical Method of the Damascus Document Reconsidered

SAMUEL IWRY

Department of Near Eastern Studies
The Johns Hopkins University
3400 N. Charles Street
Baltimore, Maryland 21218

The Damascus Document—a rare Hebrew manuscript retrieved from the Geniza in 1898 and published by Schechter in 1910 under the *ad interim* title of "Fragments of a Zadokite Work"—constitutes, in essence, the manifesto of a breakaway group in ancient Judaism who claim to have gone out from their home in the land of Judah and escaped to the North where they sojourned for some undisclosed length of time as the New Covenant Community of Damascus.

Their religious laws, designed for the members of their sectarian community and forming part of the Geniza document, were to be strictly observed under the guidance of an overseer and Zadokite priests.

In a hortatory portion of the document, however, where Amos 5:26–27 with its mention of Damascus has been slightly emended to yield a new, contemporizing interpretation, we are told that still another learned "star," the so-called "Interpreter of the Law" (*dwrš htwrh*), has likewise come to Damascus to join the leadership of the congregation and to serve as its Torah authority.

The notable preponderance of precepts regarding conduct and dealings with gentiles (*gwyym*) and the occasional warnings, such as not to get involved in brawls with the gentiles or carry off any of their possessions without the advice of the Board of Directors of the Jewish community (Habur Israel), testifies to the community's having once been a minority group in a wider diaspora.[1]

As to questions of demography and the extent of the Jewish population

---

[1] Support for this idea came from a reference in Josephus (*Ant.* XIII, 14), where we are told that the enemies of Alexander Janneus, 8,000 strong, were forced to flee the country and seek refuge outside Judea. The supposed migration was also related by some to a passage in *Megillath Taʿanith*, where it is said that "on the seventeenth of the month, the Gentiles arose against the refugee scribes (or sages) in the region of Chalcis and Beth Zabdai" northwest of Damascus. It was here, so was it commonly agreed, that a new refugee community was to arise and its members enter into a new covenant.

in the region, we now have an increasing amount of evidence (enough to fill a sizable volume) from a variety of reliable sources that a continual chain of Jewish settlements were indeed thriving in Syria and in the Hauran–in and around Damascus–both before and after the destruction of the second temple, and that Jews continued to live there up to the present time.[2] In the early centuries of the Common Era this region was the habitat of many Jewish and Christian groups as well as religious sects.

It was, therefore, common sense at the beginning of this century to maintain that the copy Schechter extracted from the Geniza was a product of Damascus that made its way to Egypt. There it was copied and recopied by scribes in the tenth and twelfth centuries C.E. until it was discarded in the Geniza store-room of the Cairo Fostat synagogue. However, when original copies of the Damascus document were found in the caves of Qumran, a disturbing crisis resulted.

In 1965, in a paper presented before the faculty of the Humanities at the Hebrew University in Jerusalem under the title "The Damascus Document after the Discoveries at Qumran," I stated that this ancient, well-preserved copy of coherent composition in pre-Christian Hebrew, which served as the indispensable catalyst for our understanding and unraveling the mystery of the Dead Sea Scrolls, is, in itself, still in a state of unyielding *crux interpretum*, just as the people who wrote it are still "Eine unbekannte Jüdische Sekte."[3]

As many as eight separate copies of the Damascus Document were found embedded in the mud of caves 4Q and 6Q, a proportion surpassing all but a few of the other non-biblical and sectarian Dead Sea scrolls. This caused all of us to believe that the Covenant of Damascus was indeed very popular in this community and seemed to be at home at Qumran.

Numerous references in this book to the flight to Damascus raised many questions. How shall we relate to the message that constitutes the backbone of the expositional portion of the book, where the author(s) recount(s) in clear, persuasive biblical phraseology the story of a group of Zadokite priests and Levites, accompanied by laymen and calling themselves *šby yśr'l*, "penitents" (?), who felt compelled to leave the land of Judah and "sojourned in Damascus"? Was it there in the land of Damascus, as we are told, that they established the new fellowship called "The Community of the New Covenant" (or "Testament"), where they continued to observe strict Biblical Law in accordance with a collection of legal stipulations and ordinances that were appended to the copy of the Geniza manuscript?

It soon dawned upon interested scholars that the claims of the group con-

---

[2] B. Z. LURIA, *The Jewish Diaspora in Syria in Post-exilic, Greco-Roman and Byzantine Times* [Hebrew] (Jerusalem, 1957).

[3] The title of Louis Ginzberg's essay in *Monatschrift für Geschichte und Wissenschaft des Judentums* (Breslau, 1912–14).

cerning their migration to Damascus, as originally understood and commented on by Schechter, Louis Ginzberg and later by Chaim Rabin, were wholly incompatible with the (archaeological) evidence from the caves in Qumran. It was natural, therefore, that a scholar like F. M. Cross could say that he felt "increasingly inclined toward those views which hold that the 'land of Damascus' (Amos 5:25) is the prophetic name applied to the desert of Qumran."[4] Even Geza Vermes, a man of prolific scholarship and meticulous interpretation of every historical allusion in the scrolls, found it very frustrating to deal with the sect's migration to Damascus, the sequences of their whereabouts before and after Qumran, and the fate of their Teacher of Righteousness. As late as 1981, he states in his *Dead Sea Scrolls — Qumran in Perspective*,[5] "In the ensuing fratricidal struggle, the Teacher and those who remained faithful to him went into exile in the 'land of Damascus' where they entered into a 'new Covenant.' There, the Teacher of Righteousness was 'gathered in,' meaning that he died." After consulting a number of scholars, including Milik, who has accepted the migration to Damascus in its concrete geographical sense, Vermes[6] turns around and says: "It is not essential to this study to solve the historical problem, *viz.*, whether the Zadokites settled in Syria or in the Qumran area. Wherever it was, their exile was interpreted as the fulfillment of the prophecy, because they firmly believed. . . . If they did travel to Damascus, it was God who decreed and foretold that they would live in that area. If, in fact, they went somewhere else, they still called that place the land of Damascus because their exegesis of holy scriptures obliged them to do so."

Faced with the desperate task of explaining a hopeless contradiction, T. H. Gaster, the first translator of the scrolls into English, strikes a rather soberly musing note by minimizing the whole Damascus affair as follows: "The members of the community . . . picture themselves as going out into the wilderness to receive a new covenant." "The text," Gaster further says, "describes their sojourn in the forbidding desert as exile in the wilderness of Damascus, therefore dramatizing it as the fulfillment of the prophet Amos who predicted that God would cause his people to 'go into exile beyond Damascus' (Amos 5:27)."[7]

Robert North uses political geography to bolster a similar hypothesis. He identifies Damascus with the Nabataean kingdom to which both Damascus and the Dead Sea region belong; hence, Damascus was Qumran.[8]

But the political geographer Robert North is not alone in claiming that "North" is "South" and "South" is "North." My good friend Shemaryahu

[4] F. M. CROSS, *The Ancient Library of Qumran* (New York: Doubleday, 1961), p. 8 n. 46.
[5] *Dead Sea Scrolls — Qumran in Perspective*, p. 143.
[6] *Scripture in Tradition and Judaism*, p. 43.
[7] *Dead Sea Scriptures in English* (A Doubleday Anchor Original, 1956), p. 4.
[8] "The Damascus of Qumran Geography," *PEQ* 87 (1955), pp. 34*ff*.

Talmon, in a circuitous but not less sophisticated manner, arrived at a similar conclusion of late, namely, that "Damascus" and the "North" in the Qumran writings should probably be understood as ciphers for the "Exile" in the desert of Judah.[9] Conceptualizing the religio-historical grasp of the covenanters, he continues to say that to them (*i.e.*, the covenanters) "life in the arid area of Qumran signified the period of exile–Egypt and Babylon rolled into one. There they located typologically the "Damascus" beyond which Israel would be exiled according to the prophet Amos (5:25): 'I shall take you into exile beyond Damascus, says God' (CD vii:13–14; *cf.* Zech. 6:8)."

How did Talmon arrive at this conclusion? The answer is: "Like the 'locust' that usually invades the land of Israel from the south, and nevertheless can represent the 'foe from the north' in the visions of the biblical prophet Joel (Joel 2:10; cp. 1:1–2:11), 'Damascus' and the 'North' in the Qumran writings should probably be understood as ciphers for 'exile in the desert of Judah.' There, in that 'Damascus,' they established the New Covenant (CD vi 19; viii 21)."

However, in a footnote in the same article Talmon remarks: "Scholars are divided on the question of whether 'Damascus' stands for the name of the well-known city or whether it is used here as a topos."[10]

In this connection, it is worth noting that while Professor Talmon is still rendering *šby yśr'l* as "the returnees [and/or repenters] of Israel," he does explain the next phrase *hywṣ'ym m'rṣ yhwdh* as "the deportees from the land of Judah, undoubtedly an allusion to the enforced deportation of Judeans in the wake of the debacle of 586 B.C.E."[11]

On the other end, J. T. Milik remains a staunch believer in a real "Damascus" and maintains that there was a migration to Damascus. He claims that at a certain time, much later, "a fairly important Essene splinter group" left the community at Qumran and settled in the region of Damascus . . . while still remaining in communion with the 'mother house.'" "The Damascus document," according to him, "was drawn up to provide an appropriate rule for the life of this offshoot in the Hauran."[12] Feeling that his attempts at bridging this controversy complicate matters even more, he makes an appeal

---

[9] *The World of Qumran from Within* (Jerusalem/Leiden, 1989), p. 285.

[10] *Ibid.*, p. 285 n. 26.

[11] See p. 40 n. 88, with which I agree that the said covenanters were Judeans who left the land probably in pre-exilic or exilic times, but I have never pinpointed any particular time in any of my writings. See also Prof. Talmon's summation on S. Iwry's theory on *šby yśr'l, ibid.*, p. 44.

S. Iwry's real-historical interpretation of the exile motif and the "return" vocabulary found in the Covenanters' literature is better attuned to the prevalent dating of the Qumran manuscripts and the emergence of the יחד [*yaḥad*] in the second century B.C.E. He opines that the Covenanters were a group of Jews who, for reasons that are no longer ascertainable, had left the Land at some juncture after Nehemiah's days. Coming from Damascus where they had established their Covenant (CD viii 35), they actually returned to Israel in the first half of the second century B.C.E.

[12] *Ten Years of Discovery in the Wilderness of Judea* (London: SCM, 1959), p. 90.

to methodology by saying: "It is methodologically unsound to take the phrase 'land of Damascus' and . . . to see in it a symbolic name for Qumran."

It was the misfortune of the previous readers, great as they were, to render the crucial phrase *šby yśʾl* as "repenters" or "penitents of Israel." As a matter of fact, the word *šāb* or *šābîm*, a derivative from the double entendre *šûb*, meaning "again, turn, turn away" or "return," does not suggest in Biblical Hebrew the term "repentee" unless it is followed by a preposition, pronoun or noun expressing that of which they repented, and more often than not, it is even capped by an adverbial phrase, *bkl lbbw wbkl npšw*, "with all his heart and soul." A somewhat later semantic equivalent for "repentance" is the word *tšwbh*, and still in religious parlance the phrase *bʾl tšwbh* for a "repentee" is regularly preferred. Again, as a matter of fact, the text of our own CD, which values among many other virtues also the need of repentance, exhibits the expression *ʾśr bʾw bbryt tšwbh* (MS B line 16), "they the princes of Judah, who once entered a covenant of repentance, but did not forsake the way of the faithless." It also exhibits the biblical phrase *šby pśʿ*, "those who turn from sin" (Isa 59:20). Basing himself on this latter phrase, Ch. Rabin in his English translation of the Zadokite Document strains to render *šby yśrʾl* all through the text "they that turned (from impiety) in Israel" (see his explanation pertaining to CD 4:2).[13]

In my lecture at the Hebrew University of Jerusalem, I stood the entire problem of leaving the land of Judah for Damascus on its head. I stated then, as I do today, that there was no migration to Damascus. The rendering of the pivotal sentence which appears seven times in CD should be: "The priests, the sons of Zadok and the laymen who joined them (*hkhnym bny ṣdwk whnlwym ʿmhm*), are the returnees of Israel (*hm šby yśrʾl*), who hail from the land of Judah (*hywṣʾym mʾrṣ yhwdh*), and have sojourned (up to now) in the land of Damascus (*wygwrw bʾrṣ dmśq*).[14] *They did not abandon or leave* Yehud country in the second Jewish commonwealth which they *nota bene* never called by the name "land of Judah" in their Dead Sea Scrolls writings. Just the opposite, this community of diaspora Jews were, indeed, the ones to make *aliya*. They came back as repatriates to the old, liberated Judea, now under the rule of the enlightened Hasmonean prince-priests, while carrying with them the books of the Torah and the books of the prophets which ancient Israel had forsaken and denigrated (CD 5:26; *cf.* 2 Chr 36:16 and the allusion in Matt 23:31).

They pictured themselves as the returnees of old Israel of the biblical age

---

[13] *The Zadokite Documents* (Oxford, 1964), p. 13, l. 2, notes 3 and 4. This is but a repetitive, build-in interpretation by the late master of Hebrew language. Otherwise (without resorting to this remedial-parenthetical arrangement), the phrase *šby yśrʾl* on the analogy of *šby pśʿ* could also mean "those who turn away from Israel."

[14] S. IWRY, "Was There a Migration to Damascus?" *Eretz-Israel* 9 [W.F. Albright Volume] (1969) 80–88.

which, for them, had not yet ended. "The Age of Wrath" (*qṣ ḥḥrwn*) was still on, and only recently had God remembered them and sent the Teacher of Righteousness (*mwrh hṣdq*, the rightful, legitimate teacher) "to lead them in the way of His heart." Although they do not mention the *šybt ṣywn*, "the return to Zion" (Psalms 126:1) of the Persian period, and they ignore completely the restoration, they use post-exilic terms such as *šbw*, *b'w*, *bnw* (with the exception of the verb *ʿlw*, which usually refers to immigrants returning from Babylon). Even their central, recurring sentence about the theme of return was modeled after the passage in Ezra 2:1 and Neh. 7:6, "Now these were the people of the province who came up out of the captivity of those exiles whom Nebuchadnezzar, King of Babylon, had carried captive to Babylon; they returned to Jerusalem and Judah, each to his own town" (RSV). The above should be juxtaposed with the CD version, which reads, "The priests are the Israel returnees . . . those who went forth, or hailed from the land of Judah and had dwelled in Damascus." Semantically, in Ezra and Nehemiah the climax is *wyšwbw*, "and they returned," while in CD *šby yśr'l*, "the returnees of Israel," is the very subject and ends with *wygwrw*, "they sojourned."

All over Ezra and Nehemiah we find the word *šbym* referring to returnees: *wy'klw bny yśr'l . . . hšbym mhgwlh*, "And the people of Israel who returned (*hšbym*) from exile ate . . ." (Ezra 6:21), *wy'sw kl hqhl hšbym mn hšby swkwt*, "And all the assembly that had returned from the captivity made Succoth" (Neh 8:17). It is from these passages that we can establish the term *šby yśr'l* in CD.

According to Ezra and Nehemiah, all the leading families were requested to present genealogical records and lists. In Ezra 2:59, we come across a case where returnees from Tel Melah and also some priests could not show any record of their descent and whether or not they belong to Israel. It was checked but not found, and they were excluded from the priesthood. Our returnees from Damascus, true to tradition, also claim to have preserved their genealogical records, and in CD 4:2 we read: "Here are the Priests, the returnees to Israel, who originate from the land of Judah and the Levites that joined them. . . . Behold the exact statement of their names according to their genealogies, the time that they served in office, the vicissitudes through which they have passed, and the years of their sojourn in exile." These last words in line 4:6, *wšny htgwrrm*, as well as *wygwrw* in the rest of the quoted passages in CD are the same words for exile used in Ezra 1:4, *wkl hnš'r mkl hmqwmwt 'sr hw' gr šm*, "and let each survivor in whatever place he sojourns" (cf. Jer 44:11–14).

Amos 5:25 is very important for our treatment of the cardinal problem of the Damascus Document. Did they leave Judea and go to Damascus, or did they return from Damascus and make Judea their abode? The authors of CD believed that it was possible to understand the message of the prophets in a contemporizing fashion—as though the prophet had alluded to their time and their historical conditions. After quoting the prophet Isaiah (7:17), about the impending catastrophe that will befall the people of Israel, the author of CD reveals to us that as a result, "those who hesitated were delivered to the sword, while those who held fast (to the commandments) escaped north."

Here the Damascus Document brings in Amos 5:25, in which in the extant MT the prophet is quoted to have said: "And I shall exile you beyond Damascus (*mhl'h ldmśq*)." The "North" and "Damascus" remained, therefore, the place of their sojourn, and all our contemporary scholars seized upon this verse to explain "how a group of Jews left the land of Judea and fled to Damascus." The scholars completely disregarded the diametrically different wording of the above quotation in the CD text. Rather, this changed wording was considered an oversight or an error committed by the medieval copyists. In fact, however, it was this "oversight" by our modern readers that sparked the controversy and discussion after the discovery of the Damascus document fragments in the caves of Qumran.

The author of the Damascus Document, indeed, did not imply that at all. On the contrary, he maintained that his people were destined by the will of God to *leave* the temporary abode of Damascus where they have sojourned for a long time, and be exiled back, or returned to their former home from where they hailed. He emended, changed, and replaced the reading *whglyty 'tkm mhl'h ldmśq*, "I will exile you beyond Damascus" (as it is found in the MT and the versions) with *m'hly dmśq*, "from the tents of Damascus," "tents" in biblical phraseology meaning a temporary, wandering home. Ch. Rabin, persistently following the old interpretation, rendered it "I will exile you from My tent to Damascus."[15] This reading is wrong and is not a "genuine variant," because had it been such, the *lamed* of *ldmśq* would not have been missing from the text of our document, if only to uphold the thesis of Dr. Rabin and, even more so, his translation. The phrase is perfectly correct as it stands without the *lamed*, and so is its meaning: *m'hly dmśq*, a construct state which means, "out of the temporary abode of Damascus and returning home."[16]

This is but a preliminary comment on the exegetical treatment of biblical quotations by the authors of the above document in places where their own identity as a providential group is concerned, or when some of their avowed principles of belief or action are in need of scriptural support.

Not only this, but by combining verses 25 and 26, the authors also intended to tell us something that went unnoticed until now—namely, that upon being exiled from the tents of Damascus, they "carried"[17] with them

[15] Rabin, *ibid*, p. 29 l. 15, note 2.
[16] *Cf.* also the reading and translation of this phrase by JOSEPH A. FITZMYER, S.J., in Schechter's *Documents of Jewish Sectaries* (Ktav Publication House, 1970), page XL (72) l. 15, note 13.
[17] Having in MT *wnś'tm*, which means they combined with MT *whglyty*.

the books of the Torah and the books of the Prophets whose words Israel had despised.[18] (Perhaps these were the priceless Dead Sea Scroll biblical manuscripts for which we shall always be grateful.)

The group of Priests and Levites "and the others who joined them"–all pious people who had once entered into a new covenant–came to the country and found conditions quite different and too liberal for them. They were given no recognition for their reputed priestly status, nor sympathy and understanding for their beliefs and practices. The priests in the Temple were no longer of the Zadokite family, and the *khny yrwšlym*, as the Hasmonean princes were referred to, were more interested in worldly things, politics, conquests, and the amassing of wealth. The calendar had changed, the authority of the Torah was in the hands of lay people. Our covenanters decided to boycott the polluted Temple, and to cease offering sacrifices. They became critical and embittered. They parted company with the establishment and became *'dt ḥyḥd*, the *sondergemeinde* or splinter group (*cf.* Ezra 4:3). Eventually, the road led to Qumran, where they were later identified as the Essenes.

Is there any allusion to Qumran in the scrolls? There certainly seems to be. In the description of the last war between the Children of Light and the Children of Darkness there is a projection of the time, the people and location of the eschatological war. This can be found in the War Scroll 1:4, which also speaks of the return by employing the words *bšwb gwlt bny 'wr mmdbr h'mym lḥnwt bmdbr yrwšlym*, "When the Sons of Light will return from the desert of the nations to camp in the desert of Jerusalem." Nowhere in the Bible is there a mention of *mdbr yrwšlym*; it only occurs here. This is the place where Qumran is located now. This is exactly where they had their camps set up, and this is where they lived their apocalyptic dreams and expectations. This is why they called themselves the "desert returnees" (*šby hmdbr*) in 1QPs37.[19]

Yigael Yadin, when commenting in his monumental work[20] on the statement in 1QM 1:4–5 on the return of the Exiled Sons of Light from the wilderness of the peoples, suggested that the reader take note of Ezek 20:34–42, the words of the preferred priest-prophet of this Zadokite group and their principal voice of inspiration.

> [35]I will bring you into the wilderness of the peoples; there I will confront you, and there I will state my case against you [36]even as I did in the wilderness of the land of Egypt. . . . [37]I will make you pass under the rod and bring you into the bond of the covenant. [38]I will rid you of those who revolt and

---

[18] See Testament of Levi 16:2.

[19] Instead of using the prevailing geographical Hebrew name of *mdbr yhwdh*, as the scholars of the Hebrew University first called the provenance of the Dead Sea Scrolls (*mgylwt mdbr yhwdh*), the authors of CD narrowed down or pinpointed the location more precisely and called it instead *mdbr yrwšlym*.

[20] *The Scrolls of the War of the Sons of Light against the Sons of Darkness* (Hebrew), Jerusalem, 1955.

transgress against me. I will take them out of the countries where they sojourn, but they shall not enter the land of Israel. Thus shall you know that I am the Lord. [42]When I bring you home to the soil of Israel.

While at it, Yadin further allowed himself to speculate on whether it would be right to assume that the people of this sectarian group, or even part of them, were compelled at a certain juncture of their experience to leave their place and emigrate or flee to Damascus; they would sojourn there for some time and afterwards come back to their abode in the region of the Dead Sea — to continue their waiting for the Messiahs of Aaron and Israel. Yadin merely speculated because at that time (1956 Hebrew edition) he, too, felt uneasy when the fragments of CD were uncovered in the caves of Qumran.

And although some years later J. T. Milik picked up the above conjecture of Yadin to make of it a strong argument for treating the land of Damascus as the identified geographical *topos* mentioned repeatedly in CD,[21] it was still prior to the time I offered to render *šby yśr'l* as the "returnees (from Damascus) who originated from (the preexilic) land of Judah," at my lecture before the Faculty of the Humanities at the Hebrew University, where Yadin and other distinguished listeners honored me with their presence.

The prophecy of Ezekiel, in addition to the above-mentioned exegetical substitution in Amos 5:25–27, served for the group as the scriptural source/approbation for the rightness of their recent action or experience. They believed that they were the recipients of the *msrt hbryt* "the bond of the covenant" when they established the New Covenant Community in Damascus, the place of the wilderness of the peoples. And since according to their best conviction they were not among the sinners and transgressors in Ezekiel, they were destined explicitly, therefore, by "the goodwill of God" to be returned to the land of Israel (*'dmt yśr'l*), calling themselves *šby yśr'l*, the returnees of Israel or "Israel returnees." Subsequently, when they later moved to camp in the desert of Jerusalem, they were called in the Pesher of Psalm 37 (1QPs37) *šby hmdbr.*

The repetitive tripartite statement, which consists of three elements of motion — *šby yśr'l — hywṣ' m'rṣ yhwdh — wygwr b'rṣ dmśq* — was intended to respond to the three cardinal questions regarding the formative stages of this esoteric movement — whence do they hail, whither did they return, and where did they sojourn in the meantime.

[21] See note 12.

DISCUSSION OF THE PAPER

HARTMUT STEGEMANN (*Göttingen University, Göttingen, Germany*): I agree with you that Damascus may be taken in the sense of the town of Damascus in the north and the surroundings. I would be glad if you would comment on one of the quotations you have printed in the handout, which is in Damascus document page 7 line 18. Is this *kokhav* of the quotation the Teacher of Righteousness, and do you mean that he went in the past to Damascus?

SAMUEL IWRY (*The Johns Hopkins University, Baltimore, MD*): I don't think that this is the Teacher of Righteousness. I have mentioned it in my paper. The *drš htwrh* joined them later on in Damascus.

NORMAN GOLB (*Oriental Institute, University of Chicago, Chicago, IL*): I agree that Damascus must mean the real Damascus because the authors of this text, whenever they have a metaphor, always signal it and explain what it is. If they had wanted Damascus to be a metaphor for something else, they would have said Damascus means, *etc.* They don't ever say that, so it cannot be anything else but the real place.

The Pesharim and the Origins of the Dead Sea Scrolls

GEORGE J. BROOKE

Department of Religions and Theology
University of Manchester
Oxford Road
Manchester M13 9PL United Kingdom

This paper addresses once again how the pesharim, especially the Habakkuk Commentary (1QpHab), should be suitably read. Ever since their publication, the pesharim have been the focus of controversy concerning the history which they may describe. The purpose of this paper is to attempt to describe something of their literary character to clarify their purpose and to put various uses and abuses of these texts in a proper methodological perspective.

As always, we must begin with the primary evidence, the texts themselves. Datable to the turn of the era, give or take a generation, they are made up of explicit quotations of scriptural texts and commentary. They are grouped together as a distinct corpus because of the use of the term פשר in various formulae which introduce the interpretation proper. The way that the scriptural text is cited has resulted in these texts being roughly classified in two groups, those that cite the scriptural extracts in the running order of the scriptural text itself, and those which are arranged in some other selective fashion (see most recently, Dimant 1992). The basis of this broad classification is very important and often forgotten. These texts are dependent on the text of Scripture in some way. Too often scholars have paid scant attention to the way the scriptural text is cited and its treatment by the interpreter, preferring rather to jump directly to their own conclusions about the significance of the commentary by itself, usually imposing on it some kind of historical reconstruction based on their own prejudices about events in some particular period from the second century B.C.E. (*e.g.*, Wacholder 1983:185–199) to the fall of the Temple (70 C.E.) (*e.g.*, Eisenman 1986).

A textual commentary in any age is a mixture on the one hand of the base text (sometimes very slightly modified) and on the other of the circumstances, exegetical techniques (Brooke 1985:166–169; Feltes 1986:205–229; Brewer 1992:189–190) and inherited traditions of the commentator. Apart from the actual choice of prophetic text, there is something very distinctive about the continuous pesharim, including 1QpHab: the scriptural text takes priority. However many other similarities there may be in matters of content, the form and structure of the continuous pesharim distinguish them in particular from all the uses of scripture in the New Testament. The continuous pesharim do not present themselves as the mere proof-texting of preconceived notions.

This attention to the form of the continuous pesharim, a form which in large measure determines their genre (Brooke 1981:494–501; Feltes 1986:162–165), has a very important corollary. When the scriptural citation is properly put first in our consideration of these texts, it immediately becomes apparent how much it determines the way the commentary runs. This in itself explains why the language of the interpretation in the pesher proper remains so stereotypical and why its possible historical referents continue to defy identification and *will continue to do so*. It is important to note that over against such tightly argued historical reconstructions as that of Stegemann (1971), which is based primarily on the pesharim, recent reevaluations of the history of the communities associated with Qumran, such as the Groningen Hypothesis (García Martínez 1988; García Martínez and van der Woude 1990), have rightly made little or no use of the pesharim. Meanwhile others persist in making historical identifications which are impossible to verify.

When considering the continuous pesharim in particular, the controlling influence of the scriptural text must be the starting point. To begin with, it is apparent that the interpreter is aware of the structure and purpose of the original context from which he is working. It is noteworthy, for example, that the structure of the Habakkuk Commentary follows the structure of Habakkuk 1–2, with the specific woes of Habakkuk directed at those the commentary despises. The controlling place of the scriptural text must also be the starting point for understanding the particular vocabulary of the sections of commentary. Usually in any section of interpretation in the pesharim it is easy to identify which elements are more or less directly dependent on the scriptural text, either through the direct reuse of particular words and phrases, or indirectly through the use of synonyms, synonyms which are often suggested by scriptural passages which have a purpose or content similar to that of the prophetic base text. Often the scriptural language is repeated, sometimes in explicit or implicit quotations, sometimes in the application of the same words or their synonyms. Many scholars have made various comments about the remaining vocabulary in the commentaries, but it is the detailed work of Callaway (1988) that has begun to clear the ground for what can and cannot be said about the relation of the interpretation to any actual history.

So, for example, it has to be noted very carefully that the figure of מורה הצדק is only mentioned in some of the continuous pesharim and, in an indefinite form, in two, or possibly three, sections of the Damascus Document (CD 1:11; 20:1, 32: ?6:11), all of which have elicited significant comments in relation to the redactional history of the pericopae in which they occur (*e.g.*, Davies 1982:61–72, 173–197; 1987). Conversely it must be stressed that, apart from this title or epithet, no form of the root צדק (צדוק,

צדיק, צדקה, צדק) is anywhere definitely used in the continuous pesharim, even when it features in the scriptural citation (as in 1QpHab 5:9; 7:[17]; 4QpPsᵃ 1–10 ii 13, 22; iii 9; iv 7) and some kind of elaborate exegesis on the term might have been expected. Anybody who bases his historical reconstruction of Palestinian Judaism on this term (Eisenman 1983) and who attempts to place the pesharim as the focus of part of such a reconstruction (Eisenman 1986) must account for the presence *and absence* of the relevant terminology in all the texts that are discussed.

In several instances in the Habakkuk Commentary, once the subject has been explicitly identified, all or nearly all of the scriptural text receives interpretation through its own reworking. More often it is necessary to look for a suitable explanation for the commentator's choice of vocabulary. As an example of what needs to be done with each pericope of pesher, we can consider the interpretation of Hab 1:17 in 1QpHab 6:8–12 (see Brooke 1991:153–155). To begin with there is a clear citation of a scriptural text other than Habakkuk in the final phrase. "Who take no pity on the fruit of the womb" is an implicit quotation of Isa 13:18, suitably part of an oracle against Babylon, according to the version of 1QIsaᵃ, as Brownlee has noted (Brownlee 1979:105).

The use of this oracle involving Babylon is supported by the use of phraseology from other similar oracles. So, for the list of those who are put to the sword three scriptural texts seem to have played some part. The difficult word אשישים, "grown men," is most closely paralleled in scriptural texts by the similar יששׁ of 2 Chron 36:17 (*cf.* 4Q502 9 4, 9, 11, 13, *etc.*). That verse describes how there will be "no compassion on young man or virgin, old man or aged" (ולא חמל על בחור ובתולה זקן וישש). Both here and in the previous half verse there are verbs that recall Hab 1:17, "slay" (הרג) and "be merciful" (חמל), further encouraging us to see an allusion to this verse in 1QpHab, though another major factor behind seeing such a connection is the use of this section of 2 Chron 36 (vs 16) in 1QpHab 4:1–3. But both those verbs also occur in Ezek 9:5–6, part of a divine command concerning the punishment (from out of the north) of the wicked, which also contains a list of those to be slain, "old men, young men and maidens, little children and women" (זקן בחור ובתולה וטף ונשים).

A second set of scriptural texts that may be reflected in this section of pesher are the sections of the Torah which discuss war. On this basis the list of victims in 1QpHab 6:11 might also reflect Deut 20:14, part of a text which may have influenced other parts of the commentary (Brooke 1991:150). In the rules for waging war in Deuteronomy 20 the males are to be put to the sword (חרב) whilst the women and little children (הנשים והטף) are taken as booty. More generally (Brownlee 1979:106), the commentary reflects Deut 28:50 and its context: a nation will be brought against disobedient Israel, which will "not regard the person of the old (זקן) or show favor to the young

(נער)." Similar stereotypical lists of the victims of war occur, for example, in Jub 23:23, Ps.Sol. 17:13 and Josephus, *Ant.* 14:480.

On this basis we may be able to account for other items in the pesher's language. It may be Deuteronomy 28 which can help explain the change of verb in the opening clause of the interpretation: ". . . the Kittim who will destroy many with the sword." In place of the "drawing" (יריק) of the sword of Hab 1:17, 1QpHab 6:10 reads "destroy" (יאבדו). According to Deut 28:51, the same nation who will show favor to neither young nor old will cause Israel to perish (האבידו). Lev 26:38 uses the same verb to describe the similar fate of the disobedient who have been exiled, not necessarily significant apart from the fact that Leviticus 26 seems to lie behind other sections of the commentary of 1QpHab, and at Lev 26:33 divine punishment comes through the unsheathed sword (והריקתי אחריכם חרב), language which parallels Hab 1:17 (יריק חרבו). A similar phrase can be found also in Exod 15:9, part of yet another passage whose phraseology lies behind several sections of pesher in 1QpHab (it is even quoted explicitly in 4Q174): the enemy said "I will draw my sword" (אריק חרבי). The idiom occurs elsewhere in scriptural texts only in Ezekiel (5:2, 12; 12:14; 28:7; 30:11).

But the issue is more complicated than noticing that the pesher alludes to particular relevant prophetic oracles and sections of the Torah. The complexity arises because other continuous pesharim also use similar stock phrases that are based in scriptural language. The relation of the various pesharim to one another becomes an issue. So, for example, in the case of the pericope under consideration, we must also take into account the evidence of 4QpPs^a 1–10 i 25–ii 1: "'[Moa]n before [Yahweh and] writhe before Him. Do not be angry with the one who makes his way prosperous, with the one [who carries] out evil plans (מזמות).' [The interpretation] of it concerns the Man of Lie, who led many (רבים) astray with deceitful words, for they chose empty words and did not lis[ten] to the Interpreter of Knowledge, so that they will perish by the sword (יובדו בחרב), by famine and by plague" (Horgan 1979: 195). The interpretation of Ps 37:7 here identifies the one who devises plots as the Man of the Lie. The specificity of this designation helps us to see that the indefinite words are probably intended as such. Thus the anarthrous "many" should probably be understood as just that and not a reference to the designation of the community as in the Manual of Discipline where it is always definite. Some of the stock phraseology of this section of 4QpPs^a is also found in the section of 1QpHab under discussion (*cf.* 4QpIsa^a 2–6 ii 8). In fact the initial phrase of the pesher proper has two elements which are also in this section of 4QpPs^a, "many" and "perish by the sword"; the word order is not quite identical and the orthography is slightly different. The frequent use of this predominantly scriptural motif with minor variations in other continuous pesharim shows that this is a standard idiom (Pardee 1973:172–173; Horgan 1979:204).

For this section on the Kittim, therefore, not only is it possible to identify several scriptural texts that have provided the vocabulary for the commentary, including one implicit quotation, but also those other scriptural texts feature in providing some of the phraseology of other sections of commentary (see Brooke 1991:143–155). In addition there is some stock interpretative language as can be seen in 4QpPs[a]. The recognition of such idiomatic material in this passage must force the modern reader to be very hesitant at identifying any particular historical experiences of the community faced by the Romans. All is controlled by the stereotypical motifs of the original contexts of the commentator's sources, though the motivation for using such sources may indeed rest in either the commentator's present experiences of the Romans (*i.e.*, approximately at the turn of the era), or in what he thought should have been the experiences of his forebears because of what the ancient texts said or implied about the Kittim. Thus little can be learnt from this pericope of 1QpHab about any particular campaign or attitude of the Roman army (assuming that in this instance they are the Kittim for the author); all one learns is that the Kittim are a stereotypical military power.

Before jumping to conclusions, therefore, about the history that may or may not be reflected in reading between the lines of the pesharim, it is important first of all to identify which literary sources are being used by the interpreter. This kind of source analysis has been variously attempted by a minority of scholars (*e.g.*, Silberman 1961; Finkel 1963) over the last forty years, but their results have not been fully appreciated. For the Habakkuk Commentary the work of Brownlee (1979) and Nitzan (1986) must be taken into account by any serious student of these texts—not that their analyses are always suitable, but because they have felt something of the literary approach of the ancient interpreter.

In looking at 1QpHab 6:8–12 we have seen that the interpretation of Hab 1:17 is made up from stock phrases which may directly reflect various scriptural passages and indirectly reflect others as these may be present in other texts from the Qumran caves. This detailed attention to the idiomatic phraseology of the interpretation means that alongside the quotation and reworking of the explicit text in any part of the commentary, an attempt should be made to identify to what other scriptural texts (and their original contexts) the commentator alludes, especially if these sources are being used through the filter of yet another text. In the thematic pesharim the quotation of several different scriptural passages discloses the cluster of traditions which are of particular concern to the author. In the continuous pesharim more subtlety is required in identifying from where the author's idioms come.

Though variously attempted over the years by a minority of scholars, only recently has a proper literary appreciation of the pesharim come to the fore (Feltes 1986:17–57; Callaway 1988:135–140). Part of this appreciation of the literary character of the pesharim has been some attention to their possible sources, both scriptural and non-scriptural. The most obvious candidate to exemplify this process is the almost certain use of a section of the Hodayot (1QH4:7–12) in 1QpHab 11:2–8. Though the parallel has often been noted, P. Davies (1987:93–97) has begun to show something of how various elements in the commentary are dependent on either the text of Habakkuk or that of the Hodayot. But, because some items occur in both sources, the matter is more complex than Davies allows. It is not as if there are two written sources, Hab 2:15 and the Hodayot, which are woven together in 1QpHab. Rather, it is because 1QH is also using Hab 2:15, that its broader context, which contains allusions to other scriptural texts, notably Ps 69:22–24, can be seen to lie behind the interpretation in the Habakkuk Commentary. In fact, Davies' source analysis is probably correct for another reason too. A thoroughgoing listing of all the small items of vocabulary which are common to both the Hodayot and the Habakkuk Commentary produces the intriguing result that the overlaps occur almost exclusively in sections of 1QpHab that discuss the Teacher of Righteousness. Here is yet another warning signal against reconstructing history out of the pesharim.

One passage in the Habakkuk Commentary is particularly distinctive for the large amount of phraseology it uses which is usually linked directly to the self-understanding of the author's community. Because this pericope may undermine the thesis of this paper, that virtually all the language of the interpretations is scripturally idiomatic, directly or indirectly, it is important to consider it in detail in all its complexity. In the interpretation of Hab 2:17 in 1QpHab 11:17–12:10 we have the clearest indication in the whole commentary that the stereotypical designations may have very specific referents. But there are still some very considerable problems in making identifications.

The interpretation of Hab 2:17 falls into two parts. In the first nearly all the phraseology is to be found also in two sections of 4QpPs^a. In fact it almost works out that the language of the first subsection of the interpretation in 1QpHab is paralleled in 4QpPs^a 3–10 iv 7–10, whereas the language of the second subsection, the interpretation of בהמות, can nearly all be found in 4QpPs^a 1–10 ii 9–16, especially 13–16. Furthermore it must be noted that these two sections of 4QpPs^a can be tied together through their common vocabulary which is not only most obviously in the scriptural רשע לצדיק, a pair of terms together in Psalm 37 only in these two places, but also is partly found in the use of עזב, a term which is used in three verses of the Psalm but only interpreted in these two places in the pesher, one of which is not even based on the use of the stem in the psalm itself. It seems as if the author of 4QpPs^a knew that these two pieces of his exegesis belonged together.

As with the interpretation of Hab 1:17 in 1QpHab 6:8–12, so with these pericopae of the Psalms Commentary it is important to see that much of the vocabulary is derived from the scriptural text: אביון (37:11), זמם (37:12), כלה (37:20), רשע (37:14, etc.), שלם (37:21). As before, too, some of the vocabulary is derived from its use in suitable scriptural contexts; so, for example the combination of נמל and שלם in Isa 66:6 and Ps 137:8 are both appropriate sources for 4QpPsᵃ 3–10 iv 9. It could be that the two commentaries are both so replete with scripturally based idioms that it is not worth pursuing whether the two are literarily related, one being dependent on the other. If the author of 1QpHab used the Psalms commentary, we need to be cautious in identifying the poor of 1QpHab as a technical self-designation of the author's community, for the term derives from the use of the text of the wisdom psalm. And the plotting is another poetic motif based in Psalm 37 itself. Or is the dependency the other way round? It is difficult to judge. If we have such difficulty knowing how to relate and understand the historical significance of two texts of the same genre, in the same language, with the same formulae and the same vocabulary, probably from the same community, in the same place, at roughly the same time, how much more problematic is discerning the relationship between the varying motifs and supposed history lying behind texts in different languages, of different genres, almost certainly from different communities and different times and places. It is only with much care in asserting how texts relate to one another that we can avoid naïve historicism, namely that wherever there are two phenomena with even the vaguest correspondences they must be related in some way in terms of cause and effect.

Whatever the case, we are dealing with an exegetical tradition which is replete with stereotypical designations. To say, as Eisenman has, that the זמם of 1QpHab here points to the conspiracy between Agrippa II and Ananus against James (1986:65), is making a scriptural motif and exegetical tradition bear too much weight of specificity, especially since the same root is used in 4QpPsᵃ 1–10 i 26 of the activities of the Man of the Lie. Eisenman has offered no supportive evidence from the exegesis within the commentary itself, only from his overall historical reconstruction, for which he considers the term suitable.

Nearly all the phraseology of the first section of the pesher (1QpHab 12:2–6) is standard scripturally derived idiom. The interpretation of Lebanon as "the council of the community" has been widely discussed in the context of the many kinds of understandings of Lebanon in literature found at Qumran and in other texts. In 4QpIsaᵃ 7–10 iii 6–7, 11–12 Lebanon seems to be identified with the Kittim (Horgan 1979:170) and in 4QpNah 1–2 ii 7 with an enemy of the elect of God. In 4QpIsaᶜ 8–10 2–3 and 21 2 it is impossible to determine the referent; there is no clear allusion to the fall of the Temple as Eisenman proposes (1986:66).

The second part of the interpretation of this pericope, after the requotation of Habakkuk, is a further replaying of stock idioms, with the notable exception of ירושלם which we need not doubt is indeed a specific geographical place. The subject matter of the first subsection concerns the abominable deeds which the Wicked Priest has committed in Jerusalem; he has defiled the sanctuary of God. In scriptural texts defilement of the sanctuary is linked to the ignoring of purification rituals (Num 19:20) and to child sacrifice (Lev 20:3), which is also clearly labelled an abomination in Ezekiel (23:38; cf. 5:11). The language of Ezekiel may well have influenced the way the phraseology of the pesher is selected and put together, but defilement of the sanctuary has yet another cause in the Damascus Document. Because of the many similarities between the Damascus Document and the pesharim, it is likely that its technical phraseology lies behind the phrasing of the commentary. In CD 4:18 defilement of the sanctuary is identified as one of the three nets of Belial. The second use of the idiom (in 5:6) explains that this defilement is because men are lying with women during their menstruation. It seems clear that the interpreter of Habakkuk uses this to understand the blood of the city and may explain why the wording of the text of Habakkuk is reordered in its requotation in 1QpHab 12:6–7. Although Eisenman is aware of the link with the Damascus Document, he simply asserts that the defilement of the sanctuary refers to the controversy over admitting Herodians into the temple and accepting gifts from foreigners (1986:67); he thus makes no attempt to appreciate the reordered מדמי of 1QpHab 12:6.

The violence done to the land is taken to refer to the cities of Judah. יהודה is a term of polyvalent significance. In the first half of the commentary there is a parenthetical pair of statements identifying the indefinite אביונים, presumably because as a standard scriptural epithet it was not necessarily obvious who they were. They are the council of the community and the "simple of Judah." Most commonly (e.g., Nitzan 1986:195–196), and probably correctly, יהודה is taken primarily as an epithet for the community which identified itself with Judah (cf. Ephraim in 4QpNah 3–4 ii 2, Ephraim and Manasseh in 4QpPs^a 1–10 ii 18, etc.; Pardee 1973:179–183). The "simple" are thus a subgroup within the community. This also makes adequate sense of the other occurrence of יהודה at 1QpHab 8:1 where we learn of כול עושי התורה בבית יהודה with עושי clearly written as a plural participle (cf. 4QpPs^a 1–10 ii 14–15: בבית יהודה אשר יזומו לכלות את עושי התורה). Once again appeal can be made to the Damascus Document as a suitable basis for appreciating the epithet. From CD 4:11 we learn that in the eschatological period there will be "no more joining the house of Judah (לבית יהודה)" (on handling sobriquets see Davies 1987:97–104).

Because it looks as if for the last letter of עושה a yod has been changed into a he, making a singular participle, Brownlee (1979:203) has proposed that it is possible to understand Judah as "the one who does the Law." Judah is then the name of an individual or his sobriquet, and Brownlee considered that we should begin trying to identify the Teacher of Righteousness at this point. This would seem to be an uncharacteristic understanding of Judah but it forces us to pay attention to a highly distinctive occurrence here of the phrase

עושי התורה (= 1QpHab 7:11; 8:1). In his identification trail Brownlee draws attention to a significant parallel to this section of the Habakkuk Commentary. In interpreting Mic 1:5c ("What is Jacob's transgression? Is it not Samaria? And what are the heights of Judah? Are they not Jerusalem?") the fragmentary 1QpMic seems to offer a two part interpretation. In the second part "the heights of Judah" are interpreted in relation to the Teacher of Righteousness (Judah?) and "the council of the community" ("the heights"). In the first more fragmentary part, before the requotation of part of Mic 1:5, it is possible to read פתאים as the last word of the interpretation. It is likely they are the object of Jacob's transgression which can be identified in the opening of the pesher as concerning someone labelled with הכזב. J. T. Milik has read the whole title מטיף הכזב (1955:78), but the first word, though suitable, is difficult to restore precisely in relation to the few traces of ink that remain. However, whatever the precise restoration should be, it looks as if the transgression of Jacob is associated with the one who has misled members of the community according to other texts. This then agrees with other references concerning Jacob and his sons in CD (CD 3:4; 20:17; also 4Q379 22 ii 13; 4Q504 1–2 v 7; when the reference is clearly to the scriptural Jacob, they are positive: CD 4:15; 4Q511 2 i 5; 5Q13 2 i 6; 11QTᵃ 29:10).

If Brownlee is right, in the second half of the exegesis in 1QpHab 12:9 the cities of Judah may then be interpreted as those cities where Judah, an individual, has influence or groups of followers. More probably, "the cities of Judah" are those where the community is represented (Nitzan 1986:196), or the settlements of the community themselves (Davies 1987:102). One is reminded of the community structures reflected in the Damascus Document, where the technical term for the location of community subgroups is "camp," but where "city" is also used for the places where group members reside (e.g., CD 10:21). If Judah is to be taken as an epithet for the community, then the *he* of עושה in 1QpHab 12:4 must be read as an example of the occasional orthographic representation of the plural construct in this way (Nitzan 1986:195).

In this pericope and the parallel in 4QpPsᵃ we are thus faced with the issue of the significance of various epithets. All modern interpreters who tackle the Habakkuk Commentary must explain how they reach their conclusions about these names. Eisenman (1986:69) proposes that "Judah" is used to stress that "the simple" are "Jews." This he adduces not from consideration of the use of Judah elsewhere but from his understanding that the epithet Ephraim, specifically identified as "those who seek after smooth things" (4QpNah 3–4 ii 2), are Gentile god-fearers. The somewhat arbitrary identification of epithets with no consideration for the complexity of the terms in relation to their scriptural usages makes one wonder also about Eisenman's identification of James the Just with the Teacher of Righteousness. On the one hand fixing on the term "righteous" opens the field to a large number of candidates, amongst which James is not a front runner, given that the earliest secure attestation of him having this label is in the writings of Origen (Hardwick 1989:83–84). On the other hand, if all the pieces of the puzzle are meant to fall as neatly into place as Eisenman urges in his reconstruction, one must wonder why he offers no consideration of all the places in the scrolls where the name of James (Ἰάκωβος) occurs. Instances such as 1QpMic 8–10 cited above lead to the probability that it is the Man of the Lie who is identified as standing at least in the tradition of the transgressions of Jacob's sons, not the Teacher of Righteousness, who is never associated with the use of the name Jacob. Without controls and without any *prima facie* identifications (Kampen 1989:297) based in the texts themselves, the identification of figures becomes at best somewhat forced, at worst merely arbitrary.

The principal players in the continuous pesharim are designated only by epithet or sobriquet (Kittim, Teacher of Righteousness, Wicked Priest, Man of Lie, Judah, Ephraim, Manasseh) and probably all we can really describe is a rift within the community and a fight that is external. These are the hallmarks of the history of religious and social groups and subgroups in any age. The work of the sociologists on the way texts reflect reality has illuminated how relatively small religious interest groups form, express their own identities over against other groups, institutionalize themselves and cope with internal disagreements, usually through the formation of splinter groups which go through the same process, decline and dissolve. To identify two communities that may be approximately contemporary on the basis of such a common behavior pattern is thus to identify clichés (White 1989:117), not historical realities.

But let us return to the second part of the interpretation of 1QpHab 11:17–12:10. We have noticed that the source for the interpretation with regard to the blood in the city is likely to be CD 5:6; CD 4:17 describes the second of the three nets of Belial as הון ("riches"), but the term גזל ("to rob") does not occur there. The theft of possessions is a replay of one item in the interpretation of 1QpHab 8:9–13, a passage which shares much vocabulary with 1QpHab 12:2–10 (עזב, הון, גזל, חמס, תועבות, פעל). The description of the Wicked Priest in 1QpHab 8:9–13 is wrapped around his betrayal of all that an officer in Israel should characterize according to Exod 18:21 (Brownlee 1979:135), but the scriptural text is not recalled directly but rather seems to be reflected as it is variously reused in the Law of the King in the Temple Scroll (11QT^a 57:8–58:17) where certain key terms occur in the same order as in 1QpHab 8:9–13. It thus seems that the description of the activities of the Wicked Priest in 1QpHab 12:10 is a reuse of such a scriptural theme (גזל and הון occur together in 11QT^a 57:21) mediated through a text like the Temple Scroll. The ideological connection between CD and the Temple Scroll should not be underestimated (Davies 1989:201–210). We can thus see that for this pericope of 1QpHab a set of texts which variously represent significant portions of scripture are the likely sources for the exegesis which lies before us.

It seems as if the two sections of the interpretation of Hab 2:17 are independent of one another, each using standard idioms from somewhat different sources. Because the abominations of the Wicked Priest take place in Jerusalem, Eisenman (1986:69–70) puts the two halves of the interpretation together and proposes that "the council of the community" is also in Jerusalem; it is another name for the Jerusalem council or the Jerusalem church. Thus, for him, the violence done to Lebanon in Hab 2:17 is the stoning of James and some of his associates in 62 C.E. At this point it seems as if Eisenman has imitated something of the methodology of the ancient commentator and is merely offering his own pesher on Hab 2:17. It's a pity that none of the early Christian sources seem to think that Hab 2:17 is particularly germane to their experiences. Where are real historical circumstances in all this?

In fact the texts do witness to history in two ways. Of primary significance must be the attempt to identify the history of the literary traditions which are discerned as underlying the exegesis in the texts and which some traditors have thought capable of mutual interpretation. To trace the history of these juxtaposed traditions will be to locate the compiler of 1QpHab in a suitable trajectory. Even in this brief survey of just two pericopae reference has been made to various traditions within scripture which the commentator utilizes for his own purposes, and often those scriptural traditions seem to be used through another textual filter. In this respect we have had cause to mention the Damascus Document, the Temple Scroll, the Hodayot, and several other of the continuous pesharim. Study of all the pericopae in the Habakkuk Commentary in terms of this kind of literary source analysis would extend this list considerably. In each case the literary analysis must take account of the genre of the source as well as the probable purpose of its use. It is our appreciation of these clusters of traditions and their varying influences which will eventually help us to suggest a suitable historical backdrop for the compiler of the Habakkuk Commentary.

The other kind of history which the pesharim barely disclose at all is the history of the events which the exegesis purports to describe. It is this kind of history which most commentators have attempted to reconstruct as the history of the Qumran community. Of the continuous pesharim, the Nahum commentary has been the key for this kind of historical enquiry since it mentions actual historical figures and hints at their actions. Those who recognize a reference to Demetrius III in 4QpNah 3–4 i 2 (Horgan 1979:160–162), which the immediate context of the pesher seems to justify, have an historical peg on which to hang the events supposedly described in the pesher. Unfortunately 4QpNah does not mention the Teacher of Righteousness, the Wicked Priest or the Man of the Lie, but it is likely (Stegemann 1971:69–87) that Ephraim (identified as "the seekers after smooth things") is an epithet for the Liar's community. For the rest of the pesharim we have no means of providing a date for their purported history without recourse to identifying some or other stereotypically described event with historical circumstances described in some other source. The variety of interpretations suggests at least for the moment that this is hazardous.

To read the pesharim primarily as literature in the way that this paper has suggested for two pericopae of the Habakkuk Commentary rather than as quarries for supporting any particular historical reconstruction means that the pesharim can only help with the identification of the origins of the Dead Sea scrolls when all the literary sources and likely allusions in each commentary are assembled. When this is done an ideological and theological *tendenz* emerges. For the pericopae discussed here, that has consisted in the first instance of prophetic oracles concerning Babylon or the Chaldeans, rules for war, the curses of Deuteronomy 28 (together with some other scriptural texts) and phrases which are very similar to those of 4QpPs^a which are derived from yet a further set of scriptural passages. In the second instance, the interpretation repeats much of the text of Hab 2:17 and identifies the various elements with sobriquets; again the language of Psalm 37 as variously interpreted within its own scriptural framework is found in the interpretation as well as echoes of scriptural material as treated in the Damascus Document and the Temple Scroll. Overall we have eschatologically relevant prophetic materials flavored with a particular view of the veracity of certain laws and various wisdom motifs that support the underdog. Piecing together the literary affiliation of the pesharim may also enable us to see that not all the so-called "sectarian" scrolls necessarily reflect a homogeneous group. We might need to distance the continuous pesharim, for example, from that part of the יחד community represented by the Manual of Discipline in its various redactions. The writer of the Habakkuk Commentary does not seem to have suffered with the עצת היחד and he uses some terms, such as רבים, in a slightly different way.

In sum, in reading the continuous pesharim two points are paramount. Firstly, to appreciate their distinctiveness, we must accept their structural self-presentation. The scriptural text takes priority. It can be played with, adjusted, punned, reordered, but it is the control. Secondly, the commentary is just such a skilled literary enterprise as the notice of some exegetical techniques points out. It is not arbitrary and should not encourage modern interpreters to treat it arbitrarily. It is carefully constructed with all manner of allusions primarily to other scriptural texts which have not only suitable vocabulary but also suitable literary contexts of their own. Furthermore, as our appreciation of the literature of the late Second Temple period increases, we can begin to see that the commentator in these texts refers to and uses his selected scriptural traditions often through the filter of their use in other texts which reflected his own ethos. To collect these texts together will be to show us in what tradition, and probably even in what place we should locate the author(s) of these exegetical masterpieces. We are still a long way from firm historical identifications, but we are beginning to trace the history of literary traditions which will eventually reveal something of the origins of the Dead Sea scrolls.

REFERENCES

BREWER, D. I.
1992 *Techniques and Assumptions in Jewish Exegesis before 70 CE.* TSAJ 30. Tübingen: Mohr.
BROOKE, G. J.
1981 "Qumran Pesher: Towards the Redefinition of A Genre." *Revue de Qumrân* 10 (1979–1981) 483–503.
1985 *Exegesis at Qumran: 4QFlorilegium in its Jewish Context.* JSOTSup 29; Sheffield: JSOT Press.
1991 "The Kittim in the Qumran Commentaries." *Images of Empire.* L. C. A. ALEXANDER, Ed.; JSOTSup 122; Sheffield: JSOT Press, 135–159.
BROWNLEE, W. H.
1979 *The Midrash Pesher of Habakkuk.* SBLMS 24; Missoula: Scholars Press.
CALLAWAY, P. R.
1988 *The History of the Qumran Community: An Investigation.* JSPSup 3; Sheffield: JSOT Press.
DAVIES, P. R.
1982 *The Damascus Covenant: An Interpretation of the "Damascus Document."* JSOTSup 25; Sheffield: JSOT Press.
1987 *Behind the Essenes.* BJS 94; Atlanta: Scholars Press, 87–105.
1988 "The Teacher of Righteousness and the 'End of Days'." *Revue de Qumrân* 13 (1988) 313–317.
1989 "The Temple Scroll and the Damascus Document." *Temple Scroll Studies.* G. J. BROOKE, Ed.; JSPSup 7; Sheffield: JSOT Press, 201–210.
DIMANT, D.
1992 "Pesharim, Qumran," *Anchor Bible Dictionary.* D. N. FREEDMAN *et al.*, Eds.; New York: Doubleday, 5.244–251.
EISENMAN, R. H.
1983 *Maccabees, Zadokites, Christians and Qumran: A New Hypothesis of Qumran Origins.* SPB 34; Leiden: Brill.
1986 *James the Just in the Habakkuk Pesher.* SPB 35; Leiden: Brill.
FELTES, H.
1986 *Die Gattung des Habakukkommentars von Qumran (1QpHab): Eine Studie zum frühen jüdischen Midrasch.* FB 58; Würzburg: Echter Verlag.
FINKEL, A.
1963 "The Pesher of Dreams and Scriptures." *Revue de Qumrân* 4 (1963–1964) 357–370.
GARCÍA MARTÍNEZ, F.
1988 "Qumran Origins and Early History: A Groningen Hypothesis." *Folia Orientalia* 25 (1988) 113–136.
GARCÍA MARTÍNEZ, F. and A. S. VAN DER WOUDE
1989 "A 'Groningen' Hypothesis of Qumran Origins and Early History." *Revue de Qumrân* 14 (1989–1990) 521–541.
HARDWICK, M. E.
1989 *Josephus as an Historical Source in Patristic Literature through Eusebius.* BJS 128; Atlanta: Scholars Press.
HORGAN, M. P.
1979 *Pesharim: Qumran Interpretations of Biblical Books.* CBQMS 8; Washington: Catholic Biblical Association of America.

KAMPEN, J.
  1989   "Review" of R. H. Eisenman, *James the Just in the Habakkuk Pesher. Journal of the American Oriental Society* **109** (1989) 297–298.
MILIK, J. T.
  1955   "Textes non bibliques," *Qumran Cave I* (DJD 1; with D. BARTHÉLEMY; Oxford: Clarendon Press), 77–149.
NITZAN, B.
  1986   *Pesher Habakkuk: A Scroll from the Wilderness of Judaea (1QpHab): Text, Introduction and Commentary.* Jerusalem: Mosad Bialik. (Hebrew)
PARDEE, D.
  1973   "A Restudy of the Commentary on Psalm 37 from Qumran Cave 4." *Revue de Qumrân* **8** (1972–1975) 163–194.
SILBERMAN, L. H.
  1961   "Unriddling the Riddle." *Revue de Qumrân* **3** (1961–1962) 323–364.
STEGEMANN, H.
  1971   *Die Entstehung der Qumrangemeinde.* Bonn: Published privately.
WACHOLDER, B.-Z.
  1983   *The Dawn of Qumran: The Sectarian Torah and the Teacher of Righteousness.* HUCM 8; Cincinnati: Hebrew Union College Press.
WHITE, R.
  1989   "Review" of R. H. Eisenman, *James the Just in the Habakkuk Pesher. Journal of Jewish Studies* **40** (1989) 117.

DISCUSSION OF THE PAPER

ROBERT EISENMAN (*California State University, Long Beach, CA*): Since my name was taken in vain on several occasions in George's paper I thought I might respond. This is not a question, this is simply a response. I think that Dr. Brooke's paper is another work of scholastic obfuscation, more obscure even than my own. He makes selective use of passages from my work.

I think what he fails to appreciate is my scientific method. I am observing absolute scientific method. You present a theory, and then you apply that theory to the facts or the data at your disposal. When Einstein presented his theory of relativity he applied that theory to the data at his disposal and tried to see if that theory fits the facts. All that I have been doing in my work is presenting a theory and applying it to the facts. I will end simply by saying that I am prepared to rely on the public's judgment. I would have the public compare my work with Dr. Brooke's and let them decide which, in fact, has a deeper and clearer understanding of the text before us.

JOHN J. COLLINS (*Divinity School, University of Chicago, Chicago, IL*): I very much appreciate the point that you're making on the need of identifying the exegetical context and so forth. My question is really one of clarification. What do you think the commentator on Habakkuk was trying to do? Do you think that there are indeed historical illusions in there, however tendentiously they may be portrayed, and however much they may be overlain with stereotypical formulations, or do you think he's doing something else?

GEORGE J. BROOKE (*University of Manchester, Manchester, U.K.*): I'm hesitant in answering your question, because this partly is a comment on Professor Eisenman as well and the statement he just made. I think it's still too early for me to offer you my historical reconstruction, but since you've tempted me, I think that I begin from the approximate date of the continuous pesharim, the turn of the era, give or take a generation. The author's group at that time may well be trying to assert itself by reclaiming the history of the community, in order to make a statement about its own position in the present. In other words, I think the author responsible for the Habakkuk commentary is lining himself up with what we can find in the Damascus Document and the Temple Scroll, but not necessarily lining himself up directly with the *Yahad* community. The terminology is fairly distinctive, which means that he may be trying to assert that his position is actually a kind of takeover, or reformation position, within the development of these communities in the last century before the fall of the Temple.

COLLINS: And thereby also lining up his opponents.

BROOKE: That's right, but where precisely they are we're a long way from being able to say.

LAWRENCE SCHIFFMAN (*New York University, New York*): This is at once a comment on the paper and a comment on Dr. Eisenman's comment. I think what we have just heard is two forms of doing what we call scholarship. One says that the public should decide, and the other says that scholars should decide. One says that one comes with a theory, puts it forward, fits all the evidence into the theory and then allows people to judge whether it's right or wrong. The other one says one starts by reading the evidence, carefully putting together a picture, saying only what we can say and what we know.

PHILLIP CALLAWAY (*Jonesboro, GA*): How do you see the relationship between the pesher Habakkuk columns 9–12, which talk about the wicked priest and the teacher, and pesher Psalms 37 4A–10? The reason I'm asking is because in the latter there's no mention of exile or a Day of Atonement, day of fasting.

BROOKE: I think the Day of Atonement is an intriguing instance, where we have something specific lying at the basis of the dispute. This may explain, in part, why we don't necessarily have it in both texts; we're just dealing with stereotypical idioms. As you felt from my paper, at the moment I don't yet know quite how I want to assert the relationship between the Psalms peshar and pesher Habakkuk. I'm inclined to think that there is some kind of literary relationship one way or the other. But it may be that this relationship can only be explained by suggesting that both texts have a prior common source. This is what New Testament scholars do to explain similar phenomena.

Theory of Judeo-Christian Origins: The Last Column of the Damascus Document

ROBERT EISENMAN

Department of Religious Studies
California State University, Long Beach
1250 Bellflower Blvd.
Long Beach, California 90840

The theory of Judeo-Christian origins does not argue that all the material at Qumran is Jewish Christian or even that most of it had to come from the first century C.E. Rather, it argues that the *last stages* of the *movement*—and contrary to some, it is a movement—responsible for the literature at Qumran is the same as or all but indistinguishable from the Jerusalem Community of James the Just from the 40s to the 60s A.D. in Jerusalem. All such terms need definition. The problem is few people have a clear understanding of what "Christianity in Palestine" means in this period; the same for terms like "Palestinian Christianity" or "the Jerusalem Church" or "the Jerusalem Community."

From the 40s to the 60s A.D., it is doubtful that the name "Christian" was even known in Palestine. By the Book of Acts' testimony (13:1–3—in this instance, probably accurate), Christians were first called "Christians" in Antioch. Here, it is clear the appellation is originally being applied to a Pauline community, including obviously "Greeks and Jews together"—one of Paul's favorite linguistic allusions—even it would appear, some "Herodians," to wit, one "Manaen brought up with Herod the Tetrarch." I take these references on the whole to be accurate because *they make sense*, a very important consideration when evaluating claims—ancient or modern—in this field.

Acts' description refers to the 50s of the Common Era. This means that "Christianity"—a Greek expression in any case—was not called this up to this point *in Palestine*. So what might "Christians" have been called in Palestine? They might have been called, "Nazoraeans" or "Nazarenes," a term with clear parallels to Qumran usages relating to the idea of "keeping," not "breaking the Law." They may have been called "Essenes" or "Jesseans," a term used by the fourth-fifth century Christian theologians, Eusebius and Epiphanius.

But "Essene" or its variations are not used at Qumran, unless Essenes are the "*'Osei ha-Torah*," *i.e.*, the "Doers of the Law," which is used at Qumran—a term with particularly pregnant meaning where the Community of James is concerned. It is possible to call the group responsible for the literature represented at Qumran, "Essene," as long as one comprehends that it was not peaceful, retiring, apolitical, and the like, which is the usual picture of Essenes, but rather something more militant.

It is possible to call it "Zealot." It also is possible to call it "Ebionite"—another little-understood term with relevance to early Christian history in Palestine, and actually used in early Church history to describe the movement and its remnants headed by or harking back to the figure of James the Just in Jerusalem. In fact, the term, *Ebion* or Ebionite, is in wide use at Qumran as a term of self-designation in numerous important published contexts and in some of the new Hymns we published in *The Dead Sea Scrolls Uncovered*, and as such would be more appropriate than many of these others.

It is also possible to call them "Zadokites" or "sons of Zadok"—even Sadducee, a derivative of this last. One of the problems, or, depending on one's perspective, one of the benefits of such a terminology, is the emphasis on words deriving from the Hebrew root for Righteousness/Righteous One/ even Justification relating to this root cluster Z-D-K at Qumran, so much so that it must always be considered whether by "son of Zadok"—again another term relating to "Sadducee"—one is actually speaking literally, *i.e.*, with reference to a genealogical "son of Zadok," or figuratively.

For two decades, I have been at pains to point out in my work the "Righteousness" implications of this word, and parallels in Christianity, when discussing "the sons of Righteousness" or "the Righteous One" and another adumbration of this linguistic cluster, the "priesthood after the order of Melchizedek" of Hebrews. I have also been at pains to point out that the Sadducees of the Herodian period are different from the kind of Sadducees we have at Qumran, *i.e.*, we have "establishment Sadducees" and "opposition Sadducees" and the operating determinant here is their attitude towards foreign rule, foreign appointment of high priests, foreign gifts and sacrifices in the Temple, niece marriage, divorce, polygamy and the like. These are the broad, over-arching categories in this as in any period—not minor nit-picking, legal quirks, though there were these as well.

In *The Dead Sea Scrolls Uncovered* (London, 1992) I refer to this corpus as the "literature of the Messianic Movement in Palestine." I also referred to it in this way in my 1983 Brill offering: *Maccabees, Zadokites, Christians and Qumran: A New Hypothesis of Qumran Origins.* In my view, that is the most appropriate way to refer to the literature we have before us, taking into account the overt Messianism of a whole range of Messianic allusions and proof texts in both previously published form and now in other more recently published ones.

What I have done in my theories—in addition to combining both "Zealot" and "Jewish Christian" hypotheses and insisting on the relation of these both, and what I call "opposition" or "Messianic Sadducees," to a pro-Maccabean viewpoint—was to recognize the parallels, particularly in terms of vocabulary and conceptualities, with materials in the New Testament, certainly in the Letters, but to a certain extent Acts and the Gospels too. I have attempted to show that these parallels, rather than being accidental or casual, are intrinsic.

In doing so, I have been able to adopt something of a *modus operandi*—that is, that the scriptural materials we have, with the exception of materials like the Letter of James, which Martin Luther and Eusebius (Constantine's Bishop) both felt should not be in the New Testament (they were right; it is much closer to Qumran ideology), Jude, 2 Peter, the last part of the Book of Acts, *etc.*, systematically reverse Qumran positions on almost every point. Instead of the militancy of Qumran, in Christianity as we know it, we have pacification; instead of intolerance and/or excommunication (though often Paul personally, if not doctrinally, adopts the absolutely unbending and intolerant attitude of his interlocutors), we have inclusion; instead of nationalism, cosmopolitanism; instead of zeal for the Law, antinomianism; compared to this-worldly Messianism, spiritualized Messianism; and an apocalyptic final war against all evil on the earth versus the *Pax Romanum*.

It is for this reason that the documents before us appear so strange. We are looking at them from the perspective of a Messianism that never existed in Palestine, that was retrospectively re-written into a Palestinian milieu. I have summed this up in the following simple manner: if you want the truth about what happened in first century B.C./first century A.D. Palestine, go to the Scrolls. The Scrolls are the documents that have come down to us almost in a time warp—unedited as it were—without any redaction tradition to speak of. All others must be treated with suspicion in direct proportion to the redaction process subjected to—particularly where an Empire as dominant, all-pervasive, and repressive as the Roman one is concerned.

This is as true for documents we call "Christian" as for those we call "Jewish," *i.e.*, Talmudic materials and the like. For instance, most heirs to the Talmudic tradition assume that the progenitors of the Rabbis—the Pharisees—were the popular party in the Palestine of their time. But this doesn't jibe with the facts. From the time of Judas Maccabee to that of his grand-nephew Alexander Jannaeus (an individual who now appears to be mentioned in an adulatory manner in new texts), to Pompey's storming the Temple in 63 B.C., to Herod in 37 B.C., through the revolts centering around opposition to the imposition of Roman tax at the turn of the eras, to the final uprising against Rome in 66–70 A.D., where Josephus tells us that the Pharisees, Sadducees, and Herodians invited the Romans into the city to suppress the uprising (the intermediary here was, surprisingly enough, an individual Josephus identifies as an Herodian named "Saulus"), on through to the Bar Kochba period—the people consistently ignore Pharisee advice. Typically, as the people generally are, they are nationalists or what I have been calling "Messianists." I admit, it is psychologically difficult—especially when personal predilictions come into play—to come to grips with the anti-nationalist policy of the Pharisees.

It has been queried how popular the movement responsible for the litera-ture at Qumran could have been, and the usual response is, it was an isolated community. But the literature represented by Qumran is as impressive as it is extensive, and this is to misunderstand the nature of the literature at Qumran. Certainly not everyone was able to live the wilderness life-style of extreme purity regulations demanded by the literature we have before us, but this does not mean that there was not a great deal of sympathy for people willing to do so throughout the commonwealth. Not everyone was willing to "enlist" as a Maccabean freedom-fighter, but this does not mean there was not a good deal of sympathy for people willing to do so. I would go further and contend, that anything less would be surprising, because this is the kind of militant, unbending, anti-foreign, Righteousness-oriented and purity-conscious movement usually appealing to the more nationalistically minded masses. If the movement represented by the literature is, in fact, what passes for "Zealot," then I would assume it is a very popular one indeed.

The inability to recognize the movement we have before us as having any-thing to do with Christianity or Christian origins in Palestine is called by some with some justice, "defending the uniqueness of Jesus," and many in the early elite in Qumran research suffered, albeit subconsciously or even what I have elsewhere termed "psychologically," from this inability. Many of the heirs to these people still do. They are looking for a familiar Jesus, but they are not going to find him in the Scrolls; therefore they automatically conclude, "the Scrolls are not Christian." However, they frame the question wrongly. What we have before us is unfamiliar almost by definition; that is what makes it so different and exciting. But it must be cautioned that it is not the documents before us that are historically defective; what is defective is the documents we are heir to and the almost childish reverence and affection with which we treat them.

It is our understanding of what is called early Christianity in Palestine that is defective, not the Scrolls. I have only tried to link the last-mentioned to familiar conceptualities and events that shine through the tradition, despite mythologization, despite quite evident overseas Hellenization, despite retro-spective Hellenistic novelizing—particularly the "Righteousness" doctrine. By tracing its relationship to the Zadokite/Sadducean movement, one is able to build up an historical picture of two groups of Sadducees, one establishment (what I later termed Herodian Sadducees) and one opposition, stemming from the more normative Maccabean tradition, but destroyed and sent into opposition with the Herodian/Roman take-over.

Those who would represent my views in a simplistic manner contend that for me all Qumran doctrines are "Christian"; this is as silly as it is inaccurate. My first book on the subject, *Maccabees, Zadokites, Christians, and Qumran*—as its title implies—traced this movement from the Maccabean into the Herodian period, and on into the early Christian era. It is too easy to reduce me to saying all these documents are "Christian," but we must speak. In fact, none of them are "Christian," as I make clear, if we mean by Christian most of the documents that have come down to us from non-Palestinian or overseas sources we call "Christian" or the religion we define by that name.

Another key usage for this period is "the Star Prophecy" of Numbers 24:18, the importance of which I repeatedly signal. Josephus designates this prophecy in a little remarked passage at the end of the *Jewish War* as the moving force behind the uprising against Rome (as it was behind the creation of Christianity). This is reinforced by the Roman historians Suetonius and Tacitus probably dependent on him. It is found in at least three places in the published corpus, including 1) in a critical section of the Damascus Document in revealing passages bearing on the "Damascus" imagery, from which the document takes its name, and the "New Covenant" to be consecrated there — imagery also paralleled in New Testament contexts; 2) in a key passage in the War Scroll leading up to an evocation of the Messiah coming on the clouds of Heaven with the Heavenly Host, as per Daniel 7, to execute Judgement on all mankind; and 3) in the collection of Messianic prooftexts named the *Messianic Florilegium* — additional indications of just how Messianic Qumran really is.

There is also "the way in the wilderness" prophecy of Isaiah 40:3, applied in Christian scripture to the activities of John the Baptist as a forerunner for Jesus. This passage is twice referred to in columns viii–ix of the Community Rule and applied there, as well as in the Damascus Document, to the group's own activities in the wilderness — in the second-named "the wilderness camps" — in preparation for the End Time and the Day of Vengeance. There are many allusions of this kind familiar to those conversant with Christian usages. This raises the question: when would a group of this kind have been applying allusions to "the way in the wilderness" to its activities? It is hard to believe any period prior to the first century, the paleography of the Community Rule notwithstanding.

There are also allusions of this kind in the well-known Habakkuk Commentary, particularly the evocation and exegesis of Hab 2:4, with which in my view the document climaxes. Along with Gen 15:6 on Abraham's faith "being reckoned for him as Righteousness" and Is 53, it is one of the foundation pieces Christian theology. My detailed analysis of it, which is beyond the scope of this presentation, can be found in *James the Just in the Habakkuk Pesher* (Leiden, 1986). Briefly, the exegesis of it in the Habakkuk *Pesher* is Jamesian, and what is more, appears to be framed with knowledge of the Pauline position in mind. Again, this is extremely telling internal evidence for a first-century provenance for this document anyhow.

This is the kind of internal data that exists placing us in the first century, as opposed to external data like paleography or Carbon 14 testing, both useful, but hardly definitive. There is no indication that materials or prophecies of this kind were popular at any period prior to the first century. Even if paleographic or carbon dating were to counterindicate this, given the imprecise nature of these two arts, I would find it difficult on the internal evidence to think that any document emphasizing such materials related to any period earlier than the first century without more internal *textual* evidence to substantiate this—this does not exist.

For instance, in columns iv–viii of the Damascus Document, there are attacks on the establishment incorporating very telling allusions for chronology at Qumran like "sleeping with women in their periods" and "marrying nieces." Since these behavior patterns are described as habitual, we have applied them to Herodians and those acquiring their pollution by intimacy with them, since Herodians were regarded as foreigners and married their nieces and close family relatives as a matter seemingly of family policy. There are also references to "vipers" and "kings of the peoples," known Roman legal terminology for petty kings in the East.

There are many more: not only has it been widely remarked, especially by the practitioners of the Zealot hypothesis some decades ago, that the military characteristics of the overseas invading armies, dubbed "Kittim" in Qumran presentations, are Roman; but in the Habakkuk *Pesher*, which uses *Ebion* to refer to the rank and file of the community—a term, of course, directly related to the name of the Jamesian tradition in early Christianity mentioned above—it is definitively stated that these Kittim "sacrifice to their standards and worship their weapons of war."

There can be little doubt, aside from the description of their overwhelming might and ruthlessness, that this is descriptive of Romans, but even more, Romans in the imperial period, not the republican, because it was during the imperial period, not before, that Roman legions paid obeisance to their standards because of the bust of the emperor upon them. There are several others even in the Habakkuk Commentary itself and interested readers should consult *James the Just in the Habakkuk Pesher* for these parallels. There is also a comprehensive and telling emphasis on "works," "justification," baptism—even Holy Spirit baptism—and the New Covenant.

It may be that the Scrolls were put into the caves in 50 B.C., the implication of much consensus theorizing—an idea I find unconvincing. Are we then to assume the people responsible for these manuscripts simply ignored 100 of the most intense and eventful years of Palestinian history—but rather were intent on pronouncements, prognostications, and historical exegeses dealing with events as ancient as George Washington or Bismarck would seem to us today? In addition to not having to answer what this fanatical and wildly apocalyptic group was doing for 100 of the most exciting years of Palestinian history, consensus scholars depend on the fact that the general public just does not read the texts, and if it does, does not feel confident enough to make any sense of them.

This is what is meant by internal data taking precedence over external, including AMS Carbon 14 tests, or the paleography of Qumran studies, which is a tissue of circularity and utterly unreliable. That is why we so much wanted to publish the *Facsimile Edition of the Dead Sea Scrolls*, to "level the playing field," so there would be no more "official" editions, which invariably contained interpretations which came to be regarded as official too–to open the debate.

The same for the library-theory of Qumran origins. The issue is not whether the materials come from Qumran or not. The group we are dealing with in these texts lives both in "wilderness camps" and in Jerusalem. That is the clear implication of the materials before us, published or unpublished. But the texts are homogeneous–the same ideas, the same concepts, the same allusions, the same unbending militancy moves from text to text across the spectrum of documents. Of course there are variations in individual style and content. For instance, one never finds a text that advocates accommodation with the Establishment or foreigners or loving one's enemies. Also too, we have, as in some mystical texts like the one incorporating the imagery of Ezekiel's "chariot," a creativity of the most intense and ecstatic kind.

It is also very clear their authors are neither Pharisees nor Pauline Christians. They would have approved neither of Herod, as both Essenes and Pharisees were said to have done–all this is clear from reading the texts–nor of the Romans, as Rabbinic Judaism and Pauline Christianity appear willing to do. In these texts, we have an unbending and militant xenophobia–the same in the more mystical texts; there is no inconsistency here. Though seemingly mired in legal minutiae that to a modern mind might appear trivial, this mind-set of extreme apocalyptic "zeal" was probably the popular one. Certainly the "Zealots" were parties to it, as probably were that group now referred to as "Jewish Christians," *i.e.*, those Jerusalem Church supporters or followers of James the Just called "zealous for the Law" in Acts 21:21. It would be like imagining, for purposes of discussion, a non-Muslim venturing into Mecca during the pilgrimage season and seeing the atmosphere of zeal and militancy reigning there. Of course, a non-Muslim could not do this; he would not be permitted. But that is just the point.

The same atmosphere held sway in Jerusalem on the Temple Mount in the period we are considering, including the same restrictions regarding "foreigners" on the Temple Mount, at least where so-called "Zealots" and the partisans of the literature we have before us were concerned. The use in other documents of the language Paul uses in Romans and Galatians to describe the significance of Abraham's salvationary state (also used in Islam with a slightly different twist to produce similar new departures), *i.e.*, delineating the minutiae of "works that would be reckoned for you as Righteousness in the end of days," or as Paul would have it in parallel, but more faith-oriented, allusions "as justifying you," are of the most fundamental importance.

Now we have this incredible denouement of the Damascus Document, found in the Cairo *Genizah* almost a century ago, the Qumran parallels to which were not released for public attention until last year. Revealingly it is an excommunication text of the most extreme and unbending kind. Not only does it thoroughly embody the mind-set we are speaking of above, but it parallels similar ones embedded in that neo-Kabbalistic mystical text referred to above, and another in columns ii–iii of the already published Community Rule, again confirming the basic homogeneity of all these documents and concepts. The words here are to be pronounced "by the Priest commanding the Many"–also referred to, as we shall see, as "the *Mebakker*" or Overseer/Inquisitor below–on "anyone who rejects these Judgements based on the (exact) sense of all the Laws found in the *Torah* of Moses" (lines 5–6). "Rebellion" is referred to in line 7 and lines 9–10, continuing the actual "curse" to be pronounced by "the Priest" (high priest?) on the rebellious person being "expelled from the presence of the Many."

The notion of "rejecting the Law in the midst of the entire Congregation" is tied to a backsliding "Liar," who is the ideological adversary of the Righteous Teacher in published texts from Qumran across the board. This adversary, who is clearly involved in a "Lying service" and whose "works" are described as being of "emptiness," contrasts with the Righteous Teacher, who both justifies the Many and whose works bring salvation. In this final column of the Damascus Document, these allusions come full circle and are accompanied by a ban on those who reject the *Torah* of Moses. Such language would certainly have been directed against a Paul, had Paul ever been to the "Damascus" this text referred to as the Damascus Document so reveres.

The text does not precisely follow any material from either of the two overlapping known manuscripts found by Solomon Schechter in the Cairo *Genizah* in 1897, though many of its allusions do. In its present form it is preserved in at least two copies. That it really is the last column of the Damascus Document can be ascertained from the blank spaces on the parchment on the left of one and the bottom of the other.

The correspondences in this last column, which make it clear, that we are continuing from earlier columns, are to columns i, viii, and xv of the Cairo version. There are also interesting new materials about a convocation of those who "dwell in camps" on the third month–in Judaism, *Shavu'ot* "the Feast of Weeks," in Christianity, Pentecost. In lines 17–19 of the text, the purpose of this very interesting convocation would appear to be not to celebrate the descent of the Holy Spirit and the abolition of the Law in favor of more Pauline Gentile-oriented doctrines and devices as in Acts 2:1ff. (see also the picture of Paul hurrying to Jerusalem to be in time for Pentecost below), but rather *to curse* all those who depart in any manner from the Law or "the *Torah* of Moses."

In lines 2–4, referring to inadvertent sin, the extant fragment begins by insisting that the penitent bring a sin or guilt offering (presumably to the Temple) to be purified (cf. Lev 4). It is worth noting, that at the time of his final Pentecost visit to Jerusalem mentioned above, James imposed a similar purification or penance procedure on Paul in the Temple. Here, in the words of Acts 21:21–24 Paul was publicly to exhibit that he was "still *walking in the way* and *keeping the Law*"–all expressions found at Qumran (italics mine).

In lines 3–5 the passages adduced to support this penance for "remission of sin," including an interlinear addition (5a), are somewhat esoteric–even a little ambiguous. Among many other key usages, one should note the reference to "the peoples" to designate those who do not follow the Law in line 10. Paul in Ro 11:13 uses a parallel term in Greek to describe himself and the people to whom he is addressing his mission, *i.e.*, "Gentiles." I cite all these examples not to belabor the point, but to show how numerous such parallels actually are. One should also note the key use of the word *ma'as*/"reject" in lines 5–6 above about "rejecting . . . the *Torah* of Moses" and a parallel word *ga'lah* in line 7 where the man "whose spirit rejects the Foundations of Righteousness" is referred to.

In the Habakkuk *Pesher* this terminology is used to describe the "Lying Spouter" who "rejects the Law in the midst of the whole congregation." The language is paralleled, too, in the Community Rule, iii–iv, which also describes the behavior of an archetypical "son of Darkness" with "a blaspheming Tongue," whose "soul rejects the Foundations of the Knowledge of the Judgements of Righteousness," whose "works are abomination, whose Spirit fornication, whose Ways uncleanness, whose service (mission) pollution . . . who walks in all the Ways of Darkness."

In i.15–16 of the Cairo Damascus Document in the midst of the long description of how the Scoffer/Comedian "poured over Israel the waters of Lying," these "Foundations of Righteousness" are "the Pathways of Righteousness." There, the allusion to "wandering astray in a trackless waste without a Way," which the last column uses to describe "the Peoples," *i.e.*, "the families (of man) and their national languages" in 10 above, is used to describe the effect of the Spouter/Scoffer's "waters of Lying."

The same is true for the connections between lines 12–13 about "the boundary markers which were laid down" and CD,i.18: "removing the boundary markers which the First (*i.e.*, the forefathers) laid down as their inheritance that He might call down upon us the curses of the Covenant." Lines 13–14 of the present text again end up by "cursing" those who "cross" or "transgress" these "boundary markers." The language parallels in these texts, as usual, are *exact*.

There are pregnant parallels of this kind in every line of the text. An interesting parallel in early Christian history would be James 2:10's assertion: "he who breaks one small point of the Law is guilty of breaking it all." In James, this passage is presented against a background of Qumranisms like "keeping" (keeping the Law), "breaking"/"Breakers" (breaking the Law), "Doer"/"doing," "Light," "Judgement," *etc.* In the context, too, of "rejecting the Judgements about the exact sense of all the Laws found in the *Torah* of Moses" in line 6, the text also uses the key word "reckoned"–used in Gen 15 in relation to Abraham's faith being "reckoned for him as Righteousness"– already mentioned above: "he will not be reckoned among all the sons of God's Truth, because his soul rejected the Foundations of Righteousness."

It would be easy to appreciate how such words could be applied in a mind-set of the kind represented by this text to a person teaching "the Many," that "the works of the Law" were "a curse" as in Gal 3:6–10–this in a section about Abraham's faith–or to someone, who, by making himself "a friend of man," had turned himself into "an Enemy of God." They increase the connections between the excommunication being pronounced in this text and information about "the Lying Spouter" in other texts.

The language at this point in the text is clearly that of Deuteronomy's "blessing and cursing." Just as in the Community Rule, v–vii, the expellee is not to participate in the pure food of the Community any longer (*i.e.*, according to another vocabulary circle, not keep "table fellowship" anymore); here one is not to "eat with him" (15). In the Community Rule no one is to cooperate with him in "common purse" or "service"/"ministry"; here one is not to "keep company with him" in any way or "ask after his welfare." Those who do so are to be "recorded" by the character known as the *Mebakker*– mentioned above–who is to make sure any additional "Judgement" with regard to such persons is carried out (16).

This *Mebakker* or "Overseer" was extensively referred to in columns, xiii–xv of the Cairo Damascus Document, as well as the same column 6 of the Community Rule mentioned above. In the latter, he is over the Community Council and functions as treasurer. In the Damascus Document he functions as a kind of "Bishop" and obviously has absolute authority over the Community and its camps. Described in earlier passages of the Damascus Document as someone, 30–50 years old, who "is the master all the secrets of men and all tongue(s) according to its (their) enumerations" (note very carefully the "tongue" and "language" significations here; CD,xiii.13–14). His word is law in everything. He is to carefully examine potential entrants, teach "the exact sense of the Law," make "Judgements," and carefully record all the matters mentioned in this document and elsewhere, particularly these "Judgements." A good example of these judgements is also provided by Document 49 of *The Dead Sea Scrolls Uncovered*, where a member of the "camps" is given a penance for masturbation. That these camps actually existed and are of fundamental importance for understanding how "the way in the wilderness" prophecy was being applied in the Qumran corpus in anticipation of the "last times" and the final apocalyptic "vengeance" on all backsliders and idolators is of no mean significance.

The usage "the priest commanding the Many" in line 8 (and probably in line 1) should be explained as well. Since he, too, makes "Judgements" (*cf.* lines 1 and 16), he is very likely identifiable with the "Bishop" just described. If they are identical—and there seems to be every reason to think they are—then this dual role is almost indistinguishable with the dual role accorded to James the Just in early Church tradition in Eusebius and Epiphanius. Even James' title, "Bishop of Jerusalem," plus the description of him in almost all early Church sources as "high priest," resonates with the materials before us here, particularly if this "priest commanding the Many" is in addition to be considered a kind of "opposition high priest."

Finally, the issue in lines 17–18 of "cursing all those who have departed to the right or to the left from the *Torah*" at Pentecost is particularly interesting. For Paul in Gal 3:11–13 above, "Christ redeemed us from the curse of the Law" by becoming "a curse" or "cursed" (*i.e.*, "by the Law") himself. To explain or show how this could be, he cites Deut 21:23 (in a discussion flanked by citation of the two key scriptural passages from Gen 15:6 about Abraham's "faith" and Hab 2:4 "the Righteous shall live by his faith"), to the effect that a man hung upon a tree is "cursed." The language of Paul's approach mirrors the language of the approach we are encountering here. Both are operating within the framework of the "blessings and cursing" from Deuteronomy.

Paul, if one can be so bold, is *reversing* the cursing language of his opponents, who, we can assume, have also "cursed" him, throwing at them the worst affront imaginable, that their Messiah, who for the purposes of argument let us say was "hung upon a tree," was "cursed" according to the very Law they cursed him with. Therefore, this Messiah has by taking this "curse" upon himself redeemed Paul (and for him and Christianity following him, all mankind as well). I have said in all of my work heretofore, that in effect the New Testament materials familiar to us—particularly the Pauline 1) show knowledge of the Qumran position on almost every point and 2) systematically reverse almost every position of Qumran in favor of a larger, more cosmopolitan, pacifistic, pro-Roman and foreign-oriented *Pax Romanum*. At the very least, this text shows that both Paul and its authors are working within the same ideological context, but at opposing ends of the spectrum. What is more, Paul is again reversing and turning positions we find here into their mirror opposite, in the process using it to develop some of the most telling theological syntheses where history of thought in the West is concerned.

The issues before us here are that momentous and one sees how important the context we are talking about in this previously unpublished fragment really is. If this suggestion has any truth to it, one can imagine how it would have enraged the interlocutors of the kind illustrated here. James 3:10, evoking as in 1QS,ii, Paul, and Lines 8–14 above, the Deuteronomic "blessing and cursing" backgrounds of the whole issue, ties, of course, this "cursing" to its nemesis "the Tongue."

The text ends, as already noted, with the evocation of an annual convocation on *Shav'uot*—in Jewish tradition, classically the commemoration of Moses' receipt of the *Torah* fifty days after going out from Egypt. Here "the Levites" and the inhabitants of all "the camps" are to gather every year for the purposes of cursing those "who depart to the right or the left from the *Torah*" (17). Again we have here a particularly vivid picture of the existence of these wilderness camps and the life led by their inhabitants in them. Parallelly in 1QS,ii.19ff. above, they are to curse "all the men of the lot of Belial . . . as long as the Government of Belial endures (Herod?) year by year in perfect order ranked according to their Spirit."

In Acts 2:1, Pentecost commemorated the descent of the Pauline "Holy Spirit" with its "Gentile Mission" accoutrements of "speaking in Tongues," *etc.* One should compare this allusion with the *Mebakker*'s abilities in this regard in CD,xiv.9 above, who is to "master . . . all Tongue(s) and its enumerations." We have already noted the revealing picture in Acts 20:16ff. of Paul hurrying to Jerusalem with his *contributions* to be on time for just such an annual convocation of the early Church (*i.e.*, Community) at Pentecost. In this context he runs into his last difficulties in Jerusalem with those within the Community of a more "Jamesian" frame of mind, who cite complaints about his activities abroad and demand absolute adherence to the Law.

In such a presentation, Acts' picture of Pentecost can be seen as the mirror reversal of the "Pentecost" being pictured here. Lines 17–18 also highlight the phrase "the exact sense of the Law"—here "Judgement"—"in all the Eras of Evil" and "Wrath" just as the Damascus Document earlier in xiii.5–6 and xiv.16ff.—these last in relation to the "Judgements" the *Mebakker*/Bishop was to make "until God should visit the earth" and "the Messiah of Aaron and Israel should rise up to forgive their sins . . ."

This language of "*doing* the exact sense of the *Torah*" is very important. It is also to be found earlier still in vi.14–15 coupled with reference to "*the Era of Evil*" and "*separating* from the sons of the Pit" (italics mine). It is also the backbone of the allusions to "doing the *Torah*" or "Doers of the *Torah*" in the Habakkuk *Pesher*'s exegesis of both Habakkuk 2:3 on "the delay of the Parousia" and Hab 2:4, "the Righteous shall live by his faith."

The text ends by evoking the phrase "*midrash ha-Torah*," *i.e.*, "the study" or "interpretation of the Law." This term also turns out to be the focal point of the critical analysis in 1QS,viii.15 of Is 40:3's "preparing a Way in the wilderness." Here, too, once again the emphasis is on *doing*, *i.e.*, *doing* the "exact sense of the Law." The actual words are: the Way "is the *study/interpretation* of the *Torah* which He commanded by the hand of Moses that they should *do* according to all that has been revealed . . . as the Prophets have revealed by His *Holy Spirit*" (italics mine).

This then ties all these documents and approaches together. Those, who in 1QS,viii.14's words, "*separate* from the habitation of the men of Evil and go out *in the wilderness* to *prepare the Way of the Lord*" (italics mine) are none other than the inhabitants "of the camps" being addressed and described in the present text. The implications, where the true nature of these wilderness camps and what was really going on in the "wilderness," are quite startling and far-reaching. One thing is certain: one has in these texts a better exposition of what was *really* going on "in the wilderness" in these times so pivotal for Western civilization than in any other more familiar literary accounts. It is *this* that the theory of Judeo-Christian origins attempts to come to grips with.

DISCUSSION OF THE PAPER

LAWRENCE SCHIFFMAN (*New York University, New York*): Just a matter of perspective. Let me begin by explaining that the issue of method here is the fundamental issue. What you essentially do is load on a whole lot of associative material that may or may not be parallel, and then deny all criteria of dating which specifies anything that we can possibly use—one by one they're all written off—then you take a fundamentally correct position (that all this stuff has got to be reevaluated and requestioned) and turn it into a bunch of jumbled information, which has nothing to do with the subject at hand. Now let's take this text that you discussed at the end. You examined a fragment, a fragment in which there is not one stitch of anything that relates to the material which you presented first. By overlaying all of that stuff, you created a false impression about the context of this fragment. This fragment needs to be studied in a context of the entire Damascus Document, then you've got to ask yourself whether it fits into some other kind of theory. As to the theory itself, as far as I am personally concerned it is a lot of nonsense.

ROBERT EISENMAN (*California State University, Long Beach*): That's not the way I talk about your work. I think you should be a little more respectful.

SCHIFFMAN: This theory is unacceptable. You may be right, in which case I apologize.

EISENMAN: Let's stop playing for the camera.

SCHIFFMAN: This theory presents the notion that the entire set of documents is talking about a certain period, whereas virtually everybody believes that it dates to another period. So you must simply write off all evidence which doesn't fit in with your view. The problem with your associative technique is that most of the things we're talking about exist in Judaism from day one. Militancy, for example, versus more accommodationist approaches, existed at day one, as they exist today in American Jewish and Israeli politics, because they're part of the different views within Judaism.

EISENMAN: Exactly, that's right.

SCHIFFMAN: You can't take different views within Judaism and then pick them out and simply say that they must be matched up with somebody who happens to fit into one or another trend, whether it be Paul, whether it be James, whether it be Jesus, John the Baptist or anyone else. These people will naturally take one or another of the trends, such as the Messianic trends which existed throughout the history of Judaism, from whenever the Qumran scrolls are until the present. That's why these associations don't seem to me to be relevant at all.

EISENMAN: One thing Prof. Schiffman does is to speak so loudly and aggressively that he tends to bulldoze all of us, whether on a podium here or in the audience. It's always difficult to respond to him. His presentation of my views is so tendentious, and it absolutely fails to come to the essence of what I'm doing. He shows no knowledge of the footnotes of any of my books, which are quite massive. All I can do is recommend that he read my books. I have extensive criticisms of the paleography and of the archeology of Qumran, I don't have to go through this kind of sophomoric criticism. What he's doing, I take as a compliment. He finally picked up my theories about this establishment/opposition Sadducee idea. You know what he's doing though, because everything he says comes from his rabbinic origins. People see this material through the myopia or the eyeglasses that they're wearing. Okay, we all have eyeglasses; you want to call mine Islamic, that may be. I think Islam relates to this material more than any of the traditions that we've been talking about, at least in ethos.

He has refashioned the theory now that the establishment Sadducees are the Maccabees. He's just pushed my ideas; I said that this is an opposition Sadducee movement stemming from the failure of the Maccabean uprising when the Herodians came in and crushed it. Prof. Schiffman just pushed it back a little further so he could also push back his Pharisee tradition, as being accurate. He continues to hold to this idea that the establishment Sadducees are the Maccabees. He thinks what we have here is a group opposing the Maccabees, i.e., an opposition Sadducee group, diverging from and attacking the Maccabees. That is total nonsense. You used that term, 'total nonsense'. This group exhibits its nationalist, xenophobic, law-oriented ethos down the line. These are consistent, and everything we know about the Maccabean family exhibits the same characteristics, except for the one exception of Hyrcanus II, which I deal with extensively in my work.

MATTHIAS KLINGHARDT (*Augsburg University, Augsburg, Germany*): Since the whole set of ideas you presented here is made up of nonspecific parallels that do not prove what they are supposed to, there is no reasonable way for me to respond. Instead, I would like to ask you a very limited question. Which texts from the Qumran caves do reflect the history of early Christianity in your opinion, and which are just traditional material? What is the criterion for determining these categories?

EISENMAN: I didn't say that we had the history of early Christianity here, I said there are parallels. You don't see what we're doing here. The parallels are strong. The thing is that the ideas are fixed, the categories are fixed, the ethos is fixed. I don't think we're ever going to agree on the dating of these materials, but like most others, I put the pesharim in the last period of the development of this group.

I can't prove that the Community Rule came from the First Century, but if it comes from any other century I would be very much surprised, given the internal data that we have there. The War Scroll evokes the Star Prophecy, as the Damascus Document does. We have from Josephus the specific information that the Star Prophecy or 'the Messianic Prophecy,' the prophecy that a world ruler would come out of Palestine, was the moving force behind the uprising against Rome. He says that at the end of the *Jewish War*. Tacitus and Suetonius, depending on him, agree with that. Christianity obviously agrees that the Star Prophecy is very important, because it is the backbone of a lot of the material Christianity is presenting. This is the kind of data that I present to you as internal data. I have discussed the paleographic, the archeological and the carbon material elsewhere. That's all that I can tell you, Dr. Klinghardt.

KLINGHARDT: So it's your point that the early Jewish Christian theology is similar to what we find in the scrolls?

EISENMAN: Jewish Christian theology, that's Second, Third Century A.D.

KLINGHARDT: No, I'm speaking about Jewish Christian theology, First Century.

EISENMAN: The Jerusalem church of James the Just, Palestinian Christianity, yes.

KLINGHARDT: I'm absolutely pleased.

EPHRAIM ISAAC (*Institute of Semitic Studies, Princeton, NJ*): I want to express some reservation about your methodology, but your material is interesting. Since you quoted Einstein's theory I will quote Darwin's theory. He wrote a book called *The Origin of Species* according to which life evolves and everything is interrelated, so to say, but even Darwin wouldn't go as far as saying different species would mix. In other words, if you start defining what you mean by Jewish-Christianity and then looking at the other thing, aren't you really mixing the different species, and confusing the picture of interrelating cultures?

EISENMAN: I don't think there was "Jewish Christianity" in Palestine in the First Century, I never imagined such a thing. However, we have to talk, yet we don't have the proper terminology. I've tried to use the terminology "Messianic Movement in Palestine," and tried to show how this developed with the demise of the Maccabean family and the evocation of a new leadership principle, revolving about prophecies like the Star Prophecy, and some of the ones in the *Messianic Florilegium*, and so on. But that terminology—I don't think there were two Messianic Movements in the First Century with totally opposing ideology; that doesn't work. "Ebionites" has connotations from the Third Century. I follow the Pseudoclementines, though the Pseudoclementines are as fictional as much of the material in the Gospels and the Book of Acts. We're talking about Hellenistic romantics across the board here. I don't think the Pseudoclementines are telling me anything particularly interesting except that there were some problems in the previous era.

So, we have to talk, and the *Ebionim* "the poor," is an actual term this group uses as self-designation. "The Poor" is a name for the current of thought moving about James continuing on into later Jewish Christian sources. It's as good a term as any other. No, I don't think we're mixing apples and oranges here. I don't think Jewish Christianity is an appropriate term. You can call them Zadokites; I prefer to call them what they called themselves, but I add the appellation "Messianic Sadducees." I like that one, I think it's creative. I'll stand on that.

Calendrical Texts and the Origins of the Dead Sea Scroll Community

JAMES C. VANDERKAM

Department of Theology
University of Notre Dame
Notre Dame, Indiana 46556

Among the many Scroll-related subjects which have been discussed in the last 45 years, calendrical issues have occupied an important place. Some of the earliest publications on the scrolls raised the issue of whether the authors of the texts followed a calendar different from the one used by their contemporaries; and some of the newly available texts which have elicited the most excitement are also calendrical in nature. In this paper I will first offer a short sketch of the history of calendrical discussion regarding the scrolls; following this I will turn to a study of two controversial issues in study of old and new calendar texts; and finally I will suggest the role that controversy about the regulation of times may have played in the origins of the group which inhabited the Qumran area.

HISTORICAL SKETCH

In the period directly after the Qumran finds became known to the scholarly world, the first (to my knowledge) expert who proposed that the בני צדוק of Qumran used a calendar at variance with that of their opponents was Shemaryahu Talmon.[1] He based his case on 1QpHab 12:4–8 in which one reads that the Wicked Priest ". . . pursued the Teacher of Righteousness to swallow him in the anger of his wrath to(?) the house of his exile; and in a time of a festival—the rest of the Day of Atonement—he appeared to them to swallow them and to make them stumble on the fasting day of the sabbath of their repose."[2] He rejected A. Dupont-Sommer's thesis that the event in question was Pompey's capture of Jerusalem in 63 B.C.E. From the text he inferred:

> The Sect's Day of Atonement did not coincide with the official Fast and had therefore no binding force for the "Wicked Priest." We might even conjecture that the Moreh Hassedek and his adherents repaired to a hidden place in order

---

[1] "Yom Hakkippurim in the Habakkuk Scroll," *Bib* 32 (1951) 549–563.
[2] Translations of Qumran texts are mine unless otherwise indicated.

to keep their Fast in the proper fashion, unmolested by their opponents. The exclusiveness of the Holy Day, incumbent only upon the Sect, is possibly expressed in the personal pronoun of יום צום שבת מנוחתם "on the Fast-day, the Sabbath of *their* rest."[3]

He goes on to deal with the way in which the interpreter deduced his pesher from the base text—Hab 2:15—and to draw attention to two other scroll passages which also point toward a differing calendar: CD 6:17–19 (". . . and to keep the sabbath day according to its interpretation and the festivals and the day of the fast according to the finding of those who enter the new covenant in the land of Damascus"); and 1QS 1:13–15 (which prohibit advancing or delaying the times when festivals were to be held). He noted, too, that CD 16:3–4 cited Jubilees and highlighted the book's accuracy respecting the divine ordinances and time-calculations. The remaining pages of Talmon's essay were devoted to other events in history in which calendrical differences were involved: Jeroboam's new festival date (1 Kings 12:32–34); and the separate Samaritan calendar and the Jewish charge that the Samaritans had interfered with the relay of fire signals from Jerusalem announcing the beginning of the month (*m. Roš. Haš.* 2). These and the episode pitting Rabban Gamaliel against Rabbi Joshua (*b. Roš. Haš.* 25ab) show the importance attaching to calendar reckoning in Jewish history. The case of the Wicked Priest and the Teacher of Righteousness adds yet another instance. "Viewed in comparison with other separatist movements, in biblical as well as post-biblical times, deviation from the official calendar is found to constitute a standard feature in Jewish sectarianism, especially during the centuries immediately preceding the Christian era and during the early Christian period."[4]

A second early writer on things calendrical was D. Barthélemy, who included several observations on such matters in a long article about recent publications on the scrolls.[5] The immediate occasion for his comments was the interpretation of the letters א, מ, and ן in 1QS 10:1–4 on which, W. Brownlee had argued, the passage forms an acrostic.[6] He agreed that the letters were symbolic but, unlike Brownlee, he found in them and the context a calendrical message related to the one in 1 Enoch 72–82: the numerical value of אמן is 91—the number of days in each quarter of the year in the Enochic 364-day scheme. He, like, Talmon, pointed to CD 16:3–4 which, in his view, demonstrated that the calendar of the sect replicated the one in Jubilees. Assuming that Jubilees, with 1 Enoch 72–82 (which Jubilees uses as a source), had months of 30 and 31 days, this calendar would place the festival of weeks on

[3] "Yom Hakkippurim," p. 552.

[4] "Yom Hakkippurim," p. 563.

[5] "Notes en marge de publications récentes sur les manuscrits de Qumrân," *RB* 59 (1952) 187–218. The calendrical section occupies pp. 199–203.

[6] W. H. BROWNLEE, *The Dead Sea Manual of Discipline: Translation and Notes* (BASOR Supplementary Studies 10–12; New Haven: ASOR, 1951), Appendix E (pp. 50–51).

3/15 and, by implication, put the *omer*-waving on 1/26 – the morrow of the sabbath that follows the week of unleavened bread. Passover and all other days would always fall on the same date, and the year would begin on a Wednesday – the fourth day of the week when the sun, moon, and stars were created (he referred to Al-Biruni who wrote similar details about the calendar of the Magharya). After mentioning the already famous letter of the patriarch Timothy about manuscripts finds in a cave near Jericho and Bar Hebraeus's account of quarrels involving Karaites who were accused of profaning the sabbath and sanctifying Wednesday, he wondered whether the authors of Jubilees and 1 Enoch, the Qumran sectaries, the Magharya, and the writers of the manuscripts found near Jericho shared the Enochic calendar. Barthélemy, too, alluded to calendar conflicts in Judaism and also in early Christianity (the quartodeciman controversy) and thought the disagreement reflected in the scrolls must have been a serious one. He raised the question whether the calendar was a utopian scheme which the sect tried to introduce into reality by relating it to Enoch and Noah, or an ancient tradition which was being defended against the influence of the Hellenistic lunar months.[7] Jubilees supports the latter option, and 1 Enoch shows that the debated issue was the four intercalary days, not the 30-day months which were at the heart of the system. In his opinion, 1 Enoch 72–82 was composed around the beginning of the Hellenistic period. Jubilees came later and opposed the lunar system which had by then gained more and more adherents. As he put it, "Finalement l'influence hellénistique aurait triomphé et le système du we-Adar en serait l'aboutissement superficiellement judaïsé."[8] Thus, the sect had its origins in the anti-Hellenistic struggle. Unlike others, the scroll writers made no calendrical compromise and retained the Jewish heritage. Barthélemy was inclined to identify the sect with the Hasidim of 1 Maccabees.

Annie Jaubert, the scholar who wrote most extensively about the calendar in the early days of the field, based her hypotheses on the foundations laid by Barthélemy. Her striking, even exciting essays were published in 1953, 1954, and 1957; they were later incorporated into her book *La date de la cène*, which appeared in 1957.[9] Leaving aside her proposal about the relation of the 364-day calendar to gospel chronology, her major points can be summarized thus:

1. The Qumran calendar is already presupposed by the late priestly writings in the Hebrew Bible (Ezekiel, P, Haggai, Zechariah, Chronicles, Ezra, Nehemiah; possibly parts of Kings).

---

[7] "Notes en marge," p. 201.

[8] "Notes en marge," p. 202.

[9] "Le calendrier des Jubilés et de la secte de Qumrân: Ses origines bibliques," *VT* 3 (1953) 250–264; "La date de la dernière cène," *RHR* 146 (1954) 140–173; and "Le calendrier des Jubilés et les jours liturgiques de la semaine," *VT* 7 (1957) 35–61. Her book *La date de la cène: calendrier biblique et liturgie chrétienne* (EBib; Paris: Gabalda, 1957) was translated as *The Date of the Last Supper* (Staten Island: Alba, 1965).

2. The calendar serves to highlight the three primary liturgical days—Sunday, Wednesday, and Friday—by placing festivals and key events of sacred history on them.

3. The 364-day calendar was the cultic calendar during the first centuries of the second-temple period but by the early second century lunar modifications seem to have entered the system.[10]

It is worth remembering that, despite all the progress these and other scholars had made in unravelling the solar calendar of Qumran, no text that confirmed the presence of the 364-day calendar among the community had yet appeared. This changed in 1956 with J. T. Milik's communication to the Strasbourg Congress; the paper appeared in print in 1957.[11] In his report Milik dealt with several texts, including the one now called 4QMMT (he cited the passage where the words מקצת מעשה התורה appear) and what he labelled the *mishmarot* texts. About his work on the latter he wrote: "Le résultat le plus important de cette étude, encore provisoire, consiste dans le fait que le calendrier de ces textes est celui des Jubilés, . . ."[12] He revealed that the *mishmarot* texts from cave 4 correlate three entities: the priestly rotation of 24 courses or divisions, a lunar calendar, and the solar one of 364 days. To illustrate he quoted בו ביחזקאל ל 29 ב22 לעשתי עשר which he interpreted as "on the sixth day in the week of the priestly division Yehezqel on the 29th in the lunar month which is the 22nd of the 11th solar month."[13] That is, a lunar calendar was also known to the writer of the text. He furnished a translation of another part of the same text which gives the festivals for the first year in a cycle and the day in the week of the priestly courses which would be on duty at the time of the festivals. The data in the text sufficed to prove that the *omer*-waving did occur on 1/26 and that the festival of weeks fell on 3/15, as Barthélemy and Jaubert had argued. A different text, he reported, contained the expression בעשרים ושנים בו מועד השמן. These words were to prove crucial in clarifying the calendar which underlies the calculations in the Temple Scroll.[14]

The 4Q calendar texts presented a system that worked only for a rotation

---

[10] For the wording of the theses and discussions of them, see VANDERKAM, "The Origin, Character, and Early History of the 364-Day Solar Calendar: A Reassessment of Jaubert's Hypotheses," *CBQ* 41 (1979) 390–411.

[11] "Le travail d'édition des manuscrits du désert de Juda" in *Volume du Congrès Strasbourg 1956* (VTSup 4; Leiden: Brill, 1957) 17–26.

[12] "Le travail," p. 24.

[13] "Le travail," p. 25. The source from which the line comes is now known to be 4Q320 (Calendrical Document A) 1 II.2.

[14] For similar information, see MILIK, *Ten Years of Discovery in the Wilderness of Judaea* (SBT 26; London: SCM, 1959) 107–110. The French original was published two years earlier: *Dix ans de Découvertes dans le Désert de Juda* (Paris: Les Éditions du Cerf, 1957). The source for the dating of the oil festival is 4Q327 (Calendrical Document E^b) 1 II.4–7.

of the 24 biblical priestly courses (1 Chr 24:7–18) in accordance with the 364-day calendar of 1 Enoch 72–82 and Jubilees. So it followed that the calendar was accepted in some sense at Qumran. The growing number of Qumran copies of 1 Enoch 72–82 and Jubilees favored the same inference. On the basis of the newly reported evidence, Talmon wrote his essay "The Calendar Reckoning of the Sect from the Judaean Desert."[15] In it he aimed ". . . to present the calendar controversy as a decisive factor in the process of the formation of the *Yaḥad* as an organized social body cut off from the Jewish community."[16] He described the calendar and found other references to the controversy in Qumran literature and reflections of it in Rabbinic texts. The evidence indicated to him not only a difference in calendar but also in the way of calculating the day—from the morning. This meant that the proper time for beginning and ending sabbath observance also entered the picture. Talmon was able to chart the periods when the priestly courses served throughout the entire year from the data supplied by Milik. He heavily underscored the social and political significance of calendar control: "The rejection of the official calculation was therefore deemed equivalent to a rejection of civil and religious authority."[17]

There were, of course, many other studies which dealt with calendrical matters, but the next major advance came with the publication of the Psalms Scroll from cave 11. The scroll was found in 1956, unrolled in 1961, submitted to the press in 1962, and published in 1965.[18] The work "David's Compositions," which occupies col. XXVII 2–11 of the scroll, contained the first explicit, published statement that a year lasts 364 days in the view of the author: David composed, among other works, "songs to sing before the altar over the whole-burnt *tamid* offering every day, for all the days of the year, 364; . . ."[19] Milik made much more evidence available when his *The Books of Enoch* appeared in 1976.[20] His principal discussion comes at the point where he is dealing with "Enochic Writings and Essene Texts from Qumrân" (59–69). There he mentions *Jub* 4:18 which details Enoch's calendrical accomplishments. He seized in particular on its reference to a week of jubilees: "This expression refers, beyond doubt in my opinion, to the most extensive cycle to be found in the calendars of 4Q, namely to the cycle of the seven jubilees.

[15] It appeared in *Aspects of the Dead Sea Scrolls* (C. RABIN and Y. YADIN, Eds.; Scripta Hierosolymitana 4; Jerusalem: Magnes, 1958) 162–199.

[16] "The Calendar Reckoning," p. 164.

[17] "The Calendar Reckoning," p. 181; *cf.* pp. 163–164.

[18] JAMES A. SANDERS, Ed., *The Psalms Scroll of Qumrân Cave 11* (11QPsª) (DJD 4; Oxford: Clarendon, 1965). See p. vii for the dates.

[19] Sanders' translation of lines 5–7. Other numbers in the same section also have calendrical significance.

[20] *The Books of Enoch: Aramaic Fragments of Qumrân Cave 4* (Oxford: Clarendon, 1976), especially pp. 61–69 and the treatment of the copies of the Astronomical chapters (273–297).

This cycle is sufficiently represented by the fragments of the calendar in a copy of the *Rule of the Community*, 4QS^b (4Q260), which dates from the second half of the second century."[21] He not only referred to this text but also gave a transcription of several important lines of it. He observed that all sabbaths, months, years, and festivals were said to be under the "sign" (אות) of a priestly division, the one on duty at the relevant time. In the lines he published, there is repeated mention of the sign of Gamul and that of Shekanyah—the two courses which serve at the beginnings of the first and second halves of the year in the first year of a cycle. In every case the sign of one comes three units after the preceding one, the seventh unit is said to be in the שמטה and the eighth unit (= first) is said to be after the שמטה. Milik took the units to be years in a seven-year cycle, and from the facts he compiled a table that covers seven jubilee units.[22] He did not examine the purpose that the document served ("Whatever may have been the reason for the invention of this cycle . . ."[23]). Later he also supplied 13 lines from 4Q317 (4QAstrCrypt)[24] which provide schematic details about the amount of the moon's surface covered by the sun's light on successive days. The fractions are those used in 1 Enoch 72–82.

When Yadin published the Temple Scroll in 1977, he showed how it, too, presupposed the 364-day calendar in its datings of the series of first-fruits festivals. As noted above, the words that Milik had quoted about the date of the oil festival were the key for unlocking the system.[25] With the recent transcription of many more calendrical texts by Wacholder and Abegg there is more hard and fast evidence that the 364-day calendar lies behind the festival dates and periods of service for the priestly groups. They have published the calendrical texts and also an intriguing document (4Q252 = Pesher Genesis^a) which treats the chronology of the flood in frg. 1 col. I and the beginning of col. II, adding these words: "On that day Noah went forth from the ark at the end of a complete year of days, 364" (1 II.2–3).[26] It has been reported

---

[21] *The Books of Enoch*, p. 61.

[22] *The Books of Enoch*, pp. 62–65.

[23] *The Books of Enoch*, p. 64.

[24] *The Books of Enoch*, p. 68.

[25] See מגילת המקדש (3 vols.; Jerusalem: IES and the Shrine of the Book, 1977) 1.95; virtually the same statement about the matter appears in the English edition (*The Temple Scroll* [3 vols.; Jerusalem: IES and the Shrine of the Book, 1983] 1.117): "We might have failed to unravel the author's system had it not been for a tiny fragment fortunately discovered at Qumran, which lists the festivals by months and days. It reads: 'on the twenty-second day of it (the sixth month) is the feast of oil (מועד השמן)'."

[26] B. Z. WACHOLDER and M. G. ABEGG, *A Preliminary Edition of the Unpublished Dead Sea Scrolls: The Hebrew and Aramaic Texts from Cave Four*, fascicles 1–2 (Washington: Biblical Archaeology Society, 1991, 1992). For the calendrical texts, see 1.60–101. For 4Q252, see 2.212–15. All of the photographs were made available in R. H. EISENMAN and J. M. ROBINSON, *A Facsimile Edition of the Dead Sea Scrolls* (2 vols.; Washington: Biblical Archaeology Society, 1991). Mention should also be made of 4Q503 ("Prières quotidiennes") which was published by M. BAILLET, *Qumrân Grotte 4 III (4Q482–4Q520)* (DJD 7; Oxford, Clarendon, 1982) pp. 105–136.

that one copy of 4QMMT begins with a complete 364-day calendar.[27] Part of a reference to 364 days as a complete year (ושלמה השנה) can be read in A.2 (שלוש מאת ושן).[28]

SOME CALENDRICAL ISSUES

There is no shortage of texts which display various aspects of the Qumran calendrical systems, but major questions remain. In this section I will deal with two of them which can be handled more effectively because of the larger textual base that is now available: was the system intercalated and thus practicable; and what does the word דוק mean especially in 4Q321. The answers to both questions, as will be seen below, may have a bearing on what role a calendar controversy played in the origins of the group.

Intercalation

Though there are statements in the texts to the effect that a year has 364 days exactly or that 364 days constitute a complete year (e.g., 4QMMT A.2; Jub 6:32, 38), scholars have concluded that if the system were to be practicable it would have to be supplemented. The calendar would fall behind the true solar year by about 1¼ days per year. After a few years the system would fail to match the agricultural cycle to which its first-fruit festivals were tied and thus prove a disaster or at least not revealed. There have been numerous proposals about how intercalation might have taken place, with the suggestion usually being made that, with the sabbatical base of the system, entire weeks would have to be added periodically. All of this has remained possible but largely speculative.[29]

Recently U. Glessmer, a member of the editorial group, has made a textually based proposal regarding intercalation.[30] He maintains that 4Q260,[31] the text which Milik published in part and which lists the times of the signs

[27] See for example, E. QIMRON and J. STRUGNELL, "An Unpublished Halakhic Letter from Qumran," Israel Museum Journal 4 (1985) 9.

[28] See EISENMAN and ROBINSON, A Facsimile Edition,[25] 1.xxxi.

[29] For a listing of some intercalary proposals, cf. VANDERKAM, "The Origin," pp. 406–407, n. 58. I wish to thank Peter Flint for his assistance in organizing and interpreting the new calendrical data from Qumran.

[30] "Der 364-Tage-Kalender und die Sabbatstruktur seiner Schaltungen in ihrer Bedeutung für den Kult" in Ernten, was man sät: Festschrift Klaus Koch zu seinem 65. Geburtstag (D. R. DANIELS, U. GLESSMER, and M. RÖSEL, Eds.; Neukirchen-Vluyn: Neukirchener Verlag, 1991) 379–398.

[31] Milik referred to the text as 4QSᵇ, but the new siglum is 4QSᶜ (Wacholder-Abegg, A Preliminary Edition, 1.96–101).

of Gamul and Shekanyah, has been misunderstood by Milik and when interpreted properly reveals the intervals at which intercalary weeks were inserted into the system. Milik thought the units mentioned in the text enumerated years within seven sabbatical cycles—that is, a jubilee. He read and restored in 1.12 a very uncertain supralinear היובל under which was הר[ביעׁ]ני. Milik translated the text (1 VI.6–13) in this way:

> [in the second (year)], the sign of Gemul. In the fifth (year), the sign of Shekanyah: after the Release (*shemiṭṭah*), the sign [of Gemul. In the fourth (year), the] sign of Shekanyah; at the Release, the sign of Gemul. In the third (year), the sign [of Shekanyah. In the sixth (year), the sign of] Gemul. In the second (year), the sign of Shekanyah; in the fifth (year), the sign of [Gemul. After] the Release, the sign of Shekanyah. In the fourth (year), the sign of Gemul; [at the Release, the sign] of Shekanyah. In the third (year), the sign of Gemul; in the sixth (year), the sign of Shekanyah. [In the second (year), the sign] of Gemul. In the fifth (year), the sign of Shekanyah: after the Release, the [sign of the beginning of the (new) Jubilee, Ge]mul. The fourth Jubilee (counts) seventeen signs; from the (last) to the Release (there remain) two (yearly) signs of (the triennial cycle of) Shekanyah . . .[32]

Glessmer notes that there are 17 signs in this section of text,[33] five of which are connected with a *shemiṭṭah* (three after and two during a "release"). The author never mentions the first or seventh unit in the sequence by an ordinal as he does with two-six; rather, they are named the unit of or the one after the "release." Thus, the word שׁמטה appears relatively frequently and is probably important to the writer. Milik's interpretation does not explain why this should be. Glessmer also alludes to a few indications in the Bible that שׁמטה can refer to a larger unit of time than the seventh year of a sabbatical cycle. His proposal ". . . geht von der Beobachtung, dass der den 'Erlass' (שׁמטה) regelnde Text Dtn 15, 1ff nicht unbedingt auf die Basis eines Sabbatjahres bezogen werden muss. So stehen zum einen die Inhalte in Dtn 15 z.T. mit denen der Freilassung in 49. Jahr, dem Jobeljahr aus Lev 25, in Beziehung."[34] While maintaining this possibility, he concludes that the real answer emerges from testing whether the word might designate a longer unit in the text.

A unit is said to be under the sign of Gamul or Shekanyah whenever that priestly division is on duty at the beginning of it. As Glessmer proposes to read the text, the first lines would mean: "In the second [sabbath of years] the sign of Gamul [that is, this course was on duty in the first week of what turns out to be the sixth year in that second sabbath of years]; in the fifth

[32] *The Books of Enoch*, pp. 62, 64.
[33] The text reads "16" in line 12, but, as Milik saw (*The Books of Enoch*, p. 64, n. a), it should be 17, as 17 are enumerated or restored according to a fixed pattern.
[34] "Der 364-Tage-Kalender," p. 393.

[sabbath of years] the sign of Shekanyah [on duty the first week of year six in the fifth sabbath of years]," *etc.* The שמטה in each case is the seventh unit of seven years within a 49-year cycle. From these givens he constructs a cycle of seven 49-year units in which there are 17 signs (the last would actually be in the eighth jubilee unit, after the seventh sabbath of years), 12 of which have no connection with a שמטה.

If one calculates the number of days that make up seven periods of 49 years each (343 years) in actual solar years of 365.25 days, the total is 125, 280.75. For the same period according to the 364-day system the total would be 124, 852. If seven days were intercalated every sabbatical period, there would be an additional 343 days, yielding 125, 195, that is, 85.75 days fewer than 343 true solar years. This is where the signs of the text fit in the picture. They indicate the points in the cycle in which an extra intercalary week is inserted. These 12 extra weeks give 84 days, 1.75 fewer than in true solar years. Even that extra amount of time could be accommodated if one added seven days at some point within four of these 343-year periods (4 × 1.75 = 7). The instances in which a sign of Gamul or Shekanyah is said to be during or after the "release" are cases in which, contrary to what one might expect, no intercalary week is added. Hence they are specially noted.

Glessmer's analysis has the advantage over Milik's of providing explanations for the repeated reference to "signs" in a fixed pattern and for underscoring the שמטה by repeating it frequently. If he is correct, then the calendar would be systematically adjusted to the true solar year, never being more than a few days at variance with it. It would, then, be a workable system and therefore a candidate for implementation over a long period. If this sort of intercalary scheme were in force, the calendar of 364-days could have been practiced for any amount of time. Publication of the full text of 4Q260 has, however, proved that Milik was correct in regarding the units as years, not seven-year entities (see, for example, 1 V 18, 1 VI 13).[35] The textual base for Glessmer's intercalary proposal is thus removed, but, as Albani maintains, Glessmer may nevertheless have found the system by which the 364-day year was adjusted to reality.[36] At the very least, his thesis shows that such accommodation is possible within the sabbatical structure. Hence, the calendar could have been intercalated in a systematic way and could have been employed.

[35] WACHOLDER and ABEGG, *A Preliminary Edition*, 1.96–97; M. ALBANI, "Die lunaren Zyklen im 364-Tage-Festkalender von 4QMischmerot/4QSᶜ," *Kirchliche Hochschule Leipzig, Forschungsstelle Judentum, Mitteilungen und Beiträge* 4 (1992) 37–40.
[36] See his discussion of the possible developments in lunar and solar calculations, "Die lunaren Zyklen," pp. 40–41. As he indicates, 4Q260 may well give the intervals at which 10 extra days were added to the 354-day lunar calendar to bring it into conformity with the 364-day system.

The Meaning of דוק

The *mishmarot* texts, about which Milik gave the essentials decades ago, are now, of course, accessible in the form of photographs and the printed edition of Wacholder and Abegg. These and other calendrical documents from cave 4 give one a fuller picture of the way in which the calendar systems of Qumran operated and seem to solve some old problems. Talmon and I. Knohl have classified the texts into six categories:

1. enumerations of months designated by ordinals;
2. calendars of sabbaths and holy seasons (texts such as 4Q326–27 include the festivals of the first fruits of wine and oil and the festival of the wood offering);
3. tables of names of the *mishmarot* in the order of their temple service;
4. lists of the *mishmarot* serving at the beginning of each month and year in a six-year cycle;
5. registers of annual festivals with reference to the *mishmarot* in which they occur; and
6. equation tables of specific dates in the solar and lunar year with the priestly course on duty.

(There are also texts that combine some of the above categories.)[37]

One prominent feature in some calendrical texts is that two regularly recurring phenomena, only one of which is named, are correlated with a day in the week-long service of a priestly division. The unnamed one of these items can be designated X; the other is called דוק (used with either the masculine or feminine singular suffix of the third person).[38] The two are separated from one another by fixed intervals: X comes 13 days after the *duq* or precedes it by 16 or 17 days.[39] There has been some disagreement about what the two entities are: Talmon-Knohl consider the X to be a point near the new moon and the *duq* to be one near the full moon (see below); Wacholder-Abegg believe the X is the full moon and the *duq* the new moon;[40] and M. Wise identifies the *duq* as the time when the moon is full and the mystery term as meaning the first day of the moon's invisibility.[41] I agree with Wacholder-Abegg that X is the full moon and *duq* a time around

---

[37] "Fragments of a Calendrical Scroll from Qumran—*Mishmarot* Ba (4Q321)," *Tarbiz* 60 (1991) 506–507 (Hebrew; an English version of the essay is scheduled for publication in the Milgrom Festschrift).

[38] "Fragments of a Calendrical Scroll," pp. 519–520.

[39] "Fragments of a Calendrical Scroll," pp. 515, 518.

[40] See, for example, their *A Preliminary Edition*, 1.68, and Appendix C.

[41] I thank Professor Wise for allowing me to see a copy of chapter 6, "Observations on New Calendrical Texts from Qumran," in his forthcoming book *Thunder in Gemini* (Journal for the Study of the Pseudepigrapha Supplement Series; Sheffield: Sheffield Academic Press), where he discusses the derivation and meaning of the term and related calendrical issues.

the appearance of the lunar crescent but think that the X (the full moon) is also the beginning of the month – the conclusion Milik had reached long ago.[42] The evidence for this conclusion should now be adduced.

1. The beginning of the system – both for the solar and lunar months – is indicated in the texts. 4Q320 (Mishmarot A) 1 I.1–5 read thus:[43]

1. [   ] to show its light from the east
2. [and] to give its light [in] the middle of the heavens in the foundation
3. [of the firmamen]t from evening until morning in the fourth (day) in the week
4. [of the sons of Ga]mul for the first month in the [firs]t year.

The restoration and reading of [הרישׁ]נה in line 5 is supported by the sequel. For example, in 1 II.4 there is mention of השׁנה השׁנית and it, like the word in I.5, is followed by a blank space marking the end of a listing for a year. Some expressions here recall Gen 1:14–19, the paragraph regarding creation of the sun, moon, and stars (ברקיע השׁמים להאיר in 1:15, 17; ויהי ערב ויהי בקר יום רביעי in 1:19). The first month of what seems to be the very first week seems to be under consideration. That the luminary in question is the moon follows from the fact that it gives its light (note: it is not dark; therefore the X cannot refer to a day of the moon's invisibility) from evening to morning.

A second passage also relates the system to creation. *Mishmarot* A 2 I.3–5 (*cf.* 4 III.1–2) says:[44]

3. [   ] the creation, holy
4. [in] the fourth (day) in the week
5. [the sons of Gamu]l, the head of all the years.

And 4QS^e 1 V.10–11 add:[45]

10. [   ] its light in (day) four in the wee[k[46]
11. [the] creation in (day) four in Ga[mul

Here again creation and the fourth day in Gamul are related.

---

[42] "Further study of the *Mišmarot* from Cave IV, not yet finished, seems to favour the assumption that the Essenes computed the beginning of *their* lunar month from the full moon, not the new moon. Nevertheless, in one of their synchronistic tables, in addition to the correspondence between the day of their solar calendar and the first day of their lunar month they also note the day of the solar month on which the *new* moon falls; this correspondence is called *dauqah* or *duqyah*, which in Rabbinic literature means 'precision (obtained by an observation)' the root *dwq* meaning 'to examine, observe'." (*Ten Years*, p. 152, n. 5).

[43] For the text, see WACHOLDER-ABEGG, *A Preliminary Edition*, 1.60. ALBANI ("Die lunaren Zyklen," pp. 24–25) also uses this text in his argument that the month begins at full moon.

[44] *A Preliminary Edition*, 1.62.

[45] *A Preliminary Edition*, 1.96.

[46] Wacholder-Abegg read בשׁבוע; in the concordance it was read as בשׁכ[ני]ה.

2. Since the order of the priestly divisions in the Qumran texts follows that in 1 Chr 24:7–18 exactly, one can plot from the starting point in the fourth day of Gamul the relations of the X and the *duq* relative to the dates in the solar and lunar months. 4Q321 provides a rather full presentation of these correlations. According to this fixed system, the X falls on the 30th day in the first solar month and the *duq* is on the 17th in the same month. That is, the X occurs at the beginning of the second lunar month (the first has 29 days), and the *duq* figures around the middle of the first one.

3. Once X is located at the beginning of the lunar month and *duq* near the middle, one can ask whether X stands for the new moon (or a point in its vicinity) or the full moon (or a point around it). Though there is no explicit statement in the texts, it appears more likely that X is near the full moon and *duq* near the new crescent than the reverse. That is, it is more likely that the system begins with a full moon as the first day of a lunar month than that it begins in the middle of the month. Several considerations support this conclusion.

One is the etymological meaning of דוק; although it is not attested elsewhere in the sense it has in the *mishmarot* texts, its meaning can be narrowed down fairly precisely to two options. First, Talmon-Knohl relate it to the geminate root דקק = to be thin.[47] As they explain, the texts indicate that the X day appears at the end of the lunar month, when the moon is dark. Hence, the דוק must come near its middle when waning begins, as it precedes the X by 13 days. The etymological sense of the word they associate with the calendrical data thus: "In our opinion, one is to identify the day of the דוקה with that day in the middle of the lunar month, in the night before the moon begins to wane, and the day X with the day at the end of the lunar month, in the night before which the moon is dark."[48] The term refers, in other words, to a point near the time when the lighted portion of the lunar surface begins to diminish or grow thinner.

This seems, however, to be highly unlikely. It would be curious to refer to a time when the moon is almost full by use of a word that means "thinness." A more likely derivation is, as Milik suggested, from the hollow root דוק which connotes careful examination and the like—an eminently suitable notion for a calendaric term.[49] This derivation leaves open, however, what it is that is being observed carefully. Wise concludes that the word designates "(astronomical) observation of the full moon"—which itself would be a novelty. In lunar systems, one makes observations of the new crescent after which the full moon follows at a fixed interval. It would be more in harmony

---

[47] "Fragments of a Calendrical Scroll," p. 519.
[48] "Fragments of a Calendrical Scroll," p. 518.
[49] See the detailed study in WISE, "Observations."

with procedures for lunar systems to associate the careful observation with a time around the first appearance of the new crescent.

It would also, however, be a novelty to begin a lunar month with the full moon. But that is what some indirect lines of evidence suggest. First, the texts cited above indicate that at the beginning of the system the moon gave light all night; hence the X day cannot be a day of lunar invisibility. Second, the standard Rabbinic story about the sun and moon at the time of their creation presupposes that the moon was created full. The story, in various forms, is transmitted in different texts. According to it, the two were created equal in brilliance but a conflict arose between them after which the moon was punished and diminished. The story makes no sense unless the moon were created full of light on the fourth day. This was the explanation for the fact that Gen 1:16 first calls the sun and moon the two great *lights* and then distinguishes them as the *greater* one to rule the day and the *lesser* to rule the night.[50]

Third, there could be a later echo of the theory that the month began on the full moon. Barthélemy and Jaubert drew the reports about a group called the Magharya into the discussion because there are some intriguing similarities with the Qumranites in their views. In his account of this group Al-Biruni says:

> Abu-'Iša Alwarrak speaks in his *Kitab-Almakalat* of a Jewish sect called the Maghribis, who maintain that the feasts are not legal unless the moon rises in Palestine as a full moon in the *night* of Wednesday, which follows after the *day* of Tuesday, at the time of sunset. Such is their New-Year's Day. From this point the days and months are counted, and here begins the rotation of the annual festivals. For God created the two great lights on a Wednesday. Likewise they do not allow Passover to fall on any other day except Wednesday. And the obligations and rites prescribed for Passover they do not hold to be necessary, except for those who dwell in the country of the Israelites. All this stands in opposition to the custom of the majority of the Jews, and to the prescriptions of the Thora.[51]

Obviously, the relation of this, if there is one, to the inhabitants of Qumran is debatable, but at least it illustrates that a Jewish group was remembered as having calculated the beginning of the months from the full moon.

---

[50] Pseudo-Jonathan Gen 1:16 reads: "God made the two great lights, *and they were equal in glory for twenty-one hours less six hundred and seventy-two parts of an hour. After that the moon spoke with a slanderous tongue against the sun, and it was made smaller. And he appointed the sun which was* the greater light to rule over the day, and *the moon which was* the lesser light <to rule over the night>, and the stars" (M. MAHER, *Targum Pseudo-Jonathan: Genesis* [The Aramaic Bible 1B; Collegeville: The Liturgical Press, 1992]). For references, see M. M. KASHER, *Torah Shelemah*, vol. 1: *Genesis* (Jerusalem: Azriel, 1938) pp. 132–137; and J. BOWKER, *The Targums & Rabbinic Literature* (Cambridge: Cambridge University, 1969) p. 105.

[51] C. E. SACHAU, Ed., *The Chronology of Ancient Nations: An English Version of the Arabic Text of the Athar-ul-Bakiya of Albiruni* (London: Wm. H. Allen, 1879) p. 278. In the context, the reference to Passover on a Wednesday must refer to the first day of Unleavened Bread.

HISTORICAL IMPLICATIONS

If the proposals made above regarding the calendar are correct, the texts from Qumran offer up systems that were radically different than any others known elsewhere in Judaism. Moreover, the number of documents which communicate calendrical information is large, probably because the issue was an important one for the community. It also seems possible that intercalation was practiced in the calendars so that they were workable arrangements. What implication may be drawn from this information in light of what is known and likely in Jewish history?

I think that the combination of data lying behind the thesis that a community began to live in the area of Qumran—a community that had brought scrolls with them, copied some, and obtained more in other ways—in the mid-second century B.C.E. and continued there until the first revolt against Rome remains convincing and that no rival theory is close to it in plausibility. The early and mid-second century would then be the likeliest time in which to search for hints in our inadequate sources for what may have caused the schism. I think, too, that calendrical issues were probably a factor from the beginning; the texts of the group at any rate place such disagreements around the time when it began (the Teacher/Wicked Priest conflict; 4QMMT, if it has been interpreted properly). The copies of calendrical texts range in date through most of the time that the site was occupied (for example, 4Q260 was copied in the second half of the second century and the 11QPsalms scroll in the first century C.E.). 1 Enoch and Jubilees, both of which antedate Qumran, show that similar systems were around well before the Qumran texts were transcribed.

As a number of scholars have noticed, there are indications of calendar problems in our meager data. Daniel 7:25, talking about what the little horn on the fourth beast would do, says that he "shall attempt to change the times and the law." This is usually interpreted in the sense that the small horn stands for Antiochus IV and the *times* intend *festivals*. From this scholars have concluded, with justification, that Daniel's cryptic words suggest a calendar change in Antiochus' time (167 B.C.E.).[52]

Some years ago I argued that another text—2 Macc 6:7a—which had not been considered in the discussions—indicated that the change in festivals entailed use of the Seleucid luni-solar calendar in the Jerusalem temple during this time. It reads: "On the monthly celebration of the king's birthday, the Jews were taken, under bitter constraint, to partake of the sacrifices; . . ." (*NRSV*). The parallel passage—1 Macc 1:59—specifies the 25th as the date of

---

[52] For a summary and references, see VANDERKAM, "2 Maccabees 6, 7A and Calendrical Change in Jerusalem," *JSJ* 12 (1981) 58–60.

the monthly royal birthday. Proper dating of the celebration required that the correct calendar be used—in this case obviously the Seleucid one.[53]

If this is true, then there was a change in cultic calendar in the 160s and the luni-solar arrangement of the Seleucids held sway in Jerusalem for some time. The priests were the group that at an earlier time had been particularly enthusiastic about Hellenistic reforms (2 Macc 4:12–17). Presumably this one was no more offensive. Also, the high priesthood remained in the hands of Seleucid appointees, among whom were the Maccabees, after 152. There may not have been much interest in rejecting the Seleucid calendar under these circumstances.

It would be a great benefit to know what happened during the intersacerdotium from 159–152, the time for which no high priest is recorded. We all know the theory associated with J. Murphy-O'Connor and H. Stegemann that the Teacher of Righteousness may have served as high priest during that time and that Jonathan ousted him when he received the office from Alexander Balas.[54] There is something very appealing about the theory, even if it is not demonstrable. It would, however, provide an appropriate setting and explanation for a physical separation of one priestly group from another. The Teacher and his followers would have been advocates of a solar calendar and perhaps of a schematic lunar one, while Jonathan, the Seleucid appointee, might have continued the practice that had prevailed during Seleucid domination. This calendar difference, coupled with the political conflict between two high-ranking priests, could have eventuated in departure by the Teacher and his followers to the wilderness of their exile.[55]

It seems that none of the Qumran texts will throw added light on these early years, while the positive reference to King Yonathan raises interesting questions about the relation between the Qumran group and the Hasmonean regime.[56] The relations between them could have changed with changing circumstances. But as far as the evidence allows us to go, the Qumran group preferred to remain in its removed place, following calendrical arrangements which were shared by no others. They were not candidates for changes of

---

[53] "2 Maccabees 6, 7A," pp. 52–74.

[54] MURPHY-O'CONNOR, "Demetrius I and the Teacher of Righteousness," *RB* 83 (1976) 400–420; STEGEMANN, *Die Entstehung der Qumrangemeinde* (Ph.D. dissertation, Bonn, 1965; privately published, 1971) 102, 212–214. See also J. G. BUNGE, "Zur Geschichte und Chronologie des Untergangs der Oniaden und des Aufstiegs der Hasmonäer," *JSJ* 6 (1975) 27–46.

[55] VANDERKAM, "2 Maccabees 6,7A," pp. 71–74.

[56] The text in question, 4Q448, was first read as referring to King Jonathan (= Alexander Jannaeus) by E. ESHEL, H. ESHEL, and A. YARDENI, "A Scroll from Qumran Which Includes Part of Psalm 154 and a Prayer for King Jonathan and His Kingdom," *Tarbiz* 60 (1992) 296–324 (Hebrew). It is possible, however, that they, like the first editor, have misread the text and that it really does not mention King Jonathan in this passage. See now G. VERMES, "Brother James's heirs?" *Times Literary Supplement* (Dec. 4, 1992) 7 who translates: "Holy City, Joy [reading עליצת instead of על יונתן] of the [divine] King. . . ." Jonathan is, nevertheless, mentioned at a later point in the text but, of course, in a very different context.

opinion in this regard because they believed God had revealed the truth to them. It was left to their opponents to change, and as far as we know they never did.

~~~~~~~~~~~~~~~~~~~~~~~~~~~~~~~~~~~~~~

DISCUSSION OF THE PAPER

MICHAEL WISE (*University of Chicago, Chicago, IL*): One comment. The text that you referred to as mentioning the *mo'ed ha-shemen* on the 22nd of the 6th month is actually, as we now know, a part of 4Q394, the first copy of *MMT.* I'm sure you knew that. That means that not only the *mo'ed ha-shemen* but also the *Qorban ha-'etzim* in the next line of that text agree between *MMT* and the Temple Scroll. They agree on these extra-biblical festivals. I find that interesting in light of the fact that some of the other *mishmarot* which espouse 364-day calendars do not list those dates, even though they go through that period of the year. I'm wondering if you would speculate as to what that might mean.

JAMES VANDERKAM (*University of Notre Dame, Notre Dame, IN*): The extra festivals are mentioned in very fragmentary bits of the mishmarot text, I don't have the number, I can look up the reference for you. As I recall they involve some reconstruction; part of the word is present, but it may well be that the two extra festivals are mentioned. I don't have any helpful thing to say about that fact, that we do have reference to these extra festivals that seem to be important in something like the Temple Scroll and have it in only a few other texts. If it is the case that these are also mentioned in these *mishmarot* texts, then they would have a more general attestation in the scrolls that perhaps wouldn't call so much attention to them. But I don't know why they're left out of some of the others. They certainly point to a biblical trigger, at least in the case of the wood festival and even, I think, in the case of the oil one.

WISE: My second observation has to do with the question of whether the moon was created full or whether it was created new. You listed some evidence with regard to the question of its being full. I've done some work on a brontologion, which is also simultaneously a lunary. It plots the movements of the moon through the signs of the zodiac. It begins with the sign of Taurus and, if I understand this text correctly, it would seem to require that the moon was created new. I want to draw that to your attention as something you might consider. It's possible, it seems to me, that, when created, the moon was 11 degrees or so removed from the sun, therefore not dark and therefore a "light," so to speak.

VANDERKAM: I ought to say first that I owe to Michael Wise the stimulation to get to work on this question of what *dwqh* meant. He sent a paper to me—I hadn't done much reflecting on it, and his paper certainly provided a lot of impetus. I think the comment you're making is in line with those other texts like 4Q317 which plot the percentages of the lunar illumination and also begin, it seems pretty clear, with the crescent. So if what I'm saying is correct, we would have differences on that. Albani has some comments about how this might fit into a historical development of debate and trial and error regarding how these calendars were to be worked out, not so much with the 364-day one, but how to work the lunar phenomena into that system. And as you know, the book of Jubilees throws the moon out, and I can understand why a person would do that. The moon really complicates any system, as we can see from these calendars. But we do have that conflict. However, I thought it would be the best methodological thing to do in reading those texts that I think clearly chart the system from a full moon, just to say "Okay, that's what they seem to do." But we have these other texts that suggest a different system to worry about later on—how the two might be juxtaposed, whether they preserve for us different points in debate about how to handle this kind of information or what.

EPHRAIM ISAAC (*Institute of Semitic Studies, Princeton, NJ*): I have a question pertaining to the issue of whether the community is separated from the other groups on the basis of calendrical matters. There is no question that calendar calculation has always been crucial in religious disputes. Nonetheless do we have any evidence whatsoever that the Qumran community celebrated the Passover at a different time from other groups? The objective of the calculation, particularly in the Jewish community at that time, was to determine to fix the date of Passover, not necessarily to determine the dates of the other festivals; the other festivals centered on dates. Perhaps even the allusion to the new moon's being at the beginning may refer to that particular date. I myself would be very skeptical that the calendar became an issue for this group unless we could determine that they had fixed a different date for the celebration of Passover.

VANDERKAM: I think it's the clear implication of the calendaric texts that we have that they are going to be celebrating Passover at a different time than other people are. If Talmon's reading of that conflict in the pesher of Habakkuk is correct, then it seems to me that that particular day would be celebrated at different times. There are several assumptions there of course, that the Wicked Priest is a high priest and his coming to where the Teacher was occurred on the Teacher's holiday, not on the priest's holiday. But if the 364-day system was practiced, then it would follow inevitably that often Passover would be celebrated on a different day, and it's dated according to that 364-day calendar. No direct evidence that I know, I'm just saying it's an implication.

WISE: I wonder if you're open to the possibility that the calendar conflict that we're talking about in the Hasmonean period in which a new, different type of lunisolar calendar took over in Jerusalem—are you open to the possibility that politically speaking, the other calendar could have come back into force again? The systems would have gone back and forth at various times, according to rulers and their political alliances.

VANDERKAM: I don't think that's impossible. I think the sort of reconstruction that I just sketched here is a plausible one, but it could have been a great deal more complicated, this back and forth on calendrical issues. Since we have so little information I don't think one can be very dogmatic about that issue.

An Annalistic Calendar from Qumran*

MICHAEL O. WISE

Department of Near Eastern Languages and Civilizations
University of Chicago
1155 E. 58th Street
Chicago, Illinois 60637

INTRODUCTION

It has been said that although the Greeks liked history, they never made it the foundation of their lives.[1] Second Temple Jews, on the contrary, did. Because they saw themselves in continuity with Abraham, Isaac and Jacob, and because for them history and religion were indistinguishable, they returned again and again to the biblical narratives. There they found not only the story of earlier generations, a record of the past as seen from a given perspective – what we today would call historical writings – but also, in a very real sense, a record of the future. For no matter what else they may have thought of the prophets of Israel, no one doubted that the essence of prophecy was prediction.[2] The Bible therefore needed very little in the way of supplementation. Wrapped together in its scrolls were history told and history foretold. Perhaps that is why the literature of the Second Temple period is so destitute of historical writings. Only 1 Maccabees and, some might argue, 1 Esdras continue the biblical tradition of historiography during these years.

The discovery of nearly a thousand literary works near the site of Qumran has done nothing but reinforce this impression, to the chagrin, naturally, of the historian hungry for new facts (or, at least, new perspectives on old facts). Most of these literary texts allude to current events, if at all, with the ambiguous generalities usual to their genres. Those Qumran texts that apparently do concern historical events and real persons, the *pesharim*, are almost equally ambiguous. Anyone who has spent time trying to decipher the coded significance of "Ephraim" and "Manasseh," of "the seekers after smooth interpretations" and "the Man of the Lie" – not to mention "the Teacher of

---

* This paper is a substantially abbreviated version of a chapter in my forthcoming book, *Thunder in Gemini*.

[1] MOMIGLIANO, A. 1990. *The Classical Foundations of Modern Historiography*: 20. University of California Press. Berkeley.

[2] See BARTON, J. 1986. *Oracles of God: Perceptions of Ancient Prophecy in Israel after the Exile*: *passim*. Oxford University Press. Oxford.

Righteousness"—is well acquainted with the frustrations inherent to the interpretation of this body of literature. With so few unambiguous statements in the sources, it is hardly surprising that historical reconstructions based on the scrolls are often convincing to none but their authors.

Apparently the authors of Qumran quasi-historical works felt no need to break away from encoded references or to use the proper names of their *dramatis personae.* Perhaps they preferred to conceal these identities. The "wise" would recognize them anyway, and it might be dangerous for their accusations to be too transparent. To this general pattern there are apparently only two exceptions. One is the well known portion of the *pesher* to Nahum that refers to an Antiochus and a Demetrius—probably, if scholarly consensus is right, Antiochus IV Epiphanes and Demetrius III Eucaerus.

The second exception was communicated by J. T. Milik early on in research on the Qumran finds. In 1957 he described a group of texts he called *mishmarot*; as their name suggests, these texts concern the priestly rotation in and out of service in the temple at Jerusalem. One of them seemed to be of outstanding importance. As Milik described it,[3]

> Un ouvrage, représenté par deux mss. différents, mais malheureusement réduits à quelques petites parcelles, s'apparente au même group de Mishmarot, mais avec des additions d'un intérêt exceptionnel . . . occasionnellement se retrouvent la mention des . . . événements historiques. Ainsi "Salamsiyon a tué . . .

Unfortunately Milik never published the fragments. Interested scholars had to wait until the recent publication of a fascimile edition to get more information. Now that the *mishmarot* text containing proper names has seen the light of day, I propose here to discuss aspects of its reading and interpretation. Rather than two manuscripts, it seems that six copies of this work have survived. Each copy is extremely fragmentary, but it may still be possible to recognize certain historical events to which reference is made, and perhaps even to show that the work contains hitherto unknown information about these events.

READING AND TRANSLATION OF THE TEXTS

The official designations of the six copies of this calendar are 4Q322–4Q324c, otherwise 4QMishmarot C^a, C^b, C^c, C^d, C^e and C^f.[4] 4QMishmarot

[3] MILIK, J. T. 1957. "Le travail d'édition des manuscrits du désert du Juda." *SVT* 4: 25–26. Milik (1959) also referred to this text in *Ten Years of Discovery in the Wilderness of Judaea*, trans. J. STRUGNELL: 73. SCM. London. Here he said, "there is an Essene calendar giving the dates of certain historical events which were celebrated annually." He seems to be thinking of *Megillat Taanit* in making this judgment about the text's function. While there are obvious analogies between the two texts, there is no evidence that the dates in the Qumran text were celebrated.
[4] I follow the index given in REED, S. A. 1991. *Dead Sea Scroll Inventory Project: List of Documents, Photographs and Museum Plates.* Ancient Biblical Manuscript Center. Claremont, CA.

Cf is inscribed in a cryptic script known as cryptic script A and is so extremely fragmentary that I will not consider it here. The other copies also include some fragments too small to yield information for the purposes at hand. The following is then my reading of the larger portions of the five texts 4Q322 (MS A), 323 (MS B), 324 (MS C), 324a (MS D) and 324b (MS E).[5]

Manuscript A (4Q322)
Fragment 1

[	א בעשר [בחודש הששי	] .1
בעשרים ואחד]	[בארבעה עשר בו ביא[ת ידעיה בששה עש]ר בו	] .2
[	[בו באית חרים בעשרים ו[שבעה בחודש [הששי	] .3
[	[התשיב ג.]	] .4
[	גו[אים וגם].	] .5
[	מ[רורי הנפש].	] .6
[	[אסורים]	] .7

Fragment 2

[	ל[תת לו יקר בערב[ים	] .1
[	ביום אר[בעה לשבט זה]	] .2
[	]ה שהוא עשרים בחודש]	] .3
[	].יסוד כאה שלמציון].	] .4
[	[להקביל את [פני	] .5
[	]ב הרקנוס מרד [על ארסטבולוס	] .6
[	[להקביל]	] .7

Fragment 3

[	]...[	] .1
[	ראש הג[ו]אים הרג ש[	] .2
[	ביום ח[מ]שי בידעיה ז.]	] .3

Fragment 4

[	].ם כרצון[	] .1

Manuscript B (4Q323)
Fragment 1

[	]ה כתשע[ה כחודש השמיני ביאת שכניה [	] .1
[בששה עשר בה ביאת אלישיב]	[ביום] [ ] בשכניה א[	] .2
[	[בעשרים תשלו[שה בה ביאת יקים <בשנים ביקים]. [<] ויום ר]ביעי ביקים	] .3
[	[בס..]. יו[ם שני בחודש הח]שיעי	] .4

[5] Since the surviving fragments lack the formulae associated with the calendar, it is not certain that 4QMishCc is a copy of the work.

Fragment 2

1. [יום רב[י]עי בחו[י]ר [זה א[חד בע[שירי]
2. [בארבעה בה ביאת הפ[צץ כאחד [ע[שר בה [ביאת פתחיה]
3. [בשמונה עשר בה ביא[ת יחזקאל בעשר[ים וחמשה בה ביאת]
4. [ו]כין   יכין הע[נ[ב]ודה [.   [
5. [בשנים כה] כיאת [גמול   [

Fragment 3

1. [[שהוא]   [
2. [   ].[[
3. [   ]ש[[
4. [   ]ות...[[
5. [   ].. אשנ]ים   [
6. [   ]. ונגד אר[סטכולוס   [
7. [א[מרו בע]   [
8. [שבעים].   [
9. [[שהוא]   [

Manuscript C (4Q324)
Fragment 1

1. [בעשרים תשלשה בה] ביאת [אלישיב בשלתשים בה ביאת יקים]
2. [אחר שבח ביקים זה אח]ד בש[שי בשבעה בה ביאת חופה]
3. [בארבעה] עשר בה [ביאת ישבאכ] ..פות בע[שרים ואחד]
4. [בה ביאת בלג[ה בעשרים [ושמונה ב]ה ביאת אמ[ר יום]
5. [רביעי באמר זה א[חד בשביעי כאר[כ]עה בה ביאת ח[ויר]
6. [יום ששי ב]חויר שהוא עשרה בשביעי שיום [הכפורים כה]
7. [   ] לברית כאחד עשר כשביעי ביאת [הפצץ   [

Manuscript D (4Q324a)
Fragment 1 Column 2

5. יום [ ]. [ ]. [ ].[בל]. [בעשרים ואחד]
6. [בו]א ביאת ש[עור]ים בעשר[ים ושמונה בוא ביאת מלכ]יה]
7. יום רביעי [כ]מלכיה זה אחד בחודש העשירי   *vacat*
8. כא[ר]בע[ה] בע[ש]ירי כיאת מי[מ]ין כאחד עשר בוא ביא[ת הקוץ]

Fragment 2

1. [כ]עשרים
2. [ואחד בוא ביאת פתחיה בעשרים ושמו]נה
3. [בוא ביאת יחזקאל ביום 3/2/1 בי]חזקאל שהוא
4. [31/30/29 בחודש הששי יום] הרג אמליוס
5. [יום רביעי ביחזקאל זה אחד בחוד]ש השביעי
6. [בארבעה בוא ביאת יכין באחד עשר בוא ב]י[את] גמול
7. [יום רביעי בגמול ש[הוא
8. [חמשה עשר בחודש השביעי חג הסכות בוא] הרג אמליוס

Fragment 3

.1 [ ]ﬠ[ ] אצל .[ ] ﬠֶ[

.2 [בﬠשרים תשמונה בוא ביאת יֹשוﬠ רביﬠ﬜י בישוﬠ זה אחד בחודש]

.3 [הﬠשירי שה]וֹא ﬠש[ו]רה [

Fragment 4

.1 [ ] [איש יהודי א]ן [

Manuscript E (4Q324b)
Fragment 1 Column 1

.1 [כוהן ﬤﬡ]וֹל כ.רי

.2 [יוחנן להבי את

Fragment 1 Column 2

.1 [ ]..

.2 [מן]

.3 [ ]

.4 [ ]

.5 [אנש]

.6 [ ].ח הו﬜.

.7 [שלמצ<י>ﬤ]

TRANSLATION

Manuscript A Fragment 1 (1) on the tenth [of the sixth month (*i.e.*, of the second year of the priestly rotation) . . .] (2) [on the fourteenth of it, the arriva]l of (the priestly course of) Jedaiah; on the sixtee[nth of it . . . on the twenty-first] (3) [of it the arrival of (the priestly course of) Harim; on the twenty]-seventh of the [sixth] month [ ] (4) he returned . . . (5) [gen]tiles and also . . . (6) [b]itter of spirit . . . (7) prisoners . . . **Fragment 2** (1) [to] give him honor among the Nabat[eans . . .] (2) [on the fou]rth [day] of this course's service . . . (3) which is the twentieth of the [ ] month . . . (4) foundation, Shelamzion came . . . (5) to visit . . . (6) Hyrcanos rebelled [against Aristobulus . . .] (7) to visit . . . **Fragment 3** (2) [the leader of the ge]ntiles murdered . . . (3) [on the fi]fth [day] of (the service of the priestly course of) Jedaiah . . . **Fragment 4** (1) according to the wi[ll of . . .] **Manuscript B Fragment 1** (1) on the nin[th of the eighth month (*i.e.*, of the second year of the priestly rotation), the arrival of (the priestly course of) Shecaniah . . .] (2) On day [ ] of (the service of the priestly course of Shecaniah, [On the sixteenth of it (*i.e.*, the eighth month), the arrival of (the priestly course of) Eliashib]; (3) [on the twenty-thi]rd of it, the arrival of (the priestly course of) Jakim;

on the second (day of the service of the priestly course of) Jakim, [ ];
and on the fo[urth] day of (the service of the priestly course of) [Jakim,]
(4) . . . the second day of the ni[nth] month . . . **Fragment 2** (1) [the four]th
[day] of (the service of the priestly course of) Hez[i]r, [this day is the fi]rst
(day) of the te]nth month (*i.e.*, of the second year of the priestly rotation);]
(2) [on the fourth day of it (*i.e.*, the tenth month), the arrival of (the priestly
course of) Happi]zzez; on the eleve[nth] of it, [the arrival of (the priestly
course of) Pethahiah;] (3) [on the eighteenth of it, the arriv]al of (the priestly
course of) Jehezkel; on the twen[ty-fifth of it, the arrival] (4) [of (the priestly
course of) Jachin; Jach]in, the se[r]vice . . . (5) [. . . on the second of it (*i.e.*,
the eleventh month)], the arrival of [(the priestly course of) Gamul . . .] **Fragment 3** (1) which is . . . (5) me[n . . .] (6) and against Ar[istobulus . . .]
(7) [and] they [sa]id . . . (8) seventy . . . (9) which is . . . **Manuscript C Fragment 1** (1) [on the twenty-third of it (*i.e.*, the fifth month of the fifth year
of the priestly rotation)], the arrival of [(the priestly course of) Eliashib; on
the thirtieth of it, the arrival of (the priestly course of) Jakim;] (2) after the sabbath, while Jakim is serving, this is the fir]st of the six[th month; on the seventh of it, the arrival of (the priestly course of) Huppah;] (3) [on the
four]teenth of it, [the arrival of (the priestly course of) Jeshebeab;] . . . on
the twen[ty-first] (4) [of it, the arrival of (the priestly course of) Bilg]ah; on
the twenty-[eighth of i]t, the arrival of (the priestly course of) Imm[er; day]
(5) [four (of the service of the priestly course of) Immer is the fi]rst day of
the seventh month; on the four[t]h of it, the arrival of (the priestly course
of) He[zir;] (6) [the sixth day of] (the service of the priestly course of) Hezir,
which is the tenth day of the seventh month, this is [the Day of Atonement;]
(7) [ ] for the covenant; on the eleventh day of the seventh month, the arrival
of (the priestly course of)[Happizzez . . .] **Manuscript D Fragment 1
Column 2** (5) day [on the twenty-first] (6) [of i]t (*i.e.*, of the ninth
month of the fifth year of the priestly rotation), the arrival of (the priestly
course of) S[eor]im; on the twenty-eighth of it, the arrival of (the priestly
course of) Malchi[jah;] (7) the fourth day of (the service of the priestly course
of) Malkijah is the first day of the tenth month. (8) On the f[ourt]h day of
the te[n]th month, the arrival of (the priestly course of) Mija[m]in; on the
eleventh of it, the arriv[al of (the priestly course of) Hakkoz;] **Fragment 2**
(1) [. . . on the] twenty-(2) [first of it (*i.e.*, of the sixth month of the sixth
year of the priestly rotation), the arrival of (the priestly course of) Pethahiah;
on the twenty-eig]th (3) [of it, the arrival of (the priestly course of) Jehezkel;
on the first (or, the second; or, the third) day of (the service of the priestly
course of) J]ehezkel, which is (4) [the twenty-ninth (or, the thirtieth; or, the
thirty-first) day of the sixth month, the Day] of the Massacre of Aemelius;
(5) [the fourth day of (the service of the priestly course of) Jehezkel is the first
day of] the seventh [mon]th; (6) [on the fourth of it (*i.e.*, of the seventh
month), the arrival of (the priestly course of) Jachin; on the eleventh of it,

the arr]iv[al of] (the priestly course of) Gamul; (7) [the fourth day of (the service of the priestly course of) Gamul, whi]ch is (8) [the fifteenth day of the seventh month, is the Festival of Booths; on that day,] Aemelius murdered . . . **Fragment 3** (2) [on the twenty-eighth of it (*i.e.*, of the ninth month of the sixth year of the priestly rotation), the arrival of (the priestly course of) Je]shua; the four[th] day of [((the service of the priestly course of) Jeshua is the first day of the] (3) [tenth month . . . wh]ich is the ten[th . . .] **Fragment 4** (1) a Jewish man . . . **Manuscript E Fragment 1 Column 1** (1) the hi[g]h priest (2) Yohanan to bring the . . . **Fragment 1 Column 2** (2) from . . . (5) a man (7) Shelamzion . . .

DISCUSSION

The regular patterning of this work, together with a knowledge of the underlying system of priestly rotation, make many of the suggested restorations certain. In common with a significant number of works from Qumran, the author reckoned by a solar calendar of 364 days. With this calendar structuring his calculations, he distributed the twenty-four priestly courses over a six year period. This is the length of time required for any given course to return to serve at the same week it had previously served. Thus, for example, the course Delaiah served in the first month of the first year of the cycle, beginning with day four of that month (1/4 Year One). Although Delaiah served twice a year, it would require six years before the course returned in month one day four. This sexennial cycle structured the recording of holy times in all the Qumran *mishmarot*. The cycle was eternal, deriving from the Creation narrative of Genesis 1. Every sabbath, month, year and festival was denominated by the name of the relevant priestly family. As the calendar under discussion shows, the system also structured chronography and, in a certain sense, historiography.

1 Chr 24:1–18 describes how the order of the priestly courses was once determined by the fall of the lot. As it is laid out in Chronicles, the order began with Jehoiarib and ended with Maaziah. The Qumran *mishmarot* use the same names for the courses–apparently indicating that their system postdates 1 Chronicles 24–but in a different order. Rather than beginning with Jehoiarib, the Qumran texts begin with Gamul.[6] Probably the reason for this change is that the list given in 1 Chronicles began the rotation in the autumn. Jehoiarib rotated into service at the beginning of the seventh month, Tishri. In contrast, the Qumran calendar texts assume a vernal New Year, beginning

---

[6] One could determine that Gamul is first simply by a complete study of the relevant texts, but one text, 4Q320 Mishmarot A, makes that inference explicit. The text reads "on the fourth, on the sabbath, the sons of Gamul (shall serve) in the first month, in the first year." See PAM 43.330, fragment 1, lines 3–5.

the year in Nisan. The different beginning derives from an understanding of the Creation narrative. The creation happened in the spring. An eternal order based on the creation must therefore also begin at that time. The vernal New Year meant that the priestly rotation would begin with Gamul.

Indications are that the Qumran calendar originally comprised one full six year cycle. The time of each course's arrival was noted, as were "New Moons"[7] and the major festivals of the religious calendar. Interwoven with these data were entries dating significant events (significant to whom is a question to which we will return). The major festivals were often double-dated using formulae introduced either by שהוא or זה. Often, but not always, the author applied the same double-dating technique to significant events. Like the New Moons and festivals, the events included in the work may have been celebrated – or, as appropriate, mourned. At the least they were memorialized. The most obvious analogy is *Megillat Taanit*, but the Qumran work was much more extensive: in addition to the 312 entries describing the rotation of the courses (52 × 6), there were entries for six years' worth of festivals and an unknown number of historical events. Assuming that the entry for each course required about half a line (the space occupied by entries in the extant portions), it is hard to believe that the complete work numbered fewer than 200 lines; it may have been much longer. Only a small percentage of the presumed original dated entries survive, and no two copies of the calendar overlap.[8] The preserved portions of the texts refer to about twenty events, some of which are dated according to the system described. The dates of others have not survived.

What was the nature of this calendar? It is notable that all the proper names preserved belong to the Hasmonean period. יוחנן is perhaps John Hyrcanus I (135/4–104 B.C.E.);[9] הרקנום is then John Hyrcanus II (63–40 B.C.E.), שלמציון is Salome Alexandra (76–63 B.C.E.), and אמליום is the Roman general M. Aemilius Scaurus. Of course, it may be fortuitous that no names from the Herodian period and later have been preserved. Any characterization of the work must be appropriately tentative, but I would hypothesize that this Qumran work was a "Hasmonean Chronicle." I base this suggestion not only on the names, but also on the fact that the few events that can be analyzed point to the Hasmonean period. It is on several of these events that I want to focus in the following discussion, in particular considering fragment 2 of manuscript A and fragment 2 of manuscript D.

---

[7] The text speaks of אחד בחודש because in the Qumran system the astronomical New Moon only occasionally fell at the beginning of the month.

[8] It is possible that D 2 immediately precedes A 2. The two mentions of Shelamzion do not seem to refer to the same event, judging by line lengths and lacunae.

[9] For the chronology of this reign and of the later Hasmoneans, see SCHÜRER I 200–202 n. 1. It is certainly possible that this "John" is someone other than Hyrcanus I, but this seems the best suggestion given the calendar as a whole.

HISTORICAL ANALYSIS

The reference to Hyrcanus in A 2:6 is the first clue to the *Tendenz* of this Qumran calendar. Provided that the reading מרד is correct, it appears that the text identifies with the supporters of Aristobulus in the civil war between the two brothers. The reading of מרד is uncertain because the final letter is damaged, but this uncertainty is not as great as it might seem. The remaining ink cannot simply be read as any letter at all; most possibilities are ruled out by the surviving traces. For example, the final letter cannot be a *waw*, thus ruling out a reading such as מרו[נרי הנפש]—a reading that one might have favored since the phrase does occur in the calendar at A 1:6.

Further, the formulaic character of the text favors the reading of a simple verb at this point. Other alternatives are conceivable, but the repeating formulae lead one to expect that the *beth* preceding Hyrcanus' name belongs to the name of a course. Given a course name in that position, either a verbless clause or a simple verb should follow almost immediately. Leaving aside the question of what letters the traces would allow for the third radical of the verb, what verbs begin with *mem* and *resh*? Considering both Biblical and Post-biblical Hebrew, the only options that come to mind are: מרה, "to rebel" (but in the Bible, only rebellion against one's father or against God); מרח, "to rob"; מרט, "to polish" (of a sword); מרץ, "to be sick" (only in derived stems); מרק, "to scour or polish"; מרר, "to be bitter"; and מרם, "to crush; to rub" (of flour or sacrificial portions). Sifted by the dual criteria of semantics and material reading, none of these options survives. Further, if it is correct to read the *beth* preceding Hyrcanus as the name of a course, a prepositional phrase beginning with מן cannot make sense. We are calculating probabilities here, of course, not solving equations. Certainty remains elusive. Nevertheless, the best option by far seems to be מרד.

Now, מרד is not a neutral term. It implies that the person carrying out the action, the "rebel," is out of power and seeking to get it. In the Hebrew Bible the term always carries that implication in the realm of human events (otherwise it describes sinful relations with God).[10] Here another question arises. Did the text link the name of Hyrcanus to מרד, or was there a syntactic break between the two words? If the author meant that Hyrcanus was re-belling, then, as noted, the text may originally have read something like ביוירי[ב] הרקנום מרד [ע]ל ארסטבולום, "in Jehoiarib Hyrcanus rebelled against Aristobulus." The general reference would be to the time when the older brother had abdicated his rights as high priest.[11] Aristobulus then became the legal resident of that office and, probably, king as well.[12] Hyrcanus

---

[10] For the first meaning, see Neh 6:6, Isa 25:5, Gen 14:4, 2 Kgs 24:20, *etc.* For the second meaning, among many possible examples note for clarity Jos 22:29 and Dan 9:5.

[11] *Ant.* 14.4–7.

[12] For Aristobulus as high priest, denied by some scholars who hold that Hyrcanus continued in that office while giving up only the throne, see *Ant.* 14.41, 97, and 20.243–44.

agreed to that arrangement at first. For a period of time, then, it was the uncontested truth that Aristobulus was ruler. When, at the instigation of Antipater, Hyrcanus later sought to annul this agreement, the situation would be described differently according to whom one supported. For those favoring Aristobulus, Hyrcanus was illegally seeking that which was no longer rightfully his; he was a rebel. For those favoring Hyrcanus, the earlier agreement ceding Aristobulus the throne had never been valid. It contradicted the absolute right of primogeniture to which Hyrcanus was heir. Aristobulus was a rebel.

Accordingly one might argue that the Qumran text be restored differently, *e.g.*, וכשיש]ב הרקנום מרד]בו ארסטבולום,[13] "and when Hyrcanus began to reign as king, Aristobulus rebelled against him." A restoration with a syntactic break between הרקנום and מרד probably would require that the text favored Hyrcanus. But we have already seen that the formulaic movement of the work does not point to such a restoration. Perhaps equally important, if one adopts that reading or something similar, the result is a literary work lacking a consistent perspective (see below on Aemilius). That is highly unlikely. All Jewish historical literature – Kings, Chronicles, Ezra-Nehemiah, 1 and 2 Maccabees, Josephus himself – seeks to fix blame and give praise, according to its author's view of which actors were faithful to God. With due regard for the hermeneutical circle, therefore, I suggest that the first restoration is more likely to represent the thrust of the missing words. In the mind of this text's author, Hyrcanus' claims were illegitimate. The author sided with Aristobulus.

Fragment D 2 is potentially the most informative portion of our text, since it may refer to details of the history of this period that were not previously known. But for precisely that reason we are on even less certain footing in attempting to interpret these lines. Both D 2:4 and D 2:8 refer to Aemilius Scaurus, and both appear to link the Roman general with the killing of some person or persons. The references raise a number of questions. Do both lines refer to the same occasion, or are two separate events in mind? In either case, is it possible to suggest what those events may be?

To consider the first question first: in accordance with the structure of the calendar, the words בחודש השביעי in line 5 logically require that the concern of lines 3 and 4 is with the sixth month. Since several lines then intervene between the mention of the seventh month and the second occurrence of הרג אמליום, as does the name of a course, גמול, which rotated in after יחזקאל of line 3, it is almost certain that two separate occasions are meant. The two occasions are presumably separated by no more than a week or two, however, because only one priestly course, Jakin, stood in the rotation between Gemul and Jehezkel. The proposed restoration accords with structural considerations

---

[13] For unqualified ישב as meaning "sit as king or ruler," see Exod 18:14, Ps 61:8, Mal 3:3, Isa 10:13, *etc.*

and the lengths of the lines.[14] (The surviving words require that this portion fit in the sixth year of the priestly cycle; see below.)

The second question is much more difficult. Josephus has a fair amount to say of the part that Scaurus played in the drama of the last years of Hasmonean rule. Nowhere is there any mention of executions or murders at the hand of the Roman general. Scaurus comes on stage at the time that Hyrcanus and Aretas had Aristobulus caged up in the temple at Jerusalem.[15] Sent to Syria as Pompey's legate, the Roman general heard both Hyrcanus and Aristobulus out, then, accepting bribes from each, ordered Aretas to raise the siege. At this time Scaurus favored Aristobulus. When Pompey himself came to Syria and decided to rehear the Judaean case, Scaurus is again mentioned as present.[16] Because Aristobulus revealed to Pompey that he had earlier bribed Scaurus, he and Scaurus became enemies. Josephus does not mention Scaurus at all in his description of the siege in Jerusalem. Nor does his name appear in the context of the slaughter in the temple when it fell to Pompey.

Where Scaurus was during all this time is not entirely clear. Presumably he was with Pompey. In *Ant.* 14.79, after narrating the fall of the Jewish nation, Josephus mentions that Pompey appointed him governor (that is, *pro-quaestore propraetore*) of Syria. Shortly thereafter, Scaurus marched against Petra. That would be in 62 B.C.E., as the parallel passage in *War* 1.159 makes clear. Petra proved a very difficult city to take, and this fact, together with a bribe from Aretas, convinced Scaurus to end the brief war. Josephus knows of no major battles. That is the last the Jewish historian has to say about his term as governor. One has the impression that he knew nothing else about that period, which was at any rate very brief—about one year. That Josephus had no sources for the period just after the fall of Aristobulus is obvious from the fact that immediately after describing the episode in Nabataea, he begins to narrate events that took place when Gabinius was governor. He places these things "sometime later" (Χρόνῳ δὲ ὕστερον).[17] Evidently, then, Josephus was

---

[14] The proposed reconstruction does not allow for the mention of the Day of Atonement. Apparently this festival was omitted by scribal error, and either was left out altogether, or was written in above the line in the missing portions. No reconstruction that mentions it can be made to fit the surviving words. That fact might seem to weaken my argument here rather badly, but such is really not the case. It must be appreciated that the Qumran *mishmarot* texts are extremely regular and formulaic in their structure. Precisely that regularity is what makes possible virtually complete restorations of many of these texts. Thus, when it is said that this fragment can only fit the sixth year of the rotation of the courses, the statement must be taken seriously: the fragment simply cannot fit anywhere else. From a scribal perspective, the regular formulae of these texts could easily result in the sort of error I am proposing. In fact, 4Q321 Mishmarot B[a] contains a scribal error that illustrates this difficulty very well. In column 3, the scribe forgot the words הואה יום הזכרון ("is the Day of Atonement") and had to write them in above the line (see PAM 43.328). I think the very same thing happened here.

[15] *Ant.* 14.29–33.

[16] *Ant.* 14.37.

[17] *Ant.* 14.82. His passage in *War* 1.160 is of course no better informed.

unaware of the two governors of Syria who intervened between Scaurus and Gabinius, L. Marcius Philippus (61–60 B.C.E.) and Cornelius Lentulus Marcellinus (59–58 B.C.E.).[18]

To what killings by Aemilius could the Qumran calendar then be referring? Any answer will be largely unsupported by evidence from Josephus. Among the conceivable answers to this question, two suggest themselves as most plausible: 1) the text refers to the siege and fall of the temple in 63 B.C.E., which culminated in the massacre of thousands of Jews; or 2) the text refers to events that took place in the year after the fall of the temple, when Scaurus was governor of Syria and may have been called upon to quell disturbances in Judaea. To my mind the first alternative is clearly preferable, since Josephus—who is at any rate well informed about catastrophic events during this period of Jewish history—knows of none during Aemilius' tenure as governor. Further, that the Qumran fragment would have referred to the fall of the temple somewhere may be taken as axiomatic given what is preserved of the text. The end of Jewish independence and of rule by the Hasmonean dynasty was a tremendous shock to Jewish life. Pompey's entrance into the Holy of Holies was a similarly powerful blow to Jewish sensibilities. Both of these disasters were remembered and echo in contemporary literature such as the *Psalms of Solomon*. It is probably best, therefore, to see fragment D 2 as referring to that time. If the second alternative (or some other) is nevertheless correct, there is no way to confirm it and little more to say. The first alternative, however, merits more discussion.

If the mention of killing in line 4 refers to the actual fall of the temple and Scaurus' involvement in the subsequent slaughter—an involvement likely in spite of Josephus' silence on the matter[19]—then הרג אמליוס in line 8 may be tied to something that Josephus mentions in passing. He reports that a short time after the temple fell, Pompey determined who had been the leaders of the revolt and had them beheaded.[20] Josephus does not say who was the actual agent of the executions, nor which officer had charge of carrying out Pompey's orders. Scaurus, as one of his principal generals, might well have been the man.

Certain Jews would have taken notice of Scaurus' actions and recorded them as found in the Qumran text. Those Jews, however, would require a particular reason to focus on Scaurus as the evildoer rather than Pompey. Josephus, relying on Strabo and Nicolaus—and in addition taking a Roman rather than Jewish perspective on these events—focuses on Pompey as the Roman leader. Which Jews might have focused on Scaurus? Those of Aristobulus'

---

[18] *Cf.* Appian, *Syr.* 51.

[19] According to *Ant.* 14.72 and *War* 1.152, members of Pompey's staff entered the temple with him. Scaurus would certainly figure as part of that group if he were at Jerusalem at all. If so, then he also would have taken part in the fighting, and with major responsibilities.

[20] *Ant.* 14.73. *Cf. Pss. Sol.* 8:20, ἀπώλεσεν ἄρχοντας αὐτῶν καὶ πᾶν σοφὸν ἐν βουλῇ.

party, naturally, those who were the victims of the Roman general. The reason for such a focus is not hard to seek: having been bribed, Scaurus had originally sided with Aristobulus. Later, when Aristobulus and Hyrcanus were pleading their case with Pompey, it is obvious that Scaurus did not speak up for Aristobulus; if he had, Aristobulus would have had no evident reason to besmirch him by revealing his graft to Pompey. From Aristobulus' perspective, then, Scaurus had committed treachery of the most contemptible sort. If it is a bad thing to be bought, it is twice as bad not to stay bought. It would be understandable if Aristobulus and his supporters considered Scaurus the principal cause of their subsequent disasters. If he had kept faith, Pompey might well have decided in favor of Aristobulus and the sequel been avoided.

Perspective is everything in historiography, of course, guiding the selection of names and events that should be mentioned. In the case of the fall of the temple in 63 B.C.E., there is quite possibly an example that parallels the highlighting of Aemilius Scaurus' role by one source in the face of complete silence about it in another. In 54 B.C.E. Aulus Plautius, *curule aedile* in that year, minted a coin on which an otherwise unknown Bacchius Judaeus strikes a suppliant pose.[21] The coin is most easily explained as commemorative of Pompey's Judaean campaign; the time lag of nine years is not problematic for Roman numismatics.[22] Bacchius was an otherwise unrecorded leader in the Jewish revolt, more prominent in the actual warfare than was the imprisoned Aristobulus. He probably led the forces within the temple. Here then is a man who was perhaps the most important Jewish leader of the war from the perspective of the Roman leadership, yet he did not merit even a mention in Josephus' accounts. That fact is a salutary reminder that we really know very little about the detailed course of these events.

If it is correct to see fragment D 2 in connection with the fall of the temple, then a most significant corollary follows: we can now be quite certain of the season when the fall occurred. The date of the fall of the temple to Pompey has long been open to question. When Josephus penned *War*, he knew no exact date for the fall. He noted merely that it was in the third month of the siege.[23] Writing *Antiquities* years later, he had done additional research on the

---

[21] The reverse side of the coin shows a bearded figure in eastern dress, kneeling with a camel at his side. He extends his right hand offering an olive branch. The inscription on the exergue reads BACCHIVS, while the right side reads IVDAEVS. See GRUEBER, H. A. 1910. *The Coins of the Roman Republic in the British Museum* 1:490, nos. 3916–3919. British Museum. London, and SYDENHAM, A. E. 1952. *The Coinage of the Roman Republic*: 156 no. 932. Spink & Son. London. SCHALIT, A. 1969. *König Herodes, der Mann und sein Werk*: 9 n. 29. Walter de Gruyter. Berlin, suggests that Bacchius was a trouble-maker in the Lebanon who was put down by Pompey along with other local chieftains. SMALLWOOD, E. MARY. 1981. *The Jews Under Roman Rule*: 26 n. 16. Brill. Leiden, argues the position adopted here.

[22] It may be significant that the reverse of the Plautius coin is adapted from that of Aemilius Scaurus.

[23] *War* 1.149.

question, having read Strabo and other historians. He was now able to specify that the temple fell "in the third month [of the seige], on the Fast Day (τῆς νηστείας ἡμέρᾳ), in the hundred and seventy-ninth Olympiad, in the consulship of Gaius Antonius and Marcus Tullius Cicero."[24] The 179th Olympiad stretched from 64–60 B.C.E.; the consulship of Antonius and Cicero was in 63 B.C.E. Therefore the temple fell sometime in 63 B.C.E., but there scholarly agreement ceases.

The first problem is Josephus' mention of "the Fast Day." In Jewish usage of the time, that expression (Hebrew צום יום) can only refer to Yom Kippur, the tenth day of the seventh month, Tishri.[25] This date would approximate to the last few days of September or the beginning of October. But modern scholarship does not take seriously Josephus' assignment of the fall to the Day of Atonement. It is considered an error, for which two explanations have been offered. Possibly he may have assimilated the date of the fall in 63 B.C.E. to that of the fall of Jerusalem to Herod in 37 B.C.E.; for the latter there exists a good explanation of an autumn dating.[26] The Jewish tendency to assimilate traditions in this way is well illustrated by the designation of 9 Ab as a day of mourning. Fully five disasters were said to have occurred on this one day. Perhaps then this is the explanation of Josephus' date. More frequently, however, scholars embrace a suggestion first made by Herzfeld,[27] who proposed that Josephus' blunder arose because he found recorded in his pagan sources that the conquest took place on a fast-day. As was natural for a Jew, Josephus supposed the phrase to refer to the Day of Atonement. In fact, however, the phrase designated a sabbath. Gentile authors often mistakenly believed the sabbath was a day of fasting.[28] Most particularly Strabo—whose narrative of the events Josephus refers to here explicitly[29]—says the final assault occurred "on the day of fasting, when the Jews abstain from all labor" (τὴν τῆς νηστείας ἡμέραν, ἡνίκα ἀπείχοντο οἱ Ἰουδαῖοι παντὸς ἔργου).[30]

Once Josephus' reference to the Day of Atonement is dismissed, the fall of the temple is no longer tied to the seventh month. It could have happened on any sabbath in any month for which there is otherwise some evidence. Modern scholarship divides at this point, some saying Pompey took the temple in the early summer, others preferring the fall. The basis for the division is how one assesses the time frame of the events between Pompey's start for Judaea and the conquest of the city. Schürer, for example, regards this

[24] *Ant.* 14.66.
[25] Note especially 1QpHab X1 6–8 and mMen 11:9.
[26] KROMAYER, J. 1894. "Forschungen zur Geschichte des II. Triumvirats." *Hermes* **29**: 569–70 n. 3.
[27] HERZFELD, L. 1855. "Wissenschaftliche Aufsätze." *MGWJ* **4**: 109–115.
[28] *E.g.*, Justinus, *Epit.* 36.2.14; Suet., *Aug.* 76.2; Mart. 4.4. 7.
[29] *Ant.* 14.68.
[30] Strabo 16.2.40.

sequence of events as "long," and says that it "cannot have happened within the space of a few months."[31] He therefore dates Pompey's triumph to the late autumn. Other scholars argue that the siege began shortly after Pompey received news of Mithridates' death, which occurred early in 63 B.C.E.[32] Since the siege lasted into the third month but was over before the fourth month began, according to this view the date of the fall was late June or early July.[33]

The Qumran text would appear to vindicate the position that argues for an autumnal dating. D 2:5 specifically refers to the seventh month, and line 6 to the course גמול. It is therefore likely that the events of lines 5–6 took place during the week when גמול was in service, and that in this particular year, that week occurred in the seventh month. According to the six-year system represented by some of the Qumran *mishmarot* texts, גמול would serve in the seventh month only once in any six year span. That would occur in the sixth year of the cycle, when the course would rotate into service on 7/11 and rotate out of service on 7/18, the "eighth day."[34] It is equally important to notice that Jehezkel, mentioned in line 3, would serve from 6/28 to 7/3 in the sixth year. Thus, if it is right to see the two instances of הרג אמליוס as involved with the fall of the temple, the following scenario results: some time in the week during which Jehezkel served, Aemilius was guilty of the first instance of killing. Perhaps that was the actual fall of the temple. Between eight and fourteen days later he was guilty of the second instance. This would be a reasonable time to allow for the identification, trial and execution of Jewish leaders such as Bacchius. In the sixth year, the sabbaths of the two priestly rotations here relevant would have occurred on 7/3 and 7/17. Each is only a week from the Day of Atonement, 7/10. Nevertheless, neither גמול nor יחזקאל ever served on a Day of Atonement at any time in the six-year cycle. Thus the text implies a date very near the Day of Atonement, but rules out the possibility that Josephus could be correct in assigning the fall to that day.[35]

A date within a week of the Day of Atonement only results, of course,

[31] SCHÜRER I: 239–240, n. 23. Agreeing with a date in the late fall is SCHÄFER, P. 1977. "The Hellenistic and Maccabean Periods." In *Israelite and Judaean History*. J. H. HAYES and J. M. MILLER, Eds: 604. SCM. London.
[32] *Ant.* 14.53.
[33] Thus SMALLWOOD, *Jews Under Roman Rule*, 565–566; R. Marcus, note *ad loc. Ant.* 14.66.
[34] *Cf.* 11QTemple 45:5. The "eighth day" was counted in terms of the old course. Thus the first day on which any course served was a Sunday and the last day was the following Sabbath. It rotated out on the second Sunday.
[35] If the fall happened only a week in either direction from that day, of course, the tendency to assimilation referred to above might well have resulted in a Jewish tradition, which became known to Josephus between *War* and *Antiquities*, in which Pompey did profane not merely the temple, but the holiest day of the year. After all, it is only a conjecture (even if a very persuasive one) that Josephus attached the fall to the Day of Atonement because of Strabo's phrase τὴν τῆς νηστείας ἡμέραν.

if one follows the solar calendar of 364 days that structures the *mishmarot* texts. The lunisolar calendar of 354 days with periodic intercalation of a month would lose ten days a year to the solar calendar until it drew even by intercalation. Every three years a month would be intercalated to synchronize the lunisolar calendar with the progression of the seasons. That, at any rate, is the way the author of 1 Enoch 74:10–16 schematized the relations between the two systems.[36] Leaving aside the vexed problem of intercalation of the solar calendar, when the seventh month of that calendar began in Year Six, the lunisolar calendar would have advanced over it by twenty-five days. A week into Tishri by the solar calendar would mean the lunisolar calendar had already entered the eighth month, Marheshvan. In terms of the solar calendar, Pompey took the temple in late September or early October 63 B.C.E.; in terms of the lunisolar calendar, the fall would equate to late October or early November of that year. Regardless of which system of dating is employed, if the Qumran text does describe the involvement of Aemilius with Pompey's conquest of the temple, then that event must now be dated to the autumn.

CONCLUSIONS

I have suggested in the foregoing analysis that the Qumran calendar refers to events involving the rebellion of Hyrcanus against Aristobulus in late 66 B.C.E.[37] and the fall of the temple to Pompey and his leading generals, especially M. Aemilius Scaurus, in the fall of 63 B.C.E. The Qumran text apparently provides new details about both situations.

What about the general character and *Tendenz* of the work? I noted above that the text was possibly a catalogue of events of the Hasmonean period. Notable is the apparent focus on national figures, not sectarian ones. Still, the work seems to represent the interests of a particular party within the political spectrum of that period. This party favored Aristobulus against Hyrcanus II in the civil war of the 60s B.C.E. They suffered, so it seems, at the hands of M. Aemilius Scaurus, and therefore focused on him rather than on Pompey

---

[36] The description is confused, however, and fails to deal with certain problems that would arise over the course of many years. The question that must be asked, however, is whether the description nevertheless represents the actual state of Jewish knowledge in the first century B.C.E. or so. The Tannaitic system, for example, lags well behind the predictive schemes of some pagan contemporaries. On the Enoch passage see NEUGEBAUER, O. 1985. "The 'Astronomical' Chapters of the Ethiopic Book of Enoch (72 to 82)." Appendix A in M. BLACK, *The Book of Enoch or 1 Enoch*: 398–401. Brill. Leiden.

[37] According to Josephus, *Ant.* 15.180, Hyrcanus ruled only three months after the death of his mother. Thereupon Aristobulus took power and ruled for three and one-half years. If the restorations of fragment A 2 above are correct, the Qumran chronicle may provide new details on the events of the year when power changed hands. It suggests that Hyrcanus rebelled sometime between 10/25–11/1 of Year Three, *i.e.*, of 66 B.C.E. That date approximates to 11/22–11/28 in the lunisolar calendar. Thus Aristobulus ruled at least ten or eleven months before Hyrcanus rebelled.

when recalling the fall of the temple and the defeat of Aristobulus' faction. Who was this faction?

Josephus locates Aristobulus' power base in two sectors of society: among powerful aristocrats, and among the priesthood. Presumably, then, the authors of our text arose from one of those groups or an amalgamation of them. These groups were essentially the same ones that had supported Alexander Jannaeus in the civil war of his reign.[38] While Alexandra ruled they were out of power. With Aristobulus at their head, they made a renewed bid for power when the queen died. Their opponents included the Pharisees. In Josephus the politics of this period focus on the Pharisees and are unusually clear: the Pharisees were out of power under Jannaeus, they came to full power under Alexandra, and they were the basis of support for Hyrcanus II.[39] During all this period they were opposed by certain of the Jerusalem élite and elements of the priesthood. I suggest, then, that it was from the ranks of these Pharisaic opponents that this Qumran calendar emerged.

Such would not be surprising in view of two considerations. First, a prayer on behalf of Alexander Jannaeus has now been identified among the Cave Four materials.[40] Clearly, its author and those who preserved the prayer favored Alexander. And second, the Qumran *pesharim* are uniformly critical of the Pharisees.[41] These authors opposed the Pharisees and, it now seems evident, supported those whom the Pharisees opposed.

These points belie what has become a commonplace in Qumran studies, namely the assertion that those who cached the scrolls opposed the Hasmonean dynasty. Matters are more complicated. In fact, the readers of these texts did not oppose all the Hasmoneans. They apparently opposed only those who countenanced Pharisaic domination of the Jerusalem power structures. Less certainly, one might argue that they opposed Hasmoneans who allied themselves with Rome or were insufficiently "nationalist."[42] Further, this Qumran calendar suggests that its authors were very much involved with national politics down to the time of Pompey's victory, if not later. It may be, therefore, that scholars ought once again to consider Dupont-Sommer's proposal identifying the "Wicked Priest" with Hyrcanus II.[43]

[38] Cf. War 1.114, Ant. 13.411 and Ant. 13.417.

[39] For a perceptive analysis of the question, "When were the Pharisees *really* in power?", note SANDERS, E. P. 1992. *Judaism: Practice and Belief, 63BCE–66CE*: 380–412. SCM. London.

[40] 4Q448. For a preliminary edition, with a few misreadings, see ESHEL, E., H. ESHEL and A. YARDENI. 1992. "A Scroll from Qumran Which Includes Part of Psalm 154 and a Prayer for King Jonathan and His Kingdom." *Tarbiz* 60: 296–324 (Heb.).

[41] Presuming, of course, that the "Seekers after Smooth Things" of those texts are correctly identified as "the Pharisees" or an important group within the pharisaic movement.

[42] One notes in this regard the absence of 1 Maccabees from the Qumran writings. Perhaps this absence is purely fortuitous, but recall that the hero of that book, Judas Maccabaeus, made a treaty with Rome (chapter 13).

[43] A. DUPONT-SOMMER, A. 1973. *The Essene Writings from Qumran*, trans. G. VERMES: 351–357. Peter Smith. Gloucester, MA.

Of course, these are narrower questions. Both here and in the broader framework of Second Temple Jewish history the Qumran calendar has a contribution to make. True, this text is not straightforward historiography; it is not, for example, a chronicle. A chronicle is interested in chronology: in sequence, in years, in eras. This text does not view time that way. It is a calendar, interested in the eternal cycles of time. Nevertheless, many of its entries presuppose one or more chronicles or the equivalent. The situation is illustrated by some modern calendars. These calendars note that February 12 is Lincoln's birthday and June 6 is D-Day. Such modern calendars presuppose a knowledge of historical personages and events. This Qumran work is analogous. Thus, while it is no annal, the designation "annalistic calendar" seems appropriate.

The work cites actual names and refers to the actions of people well known to us from other sources. Because it is so fragmentary, its contributions to historical understanding will necessarily be limited. Nevertheless, one recalls Cicero: *primo annales fuere, post historiae factae sunt.*[44] Chronicles must precede history. Not all historians will agree with Cicero's order, or even his distinctions, but none would dispute the connection of chronicle and history. To the bare facts of a chronicle's year-by-year recounting of events, a writer of history may add explanation—a particular perspective on the events. The Qumran text does not write history, but it does go beyond mere chronicling; it does add perspective. For that reason, and because—unlike the *pesharim*—it avoids encrypted references, this annalistic calendar is the nearest thing to historiography yet to emerge from the DSS. Its tantalizing remains render all the more tragic the loss of the whole work. One is reminded that, like the apostle Paul, the ancient historian must learn to be content, whether with much or, as here, with little.

~~~~~~

DISCUSSION OF THE PAPER

MOSHE BERNSTEIN (*Yeshiva University, New York*): As always, Michael, the philology stands out, something which we've heard in the past. It is always a pleasure to hear. That first line is tantalizing: you take it to mean "to give him honor among the Nabataeans." Do you believe that would be some kind of historical remark about some person whom we don't know?

MICHAEL WISE (*University of Chicago, Chicago, IL*): Yes, Moshe. I think this line may have to do with the fact that Hyrcanus II fled to the Nabataeans

[44] *De or.* 2.12.

and there found himself an ally. Of course, Antipater was very much involved in all of those events. These things may be interwoven, and it may even be possible then to give a date for the year.

BERNSTEIN: The expression *lehaqbil* and, you suggest, -'*et pene*—is this the first occurrence of this idiom?

WISE: In Qumran, you mean?

BERNSTEIN: In pre-Rabbinic literature.

WISE: That may well be.

BERNSTEIN: I know that you find the expression in Rabbinic literature. You're suggesting here that I have an earlier use of it. There's nothing wrong with that. You're suggesting an earlier attestation of the idiom than we've ever had before.

WISE: Yes.

BERNSTEIN: Finally, just a thought: although it's a very, very different kind of calendar, there is one other sort of document of this sort that in a very vague way resembles the annalistic aspect of this text. It is, of course, that very early Rabbinic document *Megillat Taanit*. It is somewhat unlike this text, but it does have a very loose similarity, in terms of recording days which were of import to the members of a particular religio-political group.

WISE: That's exactly right, Moshe. In fact, Milik in his first discussion of these portions drew that analogy also. I think it's a worthwhile analogy as far as it goes, but the difference is we don't know exactly what the people did about the events described in this calendar. Were they all celebrated or mourned? Clearly, some of them were celebrated because they're mixed in with festivals.

PHILLIP R. CALLAWAY (*Jonesboro, GA*): Mike, I think you are moving us in a good direction, but I wanted to ask something about something you said toward the end of your presentation. You said the group, or the person, that composed this annalistic calendar probably favored Alexander Jannaeus, is that correct?

WISE: No, Aristobulus.

CALLAWAY: Aristobulus, okay. How do you fit Jannaeus into this?

WISE: As I read Josephus for this period I see a correspondence between the power bases of Alexander Jannaeus and Aristobulus his son, just as there was a correspondence between the power bases of Alexandra Shelamzion and Hyrcanus II, Aristobulus' opponent at the time of the Civil War. The politics of this period, it seems to me, are breaking down along similar lines for several generations.

CALLAWAY: But you mentioned this document from Cave 4 which is a prayer on behalf of Alexander Jannaeus. I understand you were trying to say it's related in some way to the person that composed the calendar. Did I misunderstand?

WISE: The suggestion I am making is that this calendar is to be seen as favoring Aristobulus and his faction, and as upset with Scaurus. That is consistent with a poem favoring Jannaeus. The same groups were benefited by Jannaeus as were benefited by Aristobulus, and the opposite side of the coin also: the opponents of both Alexander and of Aristobulus were derived from the same sectors of society, and included primarily the Pharisees.

CALLAWAY: I just wanted a clarification because Josephus tells us that Jannaeus was a mighty murderer, killing roughly 50,000 of his own people, killing his own brother. I just wonder what kind of people we have associated with the Dead Sea Scrolls.

WISE: These were people who were happy to see those 50,000 die. That's the point I'm making, in a sense. Perspective is everything in historiography, and Josephus writes from an anti-Jannaeus perspective, apparently because he's largely following Nicolaus, Herod's historian. That's an interesting point you raise—we have no pro-Jannaeus literature. What would it look like if we did have it? It's clear that there were two sides to all of these issues, but we've only heard one generally from Josephus.

Methodology, the Scrolls, and Origins

PHILLIP R. CALLAWAY

949 O'Hara Court
Jonesboro, Georgia 30236

≈ I ≈

On this final day of the Scrolls conference we have dared to speculate on the origins of texts and, as an extension of that discussion, we hope to determine the identity of their authors-owners. Views have been advanced for Sadducean, Essene, Christian, and other origins. Because of this embarrassing array of conflicting viewpoints, for roughly a decade, I have been convinced that how we use our sources of information should ultimately supersede our desire to support any particular hypothesis. In this, I trust, we are in agreement.

I continue to believe that the historian's task is not simply to collect, arrange, and interpret "relevant" historical reports. First, we must make decisions about the intention, character, trustworthiness, significance, and usefulness of each document or portion of a document. This applies especially to fragmentary, theological writings. Too often, I contend, we fail to scrutinize the great variety of ancient sources at our disposal. The typical approach represents—in one form or another—nothing less than decorating the narrative frameworks of 1–2 Maccabees, Josephus, the New Testament, and the Rabbinic writings. To this extent, scholars admit the difficulty of understanding the Scrolls.

Six years ago, when I wrote my analysis of methodology in reconstructing Qumran history, I expressed my deep concern that the editors of 4QMMT were claiming that the author of this "letter" was none other than the Teacher of Righteousness and the intended recipient was the Wicked Priest known from a very small group of Dead Sea Scrolls. I observed at that time:

> According to their [the editors] preliminary indications ". . . there is not a shred of evidence in this document for the specific identities of the writer and the addressee of 4QMMT. It is claims such as these, which seem to persist largely unquestioned, that constitute the *raison d'être* for this investigation."[1]

---

[1] CALLAWAY, P. R. 1988. "The History of the Qumran Community. An Investigation." Sheffield: Sheffield Academic Press. *JSPSS* 3: 8.

Thus I conclude that my caveat has gone unheeded and must mention it again for the sake of the present dialogue. We still may not pretend to know the precise identity of the author of 4QMMT, and it is debatable whether we can assign it to one known Jewish group or another.

I would like to reiterate some of my observations in *The History* that I consider to be still valid and helpful for discussing the larger historical and religious context of the Scrolls. Then I shall respond directly to the views expressed at this conference. Finally, I shall offer some suggestions about where the evidence of the Scrolls and other relevant bodies of information might lead us in the future.

≈ II ≈

The following statements about the relationship between different kinds of evidence still seem to be correct.

Qumran and the caves share the same Hellenistic-Roman material culture. So-called Qumran ceramic wares are known from several non-Qumran locations for the period 31–4 B.C.E., a period when the site was presumably not occupied: Jewish Citadel C, Sam Rom Ia, Sam Vlt C2, Jer T. Val, and Bethany C 61. Herodian forms of lamps, plates, juglets, bowls, and jars were also present.[2] Cylinder jars found in the caves are known only from a tomb in the upper Transjordan at Quailba near Abila.[3] The material culture known from 'Ain Feshka and 'Ain el-Ghuweir is consistent with that at Qumran and in the caves.

P. Bar-Adon's dating of the ceramic data between 200 B.C.E. and 70 C.E., and even into the time of the Bar Kokhba revolt seems to be more acceptable than R. de Vaux and P. W. Lapp's pre-31/post-31 B.C.E. (earthquake-induced) chronological schematization.[4] R. Smith's dating of Herodian lamps from 37 B.C.E. to 135 C.E. suits better the broader periodization.[5]

The coins found at Qumran range from the reign of Antiochus III (223 B.C.E.) to the second year of the First Revolt (68 C.E.).[6] Other coins associated with stratum III, designated as a Roman occupation, date from 65 to 133 C.E.[7]

Coins found in Qumran strata I–II represent Seleucid, Jewish, and Roman

---

[2] *Ibid.*, 48.
[3] *Ibid.*, 42.
[4] *Ibid.*, 48.
[5] *Ibid.* Dr. Donceel-Voûte's contribution on the artifactual remains from Qumran urges us to explore the relationship between Qumran and its larger physical and social environment.
[6] *Ibid.*, 34–43, 46–51.
[7] *Ibid.*, 41.

mintings. These coins can certainly be traced to Tyrian, Antiochian, Caesarean, Doran, and Judaean mints. Stratum III is represented by Antiochian, Ashkelonian, and Judaean mintings.

Some Tentative Conclusions

Qumran wares were never restricted locally to Qumran alone; such forms have been found elsewhere to the north, south, east, and west. The coins also witness a broad range of mintages from the time of Antiochus III to the Second Jewish Revolt against the Romans, and this is consistent with a more flexible dating of the latest ceramic types. De Vaux's postulation of a Roman occupation of Qumran after 68 C.E. remains solidly postulated but starkly unsubstantiated. Viewed against this broader chronological range, the variety among the Scrolls makes sense. This is neither an attempt to date the origin of the Qumran community as early as the time of Antiochus III nor as late as the Bar Kokhba Revolt (or even later). It is simply a more accurate picture of the material remains.

Some scholars have used palaeography to put reconstruction of the history of the Qumran community on a scientific-quantitative basis. In general, these studies are helpful, but in terms of specific datings of individual scripts they are unsound. Almost all Qumran scholars appeal to the pioneering article written by F. M. Cross, Jr. from 1961, never inquiring into the methodological soundness of his hypothetical design.[8] Furthermore, in each case where Cross assigns dates within a certain range of years, this is a very rough approximation, perhaps nothing less than a surmise.

If my claim about Cross's hypothesis is correct, his guesswork has been compounded an untold number of times and quite simply been given an authoritative status that should have been questioned from the start. Recently, R. Eisenman and B. Thiering have accurately pinpointed several fundamental difficulties in his typology and datings.[9] The unpopularity of their versions of the history of the Qumran community among representatives of the so-called scholarly consensus has clearly detracted from discussing seriously their views on palaeography.

The following examples of allegiance to Cross's dating of Hebrew hands from the Qumran caves should illustrate the problem sufficiently. C. Newsom writes: "The hands of the Sabbath Shirot are analyzed according to the typol-

---

[8] CROSS, F. M., JR. 1961. "The Development of the Jewish Scripts." In *The Bible and the Ancient Near East*. G. ERNEST WRIGHT, Ed. :122–202. London: Routledge and Kegan Paul.

[9] EISENMAN, R. 1983. *Maccabees, Zadokites, Christians and Qumran*. Leiden. Brill :24, 32–34. THIERING, B. 1981. "Redating the Teacher of Righteousness. Theological Explorations." Sydney. *ANZSTR*: 39–45.

ogy established by F. M. Cross. . . ."[10] 4Q400 is a late Hasmonean formal hand, "earlier than the script of 4QSam^a (*ca.* 50–25 B.C.)."[11] 4Q401 "closely resembles the formal hand of 4Q400, though 4Q401 exhibits more semi-formal traits and is to be dated somewhat later than 4Q400, at the beginning of the Herodian sequence (*ca.* 25 B.C.)."[12] 11QShirShab is written in a developed Herodian formal hand with strong semiformal traits (*ca.* 20–50 A.D.).[13] MasadaShirShabb is written in a late Herodian formal hand (*ca.* 50 A.D.).[14] Masada's destruction in 73 C.E. forms the *terminus ad quem* for dating this hand.[15] As mentioned before, she originally went awry by holding to the dated typology of Cross, for even if his typology is correct (which is debatable), his datings are overly schematic. Thus, those that follow him are destined to falter as well. First, Newsom dates one manuscript within a twenty-five year range, then another to a specific year, then another to a thirty-year time-span, another to a specific year. Her use of the abbreviation *ca.* means nothing more or less than "I do not really know." Her dating of the Masada manuscript is correct based on archaeological grounds alone. But 73 C.E. is not the latest year that the script of the Masada manuscript could have been used by a Jewish scribe—unless it were a unique style that died with the inhabitants of Masada.

In her study of 4Q381, E. Schuller says: "The hand would seem to belong to 4QDeut^c and 4QSam^a (*cf.* Cross, figure 2, lines 2 and 3, p. 138), and can be dated to approximately 75 B.C."[16]

J. T. Milik's assessment of the hands of 4QEnoch appeals to Cross but is essentially vaguer than the former. The hand of 4QEn^a is

> quite archaic and is connected with the semi-cursive scripts ("semiformal") of the third and second centuries B.C. . . . However, it does not fit very well into the scribal traditions of the Jewish copyists of Judaea or even Egypt; the scribe would perhaps be dependent upon the Aramean scripts and the scribal customs of Northern Syria or Mesopotamia.[17]

Nevertheless, he cites Cross in the note, and goes on to say that 4QEn^a "is perhaps a school exercise, copied by a young scribe from the master's dictation."[18] With regard to 4QEn^b Milik's assessment is equally interesting: "The

[10] NEWSOM, C. A. 1985. *The Songs of the Sabbath Sacrifice: Edition, Translation and Commentary.* Atlanta, GA: Scholars Press :86.
[11] *Ibid.*
[12] *Ibid.*, 126.
[13] *Ibid.*, 363.
[14] *Ibid.*, 168.
[15] *Ibid.*
[16] SCHULLER, E. M. 1987. *Non-Canonical Psalms from Qumran: A Pseudepigraphic Collection.* Atlanta, GA: Scholars Press :65.
[17] MILIK, J. T. 1976. *The Books of Enoch: Aramaic Fragments of Qumran Cave 4.* Oxford: Clarendon Press :140.
[18] *Ibid.*, 141.

writing of En^b is rather archaic, probably dating from the early Hasmonean period . . ." and goes back to the first half of the second century, "perhaps exactly to the middle of the century."[19] He then says that this scribe was rather careless. 4QEn^c, he maintains, was copied by a professional and skilled scribe dating at least from the last third of the first century B.C.E.[20] This scribe had a "tendency to use the 'broken' form of the letters, a feature which recalls the North Syrian Aramaic alphabets, notably Palmyrene."[21] Milik dates the hand of 4QEn^g around 50 B.C.E., while Cross puts it within the years 50–1 B.C.E.[22] It is informative that Milik's palaeographical analyses usually refer to thirds and halves of a century. Much more instructive is his willingness to comment on skilled and unskilled hands, associating the most skilled hands with a northern Syrian-Palmyrene scribal tradition. Chronologically, therefore, his palaeographical analysis is probably no sounder than Cross's, but if he is correct about the Syrian scribal tradition then he has discovered a historical-scribal thread connecting Palmyra (or Damascus), Qumran, and Masada.

I do not have an alternative palaeographical analysis to offer, but it is obvious that Cross and Milik, two of our foremost palaeographers are grasping at chronological straws. They have no concrete idea of how rapidly Jewish scripts develop. (Nor do younger scholars.) Their periodization is artificial, based on how they thought Jews wrote in the pre-Hasmonean (Zadokite), Hasmonean, and Herodian periods. They are unable to take into consideration certain unknown factors such as age, skill, and goal in copying. The late Herodian hand is an embarrassment to any Qumran palaeographer who believes that this particular writing style went out of vogue with the destruction of Qumran and Masada. The Copper Scroll remains a palaeographical, archaeological, and historical oddity that is difficult to place in the available chronologies. I hope in a later study to discuss the palaeographical dating of the late Herodian hand at Qumran and the Copper Scroll.

The paper on dating the scrolls by carbon-14 and accelerated mass spectrometry presented at our conference was clearly written to vindicate the findings of the palaeographers of the Scrolls. The discussion after the presentation of this study predictably fell into two camps—defenders and detractors. After reading this paper, I feel compelled to make some observations about it. First of all, it is not properly documented with footnotes. Second, it is apparent that the palaeographical views of Cross are being vindicated, but this is not clearly noted. Third, C-14 in conjunction with AMS shows that the palaeographers were working in the proper historical period but that has not

[19] *Ibid.*, 164.
[20] *Ibid.*, 178.
[21] *Ibid.*
[22] *Ibid.*, 246.

been questioned recently (as far as I know). Fourth, Cross and his followers have attempted to do something much more precise than the practitioners of C-14/AMS analysis claimed to have done. According to the presentation, the latter group works within a rough range of a century, stipulating to a probability of approximately 68%. The palaeographers talk about quarter-centuries or so. In historical reconstruction missing by a year, a decade, or even by seventy-five years means quite a lot. Fifth, in cases where the C-14/AMS-dating did not clearly confirm palaeography, the evidence was characterized as tainted. Sixth, the chief problem of this study is that its sample was extremely small in comparison with the number of documents already published and much smaller when viewed in light of the great number of still unpublished texts. Neither palaeography nor C-14/AMS analysis is illegitimate when applied to the Scrolls, but one must know the interpretive limits of each approach. As it stands, C-14/AMS analysis functions as a pesher on the palaeographical analysis. In the same way, the language of this pesher, like the Qumran pesharim, is much vaguer than the source it claims to clarify.

In order to understand the Scrolls, the central issue for all of us is to place them in the proper historical context. Archaeology and palaeography point unmistakably to the late Hellenistic and Roman periods. I believe the initial disassociation of the caves and Qumran would have guided us into a more accurate and profitable historical discussion, for in that case we could have imagined more easily that the writings found in the caves were indeed brought there by persons arriving from many places—Jerusalem, the villages of Judaea, Samaria, and Syria (perhaps Damascus or Palmyra[23]). Once R. de Vaux did connect the site Qumran and the caves, scholarship began its quest to understand the isolated sectarian Qumran community that presumably had little intercourse with the outside world over a period of roughly two hundred years.

We have almost totally ignored the notion of human mobility in our discussions of the Scrolls, their authors, and their owners. One need only to think of the discovery of the Songs of the Sabbath Sacrifice and Ben Sira found at Qumran and Masada or the Damascus Document at Qumran and Cairo. For a broader picture one should only recall the mobility of Jewish leaders in 1–2 Maccabees, Josephus, of Jesus in the Gospels, and of Paul in Luke–Acts and his letters.

The Scrolls never argue for isolation. One should not mistake the apparent "monasticism" of 1QS for practical renunciation of the world and immobility down at the shores of the Dead Sea. The laws of the Damascus Document testify to "marrying" Jews, who were affiliated in some way with the group reflected in 1QS. One would expect mobility between Qumran and the various "marrying" camps throughout the countryside. This most certainly

---

[23] Prof. Dexinger's contribution to this volume encourages us to investigate possible relationships between the Samaritans and the Scrolls.

would have included messengers delivering halakhic instructions and important theological treatises.

Too often we have allowed Pliny's report about the solitary tribe of the Essenes to lure us into a mysticalization of Qumran. Few have reflected on the true value of his brief words for understanding the Scrolls. He claimed these Essenes had no women, but this is contradicted by female graves and the stance of 1QSa. He claimed they had no money, but the hoards of coins discovered on the site discount that. He claimed that the site received throngs of refugees daily whose misfortunes had tired them of living.[24] What Pliny meant by a "throng" can hardly be known. However, the inhabitants of Qumran and the neighboring settlements were never large in number. Eleven hundred graves over a period of two hundred years would average to roughly eight deaths per year, even if one starts the calculation after a lifetime of about sixty years. If two or three persons per day had sought the seclusion of Qumran over a period of two hundred years, the entire area surrounding the site would have been transformed into a graveyard for members of the sect. As we know that is not the case.

Before leaving Pliny two further points must be stated briefly. Pliny's report may accurately locate a community of Essenes in the area we now call Qumran, but he knows nothing about the structure and theology of that particular group. Furthermore, although it has been suggested that he has perhaps integrated an earlier source into his narrative, he would seem to be describing a settlement of Essenes that survived the First Jewish Revolt.[25] According to the prevailing hypothesis, the Essenes abandoned this settlement after the Romans destroyed it in 68 C.E.

The Alexandrian Jew, Philo, wrote reports about the Essenes that have often been used in discussions about the Qumran-Essenes.[26] His encomia on the Essenes were not designed to locate a particular Jewish party geographically, but rather to prove in acceptable ethnological fashion that great wisdom is not only to be found in Greece, Persia, and India, but even among the inhabitants of Palestinian Syria.[27] When he does finally describe an Essene worship-service, it looks typically Jewish and tells us nothing specifically about Essenism (*Quod* 80–82).

At the beginning of the twentieth century, and especially since the discovery of the Scrolls, scholars have basically accepted the credibility of Josephus' statements about the Essenes.[28] This is of course because of his information on the initiation procedures of the Essenes. When I wrote *The History*,

[24] *Naturalis historia* 5.17.4.
[25] VANDERKAM, JAMES C. 1992. "The People of the Dead Sea Scrolls: Essenes or Sadducees?" In *Understanding the Dead Sea Scrolls*. H. SHANKS, Ed. :5. New York: Random House.
[26] CALLAWAY, P. R. History, 65–73.
[27] Ibid., 68.
[28] Ibid., 64.

I also thought him to be our only real eyewitness to Judaean Essenes. Further study of Josephus has caused me to criticize my own initial gullibility.

In *War* 2.8.2. Josephus writes that the Essenes guard against the lascivious behavior of women and believe that none of them is faithful to a single man. I remind you that 1QSa, 1QM, 11QT, the Damascus Document, and other writings speak of the presence of women and children. He also claims that the novice received a small hatch, a girdle, and a white garment upon initiation, but no scroll makes reference to this. Of the Sadducees, Pharisees, and Essenes, only the latter group does he designate as Jews by birth. This statement conflicts with references in some of the Scrolls to proselytes (CD XIV, 3–6; 11QT LXIII, 13–14).

A much more serious problem with Josephus is his claim that the Essenes differ from other Jews in resting from all kinds of work on the sabbath (*War* 9.147–49). This behavior was in no way peculiar to the Essenes. It becomes clear that Josephus is not immune to Philo's idealism when he claims that many Essenes lived to be older than one hundred (*War* 10.150).

One of his most ludicrous claims is to have studied with the Pharisees, Sadducees, Essenes, and an ascetic named Bannus from his sixteenth to nineteenth birthday, when he suddenly decided to become a Pharisee (*Life* 12). Yet if this were true, it would easily explain why he actually knows so little about the writings and theological concerns of the Essenes.

Josephus prides himself on knowing Jewish law quite well, which he likewise admired in the Essenes and the Pharisees. If one compares his statements about Pharisees and Essenes in the *War* and the *Antiquities*, these two groups begin to look remarkably similar. In *War* 2.8.14 (*cf. Life* 38), he characterizes the Pharisees as the most exact interpreters of the laws and says that they attribute fate to God. This sounds like the Essenes in *Antiquities* 13.5.9.

In the *Antiquities*, Josephus attributes political indifference to the Essenes. I believe this is his tendency to minimize the role of Jewish nationalism for his Roman audience and to consistently present the Essenes as a Hellenistic school of philosophical thought (perhaps the Pythagorians or Stoics, although Josephus compares the Pharisees with Stoics in *Life* 2).

In *War* 2.20.2 he mentions a certain John the Essene who was given charge over the Jewish troops in Thamna, Lydda, Joppa, and Emmaus in the First Revolt against the Romans. This testimony casts doubt on Josephus' characterization of the Essenes as politically passive in *Antiquities* 18.1.18. For those who insist on using Josephus as a credible witness to the ancient Essenes (in spite of my judicious warnings), let me remind you that he also wrote that the Essenes had no particular city [of their own], but dwelled in every city. Taken together with his anecdote about Judas the Essene at the Jerusalem temple, we should wonder why Josephus had no knowledge of a Qumran-Essene community and why he had Judas predicting the death of Antigonus at the polluted temple in Jerusalem.

Now that the credibility and relevance of Pliny, Philo, and Josephus have been scrutinized and called into question with regard to the Essenes, we must turn to the Scrolls themselves in order to talk about "origins."

≈ III ≈

In contrast to my approach in *The History*, where I restricted my analysis to documentation that had any potential relevance to the history of the "Qumran" community, I now believe that any account of the origins of the Scrolls must survey the Scrolls as a whole. The failure to publish them expeditiously has handicapped all our attempts to do that.

In 1986 I included only the Damascus Document, 1QpHab, 4QpPs 37, 4QTest, and 1QH, but quickly eliminated the last two writings as unhelpful for the historical reconstruction.[29] I viewed 4QTest as an eschatological document that had nothing to do with "Qumran" history *per se*. This remains my opinion, even after reading Cross's *tour de force* based on this work and 1 Maccabees.[30] The more I read the so-called thanksgiving hymns of the Teacher, the more I am sure we are dealing with the religious poetry of a pious individual. It is simply unacceptable, however, to identify the speaker in these hymns with any known person.[31] I tend to think that P. Davies is correct in suggesting that the sufferings of the righteous one depicted in the hymns served as a literary prototype for the creation of the Teacher mentioned in the Damascus Document, 1QpHab, and 4QpPs 37.[32] Most of the Scrolls are not concerned with this figure, and I suggest that those that do are employing him as a symbol for the community of righteous individuals in Judaea.

In *The History* I never expressed doubt about the existence of the Teacher of Righteousness, the Wicked Priest, the Liar, the House of Absalom, and the Seekers-After-Smooth-Things. Instead, with respect to all the relevant documentation except for 4QpNah, I argued that the language about all these figures is notoriously vague. In the first place, it makes no sense when interpreting a prophetic passage not to supply the actual name of persons intended. 4QpNah demonstrates that personal names can be mentioned in this genre, and the Gospels do it extensively. Furthermore, if the authors of the pesharim were in fact trying to communicate something about the origins of

---

[29] *Ibid.*, 173–197. Prof. George J. Brooke in this volume argues cogently for further analyses of the relationship between biblical phraseology and the creation of the pesharim and discourages overly precise and detailed historical reconstructions based on such texts.

[30] CROSS, F. M., JR. 1992. "The Historical Context of the Scrolls." In *Understanding the Dead Sea Scrolls.* H. SHANKS, Ed. :20–32.

[31] CALLAWAY, P. R. History, 185–197.

[32] DAVIES, P. R. 1987. "Behind the Essenes. History and Ideology in the Dead Sea Scrolls." Atlanta, GA: Scholars Press. *BJS* 94: 87–105.

the Qumran community and conflicts among its leading members, why are the lemma often more vague than the preceding prophetic passages?

Let us review some of the so-called historically relevant statements in the pesharim. From 1QpHab we learn that the Liar did not listen to the Teacher's divine message (II,1–2), that the House of Absalom remained silent when the Liar flouted the Law in the midst of the community (V,9–12), and that God had given the Teacher the gift to understand how the history of God's holy people would end (VII,1–5). Furthermore, the Liar misled many people in order to build his city of vanity with blood (X,9–13). The pesher goes on to tell us that the Wicked Priest, who had been honorable until he ruled over Israel, became unfaithful, arrogant, abandoned God, chased wealth, and lived in a defiled state (VIII,8–13). This same Wicked Priest pursued the Teacher to his place of exile in order to confuse him on the Day of Atonement (XI,9–12). Within this document the author switches easily back and forth between observations about individuals and groups representing the righteous and the wicked. Undoubtedly, the writer had some sort of conflict in mind, but in my opinion it is impossible to determine with any specificity what the issue under dispute was.

4QpPs 37 reflects a similar approach, but is more clearly future-oriented and concerned with retribution for the wicked and justice for the righteous. The writer refers to the Liar, who undermined the teachings of an interpreter of knowledge (I,18–II,1). He also speaks of the wicked of Ephraim and Manasseh, who will attempt to do harm to the priest and his council (II,17–19). IV,8–10 refers precisely to the episode about the Wicked Priest and the Teacher in 1QpHab XI,9–12, but there is no mention of a place of exile or of the Day of Atonement.

The most that I am willing to say about these nebulous formulations is that they may be concerned with halakhic disputes that resulted in a split within an unidentified Jewish group. Why the antagonists must suffer a less than enviable fate merely because of differences of opinion on legal matters is not obvious to me. Only if the writer has created stereotypical individuals, imbuing them with life by assigning them code names and referring in the most imprecise fashion possible to their activities, am I able to make some theological sense of any of his prophecies. Nevertheless, I still refuse to make historical identifications based on the kind of theological mumbo-jumbo found in these two pesharim.

The language of 4QpIsa supports my view that the pesharist is concerned more with the vindication of the righteous and obedient with the aid of the messiah in the battle at the end of time than with particular known historical disputes of the past. Two passages in 4QpHos suggest that the issue is traditional Judaism versus contemporary acceptance of Gentile religious practices and laws (the commentaries on 2.11 and 6.7).

Scholars often pointed to 4QpNah as proof that the pesharim as a genre deal with history. That is true, but they are essentially concerned with the flow of Jewish history toward its inevitable divine consummation. 4QpNah I,1 points out that Jerusalem has become a dwelling-place for the "ungodly of the nations" with Jewish complicity. A concrete example is given in the case of Demetrius III, whom the Pharisees—with their concern to rule in Jerusalem—begged to take the city on their behalf. This is obviously a reference to an actual historical event recorded in Josephus, the conflict between Alexander Jannaeus and the Pharisees *ca.*90 B.C.E. (*War* 1.4.4, 6; *Antiquities* 13.14.2). In typical fashion the pesharist fails to elaborate on this event at this point. Instead, he seems to be making the observation that God had not permitted the kings of Yavan, the Seleucids, from the time of Antiochus until the coming of the rulers of the Kittim, most likely the Romans, from violating the holy city Jerusalem. (This is a prophetic claim that is at odds with the historical facts.) With the coming of the Romans God had ordained a period of irrevocable devastation.

This event involving Alexander Jannaeus and the Pharisees represents, I suspect, the initial calamities that are said will befall God's people in the coming days. In I,1 the "young lions" are interpreted as the ungodly of the nations, not as Jews. In the following pericope, I,1–2, the "lion" is none other than king Demetrius, and his "cubs" are the Jewish Seekers-After-Smooth-Things. To be entirely consistent with this exegesis, one would expect any other "young lions" to be foreigners. If our interpretation of the damaged and highly ambiguous words of I,7–8 is correct, and the "furious young lion" should be identified with Alexander Jannaeus, who crucified eight hundred Pharisees for their revolt against him, the pesharist has confounded our attempts to discover complete consistency in his exegetical logic.

In spite of these difficulties, I believe the exegetical problems can be overcome. From the perspective of the pesharist Alexander Jannaeus was no better than a foreign conqueror because of his capacity to slay his own people. This interpretation is reflected in *Antiquities* 13.14.2, where he is likened to a Thracian. During his twenty-seven year reign he had killed one brother, made slaves of the citizens of Raphia, Gaza, and Anthedon, and with the help of his foreign mercenaries had slain not fewer than fifty thousand of his people (some at Jerusalem).

Even after Demetrius had departed, Alexander pursued the Jewish rebels to Bemeselis, captured and led them back to Jerusalem, where he crucified eight hundred men and had their wives and children's throats slit. During this entire slaughter he dined and slept with his concubines. More than eight thousand of his Jewish enemies fled out of Judaea (*War* 1.4.6). When Alexander later died, these expatriates returned to Jerusalem and Judaea, and in the following scene Josephus tells us that Alexandra, the pious wife of Alexander, had taken over the kingdom and was supported by the Pharisees (*War* 1.5.1–2). Among these Pharisees were men who hated Alexander and had attempted to halt his rule by having Demetrius capture Jerusalem.

What this has to do with the history of the Qumran community I do not know, but I strongly suspect that 4QpNah was composed by a Pharisee living during the period of Roman domination, who condemned all Jewish attempts to manipulate God's evil designs for Jerusalem, the holy temple, and the holy land. The die was cast. The Romans would thwart the plans of those who by means of political machinations hoped to hinder its coming.

While I have argued that 4QpNah is concerned with history, mentioning Demetrius and Antiochus, it never names Alexander Jannaeus and his adversaries by name. Nor does it speak of the Teacher, the Liar, the House of Absalom, and halakhic conflicts. If it is concerned with Alexander Jannaeus, the pesharist is barely able to write four (now damaged) lines about this king's wicked deeds in Israel. The pesharist was not interested in the internal squabbles of a sectarian group but rather in the behavior of contemporary Jews who were acting as Gentiles do.

If one reads farther into 4QpNah, the pesharist moves away from the past to talk about similar misbehavior that God will eventually punish at the end of time. The only consistency is his use of nebulous code language about Ephraim, Manasseh, and Seekers-After-Smooth-Things. Many scholars are now identifying these sobriquets with the Pharisees based on 4QMMT and 11QT. Before addressing the potential historical context of these documents, it is necessary to make a few observations about the Damascus Document.

The Damascus Document not only refers to the mysterious Seekers-After-Smooth-Things and the Liar, but also to the origin of a Jewish association that later demonstrated its allegiance to a teacher of righteousness. The actions of these figures are described theologically, not historically. The teacher's function is simply to explain how God has and will act in history. The Liar has misled and confused the people of Israel, "abolishing the ways of righteousness" (I,15–16). His followers justified the wicked and condemned the righteous, so that God's wrath had come upon them (I,21–II,1).

As in the pesharim, this particular scenario is created out of classical biblical passages, *e.g.*, Hos 4.16, Isa 30.10, 13, and Ps 94.21. Because of the midrashic patchworking, the references to a teacher and a liar seem to be juxtaposed with no real rhyme or reason. Since they never interact, it is impossible to make a reasonable judgment about what may have transpired when their paths crossed.

The Damascus Document is a veritable tissue of biblical passages, whose dual-purpose was to explain to its readership that God always punishes the wicked and rewards the faithful and to emphasize that the Jews had failed God by not adhering to the proper interpretation of the Law as taught by the Bene Zadok.

In terms of its philosophy of history the Damascus Document is consistent with the thought of the pesharim. Unlike these writings, it preserves chronological notes that—under normal circumstances—should make the historian's task much easier. According to most translations of I,5–8, in the age of wrath God caused a plant root to grow up three hundred ninety years after Nebuchadnezzar king of Babel captured Jerusalem. If the author's calculations can be trusted, this plant root arose around 207–197 B.C.E. Twenty years later God gave this group a teacher to redirect them in God's way (I,8–11). Accordingly, this teacher lived during the time of the Maccabees.

This is the only explicit chronological evidence relevant to the origins of a Jewish remnant community in the Scrolls. It is embarrassingly easy to read. Why did the author fail over and over to tell his readers more precisely the identities and activities of the persons to whom he refers? I have no reason to doubt these chronological notes any more than the document as a whole, but doubt that the writer ever intended to narrate historical episodes. It reads more like a credo than historical fact.

III,10–16 goes beyond this chronology to suggest that after the ravaging of the land, God—as teacher—revealed to his remnant all of the hidden things in which Israel had gone astray, matters such as sabbath and festival observance, testimonies about his righteousness, and how to live with one another. The preceding homily, for which this seems to be a conclusion, lists heavenly watchers and their children who failed to heed God's commandments.

This, then, is another credo about the theological formation of a remnant group. Nevertheless, it differs from I,5–12 in that it lacks a chronology and a human teacher. The connection with the Babylonian exile and Nebuchadnezzar is by no means obvious, but the homilist's interjection of Ezek 44.15 and its interpretation might have been intended to suggest a Babylonian pedigree. This possibility is weakened by the interpretation that speaks of priests, the repentant of Israel, who left the land of Judaea. If an exile had been intended, one would have expected a reference to the *golah*. Without reference to any other passage in the Damascus Document, this one can be read as concerned with a group of priests and levites who, upon learning how polluted the holy land was and how egregiously the Israelites and Judaeans had disobeyed the Law, felt it divinely ordained to emigrate posthaste.

How do we choose between the statements in I and III? I am not sure, but do think III reflects an earlier statement than I, because of its general nature, its lack of a chronology, and its divine rather than human teacher. Generality seeks specificity rather than the opposite.

VI,2–11 presents a third variation on the same theme, which seems to supplement the claim made in III,10–16. According to this passage, God remembered his covenant and raised up wise and insightful men from Aaron and Israel. The purpose of this group, which the text says departed the land of Judaea, was to study and practice the Law seriously during the age of wrath. This passage offers two surprises. Not only does this group of wise men leave Judaea, but quite literally they sojourn in the land of Damascus. Furthermore, they must continue their legal research until a teacher of righteousness appears at the end of days.

I suggest that a synoptic reading of I, III, and VI, reveals that subsequent writers added both the chronological and geographical notes. I am unable to decide whether the chronological notes, although secondary, are still historically credible. For two reasons I think the references to Damascus should be taken seriously and literally. First, the Babylonian exile was a matter of force in the midst of defeat, not willing expatriation upon divine inspiration. Secondly, Damascus is not a symbol for Babylon or any other location, as many of my colleagues incorrectly assert based on Acts 7.43.[33] In Acts the name Babylon replaces Damascus. In the Damascus Document, the city name Damascus is merely descriptive, replacing nothing in the biblical text.[34]

Of all the scrolls, the Damascus Document alone provides references to a community that emigrated from Judaea to Damascus in order to study God's Law. As in CD I, these "historical" passages are created out of an interpretation of Num 21.18 (VI,3–5). In VI, 19 this group is admonished to adhere to the interpretation of the New Covenant in the land of Damascus. The midrash in VII, 13–19, which is based on Isa 7.17, Amos 5.26–27, 9.11, and Num 24.17, is concerned to explain and justify the religious views of this Judaean group that lived in temporary exile in Damascus. The midrashist tells us nothing about specific causes for this emigration, but it is clear that he believed that one could no longer learn the correct interpretation of the Law from the Jerusalem priesthood. This brings us to the laws of the Damascus Document, 11QT, and 4QMMT, which now serve as the chief bodies of evidence for discussing the "origins" of the Scrolls and the communities who wrote them.

≈ IV ≈

Even within the narrative of the Damascus Document the homilist notes several religio-legal issues which he felt compelled to censure (V,1–12). The first case mentioned is bigamy, which God forgave King David only because he had not read the Law. In the second reproach it is said that "they" sleep with a woman during menstruation and enter the Jerusalem temple without attending to acceptable purification procedures. Beyond that they are accused of marrying their nieces. The writer blames males and females by pointing out that while this specific law was written for men, it applies equally to females. A final accusation is made that they defile their holy spirit by speaking against the statutes of God's covenant.

---

[33] DAVIES, P. R. 1990. "The Birthplace of the Essenes: Where is 'Damascus'?" *Revue de Qumran* 14/56:511.

[34] CALLAWAY, P. R. 1990. "Qumran Origins: From *Doresh* to *Moreh*." *Revue de Qumran* 14/56:644. Prof. Samuel Iwry in this volume admonishes those who remain unwilling to accept a literal interpretation of "Damascus" in the Damascus Document.

The writer claims that the Law had been hidden from the time of the death of Eleazar and Joshua until the appearance of one Zadoq (V,2–4). Thus God forgave David's affair with Bathsheba but not the premeditated murder of her husband Uria. Presumably, the accusations mentioned are directed against known individuals, probably the leaders of Jerusalem and Judaea who lived after the time of Zadoq when the Law was revealed.

Based on Mal 1.10 the writer says further that the temple-worship is acceptable only if certain instructions are followed: avoid temple monies taken from the poor, widows, and orphans; adhere rigidly to purity laws; observe the sabbath, the festivals, and the day of fasting according to the views of the New Covenant in the land of Damascus.

It is undeniably clear that the priestly authority, at least ideologically, resides outside the Jerusalem temple. Quoting Prov 15.8, which says "the sacrifice of a wicked person is an abomination, but the prayer of a righteous person is an acceptable food offering," the writer advocates boycotting not the temple but those who are running it incorrectly (XI,20–21). XI,17–19 indicates that the writer's group did participate in worship at the temple, but required their own special purity (VI,20). Indeed, XII,1–2 prohibits a man from having sexual intercourse with a woman within the city of the temple. What has happened is that the writer's group advocates a radical system of purity from without, which they envisioned—according to the correct interpretation of the Law—should have been practiced from within. This sounds very much like the Temple Scroll.

The Temple Scroll provides an enhanced set of authoritative laws for those who intend to occupy the holy land and worship at its temple. It has often been asked whether these laws applied to the current temple or to one in the messianic age. This is a false dichotomy. The Temple Scroll was composed to demonstrate right practice and right theory for its contemporary readership. Of course, the physical temple that is described never existed and, I believe, the three-hundred-sixty-four-day liturgical calender it advocates was certainly difficult to follow in the Jerusalem context. The writer of the Temple Scroll comes closest to composing realistic law in cases of purity, impurity, and incest laws, but the practicability of said law depends ultimately on control of the temple-city, the king, and the courts. In lieu of that, a community develops its own authoritative structure, constitutional guidelines, and legal statutes.

In any case, the Damascus Document and the Temple Scroll are both concerned with purity at the temple and within one's own home. A short list should suffice: royal bigamy, violation of incest laws, defilement of the temple-city by sexual intercourse, sale of ritually pure animals and vegetable products to the Gentiles, and defilement of one's home and objects within it by an impure person or a corpse.

Which came first, the laws of the Damascus Document or the Temple Scroll? I think the former depend on halakhic instruction such as found in the Temple Scroll, but the latter are nothing short of an attempt to systematize halakhah taught in a community like the Damascus Covenant.

I share the view of many of you that the group that wrote many of the Scrolls arose because of disagreements about the correct interpretation of the Law. But I differ with L. Schiffman who writes:

> The ancient author of MMT asserts that the sect broke away from the Jewish establishment in Jerusalem because of differences involving these religious laws. He asserts that the sect will return if their opponents, who are pictured as knowing that the sectarians were right along, will recant.[35]

From what I know about the language of 4QMMT, the author claims that his group separated from the majority. Assuming that one may read this document in light of the Damascus Document, this separation was ideological, practical, and geographical. Whether one believes this group resided at Qumran, Damascus, or both—a question that begs for more serious discussion—one cannot dismiss the evidence of the Damascus Document that indicates that his group had not stopped worshiping at the Jerusalem temple. Instead, in the most important matters, such as purity, it practiced its own extremism wherever it may have been located.

Schiffman maintains that the sect offered to return, if their halakhic adversaries would "recant." From what I know of the pirated version, the writer desires to convert someone who was already somewhat familiar with the author's brand of legal interpretation. The tone of this document seems cordial and non-confrontational, not castigating as Schiffman suggests.[36]

Since first hearing that several copies of this halakhic "letter" had been discovered in cave 4, I have wondered whether it was an unposted letter or one that had in fact been sent from elsewhere to the community settled at Qumran.[37] It seems most natural to conclude that 4QMMT was written by a leader of the New Covenant in the land of Damascus. Perhaps its author had penned it to keep the Qumran branch of his community abreast of proper interpretation.

I realize that this approach may be difficult to comprehend for those who discount a literal interpretation of Damascus and hold that Qumran was the Essene headquarters. Only if one completely ignores the Damascan connection as fabricated, thus impugning the credibility of the Damascus Document in its narrative sections and trusting it in its legal sections, does the theory of splendid Qumran isolation make any sense.

---

[35] SCHIFFMAN, L. 1992. "The Sadducean Origins of the Dead Sea Scroll Sect." In *Understanding the Dead Sea Scrolls*. H. SHANKS, Ed. :41.

[36] *Ibid.*, 43.

[37] QIMRON, E. & J. STRUGNELL. 1985. "An Unpublished Halakhic Letter from Qumran." In *Biblical Archaeology Today. Proceedings of the International Congress on Biblical Archaeology*. Israel Exploration Society. Jerusalem:400–407.

Schiffman has also discovered Sadducees in 4QMMT, 11QT, and, I assume, in the Damascus Document as well. He points out that the author of 4QMMT argues in several cases against the views of the Pharisees while defending Saducean views as recorded in later Rabbinic writings.[38] According to traditional characterizations of these groups, the Pharisees had a developed oral tradition but not a written one, while their opponents, the Sadducees, maintained that "all law be based on Scripture."[39] Schiffman's argument is perplexing, for he seems to assume that even Pharisees never disagreed among themselves nor recorded their halakhah based on Scripture. The phrases "based on Scripture" and "inspired biblical exegesis" can mean almost anything to anyone. Furthermore, I wonder why Schiffman excludes the New Testament reports about the Pharisees, who are extremely concerned with Jesus' purity and violations of the Law, just as are the Damascus Document, 11QT, and 4QMMT.[40] When Schiffman writes, "The very notion of laws to be added to those of the Bible was anathema to the Qumran sectarians," I wonder whether he and I are reading the same documents.[41]

I believe that we should take the Damascan critic of the Jerusalem priesthood and leadership quite seriously. The disputes in the Damascus Document and the halakhic concerns of 11QT and 4QMMT could easily have occurred between members of the same sect or opposing sects. I doubt that the lines between groups were as hard and fast as Josephus leads us to believe. One need only recall his own experimentation with all of his contemporary religious groups.

A final note on Josephus: He consistently calls the Pharisees the most exact interpreters among his people. His Essene reports reflect a superficial and misleading understanding of the Essenes. While he is fully capable of writing about Pharisees, Sadducees, and politics, he divulges nothing about a priestly defection from Jerusalem because of halakhic disagreements. Finally, Josephus came from a priestly family, claimed to be an excellent student of the Law, saw himself as philosopher and prophet, served as military officer and diplomat, and wrote Jewish history. If he fails to inform us about the group that owned and wrote the Scrolls, how much more necessary it then becomes to treat the Scrolls, not Josephus, 1–2 Maccabees, and the New Testament, as our sources for historical reconstruction.

---

[38] SCHIFFMAN, L. 1992. "The Sadducean Origins," 41–44.

[39] SCHIFFMAN, L. 1990. "The Significance of the Scrolls." *Bible Review* :25.

[40] See Matt 3.7–10, 5.17–20, Luke 5.21, 29–30, Matt 9.11, 14–17, 12.1–14 [*cf.* Luke 6.6–11], Luke 7.36–50, Matt 12.22–24, 38–42, 15.1–20 [*cf.* Mark 7.1–23], Matt 16.1–4 [*cf.* Mark 8.11 & Luke 11.29] and parallels, Matt 22.34–40, Matt 23 [*cf.* Luke 11.37–12.1], Luke 14.1–6, 14–15, Luke 16.8 ("sons of light"), Luke 17.20–21, 18.9–14, Matt 19.1–2 and Mark 10.1–12, Luke 19.39–44, Matt 21.28–32, 22.15–22 and Mark 12.13–17, Matt 22.41–46, Matt 22.23–33 and parallels (Sadducees, *cf.* Matt 3.7–10).

[41] SCHIFFMAN, L. 1992. "The Pharisees." *Bible Review* :33.

In conclusion, I regret that I have been unable to incorporate the majority of the Scrolls into my discussion of "origins," which for me refers to beginnings and not later historical phases.

ACKNOWLEDGMENTS

I would like to express my gratitude to Ms. Tanya Persaud-White for improving my English style in many places. Factual and logical mistakes should be credited to my account.

~~~~~~

DISCUSSION OF THE PAPER

HARTMUT STEGEMANN (*University of Göttingen, Göttingen, Germany*): Dr. Callaway, thank you very much for your information and for your skepticism. I have a problem; it's a problem of consequence, and perhaps a problem of too much local Qumran orientation. I remember our book and the ways that you argued for archaeology, that the Qumran settlement is not so very old, but may have been founded or settled about 100 B.C.E. If this is right, then the oldest copy of *Serek Ha-Yahad* is from second century. Maybe similarly with the Damascus Document, which may have been written about 100. All these documents may have been written for people who did not yet live at Qumran. That's one orientation. On the other hand, everything is more or less seen from the view of Qumran. People settled there as if the books were produced by them, for them also. Could you comment on this problem?

PHILLIP R. CALLAWAY (*Jonesboro, GA*): Professor Stegemann, I think you've misunderstood what I was saying. Qumran is not at all important for me. I think it's significant that the documents were found there, but I don't think that these documents necessarily were written at that location. I have the feeling that most of them were imported. I don't find a system there, a theological system that I can talk about. I don't think that I ever argued that the Qumran settlement started in the Hellenistic period at 100 B.C.E. I think what I did was lay out what de Vaux had said so that I could try to see the various pieces of evidence. After all this time I still believe we would do better not to include Qumran in our discussions. I think in the later part of my paper I only mentioned it a couple of times, the Damascus and Qumran connection. I recognize that the connection is hypothetical with that settlement but I don't think it's hypothetical to talk about a Damascan community. I think everyone who's reading it nonliterally is misreading it.

MOSHE BERNSTEIN (*Yeshiva University, New York, NY*): I think we should talk about things that do exist as opposed to things that don't exist. When you have 6 copies of MMT and you have the Temple Scroll and you have all the other legal texts, it's time for people who are working in Qumran to find out more about how halakhic texts operate, starting with these earliest texts, and perhaps even down into the early Rabbinic period. You're right, the sources are later, but the fact is those are the only texts that you have to work with as analogs. To put aside the sizeable body of halakhic literature . . . You can't get away from the fact that one of the focal points of the literary remains that we find at Qumran, from wherever it came, are halakhic documents. The amazing thing is, there is a consistency within these documents in terms of stance, in terms of method, and in terms of the halakha itself. So you've got to take those documents as your beginning before you can start to say, "Well the tone . . . this and that." Forget about tone, read the text, study the halakha, evaluate it against other records we have of parallel halakha, and then perhaps we're going to be able to talk about tone.

CALLAWAY: Thank you, Moshe. Number one, you don't have to start with the rabbinic rites to understand what's going on in the Temple Scroll and MMT. I prefer to start with the Bible. Point two: if you keep up with what I've written on the Temple Scroll, you'll see that I have attended to the halakha.

Investigation of the Otot-text (4Q319) and Questions about Methodology

UWE GLESSMER[1]

Alttestamentliches Seminar
Universität Hamburg
Sedanstrasse 19
20146 Hamburg, Germany

MILIK'S ASSUMPTIONS IN THE RECONSTRUCTION OF 4Q319

The so called Otot-text is characterized by the repeated occurrence of the singular and plural of the word "sign," the Hebrew אות or אותות. What the signs signify I shall deal with at the end of my short communication. The designation of the manuscript fragments leads immediately to questions of methodology, however: What is the reason for the separation of these fragments from other very similar ones which belong to a copy of a *Serek-HaYachad*-version? What is meant by the designation "4QOtot" for 4Q319? Answers to both questions can be found in Milik's activities years ago, but what implications are connected with his decisions? Is Milik's perspective still methodologically valid?

The transcriptions of 4Q319 are mostly pre-published now—partly by Milik himself. Earlier—from the 1950s on—he provided some information about these calendrical texts, which are related to the 364-day calendar. This calendar was at that time debated in reaction to Jaubert's hypothesis about the use of the jubilee-calendar.[2] In 1976 Milik published one part of the Otot-text [col vi, 6–13] in his *The Books of Enoch*.[3] In 1978 in an article about "pre-Essene writings of Qumrân," he presented the transcription of some further lines of what he called column x.[4] In this contribution Milik also

[1] I wish to thank Prof. N. Golb for allowing the inclusion of this communication, which develops certain observations I expressed during the Conference. [Bibliographical references in the notes refer to the list of literature at the end of this article].

[2] Compare MILIK (1957) V.T.S. 24n3. The value of Jaubert's results in connection with the mišmarot-calendar he calls "encore provisoire" (p. 24) and leaves it as an open question: "Furent-ils réellement pratiqués par les Esséniens?" (p. 25).

[3] MILIK (1976) 62.

[4] MILIK (1978) 93; compare WOUDE (1990) *ThR* 269f and the Spanish translation in GARCÍA MARTÍNEZ ([3]1993) 76. As far as I can see this publication confused scholars. In the newest lists of already published materials it is not included. The reasons for this omission and the confusion of the different sigla I shall discuss below. I am grateful to Prof. H.-W. Kuhn (München) who in a discussion drew my attention again to this passage in Milik's article.

gave an overview of how he thought the text was arranged in the original manuscript, which at that time was called 4Q260:

col. i–iv	text which is parallel to 1QS 7,10–10,4
col. v–vii, 19	cycle of seven jubilees
col. viii, 1–7	signs of the 4 seasons in a 6-year-cycle
col. viii, 7–18	monthly signs of 6-year-cycle
col. viii, 18–ix,19	calendar of festivals in a 6-year-cycle
col. x, 2	signs of the sabbaths beginning a month
col. x, 4–8	(the above mentioned) final-passage:

.[   ]m [wl]šbtwt   [. . . and for] sabbaths/weeks
5 [ymyh]m [wl]ḥg[y]   of their days [and for] feas[ts]
[ymy]hm [wl]ḥʷdš[y šnyhm w]lʾwtwt   of thei[r days and for] mont[hs of their years and] *for signs*

[š]mt[yh]m wlywblyhm bšbt   *of the[ir re]leases* and for their jubilees in the week

[bn]y [gmw]l by[w]m hrby[ʿy]   [of the so]ns [of gamu]l on the four[th d]ay.

Milik discusses the terminology of this newly published passage with its different levels of time-divisions in light of the issue of whether the calendrical materials are to be seen as anonymous writings or as pseudepigraphs (p. 94). He connects the content of the cycle of seven jubilees with the notice of Jub 4,17.18. There the angels record that in a book they gave "signs of the sky"[5] to Enoch. With this written testimony Enoch then brought the knowledge of the structure of time-divisions and the "week of Jubilees" to mankind.

The text of Jub 4,17 for Milik "refers no doubt to En. 80-2 . . . But the text of verse 18b goes far beyond the content of our astronomical document . . . I see in this a reference to various astronomical and calendrical texts, calculated on the cycles of three, six, seven, and forty-nine years, copies of which exist among manuscripts of Cave 4 of Qumrân. . . ."[6] All these materials he sees to be in relation to the keyword אות "sign" which is also used in an Enoch-reference in Sirach.[7] In an Aramaic apocryphon–the Samaritan writing *Asaṭir*–this keyword is even used as a title of one of three books attributed to Enoch: The "book of the Signs."[8]

So Milik considers the word "sign" as a bridge to 4Q319. He remarks about the above-mentioned theory of the pseudepigraphical character: "the calendar of the seven jubilees . . . could be entitled the 'Book of the Signs.'"[9]

[5] VANDERKAM (1989) 1.24: *taʾamᵉra samāiᶜ*.
[6] MILIK (1976) 11.
[7] Compare MILIK (1976) 10f with discussion of Greek and Hebrew versions of Sir 44,16; 49,14.
[8] Citations of several passages in MILIK (1976) 64ff and the reference to this Samaritan medieval tradition.
[9] MILIK (1976) 64. Compare the sigla in FITZMYER (³1990) 57 and GARCÍA MARTÍNEZ (1989) HENOCH 200f.

He explains the separate designation of this manuscript-portion of 4QS^b in a note: "*ha-'Otot* was, in fact, the siglum which I myself gave quite spontaneously to 4Q260B."[10]

We may note in passing that after this separation from the *Serek*-manuscript was in existence, some changes in the "numerotation" took place[11] and the different labels of the ten 4Q-*serek*-manuscripts caused some irritation.[12] In the catalogue which Reed produced at the ABMC, 4Q259B is given the designation "4QCalendars A."[13]–At this time 4Q259 is the numerical counting of the fifth copy 4QS^e. But also on the next page for the sixth copy, called 4Q260A (= 4QS^F–without a corresponding 4Q260B), the publication by Milik (1976) 62 is noted.–The irritation becomes complete with the "olim-remarks" in the list of *Tov*: he noted for 4Q258 = 4QS^d (olim S^b) and for 4Q319 (olim S^b).[14]

Looking at photographs of 4Q258 and 4Q319 indicated in the last-mentioned article would not make it necessary to investigate the connection between the development of serek-manuscripts and calendrical documents. They obviously do not belong to the same manuscript. So the last step in the separation of "the book of signs" as a unity in itself could be reached.

But some fragments seen in the "Otot"-photograph PAM 43.283 (= FE 1319) prevent us from this lapse. They belong to the same manuscript–now called 4Q259 (= 4QS^e)–and posit the problem: How is the physical and internal relationship between both components of *one manuscript* to be reconstructed? So Milik's seemingly solved problem has to be reinvestigated.

Although some elements in Jub (especially "the weeks of the jubilees" in 4,18[15]) and also in 1Hen are related to the contents of 4QOtot, it should be kept in mind that no explicit identification of its provenience is attested in the text of 4Q319 itself. Should a book which is attributed to Enoch be attached to a *serek*-manuscript without any indication? Looking back, it seems suggestive to include all the calendrical material under the pseudepigraphic

---

[10] MILIK (1976) 64n1.

[11] MILIK (1977) SEM.

[12] MILIK (1978) 93n2 himself produced some misunderstanding with his remark concerning the text col. viii, 18–ix, 19 that he gave "un échantillon dans le Volumne du Congrès Strasbourg." WOUDE (1990) *ThR*, 269f took this "échantillon" in the sense: "Milik 1957 already published a fragment (in translation)" of 4Q260B. With the help of the Preliminary Edition it is possible to clear up Milik's reference. It was to a parallel of the sexennial cycle in one of the mišmarot-manuscripts; REED (1991) Fascicle 10 p. 26 calls 4Q320 "4QCalendars D^a," in the "Preliminary List of Qumran Cave 4 Documents" of 1992 p. 28 labeled as "Mishmarot A" (= PAM 43.331). Tov (1992) BA 99 [= Tov (1993) 40] gives the name as "Calendrical Doc. A."

[13] REED (1991) Fascicle 10 p. 19; on b. 26 4Q319 is called "Calendars C."

[14] Tov (1992) *BA* 98.99; compare VERMES (1992) *JJS* 300n2. In reaction to a draft of my article (1991) Prof. Talmon wrote in a private correspondence: "Ich weiss nicht was Milik dazu bewegt hat die <u>mišmarot</u> oder die <u>'otot</u> Fragmente mit der Sektenregel zu verbinden. Ich würde da vorsichtiger sein." (1 July 1991)

[15] VANDERKAM (1989) 2.26 note.

label of "Enoch." And even in Hellenistic-Roman times–in propagandistic writings of the time of cultural contact as in PsEupolemos–this label "Enoch as inventor of sciences" may be adequate for the general claim that astronomy goes back to this famous figure–and to *Jewish* tradition. But is it correct from a methodological point of view to use these references to label everything that is concerned with calendrical matters as "Enochic"? What price would we pay for doing so?

MY OWN ASSUMPTIONS ABOUT THE PLURALITY OF CALENDARS

I think the price might be that the investigator would lose his critical eye concerning the plurality and diversity of different calendrical approaches. My assumption is that there is not *one* fixed starting point in the post-exilic development of calendars but rather a *diversity* of geographical and organizational situations. The various groups only partly inherited the same textual traditions. Each group developed them further under different conditions of cultural contact. As in the wider area of the development of plural calendars in the Persian and Hellenistic and Roman periods,[16] the direction is *from diversity to unity* and not the other way round. An analogous situation forms the background of what came afterwards to be regarded as *"the Jewish calendar."*

During the first stage of the scientific rediscovery of the 364-day-year as a different system opposed to the calendar in Rabbinic literature, it might have been necessary to put all testimony together. But now that the calendrical materials from the Qumran library as well as different recensions of the *Serek-haYachad* begin to be readily available, careful distinctions should be made about the contexts in which they are imbedded–and the context brought to them. The danger of arguing in a circle is extremely great. So, I would like to base my reconstruction of 4QOtot as much as possible on hard facts, because even at this stage circular arguments seem to be possible.

A connection between 4Q319 and Enoch–which Milik saw–is indicated only by the abstraction that the general content could be labeled as "calendrical material" and the keyword "sign." Further comparisons are necessary to avoid arguments in which preconceived notions brought to the text are afterwards used to support reconstructions.

Because of changes in the Dead-Sea-Scrolls scenario within the last two years[17] nearly all calendrical texts are now available to the public in the form

---

[16] Compare GLESSMER (1993) *MuB* 12–29: "Exkurs: Der kalendarische Kontext;" see also for the "plurality of calendric traditions" in Qumran texts Callaway (1993) 29.

[17] Compare to the lists of Tov (1992) *BA* and Tov (1992) *JJS* also WACHOLDER (1993) *JJS* 129f.

of transcriptions. The earlier transcriptions of the passages now labeled as 3Q319 from the "late 50's and early 60's"[18] were reconstructed according to the entries in the privately published concordance. Wacholder/Abegg in their computer-aided reconstruction printed them under the concordance-siglum 4QS^c in the first fascicle of *A Preliminary Edition of Unpublished Dead Sea Scrolls* in 1991.[19]

Although the transcripts are pre-published and available to the public, they are to be handled with care. Some assumptions underlying the earlier re-constructions must be considered before 4QOtot is compared with other calendrical materials; for example, in the Wacholder/Abegg edition the tendency to harmonize calendrical texts is visible.[20]

THE STRUCTURE OF THE JUBILEES-CYCLE IN 4Q319

So, for 4QOtot a consideration of the interdependence between a theory about the structure of the text and the reconstruction of the full—hitherto nearly unknown—wording of the "cycle of jubilees" must have its place. I shall try to illustrate the methodological problem by using an example of different interpretations, which are dependent on structures observed in the text first published by Milik. He himself thought this structure to be extended to the text as a whole.

The arrangement seems to be clear in his base-transcription. It shows a highly structured text and a restricted vocabulary: the word אות "sign," the names of the two priestly courses נמול "Gamul" and שכניה "Schechanja," the time-related terms: שמטה "release" and יובל "jubilee," a cardinal- and some ordinal-numbers in the range from "second" to "sixth" with a certain repetition. The text-structure is further determined by use of the prepositions -ב "in/at" and אחר "after." I myself followed in some ways in Milik's footsteps in an earlier article about the interpretation of the pre-published part of what he called column vi 6–13:[21]

4Q319 [olim 4Q260B part of 4QS^b (= 4Q260A) I vi 6–13[22]

---

[18] Compare STRUGNELL in the "Preface" to the concordance RICHTER (1988) p. II.

[19] Even if not indicated by the authors in their hotly debated book under "previous discussions" EISENMAN & WISE (1992) 134 note 26, they used WACHOLDER & ABEGG (1991) as a base of their transcription. This is visible from the same filling of gaps in the manuscript (compare also p. 133 note 24 to 4Q323–324A–B).

[20] WACHOLDER & ABEGG (1991) 104ff are creating an artefact under the headlines "Luni-Solar Calendar of Qumran—First Six Year Cycle," "Calendar of Full Moons . . ., New moons . . ., and festival days . . . according to 4QMishmerot HaKohanim and 4QS^c."

[21] GLESSMER (1991) *FS.*

[22] MILIK (1976) 62f.

	ordinal-number,	sign	priestly course	cycle
A) [בשנית או]ת [נמו]ל[6]	[in 2.	sig]n	[Gamu]l	1
בחמישית אות שכניה	in 5.	sign	Schechanja	
אחר השמטה או]ת גמול[7]	after the release	sig[n	Gamul]	
[ברביעית או]ת שכניה	[in 4.]	sign	Schechanja	2
בשמטה אות גמול[8]	at the release	sign	Gamul	
בשלישית אות [שכניה]	in 3.	sign	[Schechanja]	3
[בששית אות ג]מול	[in 6.	sign	Ga]mul	
בשנית אות שכניה[9]	in 2.	sign	Schechanja	4
בחמ(י)שית אות [נמול]	in 5.	sign	[Gamul]	
[אחר] השמטה אות שכניה	[after] the release	sign	Schechanja	
ברביעית אות גמול[10]	in 4.	sign	Gamul	5
[בשמטה אות] שכניה	[at the release	sign]	Schechanja	
בשלישית אות גמול	in 3.	sign	Gamul	6
בששית אות שכניה[11]	in 6.	sign	Schechanja	
[בשנית אות] גמול	[in 2.	sign]	Gamul	7
בחמישית אות שכניה	in 5.	sign	Schechanja	
אחר השמטה א[ות][12]	after the release	s[ign (?)]		

B) [ראשית היובל]	[of the beginning of the Jubilee?]		
[ג]מ[ו]ל		[Ga]m[u]l	
(הֹיֹוֹבֵל) [הר]בֹּיֹעֹ]ין	[The fou]rt[h] ? (Jubilee?):		
אותות -/// /// \	1[7]	signs	
מ[ו]ה[13]	of this (?)		

\\ (אותות) בשמטה \\ in release   2   signs

שׁ[כניה]   Sch[echanja?]

But can we be sure that the structure (of what I call part A in the presentation of Milik's text), the separation of sentences, and the sequence of its parts – 1) preposition + ordinal; 2) word "sign"; and 3) a name of a priestly course – is correct? In their translation Eisenman/Wise indicate the same understanding as Milik by the use of punctuation-marks.[23] But since the full text in Wacholder/ Abegg's Preliminary Edition (=PE) is available I am convinced by arguments published by Albani.[24] He observed two small but important differences compared with the beginning of Milik's transcription in line 6. One new word (following the pattern of other jubilee-cycles) was added in the reconstruction of the lacuna – the word "year" [בשנה השנית]. And just before the lacuna in the PE the jubilee begins with one further instance of mentioning the name שכניה "Schechanja." So this "jubilee-opening-sentence" (as attested in the other cases) brings a variation of the pattern: the "normal-seeming" sequence of words is to be changed: 1) a name of a priestly course; 2) year; and 3) preposition + ordinal. The word "sign" seems not to be present in this case.[25] The sentence then is: "Schechanja in the second year."

The consequence of this observation is that in all following sentences the sequence should also be changed so that the temporal determination is put in the third position: 1) the word "sign"; 2) a name of a priestly course; and 3) preposition + ordinal referring to a year in a cycle of higher order (release-year). The effect is that in the text of part A which was cited above from Milik's publication, all names change their positions in relation to the release-year-cycle [given in brackets at the right hand]:

(sign?)	Schechanja	in second	year	[1. cycle]
sign	Gamul	in fifth		
sign	Schechanja	after š^emita		
sign	Gamul	in fourth		[2. cycle]
sign	Schechanja	in š^emita		
sign	Gamul	in third		[3. cycle]
sign	Schechanja	in sixth		

[23] EISENMAN & WISE (1992) 130 designate the text which Milik published as *second* column line 6–13 of what they call "Heavenly Concordances (Otot–4Q319A)." They use semicolon and comma to separate the units.

[24] ALBANI (1992) *MuB* 37ff with note 91.

[25] No complete and certain proof in one of the other opening-sentences of jubilee-units is available. In one case the jubilee-opening-sentence is preceded by a word that ends with ה. This is reconstructed in the concordance and by WACHOLDER & ABEGG (1991) 96 fr. 1 v, 18 as אות, which would fit the context, but is not attested or hypothetical in all other jubilees.

sign	Gamul	in second	[4. cycle]
sign	Schechanja	in fifth	
sign	Gamul	after šᵉmita	
sign	Schechanja	in fourth	[5. cycle]
sign	Gamul	in šᵉmita	
sign	Schechanja	in third	[6. cycle]
sign	Gamul	in sixth	
sign	Schechanja	in second	[7. cycle]
sign	Gamul	in fifth	
sign	Schechanja	after šᵉmita	

This model of one jubilee – extended to the other jubilees – produces a totally different picture than the Figure 7 presented by Milik which he calls a "Table of the cycle of seven jubilees."[26] My own tabulation of the A-element in FIGURE 1 illustrates the differences from Milik's interpretation.[27] The tabulation shows that the example passage fits into the picture presented by the Otot-text which starts the listing of signs within the week of creation "on the fourth day" with the service of the sons of Gamul. But unlike in Milik's interpretation, the cited passage does not belong to the fourth but to the third jubilee. His expectation that the preserved text (of what he considers to be the second jubilee) must be preceded by a first jubilee is shown to be unnecessary if the text is interpreted in this way. Accordingly, no further place in the manuscript must be assumed in the column which Milik counted as col. v.! The serek-text and otot-text belong to the same column.[a]

Can we then know the whole structure of the "cycle of jubilees" and its meaning, when we take into account the changed sequence? Of special interest is the following question: Is the distance of "signs" every fourth year connected with special "lunar events," i.e., "signs" in an astronomical sense? Such events of special observance are to be supposed when the 364-day-calendar is thought of against a background of coordination with a lunar calendar. Such a coordination with a special 37th lunar month preceding every fourth year is attested in those texts pre-published by Wacholder/Abegg under the designation Mišm A and Mišm B.[28] There the alternating distances of 29 and 30 days make it obvious that a lunar context is connected to the 364-day-year.[29] But is this true also for 4Q319? Or is it adequate to suppose a non-lunar re-interpretation, which uses the special counting of the "signs in the šᵉmita" in a sense of intercalation for a 364-day-year against the tropical year?

---

[26] MILIK (1976) 65.
[27] Compare the alternative tables in GLESSMER (1991) *FS* 395 and ALBANI (1992) *MuB* 47.
[a] [Note added in proof. See now Metso (1993) *JJS.*]
[28] WACHOLDER & ABEGG (1991) 60ff. 68ff.
[29] For two different models to bring lunar months into accord with the 364-day-year see GLESSMER (1993) *MuB* 45f.54–77.

1. jubilee	2. jubilee	3. jubilee	4. jubilee	5. jubilee	6. jubilee	7. jubilee
1	**1**	**1**	**1**	**1**	**1**	**1**
1. *Gamul*	1. Jedaja	1. Mijamin	1. *Schechanja*	1. Jeschebab	1. Pizez	1. *Gamul*
2. Jedaja	2. Mijamin	2. *Schechanja*	2. Jeschebab	2. Pizez	2. *Gamul*	2. . . .
3. Mijamin	3. *Schechanja*	3. Jeschebab	3. Pizez	3. *Gamul*	3. Jedaja	
4. *Schechanja*	4. Jeschebab	4. Pizez	4. *Gamul*	4. Jedaja	4. Mijamin	
5. Jeschebab	5. Pizez	5. *Gamul*	5. Jedaja	5. Mijamin	5. *Schechanja*	
6. Pizez	6. *Gamul*	6. Jedaja	6. Mijamin	6. *Schechanja*	6. Jeschebab	
7. *Gamul*	7. Jedaja	7. Mijamin	7. *Schechanja*	7. Jeschebab	7. Pizez	
2	**2**	**2**	**2**	**2**	**2**	
1. Jedaja	1. Mijamin	1. *Schechanja*	1. Jeschebab	1. Pizez	1. *Gamul*	
2. Mijamin	2. *Schechanja*	2. Jeschebab	2. Pizez	2. *Gamul*	2. Jedaja	
3. *Schechanja*	3. Jeschebab	3. Pizez	3. *Gamul*	3. Jedaja	3. Mijamin	
4. Jeschebab	4. Pizez	4. *Gamul*	4. Jedaja	4. Mijamin	4. *Schechanja*	
5. Pizez	5. *Gamul*	5. Jedaja	5. Mijamin	5. *Schechanja*	5. Jeschebab	
6. *Gamul*	6. Jedaja	6. Mijamin	6. *Schechanja*	6. Jeschebab	6. Pizez	
7. Jedaja	7. Mijamin	7. *Schechanja*	7. Jeschebab	7. Pizez	7. *Gamul*	
3	**3**	**3**	**3**	**3**	**3**	
1. Mijamin	1. *Schechanja*	1. Jeschebab	1. Pizez	1. *Gamul*	1. Jedaja	
2. *Schechanja*	2. Jeschebab	2. Pizez	2. *Gamul*	2. Jedaja	2. Mijamin	
3. Jeschebab	3. Pizez	3. *Gamul*	3. Jedaja	3. Mijamin	3. *Schechanja*	
4. Pizez	4. *Gamul*	4. Jedaja	4. Mijamin	4. *Schechanja*	4. Jeschebab	
5. *Gamul*	5. Jedaja	5. Mijamin	5. *Schechanja*	5. Jeschebab	5. Pizez	
6. Jedaja	6. Mijamin	6. *Schechanja*	6. Jeschebab	6. Pizez	6. *Gamul*	
7. Mijamin	7. *Schechanja*	7. Jeschebab	7. Pizez	7. *Gamul*	7. Jedaja	
4	**4**	**4**	**4**	**4**	**4**	(same
1. *Schechanja*	1. Jeschebab	1. Pizez	1. *Gamul*	1. Jedaja	1. Mijamin	sequence
2. Jeschebab	2. Pizez	2. *Gamul*	2. Jedaja	2. Mijamin	2. *Schechanja*	as in
3. Pizez	3. *Gamul*	3. Jedaja	3. Mijamin	3. *Schechanja*	3. Jeschebab	1. jubilee)
4. *Gamul*	4. Jedaja	4. Mijamin	4. *Schechanja*	4. Jeschebab	4. Pizez	
5. Jedaja	5. Mijamin	5. *Schechanja*	5. Jeschebab	5. Pizez	5. *Gamul*	
6. Mijamin	6. *Schechanja*	6. Jeschebab	6. Pizez	6. *Gamul*	6. Jedaja	
7. *Schechanja*	7. Jeschebab	7. Pizez	7. *Gamul*	7. Jedaja	7. Mijamin	
5	**5**	**5**	**5**	**5**	**5**	
1. Jeschebab	1. Pizez	1. *Gamul*	1. Jedaja	1. Mijamin	1. *Schechanja*	
2. Pizez	2. *Gamul*	2. Jedaja	2. Mijamin	2. *Schechanja*	2. Jeschebab	
3. *Gamul*	3. Jedaja	3. Mijamin	3. *Schechanja*	3. Jeschebab	3. Pizez	
4. Jedaja	4. Mijamin	4. *Schechanja*	4. Jeschebab	4. Pizez	4. *Gamul*	
5. Mijamin	5. *Schechanja*	5. Jeschebab	5. Pizez	5. *Gamul*	5. Jedaja	
6. *Schechanja*	6. Jeschebab	6. Pizez	6. *Gamul*	6. Jedaja	6. Mijamin	
7. Jeschebab	7. Pizez	7. *Gamul*	7. Jedaja	7. Mijamin	7. *Schechanja*	
6	**6**	**6**	**6**	**6**	**6**	
1. Pizez	1. *Gamul*	1. Jedaja	1. Mijamin	1. *Schechanja*	1. Jeschebab	
2. *Gamul*	2. Jedaja	2. Mijamin	2. *Schechanja*	2. Jeschebab	2. Pizez	
3. Jedaja	3. Mijamin	3. *Schechanja*	3. Jeschebab	3. Pizez	3. *Gamul*	
4. Mijamin	4. *Schechanja*	4. Jeschebab	4. Pizez	4. *Gamul*	4. Jedaja	
5. *Schechanja*	5. Jeschebab	5. Pizez	5. *Gamul*	5. Jedaja	5. Mijamin	
6. Jeschebab	6. Pizez	6. *Gamul*	6. Jedaja	6. Mijamin	6. *Schechanja*	
7. Pizez	7. *Gamul*	7. Jedaja	7. Mijamin	7. *Schechanja*	7. Jeschebab	
7	**7**	**7**	**7**	**7**	**7**	
1. *Gamul*	1. Jedaja	1. Mijamin	1. *Schechanja*	1. Jeschebab	1. Pizez	
2. Jedaja	2. Mijamin	2. *Schechanja*	2. Jeschebab	2. Pizez	2. *Gamul*	
3. Mijamin	3. *Schechanja*	3. Jeschebab	3. Pizez	3. *Gamul*	3. Jedaja	
4. *Schechanja*	4. Jeschebab	4. Pizez	4. *Gamul*	4. Jedaja	4. Mijamin	
5. Jeschebab	5. Pizez	5. *Gamul*	5. Jedaja	5. Mijamin	5. *Schechanja*	
6. Pizez	6. *Gamul*	6. Jedaja	6. Mijamin	6. *Schechanja*	6. Jeschebab	
7. *Gamul*	7. Jedaja	7. Mijamin	7. *Schechanja*	7. Jeschebab	7. Pizez	

FIGURE 1. Years in a "Cycle of Jubilees" and corresponding priestly courses in a six-year-cycle.

The calculation over long time spans makes this a possible solution.[30] I think that some problems remain (especially in part B)—and I shall deal with them on another occasion.[31]

This example was intended to show what makes me cautious in investigating this text. And I should also like to remind others working with it to be doubly cautious: not to build the text merely on the basis of their own theory of its content and after this not to evaluate it without considering the mental image which formed part of the input. To avoid circular methodology, the question—to which of the different possible calendrical contexts can 4Q319 be compared appropriately?[32]—must be very carefully dealt with.

Of methodological importance is that the highest level of plausibility in determining the context of the "jubilee-cycle-part" comes from the manuscript itself. There are two important factors which should be considered, the preceding text in 4Q259 and the following in 4Q319:

1. • What is the connection to the *serek*-manuscript 4QS^e?
    • How does the calendrical text fit into the developmental trend within the different versions of *serek*-manuscripts with their collections of material?
2. • What is the context following the jubilee-cycle-part that is preserved in the small fragments?
    • How are the evident parallels to *mišmarot*-texts in these parts of the manuscript to be interpreted in respect to lunar concepts?

A final answer to these questions is not possible at the moment. They are dependent especially on the hard facts of physical reconstruction of the former scroll, which I shall try to finish as soon as possible.

LITERATURE

ALBANI, M.
   1992a   Astronomie und Schöpfungsglaube : Das astronomische System im "Buch vom Umlauf der Himmelslichter" : seine religionsgeschichtliche Herkunft und theologische Bedeutung : Untersuchungen zu 1 Hen 72–82 unter Berücksichtigung der aramäischen Fragmente (4QEnastr^{a–d}), Dissertation masch : Kirchliche Hochschule Leipzig.
   1992b   "Die lunaren Zyklen im 364-Tage-Festkalender von 4QMischmerot/4QS^e" Forschungsstelle Judentum *"Mitteilungen und Beiträge"* Heft **4**: 3–47 [ISBN 3-86174-022-2].

---

[30] Compare also a Babylonian background for an intercalation which seems to reckon 364 days for a "normal year" in ALBANI (1992) DISS 180f.

[31] See GLESSMER (1993) *SBL* I shall present a modification of my working hypothesis concerning the intercalation first presented in GLESSMER (1991) *FS* in *Schriften des Institutum Judaicum Delitzschianum*, H.-J. Fabry & H. Lichtenberger, Eds. (1994).

[32] A short sketch of calendrical contexts is given in GLESSMER (1993) *MuB* 12–29.

CALLAWAY, P.
1993   The 364-Day Calendar Traditions at Qumran. In *Mogilany 1989 Vol. I (Qumranica Mogilanensia)* Z. J. Kapera, Ed. 19–29.
EISENMAN, R. and J. M. ROBINSON
1991   *A Facsimile Edition of the Dead Sea Scrolls.*
EISENMAN, R. and M. WISE
1992   *The Dead Sea Scrolls Uncovered. The First Complete Translation and Interpretation of 50 Key Documents Withheld for Over 35 Years.* [German ed.: Jesus und die Urchristen. Die Qumran-Rollen entschlüsselt. 1993.]
FITZMYER, J. A.
1990   *The Dead Sea Scrolls: Major Publications and Tools for Study.* Revised Edition. SBL Resources for Biblical Study 20.
GARCÍA MARTÍNEZ, F.
1989   Lista de MSS Proccedentes de Qumran. *Henoch* 11: 149–232.
1993   *Textos de Qumrán: Edición y Traducción.* Coleccion Estructuras y Procesos. Serie Religión.
GLESSMER, U.
1987   Das astronomische Henoch-Buch als Studienobjekt. *BN* 36: 69–129.
1991   Der 364-Tage-Kalender und die Sabbatstruktur seiner Schaltungen in ihrer Bedeutung für den Kult. In *"Ernten, was man sät"* : *Festschrift für Klaus Koch.* D. R. DANIELS, U. GLESSMER & M. RÖSEL, Eds. S. 379–398.
1993a Antike und moderne Auslegungen des Sintflutberichtes Gen 6–8 und der Qumran-Pesher 4Q252. Universität Leipzig. Forschungsstelle Judentum. *Mitteilungen und Beiträge* Heft 6: 3–79.
1993b The Otot-texts (4Q319) and the problem of intercalations in the context of the 364-day calendar (Abstract – full version forthcoming). In *SBL 1993 International Meeting*, 25–28 July, Münster, p. 49.
1993c Die biblischen Texte aus Qumran. *RdQ* 16. In press.
KOCH, K.
1983   Sabbatstruktur der Geschichte. Die sogenannte Zehn-Wochen-Apokalypse (I Hen 93,1–10 91,11–17) und das Ringen um die alttestamentlichen Chronologien im späten Israelitentum. *ZAW* 95: 403–430.
METSO, S.
1993   The Primary Results of Reconstruction of 4QS^c. *JJS* 44: 303–308.
MILIK, J. T.
1957   Le Travail d'Edition des Manuscrits du Désert de Juda. *VT.S* 4: 17–26.
1976   *The Books of Enoch. Aramaic Fragments of Qumran Cave 4.*
1977   Numérotation des feuilles des rouleaux dans le scriptorium de Qumrân. *Sem* 27: 75–81.
1978   Écrits prééséniens de Qumran: d'Hénoch à Amram. In *Qumrân. Sa piété, sa théologie et son milieu.* M. DELCOR, Ed. 91–106.
REED, S. A.
1991   *Fascicle 10: Qumran Cave 4 (4Q196–4Q363) Milik.* Dead Sea Scroll Inventory Project: Lists of Documents, Photographs and Museum Plates.
RICHTER, H.-P.
1988   *A Preliminary Concordance to the Hebrew and Aramaic Fragments from Qumrân Caves II–X including especially the Unpublished Material from Cave IV.* Printed from a Card Index prepared by R. E. BROWN, J. A. FITZMYER, W. G. OXTOBY & J. TEIXIDOR. Prepared and arranged for printing by H.-P. R.: editorum in usum – distributed by H. Stegemann.

TALMON, S.
1989   The emergence of institutionalized prayer in Israel in light of Qumran literature. In *The World of Qumran from Within*. Collected Studies. Pp. 200–243.
TOV, E.
1992a   The unpublished Qumran texts from Caves 4 and 11. *JJS* **43:** 101–136.
1992b   Qumran update: The unpublished Qumran texts from Caves 4 and 11. *BA* **55:** 94–104.
TOV, E. and S. J. PFANN, Eds.
1993   *The Dead Sea Scrolls on Microfiche. A Comprehensive Facsimile Edition of the Texts from the Judaean Desert*. Edited by E. T. with the collaboration of STEPHEN J. PFANN, with a printed Catalogue by STEPHEN A. REED. Published under the Auspices of the Israel Antiquities Authority.
VANDERKAM, J. C.
1989   *The Book of Jubilees*. Vol. I.II. CSCO 510.511 (Scriptores Aethiopici Vol. 87.88).
VERMES, G.
1992   Qumran forum miscellanea I. *JJS* **43:** 299–305.
WACHOLDER, B. Z. & M. G. ABEGG
1991/1992   *A Preliminary Edition of the Unpublished Dead Sea Scrolls. The Hebrew and Aramaic Texts from Cave Four*. Fascicle One, 1991. Fascicle Two, 1992.
WACHOLDER, B. Z.
1993   A note on E. Tov's list of preliminary editions of the unpublished Dead Sea Scrolls. *JJS* **44:** 129–131.
WEISE, M.
1961   *Kultzeiten und kultischer Bundesschluß in der "Ordensregel" vom Toten Meer*. StPB 3.
WOUDE, A. S. v. d.
1990   Fünfzehn Jahre Qumranforschung (1974–1988) (Fortsetzung). *ThR* **55:** 245–307.

Report and Discussion Concerning Radiocarbon Dating of Fourteen Dead Sea Scrolls*

DENNIS PARDEE (*Session Chairman*): The paper by Dr. Willi Wölfli that figured in the original program, *Radiocarbon Dating of Fourteen Dead Sea Scrolls*, has now been faxed to us by Dr. Georges Bonani of the Institut für Mittelenergiephysik in Zurich, and Dr. Morris Shamos, Professor of Physics at New York University, has been kind enough to agree to read most sections of the paper. Prof. Shamos is of course fully qualified to answer questions regarding the physics of the paper, but he tells me that he is clearly not the one to answer questions regarding its Near Eastern aspects.

PROFESSOR MORRIS SHAMOS (on behalf of Dr. Georges Bonani): None of the 800 Qumran manuscripts bears the date of its copying and only two have an internal terminus a quo (Milik 1959). In contrast, manuscripts found in other Judean Desert sites bear specific dates. For non-date-bearing scrolls, indirect archaeological evidence, such as pottery or coins, can be used to estimate the terminus ad quem. Paleography, the study of ancient writings, is often a more accurate method of dating. The history of Jewish scripts can be delineated in great detail, and paleographers are able to ascribe dates in the range of half, or even a quarter, century (Avigad 1958; Cross 1961; Birnbaum 1971). In the decades following the initial discovery of the scrolls, however, a number of scholars began to challenge the paleographic datings, a debate which continues up to the present (Eisenman 1983). For this reason, we felt it was necessary to check on the paleographically determined ages by using an independent method.

* This report, which was conveyed at a special session of the Conference (16 December 1992) chaired by Dr. Dennis Pardee, is extracted from a text sent via facsimile on 14 December 1992 by Dr. Georges Bonani of the Institut für Mittelenergiephysik, ETH-Hönggerberg, CH-8093 Zurich, Switzerland. Other members of the Institut who contributed to the text are Dr. Susan Ivy and Dr. Willy Wölfli. Additional contributors to the original text were Mr. Magen Broshi of the Israel Museum, Dr. Israel Carmi of the Department of Environmental Sciences and Energy Research, Weizmann Institute of Science, and Prof. John Strugnell of the Divinity School, Harvard University. The full scientific report on the tests appears in *Proceedings of the 14th International 14C Conference*, A. Long and R. S. Kra, Eds., (= *Radiocarbon* **34** [3]):843–849, 1992. For another version of the paper, see *Atiqot* **20**: 27–32, 1991.

PREVIOUS RADIOCARBON DATES

Although the radiocarbon method was developed at approximately the same time that the scrolls were discovered, too much disposable material (several grams) was required. Because of this, related material from the Qumran site was dated. Libby (1951) dated the linen wrapping of a scroll. He determined a value of 1917 ± 200 B.P. (conventional radiocarbon years), indicating that the corresponding scroll might be at least 2000 years old. In 1956 and 1960, Zeuner (1969) dated pieces of charred date palm logs excavated at the Qumran site and obtained 1940 ± 85 and 1965 ± 85 B.P. Dating of material from the scrolls themselves became feasible only after the invention of accelerator mass spectrometry (AMS) (Suter *et al.* 1984; Wölfli 1987). With AMS, samples containing 0.5–1.0 mg of carbon can now be dated with an accuracy comparable to that of the decay-counting method (Bonani *et al.* 1987).

SELECTION AND SAMPLING OF THE SCROLLS

Initial sampling of the scrolls took place on 7 July, 1990 at the Rockefeller and Israel Museums in Jerusalem. TABLE 1 lists the 14 scrolls that were finally selected for dating. A total of 20 samples (in some cases up to 3 samples from different parts of a particular scroll) were taken, photographed and weighed. Scrolls 1, 12, 13 and 14 are date-bearing documents. They span a period of 1096 years and were used to test the ^{14}C method. Detailed information on the content of the selected scrolls can be found in Bonani *et al.* (1991).

SAMPLE PREPARATION

In the laboratory, the authenticity of each sample was verified by comparison with photos taken at the sampling in Israel. The samples were reweighed and recoded. Each sample was split into subsamples, which were divided into two sets. The first set was treated and measured immediately. Treatment of the second set was deferred until the radiocarbon measurement of the first set had been completed. Three types of samples were dated: parchment, papyrus and linen threads (which were attached to Sample 5, the Testament of Levi). All sample material was microscopically examined to identify and remove any foreign material, and to evaluate the condition of the parchment.

For chemical pretreatment of the samples, we followed the standard acid-base-acid steps (see, *e.g.*, Damon *et al.* 1989). The samples were first treated in an ultrasonic bath. This was followed by hot acid, base, then acid treat-

TABLE 1. The Investigated Dead Sea Scrolls and the Results of ^{14}C and Paleographic Dating

Sample No.	ETH no.	S^a	Scroll	Material	^{14}C Ages (yr B.P.)^b	Calibrated Age Range(s)^b	P^c (%)	Paleographic or specific age^d
1	6637	3	Wadi Daliyeh	Papyrus	2289 ± 55	405–354 B.C. 306–238 B.C.	55 45	352–351 B.C.^{d}
2	6640 7082	4	Testament of Qahat	Parchment	2240 ± 39	388–353 B.C. 309–235 B.C.	34 66	100–75 B.C.
3	6639	3	Pentateuchal paraphrase	Parchment	2139 ± 32	339–324 B.C. 203–117 B.C.	12 88	125–100 B.C.
4	6651 6813	4	Book of Isaiah	Parchment	2128 ± 38	335–327 B.C. 202–107 B.C.	5 95	125–100 B.C.
5	6641 6642	5	Testament of Levi	Parchment Linen thread	2125 ± 24	191–155 B.C. 146–120 B.C.	59 41	End 2nd century– beginning 1st century B.C.
6	6643	2	Book of Samuel	Parchment	2095 ± 49	192–63 B.C.		100–75 B.C.
7	6652	4	Masada Joshua	Parchment	2086 ± 28	169–93 B.C.		30–1 B.C.
8	6812	2	Masada Sectarian	Parchment	1971 ± 46	33 B.C.–A.D.74		30–1 B.C.
9	6650 6811	5	Temple	Parchment	2030 ± 40	97 B.C.–A.D.1		End 1st century B.C.– beginning 1st century A.D.
10	6646 6647	4	Genesis Apocryphon	Parchment	2013 ± 32	73 B.C.–A.D.14		End 1st century B.C.– beginning 1st century A.D.
11	6648 6649	5	Thanksgiving	Parchment	1979 ± 32	21 B.C.–A.D.61		50 B.C.–A.D.70
12	6644	3	Wadi Seyal	Papyrus	1917 ± 42	A.D.28–122		A.D.130–131^d
13	6645	3	Murabba'at	Papyrus	1892 ± 32	A.D.69–136		A.D.134^d
14	6638	2	Khirbet Mird	Papyrus	1289 ± 36	A.D.675–765		A.D.744^d

Samples 2–6 and 9–11 are from the Qumran site. The names of the other samples are identical with the locations of their discovery. The precise location where scroll 12 was found is not known. Wadi Seyal (= Nahal Se'elim) was a general term used by Bedouin treasure hunters to mislead interested scholars.

^{a} S = Number of measured sub-samples.
^{b} Calibrated age ranges are given at the 1σ level.
^{c} P = Probability of finding the true ages in the respective time windows, when more than one calibrated range is given.
^{d} Specific age from date-bearing scroll.

ments. The material was rinsed to pH 7 with distilled water between the steps. The strength of the solution, temperature and length of time of each step depended on the ability of the material to withstand the treatment. For every sample, one subsample was only ultrasonically cleaned, while another subsample was ultrasonically and chemically cleaned. This was done to assess the removal of contaminants of each type of treatment. The samples were weighed before and after the cleaning procedures to determine the weight losses resulting from each step.

Parchment samples were affected by two complications; gelatinization (Samples 9, 10 and 11) and attachment of rice paper with glue, which had been used to reinforce scrolls in poor condition (Samples 4, 5, 7, 9 and 10). Microscopic examination revealed various degrees of gelatinization, estimated by darkening of the parchment from beige, when fresh, to dark brown and translucent, when extensively gelatinized. Gelatinization is described as the unfolding of the collagen structure to form gelatin (Weiner *et al.* 1980). This results in degradation and increased solubility of the parchment. Trial cleanings with pieces of extensively gelatinized parchment showed that most of the material had dissolved after our regular "strong" treatment (0.5 M HCl, 0.1 M NaOH and 0.5 M HCl), as well as with one-half and one-fifth strength treatments. Thus one-tenth strength (0.05 M HCl, 0.01 M NaOH and 0.05 M HCl) was used to treat all parchment samples (1st and 2nd set). Each step lasted 15–60 minutes, depending on the response of the material, in a 40–60°C water bath. Prior to cleaning, visible pieces of rice paper were removed, and the glue was scraped off under the microscope. A piece of rice paper removed from the Temple scroll (Sample 9) was cleaned and dated to estimate the effect of this contaminant.

Papyrus samples (1st set) were chemically cleaned with 0.5 M HCl and 0.1 M NaOH, at 40°C for 45 minutes for each step. The final acidification was done rapidly (10 minutes) with 0.05 M HCl, because much of the material had already dissolved. To avoid similar dissolution of samples from the 2nd set, these samples were treated with 0.25 M HCl, 0.05 M NaOH and 0.25 M HCl, at 50°C for 40 minutes (for each step). The linen threads were cleaned using 0.5 M HCl, 0.1 M NaOH and 0.5 M HCl in a 40–60°C water bath, each step lasting 45 minutes.

Following the chemical treatment, each sample was dried overnight in a 60°C oven. All of the remaining sample material, or up to 10 mg, was combusted in evacuated sealed quartz tubes, with copper oxide and silver wire. This lasted for two hours at 950°C. In the presence of hydrogen, the carbon dioxide was reduced to filamentous graphite over a cobalt catalyst using the method described by Vogel *et al.* (1984) and Vogel, Southon and Nelson (1987). The resulting graphite-cobalt mixture was pressed onto copper targets for the measurement.

MEASUREMENT, DATA EVALUATION, AND CALIBRATION

The $^{14}C/^{12}C$ and $^{13}C/^{12}C$ ratios were determined quasi-simultaneously and relative to the respective NBS oxalic acid I and PDB standard values (Bonani et al. 1987). The conventional radiocarbon ages were calculated using the procedure suggested by Stuiver and Polach (1977). They were corrected for natural fractionation and reported in years B.P. (before 1950). The results listed in Table 1 are the weighted mean values of at least two independent measurements of differently prepared subsamples. The errors quoted are at the one-sigma level (1σ), and represent the statistical error of the mean or the variance, whichever is larger.

The calibrated 1σ ^{14}C age ranges (68% confidence levels) are also listed in Table 1. They were determined from the high-precision curve of Stuiver and Pearson (1986) based on dendrochronological dating. For this transformation, we used the CalibETH program (Niklaus et al. 1991) which calculates the probability distribution, as described by Stuiver & Reimer (1987). No additional uncertainty has been added, assuming that the growth period of the papyrus and the lifetime of the animals, as well as the timespan between harvesting and writing, were short compared to the other errors involved. Because of the nature of the calibration curve, the procedure leads to double ranges in five cases. Table 1 gives the probability of finding the true age in one of the two age ranges.

RESULTS AND DISCUSSION

The specific dates of the date-bearing scrolls and the paleographically determined age ranges, given in Figure 1, were disclosed to the participants at the Zürich AMS facility only after completion of the measurements. For ease of comparison, these data are displayed together with the calibrated, 1σ ^{14}C age ranges in Table 1. The true ages of the four date-bearing manuscripts (Samples 1, 12, 13 and 14) lie within or close to the respective 1σ ranges. This indicates no significant methodological offset, either in the ^{14}C method or in the calibration curve based on measurements on American bristlecone pine and Irish oak trees. Good agreement between radiocarbon and paleographic dates is also observed in 9 of the remaining 10 samples. However, a slight systematic shift between the calibrated radiocarbon ages and the estimates of the paleographers might be inferred from the data. The calibrated ^{14}C ages are, on average, 35 years older. The statistical significance of this offset remains to be proven.

A discrepancy of approximately 200 years exists between the paleographical date and the calibrated radiocarbon dates of the Testament of Qahat (Sample 2 in Figure 1). The calibrated radiocarbon date was determined from

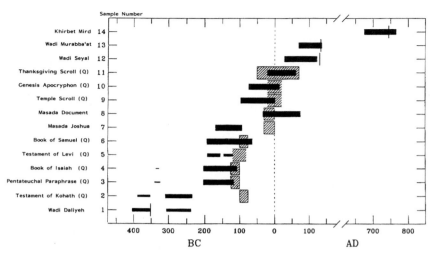

FIGURE 1. Comparison of the calibrated 1σ ^{14}C ranges (*horizontal black bars*) with paleographical estimates (*hatched areas*) and specified dates (*vertical lines*). The thickness of the black bars is proportional to the probability of finding the true age within the corresponding 1σ range.

four chemically cleaned and independently measured samples. Paleographically the Testament of Qahat has been ascribed a date of Late Hasmonean (Bonani et al. 1991). The possibility that the parchment was used for a second time (*i.e.*, a palimpsest) can also be ruled out; infrared tests do not show evidence of earlier writing (Almog, personal communication 1990). It is also unlikely that the parchment was left unused for such a long period of time. However, in this case, it is difficult to rule out chemical contamination. Two separate samples, from distinct parts of the Qahat scroll, were taken at different times. In both cases, the samples that were only ultrasonically cleaned were approximately 350 years older than the samples that were ultrasonically and chemically cleaned. Possible contaminants include castor oil (used, at one time, to improve the visibility of the writing), rice paper and glue. Castor oil and rice paper would yield younger apparent ages, as they contain modern carbon. On the other hand, the glue (a petroleum product) used to attach the rice paper to the scrolls would increase the apparent age of the scroll. Microscopic examination of the Qahat sample material did not reveal the presence of rice paper or glue; also, the parchment was ungelatinized. It is interesting to note that a sample of rice paper and glue removed from the Temple scroll (Sample 9) yielded an age of 6215 ± 75 B.P. It should be emphasized that no similar age discrepancy was found between the solely ultrasonic and ultrasonic and chemically cleaned sub-samples of the other 13 scrolls that were dated.

Parchment samples from the Temple, Genesis, and Thanksgiving scrolls were visibly the most gelatinized of the scrolls that we investigated. The parchment material was uniformly dark brown and translucent. During the initial sampling, an attempt was made to obtain ungelatinized portions in addition to samples from gelatinized edges of these scrolls. Also, additional, fresher material was requested from the Temple scroll. TABLE 3 in *Radiocarbon* (**34**[3]: 843–849) shows the results of dating gelatinized and ungelatinized samples from the same scroll. It includes the weighted averages for chemically treated and solely ultrasonically cleaned subsamples, and shows that the results agree within the stated error. This indicates that gelatinization does not affect the ^{14}C age of the parchment.

REFERENCES CITED

AVIGAD, N. 1958. The palaeography of the Dead Sea Scrolls and related documents. In *Aspects of the Dead Sea Scrolls (= Scripta Hierosolymitana IV)*. C. RABIN & Y. YADIN, Eds. Magnes Press: 56–87.

BENOIT, P., J. T. MILIK & R. DE VAUX. 1961. *Discoveries in the Judaen Desert, II*. Oxford: Oxford University Press. Pp. 93–95.

BIRNBAUM, S. A. 1971. *The Hebrew Scripts*. Leiden: Paleographic. 127 p.

BONANI, G., J. BEER, H.-J. HOFMANN, H. A. SYNAL, W. WÖLFLI, C. PFLEIDERER, B. KROMER, C. JUNGHAUS & K. O. MÜNNICH. 1987. Fractionation, precision and accuracy in ^{14}C and ^{13}C measurements. *Nuclear Instruments and Methods* **B29**: 87–90.

BONANI, G., M. BROSHI, I. CARMI, S. IVY, J. STRUGNELL & W. WÖLFLI. 1991. Radiocarbon dating of 14 Dead Sea Scrolls. *Atiqot* **XX**: 27–32.

BROSHI, M. 1990. The Dead Sea Scrolls discovery and identification. *Israel Museum Journal* **9**: 31–41.

CROSS, F. M. 1961. The development of the Jewish scripts in the Bible and the ancient Near East. In *The Bible and the Ancient Near East*. G. E. WRIGHT, Ed. :133–202. London: Routledge and Kegan Paul.

DAMON, P. E., D. J. DONAHUE, B. H. GORE, A. L. HATHEWAY, A. J. T. JULL, T. W. LINICK, P. J. SERCEL, L. J. TOOLIN, C. R. BRONK, E. T. HALL, R. E. M. HEDGES, R. HOUSLEY, I. A. LAW, C. PERRY, G. BONANI, S. TRUMBORE, W. WÖLFLI, J. C. AMBERS, S. G. E. BOWMAN, M. N. LEESE & M. S. TITE. 1989. Dating of the Shroud of Turin. *Nature* **337**: 611–615.

EISENMAN, R. 1983. *Maccabees, Zadokites, Christians and Qumran*. Leiden: Brill. Pp. 29–31.

LIBBY, W. F. 1951. Radiocarbon dates II. *Science* **114**: 291–296.

MILIK, J. T. 1959. *Ten Years of Discovery in the Wilderness of Judea*. London: SCM Press. 73 p.

NIKLAUS, T., G. BONANI, M. SIMONIUS, M. SUTER & W. WÖLFLI. 1991. CalibETH – an interactive computer program for the calibration of radiocarbon dates. *Radiocarbon* **34**(3): 843–849.

STUIVER, M. & H. A. POLACH. 1977. Discussion: Reporting of ^{14}C data. *Radiocarbon* **19**(3): 355–363.

STUIVER, M. & G. W. PEARSON. 1986. High-precision calibration of the radiocarbon time scale, AD 1950–500 BC. In Proceedings of the 12th International ^{14}C conference. M. STUIVER & R. S. KRA, Eds. *Radiocarbon* **28**(2B): 805–838.

STUIVER, M. & P. J. REIMER. 1987. User's Guide to the Program Calib and Display Rev 2.1: Quaternary Isotope Laboratory, University of Washington, Seattle.

SUKENIK, E. L. 1948. *Hidden Scrolls Preliminary Report.* Jerusalem. Mossad Bialik. (In Hebrew.)

SUTER, M., R. BALZER, G. BONANI, H. J. HOFMANN, E. MORENZONI, M. NESSI, W. WÖLFLI, M. ANDREE, J. BEER & H. OESCHGER. 1984. Precision measurements of ^{14}C in AMS—some results and prospects. *Nuclear Instruments and Methods* **B5:** 117–122.

VOGEL, J. S., J. R. SOUTHON & D. E. NELSON. 1987. Catalyst and binder effects in the use of filamentous graphite for AMS. *Nuclear Instruments and Methods* **B29:** 50–56.

VOGEL, J. S., J. R. SOUTHON, D. E. NELSON & T. A. BROWN. 1984. Performance of catalytically condensed carbon for use in accelerator mass spectrometry. *Nuclear Instruments and Methods* **B5:** 289–293.

WEINER, S., Z. KUSTANOVICH, G. A. EMANUEL & W. TRAUB. 1980. Dead Sea Scroll parchments: Unfolding of the collagen molecules and racemization of aspartic acid. *Nature* **287**(5785): 820–823.

WÖLFLI, W. 1987. Advances in accelerator mass spectrometry. *Nuclear Instruments and Methods* **B29:** 1–13.

ZEUNER, F. E. 1969. Notes on Qumran. *Palestine Exploration Quarterly* **92:** 27–36.

DISCUSSION OF THE PAPER

JOSEPH A. FITZMYER (*Catholic University, Washington, D.C.*): You mentioned castor oil. Would the use of castor oil in modern times affect the dating? The reason I ask the question is that I spent a year in the Scrollery, as they called it, in what was then called the Palestine Archaeological Museum. During the course of that year some of the fragments were cleaned with castor oil. This was something that was applied to some of those fragments in modern times, during the year 1957–58. If a fragment so treated in modern times were submitted to this process, would that effect the radiocarbon dating?

MORRIS SHAMOS (*New York University, New York*): It would, and I'm sure that's what the authors have in mind here when they mention the castor oil being used to improve the legibility of the documents. Certainly that wasn't done at the time the documents were inscribed, it must have been done subsequently.

NORMAN GOLB (*Oriental Institute, University of Chicago, Chicago, IL*): I have certain criticisms of the way this study was done, and I'd like to point out some of the difficulties.

One version of the study was published in *Atiqot* (Vol. 20, 1991, pp. 27–32)—a journal published both in Hebrew and in English in Israel. At the end of that article it states, "Our research put to test both the radiocarbon method and paleography. Seemingly both disciplines have fared well." I didn't hear that statement in the form of the article from which you read, so that's curious to me. There is another statement in the form of the study you read which is apparently not in the *Atiqot* version, so I believe, namely that there was a 35 year discrepancy. Now I am concerned about the results.

As we see from the slides being displayed, in the first article, in *Atiqot*, the statements are made that "paleography is often a more accurate method of dating," "the history of Jewish scripts can be delineated in great detail," "Paleographers are in a position to ascribe dates within a range of half or even a quarter century." I've studied the paleography of the Genizah texts for about 40 years, and I would disagree with this statement, which could not have been made by the radiocarbon people. Six scholars wrote this article, including two Qumranologists, Mr. Broshi in Jerusalem and Professor Strugnell of Harvard. This was obviously their own assertion, but according to the final paragraph of the article the research puts to rest any questions about the palaeographic results and the radiocarbon method. This is just what we want to find out, namely, if the radiocarbon datings support the assumed paleographical dating.

The *Atiqot* statement is that good agreement between radiocarbon and paleographic dates has been achieved, as though the paleographic dates are *givens* whereas they are just hypothesized. There is no way of proving those dates except by inferences from the forms of letters in similarly undated documents. We don't have *dated* documents of the scroll period. The basic trouble with the statement, as I see it, is that if the paleographical dates had been, let's say 25 or 50 years earlier, the radiocarbon dating would support it equally well. There's nothing in the radiocarbon data to show that this one particular 25-year period is the right one. The only satisfactory result is attained in the Thanksgiving Scroll, where Avigad in Jerusalem more cautiously hypothesized the date-span to be about 100 years, from around 50 B.C. to 50 A.D. There the radiocarbon dating works very nicely, because the hypothesized paleographic dating was a much broader one. Where that hasn't been the case, we have no proof that these dates are the right ones, rather than dates which would have been 75 years or so earlier.

SHAMOS: I think I might be able to contribute something to that if you allow me. I realize that it's always nice to have complete overlap of two reference points, but I must emphasize again that these are derived statistically. You know statistics have a habit of not always giving you what you want. Yes, this is excellent agreement right here, presumably. If you ask me, would I depend upon the dates or the spans of dates determined by radiocarbon dating by this particular method of radiocarbon dating, I would say, definitely yes. If you ask me if this particular institute in Zürich is known for what they do, I would say definitely yes, they're one of the best in the world.

GOLB: They alone should have written the article, without the input of those who may have felt more or less a responsibility to defend the paleographic dating.

SHAMOS: I quite agree.

LAWRENCE SCHIFFMAN (*New York University, New York*): I read this article in considerable detail and had occasion to speak to some of those who put it together. I think it is obvious that the article calls into question by a small margin the paleographic dating. The grouping of virtually all of the carbon 14 datings a little bit earlier calls that dating into question. On the other hand, the statement which is made here about paleography and its relationship to dating is intended to tell you the truth. The truth is exactly as you see it, namely that both fields, radiocarbon dating and paleography, are fields in development that cannot be depended on 100% by anybody, and they admitted this to you. They tested some dated documents as well; the sum total of the operation showed that the paleography is not a cover-up, but the paleography covered a bit later than the carbon 14 dates. Anybody with any sense reading this could raise the issue that the paleography appears to be slightly off. I think it's fairly obvious, but on the other hand it's amazing how relatively accurate it is.

It seems you're reading this article almost to ask why didn't they do one of two things, either cover it up or tell me the whole paleography is worthless. What we learned is that we can't overstate the validity of paleography, as you correctly stated; on the other hand it's not a worthless science. From the Testament of Kohath I learn that carbon 14 dating, paleography, and all of our sciences may tell us that not everything is the way we thought it was, and we better be more humble than we tend to be in the way we state our conclusions.

I think this article makes very clear that this field of carbon 14 dating, just like the field of Dead Sea Scroll studies, is a field which is progressing. They came to our material as a help to refine their own science.

GOLB: To the statement of Dr. Schiffman I must certainly object. It says at the beginning of the *Atiqot* article that paleography is often a more accurate method of dating: "The history of Jewish scripts can be delineated in great detail and paleographers are in a position to ascribe dates within ranges of a half, or even a quarter, century." *etc.* I object to this statement. There is no proof in the case of the paleography of the Dead Sea Scrolls that 25 year dating spans are correct. The radiocarbon results do *not* support such a narrow dating. The results support an ancient dating within a range of approximately a century. That's fine, but we can't get any closer on the basis of paleographic analysis. We don't have dated documents of the period. In the Cairo Genizah we do have many dated documents, which makes it possible for us to date other texts of similar or the same handwriting. But I would never dare to date a Genizah document (written a thousand years after these texts) to within a span of less than 100 years.

We once had a lecture at the Oriental Institute by a very eminent Hebrew paleographer, Dr. Birnbaum of London, and after his lecture he came to my office. I showed him a big stack of Cairo Genizah documents which were dated. I said, "Let's play a game. I'll cover up the dates, and let's see how close you can get." He didn't want to do it, and there is good reason why not. He was prudent.

CHAIRMAN DENNIS PARDEE (*Oriental Institute, University of Chicago, Chicago, IL*): Would you subscribe, Dr. Shamos, to that description from a physicist's point of view, that these two charts superimposed one on the other, the paleographic and the ^{14}C, no longer allow one to date a Hebrew manuscript within 25 years, but rather closer to 100 years?

SHAMOS: To me it would be a safe statement, yes. But I would like to add something to a comment of Dr. Schiffman's, because I think he's perfectly correct. In the science of radiocarbon dating we have moved by a factor of 1000, roughly, in sensitivity over a period of 40 years or so. In the future I think you will have a more sensitive method of distinguishing between the paleography and the carbon dating.

HERSHEL SHANKS (editor, *Biblical Archaeology Review*): Professor Fitzmyer asked you, Dr. Shamos, about the contamination from castor oil, and I thought you said that might indeed change the result. The reason I'm going into this is because of sample #2, the Testament of Kohath. I don't know if you meant to leave the impression from your answer to Joe Fitzmyer's question, that maybe that accounts for the discrepancy on #2, but I think the paper itself said that they had no idea, they couldn't account for the discrepancy in #2.

SHAMOS: I didn't intend that. It would have interfered with the result if the castor oil had not been cleaned off properly. I'm assuming that in the cleaning of the sample that castor oil was removed.

SHANKS: You also said that the castor oil would make it appear younger, not older.

SHAMOS: That's right.

SHANKS: A gentleman wrote to *BAR* asking if we could have more tests. He was willing to pay for them. I transmitted that letter to the Israel Antiquities Authority and received a reply that they were going to submit this question to the Archeological Council. Recently I received a reply that the Archeological Council has authorized additional carbon 14 tests. Included in the new tests would be the last part of the Damascus Document. If any of you have critical documents where you think that a carbon 14 test would be useful I'd love to hear from you. I will transmit that to the Israeli authorities.

FITZMYER: I disagree with the way Professor Golb is interpreting this material. I would agree with him, however, that it would have been better had the people in Zürich written this article on their own, without any contribution from either Broshi or Strugnell. I can see the conflict of interest. I can also agree that, the way the thing is described, claims are being made that are not necessarily based on the evidence of the radiocarbon dating itself. But I would tend to agree with the paleographers, even with their claim about 50 or 25 years. I think they're within their rights to establish that kind of plus or minus.

Except for the Testament of Kohath, which is creating the problem, in all the other cases radiocarbon dating has confirmed what the paleographers have said. I think that's what we should be looking at, apart from the charges and the claims that are being made here as far as the article itself is concerned.

GOLB: Dr. Shamos just said, however, in response to my question that we should enlarge our dating range to closer to a century instead of a quarter century. That is what I heard him say as a physicist's remark to that answer.

FITZMYER: What I'm saying to you, though, is I don't find the paleographical margin of error that much out of key with what the radiocarbon dating has come up with.

GOLB: No, it overlaps, except that the margin of error of 25 or 50 years is a good deal less then the carbon 14 people would claim.

FITZMYER: I realize that, that's the claim that the paleographer makes. You must remember that the estimate has been based on a lot of material that the paleographers have. I personally tend to respect that.

GOLB: If you wish to defend paleographers in a certain way you're certainly entitled to. In my experience in a paleographical investigation of the Cairo Genizah documents, however, I do not find it possible to date Hebrew texts to within periods of less than 100 years. (If you care for a detailed discussion on my part of paleographical considerations, you might look for example into my *Khazarian Hebrew Documents of the 10th Century*, where I have a very detailed paleographical discussion.) I haven't produced charts for a paleography of Cairo Genizah texts because we're not yet in a position to do that; there are too many manuscripts. Maybe in 100 years we'll have all of them accurately dated.

AL WOLTERS (*Redeemer College, Ancaster, Ont., Canada*): If those black lines representing the carbon 14 dates were to represent a 90% probability, how much longer would they be?

SHAMOS: Should I make a little calculation? 95% would be twice as long, so 90% would be a little less than twice as long.

WOLTERS: And would it go from the middle?

SHAMOS: Yes, from the middle.

FERDINAND DEXINGER (*University of Vienna*): Being neither a paleographer nor an expert in carbon-dating methods, for me this chart shows one thing: The paleographic dating lies, statistically speaking, within the physical possibilities. In that sense it is correct and it's not wrong. For me as a historian, that says that, using these texts, I have to interpret them or use them within the radiocarbon possibilities.

SHAMOS: I think I would agree with that.

PARDEE: If I may inject my view, it shows that the paleographers weren't out to lunch. On the other hand, it does not show that their claim to be able to date manuscripts within 25 years is supported.

SHAMOS: No, it doesn't do that.

PARDEE: Neither more nor less.

JEFF ROGERS (*Furman University, Greenville, NC*): From what I hear people saying, one looks at the chart and says I'm still comfortable, another looks at the chart and says I'm still not comfortable. I think one of the things to look at is the range where we do have internal dates and that suggests to us that we're not going to get the kind of precision that all of us would like from the correspondence of these two methods of dating, certainly because of the statistical issues and perhaps as well because of errors which we might make.

PARDEE: Dr. Shamos, would you care to remark on the fact that the dated document is always to the left of the bar. Does that mean anything to you?

SHAMOS: One might think that there's some kind of systematic deviation on the part of the radiocarbon dating, and that the deviation is always toward the older document age. That's a conclusion one's tempted to make, but I would hesitate to do that. There may be a systematic error in the radiocarbon dating. They continue to explore that possibility all the time. I would suggest that, but I won't claim it.

SCHIFFMAN: We're talking about the date of death of the animal whose skin appears here. I don't think people kept it on parchment for too long, but just remember we're talking about the death of the animal, not the writing of the scroll.

If we speak about Hebrew paleography in samples 12 and 13 (and admittedly we need more samples to prove what I'm saying), it appears to be quite clear that the paleographers did a very good job but they were off by a few years and we have to simply move everything back a little bit in age as a result of carbon 14. That's possibility number one.

Possibility number two is that as the carbon 14 people continue to refine their work with both our samples and other samples we may find out that that's not totally the case. In other words, we're not dealing here with paleography being no good and you can't do it, and we're not dealing here with carbon 14 being perfect and it proves everything. We're dealing with working together between two different methodologies for dating which are getting us a lot closer to where we are. And one of the things that seems to emerge from all this evidence is that the paleographers dated things a bit too late and their work will have to be refined in light of the carbon 14, unless there are further surprises for us in the future of carbon 14 dating.

PAUL GARNET (*Concordia University, Montreal, Que., Canada*): I would be intrigued to know how soon after the death of an animal can one write on its skin, and how long will that skin keep before it's no longer usable for such purposes?

Ethics of Publication of the Dead Sea Scrolls: Panel Discussion*

PANELISTS: Eric Meyers (*chairman*), Norman Golb, Lawrence Schiffman, and James VanderKam. In addition, a prepared statement from James Robinson was read by Chairman Meyers. Open discussion follows the presentations.

CHAIRMAN MEYERS: At this time we will begin our session on the ethics of archaeology and publication. We're going to keep to the schedule as previously announced, with some flexibility, but with greater strictness than this morning.

I will be serving as chairman again. I will be speaking on some background with reference to the adopted statement of the American Schools of Oriental Research (ASOR) at our recent convention. The Chairman of the ASOR subcommittee, James VanderKam, will be second; he will also be presenting the document adopted by the Society for Biblical Literature and will be making a statement on behalf of Emanuel Tov and the Israel Antiquities Authority. Dr. Schiffman will come third, a statement from James Robinson sent to me by fax will follow, and Dr. Golb will be the fourth panelist to speak.

With your permission, we will call this session to order.

While we all regret how difficult it has been to access some of the Dead Sea Scrolls, some of us, myself included, have applauded the open access that today willy-nilly exists. However, if we had it to do all over again, no one, I believe, would do it quite the same way.

Many groups have made mistakes—of that, there is no doubt. The Jordanians erred when they assigned a group of scholars projects that were unrealistic and then again permitted an excavation on the site to go forward and to not truly require a final report. The Israelis were trying to do good in the eyes of the world after 1967 but did not press to change the assignments for fear of arousing negative world opinion. Ironically, they let the Jordanian guidelines exist until the mid-1980s when John Strugnell was appointed chief editor and a new broadened group of scholars was invited to participate in the scholarly presentation of the data.

Only after his notorious interview with Avi Katzman reprinted in the BAR did Strugnell's plan come to public scrutiny. The Israel Antiquities Authority

---

* Names and affiliations for all panelists and speakers from the floor will be found in an APPENDIX to this panel discussion.

ultimately removed John Strugnell and appointed a new team with 40+ scholars assigned to complete the work of the original discovery by circa 1997. However, the stand taken by the Huntington Library of September 1991 with regard to access made many of the previous arrangements moot.

Indeed, the stand of the Huntington Library after the publication of the Abegg-Wacholder manuscripts, the BAR facsimile edition, with and without the Qumran MMT, and most recently the Eisenman-Wise volume, which has to all intents and purposes placed the entire Dead Sea Scrolls corpus into the public hands for full review and scrutiny, has fulfilled the desires of many including Drs. Golb, Shanks, Wacholder, Eisenman, and others to place these treasures into the hands of all who desired them.

In my view, having seen all the new publications, I'm not convinced that the way that this corpus has come to light serves either the public's interest or the scholarly desire to know what exists. Let me explain.

There is no doubt that the entire history of trickle-down publication of Dead Sea Scrolls is unfortunate. But, let us recall some relevant and not unimportant historical data. There was the War of Israel Independence that followed shortly after the discovery of the Dead Sea Scrolls and the founding of the state of Israel in 1948. The Scrolls were found in what was to become the Hashemite Kingdom of Jordan and the subsequent excavations of the École Biblique were carried out under its auspices.

While there was in 1956 the Suez War, the most important political development affecting the Scrolls was the 1967 June war, which placed the Rockefeller Museum and Antiquities Authority completely under the control of the Israeli authorities. This included virtually all of the Scrolls except the Copper Scroll and other fragments as well as archaeological data which stayed in Jordan in the Amman Museum.

No significant changes were undertaken by the Israel Department of Antiquities at the time, and the old assignment schedules of Jordan and the assignment of the excavation report to the École Biblique were honored by Israel with every good intention.

The results of this laissez faire attitude or approach by Israel, however, were all too modest and slow: very little new publication occurred after 1967, although much had appeared through the years on the Scrolls themselves, especially in the Oxford DJD editions, which continue to appear to this day, and the numerous articles on the archaeology of Qumran (cited in this morning session) by de Vaux and others and the interim reports that were produced in that connection.

It was inertia, tradition, and, ironically, desire by the Israelis not to rock the boat that allowed existing understandings to continue through the 1970s and into the mid-1980s under Israeli supervision. In hindsight, it appears to have been a policy too benign and too tolerant. At the time, however, the majority view was that this was the best course of action. When certain individuals already mentioned began lobbying in public for greater access to the Scrolls and began attacking the official team of scholars as the cartel, a largely sympathetic public affirmed their feelings of outrage and disappointment.

Newspapers, TV, and the media here with us again today jumped on the bandwagon, stating that the official team of the Israel Antiquities Authority was conspiring to cover up historical information of all sorts and was complicitous in an Israeli coverup. That the public believed this is not surprising. But, that the cover-up theory gained currency and the concomitant belief that the delay was deliberate is most unfortunate. A myth was thus created by the American public in this connection, regarding the unreliable and irresponsible scholarly community. This myth is documented in a film that I helped produce with Biblical Productions which is now available through Filmmakers Library in New York City.

Neither the Israel Antiquities Authority nor the official team, either before or after John Strugnell's leadership desired, attempted or participated in any conscious delay of publication let alone in the cover-up of materials thought to be too sensitive for public consumption, in my opinion. This group does not need me to rehearse the complexity of the preparation of Cave 4 plates, given the hundreds of thousands of fragments that are associated with it.

There was and is a decent if not defensible and distinguished record of publication of the major documents of the Dead Sea Scrolls. That some surprises were to be found in the unpublished texts is not at all to be unexpected. That they have come out only since the availability of the negatives through the Huntington Library is something worth talking about and it is to this issue that I now turn.

The underlying and still unanswered question of the ethics of publishing the Dead Sea Scrolls to me seems to be whose scrolls are they? Under whose legal jurisdiction do they fall? And, what connection do they have to the approved excavations of the Dead Sea Scroll cave site and its environs?

Unfortunately and predictably, the answers to these questions are complex. Israel did not become a major player in the picture until 1967 when it annexed the Rockefeller Museum in which the scrolls were housed and stored. As I have said, even then, Israel did not exert any pressure on the international team, even though many Israeli and Jewish scholars had not been included in that team and the team itself was well known to be delinquent in publishing and not open to broad Jewish participation.

Until Strugnell's infamous interview and until the late 1980s, not many in academia or in publishing seemed to mind that the corpus was still incompletely published and that there were some important manuscripts still to be published also—especially MMT which had circulated unofficially for some time and had appeared in a pirated Kapera edition in Poland.

Be this as it may, in 1980, Miss Elizabeth Hay Bechtel won agreement from the Israel Department of Antiquities to rephotograph the entire Dead Sea Scroll corpus for the purpose of proper preservation in a variety of locations in the United States. Apparently there was some understanding that the Ancient Biblical Manuscript Center at Claremont would be the official repository, along with Oxford University, Hebrew Union College, and other places as well.

Unbeknownst to Israel and to the others, however, was the fact that Ms. Bechtel had printed an additional set of negatives which she deposited in the Huntington Library for safekeeping (and I might add parenthetically they almost came to Duke University). When she died in 1987, her will declared the Huntington Library Depository to be the sole owner of the library of the Qumran negatives. The original intent had been that Claremont, the Ancient Biblical Manuscript Center there, was to have been the place, but a falling out between Ms. Bechtel and Professor James Sanders there made that impossible. Obviously, the IAA was upset that the Huntington chose to ignore the conditions set on the 1980 photographic mission, which had specified that negatives were to be used with the Israel Antiquities Authority's agreement and approval.

The recent spate of lawsuits, however, over MMT and surely others that will follow casts a cloud over the entire issue. Because there were so many fragments, the special configuration of small negatives by assigned scholars has become an issue of intellectual property. The Jerusalem Court for example is now involved at one level in deciding on the case of MMT regarding the Shanks-Eisenman edition and its legality, as well as a Philadelphia court also *vis-à-vis* Professor Qimron. I understand Professor Alan Dershowitz and another attorney are defending Professor Qimron in the Philadelphia suit.

The fact of the matter is that since the deposition in 1982 of the complete photographic archives at the Huntington Library and several other places, which I mentioned, the Scrolls have been accessible to anyone interested enough to read them. There is no doubt that the Israel Antiquities Authority and the Rockefeller Museum of Jerusalem that houses them own the Scrolls, unless one would challenge the Israeli annexation of East Jerusalem and its appropriation of the Palestine Archaeological Museum (the Rockefeller).

The question is how ownership of a manuscript in which a text is embodied passes from one body to another. To put it differently, when is a text no longer under copyright protection? But, since many texts were not published, do the laws of copyright apply?

At the most recent ASOR (American Schools of Oriental Research) meeting in San Francisco two weeks ago, the society reaffirmed the right of the Israel Antiquities Authority to manage and regulate cultural resources, both written and nonwritten. The ASOR statement differs from other existing statements in that it takes into full account both the written textual remains and all of the archaeological remains. Moreover, ASOR reaffirmed the principle of reasonable time for publication with respect to both written and non-written finds. In addition, with regard to access, ASOR reaffirmed the right of the host government in which land the discovery was made to regulate access and to secure proper preservation of the finds. This is key. ASOR also reaffirmed that after reasonable time limit, the material, photographs and documentation should be made generally accessible to interested parties within the limits of the requirements for preservation.

Now, this may not seem earthshaking to many of you, but it does say something very significant. First, ASOR does not distinguish between written and nonwritten remains as I have indicated, with respect to either access or timely publication; for those of you who are archaeologists know that were we to provide full access to archaeological data, following soon upon excavation, it would be catastrophic for many projects.

Second, ASOR recognizes the authority and jurisdiction of the host country in such matters.

Third, access obviously can mean one thing for artifacts and another for written remains. The host authority should facilitate such collaboration where possible and appropriate.

Finally, it is the opinion of ASOR scholars that the host country must come to grips with the issue of what constitutes a reasonable time for publication. If you were to look up the parliamentary law in Israel regarding timely publication, it would be very very vague. If you were to look up the equivalent law in the Hashemite Kingdom of Jordan it would be sufficiently vague, and also in Cyprus. I think it's time now for the host countries to refine the laws that they pass regarding reasonable time for publication.

However, these guidelines apply to the present controversy. First let me say that over the past 45 years, full access to the corpus was not provided by Jordan or Israel or by the International Team. Also, it is obvious that more than a reasonable time has elapsed between discovery and publication. Am I happy with the Huntington Library decision or the facsimile edition of the BAS, or the recent Eisenman-Wise publication? No, I am not. The new team and timetable imposed by the Israel Antiquities Authority two years ago, circa 1997, should have been allowed an opportunity to complete official publication. The imminent release through E. J. Brill of the Israel Antiquities Authority copies of negatives shows good intent, albeit tardy and in response to international pressure.

However, when truth be told, many older scholars have now been hurt in the process and their efforts of years have not been recognized by the people publishing unauthorized texts. Now the matter has been thrown into the courts where it will probably remain for years to come. This is unfortunate and too bad. No doubt new lawsuits will follow.

Once the team was reorganized and a timetable established, protocols for access should have been immediately worked out, and they were being worked on at the time of the Huntington Library decision. The Huntington Library obviously consulted lawyers, however, before going public, and those lawyers apparently advised them that they could open up the Bechtel Qumran photo archives to the public without fear of legal interference from Israel. This precedent, in my opinion (not speaking on behalf of ASOR), is idiosyncratic and it seems to me should not serve as a basis on which to guide future discoveries.

Such specific protocols, if and when they are established, must take into account the patrimony of the country in which the discovery is made. Otherwise, it seems to me, there would be chaos. I don't see pressure being placed on Syria to hurry up with the publication of the Ebla cuneiform archives. I don't see pressure on Israel to publish and provide full access to all of the unpublished digs that have occurred there. I don't see pressure on Jordan for the same issues. And, I don't see pressures in Cyprus either.

In short, I'm happy that we have full Qumran photo archives available today, but I am not happy with the first results and I hope that no precedent is seen in these actions.

In conclusion, I call upon all of our academic societies, not just ASOR and the SBL, but AJS as well as other interested parties and groups to lobby with the antiquities authorities in separate countries to uphold the laws of their land in this connection and to spell out in greater detail what constitutes access and how one realizes it and what constitutes a reasonable time limit for publication, either of written or nonwritten remains, either excavated or discovered by chance or even purchased from dealers or from an anonymous source.

JAMES VANDERKAM: I have been asked to do two things that are related and both somewhat out of date, I suspect. They both relate to 1991 which is a long time ago in this field.

The first is to relate a communication from Emanuel Tov to Professor Golb. Professor Golb asked Tov to submit a statement that Tov had given at the Society of Biblical Literature Annual Meeting a year ago in Kansas City. And, Tov responded that he apparently did not have a written copy of his address at that time, and also that the context had changed somewhat. But, in response, this is what Tov wrote and he has indicated that it is permissible to use this in public.

Tov writes: "I did find a hand-written copy of my address to the panel discussion at the Kansas City meeting. That discussion incidentally was organized by the Society of Biblical Literature and on that panel several people gave statements." (They included Tov, Eugene Ulrich, Martin Abegg, William Moffett of the Huntington Library, James Sanders and myself.)

In his address, Tov touched on a number of issues that he was asked to summarize here. He says he did think this would be worthwhile, but he did not think it would be worthwhile to send the text as a whole, which should be viewed in the light of the then-heated discussion about the issue of free access to the Scrolls. That issue, he writes, was settled more than a year ago with the press release of the Israel Antiquities Authority of October 27, 1991, allowing that access.

Tov writes,

In my talk, I quoted that press release which starts off in the following way. "The Israel Antiquities Authority has decided to grant access to photos of the Judean desert scrolls at the Rockefeller Museum Building. In unanimous agreement, the three authorized institutions abroad—Hebrew Union College at Cincinnati, the Ancient Biblical Manuscript Center at Claremont, and the Oxford Center for Postgraduate Hebrew Studies at Yarnton—where photos were officially deposited will also permit access to their photo collections." That's the end of that statement.

Then Tov adds that he included the following statement which was new at the conference as it was based on an IAA decision of November 11, 1991.

At that stage [that is, the stage when the October 27 statement was issued] it was expected from the users of photographic images that they would sign a declaration stating that the content of the texts may be quoted in all publications, but not including a text edition. At a second stage, which has not been widely publicized, the IAA realized that this request was not practical. Thus, two weeks after the first new release, the IAA relieved the institutions holding the photographs from the request to institute such a declaration. That is, anyone asking for access to any or all of the photographs will automatically get permission to do so without any limitation both in Israel and at the institutions abroad.

Tov continues,

Since you ask for these statements, I send them to you hoping that you had this in mind. At the same time I respectfully submit that the issues raised in recent weeks by the publication of the book by Eisenman and Wise are not related to the statement you asked for, nor do they seem to be related to the other statements referred to in the first paragraph of Professor Golb's letter. At stake are different matters, mainly scholarly honestly and unauthorized and inappropriate quoting from unpublished and published transcriptions and scholarly discussions, which are the intellectual property of the scholars who had carried out the research and who now see their work in print without their names attached or improperly quoted.

A letter of protest concerning these unacceptable procedures signed by many members of the international committee publishing the scrolls is being dispatched in these days (also to you in the congress). I hope that you and the distinguished members of the panel realize that different issues are involved and I hope that at the panel the right issues will be addressed; that is, the matters mentioned in the preceding paragraph and in our letter of protest, all of which instigated the organizers of the New York Academy of Sciences Conference to institute the panel discussion. The issue of the general approach to the scrolls is an important issue, as well; but, that has been settled in October–November 1991.

These are the contents of Dr. Tov's letter.

The second item that I was asked to present to you is the statement by the Society of Biblical Literature adopted in 1991 regarding access to manuscript discoveries. Briefly, let me sketch the history of that document. The American Schools of Oriental Research appointed a committee, the Ancient Manuscripts Committee, to look into this issue and to attempt to come up with a statement. The Society of Biblical Literature heard of this and decided it was a good idea to do the same. So, through the Research and Publications Committee of the SBL, a statement was drawn up in 1991. It was presented to the Research and Publications Committee, to the SBL Council, and to the SBL business meeting. It was meant to be a strong statement, raising the question of who if anyone had rights in this area and aiming to avoid another scroll situation. It was hoped that the SBL could use whatever moral authority it has to urge people who hold power in these areas to act in accord with it. This same statement (after it was adopted by the SBL) was then presented to ASOR, whose Ancient Manuscripts Committee had of course originated the process. That Ancient Manuscripts Committee approved it a year ago, but the trustees of ASOR did not accept it and returned it for committee discussion, as well as discussion within the wider context of archaeological policy. So ASOR has come up with a statement, as Eric Meyers indicated, in this past year.

The SBL statement which I will read to you could be characterized as an ideal statement, adopted by a group that does not conduct digs or own property in countries where digs are conducted. Hence, it is different in those regards than ASOR is. But, the statement operates on the principle that having more people working on a text should, in most cases, be a better situation than just a single person or a small number, in that no one has exclusive rights to finds of manuscripts: all scholars do, and others as well.

The statement I am going to read has been called naïve, and there may be some naïveté in it. But it has some virtue, too.

The Society of Biblical Literature wishes to encourage prompt publication of ancient written materials and ready access to unpublished textual materials. In order to achieve these ends, the Society adopts the following guidelines: First, recommendation to those who own or control ancient written materials. Those who own or control ancient written materials should allow all scholars to have access to them. If the condition of the written materials requires that access to them be restricted, arrangements should be made for a facsimile reproduction that will be accessible to all scholars. Although the owners or those in control may choose to authorize one scholar or preferably a team of scholars to prepare an official edition of any given ancient written materials, such authorization should neither preclude access to the written materials by other scholars nor hinder other scholars from publishing their own studies, translations or editions of the written materials.

Second, obligations entailed by specially authorized editions. Scholars who are given special authorization to work on official editions of ancient written materials should cooperate with the owners or those in control of the written materials to ensure publication of the edition in an expeditious manner and they should facilitate access to the written materials by all scholars. If the owners or those in control grant to specially authorized editors any privileges that are unavailable to other scholars, these privileges should by no means include exclusive access to the written materials or facsimile reproductions of them. Furthermore, the owners or those in control should set a reasonable deadline for completion of the envisioned edition (not more than five years after the special authorization is granted).

Perhaps your reaction to that is that it looks like a committee wrote it, and it certainly does in some way. But, it does make the strong statement that access to such materials must be made available to all. Thank you.

LAWRENCE SCHIFFMAN: If I may pick up on Emanuel Tov's words, it now falls to me to address some of the real issues. I begin with theoretical considerations. The academic enterprise requires that a delicate balance be maintained between two competing interests which appear on the surface to be contradictory: the free exchange of information and the rights of an individual to his or her intellectual property.

The free exchange leads to the availability of the results of others' research in the same or related fields. It is obvious that without such a flow, scholarly progress would be much slower and widespread duplication of efforts would ensue. Further, excessive restriction of the flow of information would impede our entire raison d'être: teaching in the wider sense of the word, that is, the dissemination of a combination of ideas, data, methods, and results which make up in our case what is generally termed humanistic research.

At the same time, the free exchange of information cannot be left unhindered by ethical or legal restrictions. First, our society and our academic community recognize the notion that people have the right to be given credit for their work. Every scholar has the right to publish his or her own work under his or her own name first.

Second, some research results or literary creation have monetary value and may be the result of great personal or financial investment. Accordingly, our society and our legal systems recognize the rights of scholars to the results of their creative work. Nevertheless, academics generally want to share their results before publication in the form of conference papers. Professors discuss their research with students and colleagues and they publish preliminary results in articles eventually intended to appear in books. Therefore, the insistence on complete documentation and full rights of the scholar to publish his or her own research first usually is intended to encourage the exchange of information. Otherwise, all scholarly exchange would grind to a halt and scholarly progress would proceed at a snail's pace.

It is in this theoretical framework that one can look at the past history of publication of the Dead Sea Scrolls as well as more recent issues. I will simply touch right now on a few problematical things that have happened over the years, some of which are known, some of which are not known, which have created the difficult climate in which we are operating today.

For example, we can begin with the case of the Zadokite fragments found in two partial manuscripts by Solomon Schechter. Schechter secured an agreement with Cambridge University Library so that others could not make use of this manuscript for five years after its publication in 1910. The result of this arrangement was that when Louis Ginzberg published his very important work, *An Unknown Jewish Sect*, he did not have the benefit of use of the manuscript and made all kinds of unnecessary emendations.

When the actual scrolls were found, the initial scrolls were published quickly. After these publications, however, the problems began. I will not rehash these problems here. I do want to point out that I take great exception to this behavior as well as that of those I will talk about later. I want that very clear for the context of what we were discussing today. I'm not starting my criticism in 1992. I strongly criticize those who did not publish the material, but kept it under wraps for whatever reasons.

A different kind of conflict, still well known, occurred after the publication of Wacholder's *The Dawn of Qumran* in 1983. Yadin published his Hebrew edition of the scrolls in 1977. He was still working on the details of the English edition when the English-speaking world received the Wacholder book. Yadin wrote a letter to 60 people claiming plagiarism. At that time, I wrote to Yadin to say that there was in my view no actual plagiarism. Wacholder had made various arguments in which after misinterpreting Yadin, he would then end up by accepting Yadin's actual view. This is what I would call the kind of misunderstanding that academics are used to and which is hopefully dealt with with a shrug of the shoulders.

A different set of issues is involved in the unauthorized publication of MMT, the Wacholder-Abegg edition, and the Huntington Library edition and facsimiles. Briefly, my opinion is that those who published the material may have done so on the assumption that the need to secure the freedom of access to information outweighs the intellectual property rights of those scholars who had assembled the jigsaw puzzle and prepared the final transcription. It was in accordance with such an assumption that a variety of individuals and a variety of forces did undertake those actions, the ethics of which to some extent are the subject of our discussion today.

Instead, however, I should like to focus on the problem of the Eisenman-Wise volume. Let me again emphasize that I address it within the context of the history of problematical issues in our field and not as the first time that any such problem has arisen.

It is at this point (namely, after the "liberation" of the scrolls) that Robert Eisenman and Michael Wise published their volume, *The Dead Sea Scrolls Uncovered*. At this time, it must be remembered free access had finally been secured and the monopoly on Qumran texts had been broken. I call attention to the fact that in addition to the SBL statement that Jim VanderKam just read to you, in the statement on the publication of *The Dead Sea Scrolls Uncovered* which was originally signed by 19 scholars, there is found the following:

> . . . we should like to emphasize that the objections we are raising about this volume do not in any way stem from the desire on the part of the editorial team to maintain a monopoly or to forestall the publication of texts by others; as is well known the photographs of the scrolls are now available to all researchers and no monopoly exists.

Before detailing the particular objections, I want to emphasize that the complaint does not stem from the fact that these authors have published documents which others are preparing for the Oxford edition. No one on the editorial team preparing the Oxford editions is trying to stop others from publishing. Any attempt to claim that such a monopoly may still exist represents a smoke screen and its discussion is really a waste of time.

My criticism of the Eisenman and Wise volume is that in my opinion the authors do not cite the sources of their work accurately and sufficiently. Credit is not sufficiently given to all of the scholars whose work was used in preparing the volume. Even if they repeated much of the same work as those other scholars, they owed their predecessors fair credit for their contributions.

I will now go through specifics.

A) The volume claims to publish 50 previously unpublished texts. Its subtitle reads, "The First Complete Translation/Interpretation of Fifty Key Documents Withheld for over Thirty-Five Years." In describing their work, the editors write, "Two teams immediately set to work. . . . their aim was to go through everything, every photograph individually to see what was there, however long it took, leaving nothing to chance and depending on *no one else's work*" (page 4; emphasis in original). In actuality, of these texts about half were previously published before this volume appeared, some of them years ago. Of the remaining half, 50% of those, about 1/4th of the total, were partially published previously. This means that only a minority of the texts is new.

B) The authors do state in the introduction that some of the material may have been published (page 13). But, in their bibliographic note at the end of each chapter, they mention "previous discussions" of texts. Under this rubric, they list full-scale scholarly editions which include translations and commentaries, along with articles containing only brief allusions. No distinction between these types of contributions is made. This technique conceals from the reader that a substantial number of the citations are to full definitive publications which the authors used in preparing the volume. They sometimes copied the original transcriptions with minor modifications. In my opinion, these practices do not accord with normally accepted rules of academic documentation. I do not care how many examples of this behavior can be cited by anybody. It has absolutely nothing to do with whether it accords with the normally accepted rules – even if I did it.

C) In several easily identifiable cases, despite their claims to have deciphered the materials and the photographic plates themselves, the authors depended on handouts distributed at conferences, the existence of which they appear to hide from the readers in order to portray themselves as producing the *editio princeps* of the text in question. Every scholar has a right to see his/her work appear for the first time under his/her own name. Citing a forthcoming article from which a handout constituting a full-fledged text edition is used without acknowledging the existence of such a handout is not appropriate scholarly practice. Let me refer to specific examples to prove this point.

On page 55, the authors provide their edition of 4Q390. Under their list of previous discussions of this text (page 73ff.) was the paper presented by Dimant at the Madrid Conference which is forthcoming in that volume (which is currently in production [the volume has since appeared]). Wise and Eisenman, neither of whom attended the conference, apparently obtained a copy of Dimant's handout containing a rendition and translation of the text to be published in the Conference volume. As can be demonstrated, they used it as a basis for their supposedly original edition. Their 4Q390 contains errors which appeared in Professor Dimant's handout and have since been corrected by her for the conference volume, including the omission of an absolutely clear letter in one case that anybody would have noticed in two seconds. In addition, they explained that the text is really three different texts, a discovery made by Dimant in the course of her work. But, they do not give her credit for the idea.

In the case of another text worked on by Dimant, the editors made use of the edition she printed without proper citation – unless you really think that previous discussion is a fair description of a full edition, translation, and commentary.

D) The editors claim they have not used the previously circulated edition of 4QMMT prepared by J. Strugnell and E. Qimron. They write, "We have gone through the entire corpus of pictures completely ourselves, depending on no one elses' work to do this. Our reconstructions, transliteration" – which means transcription—"and translation here *are completely new*" (emphasis in original). "We have not relied on anyone or any other work." They go on to claim that the reconstructing of the fragments was easy. I have investigated this. I find it hard to believe that the task was "easy," but that's a matter of scholarly judgment—and perhaps I am not so smart.

It is clear that the transcription of Qimron and Strugnell was used. I will now give my view as to the proof. Qimron and Strugnell hand-wrote the MMT which has circulated since 1984, Strugnell wrote the word *biyadenu*, *beth-yodh-daleth-nun-waw*, such that *daleth-nun* appeared to run together. This produces the impression to one not used to his handwriting that the text says *beto*. The authors read *beto* and translate "his temple," whereas the syntax would in fact require *be-beto*.

Looking at the photograph of this manuscript, one can easily tell that the letters are *be-yadenu: welo-yimmaṣē' biyadenu ma'al wešeqer wera'ah*. The error the authors made is only possible if they were working from the handwritten copy of Strugnell-Qimron, and not from a photograph or manuscript of the original text. Furthermore, Eisenman and Wise's edition makes all the same joins—the transitions between fragmentary manuscripts—that Strugnell and Qimron had made. I want to add that this does not mean that these authors did no work. What I am arguing is simply that they used these works, not that they did not do anything on their own.

E) The authors do not sufficiently document the contribution of others whose ideas they made use of throughout the volume. They do not acknowledge much of the important research on the scrolls which has taken place in the last 40 years. They made use of important discoveries by reputable scholars, presenting them without proper credit given to those who truly discovered them. The authors did indeed edit and translate the "Jonathan the King" text (4Q448) on their own, but only cited an article from the Jerusalem Post, failing to mention the scholars identified there as those whose work led to the major discovery of the words "King Jonathan" in this text, namely Ada Yardeni for the decipherment, Hanan and Esther Eshel for the interpretation. Minimizing previous scholarship has the effect of making the book innovative, even explosive, and is intended to provide some explanation of why these documents (some published decades ago) were kept secret.

The standards of academic discourse demand that the contributions of others are always to be acknowledged fairly and openly. This principle should never be sacrificed for sales or sensationalism.

Concluding Remarks

We are all poorer for the uncovering of the Dead Sea Scrolls. What has truly been uncovered is one more instance in the long line of questionable actions which plague our field. I wish I had not found it necessary to stand before you with this message today. Our field is experiencing the loss of the credibility of its most outspoken gadfly and one of its most promising young scholars. I wish that they had sought the advice of other professionals who might have helped them avoid these criticisms. I cannot tell you how many nights were spent at 1, 2, and 3 in the morning at home discussing whether any of these words should ever be uttered.

I cannot accept the excuses which the authors offer. One author blames the other for commentary. The second blames the first for the text. Graduate students have been put forward as the real culprits. When a scholar signs his name or her name to a book, either as its author or coauthor, that scholar undertakes full responsibility for every word. And, when we sign our names our ultimate responsibility is to the readers and to our colleagues to fully account for all the sources we use and for the interpretations we espouse.

The book of Deuteronomy tells us that we are given a choice between life and death, blessing and curse. According to the Rule of the Community, Deuteronomy is here referring to the choice between light and darkness. We have to decide if we want to "enlighten the heart of mankind and teach the ways of truthful righteousness with a spirit of understanding in all the plans of our actions." This is our responsibility as scholars. Thank you very much.

CHAIRMAN MEYERS: Professor James Robinson has not been able to attend this afternoon's colloquium and we have just received by fax the following statement, which I will read before Dr. Golb's presentation.

(This is the statement of James M. Robinson of Claremont Graduate School.)

Ethics in Publishing Manuscript Discoveries

The question of what the ethics should be regarding the publication of important manuscript discoveries has been posed acutely by the experience we have shared over the past generation regarding the publication of the Dead Sea Scrolls. What began as a rather normal, standard procedure in our discipline became, with the passage of time, an ethically repugnant monopoly that finally had to be broken by force. Those who were collaborators or fellow-travellers in that monopoly, who would still be enjoying its advantages had it not been destroyed, are hence the most obvious persons not in an ethical position to be involved in making ethical criticisms of their colleagues whom they intentionally excluded.

There has emerged universal agreement among all (except the cartel itself) that the publication policies of the Dead Sea Scroll editors had, after the lapse of a generation, become unethical. This conclusion is based not only on the practically unanimous acclaim in the press and the academic community for the steps taken to break the monopoly in 1991: A first fascicle of *A Preliminary Edition of the Unpublished Dead Sea Scrolls* reconstructed with the help of a computer from an unpublished preliminary concordance that became available to persons outside the cartel, by Ben Zion Wacholder and Martin Abegg of Hebrew Union College, Cincinnati, on 4 September 1991; the release to the scholarly public, without restrictions on their use, of the microfilms stored a decade ago by Elizabeth Hay Bechtel at the Huntington Library, by William A. Moffett, Director of the Huntington Library, on 22 September 1991; and *A Facsimile Edition of the Dead Sea Scrolls*, a two-volume publication at the Biblical Archaeology Society of 1,787 mostly unpublished photographs of fragments, by Robert H. Eisenman and myself, on 19 November 1991. These three actions, taken independently of each other, indeed in unawareness of each other, are cumulatively an indication that the academic community was no longer willing to tolerate the situation, as was confirmed by the overwhelmingly positive response by the press and academia.

Perhaps most telling is the fax sent on 6 October 1991 by Emanuel Tov, head of the official editorial team, to Moffett, when he made the concession that "the criticism was correct twenty years ago, ten years ago, and even five years ago." Thus the new team has joined the chorus of those who repudiate the old team, thus for all practical purposes making the criticism a consensus.

Of course Tov's criticism of the past was presented in the context of his effort to gain acceptance for continuing the same policy with a new team in the present and future, as became evident from the conclusion of the sentence quoted above: "but it is not correct for the situation prevailing as of some five years ago." He went on to explain: "Again, criticisms of the speed of publication were certainly in order, but they do not pertain to the present situation in which we have, I hope, everything under control. A timetable agreed upon between my predecessor and the IAA for the publication of all the material by 1996 is being adhered to." Presumably Moffett was being requested to expect the new team to do what the old team had failed to do, in terms of timetable, and to wait until 1996 to see if such an optimistic prediction would be fulfilled.

One can already make a spot check on the basis of preliminary results: The catalogue "News from Brill 92/4" announces proudly *The Dead Sea Scrolls on Microfiche*: "A Comprehensive Facsimile Edition of the Texts from the Judaean Desert With a Printed Catalogue by Stephen A. Reed Published under the Auspices of the Israel Antiquities Authority Edited by Emanuel Tov." This will no doubt be superior to the microfiche edition of largely unpublished fragments (supplied by Robert W. Eisenman and prepared for publication by myself), for whose publication Brill signed a contract on 15 February 1991, but then, out of fear of repercussions comparable to those suffered in April 1991 by Zdzislaw J. Kapera at the Dead Sea Scrolls convention in Salamanca, Spain (for making available the much-discussed but unpublished text 4Q MMT), Brill broke the contract with us in April 1991, less than a month before the projected publication date of 3 May 1991. The main difference however between that incomplete and unauthorized microfiche edition and the complete and authorized microfiche edition, other than the fact that our edition would have broken the monopoly and Tov's edition will have no significant effect on the history of research, is that our edition was on schedule (the microfiche negatives are today collecting dust in the Netherlands), and would in fact have been published on schedule 3 May 1991, had Brill not broken its contract, whereas the official microfiche edition, promised in the Brill catalogue for "December 1992," is, as of mid-December 1992, still far from publication. The Ancient Biblical Manuscript Center, which is supplying the catalogue and a number of the photographs, and hence is familiar with publication plans, estimates at least a six months delay. This amounts to doubling the production time. We will see.

Now that the reorganized official team begins by not meeting its first deadline, what is the ethical justification for asking others to wait trustingly, not to say naively, for the assigned editors to abide by their deadlines, rather than going ahead and publishing what one can? Already, in anticipation that the final 1996 deadline will not be met, blame is being shifted to Oxford University Press, which understandably cannot publish at the last minute the quantity of volumes due to be submitted for publication within the tight schedule Tov has promised. Are we to assume that such realities of publication were not known when the promises were made?

Tov pled the case for the new team in touching terms: "The international team now consists of some 30, and soon 40, scholars actively involved in the publication. Many of them are young scholars who received their texts only three, two or one year ago with the understanding that they would publish the first editions of these texts." This means that the monopolizing disease, originally confined to a handful of aging experts, has reached epidemic proportions, which we should, as our ethical duty, aid and abet. Why did not those young scholars, with the lessons of the past generation staring them in the face, face up to their ethical responsibilities to their excluded colleagues, rather than excluding them still again so as to advance their own careers at the expense of the rest of the academic community? Tov did not fail to point out that unauthorized publications "would hurt the academic careers of many Qumran specialists." But he completely overlooked what his policy was doing to the academic careers of all the other specialists not included within the circle of 40!

Tov's defense of his inner circle went on: "These scholars should certainly not suffer from the sins of a previous generation, I believe." Since they entered voluntarily into the monopoly, it is their own sin that is in question, when they "suffer" from the same kind of academic competition, the give and take, that all the rest of us consider normal intellectual dialogue. But even apart from their own ethical responsibility, it is hardly legitimate to abstract away from the actual intolerable situation in which we find ourselves. One need merely think of the rationale our academic community has accepted for affirmative action in hiring: Given the fact that, in the past, prejudices ("sins of a previous generation") led to women and minorities being under-represented, we must commit ourselves now to aggressive policies to seek out women and minorities to appoint, to redress the situation. This will make it hard on young white male academics for years to come. Is this a valid reason for renouncing affirmative action? "These scholars should certainly not suffer from the sins of a previous generation," Tov believes. American higher education has however once and for all decided that this way of reasoning is not ethical.

NORMAN GOLB: Ladies and gentlemen, we had hoped to have someone besides myself on this panel, because I did organize the conference with my colleagues; but it was decided by the organizing committee that I should make a statement. I and my colleagues had hoped that this discussion would be on a high level and free of personal attack and invective, but that hasn't been the case. I had intended, hoping that there would not be this invective, to speak about my experience in manuscript studies in the Cambridge Cairo Geniza collection for over 30 years and to describe the customs and actions that we have or have not taken there. Among other matters I intended to talk about the question of republication of manuscripts by scholars other than original editors, the nature of errors in manuscript editions, uncorrected re-editions and corrected re-editions, and assignments of manuscripts to students for dissertations, which is a very serious ethical issue. But, the intemperate attack by a group of scholars, repeated this afternoon by one of them, on our colleagues, Professors Wise and Eisenman, makes it essential that I give you my response to the statements that were made.*

The attack against our aforementioned colleagues' recent publication of Dead Sea Scrolls is not only remarkable for its invective tone, but also in its egregious departure from the civilized and well-established custom of review of books in appropriate pages of journals and newspapers by individual critics. The obvious polemical thrust of this group effort to discredit the book in question raises questions not so much about the book as about the fundamental motive of the writers of the statement in promulgating it.

* [See résumé of the attack in *The New York Times*, 13 Dec. 1992; and *Biblical Archaeology Review*, March/April 1993, pp. 66–67.]

It must be pointed out that the signers were either themselves involved in the lengthy and eventually unsuccessful effort to prevent release of the scrolls or beneficiaries of that failed policy (and that means everyone who signed the statement). This attack on my colleagues, Drs. Wise and Eisenman, dated December 9, was sent to us at Chicago virtually on the eve of our departure to participate in the conference on the scrolls beginning today [14 December 1992]. We observe in it the continuing manifestation of what may be properly called McCarthyism in the investigation of the scrolls. I make this statement in an ethical sense, consonant with the theme of this panel.

The present stage of the malaise in Qumran studies revealed by this intemperate outburst, coming from Qumranologists allied with the official committees, began with the struggle over the freeing of the scrolls during the past few years. I refer to the innuendos, half truths, calumnies, fallacious claims and misuse of authority that seemed to characterize the actions of members of those committees as the struggle developed over the freeing of the scrolls, which all of us striving for mutual collegiality among Qumran scholars hoped to have come to an end with the freeing of the scrolls and the editor-in-chief's welcome announcement of November 1991 acknowledging the rights of scholars to publish their own editions of Qumran manuscripts without regard to assignments made to others.

A number of these ill-conceived actions were personally directed against scholars, including myself, who had pressed for the freedom of the texts while at the same time disagreeing with the traditional interpretation of Qumran origins favored by the central committees.

Among the actions and statements that occurred (which are all documented) were the quiet awarding of editorships of individual scrolls to students of those in positions of control. Why, for example, were texts being given to students at Harvard University and not the University of Chicago? This is inexcusable.

Other actions include the characterization of the successful efforts of two Cincinnati researchers, during the battle to free the scrolls, to reconstruct previously unpublished texts as a "violation of international law" and "thievery"; the spurious claims, in advance of actual publication, that the results of radiocarbon tests proved that Essenes had written the scrolls and that the hypothetical paleographical datings of the manuscripts were accurate (which they are not); and the published portrayal of me by a member of the Scrolls Oversight Committee as, "a revolting argumentalist, a polemicist and troublemaker," who had "filled the world with his dirt and from whom the world will be free when he is dead."

In America, a member of the same group prominent in the effort to compose and disseminate the attack presently under discussion was not above appropriating and republishing notable parts of my own hypothesis of Qumran origins as his own without attribution, while simultaneously making demonstrably fallacious claims, in the context of invectives directed against me personally, about the nature of the theory of Jerusalem origin and the evidence supporting it.

I have never responded to these and other unfortunate statements, always hoping that those who produced them, like others engaged in the pursuit of learning, would eventually have the strength to reclaim their innate sense of honor. With the astonishingly deceitful attack on my colleague, Dr. Wise, produced with the hope and intention of destroying the career of an outstanding and brilliant scholar of the Qumran texts, I now despair of seeing that honor reclaimed, but will continue to hope for the miracle of friendly and collegial relations amongst scroll scholars within the necessary context of their notable and extreme differences with one another. It is these differences that lie at the bottom of the attack under discussion, no matter what statements are made to the contrary by its promulgators.

While claiming that they are in no way opposed to the publication of Qumran texts by others, the signers of the document by this and previously well-known efforts attempt to discourage precisely such publication by those whose views on Qumran origins differ radically from their own. In his commentaries on Dr. Wise's editions and translations, Dr. Eisenman attempts to strengthen his own well-known view that the texts have a Judeo-Christian origin. These commentaries, appearing as they do with a group of new Qumran texts conveniently attainable by the public, may well strengthen his hand in coming months in the court of public opinion.

I do not personally share Dr. Eisenman's views on the origin of the Qumran texts, but in my perception they are no more untenable than the traditional view espoused by the writers of that statement—and he has just as much right to defend and develop his thesis as do they their own. The effort to discredit this interpretation is what lies at the bottom of the writers' polemical statement, not an interest in encouraging perfect editions of texts.

Since the attack unfairly and unjustly damages the name of two independent scholars of the Qumran Scrolls and will necessarily (despite the inevitable disclaimers) tend to discourage future efforts by other independent scholars to investigate the scrolls without regard to the overarching sectarian hypothesis that the writers of the letter support, I have no choice but to offer this response to a statement that would otherwise not merit a reply.

Among the most surprisingly untrue assertions made in the present attack is the writers' claim in paragraph 4 that the text known as 4QMMT, a fragmentary work representing legal views of a separatist group, was copied by the two authors of the recent book from an earlier unpublished transcription of this work done by other scholars that had been widely circulated beforehand. (It may be noted that this text was described by still another scholar in the 1950s.) That this earlier transcription became well known during the 1980s is quite true; however, in the winter of 1991, I and Professor Wise, who (together with several of our graduate students) was responsible for all of the texts and translations published in *The Dead Sea Scrolls Uncovered*, held a seminar on this and other Qumran texts at the University of Chicago. We spent several weeks on this particular text, ourselves reconstructing it from photographs of the manuscripts that had become available to us. And it was Dr. Wise himself who took the major lead in this reconstruction.

Dr. Wise's edition of the text contains approximately 90 new readings and restorations plus an entirely new section of over 160 lines that was not as much as included in the earlier transcription. It is moreover essential to indicate that the earlier transcribers of this text announced in an article published already in 1985 the hope "that a preliminary edition of the whole document will be finished in a year or so." The edition never appeared. Pressure for the release of the Scrolls subsequently built up and the freeing of the texts ensued in the autumn of 1991. Dr. Wise's eventual edition of the fuller text of MMT is not only of a high standard of scholarly excellence for a popular book, but fully conformed to the ethical guidelines for publication of ancient texts announced by the Society of Biblical Literature in the autumn of 1991, which Dr. VanderKam has just read to us.

The underlying issues raised by the writers of the attack in effect concern the rights of independent scholars to edit, translate, and publish Qumran Scrolls without interference, harassment, or accusatory challenges regarding rights of publication of ancient texts. The earlier transcribers of a part of the MMT did not expeditiously publish their transcription, which was itself grossly incomplete, and cannot conceivably lay claim to an exclusive right to publish the text.

The writers' reference to a lawsuit involving 4QMMT is particularly inappropriate insofar as it implies odiousness or illegality where none has been demonstrated. The lawsuit was brought by the very party who now claims wrongly that his transcription was appropriated by Drs. Wise and Eisenman. In this respect, I must emphasize that several days before the distribution of the attack I spoke with two of its writers and made clear to them precisely what process had been followed by us in our study of the MMT text at Chicago. At that time, I was ignorant of any intention on their part to compose such an attack. Yet, making no apparent attempt to confirm the facts independently, they thereafter issued their statement without any allusion to our conversation or to the work accomplished during the seminar at Chicago. The untrue and indeed reckless assertions directed against the two authors extend to every other paragraph of the statement under discussion. For example:

A) The writers assert in paragraph 1 that the volume claims to publish fifty previously unpublished texts. I am unaware of any statement in the book that makes this claim. The publisher's statement on the front cover is to the effect that the book contains "the first complete translation and interpretation of 50 key documents withheld over 35 years," a statement of an entirely different order. The texts were indeed withheld for the time indicated from the scrutiny of many scholars—that is from 1955 through 1990, *i.e.* 35 years. During the past two years various Qumran scrolls have been worked on by others, but this is not substantively pertinent to the statement made that the work embodies 50 Qumran texts in a single volume—texts, we may note, that are either published for the first time or represent new editions, in many cases more complete, and in all cases, to the best of my knowledge, improved editions. The description accompanying the book is substantially correct and calls for no apologies either by the authors or publisher.

I can personally attest to the fact that Dr. Wise, with the aid of an outstanding group of our graduate students, did indeed study photographs of the Qumran texts *ad fontem*, from the source, and that his selection of texts eventually published was made on the basis of his own intensive perusal of those photographs.

The writers of the statement appear surprised by this unusual productivity and the paleographic skills that it betokens, but rather than congratulating Dr. Wise upon seeing the evidence of it, they attribute his contributions to wrongful actions by seeing sinister implications in the perfectly normal rubric "Previous Discussions" accompanying the bibliographies. They claim without a semblance of proof that prior "definitive publications" underlie the Eisenman-Wise editions of texts throughout the new volume. (We are reminded of the regrettable statement about "definitive interpretations" once used by the Antiquities Authority to defend the withholding of the texts from scholars. It is almost superfluous to add that the writers of the attack themselves often present interpretations of the Qumran texts and the Qumran origins that appear on objective grounds to be almost totally unconvincing.) The writers of the statement moreover make the claim that the authors base themselves on "several unnamed publications," once again without offering the slightest proof of this additional allegation. They then suggest that the authors are guilty of "often copying the original transcriptions with only minor modifications," whereas in each of the several cases to which the writers apparently allude, Dr. Wise did not copy from other transcriptions but himself transcribed the texts painstakingly from the photographs. I am a witness to this activity. The authors seize upon a common and entirely legitimate phenomenon in the continuous process of the editing of ancient manuscripts, and attempt to turn it into a manifestation of wickedness. Professor Wise has made changes or improvements in the wording of several of the texts in question as compared with earlier editions. This is reason enough for their inclusion in a volume of this kind, and calls for no apologies or justification.

B) Throughout their attack, the writers fail to distinguish between two entirely different modes of investigation of ancient manuscripts. The first is characterized by free and open research in manuscript collections by any scholars in pertinent fields of study who may wish to engage in that research.

In this kind of research, important discoveries by individuals take place under dynamically competitive circumstances, as in the case of the study of the Cairo Geniza documents.

One scholar may see in a manuscript what others have not, and legitimately lay claim to a new discovery based upon those special skills that had enabled him to produce his finding. Others, having the opportunity to peruse the same manuscript without having seen its particular importance, will then (under the normal rules of fair play) acknowledge the discoverer's right to prior publication of his finding in an expeditious manner.

The other mode of manuscript investigation is, by contrast, not characterized by these elements, but consists in the control of collections of manuscripts by individuals or groups who assign particular texts to researchers of their choice hoping that they will find information of importance in the assigned texts and then publish them. It was the second mode of operation that characterized the official editorial team's policy before the texts were freed in the autumn of 1991. By that time, they had already assigned most of the texts to over 50 hand-picked individuals. A list of these assignments was published in the spring of 1992 by the new editor-in-chief of the project, who did not, however, publish his statement to the press of November 1991 acknowledging the rights of other scholars to publish their own editions of Qumran manuscripts without regard to their prior assignments. Why is it that, when Professor Tov published the list of the 50 scholars who were assigned texts, he did not include an appendix consisting of the statement he read at the SBL meeting in 1991? The SBL saw to it that their own statement was published. Why wasn't this one?

The basic contents of the texts were in most cases known as of the time the assignments were made. The publication of the editor-in-chief's list of assignments without the accompanying statement earlier given to the press had the effect of implying a certain right of priority by the assignees to publish the texts handed over to them. And this prior right has been further implied by the distribution at scholarly meetings of handouts of preliminary editions of certain texts assigned in this way.

Under these circumstances, the readings arrived at by the individual members of the group in question, to whom the texts had been assigned as much as a year and in certain cases several years before the texts were freed, were not achieved under competitive circumstances. Any claims to "discoveries" made by them must be qualified by this fact and by the further truth that the basic contents of many of the texts had been determined by earlier editors in the 1950s.

Now the dubious prior right of publication is asserted several times over in the writers' attack on the Eisenman-Wise book, thus revealing continued resistance to the principle of open access to the scrolls and competitive study of their contents by all scholars engaged in relevant fields of learning. It must be borne in mind that the assignments in question were not made under competitive conditions. Many scholars were prevented from seeing these texts, while at the same time they were being handed out to a chosen group for study and publication. Under these circumstances the assignees have of course every right to publish their own work, but can make no legitimate claim to a prior right of publication, handouts or no handouts, lists of assignees or no lists of assignees.

This applies not only to the so-called MMT text, but to others as well. In the case of a major discovery by several graduate students referred to in paragraph 5 of the writers' attack, Drs. Wise and Eisenman do indeed refer to the very lengthy and detailed description of the text's discovery that appeared in the magazine section of the *Jerusalem Post* while they were engaged in completing their book. Since the magazine article in question, written by a newsman who habitually reports on developments in Qumran research, does give the names of the researchers who produced their finding, the attack on Drs. Wise and Eisenman for not giving fuller information in their bibliography is arbitrary and without merit.

We moreover observe that the writers first attack the authors of the book "for making use of important discoveries by reputable scholars and presenting them as if they are their own original ideas," but the only instance they cite of this alleged wrongdoing is that involving the three graduate students' abovementioned findings. Since the authors clearly document the source of the finding by their black and white reference to the magazine article containing the pertinent information, and since Dr. Wise in addition has produced an independent version and translation of this text with various new readings and interpretations, no stigma whatever can legitimately be attached to the authors regarding their manner of dealing with this text. They are doing precisely what scholars should do in attempting to cast light on the Dead Sea Scrolls. It is the writers of the circulated statement who, by constantly resorting to invective, unproven assertions and demonstrable untruths in their effort to discredit the authors, are themselves the ones seriously at fault.

C) The extent to which this is the case is seen from still another statement of the writers. Although claiming that their objections relate to "ethics and integrity," they do not find it inappropriate to claim in addition that the "volume abounds with errors and imprecisions in the transcription of the Hebrew and Aramaic documents and in translating and interpreting them."

This statement represents the nadir of the writer's effort to discredit the book's authors. They cannot but be aware of the fact that editions of Qumran texts always contain errors. It is a truism of manuscript investigation that full understanding of ancient texts is achieved, if ever, only after decades of study and restudy—and the Qumran Scrolls are no exception to this rule.

I challenge the writers to do as well as Dr. Wise has in his transcription and translation of almost 30 entirely new texts never before published. Has any of them done such a thing, or published even half that number? And as well as he has? Some of them are of great difficulty, but he has been more than up to the task without the aid of editorial committees or specially appointed palaeographers to help him. When, finally, the writers further claim that the volume abounds with errors of *interpretation*, they distance themselves still further from the ideals and standards of humanistic learning. What they would like us to believe is that they have true interpretations of the Qumran manuscripts, in contrast with those they collectively label false. And by this assertion, they degrade the very scholarship that they claim to represent.

OPEN DISCUSSION

MICHAEL WISE: I would like to read portions of a longer response to some of the things that were said in this circular letter that was sent out by a group of Qumranologists that served as the basis for an article that appeared in *The New York Times* yesterday. I will address myself to certain points that are brought out.

I want to point out first of all that what we've done in this book is attempted to produce preliminary editions, not scholarly editions. In this sense, a recognition of the book's intended audience is mandatory and goes a long way towards explaining many of the aspects of its format that my colleagues are finding so objectionable.

The production of preliminary editions was in keeping with the recent statement on publication and access referred to today proposed by the Society of Biblical Literature. That statement provides that while the owners of manuscripts may wish to assign them to certain scholars for "official editions," "such authorizations should neither preclude access to the written materials by other scholars nor hinder other scholars from publishing their own studies, translations or editions of the written materials." Further preliminary editions were specifically allowed for despite disclaimers in the statement made by Tov, the editor-in-chief of the scrolls publication project, and quoted in an article in *The New York Times* on 27 November 1991, wherein he also noted that his team, instead of pursuing preliminary editions, would continue their stated intention of producing scholarly editions.

In the spirit of cooperation thus envisaged, we offered our preliminary and doubtless acknowledged imperfect first attempt at understanding these texts. On the points raised in the regrettably libelous letter signed by several prominent Qumranologists, let me address myself in order:

1) The letter states that we claim to publish 50 previously unpublished

texts. In fact we nowhere make that claim. And to say that we do so only demonstrates the letter's propagandistic intent. We say forthrightly, page 13, that not all the texts are new. As we indicate, we have included texts that, A) were previously published in a less complete form, or B) lacked English translation. Remember the intended audience was a popular audience. They can't read French translations that appear in scholarly journals. Other texts C) were published in the interim while we were at work on our collection, or D) are entirely new.

For previously published materials we offer suggested improvements of reading, translation or interpretation, not necessarily all three. That is all we say that we intend. As to the percentage of new material, counting tends to be subjective. If so inclined, one can assert that a text is not new if a single line, even a single word has previously appeared. But, a less legalistic assessment would indicate that we have published 29 texts that are either completely or virtually completely new.

2) The letter states that our categorization of all previous scholars' works under the single rubric "Previous Discussions" is "clearly calculated to hide from the reader" our indebtedness to such work. The letter calls this description "fraudulent."

Now perhaps our choice of terminology here was not the most felicitous, but why should the letter draw such malicious conclusions from it? By what right would authors presume to know and label what was in our minds? To the extent that our book is useful to scholars, it is at most in the form of a handbook. Other such handbooks in the field (I might note many, but for example Fitzmyer and Harrington's *Manual of Palestinian Aramaic Texts*) similarly simply list relevant bibliography without always specifying what they have derived from where. To do so by means of footnotes would be to change the nature of the book entirely. Fulsome is for scholarly publications. Anyone doubting what our book is ought to read the first page, which explains what 1Q means, what 2Q means, *etc.*, *etc.* No scholar needs such explanations. So, again, we draw attention to our volume's intended audience.

3) The letter states that in several cases, we have lied about our claim to have deciphered material from the photographs and have instead simply copied with "minor modifications" handouts from scholarly conferences. Further, it is said that we hide the existence of these handouts from the readers in order falsely to appear to produce *editio princeps*. Neither charge is true. It is a fact that we have twice consulted handouts, but only after having first produced our own editions of the texts in question and only because it was announced the handouts would be a part of published proceedings due out fully a year before our own book. In that belief, we read the handouts and clearly labeled the forthcoming articles to which they belonged. Unfortunately, the publication of the articles associated with the handouts was greatly delayed.

One example should suffice to put the lie to the letter's charge of mere copying. Our version of 4Q Aaron A or 4Q541, one of those in question, deviates at 34 points from the version of the handout, including differences of both readings and joins. Such differences cannot be considered minor and amount to, in fact, a different edition of the text.

Lastly, we neither believe nor claim to have produced a single *editio princeps* in our book, as should be obvious to anyone who knows how that term is used in scholarly parlance.

4) The circular asserts that we have published a work known to some as MMT based not on our own work, but on a previously circulated "edition" by J. Strugnell and Elisha Qimron. Our statement that we have done our own work is labeled "laughable and manifestly dishonest."

Now, no one in the field can deny having read the Strugnell-Qimron version, and we don't, either. But, does that mean that any subsequent edition produced by others is *ipso facto* stolen? Our work on what we regard as two separate letters on righteousness derives from our own long and close study of photographs. This work began in a seminar, as Professor Golb has mentioned, devoted to those photographs held at the University of Chicago from January through March 1991. Together with several advanced graduate students and my colleague, Norman Golb, I went through virtually all of the relevant photographs in that period of ten weeks, noting readings and joins. Hundreds of hours of work were expended by all of us on those photographs during the period and later I spent hundreds more in November and December of 1991. I might note that those at the University of Chicago seminar can attest to these facts.

The result is an edition of two letters that differs in dozens of places in readings, reconstructions and manuscript base. In fact, the first 175 lines of the approximately 300 lines of our letters never circulated and can by no means be attributed to theft. For the other lines, the letter finds it "a miracle" that our edition "made all the same joins and transitions between fragmentary manuscripts" that Strugnell and Qimron had made.

First, it is not true, as far as I can tell, that we have made all the same joins, but to the extent that the two editions resemble each other, that is a function of the evidence itself. It should be appreciated that six copies of the portions in question have survived, and that by the standards of the Cave 4 materials, three are very well preserved, virtually intact for long stretches. The circular seeks to emphasize the fragmentary state of the texts, but of about 120 lines in question, 53 lines can easily be read virtually complete and about 70 lines—often different from those 53 just noted—are contained in more than one manuscript.

Actually, with all of these copies, an editor is forced by the evidence to follow certain lines. In terms of transitions between manuscripts, it only makes sense to follow at each point the best preserved manuscript. Who would do otherwise? Concordance on this point is hardly miraculous.

As to joins, once again the evidence decides the issue and any competent editor would see where it leads. For example, the photograph 43.476 contains among others eight very small fragments whose reading and relationship might be impossible to discover, except for the fact that the fragments contain text that overlaps with the second copy of the letters. Once the overlaps are noted, the portions can be reconstructed and yield about a dozen valuable readings otherwise lost. Such a discovery is not at all miraculous. It is just a matter of hard work.

At other points where line lags in the placement of fragments might be impossible to discern, biblical quotations partially preserved in different fragments guide the editor.

The lawsuit reference by the circular involves different issues and is irrelevant to the matters at hand. It should not even have been mentioned, and the fact of its mention underlines again the misleading character and flawed reasoning of this circular.

5) Point five of the circular letter returns once again to the matter of documentation. Therefore, once again it is necessary to state that this book is essentially a popular volume. It is so marketed. It was so conceived. Some scholars seem to feel that one cannot publish a preliminary edition of a Qumran text without extensive documentation and interaction with secondary literature. Perhaps, but that has never been the standard in the field before. The lack of such documentation has never before been labeled unethical. Why should it be concluded that because the commentary assumes certain ideas that have become standard in the field that we are claiming these ideas as our own discoveries? Such a charge is absurd.

In fact, our use of these ideas as axiomatic amounts to an acknowledgment of their fundamental importance. They're not after all new ideas with which some specialists might be unfamiliar. All scholars in the field would recognize whence these ideas come.

The case cited involving a different type of acknowledgment, that of the Alexander Jannaeus text, is perhaps different. To be sure, we plainly state, page 276, that this text was discovered by "a young Israeli scholar" and indicate in the bibliography where the reader can find that discovery first described. But, we neglect to mention the name of that scholar, Ada Yardeni in particular, who found the text. That is a regrettable oversight that happened because the editor who wrote the commentary had not himself seen the item in the bibliography and did not know the Israeli's name. But, there was nothing malicious in this oversight. It was not part of some grand scheme, as the letter implies, aimed at "intentional hiding of the debt" due to other Qumran scholars.

6) The letter then finds fault with the book's subtitle, *The First Complete Translation and Interpretation of Fifty Key Documents Withheld for Over Thirty-Five Years*. First it must be stated that the choice of the subtitle was a matter

of marketing. By the terms of the book's contract, totally in control of the publisher, the wording is intended to strike the general reader and gain his or her interest. As you know, that has to be done sometimes in a way that doesn't necessarily appeal to scholars.

But strictly speaking, every word of the subtitle is correct, and while perhaps offensive to some, it is not thereby unethical. Our book does indeed mark the first time that these 50 texts has been available in such complete form and with an interpretation aimed at the general reader. Since the photographs containing these texts in the form we give them were not accessible until 1991, a figure of 35 years is not wrong. Since access to these texts in their complete form was intentionally denied the generality of scholars during that period, the use of the term "withheld" is surely accurate, even if again offensive to some. We do not imply in this subtitle that the situation thus described still continues.

Finally, the letter charges that our book contains errors. Here at last we may agree, for such is certainly the case. It is impossible to produce an *editio princeps*, much less preliminary editions such as we present, without errors. It simply doesn't happen. The history of manuscript research generally and the Qumran field specifically proves this fact. The official series in which the scrolls are being published itself abounds with errors of every sort which subsequent scholarship has never ceased to point out.

For example, according to Al Wolters, J. T. Milik's edition of the Copper Scroll contains no fewer than 70 misreadings. That is not to say that Milik did not do exemplary work. It is only to say that he began the process of understanding the text and that Wolters is advancing it.

The only way to avoid error is not to publish. We have published a volume of preliminary editions, all-around work in the terms indicated hoping to advance knowledge in the field. We invite our colleagues to improve our work and I'm sure that they will. In the meantime, the general reader will have at least some idea of what these new texts say. Thank you.

ROBERT EISENMAN: I have heard my name taken in vain a little bit here and I would like to have my say. I don't know that I can collect my thoughts to say what I want to say, but I must say, mention of Alan Dershowitz by Eric Meyers was very significant. I hate to say this, but I do believe that both his and Lawrence Schiffman's presentations are related to that phenomenon. I say it with heavy heart, because this panel just sounds to me to a certain extent like a lawyer's brief. Even Eric's presentation dovetailed very nicely with the Israel Antiquities Authority's stand. Suddenly, he tells us he is aware of further legal action being contemplated. So he then knows a lot more than I know, or would even have suspected. I don't say that he knows this for certain, but he has heard or thought about this. This does make me concerned that what is happening here is not exactly what it seems.

I too would like to talk about ethics, because I think I have the right. Talking of ethics, Prof. Schiffman, the author of many of these accusations, called the public relations person in New York who was in charge of giving out copies of our book, and asked for a *free* copy, so he could look at it in advance. I hadn't heard about that. If I had, he would never have gotten a free prepublication copy from me. I would have asked him to go out and *buy* his own copy. In my view, the ethics of that is similar to boiling a kid in its mother's milk, and he of all people should know very well what that entails. That's a *moral statement*, Larry, in case you didn't recognize it.

Now, I would also like to read a portion from our book that Michael Wise didn't read. On page 13, our book states (and I think it is totally accurate), "Since the situation in this field is so fluid, it is always possible that a text included in this work may have been published elsewhere or be in the process of being published, and parts of text or a whole text included in this work, in fact, were already published and were published after we began working on them. Since we were already working on the text (or texts) in any event and since no complete English translation was readily available, and it was important to have a full literary context by which to judge the text, we have included them. We have also provided a section at the end of each chapter containing publication and technical information."

Now our interlocutors cavil about that section at the end called "notes" or "previous discussions." Frankly I hadn't even noticed what the title of that section was, and there certainly was never any intent on my part to deceive them. The strange thing here about these things is that I am always called 'idiosyncratic' and a 'maverick'. They all know very well I don't read their works. I never read their works—or hardly ever—because, quite frankly, I don't want my brain to be addled. I'm not invited to their conferences and I don't get their handouts, and when I submit my papers to them, they don't publish them.

So, if you want to talk about ethics, let me tell you about an incident when I was invited by the 'official team' to the Groningen Conference in Holland. At the time, I guess, they didn't suspect my heterodox position. The arrangements at that conference were that every paper, pro and con, was supposed to be published. I submitted a paper that I thought was one of the best papers that I had ever written. As far as I am aware, every paper given at that conference was published in the *Revue de Qumran* (a journal controlled by the École Biblique), except mine.

Professor Schiffman cooperated with that. He allowed his paper to be published, knowing that my paper wasn't going to be published. We're supposed to be talking about ethics here. Was that ethics? Was that ethical?

This is the kind of thing that we have been subjected to. So, for me personally to hear that I have borrowed from other people's works staggers me. Everybody in this room, everybody in the world knows that my theories don't resemble anyone else's theories, and that I don't borrow from anybody, and that that is the most preposterous accusation. You see, if you were going to dream up an accusation, quite honestly you couldn't dream up a falser one as far as where I am concerned.

Now let me tell you about this work, *The Dead Sea Scrolls Uncovered*. It consists of three sections. There is a transcription. There is a translation. And, there is an interpretation. The thing that was most thrilling to me personally about this work, as Professor Golb intimated, was to be able to be the first one out there with an *interpretation*. That's what I really loved about this book: for the first time we were going to be able to comment first. Because, if you've been following my ideas, you know that I have been saying all along that the *editio princeps* official editions–ever so subtly–slide in an official interpretation that, to a docile and unsuspecting public, becomes orthodoxy. I have said–and Hershel Shanks knows this because he wouldn't let me put it in my introduction–that the reason that I participated in the *Facsimile Edition* was to level the playing field, to get away from the official interpretations of the text, to let, as it were, 'a thousand voices sing.'

So when this chance came to be out there first with the 50 texts that we sent to the publisher–the best documents from the unpublished corpus (something like this is how we privately described our work)–frankly, I felt that most of that material was unpublished. I was really quite astonished by Michael's publication notes. I thought he was being very generous. He gave credit beyond what most people would be called upon to do.

In any event, there were three parts to the book. Michael's team did the transcriptions. I will take issue with Professor Golb on one thing. Our team found the masturbation text. So in any case that's one text that we will take credit for. The rest I would say that the Chicago team did the work for. The transcriptions were provided as a public service, as few popular books of this kind ever have them, so people would know our translations were accurate. And isn't it strange that this is just the part of the book our critics zero in on?

As far as the translations go, both groups worked on these. The Chicago team did the preliminary translations, and came back with what I considered in some cases to be very rough, crude, inexact and unpoetic English translations of the Hebrew. I can tell you that I personally went over every text from the Hebrew transcriptions they gave me, but not the Aramaic ones. I never looked at anyone else's work. I don't care about these people's work. I do not look at it in order to get inspiration. I go to first sources; I am only interested in primary sources. Therefore I consider Professor Schiffman's attack total and complete slander. He knows very well that I don't do the things he alleges, because I told him so personally before he ever wrote these charges and fully described our working method to him in San Francisco last month.

When we went through these materials, being the person giving over the manuscripts to Michael and his team, I very carefully instructed Michael and his teams to go through everything afresh and rely on no one else's work. They assured me, as he has assured you today, that that is what they have done, and I believe them. I believed them then and I believe them now.

Let me just make two final points, although I could say much much more. I don't think we should get into a debate with our critics. I think what has been said is sufficient. He's had his say. We shouldn't go back for more replies, and another circle of criticisms. It should be cut at some point, because this just gets into nastiness, and it can get a lot nastier.

But, let me state this. As Michael pointed out, and I agree, approximately thirty new texts were found. You know and the public knows, we found the text Shanks' magazine is now calling 'the Pierced Messiah text.' Everybody knows that. Whether we interpreted it correctly or not isn't the point. We also found the Messiah of Heaven and Earth text. I was the first one to publish the Kohath text. I had no idea Puech was working on that. We published the Kohath text in *BAR*. We also found those extra passages in what we named the Genesis *Florilegium* and reconstructed a beautiful text, superior to the Oxford reconstruction of it. That they published before us doesn't mean we didn't find it before them. We published that text in National Geographic a year and a half ago. So we have been finding these texts all along. We reconstructed a beautiful text which we called the Children of *Yesha'*, the Children of Salvation text. We found that marvelous text about masturbation. We didn't need anyone else's help to find these texts. We didn't need anyone's help in finding the two copies of the last column of the Damascus Document, and we got out there first with our own translation. That's what free competition and scholarship are all about.

Now, I submit to you, if we could do all that by ourselves, why do you think we would have needed to rely on these people's work to do these other things? In fact, I submit, we didn't. We didn't need to rely on anyone else's work. We could do it *all by ourselves*, and as far as I am aware, we did do it all by ourselves.

In any event, if this position is recognized, it would mean that we have copyright over these additional 30 or so texts, which would be an absurdity.

The last point is about whether this has to do with the issue of transcriptions or whether it has to do with an old establishment attempting to reassert control over the field again, to go back to the old situation of official editions; let me point out that when the Abegg-Wacholder publication came out, no one particularly caviled that that work came from someone else's—namely Professor Fitzmyer's—work, and I disapproved of what they did there. But, I didn't hear the caviling we are hearing now, even though not one single item in that book is really an original item. It all came from a concordance assembled in the 1960s. They reconstructed the transcriptions completely from other people's texts.

We don't hear the same viciousness and animosity as we are hearing here.

So why are we hearing it here? I submit it is because of the new translations and the new interpretations, the new spin we – Professor Wise with his own hypothesis, mine with the Jewish-Christian one – are giving these things. Also, since we got out there first with it, that infuriates a lot of people. They feel that by discrediting us, they discredit our interpretations.

I submit that it won't work. The game is up, Larry. Even though you have now joined the 'official team,' you remember when you told me in San Francisco you did not understand what was meant in the *Vanity Fair* article when you were termed a 'running dog of the Establishment'? I'm not surprised you did not understand then. In any case, I submit that the game is up. There are no more official editions, no more teams. What we have is free competition and free thinking and that's what should have been in the first place.

CHAIRMAN MEYERS: I would like to comment, not on your statement, Robert, but on the meaning of the ASOR policy. If what has been proposed here for manuscript or written evidence were extended as well to nonwritten remains, I think it would create chaos in the entire field of archaeology – should someone's dig be immediately made available for anyone to publish and work through indiscriminately? I think this is the obligation of the local, national powers to negotiate. Those of us who work more in the field than in the papyrological, epigraphic area are very sensitive to these matters, and I think that is the issue of principle that ASOR has raised.

HERSHEL SHANKS: I fear that the way I intended to begin my remarks would almost sound irrelevant today. I want to make a plea – it seems almost too late to do it – for reconciliation. We are tearing ourselves apart. I have good friends, very good friends, among the 19 scholars who signed this statement. I have friends on the other side. We're playing in a game, in a field where we're unleashing forces that we have no control over. I beg of us, if I can call you colleagues, to reconsider.

I think we have to look at what's happened in context. The first context, as has been repeatedly mentioned, is "relevance." This Dead Sea Scroll material is special. It is unique. We're talking about scrolls that have been unavailable to scholars generally for 40 years now, and the same rules therefore don't necessarily apply.

The second thing, in the context of what's occurred, are the battles and the fights and the wrongs. It was easily predictable that this kind of statement that was signed by the 19 scholars would be used as a way to fight substantive battles, not ethical battles, not procedural battles, but really to give exposure to substantive positions that are not its real concern.

I have to say that despite the fact that I have such good friends who have signed that letter, I'm sorry it's been signed. I think a couple of things are wrong with it. It is signed by 19 of the most prominent Qumran scholars in the world, and it looks like a gang-up. It is like we're going to get this one little untenured professor and ruin his life. It accuses him of lying, of cheating, of dishonesty. I wonder, did all of the signers of this letter look at the matter and assess the evidence, or was it, "Gee whiz, Larry Schiffman and Jim VanderKam and Frank Cross signed it. Even Joe Fitzmyer." I'll tell you, it really incites me with a little compassion for Michael Wise. This is a man's life that's at stake, and there seems to be no reluctance to tear it apart.

Another thing about the affair that concerns me is that apparently nobody went to Michael, who prepared these transcriptions, and said, "Michael we know your reputation. We know of your fine scholarship. We admire and respect your work. We're stunned at this. Tell us about it. What happened? Let's hear your side of the story." No one went to Michael Wise. They just signed as if it didn't matter. You're ruining a man's career.

At a private press conference which I was allowed to attend, I put some tough questions to Michael. I said, "Michael, you said in this book that everything about MMT was new and you didn't use anybody else's work. You didn't use Strugnell and Qimron. Is that accurate?" And, he said plainly and firmly, "Yes, it is accurate. We did not." And, I said to him, "Michael, if you are telling the truth, these people owe you a terrible apology." I said, "If." Now, Larry says that there is a mistake in there that shows that Wise was misreading Strugnell's handwriting. I don't know the answer. Maybe you're right, Larry. Maybe Michael's right. But, I want to know more before I throw this man's career in the drain.

There are really two specific issues involved. One is, can you use handouts? Can you use unpublished materials? And, two is, do you give credit? Now, the second one is easy. You give credit. We always try to give credit. If we make a mistake, we'll make it up. We'll apologize, and cite you in the next edition. But, I'm not sure you ruin a man's life over it. I'm not sure you gang up, 19 of the greatest scholars in the world. I'm not sure you bring a lawsuit. Before you accuse someone of bad intention, maliciousness, hesitate. We're all fine people. I don't think that anybody here is an evil person. If we don't give an adequate citation, it is not because we're evil people. We should correct it. But, let's not cut people off at the knees or put them in jail.

There is more debate about the first issue. Larry said in his statement—it was stated in the letter signed by the 19 scholars—that a scholar has a right to get his ideas out under his or her own name. That's a difficult issue. There are things to be said on both sides of that.

I think in the context of Qumran, however, it is clear. Today we know that there is no patience left. When we get information, we publish it, and we try to give credit where credit is due. On the issue of the handouts, consider the case of Joe Fitzmyer, a man whose great scholarship and integrity I greatly admire. When Milik lectured on 4Q246 at Harvard in 1972, he mentioned some of the material which Fitzmyer later published. I think Fitzmyer's action was perfectly proper, and I think it is perfectly proper to publish information that you get about what's in these scrolls, especially given the context.

A word about how we reconstruct texts and use other people's work. I'm no scholar, as you know, but I know enough to know that when you see an arrangement of some fragments you can't put that out of your mind. It's there. If he or she did it correctly, then you can't do it over. It's right. It fits. And it's the same thing with a reconstruction. If you've got a few letters that are missing in a word, then you might not have immediately thought of it, but you read it. You immediately know that those are the right letters and even the words. And, so to this extent if you are to publish, you have to use, in that sense, previous scholarship.

I hope we're all colleagues. I mean, we come to these conferences, we socialize, we kibbitz, we talk, we gossip, we enjoy ourselves, we contribute to knowledge. Or in my case, at least I disseminate it a little bit.

I would end where I began, with a plea for reconciliation, a plea for a cessation of accusations about people's intentions, and to understand that we're operating in a terribly public forum where the stakes are very high, where people's careers are at stake, and a little more compassion than punctiliousness is needed. Let's realize where we are and go forward together.

LAWRENCE SCHIFFMAN: I just wanted to make two statements if I could. The first is as I say almost a trivial point. When I heard this book came out, I thought it was phenomenal. I was doing a review of all the texts that have been published and the facsimile edition, and I wanted to include this book. I, therefore, called the publisher and asked for a copy. As was the case with others, I found a need to respond. I just felt that piece of trivia should be clarified.

Second of all, I want to say that, Herschel, your very beautiful and I think correct comments have not escaped anyone in this. I alluded before to nights of being up all night discussing what is the right course, what is not the right course. There were various conversations as were alluded to before. Many, many people's advice was gotten. Many scholars were shown the examples.

I had a line in here which is not in my final version and I want to say it, even though I don't have the text. I said in the original version that I come to give these remarks mindful of a Jewish tradition which says that if you embarrass someone in public, even if you have to do so, even if it is the right thing to do so, you still have to repent, which I will have to do. So, I would say to you that to my mind what's happening here is a tragedy.

We heard in the remarks that indeed some of this material was used in one way or another. I think it is necessary that our field begins at some point to function according to the standards by which other fields function. We have to do it immediately. Whether we draw the line on book A or book B or book C, we had better start doing it, because of precisely the things you said, with which I agree. Thank you for the chance to add those remarks.

ROBERT EISENMAN: Eric, if I may just add one word. Dr. Schiffman, you willfully with these other scholars sent out this letter to various representatives of the press, and there is no excuse for a scholar to do such a thing. It is unwarranted by the quality of this work. I am shocked and amazed by it. And, of course, we want to have friendly relations, but we have to do it on that basis of truth. There was no reason for such a statement.

HARTMUT STEGEMANN: I have been working on the scrolls for 38 years and since the year 1964 I have always had free access to every document from the Dead Sea Scrolls in the Israel Museum and the Rockefeller Museum. I'll comment on the discussion on one point, the scientific point of view. There is a great difference between the things which are related by Mr. Shanks and with this new book, with the 50 texts, from the point of view of science. What Mr. Shanks did by publishing the first two volumes of photos is criticized by some people, particularly regarding his sources. Everybody knows who the sources were. He says these are the plates from the Rockefeller Museum. He does not say from whom he got them (at least they are Professors Eisenman and Robinson), but the sources are clear.

The same is the case with the volumes where he started to publish unpublished texts. He says they are from a concordance. Some people again may be angry at this, but from the scientific point of view, you know the way. It's different in the new book. Let me tell you of three instances, one of which was already mentioned. The first case is the so-called MMT text. In the arrangement of fragments which was made at first by Professor Strugnell (which was afterwards changed by Qimron) there are three major mistakes. Just the same, these mistakes are now in the new book.

If you look at the text of the fragments, there are many lacunae. Some of the lacunae were incorrectly filled in by Strugnell and Qimron. But it is just those wrong reconstructions of lacunae that appear in this book. Why? It is not possible to come to the same errors when only studying the fragments.

Second. Another text is the end part of the so-called Damascus Document. This is just the version which was printed in the first volume of not-yet published texts by Hershel Shanks in September of last year. It is the very same text. Everybody knows it was done by Milik, put into the concordance about 1960, but here it is again, without naming Milik or Bernstein, Wacholder, or anybody who was involved.

Last example. At the end of the volume, text #50 is of interest only because the name "Jonathan" appears there twice. There were three people responsible for this reading: Ada Yardeni and Hanan and Esther Eshel. They were never published in a scientific journal, although they told about the text at Paris this summer. Why are they not given credit for their scientific labor on this very important text? This is not good academic practice to publish 50 texts as if you had deciphered them alone. Indeed, the sources are not named. Therefore, I protest against such a way of publishing.

MICHAEL WISE: I already knew about this mistake that Larry Schiffman has referred to in the MMT transcription—that is, the reading of *biyadenu*, which is clear on the photograph, rather than *beto*—because he told me about this a week ago. It caught me completely by surprise. I went back and checked the photos, and indeed he was right. There was no question that the reading is *biyadenu*. The only thing I could think at the time was that there was no way I could have claimed to have looked at these texts and worked from the photos. It would appear that there was nothing I could say even if that were true, because of this error. So, I called my colleague, Norman Golb, more or less in despair and told him about this instance. He told me that this exact same phenomenon has occurred repeatedly in the editing of manuscripts, where one scholar has read the edition of another but then subsequently goes to the photographs and produces his own edition. In fact, this happened to Norman himself, as he has said. He can give examples, which I don't recall off the top of my head.

I believe it was necessary to state this. It doesn't invalidate what we've said. It is a psychological phenomenon in the editing of texts.

MOSHE BERNSTEIN: I am not an editor of texts. I am in possession of no unpublished texts. Indeed, I am currently engaged in commenting and writing about certain texts which have not yet reached official publication. The questions that have been raised here are, of course, very serious. I don't think anyone has greater respect for Michael Wise's work than I. He has delivered distinguished papers in sessions which I have chaired at SBL. But, I think there is perhaps something that we can all learn from this situation which might redound to all our benefit.

I say this being in almost total disagreement with every page of this book, because I think the interpretations in it are wrong. We shouldn't get away from the question of having people write proper reviews of this book when the dust of the debate over proper use of sources has been completed, because on the presumption that Professors Eisenman and Wise are innocent, then we have the job of sitting down, sifting through this material and in my opinion consigning it to its proper place.

But, what we can learn from this is the need to work together. The need to work in consonance, not to work in isolation of other scholars. That reminds me of the work of that quick-to-publish Dead Sea Scroll scholar, John Allegro, who got his stuff out before anybody else. John Strugnell then had to write a review longer than the volume, which is probably more valuable than the volume, but Allegro got his work done. And, Allegro also was guilty of the wrong kind of popularization.

So what we may have in front of us here is a kind of dual "allegroism," a popular work with texts that were published much too quickly, without consultation with colleagues. Perhaps the most important thing that we can learn to do is to share our interpretations with colleagues before they reach public fora, whether in scholarly journals or books. We should take rather as our example the work of somebody like Yigael Yadin, who in the production of his massive and exemplary commentary on the Temple Scroll, made sure to address those questions about which he had doubt to the most eminent scholars in the relevant fields.

As a result, Yadin's *Temple Scroll* stands as the right way to write a Qumran commentary. I'm not sure that we should be writing popular books before the proper scholarly material has been worked through. I think it is only after we've done the proper kind of analysis, shared work, settling of thorny textual questions and the like that we are going to be ready to put material like this before the public. To put it before the public in its unfinished state, in its preliminary state actually may do a disservice to all of us as scholars in the long run.

So my own plea, if I can add it to that which Hershel Shanks made before, is let's learn from this to share our work with others, to disseminate it, making sure that it will only appear in our name eventually, but nevertheless to disseminate it, to share it with others, and in that way the product that we are going to be able to put before the public, both the scholarly one and the popular one, will be far better as a result.

JOSEPH PATRICH: I want to add another dimension to this ethical discussion which is very important, and this is archaeology. We heard this morning several lectures that demonstrated the importance of proper archaeological work and of proper documentation, not just to run wild, to survey caves, to go into an area, to come without license, and to claim then new results and to bring all kinds of sophisticated equipment without a license from the Israeli authority, and then go and try again to build some kind of sensational claim for new discoveries. This is very sensitive, no less sensitive than what you're discussing here about publishing unauthorized versions and editions and so on. I think that all of you should be aware about these things, because it happened in the past and it may happen again in the future. The Israel Department of Antiquities is trying to control these things as well, and stands against all kinds of media pressure in this domain as well. Thank you very much.

RAYMOND EDGE: Perhaps we should have changed this from the ethics of publication to the fight over the publication of the Dead Sea Scrolls, because that's what it sounds like to me. So, I'd like to get back to the ethics of it, especially with follow-up of what's just been said about what's going to happen after this.

A couple of questions to the ASOR representative as well as to the Society of Biblical Literature. You mentioned that the host country should decide, and within a reasonable time. Is that host country to be interpreted as Israel?

Or, since it is occupied territory according to some, Jordan? So, therefore, we're still in a stalemate.

To those of the Society of Biblical Literature, how do you interpret "all scholars," because I sit here as a person who is quite qualified but yet was unable to see them until September 1991.

In addition to that, you said five years would be a reasonable time for publication. Why don't we apply that rule now? It has now been 30 years past that five years, so let anybody and everybody decide to publish. Their interpretations will fall or not. Let the public as well as the scholarship decide that.

We've already gone over five years. Why not allow it to happen now? I would like those particular questions to be answered. Then perhaps we can get back to the ethics of it.

CHAIRMAN MEYERS: I'll respond as best I can to part of that and let you, Jim, respond for SBL.

The archaeologists, particularly those in ASOR, recognize the jurisdiction of the government of Israel in this regard, and it has not been challenged by Jordan. So in this regard the scholars working in Israel and working in Jordan recognize the licensing authorities in either country. We work through the official representatives—that is, the directors of antiquities in each of these bodies. It is their job to see that this material is properly preserved and properly published within reasonable time and to allow access to occur.

So, I think a lot of these questions should be directed to those authorities. I personally feel that reasonable time has passed, and therefore the fact that this stuff is out there is okay. I have personally rejected the notion that the current *modus operandi* should be taken in any way as a precedent for future deliberations. That, I think, fairly represents the archaeologist's position.

I'll let Jim, who is on both committees, speak to that as well.

JAMES VANDERKAM: The Society of Biblical Literature adopted the statement that said, "accessible to all scholars" because it is a society of scholars of the biblical material and really is not in a position to deal with questions affecting the wider populace.

As far as the five-year limitation, I hope that no one gets from this discussion, despite some of the assertions that have been made, that there is any objection to publishing any text from Qumran. Certainly the Society of Biblical Literature statement encourages anyone to publish texts. Some people publish official versions, but anyone has a right to publish texts. That's not what is at issue here.

RAYMOND EDGE: So, therefore, who decides who is a scholar?

JAMES VANDERKAM: If you are a university scholar in the field of knowledge, you have the right to see the text that pertains to your field.

RAYMOND EDGE: That's what we did not have until September 1991. Having talked to Mr. Moffett, of course, there was a lack of ethics on both sides, specifically from those that requested the pictures be sent to them, and for him not to keep any copies whatsoever. So there have been problems on both sides. I think what we need to decide is what's going to happen with texts that perhaps may be discovered in the future and not what's already been done.

CHAIRMAN MEYERS: Yes, and there is no consensus on that at the moment.

RAYMOND EDGE: That's what we need to get to as far as the ethics, because that's where it is going to follow up with me and others of my generation—what will happen after this? That's the question, not what has happened with the book that's been published.

ROBERT EISENMAN: Just quickly as concerns our expeditions, Dr. Patrich made these false accusations to the Antiquities Department several years ago. They were not entertained then because there was a lot of testimony to the contrary. Furthermore, we were given a license for our survey this past year and for our radar ground scan by the Israel Antiquities Authority. We were not given a license for excavations to check these results. We are still seeking that. However, we didn't do any excavating, and he charged that we did. In fact, we never have.

DAVID PATTERSON: I am not a scholar in the field of Qumran, although I've been interested in it since about 1954 or 1955 when on the faculty of Manchester University, where I saw the Copper Scroll after it had been cut up. It was quite a remarkable experience. I also saw in the house of John Allegro a jar in which part of the scrolls had been found. How he got it, I never asked.

I really want just to make a statement of fact and to correct something which has appeared incorrectly in a number of places and which our Chairman in all innocence repeated in his introduction. That is that the Oxford Center for Postgraduate Hebrew Studies does possess a complete photographic copy of all the Qumran materials and we have 3300 photographs. These were not, as seems to be generally supposed, obtained at the time when the three microfilm copies were deposited in the United States, which I think was in the early 1980s. We actually got these new photographs in the years 1990 and 1991.

The negotiations were carried out by Professor Allan Crown who was acting president of the center when I was on sabbatical leave. When I came back, we both went to Jerusalem and made an agreement with the Israel Antiquities Authority that a complete copy of the Qumran materials be deposited in the Oxford Center. And, that was done over the course of a year.

At that particular time, we had to sign an agreement to say that whereas we could allow free access to the published materials, we could not allow access to the unpublished materials without the permission of the editor-in-chief at that time, John Strugnell, and the particular editor of the material being worked on.

We signed this agreement because we had no alternative and we hoped that we would be able in the course of time to work for open access. Fortunately, this came about much more quickly than we had ever hoped, because of the action of the director of the Huntington Library. What I want to say is that these photographs are now available to any bona fide scholar who would care to consult them. But, we do have state of the art machinery which enables us to blow up any little bit of it 2–3–4 times its size and makes it much easier to read in many ways. So, if there are scholars here who are not yet aware of that, I hope that in the course of years they will make use of it.

CHAIRMAN MEYERS: Duke was also given a complete set by Bill Moffett, and we have a complete set at our library. They are also available to anyone without restriction.

HERSHEL SHANKS: There has been a lot of talk just in the last remarks by David Patterson that the photos were taken in 1991 and given to them. That's accurate. But, the actual photographing of the scrolls was done pre-1967. The bulk of the scrolls were photographed only once by a great aero-photographer by the name of Nagib Albina. Recently there has been some rephotographing, but not the whole set. When Ms. Bechtel made her arrangements, photographs were not taken in the 1980s, copies were made of the Albina negatives. That's true of the collections at HUC, at ABMC, at Huntington, and at Oxford. In addition there are other more recent pictures, but the corpus as a whole is largely dependent on the Albina photographs. Unfortunately, those have not always been taken well care of and some of them have crumbled.

DAVID PATTERSON: I must take issue with Mr. Shanks with the greatest respect because I'm sure he speaks out of sincerity and sincerity of belief. But, in fact, the set of photographs that we have are completely new and the photographer in Jerusalem made a completely new photograph of every piece of the material both at the Rockefeller Museum and at the Shrine of the Book. The 3000 in the Rockefeller Museum, and the 300 of the Shrine of the Book. They are new photographs. We had to pay for every one of them.

JODI MAGNESS: Actually, I can attest that those photographs were retaken in the 1980s in Jerusalem, because I was friends with the photographer, Bob Schlosser, who stayed at the Albright in the summer of 1986. I personally saw him in the dark room developing those photographs. He would go to Magen Broshi and photograph the Dead Sea Scrolls and develop them in the dark room at the Albright Institute. I don't know if it was all the scrolls, but it was some of them.

HERSHEL SHANKS: I talked to Bob Schlosser also. That's what he told me. But, it is not the whole corpus, but I'm glad to be corrected by David Patterson.

CHAIRMAN MEYERS: I just want one second to say that there have been several different accounts here. I'm not going to go into it, because there is no time. They're all incomplete. They're all confused and none of them exactly correct. For example, Jodi was talking about the development of Schlosser's copies of the negative which were copies of the original negatives. Everybody is talking about something different. So, let's not talk about it, but it is all a little bit confused.

APPENDIX 1

STATEMENT OF MICHAEL WISE, 12/17/92

Having been responsible with my team for the transcriptions in the volume, *The Dead Sea Scrolls Uncovered*, I wish to state that, after fruitful discussion with my colleagues, I have come to understand their position more fully. I regret the impression, unintended by me, which emerges from the introduction concerning the degree to which some parts of the work were done independently. I am sorry that the documentation for certain portions of the book for which I was responsible was incomplete, and that I did not more fully express indebtedness to colleagues whose work I consulted and whom I admire, including Professors Devorah Dimant, Emile Puech, Elisha Qimron, and Shemaryahu Talmon. It is moreover regrettable that I did not have adequate input into the final form of the book, and that is something that should not have happened. I hope that there will be future editions of the book so that these deficiencies can be corrected, and look forward to creative work with my colleagues in the months ahead.

STATEMENT OF QUMRAN SCHOLARS
Gathered at the New York Academy of Sciences, 12/17/92

We wish to communicate the understanding which we, colleagues in the study of the Dead Sea Scrolls, have reached after publication of the Eisenman-Wise volume, *The Dead Sea Scrolls Uncovered*, the statement of protest by scholars, and further discussion at the New York Conference on "Methods of Investigation of the Dead Sea Scrolls and the Khirbet Qumran Site."

In light of Prof. Wise's statement and after obtaining additional information about the production of the book, those of us who were signatories to the statement of protest hereby retract the statement and all it implies.

All those present at this conference join in supporting this agreement. We reaffirm the authors' right and that of all scholars to publish Qumran texts and to make properly acknowledged use of the work of others. We join together in the spirit of collegial friendship and look forward to future cooperation in the domain of studies on the Dead Sea Scrolls.

Appendix 2

Participants in the panel discussion were Eric Meyers (*Duke University*), James VanderKam (*Notre Dame University*), Lawrence Schiffman (*New York University*), Norman Golb (*University of Chicago*), and (*in absentia*) James Robinson (*Claremont Graduate School*). Participants in the ensuing debate included, in addition to the above, Michael Wise (*University of Chicago*), Robert Eisenman (*California State University*), Hartmut Stegemann (*Göttingen University*), Moshe Bernstein (*Yeshivah University*), Joseph Patrich (*Haifa University*), Raymond Edge (*University of Texas at Austin*), David Patterson (*Oxford University*), Jodi Magness (*Tufts University*), and Hershel Shanks, Editor of the *Biblical Archaeology Review*.

Author Index*

* Page numbers in italics represent comments made in discussions.

Subject Index